Eating & Drinking

in Great Britain & Ireland

timeout.com

Penguin Books

Edited and designed by
Time Out Guides Limited
Universal House
251 Tottenham Court Road
London W1T 7AB
Tel + 44 (0)20 7813 3000
Fax + 44 (0)20 7813 6001
Email guides@timeout.com
www.timeout.com

PENGUIN BOOKS

Published by the Penguin Group
Penguin Books Ltd, 80 Strand, London WC2R ORL, England
Penguin Books USA Inc., 375 Hudson Street, New York, New York 10014, USA
Penguin Books Australia Ltd, 250 Camberwell Road, Camberwell, Victoria 3124, Australia
Penguin Books Canada Ltd, 10 Alcorn Avenue, Toronto, Ontario, Canada M4V 3B2
Penguin Books (NZ) Ltd, cnr Rosedale and Airborne Roads, Albany, Auckland, New Zealand

Penguin Books Ltd, Registered Offices: Harmondsworth, Middlesex, England

First published 2003

10 9 8 7 6 5 4 3 2 1

Reviews in this guide were written by:
London taken from the *Time Out Guide to Eating & Drinking in London*; Jim Driver (*Pub crawl: London*); Andrew Humphreys (*Bar crawl: London*). **England** Jennifer Alexander (Hampshire); Patricia Ambrose (Suffolk); Abby Aron (Kent, Hampshire); Ismay Atkins (Cornwall, Somerset); Roslyn Atkins (Cornwall); Willa Bailey (Cornwall, Devon); Helen Barnard (Berkshire, Buckinghamshire); Sophie Blacksell (Bristol, *Bar crawl: Bristol*); Dorothy Boswell (Hampshire, Sussex); Anna Britten (Somerset); Elizabeth Carter (Kent, Yorkshire); Robert Cockcroft (Yorkshire); Jonathan Cox (Birmingham, Lancashire); Peterjon Cresswell (Sussex); Simon Cropper (Herefordshire); Fiona Cumberpatch (Lincolnshire, Northamptonshire); Christi Daugherty (York); Sally Davies (Gloucestershire); Alison Davison (Birmingham, Leicestershire, Shropshire, Staffordshire, Warwickshire, Worcestershire); Guy Dimond (Sussex); Eli Dryden (Cheshire); Dominic Earle (Northamptonshire); Sarah Ewbank (Yorkshire); Peter Fiennes (Devon, Cornwall); Michael Flexer (Hampshire, Surrey); Will Fulford-Jones (Wiltshire); Janice Fuscoe (Cambridgeshire, Sussex); Juliet Gardiner (Cambridgeshire, Norfolk, Scotland); Helen Gilchrist (Cornwall); Charlie Godfrey-Fausset (Devon, Somerset); Hugh Graham (Dorset); Viv Groskop (Cambridgeshire, Cornwall, Lancashire, Somerset); Roopa Gulati (Cumbria); Sarah Guy (Lincolnshire, Surrey, Sussex, Yorkshire); Susan Guy (Lincolnshire); David Hall (Essex); Derek Hammond (Rutland, Warwickshire); Lindsay Harriss (Cornwall); Phil Harriss (Norfolk, Oxfordshire, *The best: Markets for food*); Will Hodgkinson (Kent); Jane Howard (Dorset); Richard Howe (Bedfordshire); Dean Irvine (Gloucestershire, Sussex); Sarah Jacobs (Kent); Arabella Keatley (Berkshire, Oxfordshire); Sarah Kent (Norfolk); Melanie Leyshon (Cornwall); Cathy Limb (Hertfordshire, Sussex); Susan Low (Bristol, Cornwall); David Lloyd (Cheshire, Derbyshire, Lancashire, Manchester, *Bar crawl: Manchester*); Sharon Lougher (Surrey); Jane Marshall (Norfolk); Natalia Marshall (Hertfordshire, Wiltshire); Lesley McCave (Kent); Chris Moore (Sussex); Chris Moss (Liverpool & Merseyside); Tony Mudd (fish & chips, Essex, Suffolk); Lisa Mullen (Buckinghamshire); Lucy Muss (Gloucestershire); Anna Norman (Kent); Frances Paffard (Suffolk); Grace Parker (Hampshire); Emma Perry (Suffolk); Cath Phillips (Wiltshire, Yorkshire); Susan Pollack (Birmingham, Oxfordshire, Sussex); Sam Le Quesne (Jersey); Simon Radcliffe (Kent); Nick Rider (Warwickshire); Nicholas Royle (Manchester); Rosamund Sales (Gloucestershire); Chris Salmon (Derbyshire, Manchester, York); David Sandhu (Nottinghamshire, *Bar crawl: Nottingham*); Cyrus Shahrad (Berkshire, Buckinghamshire, Gloucestershire); Andrew Shields (Essex, Rutland); Anna Smith (Lincolnshire); Sue Smith (Cornwall); Derryck Strachan (Devon); Caroline Taverne (Hampshire, Suffolk); Jill Turton (Leeds, Yorkshire, *Bar crawl: Leeds*); Peter Watts (Oxfordshire, Wiltshire); Sue Webster (Berkshire, Hampshire, Norfolk); Andrew White (Berkshire, Oxfordshire); Mario Wynn Jones (County Durham, Cumbria, Gloucestershire, Northamptonshire, Northumberland, Newcastle, Tyne & Wear, Wiltshire); Yolanda Zapaterra (Kent). **Scotland** Keith Davidson. **Wales** David Lloyd, Philip Moss. **Ireland** Caroline Workman (Northern Ireland, *Bar crawl: Belfast*); John McKenna (Republic of Ireland).

Maps JS Graphics (john@jsgraphics.co.uk).

Cover photography Adrian Briscoe at The Leatherne Bottel. Styling by Rebecca de Boehmler. The following items were provided by; wooden table/Chelsea Gardener; large wine glass,white plates, napkins and cutlery/Conran Shop; silver plate/Harrods; smaller wine glass and decanter/Purves and Purves.

Photography page iii Adrian Briscoe; pages 1, 6, 41, 65, 90, 91, 98, 101 Alys Tomlinson; pages 11, 13, 17, 37, 105, 118, 166, 167, 183, 187, 189, 192, 193, 194, 195, 201, 203, 305, 306, 309, 311-316, 358, 361, 367 Heloise Bergman; pages 28, 58, 59, 61, 68 Tricia de Courcy; pages 73, 78, 79 Paul Carter; pages 110, 111 Don Last; pages 123, 129, 137, 143 Alan McNamee/Riverside Pictures; pages 147, 153, 156, 161, 170-177 Mike Carsley; pages 180, 181 Nick Smith; pages 205, 211, 216, 217, 227, 231, 234, 235, 267, 270, 271, 279, 288, 289 Ian Stuart; page 219 Neville Chadwick; page 238 Paul Burroughs; pages 239, 246, 251, 256, 257, 263, 264, 265 Paul McDonald; pages 295, 322, 347-354 Phil Taylor; pages 299, 322, 324, 325 Walter Neilson; page 319 Donald Stewart; pages 327-344 Paul Avis. The following images were provided by the featured establishments: pages 125, 357, 365.

The Editor would like to thank Kathleen Guy, Rachel Harvey, David Marshall, Heather Munn, Megan Slyfield.

London

London Overview

Central London

Marylebone

Fairuz ★

3 Blandford Street, W1U 3DA (020 7486 8108/ 8182). Baker Street or Bond Street tube. **Meals served** noon-11.30pm Mon-Sat; noon-10.30pm Sun. **Main courses** £9-£13. **Set meals** £17.95 meze, £24.95 3 courses. **Cover** £1.50. **Credit** AmEx, DC, MC, V.

An informal atmosphere, welcoming staff and top-class Lebanese food make Fairuz a perennial favourite. Eschewing the formality that's so often the way with Lebanese restaurants, this little place is painted a warm Mediterranean yellow, and there's a fold-back frontage and pavement seating for summer dining. The meze dishes are prepared with precision and care: highlights include zesty fuul moukala (green fuul beans cooked with coriander and lemon), perfect falafel and a finely chopped tabouleh. Of the mains, the mixed fish grill is a generous portion of the freshest fish, all beautifully cooked; a Ksara rosé makes a fine accompaniment.

La Galette ★

56 Paddington Street, W1U 4HY (020 7935 1554/ www.lagalette.com). Baker Street tube. **Meals served** 8.30am-11pm Mon-Fri; 10am-11pm Sat, Sun. **Main courses** £5.60-£8.50. **Set lunch** (noon-5pm Mon-Fri) £6.95 2 courses. **Credit** AmEx, MC, V.

This light, bright, well-run place is as delightful as a crêperie can be, with a great sense of purpose and confidence. The convivial atmosphere makes the earthenware bowls of Breton cider fun rather than kitsch – and the freshness and quality of the ingredients make the simple galettes seem luxurious. The galette complete is filled with caramelised onion, rich ham, intense mushrooms and an egg with its soft yolk peeping out of the middle; the paysanne is covered with a mix of leeks, bacon, parsley and cream. Sweet crêpes are as crisp and bulky as the galettes and have toppings from lemon and sugar to chestnut cream.

Golden Hind ★ ★

73 Marylebone Lane, W1U 2PN (020 7486 3644). Bond Street tube. **Lunch served** noon-3pm Mon-Fri. **Dinner served** 6-10pm Mon-Sat. **Main courses** £5-£10.70. **Credit** AmEx, JCB, MC, V.

Dominated by buttercup-yellow walls, signed celebrity photos and a decommissioned art deco fish fryer, this unassuming little restaurant has been serving good stuff to the people of Marylebone since 1914. Now in the able hands of Mr Christou, the menu mixes the traditional delights of fish cakes, cod, haddock and skate with the more exotic likes of mussels in batter and king prawns in garlic. When haddock and chips is available, it's among the very

best around. Fresh, white, flaky fish is housed in a scrumptious thin batter, while the chips come about as near to perfection as God will allow. The mushy peas and own-made tartare sauce are divine. With service that's prompt, friendly and efficient, this is one satisfying fish and chip joint.

Levant

Jason Court, 76 Wigmore Street, W1U 2SJ (020 7224 1111/www.levantrestaurant.co.uk). Bond Street tube. **Bar Open** noon-1am daily. **Bar snacks** £3-£5.75. *Restaurant* **Meals served** noon-11.30pm Mon-Thur, Sun; noon-midnight Sat, Sun. **Main courses** £12.50-£22.50. **Set lunch** (noon-6pm daily) £8.50 2 courses; £11.50 3 courses. **Set dinner** £24.50-£65. **Credit** AmEx, DC, JCB, MC, V.

From the dramatic entrance (down stone-clad stairs strewn with rose petals, lit by lanterns) to the entertainment (belly dancers), Levant boldly strives for the exotic eastern effect. The interior is a Moorish fantasy of mashrebeya screens, more Moroccan lanterns and low seating. It's all very partyish and pricey. Food is a combination of standard Lebanese meze dishes and main courses, plus some European-inspired plates with a Lebanese slant. Particularly good is the tangy fried aubergine with pomegranate, and the nutty muhummara (chopped nuts mashed with chilli and oil). Own-made breads include a featherweight pitta. The only downsides are the two sittings policy and the noise level; the music is turned up even louder for the belly dancer, who makes her first appearance at around 8.30pm.

Locanda Locatelli ★

8 Seymour Street, W1H 7JZ (020 7935 9088/ www.locandalocatelli.com). Marble Arch tube. **Lunch served** noon-3pm Mon-Sat. **Dinner served** 7-11pm Mon-Thur; 7-11.30pm Fri, Sat. **Main courses** £16-£30. **Credit** AmEx, MC, V.

Giorgio Locatelli's glamorous Italian restaurant is a sleek operation, with an elegant interior by David Collins, a suave crew of waiters and a menu that, like the diners, runs from robust to ladies-who-lunch. Follow melt-in-the-mouth pasta (maybe orecchiette with turnip tops and chilli), or a starter such as ox tongue with parsley sauce, with one of the wonderful fish dishes (roast brill with green olives and tomato) or the likes of grilled baby chicken with roast potatoes and spinach. Top it all with tart of the day (pineapple was wonderful) and you'll realise the hype surrounding this place is true.

Mandalay ★

444 Edgware Road, W2 1EG (020 7258 3696). Edgware Road tube. **Lunch served** noon-2.30pm, **dinner served** 6-10.30pm Mon-Sat. **Main courses**

£3.90-£6.90. **Set lunch** £3.70 1 course, £5.90 3 courses. **Credit** AmEx, DC, JCB, MC, V.

The capital's only Burmese restaurant is modestly housed in cosy premises on the northern stretch of Edgware Road. Burmese cuisine, as the owners (the gracious Ali brothers) are happy to explain, is influenced by Chinese, Indian and Thai cooking yet offers its own distinctive dishes. So, for example, the extensive menu includes both spring rolls and samosas, and stir-fried dishes sit alongside curries. A typical meal might start with deliciously crisp and ungreasy shrimp and bean sprout fritters, or a refreshing chilli-spiked raw papaya salad, before moving on to, perhaps, soothing chicken with lemongrass in a fragrant coconut milk sauce or 'twice-cooked fish curry' – a generous portion of fried fish in a rich tomato gravy, set off nicely by spinach with garlic and ginger.

Maroush Gardens

1-3 Connaught Street, W2 2BH (020 7262 0222/ www.maroush.com). Marble Arch tube. **Meals served** noon-11.30pm daily. **Set menu** £20-£25 (minimum 2 people). **Credit** AmEx, MC, V.

This, the newest branch of the Maroush chain of Lebanese restaurants, sticks pretty much to the formula that has served so well. Fresh fish is a feature here, but not at the expense of the time-honoured combination of meze dishes and grills. Fattoush is a large bowl of crunchy mixed salad, along with croutons of pitta for added bite. Accompany it with some tangy chicken liver sautéed in lemon and butter, crumbly hlaywat (sweetbreads) and mellow, well-spiced fuul. Dark wooden columns give the restaurant the air of an old-fashioned bank. If you want to enter a different world, go to Maroush I (a few yards down Edgware Road at No.21) in the evening – preferably at the weekend. In the basement there you'll find a cosmopolitan party in full swing, with singers, electric organ and a belly dancer. Ranoush Juice Bar (*see below*) is also part of the group.

Orrery ★

55 Marylebone High Street, W1M 3AE (020 7616 8000/www.orrery.co.uk). Baker Street or Regent's Park tube. **Lunch served** noon-3pm daily. **Dinner served** 7-11pm Mon-Sat; 7-10.30pm Sun. **Main courses** £14.50-£26. **Set lunch** £23.50 3 courses. **Set dinner** (Sun) £30 3 courses incl glass of champagne. **Credit** AmEx, DC, JCB, MC, V.

This upmarket Conran eaterie is a class act – with an appetising francophile menu that changes often, a top-notch wine list and prices that reflect its haute cuisine aspirations. Starters are little miracles of taste and texture – the likes of watercress velouté with poached duck egg and truffle or lasagne of Dorset crab with courgette. Mains might be a perfect lemon Dover sole with broad beans, mussels and clams in a light but rich sauce or rabbit stuffed with wild mushrooms, accompanied by parmesan tuile and blobs of carrot purée. Finish with, perhaps, an apricot-themed dessert consisting of a delicate, cloud-like soufflé and a stronger-tasting sorbet. Service is efficient if sometimes over-attentive.

Phoenix Palace ★

3-5 Glentworth Street, NW1 5PG (020 7486 3515). Baker Street tube. **Meals served** noon-11.30pm Mon-Sat; noon-10.30pm Sun. **Main courses** £5-£30. **Set meals** £10-£20. **Credit** AmEx, MC, V.

Now firmly established as one of the best Chinese restaurants in town, Phoenix draws nightly crowds of urbane Cantonese and other discerning Londoners. The atmosphere is smart Hong Kong: that is, very Chinese, but without the kitsch razzle-dazzle of Chinatown. Food is consistently excellent – go for something from the monthly specials menu, where you'll find unfamiliar dishes and more unusual ingredients. Begin with soup of the day: on our last visit a mellow brew of chicken and pork ribs with salted greens. The special of baked crab with sizzly garlic and fiery chillies is deliciously fragrant, and they'll even rustle up off-menu treats on request, such as a stir-fry of bitter melon and salted duck-egg yolk. Complimentary desserts are given to Chinese customers and others who request them: perhaps a sweet soup of silver ear fungus and crisp rice balls. Service doesn't always live up to the food.

The Providores & Tapa Room ★

109 Marylebone High Street, W1U 4RX (020 7935 6175/www.theprovidores.co.uk). Baker Street or Bond Street tube. The Providores **Lunch served** noon-2.45pm daily. **Dinner served** 6-10.45pm Mon-Sat; 6-10pm Sun. **Main courses** £15-£19. *Tapa Room* **Breakfast served** 9-11.30am Mon-Fri; 10am-3pm Sat, Sun. **Meals served** noon-10.30pm Mon-Fri; 4-10.30pm Sat; 4-10pm Sun. **Tapas** £1.50-£9. **Credit** AmEx, MC, V.

This impressive operation combines café and wine bar with first-class fusion restaurant. The premises are cramped, with a lively crowd squeezed in at shared bench tables in the ground-floor Tapa Room. Here you can munch on brunchy snacks and global tapas, from grilled chorizo to salted steamed edamame, and more elaborate dishes like beetroot, sorrel and parmesan risotto. Upstairs at the Providores, another minimally decorated space, all colour is provided by the inspired cooking. Expect bizarre-sounding ingredients in freaky combinations that somehow meld into a tastebud-entrancing whole. Grilled scallops on a plantain fritter with sweet chilli sauce and salted coconut milk are savoury-sweet and fiery-salty. Save room for desserts, particularly if atari goma (an Asian sesame paste) panna cotta with Monbazillac and elderflower jelly is on the menu – it's a dish of genius. The wine list is dominated by choice Kiwi bottles.

Ranoush Juice Bar ★

43 Edgware Road, W2 2JR (020 7723 5929/ www.maroush.com). Marble Arch tube. **Meals served** 9am-3am daily. **Main courses** £3-£12. **No credit cards.**

The Edgware Road's landmark snack and juice bar is an authentic Beirut-style hangout of polished brass, marble tops and harsh lighting. As much social centre as eaterie, it's busy throughout the day with local, expat and visiting Middle Easterners rendezvousing over coffee or freshly squeezed juice (any fruit you can think of, £1.75). Patrons graze from the enticing glass-fronted counter display of fast food Arabic-style: tabbouleh, houmous, labneh, falafel, stuffed vine leaves, plus excellent warm chicken liver sandwiches and garlicky shawarma (lamb or chicken, £3). With four people competing for every one of the handful of chairs and stools the place sometimes feels like a tube carriage at rush hour, but nobody seems to mind. By night the neon-lit Ranoush really buzzes when it becomes a West London alternative to Soho's Bar Italia for a post-pub/club caffeine fix or munchie binge.

Satay House

13 Sale Place, W2 1PX (020 7723 6763/ www.satayhouse.com). Edgware Road tube/ Paddington tube/rail. **Lunch served** noon-3pm, **dinner served** 6-11pm daily. **Main courses** £5-£18.50. **Set meals** £13.50, £18, £25 (minimum 2 people). **Credit** AmEx, DC, MC, V.
A laid-back restaurant that's a homely haven attracting Malay, Indian, Chinese and English diners. Refreshingly, the extensive Malay menu offers both standard and less common dishes, including fermented durian, curried pineapple and sago gula melaka (a sago and coconut milk dessert). Appetising smells waft from the kitchen and the pause between orders being taken and dishes arriving points to freshly cooked food. Satay and roti canai make a tasty first course. It could be followed by a spanking-fresh grilled mackerel, kangkong blachan (with an authentic fishy flavour) and richly spiced prawns and petai beans, which add a distinctive fermented flavour. Given the quality of the cooking and the generosity of the portions, prices are very reasonable – this is a great place to enjoy authentic Malay cuisine.

Six-13

19 Wigmore Street, W1U 1PH (020 7629 6133/ www.six13.com). Bond Street or Oxford Circus tube. **Lunch served** noon-3pm Mon-Thur. **Dinner served** *summer* 5.30-10.30pm Mon-Thur; (prepaid only) from 7.30pm Fri; *winter* 5.30-10.30pm Mon-Thur. **Main courses** £17-£24. **Set lunch** £20 2 courses, £24 3 courses. **Credit** AmEx, MC, V.
The only London restaurant offering sophisticated, modern kosher cuisine (consommé of chicken soup with paysanne vegetables gives just the slightest nod to tradition), Six-13 has unfussy pale-green walls and furnishings and smooth service. The New Zealander chef presents his dishes with style and (mainly) success, given the limitations of kashrut. The confit duck salad is not one of his best, but spiced pears with chopped liver are inspired. Salmon ceviche, Mediterranean vegetable terrine or foie gras are all tempting. Sea bass on lemongrass mash with pak

choi is good; veal on roasted root vegetables with a sweetish sauce is faultless. Over-sweet desserts are the weak point. With a broad wine list (£16.50-£95), it all adds up to a pleasurable, if expensive, experience. Try the weekly changing set lunch for better value. (Kosher supervised – Beth Din.)

Villandry

170 Great Portland Street, W1W 5QB (020 7631 3131/www.villandry.com). Great Portland Street tube. **Breakfast served** 8am-noon Mon-Sat. **Brunch served** noon-3pm Sat, Sun. **Lunch served** noon-3pm Mon-Fri. **Dinner served** 6-10.30pm Mon-Sat. **Main courses** £10.50-£19.50. **Credit** AmEx, DC, JCB, MC, V.
A charcuterie bar has been added to a line-up that already combines a restaurant, foodstore and bar on the same (spacious) ground floor premises. Staff in the shop can be a bit slow; the tempo in the restaurant is nicely efficient. A menu of modish but unfussy dishes changes twice a day: sliced pork salad with apples and quince jelly or chilled provençal soup with black olives might be followed by fish pie with spinach or grilled lamb with merguez sausage, couscous and harissa. Desserts run from elderflower, strawberry and champagne jelly to chocolate cake with crème chantilly, though there's always temptation to sample one (£5.50) or five (a stiff £11.50) of the splendid European cheeses.

Wagamama ★

101A Wigmore Street, W1H 9AB (020 7409 0111/ www.wagamama.com). Bond Street or Marble Arch tube. **Meals served** noon-11pm Mon-Sat; 12.30-10.30pm Sun. **Main courses** £5.25-£8.50. **Set meals** £9.95-£10.95 2 courses. **Credit** AmEx, DC JCB, MC, V.
Less a restaurant, more a way of life, Wagamama offers cheap, filling, healthy food in a bustling, smoke-free environment. Your order may arrive before or after that of others in your party, as dishes are delivered the moment they're ready. There are no starters. Go for a main, plus a side dish if you've got an appetite. Edamame, steamed green soya beans squeezed from pods directly into the mouth, are superb and plentiful. Also unreservedly recommended are the chicken katsu curry (chicken fillet fried in crispy breadcrumbs with curry sauce and red pickles) and the kare lomen (a bowl of spicy ramen with lemongrass, coconut milk and ginger garnished with char-grilled king prawns). The drinks list rounds up beers, wines and soft drinks alongside saké, plum wine and (free) green tea.

Also in the area

Carluccio's 12 Great Portland Street, W1W 8QN (020 7580 3050); **Carluccio's** St Christopher's Place, W1U 1AY (020 7935 5927); **De Gustibus** 53 Blandford Street, W1U 7HL (020 7486 6608); **Giraffe** 6-8 Blandford Street, W1H 3HA (020 7935 2333); **Paul** 115 Marylebone High Street, W1U 4BS (020 7224 5615); **Royal China** 40 Baker Street, W1M 1DA (020 7487 4688).

Mayfair & St James's

Le Caprice ★

Arlington House, Arlington Street, SW1A 1RT (020 7629 2239). Green Park tube. **Lunch served** noon-3pm Mon-Sat; noon-3.30pm Sun. **Dinner served** 5.30pm-midnight Mon-Sat; 6pm-midnight Sun. **Main courses** £12-£23. **Credit** AmEx, DC, MC, V.

Stuck at the foot of a nondescript modern office building, Le Caprice does little to pull in passing custom. It's just as well; passing customers would have to wait a month for a table. For more than 20 years, this influential, utterly reliable restaurant has been knocking out simple but beautifully executed bistro dishes. If you crave a classic caesar salad, a spicy steak tartare, or even a superior burger and chips (sorry, chopped steak Americaine with pommes allumettes), you won't find better versions in London. Signature desserts include Scandinavian iced berries with white chocolate sauce and ambrosial wild strawberry and champagne jelly. The prices may seem high for bistro food, but for a near-perfect meal served by effortlessly professional staff in a place as buzzy as Le Caprice, they're a steal. It's worth calling on the day for lunch availability.

Chintamani

122 Jermyn Street, SW1Y 4UJ (020 7839 2020). Piccadilly Circus tube. **dinner served** 6-11.30pm Mon Sat. **Main courses** £14-£22. **Set meals** (lunch, 6-7pm) £16.95 2 courses, £19.95 3 courses. **Credit** AmEx, DC, JCB, MC, V.

Chintamani redefines top-end Turkish dining. The clientele is young, and light, clubby music plays in a luxurious (marble toilets), relaxed setting. This is a designer space, with a great red chandelier and a sweeping cloth across the ceiling creating a 'tent' feel. The wine list is global and extensive. The menu is relatively short but adventurous, with seafood dishes, a fair amount of beef (common in Turkey, but not in Turkish restaurants here) and pork. Starters of börecik (crispy veal dumplings in loads of yoghurt) and midye dolma (mussels with rice and pine kernels) both impressed; texture and freshness were to the fore. Morina (harissa-crusted cod) main was superb, with spinachy rice, potato, lentil and parsley sauce, and islim kebab (aubergine rolled around diced veal) was exquisite. An upmarket restaurant where food lives up to the surroundings.

Criterion

224 Piccadilly, W1J 9HP (020 7930 0488/ www.whitestarline.org.uk). Piccadilly Circus tube. **Lunch served** noon-2.30pm, **dinner served** 5.30-11pm Mon-Sat. **Main courses** £10.50-£22.50. **Set meals** (noon-2.30pm, 5.30-7pm) £14.95 2 courses, £17.95 3 courses. **Credit** AmEx, DC, JCB, MC, V.

With a gilded neo-Byzantine interior reminiscent of a Klimt painting and a nicely balanced, well-executed French menu, the Criterion has a flying start. Its location makes it the perfect pre-theatre stop, and there's a bargain-priced set lunch to keep the business diners happy. Owner Marco Pierre White has revamped and simplified the menu, leaving plenty of choice among a roster of French classics spiced up with the occasional Mediterranean influence. Hors d'oeuvres are firmly in the classic camp, with simple French onion soup, sardines grillées, eggs benedict with perfect hollandaise, a creamy parfait of foie gras or a frothy cappuccino of mushrooms all on offer. Mains are divided up into the traditional fish and crustaceans, meat and a range of Aberdeen Angus ribeyes.

Le Gavroche ★

43 Upper Brook Street, W1K 7QR (020 7408 0881/ www.le-gavroche.co.uk). Marble Arch tube. **Lunch served** noon-2pm Mon-Fri. **Dinner served** 7-11pm Mon-Sat. **Main courses** £27-£39. **Minimum** £60 dinner. **Set lunch** £40 3 courses incl coffee, half bottle of wine, mineral water. **Credit** AmEx, DC, JCB, MC, V.

From the hassle-free moment of booking, Le Gavroche's staff are politeness personified. The only downer is the bill. Well, for once, hang the cost and give yourself up to the experience of exceptionally fine dining. Le Gavroche's dark, clubby dining room is subterranean and always strikes a sombre note because of it, but pictures, table ornaments and the fairly ready smiles of the waiters hint at a sense of fun not far beneath the serious surface. Pre-dinner, pre- and post-dessert nibbles are gorgeous. The meal proper might begin with a light yet richly flavoured cheese soufflé floating on a lake of seasoned cream, or tiny bowls of tender tomato stew, frog's legs and snails. Main courses like wild roasted salmon with summery vegetables or buttery turbot with razor clam, prawns and squid ink risotto are unmitigated delights. Desserts like featherweight soufflé Rothschild and a wild strawberry millefeuille with mascarpone sorbet are faultless.

Gordon Ramsay at Claridges ★

55 Brook Street, W1A 2JQ (020 7499 0099). Bond Street tube. **Lunch served** noon-2.45pm Mon-Fri; noon-3.30pm Sat, Sun. **Dinner served** 5.45-11pm Mon-Sat; 6-11pm Sun. **Set meal** (lunch, 5-7pm) £25 3 courses. **Set dinner** £50 3 courses; prestige menu £60 6 courses. **Credit** AmEx, MC, V.

Claridges is a gorgeous hotel on any occasion. The glamour steps up as you pass through the darkly gleaming bar and on into the plush, peachy enclave

of the restaurant. Less daunting than it might sound, the six-course 'prestige' menu is a light, modestly portioned affair designed to offer as many flavour contrasts as possible. The session might begin with velvety pumpkin velouté shot through with tiny nuggets of parmesan, artichoke and truffle, perhaps followed by a lesson in smoothness like ballotine of foie gras served with saffron and pear chutney. Dishes are accomplished, though there's the odd quibble, such as chutney that's delicious but overpowers the liver. Hang on, because there's better to come: a paper-thin tiger prawn and scallop raviolo, for instance, served on creamy lemongrass and chive sauce. Mains like melting belly pork and Cornish cannon of lamb are faultless, too. And little pre-desserts and desserts proper are light and sweetly presented. The Connaught (Carlos Place, W1K 2AL; 020 7592 1222) is another stately Mayfair hotel to benefit from a Ramsay makeover – this time with protégée Angela Hartnett at the stoves.

Kaya

42 Albemarle Street, W1S 3FE (020 7499 0622/ 0633). Green Park tube. **Lunch served** noon-3pm Mon-Sat. **Dinner served** 6-11pm daily. **Main courses** £7.50-£17. **Set lunch** £12-£15. **Credit** AmEx, DC, JCB, MC, V.

Kaya is the most formal – and most expensive – of London's Korean restaurants. The look is easy on the eye: spherical paper lanterns hang low over the tables and oriental prints adorn the walls. Korean music plays in the background as staff rustle past, decked out in voluminous traditional garb. Table-top grilling is popular. Among dishes prepared in the kitchen, panch'an – kimch'i, sesame (perilla) leaf and salty fried squid pickles – whets the appetite. A starter of jellyfish and seafood in mustard sauce features thin lacy frills of jellyfish, crabsticks, thinly sliced cucumber and carrot, topped with piquant mustard sauce. Yuk hwe, a Korean version of steak tartare, is subtly flavoured and tender.

Kiku

17 Half Moon Street, W1J 7BE (020 7499 4208). Green Park tube. **Lunch served** noon-3pm Mon-Sat. **Dinner served** 6-10.30pm daily. **Main courses** £3-£28. **Set lunch** £12-£25 incl miso soup, pickles, rice. **Set dinner** £40-£60 incl miso soup, pickles, rice and dessert. **Credit** AmEx, MC, V.

Kiku is spotless and bright with blond wood, ikebana (flower arrangements) and tinkling background music. An appetiser (courtesy of the chef) of baby anchovies on grated daikon sounded the only poor note of the evening: the tiny fish morsels were lost in a bland mush of too-dry daikon. The meal picked up with some fine sushi. Tuna, scallops and ikura (salmon roe) burst on the tongue with a sharp tang. Deep-fried aubergine with miso sauce was rich, warm and nutty; agedashidofu was a wonderfully light, bouncy treat. Refreshing anmitsu (sweet red azuki beans, cubes of agar-agar and ice-cream) and champagne sorbet rounded off a thoroughly enjoyable meal.

Mirabelle

56 Curzon Street, W1Y 8DL (020 7499 4636/ www.whitestarline.org.uk). Green Park tube. **Lunch served** noon-2.30pm Mon-Sat; noon-3pm Sun. **Dinner served** 6-11pm daily. **Main courses** £14.50-£25. **Set lunches** (Mon-Sat) £16.50 2 courses; £19.50 3 courses. **Credit** AmEx, DC, MC, V.

In the 1950s and 1960s, Mirabelle was one of London's most stylish dining rooms, and Marco Pierre White has done an impressive job at reinstating that reputation. The bar area has an irresistibly glamorous feel, with splendid mirrored and beaded screens. The dining room itself is a crisper affair, featuring white linen, neat fresh flowers and skylights. From a menu of French classics, try an ornately presented cylinder of dressed crab served simply with melba toast or lightly seared succulent scallops atop a tarte tartin of sweet, caramelised endive. Follow with melt-in-the-mouth daube of Aberdeen Angus à l'ancienne, or a rich cut of roast peppered venison. Desserts stick with old faves: a devilishly creamy crème brûlée and a fluffy soufflé Mirabelle. The wine list is long and expensive; service unfalteringly smooth.

Miyama

38 Clarges Street, W1Y 7PJ (020 7493 3807/7499 2443).Green Park tube. **Lunch served** noon-2.30pm Mon-Sat. **Dinner served** 6-10.30pm daily. **Main courses** £9-£25. **Set lunch** £13-£22 incl miso soup, pickles and rice. **Set dinner** £35-£45 incl miso soup, pickles, rice and dessert. **Credit** AmEx, DC, MC, V.

The black floor tiles and mirrors suggest Miyama is the haunt of Japanese suits knocking back saké, but there's more to it than that. Waitresses in kimonos guided us to a table, where an appetiser of seaweed with sesame seeds started proceedings. Atsu-kan (hot saké) came with individually decorated cups. A platter of sushi and sashimi followed: melting slivers of tuna, salmon and sea bass; the California roll and prawn and cucumber nigiri were firm and fresh. Our next treat was grilled black cod in sweet miso sauce, but sea bass in teriyaki sauce was bland. Service was demure and seamless. There's a large selection of lunch menus and a basement sushi bar.

Momo

25 Heddon Street, W1B 4BH (020 7434 4040). Piccadilly Circus tube. **Lunch served** noon-2.30pm daily. **Dinner served** 7-11pm Mon-Sat; 6-10.30pm Sun. **Main courses** £9.75-£19.50. **Set lunch** £17 2 courses. **Credit** AmEx, DC, MC, V.

The furore surrounding Mourad Mazouz's showy, exclusive money's-no-object venture Sketch (9 Conduit Street, W1; 0870 777 4488) puts his original London restaurant Momo in the shade, but a recent revisit reminds us what a piece of theatre this is too. It's a big place with twinkly brass lanterns and filled every night with chattery action. Good-looking staff in kasbah pop art T-shirts flit between tables with water jugs and bowls for ritualised handwashing, proffering menus and delivering dishes as though part of some conjuring

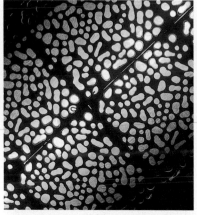

Chintamani. *See p25.*

act. The food doesn't live up to the presentation. It's simply good Moroccan: lamb, chicken, couscous and tajine. Order mint tea and (pricey) pastries to reinject the flair and ooh and aah as your server pours with the teapot nose high and the cup down by their knees. One final bit of slick presentation: after exactly two hours (the time allocated for each sitting) your coats appear, unasked for, as if by magic.

Nicole's

158 New Bond Street, W1Y 9PA (020 7499 8408). Bond Street or Green Park tube. Bar **Open** 10am-10.45pm Mon-Fri; 10am-6pm Sat. **Meals served** 11.30am-5.30pm Mon-Sat. **Main courses** £9.75-£11.25. *Restaurant* **Breakfast served** 10-11am Mon-Fri; 10-11.30am Sat. **Lunch served** noon-3.30pm Mon-Fri; noon-4pm Sat. **Afternoon tea served** 3-6pm Mon-Sat. **Dinner served** 6.30-10.30pm Mon-Fri. **Main courses** £18-£21. **Credit** AmEx, DC, JCB, MC, V.

All the ladies-who-lunch clichés come true here – this delicately decorated basement restaurant beneath the Nicole Farhi boutique is packed with women toying with just one dish – perhaps pan-fried, herb-stuffed red snapper with orzo, feta, mint and lemon salad. But they're fools to deny themselves, because this is seriously good food. Follow seared tuna, roast cauliflower, lemon and green olive salad with grilled Moroccan-spiced chicken with tabouleh and spicy aubergine salad and you'll be a very happy diner. Until you see the bill, of course; most starters are around £8, mains £20 and side orders £4-£7.50. Staff are amazingly sweet-natured in the face of such faddy eaters.

Nobu

Metropolitan Hotel, 19 Old Park Lane, W1K 1LB (020 7447 4747). Hyde Park Corner tube. **Lunch served** noon-2.15pm Mon-Fri. **Dinner served** 6-10.15pm Mon-Thur; 6-11pm Fri, Sat; 6-9.30pm Sun.

Main courses £5-£27.50. **Set lunch** £50 chef's selection, £25 bento box, £25 sushi box. **Set dinner** £70-£90 chef's selection incl green tea. **Credit** AmEx, DC, MC, V.

Celebrity patronage has kept Nobu in the news, but when we visited it was packed with families and tourists. Occupying a floor of the Metropolitan Hotel, Nobu's decor is minimalist blond wood and cream leather; service is slick but friendly. We kicked off with a Pisco Blood Orange cocktail, made with umeshu (plum wine). Tuna tempura roll was sublime: cool tuna and warm, crisp batter. Less rewarding were hot miso chips with tuna and scallops. Sashimi salad (wafer-thin salmon, tuna and scallops) was delectable. The famous black cod with miso burst with flavour, and beef 'toban' yaki arrived sizzling and tender. Honey ice-cream with fruity sauce cleansed the palate beautifully.

Patara Thai

3&7 Maddox Street, W1S 2QB (020 7499 6008). Oxford Circus tube. **Lunch served** noon-3pm, **dinner served** 6-10pm daily. **Main courses** £10.95-£15.50. **Set lunch** £10.95 2 courses; £13.95 2 courses. **Credit** AmEx, DC, JCB, MC, V.

The latest London branch of this Thai restaurant group lives up to its Mayfair location. The place is pure class, from its chill-out remix music to its graceful serving staff in Armani-does-Thailand silk. An intelligent menu combines classics with inspired contemporary offerings. Start with ornate pork and chicken dumplings, some of which are coloured a fetching (and traditional) pale purple. Also good are the black cod broth with ginger or the zingy tuna tartare spiked with lime juice and lemongrass. Prad prig khing (sweet, spicy sugar snap peas and prawns in a kaffir lime-strewn sauce) has real gravitas, while wok-fried egg noodles with soft-shell crab tempura and a feisty black pepper sauce has a reassuringly down-home quality. Desserts are equally sophisticated, especially the coconut ice-cream served with coconut flesh and fresh fruit.

The Quilon

St James's Court Hotel, 41 Buckingham Gate, SW1E 6AF (020 7821 1899/www.thequilonrestaurant.com). St James's Park tube. **Lunch served** noon-2.30pm Mon-Fri. **Dinner served** 6-11pm Mon-Sat. **Main courses** £7.50-£20. **Set lunch** £12.95 2 courses, £15.95 3 courses. **Credit** AmEx, DC, MC, V.

Never mind the less-than-tropical feel to this business hotel dining hall – Quilon's South Indian coastal cooking is a saviour for Indians (and others) blessed with good taste and deep pockets. Service is spot-on. Steamy complimentary glasses of rasam (hot peppery consommé flecked with warming spice) whet the appetite, while starters like sumptuous mussels mappas, served on the shell in an intense broth of pounded ginger, or tart kodampulli (sun-dried fish tamarind) and coconut milk, are top-drawer stuff. Our gold star goes to the mango curry; this remarkably fruity base is tempered with the tang of yoghurt, mustard seeds and crackling curry

leaves, and sparkles with sweet-sour savours. South Indian-style meaty biriani doesn't quite make the grade, swamped in an overdose of masala. In all, though, Quilon is a haven for balmy flavours.

The Ritz

150 Piccadilly, W1J 9BR (020 7493 8181 ext 3370/www.theritzlondon.com). Green Park tube. **Bar Open** 11am-11pm Mon-Sat; noon-10.30pm Sun. **Restaurant Lunch served** 12.30-2.30pm daily. **Dinner served** 6-11pm Mon-Sat; 6.30-10pm Sun. **Main courses** £25-£56. **Set lunch** £37 3 courses. **Set dinner** (6-7pm) £43 3 courses; (Mon-Thur) £55 4 courses; (Fri, Sat) £65 4 courses. **Credit** AmEx, JCB, MC, V.

Pink by day and gold by night, the gilded dining room at the Ritz never fails to impress. Celeb-spotting isn't usually a problem. The à la carte menu is presented in traditional French style – multiple courses without headings – which can be confusing, so aim for something near the top, middle and end if in doubt. Price is no guide, as starters range from £10 to £30, main courses from £25 to £56, and desserts to a whopping £48 for two. Quality has improved recently, with a number of unashamedly delicious items in the set dinners, along the lines of asparagus and morel risotto, ballotine of ham hock with white beans, sea bass with fennel and vanilla, plus the bread, cheese, coffee and petits fours. Other dishes, though, look the part but lack character. Dining at the Ritz is fun and doesn't have to cost a fortune, so pick a sunny day and dress up.

Tamarind

20 Queen Street, W1J 5PR (020 7629 3561/ www.tamarindrestaurant.com). Green Park tube. **Lunch served** noon-3pm Mon-Fri; noon-2.30pm Sun. **Dinner served** 6-11.30pm Mon-Sat; 6-10.30pm Sun. **Main courses** £14.50-£22. **Set lunch** £14.50 2 courses, £16.50 3 courses. **Set dinner** (6-7pm) £22 2 courses. **Credit** AmEx, DC, JCB, MC, V.

This dignified basement restaurant sets the scene for Alfred Prasad's softly-softly approach to stylish dining. Cooking is mainly North Indian, with an emphasis on gentle, freshly pounded spices. Tandoori kumbh chaat, a medley of mushrooms dipped in ginger-infused yoghurt and seared in the tandoor, is delicious; it comes with a tart finishing of lime juice and toasted tangy spice. Delicate roomali rotis thin as huge folded handkerchiefs are rippingly good and ideal for dipping into frontier-style makhani dahl – creamy lentils tastefully simmered with tomatoes, cream and weighty butter. Diners on elastic expense accounts are entertained by roti-tossing chefs through the frosted kitchen window.

Also in the area

Bank 4 Buckingham Gate, SW1E 6BS (020 7979 9797); **Carluccio's** Fenwick, 60 New Bond Street, W1S 1RJ (020 7935 5927); **Quod** 57 Haymarket, SW1Y 4QX (020 7925 1234); **Rasa** 6 Dering Street, W1S 1DA (020 7629 1346); **Strada** 15-16 New Burlington Street, W1X 1FF (020 7287 5967).

Soho & Fitzrovia

Back to Basics

21A Foley Street, W1W 6DS (020 7436 2181/
www.backtobasics.uk.com). Goodge Street or Oxford
Circus tube. **Lunch served** noon-3pm, **dinner**
served 6-10.30pm Mon-Sat. **Main courses**
£12.75-£15.95. **Credit** AmEx, DC, MC, V.
Back to Basics has two contrasting personas, the
summer lunchtimes when the tables are streetside,
and the (more usual) chillier evenings, when it is
intimate, quiet and romantically lit. The menu,
chalked up on the board, changes daily and
maintains a high standard: big dishes of expertly
cooked fish with delicious flavour combinations,
such as sea bass with Asian greens and a Thai-
infused sauce or the more robust cod with feta and
sun-dried tomatoes. Dishes are served in big white
bowls with plenty of salad and tasty extras. A
highlight of the meal is the bread – half a white loaf,
warm from the oven and served on a wood board
with flavoured butters: garlic, sun-dried tomato and
mushroom. And wine is served in big goldfish bowl
glasses. One drawback – service is a bit brusque.

Bodean's

10 Poland Street, W1F 8PZ (020 7287 7575/
www.bodeansbbq.com). Oxford Circus or Piccadilly
Circus tube. Deli **Open** noon-11pm daily. *Restaurant*
Lunch served noon-3pm, **dinner served** 6-11pm
Mon-Fri. **Meals served** noon-11pm Sat; noon-
10.30pm Sun. **Main courses** £6-£25. **Credit**
AmEx, MC, V.
This is one of those establishments that makes your
heart jump – a good barbecue in Soho at a
reasonable price. We never dared dream it was
possible. But it is, and we'll be damned if it's not
done right. Our waiter was working his first night
and we loved him instantly for being the provider
of a rich bowl of chowder thick with clams and
potatoes as a starter. A main course of an entire set
of baby back ribs was huge, flavour-packed and so
tender it fell off the bone. A half-slab of pork ribs
was equally perfect. Side dishes of western-style
beans (in a spicy tomato sauce) and crisp coleslaw
were excellent. A couple of bottles of ice-cold beer
on the side and we were in heaven.

Busaba Eathai ★

22 Store Street, WC1 7DS (020 7299 7900/
www.basuba.com). Goodge Street or Tottenham
Court Road tube. **Meals served** noon-11pm Mon-
Thur; noon-11.30pm Fri, Sat; noon-10pm Sun. **Credit**
AmEx, JCB, MC, V.
With a sleek, woody interior packed with large
communal tables, all full of diners, Busaba is a brisk
place for busy people to eat great food. This new
branch is, so far, less crowded than the very

successful Wardour Street original. The menu's
options range from spring rolls to noodles and rice
dishes in diverse vegetarian and meaty versions. All
layer flavour without ever letting the fresh
ingredients – juicy oyster mushrooms, plump
prawns, crisp asparagus and succulent greens – be
dominated by dark sauces or crunchy peanut
dressings. Green veg curry was good, though pad
Thai jay was slightly dull. After a mountain of
noodles and a side order of 'morning glory' green
beans, you'll be quite content with the many fruit
and vegetable juices offered as an alternative to a
dessert menu, or lemongrass tea with honey.

Chowki ★

2-3 Denman Street, W1D 7HA (020 7439 1330).
Piccadilly Circus tube. **Meals served** noon-11.30pm
Mon-Sat; noon-10.30pm Sun. **Main courses** £5.95-
£8.95. **Set meal** £10.95 3 courses. **Credit** AmEx,
DC, MC, V.
An uninspiring location, on a side street within a
roti's throw of Piccadilly Circus, doesn't deter diners
from enjoying homely Indian meals here. Maroon
leatherette banquettes and dark formica-topped
tables are a tad gloomy, but what's lacking by way
of decor is made up for by some jolly decent cooking.
Kuldeep Singh, the owner, draws upon different
areas of India each month to produce traditional
specialities with delightfully varied cooking styles.
Friendly waiters will happily offer pearls of wisdom
when you're making decisions. On our last visit, the
cooking of Mangalore, Benares and the Parsee
community inspired chefs to recreate delectable
dishes. Sweetly spiced banana fritters rolled in
crunchy poppy seeds were top-notch and made an
unusual Parsee starter. Equally satisfying was a
main of warming chicken curry, seasoned with nutty-
tasting Mangalorean spices from West India.

Eagle Bar Diner

3-5 Rathbone Place, W1T 1HJ (020 7637 1418/
www.eaglebardiner.com). Tottenham Court Road
tube. **Meals served** 8am-11pm Mon-Fri; 11am-11pm
Sat; 11am-7pm Sun. **Main courses** £4-£8.75.
Credit MC, V.
The Eagle is a postmodern all-day diner that, come
sundown, seamlessly morphs into a cocktail bar of
distinction. This is achieved by classy design – high-
backed green snugs fronted by brown sofas facing
a long zinc bar with fluorescent pink back shelving
– and by imaginative touches like a gutted old Coke
machine offering the day's papers. This is diner chic:
it looks, tastes (and hits your wallet) like the Beverly
Hills version of an American roadside diner. Burgers
are big, made of prime beef and served with gourmet
cheeses and excellent bread; the 8oz rump steak

Fino

burger was a tad dry, but very good. A grilled tuna burger, covered in monterey jack cheese, was the stuff of dreams. Ditto an excellent bowl of fat chips. We loved the American-themed cocktails, Martinis (complete with marshmallows, peanut butter and liquorice) and milkshakes (banana and peanut butter!), plus a selection of little-seen Atlantic-crossing beers including fine Brooklyn Lager. Service is friendly and it's a handy refuge from the ugly end of Oxford Street.

Fino

33 Charlotte Street, W1T 1RR (7813 8010/ www.finorestaurant.com). Goodge Street tube. **Lunch served** noon-3.30pm Mon-Fri. **Dinner served** 6-10.30pm Mon-Sat. **Tapas** £3-£12. **Set meal** £17.95 5 tapas. **Credit** AmEx, MC, V.

Opened in March 2003, Fino is the latest in a line of efforts to serve high-quality tapas in a sophisticated setting. The blond wood-panelled dining space is spacious and airy, despite being in a basement. It and an accompanying cocktail bar fill regularly with well-heeled customers. Carefully sourced fresh ingredients are key to the tapas-only menu, but dishes are also cooked and presented with flair. High points included succulent tiger prawns with aïoli and smooth, creamy wild mushroom croquettes; a tortilla featured unusually subtle chorizo; chickpeas with spinach and bacon were a smooth urban version of a rustic standard. The only disappointment was the Jabugo ham, which fell short on flavour. Sherries headline the drinks list, but there are also select modern Spanish wines. Friendly young staff keep diners happy. The main hitch is the price: a full meal with wine easily reaches £40 per head.

Hakkasan ★

8 Hanway Place, W1P 9DH (020 7907 1888). Tottenham Court Road tube. Bar **Open** noon-midnight Mon-Wed; noon-2am Thur-Sat; noon-11.30pm Sun. *Restaurant* **Lunch served** noon-3.30pm Mon-Fri; noon-5pm Sat, Sun.

Dinner served 6pm-midnight Mon-Sat; 6-11pm Sun. **Main courses** £5.90-£40. **Dim sum** £3.50-£16. **Credit** AmEx, MC, V.

Alan Yau's basement bar and Michelin-starred restaurant must be one of the most stylish venues in town: a slinky assembly of black furniture on black tiles, with black wooden structures framing the bar and partitioning the dining area. Shadowy figures can be spotted in the kitchen, through a turquoise haze of misted glass. Service and food usually live up to the setting. Both dim sum and full menus are brim-full of novel interpretations of traditional dishes. Not everything works, but much does – meltingly light taro croquettes; delectable Chinese chive dumplings, beautiful in green translucent wrappers; stir-fried watercress with salty, pungent century eggs and exquisite stock; roasted silver cod with champagne and Chinese honey. Prices are high at Hakkasan, but you get what you pay for.

Lindsay House

21 Romilly Street, W1V 5AF (020 7439 0450/ www.lindsayhouse.co.uk). Leicester Square tube. **Lunch served** noon-2.30pm Mon-Sat. **Dinner served** 6-11pm Mon-Sat. **Main courses** (lunch) £18-£22. **Pre-theatre set dinner** (6-6.45pm Mon-Sat) £24 2 courses, £29.50 3 courses. **Set dinner** £48 3 courses. **Credit** AmEx, DC, MC, V.

Behind a discreet front door (kept firmly shut – you'll need to ring the bell), this sophisticated townhouse restaurant has two small dining rooms on two floors. Colours are muted, table settings are simple and floors are bare; the focus is kept squarely on the food, with outstanding results. Chef Richard Corrigan makes great use of market-fresh ingredients in dishes like fat scallops teamed with salty pork belly and spiced carrots. While the Irish influence seems less prevalent than it once was, his cooking has a restrained elegance that's truly memorable – roast organic chicken with lasagne of asparagus and caramelised ceps was among the most satisfying dishes we tried all year. Portion sizes

leave room for superb puddings: vanilla crème brûlée with Granny Smith sorbet and caramelised apple had us slumped in cross-eyed ecstasy. The friendly staff, the unobtrusive clientele and, above all, the wine list add to the enjoyment.

Maison Bertaux ★

28 Greek Street, W1V 5LL (020 7437 6007).
Leicester Square or Piccadilly Circus tube.
Food served 8.30am-8pm daily. **No credit cards**.
The rivalry's not quite Arsenal/Spurs, but true Sohoites tend to be either Pâtisserie Valerie (*see p35*) people or Maison Bertaux people; the twain rarely meet. Nothing ever seems to change at this gem. Happily, the stasis extends to the food (as ever, magnificent) and the welcome (wonderfully warm). Savoury snacks stretch to slices of pizza and terrific quiches; sweet things range from the fruity to the creamy (the eclairs here positively define naughty but nice). The croissants are legendary.

Mar i Terra ★

17 Air Street, W1B 5AF (020 7734 1992/
www.mariterra.co.uk). Piccadilly Circus tube. **Lunch served** noon-3pm, **dinner served** 5-11pm Mon-Fri. **Meals served** noon-11pm Sat; 1-10pm Sun (closed Sun July-Sept). **Tapas** £1.50-£8.50. **Credit** AmEx, DC, MC, V.
The Mar i Terra ('sea and land' in Catalan) enthusiastically waves the flag for modern tapas. The turquoise walls and shiny surfaces are a blessed relief from dark, smoky tapas joints. The largely Catalan-inspired menu contains a section devoted to nueva cocina – 'modern' tapas. Many feature honey: chicken is baked with it, fried aubergines are drizzled with it (and somewhat overpowered). A delicately flavoured pork dish was cooked with orange and served with rice. Jamón de Teruel, while without the lofty provenance (or jaw-dropping price tag) of Jabugo ham, was sliced paper-thin and drizzled with good olive oil. The wine list is worth a look. Add a Spanish soundtrack and polite service and we were impressed. Boring white bread lets things down a bit, but that's a minor grumble.

Masala Zone ★

9 Marshall Street, W1F 7ER (020 7287 9966).
Oxford Circus tube. **Lunch served** noon-2.45pm Mon-Fri; noon-3pm Sat; 12.30-3.30pm Sun. **Dinner served** 5.30-11pm Mon-Fri; 5-11pm Sat; 6-10.30pm Sun. **Snacks served** 3-5pm Sat. **Main courses** £5-£11. **Set thali** (not available 3-5pm Sat) £6.25-£11. **Credit** MC, V.
This large, Wagamama-esque dining hall is an immense and deserved success. Its owners have produced a pan-Indian menu that encompasses meal-in-one dishes, 'grazing platters', snacks (of the Bombay beach-food ilk) and thalis. Rarely seen ingredients and authentic regional dishes also pop up. The huge helping of the malabar seafood bowl, with flat noodles, tender squid and big prawns in a coconut milk-based soup, is more Singaporean laksa than Keralan stew, but marvellous nonetheless.

Samosas come freshly fried, round kebabs feature mousse-light flavoursome meat, and green lamb masala is a richly enjoyable curry. Equally praiseworthy are the side dishes at only 75p a throw: thali-sized pots of dahl, vegetable curry (perhaps containing tinda, which are like little cucumbers) and raita. Swift young staff cope well, and the Zone is constantly abuzz with enthusiastic diners.

Mr Kong

21 Lisle Street, WC2H 7BA (020 7437 7341/9679).
Leicester Square tube. **Meals served** noon-2.45am daily. **Main courses** £5-£26. **Minimum** £7 after 5pm. **Set meals** £10 (minimum 2 people), £22 (minimum 4 people). **Credit** AmEx, DC, MC, V.
This cheerful, unpretentious restaurant with friendly service and generous portions is renowned for steamed crab – a messy dish if you're not au fait with the cracking and extracting implements. Steamed crab is very fresh and comes soused in sour-sweet Shaoxing wine, which complements the flavours wonderfully. It's a strong and unusual taste, though, and beginners might prefer the more standard steamed crab with ginger and spring onion. The chef's specials include pearls such as steamed scallops with glass noodles (a delicious start) – tender and fresh, and served with a bowl of soy and chilli for bite. The 'sand' in the sand storm aubergine and bean curd is a mound of crispy, golden fried garlic almost burying the melting chunks of aubergine. The 'dragon whistlers' of the dragon whistlers with dried scallops are delicate green pea leaves, flavoured with tons of scallops.

Navarro's

67 Charlotte Street, W1T 4PH (020 7637 7713/
www.navarros.co.uk). Goodge Street tube. **Lunch served** noon-3pm Mon-Fri. **Dinner served** 6-10pm Mon-Sat. **Tapas** £3-£18.95. **Credit** AmEx, DC, MC, V.
For the past decade, tremendously atmospheric Navarro's has been one of London's top Spanish eateries – and it shows no sign of flagging. The decoration is a treat, of both the staff (in jaunty traditional costumes) and the dining areas (with bright wooden furniture and tiled walls). Yet the beauty is more than skin deep – you can enjoy some of the best, and most unusual, tapas in town here. From the classically simple (just try to find a better tortilla) to the rarely seen (such as a rich, satisfying chicken-and-prawns combo in an oloroso sherry and paprika sauce), there's scarcely a dud on the menu. Prawns are always good, whether dangling theatrically from a skewer on a stand at your table or char-grilled and paired with wild mushrooms. The wine list mixes classics with the unfamiliar. We defy you not to have a great evening here.

New Mayflower

68-70 Shaftesbury Avenue, W1B 6LY (020 7734 9207). Piccadilly Circus tube. **Meals served** 5pm-4am daily. **Main courses** £6.50-£45. **Minimum** £8. **Set dinner** £12, £22 (minimum 2 people). **Credit** AmEx, MC, V.

Harry Ramsden's has come to London!

Enjoy a great British tradition with Harry Ramsden's World Famous Fish and Chips in our new comfortable restaurant in the heart of London's Piccadilly.

Our menu offers a superb choice of dishes to suit all tastes. Plus there are special menus for young children, the over sixties and group bookings.
You can even enjoy a glass of wine or a beer with your meal.

When you are in a hurry, just pop into the Harry Ramsden's Express.

To make a booking, or for more information, simply call:-

0207 287 3148

or visit our website:
www.harryramsdens.co.uk

You will find us in all the right places.

Harry Ramsden's
WORLD FAMOUS FISH & CHIPS

Regent Palace Hotel, Sherwood Street, Piccadilly Circus London W1A 4BZ

The location and dark windows of this bustling, warren-like restaurant could put you off. Inside, every nook and cranny is crammed with tables and the decor is functional and bright. A carnival atmosphere often prevails thanks to big, cheerful family groups of local Chinese and jolly Chopin waltzes on the sound system. The aromatic duck with pancakes is finely crisped and not at all greasy. The steamed sea bass with spring onions (a favourite) and piquant sauce is excellent value, as well presented as at fancier restaurants charging three times the price. Crab meat with Chinese mushrooms and vegetables is a beautiful tricolour of dark, meaty mushrooms, crunchy green broccoli and pink slivers of crab. At the New Mayflower Chinese diners are often given complimentary extras: sweet pickled vegetables as an entrée and a sweet soup with white fungus to finish; non-Chinese can have them too if they ask!

Özer

5 Langham Place, W1B 3DG (020 7323 0505). Oxford Circus or Regent's Park tube. Bar **Open** noon-11pm daily. *Restaurant* **Meals served** noon-midnight daily. **Main courses** £7.50-£17.50. **Set lunch** (noon-7pm) £8 2 courses. **Set dinner** (7-11pm) £10 2 courses, £13 3 courses. **Credit** AmEx, DC, MC, V.

Proceed through the seductive front bar to the spacious eating area, thoroughly designed from the red decor and black uniforms to the glass tiles used as starter platters. Start with freshly baked pide accompanied by enormous olives and tasty, but over-refined houmous. Move on to dolma and bakla beans in yoghurt. The Özer special main is a beautiful lamb stew with aubergines and lots of nuts, and monkfish guvech is succulent rings of fish in a rich sauce. Each comes with excellent basmati rice and vegetables. Service is exceptionally attentive. Even the loos are lovely.

Patisserie Valerie ★

44 Old Compton Street, W1D 4TY (020 7437 3466/ www.patisserie-valerie.co.uk). Leicester Square, Piccadilly Circus or Tottenham Court Road tube. **Open** 7.30am-8.30pm Mon-Fri; 8am-8pm Sat; 9am-6.30pm Sun. **Main courses** £3.75-£7.95. **Credit** AmEx, DC, MC, V.

A much-loved Soho institution, and deservedly so, Valerie's has been in the area since 1926. A mouth-watering display of croissants, fruit tarts and authentic French gateaux fill the window, while chocolates, marzipan figures and other sweet treats occupy more display cases inside. Red formica-topped tables and Toulouse-Lautrec cartoons lend a 1950s Parisian café vibe to the ground floor; upstairs is lighter and less cramped (and serves wine and beer), though also less characterful. The menu offers more than just coffee and pastries. Breakfast (served until 4pm) includes fruit salad or smoked salmon and scrambled eggs; there's also a variety of toasted sandwiches (served with crisps and salad) and grilled snacks.

Pied à Terre ★

34 Charlotte Street, W1T 2NH (020 7636 1178/ www.pied.a.terre.co.uk). Goodge Street or Tottenham Court Road tube. **Lunch served** 12.15-2.30pm Tue-Fri. **Dinner served** 6.15-11pm Mon-Sat. **Main courses** £27. **Set lunch** £19.50 2 courses, £24 3 courses. **Credit** AmEx, MC, V.

In keeping with the understated decor, there's nothing glitzy about Shane Osborn's cooking: good ingredients are ideally partnered and creatively presented. It sounds easy, but what sets Pied à Terre so far apart from other restaurants is the clarity and consistency of such simple brilliance. For example, spätzle was pillow-light, glossed in a buttery hazelnut emulsion, studded with dark and luscious trompettes de la mort and topped with a soft poached egg that burst its huge golden yolk over the whole lot to exquisite effect. Likewise, pearl-white crisp-edged halibut was utterly compelling on its vividly coloured yet harmonious bed of smoked bacon and mushroom risotto, punctuated with bright froths of garden pea. So, subdued surroundings, but really great food.

Red Fort ★

77 Dean Street, W1D 3SH (020 7437 2115/ www.redfort.co.uk). Tottenham Court Road tube. **Lunch served** noon-2.15pm Mon-Fri. **Dinner served** 5.45-11.15pm Mon-Sat. **Main courses** £12.50-£28. **Set lunch** £12 2 courses. **Pre-theatre dinner** (5.45-7pm) £16 2 courses incl tea or coffee. **Credit** AmEx, DC, MC, V.

A distinctive water feature set against the back wall, brass artefacts in alcoves and marigolds floating in urns create a dramatic backdrop for utterly authentic cooking at this luxurious Soho restaurant. Chef Mohammed Rais, a top culinary name in India, has experience in cooking for maharajas, and takes pride in recreating refined spice blends from the royal kitchens of Awadh – the historical region around Lucknow. Dried rose petals sprinkled with sweet spice and lemony cardamoms paired with pounded mace are typically aromatic seasonings. Highlights of the menu include biriani samudra (seafood rice, scented with saffron and cooked in steam within a sealed clay pot) and palak ki katli (spinach leaves flash-fried with mild chilli powder, garlic and onions). Service is slick, unobtrusive and doesn't get flustered, even when busy. Red Fort's attention to the finer aspects of traditional cooking sets it apart as London's top Indian restaurant.

Sardo

45 Grafton Way, W1T 5LA (020 7387 2521/ www.sardo-restaurant.com). Warren Street tube. **Lunch served** noon-3pm Mon-Fri. **Dinner served** 6-11pm Mon-Sat. **Main courses** £8.90-£18. **Credit** AmEx, DC, MC, V.

That such a simple-looking restaurant can be full-to-bursting on a Monday night indicates the respect Sardo has garnered since it first opened just a few years ago. The shift from friendly posh pizzeria to high altar of Sardinian cuisine is clearly paying off.

Try dishes like artichokes and thinly shaved Sardinian bottarga (dried mullet roe); sun-dried tuna fillet with fresh beans and sun-dried tomatoes; fregola cooked with courgette, sprinkled with exquisitely fresh white crab meat; and aromatic char-grilled own-made Sardinian sausages, served with delicious mostarda di frutta. On the subject of wines, your best move is simply to be guided by the gregarious owner, who is constantly looking for bottles to tantalise customers with and offers many reasonably priced options from his beloved homeland.

The Sugar Club ★

21 Warwick Street, W1R 5RB (020 7437 7776/ www.thesugarclub.co.uk). Oxford Circus or Piccadilly Circus tube. **Lunch served** noon-3pm Tue-Fri. **Dinner served** 5.30-11pm Mon-Sat; 6-10.30pm Sun. **Main courses** £13.90-£22. **Set menu** (lunch, 5.30-6.30pm Mon-Sat) £15.50 2 courses, £19.50 3 courses. **Credit** AmEx, DC, JCB, MC, V.

Little to look at, decor-wise, and not inconsiderable prices ('organic and wild produce used where possible') mean that the food here has to be pretty special. And it is. Even a simple sounding starter such as rocket and parmesan salad with sage anchovy fritters will be more than the sum of its parts. Typical mains might be ginger-steamed John Dory and queen scallop wun tun with Siamese watercress, chilli and fermented yellow bean stir-fry. or grilled rump steak on yakisoba noodle pancake with soy-braised Asian mushrooms. Puds are the likes of maple syrup crème brûlée with peaches or Valrhona chocolate mousse cake with blueberries and whipped cream. The lively ground floor is considered more 'fun', but diners who wish to talk will be more interested in the basement. Service is utterly charming.

Table Café ★

Basement of Habitat, 196 Tottenham Court Road, W1P 6LX (020 7636 8330). Goodge Street tube. **Breakfast served** 10-11.45am, **lunch served** noon-4pm, **tea served** 4-5.30pm daily. **Main courses** £6.60-£8. **Set lunch** £7.50 2 courses. **Credit** MC, V.

A thriving daytime destination in the basement of Habitat. The appeal lies partly in the wholesome Italian-biased menu, which focuses on fresh ingredients simply prepared. Chicken and vegetable salad is a moist, moreish pyramid of finely chopped health. For dessert, try creamy, very sweet torrone semifreddo, or the coconut loaf cake that arrived in hefty slices. There's a good choice of soft drinks – freshly squeezed carrot juice, traditional lemonade, Big Tom and elegant apple juices – plus coffees. Be sure to arrive early or late during the week; at peak times it's packed.

La Trouvaille ★

12A Newburgh Street, W1F 7RR (020 7287 8488/ www.latrouvaille.co.uk). Oxford Circus tube. **Lunch served** noon-3pm, **dinner served** 6-11pm Mon-Sat.

Main courses £12.50-£17.95. **Set lunch** £16.95 2 courses, £19.75 3 courses. **Credit** AmEx, DC, JCB, MC, V.

La Trouvaille is some find: slightly crazy, thoroughly inspired French food served by slightly crazy, adrenaline-fired French staff. How about a flower salad with fiddlehead fern fritters, liquorice bisque with beef skirt or a mature cheddar milkshake with strawberry charlotte? Suspend your disbelief, and ask for the waiter's recommendations – this should produce a memorable meal, starting perhaps with three tender cubes of marinated duck magret, each topped with a different seed coating (dill, poppy and celery), skewered ready to be dipped in herb fromage frais; followed by rich, flavour-dense Herdwick mutton fillet (how often do you find mutton?) with a lilting lavender sauce, garlic and grilled courgettes; and crowned by a transcendent chocolate and violet coulant, wild cherry and goat yoghurt. It's all very witty yet ungimmicky food cooked by an assured, inventive hand; paired with a casual, relaxed atmosphere and highly enthusiastic Antoine de Caunes-like staff, you have a winning restaurant.

YMing

35-36 Greek Street, W1D 5DL (020 7734 2721/ www.yming.com). Leicester Square, Piccadilly Circus or Tottenham Court Road tube. **Meals served** noon-11.45pm Mon-Sat. **Main courses** £6-£12. **Set lunch** £10 3 courses (noon-6pm). **Set meals** £15, £17, £20 (minimum 2 people). **Credit** AmEx, DC, MC, V.

An enticing menu, unfailingly helpful staff and a serene atmosphere make YMing a welcome refuge from the hurly-burly of nearby Chinatown. Owner Christine Yau, one of the leading lights in London's Chinese community, offers delicious regional dishes you're unlikely to find elsewhere in London, but in a European-style restaurant ambience. On our last visit, we enjoyed the scrumptious 'village duck', a Hakka concoction of duck, lily flowers and shiitake mushrooms in a sauce luxuriant with fermented beancurd, and a fine spicy-sour stir-fry of Chinese cabbage. The fish in Chinese rice wine sauce with wood ear fungus was superbly seasoned. Deep-fried starters are usually well done: try the yummy 'aubergine delight' topped with a smidgeon of black bean sauce. Dine in the peaceful upstairs dining rooms with someone you really want to talk to, or throw a private dinner party in the dramatic purple chamber downstairs.

Also in the area

Busaba Eathai 106-110 Wardour Street, W1F 0TR (020 7255 8686); **Café Lazeez** 21 Dean Street, W1D 3RS (020 7434 9393); **Carluccio's** 8 Market Place, W1W 8AG (020 7636 2228); **Livebait Café Fish** 36-40 Rupert Street, W1V 7FR (020 7287 8989); **Rasa Samudra** 5 Charlotte Street, W1T 1RE (020 7637 0222); **Strada** 9-10 Market Place, W1W 8AQ (020 7580 4644); **Wagamama** 10A Lexington Street, W1R 3HS (020 7292 0990).

Covent Garden & Bloomsbury

The Admiralty

Somerset House, The Strand, WC2R 1LA (020 7845 4646). Charing Cross tube/rail. **Lunch served** noon-2.30pm daily. **Dinner served** 6-10.30pm Mon-Sat. **Set meals** (lunch, 6-7pm Mon-Fri) £28 4 courses. **Set dinner** £28 2 courses, £33 3 courses, £37 5 courses (vegetarian), £42 5 courses (dégustation). **Credit** AmEx, DC, JCB, MC, V.

The Admiralty's dining room is gorgeous – restrained nautical decor and fantastical chandeliers – and the food hovers between good and great. The menu is nicely conceived, comprising a tasting menu, a short à la carte with an interesting fish section, and a vegetarian menu. A typical winter dish would be snail ravioli with artichokes, poached garlic and wine butter, or pigeon with puy lentils, pommes Anna, onion soubise and red wine jus, served neat on the plate and distinct in every ingredient (the food all comes from French markets, and it shows). The wine list is well constructed, and the positively Mephistophelean dessert list guarantees that you shortly will be. Staff, while skilled, can be a little lackadaisical.

Christopher's

18 Wellington Street, WC2E 7DD (020 7240 4222/ www.christophersgrill.com). Covent Garden, Embankment or Temple tube/Charing Cross tube/rail. **Bar Open** 11.30am-11pm Mon-Sat. *Restaurant* **Brunch served** 11.30am-4pm Sat, Sun. **Lunch served** noon-3.45pm Mon-Fri. **Dinner served** 5pm-midnight Mon-Sat. **Main courses** £12-£28. **Set dinner** (5-7pm, 10pm-midnight Mon-Sat) £12.95 2 courses, £16.50 3 courses. **Credit** AmEx, DC, MC, V.

A recent and long overdue renovation has transformed Christopher's from faded glory to modern beauty. In particular, the ground-floor bar is elegant, sleek and (so far) largely undiscovered. The first-floor restaurant has been tactfully done up in neutral colours, with modern touches and classy fixtures. At last the look of the place fits the menu and service, both of which are excellent. Starters might be a light and airy goat's cheese mousseline or a divinely dark, rich, heavy pheasant ravioli. It's hard to beat a main of classic ribeye with chips, and then an indulgent chocolate soufflé for pudding. The quality wine list only enhances the experience.

Cigala ★

54 Lamb's Conduit Street, WC1N 3LW (020 7405 1717/www.cigala.co.uk). Holborn or Russell Square tube. **Lunch served** noon-3pm Mon-Fri; 12.30-3.45pm Sat. **Dinner served** 6-10.45pm Mon-Sat. **Meals served** 12.30-9.30pm Sun. **Main courses** £11-£17. **Tapas** £2-£8. **Set lunch** (Mon-Fri) £15 2 courses, £18 3 courses. **Set dinner** £30 6 courses. **Credit** AmEx, DC, MC, V.

Cigala is a slick operation, with attentive service, high-quality food and classy surroundings. Black-clad waiting staff whisk around the smart white and pine restaurant with an air of tremendous efficiency and, even better, they actually know their stuff. Tapas high notes include cecina (oak-smoked cured beef) served with mini gherkins, and moreish king prawns al pil pil served in a bread-dippingly good white wine, parsley, garlic and chilli sauce. A main course of grilled sea bass was marred only by the bland accompanying escalivada (Catalan-style

Savoy Grill. *See p43.*

ratatouille). The wine list has plenty of characterful vintages under £30. Beware the ultra-filling own-made bread while waiting for your food and note that tapas can only be eaten in the basement tapas bar or at the outside tables.

Food for Thought ★

31 Neal Street, WC2H 9PR (020 7836 9072).
Covent Garden tube. **Breakfast served** 9.30-11.30am Mon-Sat. **Lunch served** noon-5pm daily. **Dinner served** 5-8.30pm Mon-Sat. **Main courses** £3-£6.50. **No credit cards**.

This café has been dishing out tasty, inviting fare in unpretentious surroundings for nigh on three decades. Snagging a seat in the basement usually leads to table-sharing, lunchtime takeaway queues are long and dishes sometimes run out, but these are testament to the enduring popularity of the place. The reliably good, daily-changing global menu might include Indonesian curry and noodles; Middle Eastern bake with roasted veg, minted yoghurt and almonds; or portobello mushrooms stuffed with rocket pesto risotto and served with saffron chickpea stew and salad. Stir-fries, soup, quiche and salads are further options. Desserts (crumbles and fruit salads), cakes and bread (lemon and poppyseed scones, doorstop flapjacks) also rate highly. There are always vegan, wheat- and dairy-free choices.

The Gaucho Grill

125-126 Chancery Lane, WC2A 1PU (020 7242 7727/www.thegauchogrill.co.uk). Chancery Lane tube. **Meals served** noon-11pm Mon-Fri. **Main courses** £9-£20. **Credit** AmEx, DC, JCB, MC, V.

Only the cowskin seats evoke the pampas at these upscale grill houses; the Holborn branch is a super-slick lounge of cool black-and-white spaces. The Argentinian food is usually classy (though it occasionally slips) and the prices are aristocratic. The sweetbread and black pudding starters are small but tasty, while the steaks are petite compared with their equivalents in the homeland, though of excellent quality. The carbonada is sweet to taste, but more a refined soup than a hearty stew. Desserts include dulce de leche crêpe – a melt-in-your-mouth experience – or a trad Argentine ice-cream and whisky finisher called Don Pedro.

Hazuki ★

43 Chandos Place, WC2 4HS (020 7240 2530). Charing Cross tube/rail. **Lunch served** noon-2.30pm Mon-Fri. **Dinner served** 5.30-10.30pm Mon-Sat; 5.30-9.30pm Sun. **Main courses** £5-£11. **Credit** AmEx, JCB, MC, V.

Hazuki offers a handy central location, classy but accessible surroundings and good, affordable Japanese food. White walls, soft lighting and a dark-floored, low-ceilinged mezzanine decorated with zen-like flower arrangements and pebbles make a soothing setting for a meal. A typical lunch might consist of boiled daikon in a 'Japanese citrus' sauce, fresh, flavourful and artfully arrayed sashimi, horenso goma ae (spinach in a sesame sauce), and

tori karage (small savoury chunks of chicken fried in flour). The nest of green tea-flavoured seaweed filaments served beside the sashimi makes an interesting counterpoint of flavour and texture to the fish. A refreshing accompaniment is the sweet drink calpico, made from fermented milk.

The Ivy ★

1 West Street, WC2H 9NQ (020 7836 4751). Leicester Square tube. **Lunch served** noon-3pm Mon-Sat; noon-3.30pm Sun. **Dinner served** 5.30pm-midnight daily. **Main courses** £8.75-£21.75. **Set lunch** (Sat, Sun) £18.50 3 courses. **Cover** £1.50 (lunch). **Credit** AmEx, DC, JCB, MC, V.

The difficulty of booking a table at the Ivy is almost as legendary as the restaurant itself (phone several months ahead and cross your fingers). Once inside, however, any hasssle is forgotten as the wonderfully courteous staff take your coats and see you to your table. In spite of all the hype and the tedious celebrity association, the Ivy really is a lovely place to eat. The dining room is smart, but understated; latticed windows dotted with panes of coloured glass allow light in but keep the world at bay. A long, tempting menu offers brilliant but unpretentious renditions of traditional French and British fare, with a scattering of fusion dishes. Start, perhaps, across the Channel with a sautéed foie gras on an apple tart with a ragged halo of dark raisin jus, before returning home for a classic shepherd's pie, and then finish with warm, caramelised apricots with elderflower ice-cream. A treat.

Orso

27 Wellington Street, WC2E 7DB (020 7240 5269/ www.joeallen.co.uk). Covent Garden tube. **Meals served** noon-midnight daily. **Main courses** £8.50-£16. **Set lunch** (noon-5pm Sat, Sun) £18.50 2 courses, £20.50 3 courses incl glass of champagne or Bloody Mary. **Set dinner** (5-6.45pm Mon-Sat) £16 2 courses, £18 3 courses incl coffee. **Credit** AmEx, MC, V.

Although long established and showing signs of wear, Orso still has a smart image. A short list of pizzas and all-day opening makes this colourful basement restaurant appeal to families and American tourists in particular, and to suit the clientele portions are typically generous and service outgoing and friendly. Palate-pleasing dishes include crab meat, courgettes and lemon risotto; hearty soups of the day (white bean with purple sprouting broccoli, for instance); rich slow-roast pork with wonderful crackling, sagey roast potatoes and baked apple; grilled seafood with rocket and peppers; and desserts like pear and almond tart or strawberries with pepper and balsamic. The wine list is notable for its small-jug options, which include 500ml of house wine for customers who can't decide whether to have a glass or a bottle.

Paul ★

29 Bedford Street, WC2E 9ED (020 7836 3304). Covent Garden tube. **Meals served** 7.30am-9pm Mon-Fri; 9am-9pm Sat, Sun. **Credit** AmEx, JCB, MC, V.

Bar crawl: London

Exciting times these. While London pubs struggle against closure, cack-handed conversions and corporate mismanagement, the capital's bar scene flourishes. There's not a week goes by without a thud on the desk announcing the arrival of some overstuffed package filled with PR guff trumpeting the opening of the capital's newest best bar. Actually, a surprising number of these places are good, going on very good.

The reasons for this are no great mystery. Whereas pubs tend to be owned by multi-tentacled conglomerates, misled by marketing teams and answerable only to shareholders, bars are largely one-offs, or the work of small independent enterprises that typically make up in vision and enthusiasm what they lack in cash. Bar operators are quick to spot new trends, identify niches and break ground in up-and-coming areas. With no real blueprint for what a London bar should be, reinvention is rife. The last 12 months alone have added notable new venues in the diverse forms of the American diner-cum-cocktail bar **Eagle Bar Diner** (3-5 Rathbone Place, W1; 020 7637 1418), the South Seas theme bar **South London Pacific** (340 Kennington Road, SE11; 020 7820 9189) and an American Deep South juke joint **Boogaloo** (312 Archway Road, N6; 020 8340 2928).

DJ bars continue to proliferate at a giddy rate, both in the form of new start-ups and clubby revamps of existing old drinking dens. However, they've transformed from pre-club hangouts to buzzy destinations in their own right. The best, like **Market Place** (11 Market Place, W1; 020 7079 2020) and **The Social**, pictured (5 Little Portland Street, W1; 020 7636 4992), are intimate, convivial places to drink, eat and mingle until late. They also offer diverse music that appeals to a broad church, far beyond hardcore clubbers. Prime DJ-bar territory remains the electro swamps of Hoxton/Shoreditch and, south of the river, Brixton, but good venues are now scattered throughout the A-Z.

If there's a prevailing theme right now, it's glamour. Recent openings like Notting Hill's **Lonsdale** (44-48 Lonsdale Road, W11; 020 7228 1517) was winner of the *Time Out* Eating & Drinking Best Bar Award 2003. It razzles and dazzles with walls studded by rows of aged bronze hemispheres like some oversized

Paracetamol foil packaging, lush red carpets and patterned, fake fur upholstery. **Aura** (48-49 St James Street, SW1; 020 7499 6655) mixes the glam (plum-coloured leather banquettes and cut-glass chandeliers formerly of Claridge's ballroom) with the kitsch (a fresco of topless ladies at the entrance and comic book panelling behind the bar). But even this pales beside the high camp excess of **Loungelover** (1 Whitby Street, EC1; 020 7012 1234), which boasts gaily coloured anatomical models, a decaying doll's house, small stuffed mammals, mounted marlin heads, painted fairground gallopers and myriad light fittings – from Chinese lanterns to starburst chandeliers and glowing-tipped crowns.

In such high-gloss settings, a weak, auntyish tumbler of G&T just doesn't cut it and drink of choice is the cocktail. Nothing new in that; Londoners have been mixing their drinks since the 1920s, when sensible barmen fled Prohibition-era America for Europe, some of them setting up over here to continue their demon dabbling in alcohol. **The American Bar** (Savoy Hotel, Strand, WC2; 020 7836 4343) was one of the first to serve cocktails in England and it still lays claim to the best vodka Martini in town. These days it's easier than ever to get a properly made, innovative booze fusion. The current crop of barmen who take their craft very seriously indeed are led by the likes of Dick Bradsell, who has consulted to more bars than most of us have had hangovers – notably the award-winning **Match** trio (37-38 Margaret Street, W1, 020 7499 3443; 45-47 Clerkenwell Road, EC1, 020 7250 4002; 2 Tabernacle Street, EC2, 020 7920 0701). But there's also Douglas Ankrah, the creative barman behind the excellent **Akbar** (77 Dean Street, W1; 020 7437 2525) and **Townhouse** (31 Beauchamp Place, SW3; 020 7493 8000). Even the staff of the grottiest old man's boozer are now expected to be able to shake, stir, blend and muddle to order, with the ability to concoct a kick-ass Bloody Mary being a minimum job requirement.

Modern London bars are also specialists. Vodka fans can travel to **The Baltic** (74 Blackfriars Road, SE1; 020 7928 1111) or favour the Polish product at **Na Zdrowie** (11 Little Turnstile, WC1; 020 7831 9679). For bourbon, there's

EST. LONDON 1997

Grand Central (93 Great Eastern Street, EC1; 020 7613 4228) and **Rockwell** (Trafalgar Hotel, 2 Spring Gardens, SW1; 020 7870 2959). The latter is a purveyor of over 80 varieties of bourbon, to be served straight or on the rocks, added to mixed specials or delicately dripped into antique brand-tasting glasses. If gin's your thing, get up to **Steam** (1 Eastbourne Terrace, W2; 020 7850 0555) at Paddington. Here, they have their own take on the Bloody Mary, which replaces tomato juice with San Franciscan Anchor Steam beer and vodka with mother's ruin.

Visitors to the capital might not even have to stray much further than a corridor crawl from their bedrooms to find a stylish spot for a short, shot or long drink. A handful of the smartest bars in town are attached to hotels. Some of these are old school, such as the aforementioned American Bar at the Savoy (home of the White Lady, but welcoming of any suitably attired), and **Claridge's Bar** (Claridge's Hotel, 49 Brook Street, W1; 020 7629 8860) which, despite a recent revamp, remains an absolute classic. However, you may need to send up flares to secure the attention of snooty staff. Spirit specialist **Rockwell** (*see above*) is more typical of the

modern hotel bar, joined as it is to the hip Trafalgar Hotel. Berkeley Hotel's **Blue Bar** (Wilton Place, SW1; 020 7235 6000) is an *Ab-Fab* gossipy den of Wedgwood-hued boho chic (Madonna liked it so much she had her living room done up just like it). Meanwhile **mybar** (11 Bayley Street, WC1; 020 7667 6000) perfectly fits the feng shui ambience of its host myhotel. This is lifestyle accommodation designed 'with cutting-edge philosophers, sensitive aromatherapists and seasoned world travellers' in mind. Get past the verbosity and it's just a cool little bar that knows how to fix a fine drink.

Not everything is ring-a-ding-ding. Drinks can be laughably expensive. Someone has to foot the interior designer's bills and fork out for the PR company's retainer – and it's likely to be you, the punter. And if a place is good and gets too much trade, there's always the threat of the membership bar descending. That means your new favourite bar suddenly closes its doors to all but those invited to cough up several hundred pounds per annum for the privilege of continuing to drink there. What to do? Easy: just shrug your shoulders and wait – this is London, there'll be another place opening any minute now.

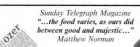

The smart black exteriors of this quality French chain are now starting to be recognised in cities worldwide as it expands globally. Paul's deserved popularity is due to the quality of its superbly fresh pâtisserie and bakery goods, coupled with upmarket design and utterly classic interiors. The café area in this branch is surprisingly welcoming and relaxed, despite the grandiose decor. The menu could be straight from a Paris café. Dishes on offer include omelettes (mushroom, ham, cheese, or 'complet'), gratins, soups and generous-sized salads, each for around £5; or you could choose a sandwich, quiche, or tempting cake or fruit tart from the takeaway counter to eat in. The only un-Parisian element of the experience is the gracious service.

Prospect Grill ★

4-6 Garrick Street, WC2E 9BH (020 7379 0412). Covent Garden or Leicester Square tube. **Lunch served** 11.45am-3.30pm, **dinner served** 5.45-11.45pm Mon-Fri. **Meals served** 11.45am-11.45pm Sat. **Main courses** £9.95-£15.95. **Set lunch** £14.95 2 courses, £16.95 3 courses. **Credit** AmEx, MC, V.

For several years running the Prospect has been our favourite North American restaurant in London, and it remains so today. The atmosphere is classy without being stuffy; the look is low-key private club. Service is attentive without being obsequious or intrusive; food is simple and good, and often organic and free-range. We started with raspberry Martinis and classic pâté served with thin slices of toast – the drinks were fruity, the pâté creamy and rich. Next, fillet steak (grass-fed) with béarnaise sauce was tender and well cooked, the sauce served on the side so we could use as much as we wanted. Another main of grilled free-range pork chop was thick and tasty, with a side of fried mixed peppers. Ice-cream and sorbet provided a smooth end.

Rules

35 Maiden Lane, WC2E 7LB (020 7836 5314/ www.rules.co.uk). Covent Garden tube. **Meals served** noon-11.30pm Mon-Sat; noon-10.30pm Sun. **Main courses** £16.95-£22.50. **Credit** AmEx, DC, MC, V.

A restaurant that wears its history on its sleeve, Rules has no shortage of tourist diners marvelling at the solid tradition of its dining room (comfortably upholstered banquettes, walls cluttered with pictures, stuffed animal trophies) or cooing over the wood-panelled Edward VII private room. But despite all this, a meal here is never less than enjoyable, and at times even sublime. Meat and game are carefully sourced (sometimes from the restaurant's own estate in the high Pennines), and the quality shows in excellent starters like thickly sliced smoked salmon or rich stilton-and-walnut tart. Among the mains, grilled rump steak comes exactly as ordered, while succulent duck breast is pepped up by tart five-spice chutney. Desserts suit the tastes (and are probably responsible for the waistlines) of many of the old-school gents who like to eat here. Staff treat all-comers with polished efficiency, and the wine list has something for everyone.

The Savoy Grill

The Savoy Hotel, Strand, WC2R 0EU (020 7420 2065/www.savoy-group.com). Covent Garden or Embankment tube/Charing Cross tube/rail. **Lunch served** noon-2.45pm Mon-Fri; noon-3.15pm Sat, Sun. **Dinner served** 5.45-11pm Mon-Sat; 6-10.30pm Sun. **Set dinner** (5.45-6.45pm Mon-Sat) £25 3 courses; £35 3 courses; (7-11pm Mon-Sat) £45 tasting menu. **Credit** AmEx, JCB, MC, V.

Like a gouty old major sleeping off his lunch, the Savoy Grill has always left new-fangled living to the youngsters. Until now. A light redesign and the arrival of new chef Marcus Wareing has brought this great British restaurant blinking into the 21st century. The shimmering staff and clubby vibe of the dining room, with its boldly striped liquorice and caramel banquettes, remain, as do the old-world clientele, but the menu has distinct haute cuisine overtones. Starters like roast scallops with fresh pea purée or caramelised calf's sweetbreads on pancetta and onion marmalade bear the hallmarks of a deft hand. Mains still offer extra padding in the carvery and grill section, but the lion's share are delicate, inventive dishes like delicious braised pork belly with sautéed Jerusalem artichoke. Puds are similarly accomplished and quite fun (rum baba macerated in Malibu). As for the wine list, you may find yourself looking long and hard for affordable bottles.

J Sheekey ★

28-32 St Martin's Court, WC2N 4AL (020 7240 2565). Leicester Square tube. **Lunch served** noon-3pm Mon-Sat; noon-3.30pm Sun. **Dinner served** 5.30pm-midnight Mon-Sat; 6pm-midnight Sun. **Main courses** £9.75-£29.95. **Set lunch** (Sat, Sun) £14.75 2 courses, £18.50 3 courses. **Cover** £1.50. **Credit** AmEx, DC, MC, V.

Dining at J Sheekey is a special experience. Similar to its better-known sister the Ivy, it has a beautiful interior, food that's simple but of the highest quality, and surprisingly reasonable prices. But here you're less likely to have Simon Callow on one side of you and Patsy Palmer on the other – which means you won't have to book months in advance to get a table. The menu is a mix of traditional dishes and more experimental ones: sublime fish pie next to squid with chorizo or wafer-thin tuna carpaccio with fennel. Desserts are also perfect: familiar apple crumble next to extravagant zabaglione. Staff are exceptionally professional, but relaxed and friendly at the same time. Sheekey has all the qualities of an über-smart eaterie, but without bad-taste decor and stuffiness. One of London's best.

Also in the area

Bank 1 Kingsway, WC2B 6XF (020 7979 9797); **Livebait** 21 Wellington Street, WC2E 7DA (020 7836 7161); **Loch Fyne** 2-4 Catherine Street, WC2B 5JS (020 7240 4999); **Strada** 6 Great Queen Street, WC2B 5DH (020 7405 6293); **Wagamama** 4A Streatham Street, WC1A 1JB (020 7323 9223); **Wagamama** 14A Irving Street, WC2H 7AF (020 7839 2323); **Wagamama** 1 Tavistock Street, WC2E 7PG (020 7836 3330).

Clerkenwell & the City

Arkansas Café ★

Unit 12, 107B Commercial Street, Old Spitalfields Market, E1 6AA (020 7377 6999). Liverpool Street tube/rail. **Lunch served** noon-2.30pm Mon-Fri; noon-4pm Sun. **Dinner served** by arrangement. **Main courses** £5-£14.50. **Credit** MC, V.

Barbecue, steaks, roasted duck – what more could you want? Well, you might want comfortable seats, Mozart on the sound system and bottles of Châteauneuf-du-Pape slowly decanted, but that just ain't gonna happen here. The Arkansas Café is a rough and ready sort of place tucked away inside Spitalfields Market, but the food could not be better if it were served in Chelsea by a waiter with a PhD. Bubba, the Yank owner-chef, is loud-mouthed, friendly and funny, and he knows his meat and how to cook it. His barbecue platter features succulent roast chicken, tender brisket and sagey sausage with beans, tart coleslaw, purple cabbage and mash – all for less than a tenner. A slice of pecan pie for dessert is almost too sweet to eat, but so very good.

Aurora

Liverpool Street, EC2M 7QN (020 7618 7000/ www.aurora.restaurant.co.uk). Liverpool Street tube/rail. **Lunch served** noon-2.45pm, **dinner served** 6.45-10pm Mon-Fri. **Main courses** £15.50-£29.50. **Set lunch** £28 3 courses. **Set meal** £45 (£65 with wine) 6-course tasting menu. **Credit** AmEx, DC, MC, V.

This restaurant, the grandest in the plush Great Eastern Hotel, displays a winning combination of top-drawer food and a relaxed atmosphere. Sure, there's a sommelier – but he turns out to be very chatty; like the rest of the staff, he gives the impression that although he knows a lot, he wants you to enjoy yourself. Prices, as you'd expect, are high but it's hard to fault the kitchen. For example, roast sea scallops with braised calamares and pea purée is an exquisite way to start a meal. Poached lobster with tarragon polenta and pumpkin fondant looks and tastes sensational; caramelised calf's sweetbreads with romaine lettuce and morels is plate-lickingly good. Puddings (espresso coffee chocolate mousse, lime sorbet with compote of red fruits) don't, perhaps, quite match the richly rewarding cheese trolley.

Cicada

132-136 St John Street, EC1V 4JT (020 7608 1550/ www.cicada.nu). Farringdon tube/rail/4, 55, 243 bus. **Lunch served** noon-3pm Mon-Fri. **Dinner served** 6-11pm Mon-Sat. **Dim sum served** noon-11pm Mon-Fri; 6-11pm Sat. **Main courses** £8-£11. **Credit** AmEx, DC, JCB, MC, V.

This busy, buzzy Clerkenwell hangout is a haunt of City suits and EC1 media types, who co-exist as amicably as the civilised mix of parquet flooring and leather banquettes. A horseshoe bar area sits astride a drinking and dining area. The oriental menu encompasses Thai, Japanese and Chinese dishes, all executed with no mean skill. Starters of fried prawn sesame rolls, avocado and sweet potato tempura or a sashimi plate with citrus soy are impressively light, fresh and well flavoured. Main courses aren't always a success. Pad Thai with prawn comes with the prawns, tofu and chillies plonked on each side of a wodge of noodles. Thai green curry with chicken is more successful and portions are very generous.

Club Gascon

57 West Smithfield, EC1A 9DS (020 7796 0600). Barbican tube/Farringdon tube/rail. **Lunch served** noon-2pm Mon-Fri. **Dinner served** 7-10pm Mon-Thur; 7-10.30pm Fri, Sat. **Tapas** £4-£15. **Set meal** £35 5 courses. **Credit** AmEx, MC, V.

Not content with serving fine French food tapas-style, Club Gascon offers a certain amount of culinary quirkiness too. Sometimes the experimentation falls flat, but when it works – as in wild smoked salmon wrapped around a pine twig, served on a piece of slate with a herbed sorbet and pine nuts – it's pretty memorable. A regular meal is easy to order: excellent dark chips, one of many foie gras choices, cassoulet and so on. But don't miss such offbeat offerings as smoked zander on a hot stone or crispy wild sea bass with 'surprised turnip' (a small turnip covered in foam). Service is reassuringly French, although not without glitches. The wine list, also French, is unlikely to disappoint. The location means a preponderance of male diners in suits, but this isn't a stuffy establishment – just look at the flower displays for a clue to the style of the place.

Le Coq d'Argent

No.1 Poultry, EC2R 8EJ (020 7395 5000/5050/ www.conran.com). Bank tube/DLR. **Bar & Grill Open** 11.30am-4pm; 5-10.30pm Mon-Fri. **Main courses** £12-£15. *Restaurant* **Breakfast served** 7.30-10am Mon-Fri. **Brunch served** noon-3pm Sun. **Lunch served** 11.30am-3pm Mon-Fri. **Dinner served** 6-10pm Mon-Fri; 6.30-10pm Sat. **Main courses** £15-£20. **Set lunch** £25 2 courses, £29.50 3 courses. **Credit** AmEx, DC, JCB, MC, V.

The setting of this Conran joint is undoubtedly striking – atop the postmodern striped behemoth that so outraged Prince Charles, with a circular roof garden-cum-bar and adjoining wedge-shaped lawn offering fine skyline views. The restaurant is big, stylish and impersonal, with the corporate feel that afflicts most of Conran's restaurants, no doubt exaggerated by the preponderance of besuited Square Mile males. The menu majors on shellfish and classic French dishes, some of which are more successful than others. Starters might be goat's cheese, tomato and aubergine tart or a salad of soft, creamy quail, grapes and pine nuts. Move on to a macho Scottish beef fillet in a rich bacon and artichoke gravy, or maybe a thick slab of tuna. The vegetable side dishes tend to lack finesse, which isn't what you'd expect with expense account prices and classy surroundings. Top marks, though, to the superlative wine list. Service is discreetly efficient.

De Gustibus

53-55 Carter Lane, EC4V 5AE (020 7236 0056).
St Paul's tube/Blackfriars tube/rail. **Open** 7am-5pm
Mon-Fri. **Credit** MC, V.
De Gustibus does a thriving lunchtime trade from city workers who come to savour its delicious artisan breads; it's the flavours and textures of these breads that make the sandwiches here so good. Choose from a wide range of varieties, including focaccia, rye and ciabatta. The fillings (cheeses, salamis, Mexican tuna, salt beef), although secondary considerations, are good too, and there's a selection of salad leaves and pickles, as well as hot dishes and pizza. The rushed service means that choosing what to go for can be a bit stressful, but it's hard to go far wrong. Indoor seating consists of communal window tables with high stools, and the canary yellow and metallic grey interior gives the place an airy industrial feel.

Eagle

159 Farringdon Road, EC1R 3AL (020 7837 1353).
Farringdon tube/rail. **Open** noon-11pm Mon-Sat;
noon-5pm Sun. **Lunch served** 12.30-2.30pm Mon-Fri;
12.30-3.30pm Sat, Sun. **Dinner served** 6.30-10.30pm
Mon-Sat. **Main courses** £5-£15. **Credit** MC,V.
Gastropubbery at its most satisfyingly basic. The single-room corner boozer has an interior that's all hard surfaces, well scuffed and worn. There's no reserved dining area because the place is too small to subdivide and, besides, everybody is eating anyway. A polished wooden bar runs the length of the back wall. Part is given over to booze (Charles Wells beers on draught, continental white beers and a decent array of wines) while the rest is the domain of a couple of glistening-browed chefs attending a big open grill. Much of the chalkboard menu focuses on that grill, so expect hefty steak sandwiches, hulking sausages and, on our last visit, a super-sized half of guinea fowl tarted up with own-made preserved lemons. Lighter options included a roast beetroot and goat's curd salad.

Flâneur

41 Farringdon Road, EC1M 3JB (020 7404 4422).
Farringdon tube/rail. **Open** 9am-10pm Mon-Sat;
9am-6pm Sun. **Brunch served** 9am-4pm Sun.
Lunch served noon-3pm Mon-Sat. **Dinner served**
6-10pm Mon-Sat. **Main courses** £9-£11.90. **Credit**
AmEx, DC, JCB, MC, V.

This food hall and restaurant is an unexpected treasure in a grim part of the Farringdon Road. Huge windows show off the comestibles; the deli extends back into the dining room, where the tables are squashed in among further aisles of goodies. The menu makes tempting reading: follow pea, mint and crispy pancetta soup with braised shoulder of Gloucester Old Spot with cream, sage and new potato. Or start with a warm salad of duck confit, green beans, frisée and pequillo peppers, and move on to pan-fried fillet of cod with lentils and salsa verde. Cakes (notably cheesecakes), compotes and fools form the backbone of the dessert list – try nectarine upside-down cake for size. We have a couple of quibbles – those oversized chairs don't work in the cramped space, however handsome they look; and service can be very slow when the place is busy. But, overall, a super and individual restaurant.

Gaudí

63 Clerkenwell Road, EC1M 5NP (020 7608 3220).
Farringdon tube/rail/55, 243 bus. **Lunch served**
noon-2.30pm Mon-Fri. **Dinner served** 7-10.30pm
Mon-Sat. **Main courses** £12-£23. **Set lunch** £12.50
2 courses, £15 3 courses. **Credit** AmEx, DC, MC, V.
You wouldn't necessarily expect much from a place that's part of a nightclub complex, but Gaudi just might be the best Spanish restaurant in London. With Catalan Josep Carbonell in charge of the kitchen, modern Catalan cooking comes to the fore. His ham salad combines superb pata negra Spanish ham, walnuts, balsamic dressing, vibrantly fresh figs and a fabulous manchego cheese mousse, while Catalan-style cannelloni is stuffed with escalivada, manchego and a saffron béchamel sauce. Main dishes might include Iberian pork fillet with a rich mix of poached potatoes, shallots and cabbage in port sauce, or wonderful grilled swordfish offset by a complex blend of wild mushrooms, beansprouts, aïoli and red pepper sauce. Desserts tend to be more elaborate still – the 'chocolate contrast' includes decadently rich profiterole-like pastries and a goat's cheese ice-cream. Special mention goes to the wine list, a monumental collection of fine modern Spanish labels.

Little Bay ★

171 Farringdon Road, EC1R 3AL (020 7278 1234).
Farringdon tube/rail. **Meals served** 10am-midnight
Mon-Sat; 10am-11pm Sun. **Main courses** £5.45-
£7.95. **Credit** MC, V.
This fun, friendly and funky establishment stands out with some of the best cheap eats in London. Decor is unfussy (upstairs white, downstairs red), and tables are packed in like the proverbial fish. But none of this matters, because Little Bay provides decent food at a third of the price you'll find in most of the capital's restaurants. Pig's cheek with chorizo mash and asparagus in hollandaise sauce showcases fresh ingredients and sophisticated flavours, while mains include the likes of barbary duck with a filo parcel. The Jamie Oliver-style chips (cooked in goose fat) are fab, and sides of veg come the way God intended – crisp and green.

Moro ★

34-36 Exmouth Market, EC1R 4QE (020 7833 8336/www.moro.co.uk). Farringdon tube/rail. **Bar Open** 12.30-10.30pm Mon-Fri; 7-10.30pm Sat. *Restaurant* **Lunch served** 12.30-2.30pm Mon-Fri. **Dinner served** 7-10.30pm Mon-Sat. **Main courses** £13.50-£16.50. **Credit** AmEx, DC, MC, V.

Few restaurants have received the volume of positive press that has been heaped on Moro over the past few years. And few have deserved it as much. Don't go, though, expecting traditional Spanish food. You can get decent tapas at the long bar, but the menu owes as much to North Africa and the Middle East as to Spain. Starters might be salads of runner beans topped with grated mullet roe, or with morels, tomatoes and judion beans. Mains tend to be equally simple but carefully sourced and beautifully cooked – maybe courgette and feta cheese fritters or melt-in-the-mouth pot-roasted pork, served with luxuriant sherry vinegar with a side of white beans. Rosewater and cardamom ice-cream, and yoghurt cake with pistachios for dessert are perhaps more acquired tastes. The atmosphere is very relaxed and very media (the offices of the *Guardian* are nearby).

The Place Below ★

St Mary-le-Bow, Cheapside, EC2V 6AU (020 7329 0789/www.theplacebelow.co.uk). St Paul's tube/ Bank tube/DLR. **Breakfast served** 7.30-10.30am, **lunch served** 11.30am-2.30pm, **snacks served** 2.30-3.30pm Mon-Fri. **Main courses** £5.50-£7.50. **Credit** MC, V.

A deservedly popular lunch spot with City workers, both outdoors in Bow Churchyard and down in the dramatic Norman crypt. The daily changing menu features leafy salads, a 'health bowl' (organic brown rice, lentils and seasonal veg with a ginger and sesame dressing), red pepper and pesto quiche, and soups such as split green pea and mint with own-made bread. Hot specials are equally good: sweet potato and caerphilly pie is a nice balance of flaky filo pastry and rich, but not heavy, savoury filling, accompanied by just-right, buttered greens. Eat between 11.30am and noon, or from 1.30pm to 2.30pm, and main courses cost £2 less. There's also a takeaway lunch counter for picking up filled ciabatta rolls, Comptoir Gascon pastries and divine Valrhona chocolate flapjacks.

Potemkin

144 Clerkenwell Road, EC1R 5DP (020 7278 6661/ www.potemkin.co.uk). Farringdon tube/rail. Bar **Open** 11am-11pm Mon-Fri; 6pm-midnight Sat. *Restaurant* **Meals served** noon-10.30pm Mon-Sat. **Main courses** £9.50-£18. **Credit** AmEx, DC, JCB, MC, V.

With its plush interior, Soviet-era posters and red velvet seating, Potemkin knows how to create atmosphere. The menu is beautifully written and presented and features Tsarist Russian classics with a few exotic Caucasian dishes thrown in.

Service (from Russian staff) is charmingly enthusiastic. Everything tasted great, but not for the prices we paid: starters of oscietra caviar with blini were way off at £30 a go. The blinis were thin and too few. Main courses were better: Georgian pork shashlik was superb. Sturgeon with asparagus in a béarnaise sauce was a rare treat, but could have been pepped up with herbs and the fish was slightly overcooked (and a tad overpriced at £18). Things picked up with dessert: chocolate truffle cake was worthy of any French restaurant and the blinchik tvorogom pancakes oozed creamy custard sauce. There's superb dry Georgian white by the glass and cocktails are fantastic. Potemkin remains the best Russian restaurant in London.

Quality Chop House

94 Farringdon Road, EC1R 3EA (020 7837 5093). Farringdon tube/rail/19, 38, 341 bus. **Lunch served** noon-3pm Mon-Fri; noon-4pm Sun. **Dinner served** 6.30-11.30pm Mon-Sat; 7-11.30pm Sun. **Main courses** £6.75-£24. **Credit** AmEx, MC, V.

First, a word to the long-legged: the cramped booths that constitute most of the seating in this quaintly converted, snappily updated working men's canteen will leave you walking like Bambi. But despite its humble heritage, the Chop House is the favourite choice of local new-media bods and creative types who like its mellow ambience. For some, the idea of 'progressive working class' cuisine might be stretching it a bit – do many people really order the jellied eels? – but most punters tuck into their crab salads, corned beef hashes and duck confits with enthusiasm. Wines are also great (and affordable), and staff are never less than charming.

St John ★

26 St John Street, EC1M 4AY (020 7251 0848/ 4998/www.stjohnrestaurant.com). Farringdon tube/rail. Bar **Open** 11am-11pm Mon-Fri; 6-11pm Sat. **Main courses** £3-£10. *Restaurant* **Lunch served** noon-3pm Mon-Fri. **Dinner served** 6-11pm Mon-Sat. **Main courses** £10-£18. **Credit** AmEx, DC, MC, V.

Fergus Henderson's unflinching, restlessly inventive approach to British cuisine continues to attract the culinarily curious from near and far with the promise of well-rendered, often offaly dishes. But it's not all chitterlings and chicken necks. The menu also puts fine seasonal produce to gentler use in dishes like succulent squid served cold with fennel or roast chicken in a delicious pool of broccoli vinaigrette. Portions are simply presented, rather like the restaurant itself, which has retained much of its austere, masculine character from its days as a smokehouse. There are daily changing fish dishes – say, a brace of delicate slip soles – and a vegetarian dish too. Puds are hearty, wines are thoroughly decent (and affordable) and staff are pleasant. St John Bread & Wine (a wine bar and bakery offshoot) has recently opened at 94-96 Commercial Street, E1 (020 7247 8724).

London

Smiths of Smithfield

67-77 Charterhouse Street, EC1M 6HJ (020 7251 7950/www.smithsofsmithfield.co.uk). Farringdon tube/rail. Ground floor bar **Meals served** 7am-5pm Mon-Fri; 9am-5pm Sat, Sun. **Snacks** £2.25-£5.50. *Dining room* **Lunch served** noon-3pm Mon-Fri. **Dinner served** 6-11pm Mon-Sat. **Main courses** £10.50-£11.50. *Top floor* **Lunch served** noon-3.30pm Mon-Fri, Sun. **Dinner served** 6.30-11pm Mon-Sat; 6.30-10.30pm Sun. **Main courses** £13-£28. **Set lunch** (Sun) £25 3 courses. *Cocktail bar* **Snacks served** 5-11pm Mon-Wed; 5pm-1am Thur-Sat. **Snacks** £5-£6. **Credit** AmEx, MC, V.

The ground floor bar is a great spot for breakfast or a light lunch, and weekend brunch is very family-friendly. The menu chalks up favourites: burgers, soup, eggs, all served in homely style. A juicy fillet of organic chicken in a big salady roll makes a perfect lunch. Full cream milkshakes or waffles, strawberries and ice-cream make delicious puds. There's a cocktail bar and a dining room on the next floor, serving superb char-grills counterpointed by piquant delights such as spiced duck salad with green papaya, Thai herbs and chilli dressing. As if this wasn't enough, the top floor restaurant goes one notch higher in terms of price and quality. Expect the likes of longhorn sirloin steak or roast Dover sole with herb and Morecambe Bay brown shrimp butter.

Strada ★

8-10 Exmouth Market, EC1R 4QA (020 7278 0800/ www.strada.co.uk). Farringdon tube/rail. **Meals served** noon-11pm Mon-Sat; noon-10.30pm Sun. **Main courses** £5.50-£12.95. **Credit** AmEx, DC, JCB, MC, V.

If you want an example of how to do a chain restaurant well, look no further than Strada. The formula's simple: fresh ingredients, freshly cooked; a straightforward but interesting menu; and a firm commitment to friendly and flexible service (it's hugely popular with families). Big baskets of flat, crunchy garlic bread, huge pizzas from the wood-burning ovens and nicely cooked pastas and risotto are the staples here, and it's hard to find fault with any of it. Mineral water arrives free on every table, and a short list of very acceptable Italian beers and wines smoothes everything along nicely. Bookings are not accepted. Pizza is available to take away.

Sutton Arms

6 Carthusian Street, EC1M 6EB (020 7253 0723). Barbican tube/rail. *Bar* **Open** noon-3pm, 5-11pm Mon-Fri. *Restaurant* **Lunch served** 12.30-2pm Tue-Fri. **Dinner served** 6-10pm Mon-Fri. **Main courses** £10-£14. **Set lunch** £12.50 2 courses, £15.50 3 courses. **Credit** AmEx, MC, V.

Free from the creaking timbers, nooks and snugs that haunt most of the pubs in this Dickensian quarter, the Sutton Arms has a real sense of restrained elegance. The ground-floor bar is cosy but uncluttered (three superb busts and a wonderful vintage poster add character), while the dark wood and simple furniture in the small upstairs room allow diners to concentrate on accomplished, inventive cooking. Squash soup has a zingy twist of fresh mint, tender roast chicken comes with fennel and rich livers. Wines, too, are interesting and staff are charming.

Sweetings

39 Queen Victoria Street, EC4N 4SA (020 7248 3062). Cannon Street tube/rail/Bank tube/DLR. **Lunch served** 11.30am-3pm Mon-Fri. **Main courses** £11-£21.50. **Credit** AmEx, JCB, MC, V.

Sweetings is so traditional it deserves to be made a museum. Virtually unchanged since it started business in 1889, it still operates only at weekday lunchtimes, takes no bookings and has only recently started to take credit cards. The interior is all tiles and tablecloths, the tables adorned with jugs of tartare sauce and buttered, sliced bread; the café feel is smartened by heavy cutlery and napkins. Seating is either on high benches or crammed in at long tables at the back. The menu is to the point – starters of potted shrimp, gravadlax and roll-mop; mains of skate wing with black butter, smoked haddock with poached egg, and turbot with mustard sauce – but the fish is of a high quality.

Les Trois Garçons

1 Club Row, E1 6JX (020 7613 1924/ www.lestroisgarcons.com). Liverpool Street tube/rail/8, 388 bus. **Dinner served** 7-10pm Mon-Wed; 7-10.30pm Thur-Sat. **Main courses** £12.50-£22. **Set dinner** (Mon-Wed) £20 2 courses, £24 3 courses. **Credit** AmEx, DC, JCB, MC, V.

A menagerie of stuffed dining companions, from a croc in a crown to a tiger in a tiara, resides in this theatrical restaurant adorned with Murano chandeliers and jewelled drapes. The French cuisine is costly, but first-rate and remarkably unfussy, and there's unobtrusive service to boot. Melting, silky foie gras is enhanced rather than overpowered by black truffles, while toasted goat's cheese salad uses the fruity burst of grapes as a potent counterpoint. Four fish mains present a worthy choice, while among the meaty offerings is an earthy rump of lamb with herby mash. Conclude with a classic lemon tart or yield to chocolate pudding with own-made ice-cream and you'll leave these extravagant rococo surroundings on a sparkling note.

Also in the area

Café Lazeez 88 St John St, EC1M 4EH (020 7253 2224); **Carluccio's** 12 West Smithfield, EC1A 9JR (020 7329 5904); **Gaucho Grill** 12 Gracechurch Street, EC3V 0BL (020 7626 5180); **Livebait** 1 Watling Street, EC4M 9BP (020 7213 0540); **Livebait** 1 Plough Place, EC4A 1HY (020 7842 0510); **The Living Room** 2-3 West Smithfield, EC1A 9JX (0870 442 2541); **The Real Greek Souvlaki & Bar** 140-142 St John Street, EC1V 4UA (020 7253 7234); **S&M Café** 48 Brushfield Street, E1 6AG (020 7247 2252); **Wagamama** 1A Ropemaker Street, EC2V 0HR (020 7588 2688); **Wagamama** 109 Fleet Street, EC4 2AB (020 7853 7889).

Chelsea, Knightsbridge, South Kensington & Victoria

Aziz

30-32 Vanston Place, SW6 1AX (020 7386 0086).
Fulham Broadway tube. **Lunch served** noon-3pm
Mon-Fri; noon-4pm Sun. **Dinner served** 6.30-
10.30pm Mon-Fri. **Meals served** noon-10.30pm Sat.
Main courses £8.50-£15.50. **Set brunch** £22
4 courses. **Set lunch** £10 incl a glass of wine.
Credit AmEx, MC, V.
A first London venture for Iranian couple Shahrock
and Zehra Parvin, with former Momo head chef
Michel Giraud. Meze supplements the familiar with
little-seen (in London) items like chakchouka, a
Tunisian dish of soft fried peppers, sweetcorn
fritters and gooey tulum cheese. Gorgeous breads
might include olive, sesame or apricot and walnut.
Presentation is stunning. Tuna is propped against
a cone of saffron rice; monkfish is served inside a
pastry pillow on a petal-strewn plate. Muhallabia,
usually a simple milky pudding, tastes of burnt
sugar, cardamom, mint, orange, raspberry,
rosewater and sesame and looks fabulous. The
restaurant is smart, but a coat rail and highchair are
the first things guests see as they walk in.

Bibendum

Michelin House, 81 Fulham Road, SW3 6RD
(020 7581 5817/www.bibendum.co.uk). South
Kensington tube. **Lunch served** noon-2.30pm
Mon-Fri; 12.30-3pm Sat, Sun. **Main courses**
£15.50-£26.50. **Set lunch** (Mon-Fri) £25 3 courses;
(Sat, Sun) £28.50 3 courses. **Dinner served** 7-11pm
Mon-Sat; 7-10.30pm Sun. **Main courses** £19-£26.50.
Credit AmEx, DC, MC, V.
This is one classy dining room. Set on the first floor
of the Michelin building – which also holds the
Bibendum Oyster Bar (*see below*) and the Conran
shop – the restaurant is cream, with colour from the
impressive Michelin man stained glass and the blue
chair covers. Much of the menu is urbane, crowd-
pleasing territory: summer vegetable and lettuce
heart salad, followed by haddock and (thin, golden)
chips was top-notch comfort food. More robust
choices might be brawn salad, deep-fried calf's
brains with sauce gribiche or salt cod ravioli with
summer truffles and peas. Finish with chocolate and
praline parfait or the bullishly priced cheese
selection (£9.50). The French-leaning wine list takes
some reading, but the sommelier is happy to help.

Bibendum Oyster Bar

Michelin House, 81 Fulham Road, SW3 6RD (020
7581 5817/www.bibendum.co.uk). South Kensington
tube. Bar **Meals served** noon-10.30pm Mon-Sat,
noon-10pm Sun. **Main courses** £10-£28.50.
Restaurant **Lunch served** noon-2.30pm Mon-Fri;
12.30-3pm Sat, Sun. **Dinner served** 7-11.30pm
Mon-Sat; 7-10.30pm Sun. **Main courses** £16.50-
£28.50. **Set lunch** (Mon-Fri) £25 3 courses; (Sat,
Sun) £28.50 3 courses. **Credit** AmEx, DC, MC, V.
While Michelin House's restaurant looks after
serious diners, its Oyster Bar is more a smart café
frequented by people after caviar, oysters and
seafood platters for lunch (it's open in the evenings,
but generally quiet). The situation is fine: mosaic
floor, tiled walls, reminders of the Michelin man; it's
lovely on warm days, when the doors are open. The
menu caters to lunchtime diners with small, simple
dishes: crostini and egg mayonnaise sit alongside
poached salmon with pickled cucumber and salade
niçoise. And then, of course, there are the oysters
and shellfish. Portions are big and prices less posh
than the clientele. A great place for people-watching.

Blue Elephant

4-6 Fulham Broadway, SW6 1AA (020 7385 6595/
www.blueelephant.com). Fulham Broadway tube.
Lunch served noon-2.30pm Mon-Fri; noon-4pm
Sun. **Dinner served** 7pm-midnight Mon-Thur;
6.30pm-midnight Fri, Sat; 7-10.30pm Sun. **Main
courses** £9.50-£19.60. **Set meals** £32-£51
3 courses. **Set buffet** (lunch Sun) £22 adults, £11
children. **Credit** AmEx, DC, MC, V.
It's a magical mystery tour to your table over fish
ponds and through dense foliage to a series of Thai
pavilions. Food is kitschly presented with carved
fruits. Starters were disappointing: little cakes of
corn and prawn looked tired, and a 'sunburst'
pomelo salad was clumpy with extremely crunchy
dried prawns. After that, things looked up, with a
powerful dish of minced chicken (laab kai), hot with
chilli. Pad Thai – rice noodles studded with soft eggy
bits and crunchy beansprouts – was suitably gentle,
while a moderately hot (one elephant on a scale to
three) lamb massaman curry was all flavour. Part of
an international chain of 12, the Blue Elephant
attracts everyone from first dates to families with
wide-eyed children. A full-on jungle experience.

Chutney Mary ★

535 King's Road, SW10 0SZ (020 7351 3113/ www.realindianfood.com). Fulham Broadway tube/West Brompton tube/rail/bus 11, 22. **Lunch served** 12.30-2.30pm Sat; 12.30-3pm Sun. **Dinner served** 6.30-11pm Mon-Sat; 6.30-10.30pm Sun. **Main courses** £12.50-£24. **Set lunch** (12.30-3pm Sun) £16.50 3 courses. **Credit** AmEx, DC, MC, V.

Chutney Mary's basement restaurant is a lovely spot, with leafy conservatory, flickering candles, purple ceiling and Indian prints. Chef Nagarajan Rubinath gives street food a glam makeover, sitting raunchy salads next to delicacies from royal Indian palaces. Especially memorable is the nihari soup: a robust lamb stock infused with cardamom and topped with a veil of puff pastry. Goan green chicken curry is a tongue-tingling rendition of pounded herby greens, chillies and onions, simmered with sizeable chunks of boneless chicken. Desserts are outstanding – delicately spiced garam masala brûlée, served with a dab of cardamom-scented custard. Service is faultless, as is the wine list.

Drones ★

1 Pont Street, SW1X 9EJ (020 7235 9555). Knightsbridge tube. **Lunch served** noon-2.30pm Mon-Sat; noon-3.30pm Sun. **Dinner served** 6-11pm Mon-Sat. **Main courses** £9.50-£22. **Set lunch** (Mon-Sat) £14.95 2 courses, £17.95 3 courses; (Sun) £19.50 3 courses. **Credit** AmEx, DC, MC, V.

A Marco Pierre White restaurant in Knightsbridge is always going to involve a loosening of the purse strings, but Drones justifies a big bill. The gentle amber lighting and 1930s stills on the wall give a swish but relaxed feel, and the service is attentive and good-humoured. Starters such as asparagus, and omelette cardina demonstrate the kitchen's ability to handle the simple and the complex with equal skill. Delicious lemon sole is seasoned delicately, with a richer element added by a sensuous creamed mash. To finish, it's hard to beat the beautifully fruity rice pudding and supreme crème brûlée. A wonderful experience.

Hunan

51 Pimlico Road, SW1 8NE (020 7730 5712). Sloane Square tube. **Lunch served** noon-2.30pm, **dinner served** 6-11pm Mon-Sat. **Main courses** £9-£30. **Set meals** £30-£200 (minimum 2 people). **Credit** AmEx, DC, MC, V.

Go for the 'leave it to us feast' at Hunan. The resulting gastronomic journey will be in the classic Chinese idiom: dish after exquisite, bijou dish of enticing delicacies. Hunan, the western Chinese province, is renowned for its spicy cuisine; Hunan the restaurant, is London's only venue dedicated to this cooking. It's a small place where expensive Chinese figurines enliven a magnolia-walled and wooden-floored interior. Mr Peng, the wry proprietor, guides you through a meal, the hallmarks of which are chillies, sesame seeds, copious chopped garlic and elaborate preparation. The highlights of the dozen or so dishes might be the piquant pickles, stuffed baby squid with bitter melon, salmon and white fish rolls or crisp wun tuns with a fennel-tinged aubergine filling. Dinners are still more varied, Mr Peng assured us.

Lots Road Pub & Dining Room

114 Lots Road, SW10 0RJ (020 7352 6645). Fulham Broadway tube, then 11 bus or Sloane Square tube, then 11, 19, 22 bus. **Open** 11am-11pm Mon-Sat; 11am-10.30pm Sun. **Lunch served** noon-3pm Mon-Fri. **Dinner served** 5.30-10pm Mon-Thur; 5.30-10.30pm Fri. **Meals served** noon-10.30pm Sat; noon-10pm Sun. **Main courses** £8-£13. **Set dinner** (Mon-Sat 5.30-7.30pm, 5.30-10pm Sun) £12.50 2 courses. **Credit** AmEx, MC, V.

An airy, comfortable gastropub star with stripped wood, cream walls with magenta details and flowers on the tables. The staff are ready to please, and the atmosphere is laidback. Fresh ingredients are cooked to order, so some dishes take time. A starter of marinated squid with spinach and a coriander-based dressing was delicately tangy, and meat mains were

The best London...

Family refuelling

Dexter's Grill (*see p61*), **Giraffe** (*see p67*), **Gourmet Burger Kitchen** (*see p62*), **Masala Zone** (*see p33*), **Mosaica @ the factory** (*see p69*), **Orso** (*see p39*), **Strada** (*see p47*), **Table Café** (*see p36*), **Victoria** (*see p59*), **Wagamama** (*see p24*).

Fish & chips

Brady's (*see p60*), **Golden Hind** (*see p22*), **Olley's** (*see p62*).

Meat joints

Arkansas Café (*see p44*), **Bodean's** (*see p30*), **Gaucho Grill** (*see p39*), **Mangal Oçakbasi** (*see p69*), **Rules** (*see p43*), **St John** (*see p46*), **Savoy Grill** (*see p43*), **Smiths of Smithfield** (*see p47*).

Outdoor eating

Canyon (*see p60*), **Coq d'Argent** (*see p44*), **Ransome's Dock** (*see p63*), **Royal China** (*see p66*).

See-and-be-seen

Bibendum Oyster Bar (*see p48*), **E&O** (*see p54*), **Hakkasan** (*see p31*), **The Ivy** (*see p39*), **Locanda Locatelli** (*see p22*), **192** (*see p55*), **Trois Garçons** (*see p47*); **Zuma** (*see p51*).

Views

Blue Print Café (*see p52*), **Depot** (*see p56*), **Riverwalk** (*see p53*), **Oxo Tower** (*see p53*).

spectacularly good. The beef in a ribeye steak sandwich with green salad and chips was juicy and cooked exactly as ordered, and the Lots Road burger with big chips is a clear candidate for London's best burger. Worth a detour.

Mr Chow

151 Knightsbridge, SW1X 7PA (020 7589 7347). Knightsbridge tube. **Lunch served** 12.30-3pm, **dinner served** 7pm-midnight daily. **Main courses** £12.50-£32. **Set lunch** £15 2 courses, £18 3 courses. **Credit** AmEx, DC, MC, V.

A near perfect combination of fine food, faultless service and delightful ambience. The lighting and atmosphere are discreetly glamorous, and oriental touches add a quirky feel. The menu is scattered with dishes you won't find elsewhere – try the glazed prawns with walnuts, a fabulous dish combining a dry, crisp bite with inner succulence, or steamed scallops speckled with garlic, spring onion and red pepper. Move on to fragrant lacquered pigeon with plum sauce or the luscious 'green prawn' stir-fry. Order the hand-pulled noodles and you get the full spectacle: a chef whipping a lump of dough into spaghetti-fine strands to general applause. Mr Chow has been going since 1968 and it's a joy to eat here.

Nahm ★

Halkin Hotel, Halkin Street, SW1X 7DJ (020 7333 1234/www.halkin.co.uk). Hyde Park Corner tube. **Lunch served** noon-2.30pm Mon-Fri. **Dinner served** 7-11pm Mon-Sat; 7-10pm Sun. **Main courses** £24-£29. **Set lunch** £18-£26 2 courses. **Set dinner** £47 4 courses. **Credit** AmEx, DC, MC, V.

David Thompson has been garlanded with awards since setting up Nahm. His startling interpretations of 'royal Thai' cooking are extraordinary, unlike the airport mall decor. The £47 set meal brings a wave of revelatory dishes. Tiny miang (betel leaf-wrapped savoury confections) were unexpected assemblies of ingredients that assaulted the tastebuds. 'Sour orange curry' of halibut burst with hot spices. And then there's 'caramelised' shredded beef with oysters marinated in kaffir lime juice and ginger. Elaborate preparation is apparent at every stage. The service can be didactic and inflexible, but this time our waiter was helpful in accommodating our vegetarian guest, who received the gamut of stunning dishes.

Olé ★

Broadway Chambers, Fulham Broadway, SW6 1EP (020 7610 2010/www.olerestaurants.com). Fulham Broadway tube. Tapas bar **Open** noon-12.30am Mon-Sat; *summer* noon-12.30am daily. **Tapas** £1.55-£6. *Restaurant* **Meals served** noon-10.30pm daily. **Main courses** £6.50-£10.50. **Credit** AmEx, DC, MC, V.

Olé is several cuts above the standard London tapas bar. It's a cool, elegant, white-walled space; the food is carefully prepared and artfully presented. Most of the menu sticks to traditional dishes (excellent jamón serrano and albóndigas – meatballs in a tomato sauce). Tortilla is served five ways: plain, with ratatouille, chorizo, tuna or spinach. Our

chorizo version was beautifully done. There are modern tapas, too, such as pork loin with roast vegetables and 'mustard essence'. Even croquetas, a tired cliché in many tapas places, are done well; two types, Iberico ham or egg and spinach, are served with a garlicky mayonnaise. Olé!

The Painted Heron

112 Cheyne Walk, SW10 0TJ (020 7351 5232). Bus 11, 22. **Lunch served** noon-2.30pm Mon-Fri. **Dinner served** 6-11pm Mon-Sat. **Meals served** noon-10.30pm Sun. **Main courses** £10-£12. **Set meal** £15 3 courses. **Credit** MC, V.

One of Chelsea's hidden gems, the Painted Heron has become a honey-pot for fans of new-wave Indian cooking. Yogesh Datta treats customers to tempting teasers such as peppery radish relish, and garlic pickle, which hits the spot in a way bottled mango chutney never could. Starters include spinach and sweet potato cakes filled with meltingly soft goat's cheese. Equally delectable is the main course of scallops in hot Keralan red curry. The young service team is slick. Datta's cooking has travelled well.

Racine ★

239 Brompton Road, SW3 2EP (020 7584 4477). Knightsbridge or South Kensington tube/14, 74 bus. **Lunch served** noon-3pm Mon-Fri; noon-3.30pm Sat, Sun. **Dinner served** 6-10.30pm Mon-Sat; 6-10pm Sun. **Main courses** £9.50-£18.75. **Set meal** (noon-7.30pm) £14.50 2 courses, £16.50 3 courses. **Credit** AmEx, DC, MC, V.

Racine is pretty much the ideal restaurant. True to its roots (a hearty salade Lyonnaise pulls no punches), but prepared to be accommodating (there's always an imaginative vegetarian main course). Staff are perfectly drilled but relaxed; in the kitchen, Henry Harris produces high-calibre dishes. Tomatoes with basil, crème fraîche and toasted brioche were a light, subtle precursor to grilled calves' kidneys with cabbage, onion and emmenthal mash. French farmhouse cheeses and puddings such as pot de crème de vanille aux pruneaux are hard to pass up. The prix-fixe menu is an unmissable bargain. London needs more restaurants like this. Racine was *Time Out*'s Best New Restaurant in 2003.

Tom Aikens

43 Elystan Street, SW3 3NT (020 7584 2003). South Kensington tube. **Lunch served** 12.30-2.30pm, **dinner served** 7-11pm Mon-Fri. **Set lunch** £24.50 3 courses incl coffee. **Set dinner** £49 3 courses incl coffee, £59 7 courses incl coffee. **Credit** AmEx, MC, V.

In the late 1990s gifted young chef Aikens turned his back on the glare of publicity. Now he's back with his own fabulous place. In contrast to the stark, minimalist dining room, Aikens's food provides colour, texture and interest. Some dishes verge on the absurd: rabbit confit was fenced in by a pallisade of baby carrots; frog's legs had the bones pointing skywards and the flesh squashed against the plate. But dishes were revelatory, punctuated by delightful appetisers. Service was professional and charming.

Racine

Zafferano

15 Lowndes Street, SW1X 9EY (020 7235 5800). Knightsbridge tube. **Lunch served** noon-2.30pm daily. **Dinner served** 7-11pm Mon-Sat; 7-10.30pm Sun. **Set lunch** £21.50 2 courses, £26.50 3 courses, £30.50 4 courses. **Set dinner** £29.50 2 courses, £37.50 3 courses, £41.50 4 courses. **Credit** AmEx, DC, MC, V.

One of London's premier Italian restaurants, Zafferano is set across two shop fronts in a small, quiet shopping area. The lunch menu is terrific value though you may swallow harder at the bill for dinner, when three courses cost £37.50 and the specials may entail £10 supplements. Classic dishes, bursting with clear, intense flavours, include ochre-red crayfish risotto; pasta parcels filled with tender osso bucco and doused with saffron-flavoured jus; and char-grilled lamb with aubergine. But desserts are usually the highlight: warm, dark chocolate fondant with gianduja ice-cream, and pink grapefruit sorbet with basil syrup. Don't skip the amaretti or truffles with coffee.

Zuma

5 Raphael Street, SW7 1DL (020 7584 1010/ www.zumarestaurant.com). Knightsbridge tube. **Lunch served** noon-2pm Mon-Sat; noon-4pm Sun.

Dinner served 6-11pm Mon-Sat. **Main courses** £3.50-£28.50. **Set lunch** £8.50-£14.80. **Credit** AmEx, DC, MC, V.

Probably named after the propensity of your bill to reach giddy heights, Zuma is doing well. The dining area is bound by a golden screen, a glass-fronted kitchen and a robatayaki and sushi counter. Start with a bowl of edamame 'Zuma style' – it's too big to finish. Then work your way through the upmarket pick-and-mix menu. As well as wasabi in the nigiri, there were intriguing dabs of other, invariably hot, ingredients. Spicy beef was meltingly soft; equally joyous were tuna tataki (small rolls of flash-grilled tuna in ponzu), cosmopolitan vegetable tempura and a raspberry chawan mushi. Book well in advance for this fashionable place.

Also in the area

Café Lazeez 93-95 Old Brompton Road, SW7 3LD (020 7581 9993); **The Gaucho Grill** 89 Sloane Avenue, SW3 3DX (020 7584 9901); **Giraffe** 7 Kensington High Street, W8 5NP (020 7938 1221); **Loch Fyne** 676 Fulham Road, SW6 5SA (020 7610 8020); **Wagamama** Lower ground floor, Harvey Nichols, SW1X 7RJ (020 7201 8000); **Wagamama** 26A Kensington High Street, W8 4PF (020 7376 1717).

Waterloo & South Bank

Arancia ★

52 Southwark Park Road, SE16 3RS (020 7394 1751/www.arancia-london.co.uk). Bermondsey tube/ Elephant & Castle tube/rail then 1, 53 bus/South Bermondsey rail. **Lunch served** 12.30-2.30pm Wed-Sun. **Dinner served** 7-11pm daily. **Main courses** £8.80-£9.20. **Set lunch** £7.50 2 courses, £10.50 3 courses. **Credit** MC, V.

You can tell Arancia was once a corner shop from the design of the building, but today it's a low-key restaurant with cheerful tangerine curtains, paper tablecloths, abstract art and bare floorboards. The kitchen majors on fresh ingredients, especially vegetables, and fairly humble recipes, but executes them better than most people could at home. The roast chicken is very good, fish cakes are another popular inclusion, and there is inevitably something intriguing for vegetarians. Arancia's chocolate 'semifreddo' is more like a cake than the half-frozen parfait it should be, but tastes good nevertheless. And when the desserts are priced around £3.50, who's complaining? The wine list is also a steal.

Baltic

74 Blackfriars Road, SE1 8HA (020 7928 1111/ www.balticrestaurant.co.uk). Southwark tube. **Lunch served** noon-3pm Mon-Fri, Sun. **Dinner served** 6-11pm Mon-Sat; 6-10.30pm Sun. **Main courses** £11-£12.50. **Set meal** (noon-3pm, 6-7pm) £11.50 2 courses, £13.50 3 courses. **Credit** AmEx, MC, V.

An attractive venue with an airy dining space, amber sculptures, pristine white tables, and an equally seductive bar with velvet curtains and alcove banquettes. The menu can't be faulted for its take on modern Polish and Eastern European: classic blinis and herring alongside adventurous Georgian lamb and Latvian fish dishes. Creamed mushrooms with potato pancake was huge but delicious. Pyzy, potato dumplings with spiced veal and wild mushrooms, were slightly more delicate and perfectly flavoured. Salmon steak with mizeria (cucumber salad) was simple but excellent; marinated paprika chicken was tender and came in a wonderful spicy adjika-style sauce. Desserts are legendary, especially the addictive white chocolate cheesecake. Service lets the side down. Still – their sense of occasion keeps them top of the Eastern European league.

Blue Print Café

Design Museum, Shad Thames, SE1 2YD (020 7378 7031/www.conran.com). Tower Hill tube/Tower Gateway DLR/London Bridge tube/rail/47, 78 bus. **Lunch served** noon-3pm daily. **Dinner served** 6-11pm Mon-Sat. **Main courses** £11.50-£22. **Credit** AmEx, DC, MC, V.

Few sites in London can beat the Blue Print Café for a river view. The blue binoculars are a nice acknowledgement that this is what a lot of people are here for, and the room is decorated in a modern, pared-down style that doesn't try to compete with the Thames. The kitchen here has had its ups and downs over the years, but is currently on good form – dishes are interesting, but not trying too hard; the menu changes twice daily. Salad of beetroot, soft boiled egg, horseradish and mustard makes a colourful and refreshing summer starter; smoked eel with potato and french beans is good stuff too. Onglet with chorizo and salsas verde and rosso or a whole bream with a sharply-dressed cucumber salad are winning choices from a tempting list of mains. Service comes with a smile and the atmosphere is unhurried.

Champor-Champor

62 Weston Street, SE1 3QJ (020 7403 4600/ www.champor-champor.com). London Bridge tube/rail. **Lunch served** by appointment Mon-Fri. **Dinner served** 6.30-10.30pm Mon-Sat. **Set meals** £19.90 2 courses, £24.50 3 courses. **Credit** AmEx, JCB, MC, V.

In the grey backstreets of SE1 sits this tiny burst of colour. Candles and vibrant fabrics add intimacy to the friendly welcome. Regulars eagerly order fish and meat dishes from the original, seasonal menu. Perhaps they'll start with stir-fried scallops with salted duck egg and julienne of bangla betel leaf, then follow with miso and honey-glazed duck breast with red onion, pumpkin and paw-paw compote and crispy noodles. Vegetarians also get their share of Malaysian delights. The purple sweet potato and water-chestnut soup is a warming starter, while the chilli oil and tangy dressing on the cold starter of wild mushroom and paneer kerabu also turn the heat on. Non-meat main-course flavours and textures range from the subtle creaminess of Malay lodeh and gado gado sauce to the oozing, crunchy black rice, cassava and herb-stuffed coconut. Leave space for luxurious smoked banana steam pudding.

Delfina

50 Bermondsey Street, SE1 3UD (020 7357 0244/www.delfina.org.uk). London Bridge tube/rail. **Open** 8am-5pm, **coffee served** 9am-noon, 3-5pm, **lunch served** noon-3pm Mon-Fri. **Main courses** £9.95-£12.95. **Credit** AmEx, DC, JCB, MC, V.

Don't be put off by the rather dismal surroundings of London Bridge station – carry on to this delightful studio café. It's a lovely airy space (functioning as an art gallery by night), with a sensibly brief, course whenever possible. Enjoy the likes of subtle, tender seared tuna in sesame with avocado, watermelon, soy and sprout salad, followed by radicchio risotto paired, daringly, with sliced strawberries in balsamic vinegar or tamarind-glazed tilapia with spicy pakoras and a yoghurt sauce. Service is friendly and there are plenty of wines by the glass – always important at lunchtime.

Fina Estampa

150 Tooley Street, SE1 2TU (020 7403 1342). London Bridge tube/rail. Bar **Open** noon-10pm Mon-Fri; 6-10pm Sat. **Lunch served** noon-3pm Mon-Fri. **Dinner served** 6.30-10.30pm Mon-Sat. **Main courses** £7.95-£14.95. **Credit** AmEx, DC, MC, V.
On leaving the smart-but-gloomy cocktail lounge the scent of coriander, garlic and sweet spices makes for a promising introduction to Peruvian food. The ceviche (the South American take on sushi) and sweet potato starters confirmed this and the waiters proved their authentic, if upmarket, credentials. The two classics, lamb seco and carapulcra, built around pork and cassava and Incan dried potatoes, were both fantastic, and excellent heavy Argentine reds complemented the tastes. There's no dessert as such, bar the not-always-available alfajor biscuits, ice-cream or fruit. The musical menu of boleros, gushy romance numbers and a smattering of Manu Chao, and the wonderful view – Tower Bridge sitting in a halo of lamplight – make you want to stay put. If the bar downstairs were better used, this could be the ultimate Peruvian night.

Oxo Tower Restaurant, Bar & Brasserie

Oxo Tower Wharf, Barge House Street, SE1 9PH (020 7803 3888/www.harveynichols.com). Blackfriars or Waterloo tube/rail. Bar **Open** 11am-11pm Mon-Sat; noon-10.30pm Sun. *Brasserie* **Lunch served** noon-2.45pm Mon-Sat; noon-3.45pm Sun. **Dinner served** 5.30-11pm Mon-Sat; 6-10.15pm Sun. **Main courses** £10.25-£17. **Set meal** (lunch, 5.30-6.45pm Mon-Fri) £19.50 2 courses, £23.50 3 courses incl glass of wine & coffee. *Restaurant* **Lunch served** noon-2.30pm Mon-Sat; noon-3pm Sun. **Dinner served** 6-11pm Mon-Sat; 6.30-10pm Sun. **Main courses** £17.50-£26. **Set lunch** (Mon-Fri, Sun) £23.50 2 courses, £28.50 3 courses. **Credit** AmEx, DC, MC, V.
Perched atop the Oxo Tower with sweeping views along the Thames, this must be one of the best dining settings in London – especially at sunset. Lifschutz Davidson's design is elegant, with glass walls and a swooping louvred ceiling. The design of the food is key, too. A starter of crab on yuzu jelly (tasting of mandarin and grapefruit) was delicately delicious. Mains included venison and guinea fowl, but we went for less hearty options. Grilled dorade, salt cod and red pepper with squid showcased top-class ingredients – but wasn't outstanding. Spiced lamb tenderloin with peas, mint and coriander similarly lacked oomph, but a side of mash was creamy heaven. Best was a luscious lemon sponge pud with a lightly perfumed rosewater sorbet:

perfect. Service is attentive without being irritating, and the long wine list includes fine choices for under £30 as well as a Chateau Petrus for £1,800.

Riverwalk

Second Floor, Oxo Tower Wharf, Barge House Street, SE1 9PH (grill 020 7928 2864/restaurant 020 7928 2884/www.riverwalk.co.uk). Blackfriars tube or Waterloo tube/rail. Grill **Brunch served** noon-5pm Sun. **Lunch served** noon-3pm Mon-Sat. **Dinner served** 6-10.30pm daily. **Main courses** £13.50-£19.50. **Set meals** (6-7pm Mon-Fri) £12.50 2 courses, £15.50 3 courses. *Restaurant* **Lunch served** noon-3pm Tue-Fri. **Dinner served** 6-10.30pm Tue-Sat. **Main courses** £5.50-£13. **Set meals** £12.50 2 courses, £19.50 3 courses. **Credit** AmEx, DC, MC, V.
The Oxo Tower is currently the best eating spot on the South Bank, with the Oxo Tower Restaurant (*see above*) on the top floor and the cheaper but similarly accomplished Riverwalk on the second floor. It offers a choice of bar with the emphasis on Martinis and champagne; restaurant (featuring pick-and-mix pan-Asian dishes like black salmon with pickled veg or seared ginger beef with crispy noodles) or grill. The latter serves a modern European menu with more impact than most. Spring pea and green scallion risotto with pecorino followed by brochette of grilled Orkney lamb and bell peppers with orange-infused vanilla couscous was an assured offering. A river view seems to be guaranteed wherever you sit, and the venue is handsome – unfussily contemporary, with comfortable seating and natural light.

Tas Pide ★

20-22 New Globe Walk, SE1 9DR (020 7633 9777). **Meals served** noon-11.30pm Mon-Sat; noon-10.30pm Sun. **Main courses** £5.25-£8.95. **Set meal** £7.45 2 courses, £17.45 3 courses. **Credit** AmEx, MC, V.
Abandoning the modernism of the other Tas restaurants for a more classical feel, Tas Pide is pleasantly intimate. Heavy wooden beams echo the Globe theatre across the road and a musician plucks at an oud (Turkish lute). On being seated we were presented with a complimentary, richly textured lentil soup along with olives, dips and fine home-made pide. Swordfish baked in foil, with potatoes, red onion, tomato and coriander was excellent, a tasty, solid steak in a mouthwatering sauce. Traditional Turkish pizza with mushrooms, tulum cheese and oak-cured beef also went down well. A side salad of incir salatası (sun-dried figs, goat's cheese and balsamic vinegar) provided a good mix of modern and traditional ingredients. For dessert, kaymaklı kayısı (purée of candied chestnut with pistachio) is worth trying. We closed with fine Turkish coffee and ıhlamur (lime tree tea with honey). Recommended.

Also in the area

Livebait 41-45 The Cut, SE1 8LF (020 7928 7211); **Tas** 33 The Cut, SE1 8LX (020 7928 1444); **Tas** 72 Borough High Street, SE1 O2E (020 7403 7200).

Bayswater & Notting Hill

Al Waha

75 Westbourne Grove, W2 4UL (020 7229 0806). Bayswater tube. **Meals served** noon-midnight daily. **Main courses** £9-£18. **Set lunch** £12.50 5 courses. **Set meal** £20 3 courses incl coffee. **Credit** AmEx, DC, MC, V.

Al Waha ('the oasis') is busy and reliable. It's a smart little place, done out in a warm, mellow yellow and tables are separated by potted greenery. Meze choices are legion, running to 50-plus. Relieve the burden of choice by opting for the set menu, which delivers a large dish of creamy houmous kawarmah (served warm, topped with chopped lamb and pine nuts) and a generous fattoush salad, plus excellent moist falafel and crisp kibbeh. Accompany this with the dish of the day, which might be kharoof mahshi (slices of lamb on a bed of rice, heavily spiced with cinnamon and studded with pistachios and sliced almonds). Great food, fantastic value.

Clarke's

124 Kensington Church Street, W8 4BH (020 7221 9225/www.sallyclarke.com). Notting Hill Gate tube. **Lunch served** 12.30-2pm Mon-Fri. **Brunch served** 11am-2pm Sat. **Dinner served** 7-10pm Tue-Sat. **Main courses** £14-£21. **Set dinner** £48 4 courses incl coffee, service. **Credit** AmEx, DC, JCB, MC, V.

A very civilised restaurant, with a sedate well-heeled clientele. There's a short menu at lunch (and brunch), but it's no choice at dinner (vegetarians should check ahead). The emphasis is on top-quality ingredients simply served; this approach is matched by discreet decor. San Daniele ham with organic leaves and pomegranate-chive dressing could be followed by perfectly cooked roasted monkfish with rappini (a bitter broccoli) and roast potatoes, with anchovy and tarragon mayonnaise. Montgomery cheddar and a luscious lemon pot might round things off. Details can go awry – not really acceptable at these prices – but when it all works, you're in clover.

Cow Dining Room

89 Westbourne Park Road, W2 5QH (020 7221 0021). Royal Oak or Westbourne Park tube. **Open** noon-11pm Mon-Sat; noon-10.30pm Sun. *Bar* **Lunch served** noon-3.30pm daily. **Dinner served** 6-10.30pm Mon-Sat; 6-10pm Sun. **Main courses** £8-£13. *Dining Room* **Lunch served** 12.30-3.30pm Sun. **Dinner served** 7-11pm Mon-Sat; 6-10pm Sun. **Main courses** £13-£18. **Credit** JCB, MC, V.

Above this popular pub, the Cow's dining room is more restaurant than gastropub (as reflected in the prices), boasting its own entrance and steep stairs. The white and maroon decor and artists' prints give the small but airy space a Swinging London look, which suits the media crowd. The regularly changing menus are fashionable, eclectic and British, with, as a lux speciality, oysters from £8.50 for six. Typical dishes are asparagus with balsamic vinegar and parmesan, lamb cutlets with a lusciously rich ratatouille or nettle and ricotta ravioli; on the whole they deliver. A sophisticated wine selection is a plus, as is the easygoing but efficient service. The pub offers an upscale bar menu.

E&O

14 Blenheim Crescent, W11 1NN (020 7229 5454/ www.eando.nu). Ladbroke Grove tube. *Bar* **Open** (dim sum) noon-11pm Mon-Sat; noon-10.30pm Sun. *Restaurant* **Lunch served** noon-3pm Mon-Sat; 1-3pm Sun. **Dinner served** 6-11pm Mon-Sat; 6-10.30pm Sun. **Main courses** £6-£19.50. **Credit** AmEx, DC, MC, V.

Although it's not an exclusively vegetarian eaterie, E&O's non-meat selection is so good that it won the Best Vegetarian Restaurant gong at the 2003 *Time Out* London Eating & Drinking Awards. With dark wood furniture, beautiful staff and the kind of front bar you can imagine LA film stars draping themselves over, you might expect this restaurant to be all style and little content. Think again. The menu is varied and full of vegetarian options, and what you get is course after course of fabulous fruit and veg mixed to create refreshing and flavour-packed dishes. Nibble on some edemame (cooked soy beans still in their pods) in soy and mirin sauce while you select from dim sum, tempura, curries and other oriental specials.

Kensington Place ★

201-209 Kensington Church Street, W8 7LX (020 7727 3184/www.kensingtonplace.co.uk). Notting Hill Gate tube. **Lunch served** noon-3.30pm daily. **Dinner served** 6.30-11.45pm Mon-Sat; 6.30-10.15pm Sun. **Main courses** £14-£18.50. **Set lunch** (Mon-Fri) £16.50 3 courses; (Sun) £18 3 courses. **Credit** AmEx, DC, JCB, MC, V.

A longtime favourite and now into its 16th year of operation under the stewardship of Rowley Leigh, Kensington Place continues to please with a formula that combines good-looking, special occasion surroundings, amiably professional service and consistently excellent cooking. Sunday lunches are particularly relaxed. Start, perhaps, with a head-clearing Bloody Mary, followed by a dish of petite fried mullets accompanied by a crunchy, punchy salsa verde. Then get to grips with a classic roast beef with all the trimmings, the meat perfectly pink and tender. While the old favourites such as griddled fois gras with sweetcorn pancake remain, the kitchen continues to innovate and expand its version of the modern British repertoire.

Magic Wok ★

100 Queensway, W2 3RR (020 7792 9767).
Bayswater or Queensway tube. **Meals served**
noon-11pm daily. **Main courses** £5-£12.50. **Set
meals** £11.50-£24 per person (minimum 2). **Credit**
AmEx, MC, V.

A pioneer in translating its menu of speciality dishes
into English, Magic Wok remains one of the best
places to introduce non-Chinese to proper Chinese
food. It's a small, usually crowded venue, narrow at
the front and opening up just enough at the back to
allow for two round banqueting tables. Culinary
adventurers need to scrutinise the specials list. Spin
doctors have had little hand in the translations;
witness the 'stir-fried goose web with dried fish lip
mew and sea cucumber' and 'crispy pig's intestine'.
Main courses are magnificent: 'stir-fried seafood
with egg white and fresh milk', for instance, is a
light, scrambled egg mix and comes with toasted
pine nuts as a textural counterpoint; steamed belly
of pork in hot-pot is a comforting, flavour-packed
stew; the huge portion of lotus leaf rice is full of
enticing titbits. Fairly priced wines, enthusiastic
service, and fresh orange and fortune cookies with
the bill increase our admiration for this place.

Mandarin Kitchen

14-16 Queensway, W2 3RX (020 7727 9012).
Bayswater or Queensway tube. **Meals served**
noon-11.30pm daily. **Main courses** £5.90-£25.
Set meal £10.90 per person (minimum 2). **Credit**
AmEx, DC, JCB, MC, V.

They say more lobsters are served (and eaten) at the
Mandarin Kitchen than at any other restaurant in
Britain, and you might believe it looking at the
number of these magnificent creatures emerging
from the kitchen. This is the place for a seafood
extravaganza, with specialities including steamed
scallops, razor clams, sea bass and roast baby squid.
Customers include smart Cantonese and Japanese,
European chefs and discerning eaters in general. The
decor is nothing to write home about and
reservations are not always honoured in a timely
manner, but service is much improved, with friendly
and attentive waiters.

Nipa

Royal Lancaster Hotel, Lancaster Terrace, W2 2TY
(020 7262 6737/www.royallancaster.com).
Lancaster Gate tube. **Bar Open** 11am-11pm Mon-Sat;
11am-10.30pm Sun. *Restaurant* **Lunch served**
noon-2pm Mon-Fri. **Dinner served** 6.30-10.30pm
Mon-Sat. **Main courses** £8.50-£13.50. **Credit**
AmEx, DC, JCB, MC, V.

'Thai green curry is the new chicken tikka,' says one
of the suits at the next table, pretty much summing
up the mood of a nation. 'Especially with a bottle of
Sancerre.' He's in luck. This clubby, formal
restaurant serves one of London's best Thai green
curries – either with chicken, or with tender house-
made fish balls and two types of Thai aubergine –
and the large wine list includes a half-decent
Sancerre. The decor is a bit tourist-Thai with its

oriental motifs, purple cloths and woven fabrics, and
the Thai staff are an uncharacteristically unsmiling
lot, but the food is the real McCoy. Dishes include
sweet chicken dumplings wrapped in gloriously,
glutinously sticky rice flour skins, and a crisp Thai
omelette studded with slices of salty turnip, red chilli
and fried basil. Nipa just needs a few smiles and a
bit of life, and it would be very good indeed.

192

*192 Kensington Park Road, W11 2ES (020 7229
0482). Ladbroke Grove or Notting Hill Gate tube.*
Lunch served 12.30-3pm Mon-Fri; 12.30-3.30pm Sat,
Sun. **Dinner served** 7-11.30pm Mon-Sat; 7-11pm
Sun. **Main courses** £12-£17. **Set lunch** (Mon-Fri,
Sun) £15 2 courses, £18 3 courses. **Credit** MC, V.

Notting Hill's number-one vanity spot is all too often
disfigured by braying media goons, but the quality
of the food usually offers more than adequate
compensation. The menu is varied and appealing –
start, perhaps, with a simple gazpacho or a flasher
fennel soup with scallop tortelloni, then take your
pick from a selection of pastas and risottos. Or head
straight for the mains, such as a great surf 'n' turf
combo of roast turbot and three juicy hunks of
charred beef served on a thick bed of perfect spinach.
For the quality and variety of wine by the bottle and
glass, 192 still leads the pack. The only surprise
remains the ordinary decor: little more than red
upholstered benches with run-around mirrors to
help customers keep an eye on which celebs are in.

Pharmacy Restaurant & Bar

150 Notting Hill Gate, W11 3QG (020 7221 2442).
Notting Hill Gate tube. **Bar Open** noon-3pm, 5.30pm-
1am Mon-Thur; noon-3pm, 5.30pm-2am Fri, Sat;
noon-midnight Sun. *Restaurant* **Lunch served**
noon-3pm Mon-Fri. **Dinner served** 7-10.30pm Mon-
Sat. **Main courses** £14-£26. **Set lunch** £16.50 2
courses, £18.50 3 courses. **Credit** AmEx, DC, MC, V.

Seemingly moribund not long ago, medical-themed
Pharmacy has been injected with new life by the
arrival of chef Hywel Jones. The first-floor dining
room offers diverting views over bustling Notting
Hill Gate, though they're unlikely to distract from
the hefty prices, but pulses may return to normal
when the food appears. Presentation is exquisite –
starters like cornish crab cake, avocado salad and
saffron vinaigrette are works of art and taste as good
as they look. Mains are equally classy: try Welsh
lamb with sweet onion tatin and provençal
vegetables. Save room for the sensational
cheeseboard and eccentric puddings like meringue,
spearmint ice-cream and raspberries. The wine list
is an impressive fusillade of pricey vintages; the hip
young staff are cheerful and sweet.

Also in the area

Fairuz 27 Westbourne Grove, W2 4UA (020 7243
8444); **Livebait** 175 Westbourne Grove, W11 2SB
(020 7727 4321); **Royal China** 13 Queensway, W2
4QJ (020 7221 2535); **S&M Café** 268 Portobello Road,
W10 5TY (020 8968 8898).

West

Chosan

292 Upper Richmond Road, SW15 6TH (020 8788 9626). East Putney tube. **Lunch served** noon-2.30pm Sat, Sun. **Dinner served** 6.30-10.30pm Tue-Sat; 6.30-10pm Sun. **Main courses** £3.30-£19.90. **Set lunch** £7.90-£13.90 incl miso soup & rice. **Set dinner** £17.90-£19.90 7 courses; £24.90 bento box. **Credit** MC, V.

There's an intimate, family feel about Chosan that is warm and welcoming. Mellow lighting and red lanterns enhance the cosy ambience. The menu is huge and the extensive saké list features such rarities as the pongy fish-fin saké. The à la carte sushi and sashimi menu also boasts some unusual finds such as cuttlefish, brill and green mullet. The seven-course dinners are good value; they include spinach and sesame salad, deep-fried tofu and a fruit dessert alongside the mains. Moist, moreish sashimi arrives on a wooden platter. Salmon foilyaki (wrapped in foil) is baked to perfection. There's only the odd let-down, like a side order of soggy shumai. In all, a charming, impressive neighbourhood eaterie.

The Depot

Tideway Yard, 125 Mortlake High Street, SW14 8SN (020 8878 9462). Barnes Bridge or Mortlake rail/209 bus. **Open** 10am-11pm Mon-Sat; 10am-10.30pm Sun. **Lunch served** noon-3pm, **dinner served** 6-11pm Mon-Sat. **Meals served** noon-4.30pm, 6-10.30pm Sun. **Main courses** £9.95-£15.50. **Set lunch** (Mon-Sat) £10.25 2 courses. **Set dinner** £14.50 3 courses. **Credit** AmEx, DC, MC, V.

Housed in a former council stables, with the Thames on one side and a courtyard on the other, the Depot is a charming spot. Mediterranean and oriental influences mingle in the tempting seasonal menu. Mains include steak and chicken as well as more idiosyncratic combinations, such as roast salmon, wedged between a delicious houmous pancake, with baba ganoush. Roast peppers, asparagus and a mini crab tartlet are fine partners for a hefty slab of tuna. You might be too full to try the puds, including concoctions like passion-fruit crème brûlée with elderflower and coriander jelly. Next time, perhaps.

Enoteca Turi

28 Putney High Street, SW15 1SQ (020 8785 4449). East Putney tube/Putney Bridge rail/14, 74, 270 bus. **Lunch served** 12.30-2.30pm Mon-Sat. **Dinner served** 6.30-11pm Mon-Thur; 6.30-11.30pm Fri, Sat. **Main courses** £14-£17. **Credit** AmEx, DC, MC, V.

Formerly a cosy, wood-panelled tratt, Enoteca Turi is now a spacious and cosmopolitan restaurant that could hold its own in the West End. There's bold modern art, good linen and cutlery, and a sophisticated list of seasonal foods, but perhaps most notable is the huge wine selection and the careful matching of wines to dishes. Typical dishes include seared tuna with peas and artichokes; grilled squid with tomato, carrot salad and toast; own-made gnocchi with courgettes and prawns; and pasta with samphire, potatoes and pesto. Desserts include Tuscan chocolate cake with pine kernels.

Fish Hoek

8 Elliott Road, W4 1PE (020 8742 0766). Turnham Green tube. **Lunch served** noon-2.30pm. **Dinner served** 6-10.30pm Tue-Thur, Sun; 6-11pm Fri, Sat. **Main courses** £9.75-£34. **Credit** MC, V.

Fish Hoek comes to us from the owners of the late Springbok Café – both bold and unusual local restaurants. Like Springbok, everything is lovingly presented, from the attractive interior to the exciting dishes and enthusiastic staff. The confusing menu (over 30 dishes of small or large portions in very small type) offers a bizarre range of fish. Kingfish was strongly flavoured and offset by a paw-paw and lime salsa. The best dish was mussels so drenched in chilli that we needed a minute to collect ourselves afterwards. It's a small, cramped space, booked up most nights, but the staff cope brilliantly.

The Gate ★

51 Queen Caroline Street, W6 9QL (020 8748 6932/ www.gateveg.co.uk). Hammersmith tube. **Lunch served** noon-3pm Mon-Fri. **Dinner served** 6-10.45pm Mon-Sat. **Main courses** £7.95-£11.50. **Credit** AmEx, DC, JCB, MC, V.

This long-established, classy venue has opened a sister restaurant in Belsize Village, but you can't beat the original for its setting. Dine in the secluded, leafy courtyard, or the airy converted artist's loft. Food, too, wins the sibling rivalry stakes. Spinach, blue cheese and walnut tart might precede baby aubergines stuffed with pine nuts, goat's cheese, spinach, puy lentils, tomatoes and olives, served with a duxelle of wild mushrooms and polenta cake. Savoury jams and dressings add a special touch to beetroot and goat's cheese tortillas, halloumi kebabs, strudels and pasta dishes. There are vegan dishes and wines too. Desserts, including a creamy cappuccino brûlée, are good. The Gate proves that it is possible to run a fabulous vegetarian establishment.

Golden Palace

146-150 Station Road, Harrow, Middx, HA1 2RH (020 8863 2333). Harrow-on-the-Hill tube/rail. **Meals served** noon-11.30pm Mon-Sat; 11am-10.30pm Sun. **Dim sum served** noon-5pm Mon-Sat; 11am-5pm Sun. **Main courses** £5.20-£7.50, **dim sum** £2.20-£3.20. **Set meals** £18-£24.50 (minimum 2 people). **Credit** AmEx, DC, MC, V.

This large suburban restaurant offers dim sum to rival the best in the city centre, and is usually thronged with customers, many of them Chinese. The dining rooms are smart and comfortable, staff are helpful and the full-colour illustrated dim sum menu makes ordering easy. We love the fried chive dumplings – their prawn filling laced with teasingly pungent Chinese chive – and the steamed seaweed rolls clad in a wispy sauce. Slabs of golden-crisp taro cake are studded with dried shrimp and infused with five spice, and the prawn cheung fun is exemplary. There are excellent Buddhist-style vegetarian snacks, a rarity in dim sum places (try the 'roast duck' made from beancurd skin).

The Green Olive

5 Warwick Place, W9 2PX (020 7289 2469).
Warwick Avenue tube/6 bus. **Lunch served**
12.30-2.30pm Mon-Sat; 12.30-2.45pm Sun. **Dinner served** 7-10pm Mon-Sat; 6.30-10.15pm Sun. **Set lunch** £18 2 courses, £23 3 courses, £26 4 courses. **Set dinner** £21.50 2 courses, £26.50 3 courses, £30 4 courses. **Credit** AmEx, JCB, MC, V.

A lick of paint and sheer apple-and-cream curtains have brought a spring-like mood to this intimate restaurant in quiet Warwick Place. There have been changes behind the scenes too but the output is as good as ever. Exquisite smoked swordfish carpaccio was decorated with pomegranate and sultana salad, while a crown of green beans and caperberries regaled delicious vitello tonnato. For mains there was tastily herb-crusted mackerel and excellent roast lamb with aubergine caviar and the creamiest celeriac purée. The cheese plate was well selected and served with mostarda di Cremona, but stunning roast pineapple with saffron and chilli won the Best Afters trophy. The courteous maître d' doubled as sommelier and could recite the wine list backwards.

Jashan ★

1-2 Coronet Parade, Ealing Road, Wembley,
Middx HA0 4AY (020 8900 9800/www.jashan
restaurants.com). Wembley Central tube. **Lunch served** noon-3.30pm, **dinner served** 6-11pm Mon-Fri. **Meals served** noon-11pm Sat, Sun. **Main courses** £3.50-£4.95. **Unlicensed** no alcohol allowed. **Credit** AmEx, JCB, MC, V.

The name of this cheerful-looking café means 'celebration' and, indeed, fenugreek leaf and paneer pilau, saffron falooda and mango lassi are worth celebrating. A platter of fried savouries, however, was pretty but samey and subzi makhani (vegetables in buttery tomato sauce) was bland. Service can range from near-comatose to overly rushed. Jashan parallels a current Bombay trend, with vegetables cooked in 'European-style' tomato or cream sauces, cheddar-like cheese used in traditional dishes and regional recipes given a Gujarati spin.

Karahi King ★

213 East Lane, North Wembley, Middx HA0 3NG
(020 8904 2760/4994). North Wembley tube/245 bus.
Meals served noon-midnight daily. **Main courses** £3.50-£12. **No credit cards.**

On an uninspiring stretch of North Wembley road, Karahi King dishes out earthy Punjabi fare with back-slapping camaraderie to local Indian families. Functional, with wobbly, wipe-clean tables, parquet flooring and blasts of Bollywood music, this spot looks like any other Indian high street joint. Unlike at most clones, though, cooking here really delivers the goods. Deliciously crisp, meaty samosas served straight from the pan are packed with juicy, cumin-scented lamb mince. Karahi methi gosht – lamb curry, simmered with generous helpings of ginger, chillies and chopped fresh fenugreek leaves – is fabulous value at £5.90.

Madhu's ★ ★

39 South Road, Southall, Middx UB1 1SW (020
8574 1897/6380/www.madhusonline.com). Southall
rail. **Lunch served** 12.30-3pm Mon, Wed-Fri.
Dinner served 6-11.30pm Mon, Wed, Thur, Sun; 6pm-midnight Fri, Sat. **Main courses** £6-£12. **Credit** AmEx, DC, MC, V.

Refurbished, family-run Madhu's makes a sizzling statement in Southall's Punjabi heartland: North Indian cooking with a Kenyan twist. Shiny black granite, light wooden flooring and a water feature make this the dressiest Indian restaurant in the area. Pungent red pili pili chillies pack power into a main of machuzi kuku – a delicious Indo-Kenyan chicken dish simmered in a cinnamon- and clove-spiked broth. Madhu's does a selection of brilliant desserts: carrot halwa – a fudgy, cardamom-scented hot pud made from grated carrots – could be the best you'll taste outside India. Service can be a tad chaotic, but smiles never slip.

New Asian Tandoori Centre Roxy ★

114-118 The Green, Southall, Middx UB2 4VQ
(020 8574 2597). Southall rail. **Meals served**
8am-11pm Mon-Thur; 8am-midnight Fri-Sun.
Main courses £3-£7. **No credit cards.**

Popular with Indian families, this Sikh-run caff dishes out some of the most scrumptious Punjabi street snacks going. Playful banter between waiters and customers adds to the sense of community. Though busy as a takeaway, it's more fun to sit in the airy dining hall and begin a meal with pitchers of lovely lassi. Channas – tart chickpeas cooked with tons of onions and sharpened with pounded pomegranate seeds – couldn't be better from an Indian street stall, and in true Punjabi tradition they come with hot baturas (puffed, spongy bread). Authentic veggies, meaty kebabs, samosas and above average curries mark this place as a landmark for wholesome Punjabi grub.

Redmond's ★

170 Upper Richmond Road West, SW14 8AW
(020 8878 1922). Mortlake rail then 337 bus.
Lunch served noon-2.30pm Sun. **Dinner served** 6.30-10.30pm Mon-Thur; 7-10.30pm Sat, Sun. **Set lunch** £17 2 courses, £21 3 courses. **Set dinner** £26 2 courses, £29.50 3 courses. **Credit** AmEx, MC, V.

Redmond's is humming on Saturday nights. The one-room space, full of locals, is decorous, service is polished and the wine list a treat. The cooking is fine indeed. First-rate, often seasonal, ingredients are handled with a delicacy of touch lacking from many more highly praised restaurants. Highlights of a set dinner included succulent tuna carpaccio; a summery main of pea, mint and red onion risotto; and poached rhubarb with a blood orange sorbet. But every dish was a winner: we could have singled out the crab ravioli starter or the superb British farmhouse cheeses. Redmond's is always good, barring the odd hiccup. This time it was faultless.

Riva

169 Church Road, SW13 9HR (020 8748 0434).
Barnes or Barnes Bridge rail. **Lunch served** noon-2.30pm Mon-Fri, Sun. **Dinner served** 7-11pm Mon-Sat; 7-9.30pm Sun. **Main courses** £11.50-£19.50.
Credit AmEx, MC, V.
Riva is an Italian favourite of many years' standing. A typical meal might be linguine with queen scallops and langoustine, followed by calf's liver with polenta or grilled squid with wild herbs, and finished off with panna cotta with mixed berries. Like the rest of the operation, the wine list is fairly priced. Efficient, meticulous staff add to the understated charm of the long room. In all, good value for money in an elegantly tranquil setting.

The River Café

Thames Wharf, Rainville Road, W6 9HA (020 7386 4200/www.rivercafe.com). Hammersmith tube.
Lunch served 12.30-3pm daily. **Dinner served** 7-9.30pm Mon-Sat. **Main courses** £23-£30. **Credit** AmEx, DC, MC, V.
Sitting outside among the verdant herb pots here is one of the most pleasant ways to spend a sunny day in London. Yet complete relaxation is elusive: the clock is ticking and soon other diners will arrive to claim the table. Choosing quickly is hard, so tempting is the menu. Hearty options, simply presented but spot-on for flavour, might include mixed seafood risotto with tiny nuggets of lobster, or own-made tagliatelle with Scottish chanterelles, parsley and cheese. Though food is pricey, the excellent wine list offers good bottles for as little as £10.50. Some desserts, such as vin santo ice-cream with pressed chocolate cake, highlight a meal but others disappoint. From the booking person to the valet, staff are confident and gracious. Expert macchiato brings things to a swift conclusion, but it's hard not to like this place, hyped though it is.

Royal China

3 Chelverton Road, SW15 1RN (020 8788 0907).
East Putney tube/Putney rail/14, 37, 74 bus. **Lunch served** noon-3.30pm Mon-Sat; noon-4pm Sun.
Dinner served 6.30-11pm Mon-Thur; 6.30-11.30pm

Sagar

Fri, Sat; 6.30-10.30pm Sun. **Main courses** £5.50-£40. **Set meals** £23, £26 (minimum 2 people). **Credit** AmEx, DC.

Situated in an old synagogue, this restaurant was once part of the Royal China chain but went it alone some years ago. The gold and black lacquered interior remains, as does the high standard of cooking. Recommended are the golden, light mixed meat croquettes, steamed prawn dumplings, baked roasted pork puffs and jumbo scallops steamed in their shells. There's also a wide selection of Cantonese classics. Finish up with a creamy mango pudding. Service is friendly and attentive, and, mercifully, the plinky keyboard muzak was almost inaudible above the noisy chatter of mainly Chinese patrons.

Sagar ★ ★
157 King Street, W6 9JT (020 8741 8563).
Hammersmith tube/299 bus. **Lunch served** noon-2.45pm, **dinner served** 5.30-10.45pm Mon-Wed. **Meals served** noon-10.45pm Thur-Sun. **Main courses** £5-£10. **Credit** AmEx, JCB, MC, V.
Specialising in the vegetarian cuisine of Udupi, a coastal town in Karnataka, Sagar (meaning 'ocean') is a rare treat. The twin themes of 'pale wood' and 'minimalism' characterise its furnishings and the food is outstanding. Idli, soft and light, falls off the fork. Sambar is near perfect. Paper masala dosai has authentic fenugreek undertones. Suki bhajee and

vegetable kootu feature daily-changing seasonal vegetables – the former stir-fried with spices, the latter cooked in a coconut and yoghurt sauce. Sheera, a rich, saffron-suffused semolina dessert, has the texture of freshly baked sponge cake. Only chutneys and pickles are mundane. Otherwise, Sagar's two talented chefs produce a culinary sensation.

La Trompette ★
5-7 Devonshire Road, W4 2EU (020 8747 1836).
Turnham Green tube. **Lunch served** noon-2.30pm Mon-Sat; 12.30-3pm Sun. **Dinner served** 6.30-10.30pm Mon-Sat; 7-10pm Sun. **Set lunch** £21.50 3 courses; (Sun) £25 3 courses. **Set dinner** £30 3 courses. **Credit** AmEx, JCB, MC, V.
The 2002 winner of *Time Out's* Best New Restaurant award, La Trompette continues to build on its success and is often packed. No surprise, perhaps, when it's part of the same stable as Chez Bruce (*see p60*) and the Glasshouse (*see p61*). The room, with leather banquettes and soft lighting, is discreetly luxurious, and staff are super-efficient. The modern French menu offers a mix of summery dishes and heartier options. Starters like rock oysters topped with plump scallops in a pool of tomato jelly and gazpacho vinaigrette are hard to resist. Mains might include ragoût of sea bream and shellfish in a fragrant crème fraîche and champagne broth or calf's kidneys and sweetbreads with Madeira sauce. A sleek operation, with a good-value set dinner.

The Victoria
10 West Temple Sheen, SW14 7RT (020 8876 4238/www.thevictoria.net). *Mortlake rail.* **Open** 8am-11pm Mon-Sat; 8am-10.30pm Sun. **Breakfast served** 8-9.30am Mon-Fri; 8-10am Sat, Sun. **Lunch served** noon-2.30pm Mon-Fri; noon-3pm Sat, Sun. **Dinner served** 7-10pm Mon-Sat; 7-9pm Sun. **Main courses** £9.95-£16.95. **Credit** AmEx, MC, V.
A pub renowned as a weekend lunch spot, with an attractive children's play area and a conservatory overlooking it. It's very family-friendly and waiting staff gently suggest younger children might prefer small portions of the plainer items on the changing menu – grilled chicken with chips, perhaps, or just the one boar and apple sausage with mash. The imaginative dishes use top-class ingredients. Beetroot risotto with spinach was rosy-hued, nutty and creamy. Desserts are glorious. We still dream of the chocolate pudding with seville orange ice-cream.

Also in the area
Bar Estilo 2-3 Rocks Lane, SW13 0DB (020 8878 2122); **Carluccio's** 5-6 The Green, W5 5DA (020 8566 4458); **FishWorks Seafood Café** 6 Turnham Green Terrace, W4 1QP (020 8994 0086); **Gilbey's** 77 The Grove, W5 5LL (020 8840 7568); **Giraffe** 270 Chiswick High Road, W4 1PD (020 8995 2100); **Sonny's** 94 Church Road, SW13 0DQ (020 8748 0393); **Strada** 237 Earl's Court Road, SW5 9AN (020 7835 1180); **Strada** 175 New King's Road, SW6 4SW (020 7731 6404); **Strada** 375 Lonsdale Road, SW13 9PY (020 8392 9216).

South

Asadal

180 New Malden High Street, New Malden, Surrey KT3 4ES (020 8942 2334/8949 7385). New Malden rail. **Lunch served** noon-3pm Mon-Fri. **Dinner served** 6-11pm Mon-Fri; 5-11pm Sun. **Meals served** noon-11pm Sat. **Main courses** £7-£25. **Set dinners** £15 2 courses, £50 5 courses (minimum 2). **Credit** AmEx, MC, V.

One of the few 'fancy' Korean restaurants in Greater London, where the cooking, though not cheap, is exemplary. Even simple dishes, like sesame-flecked spinach namul served with kimch'i as part of the panch'an selection, are spot-on. Bindaedok, a thick fried pancake with red and green pepper and minced beef, is perfect: crisp, hot and not a spot of stray grease. There are dishes you won't find elsewhere, such as raw abalone in the shell, sliced paper-thin and tasting of the sea. Galbi, beef spare ribs served off the bone and marinated in a sweet, garlic-laced sauce, is barbecued at the table. It's superb – tender, succulent and full of flavour. Bibimbap, packed with vegetables and topped with raw egg, arrives in a hot bowl, so the rice gets crunchy on the bottom. Staff are eagle-eyed and friendly, even when it's busy.

Brady's ★

513 Old York Road, SW18 1TF (020 8877 9599). Wandsworth Town rail/28, 44 bus. **Dinner served** 6.30-10pm Mon; 6.30-10.30pm Tue, Wed, Sat; 6.30-10.45pm Thur, Fri. **Main courses** £6.35-£8.95. **No credit cards**.

There's something reassuring about a posh fish-and-chip restaurant, especially one as far from the seaside as this. Brady's middle-class chic incorporates rickety tables, hand-painted mermaids and green-and-cream wall menus. Starters encompass divine potted shrimps with toast, flaky salmon fish cakes and a refreshing plate of anchovies and sweet herring. Mains take in the usual suspects, and specials like conger eel and lemon sole. Full marks to the own-made relishes (tarragon mayonnaise is a must) and large-cut, just-right chips. The fish was great, but portions could be bigger: the large haddock could better be described as medium and the small as child-size.

Cah Chi ★

34 Durham Road, SW20 0TW (020 8947 1081). Raynes Park rail/57, 131 bus. **Lunch served** noon-3pm, **dinner served** 5-11pm Tue-Fri. **Meals served** noon-11pm Sat; noon-10.30pm Sun. **Main courses** £4.50-£14. **Set dinner** £15. **No credit cards**.

New Malden is undoubtedly the place to find authentic Korean restaurants, but stray towards Central London and you'll come across this gem. It's plain in decor, but as friendly as they come, with children's drawings and pictures of customers on the walls. The food is fantastic, as is the service – let staff steer you round the sizeable menu. High points include kun man du (hot, juicy steamed and fried dumplings), and a gob-smacking stir-fry of soondae (black pudding made with rice vermicelli: you can see its tracery-like lines through the skin) flavoured with perilla leaves and seeds and cooked in a wok at the table. Panch'an are also a treat – a selection of kimch'i, pickled cucumber and sticky-sweet soy beans. Less impressive is an oily bindaedok pancake, but the food generally hits the high notes. Cah Chi is deservedly popular, so book ahead. Oh, and it's BYO.

Canyon

The Tow Path, Richmond Riverside, Richmond, Surrey TW10 6UJ (020 8948 2944). Richmond tube/rail. **Brunch served** 11am-3.30pm Sat, Sun. **Lunch served** noon-3.30pm Mon-Fri. **Dinner served** 6-11pm Mon-Sat; 6-10.30pm Sun. **Main courses** £10-£18. **Credit** AmEx, DC, MC, V.

With its big terrace overlooking the river, wide windows and sweeping views, Canyon has long been the perfect fair weather restaurant for those for whom money is little object and good food matters. In far west London, and a good walk from the tube, this is destination dining worth the trip for starters like Asian pear salad (buttery slices of sweet pear, roast pumpkin seeds and avocado) and mains like oriental marinated steak with a savoury sauce married to brightly flavoured spring greens. Dishes like basil-stuffed chicken breast with herb couscous are anything but ordinary: rich flavours transform the chicken into something special. Puds like blackcurrant cheesecake are just right – tart and sweet in equal measure. Staff are accommodating.

Chez Bruce ★

2 Bellevue Road, SW17 7EG (020 8672 0114). Wandsworth Common rail. **Lunch served** noon-2pm Mon-Fri; 12.30-2.30pm Sat; 12.30-3pm Sun. **Dinner served** 7-10.30pm Mon-Thur, Sun; 6.30-10.30pm Fri, Sat. **Set lunch** (Mon-Fri) £23.50 3 courses; (Sat) £25 3 courses; (Sun) £27.50 3 courses. **Set dinner** £30 3 courses. **Credit** AmEx, DC, MC, V.

Chez Bruce is as popular as ever, so much so that you can now dine at one of six tables in a tiny upstairs room, although we can't recommend it if you want to feel part of the main event. This happens downstairs, in a long, white room, among the mirrored pillars, drab art and a wealthy Wandsworth set, enjoying fine views over the common and the enthusiastic attentions of the numerous staff. On a hot summer's evening a starter of gazpacho Andalus is fabulously cold and intense.

Gourmet Burger Kitchen. *See p62.*

The choice might also include tomato tartlets and deep-fried turbot goujons or herb salad with griselles and a walnut oil dressing. Just as good are main courses like roast cod on olive oil mash with a red pepper compote and a dashing parsley and lemon sauce, though very occasionally you do get a duff dish. If it's on, don't pass by the stupendous lemon posset with shortbread for dessert. The mighty, 28-page wine list is also a highlight.

Dexter's Grill

20 Bellevue Road, SW17 7EB (020 8767 1858). Wandsworth Common rail. **Meals served** noon-11pm Mon-Fri; 10am-11pm Sat; 10am-10.30pm Sun. **Main courses** £7-£15. **Credit** AmEx, MC, V.
A big-hitter in the family-friendly stakes at weekends (and winner of the Best Family Restaurant category of the *Time Out* London Eating & Drinking Awards 2003), Dexter's endears itself to big eaters of all ages – especially those into burgers, steak or chicken. It's an attractive, friendly place, adept at providing the cheery greeting you associate with down-home diners. A big jug of iced water appears as soon as you sit down, though we had to sample the excellent blueberry and apple smoothie as well. The burgers are something to write home about: extremely lean, with juices leaking into a soft bun. Relishes are served separately; chips are delicious. We regretted ordering cheesecake, which was run-of-the-mill, but rate the ice-cream and milkshakes highly.

The French Table

85 Maple Road, Surbiton, Surrey KT6 4AW (020 8399 2365). Surbiton rail. **Lunch served** noon-2.30pm Wed-Fri, Sun. **Dinner served** 7-10.30pm Tue-Sat. **Main courses** £10.80-£14.80. **Set lunch** (Wed-Fri) £12.50 2 courses; £15.50 3 courses; (Sun) £16.50 3 courses. **Credit** MC, V.
On a Surbiton site that's seemed strangely cursed (few restaurants have lasted here more than a couple of years), Eric and Sarah Guignard have established an enthusiastic local following since opening in 2001.

There are no culinary fireworks, and an occasional dish doesn't work, but the crowds return for the warm atmosphere and reliable French repertoire with the odd twist. The 'duo of foie gras' comes, unusually, on warm mozzarella and in the form of a 'ballotine with four spice' (a terrine). Fish figures heavily among the mains – such as baked cod with scallop mousse, courgette fondue and fresh pea sauce. Menu regulars include the superb caramelised pork belly in red wine, with glazed turnips and a 'pastilla' of dried figs and apricots. Try the small but perfectly formed cheeseboard, or the cocoa overload of the chocolate and praline gateau with cherry sorbet. The wine list is interesting and fairly priced (lots under £20). The service is lovely.

The Glasshouse ★

14 Station Parade, Kew, Surrey TW9 3PZ (020 8940 6777). Kew Gardens tube/rail. **Lunch served** noon-2.30pm Mon-Sat; 12.30-2.45pm Sun. **Dinner served** 7-10.30pm Mon-Thur; 6.30-10.30pm Fri, Sat; 7.30-10pm Sun. **Set lunch** £17.50 3 courses; (Sun) £25 3 courses. **Set dinner** £30 3 courses. **Credit** AmEx, MC, V.
One of London's most genteel neighbourhoods is the ideal location for a restaurant as sophisticated and unassuming as the Glasshouse. The elegant wedge of a dining room is rarely less than full; it's easy to see why. The cooking is ambitious, modern and largely free of showboating flourishes (and excessive price tags). Pea soup with smoked bacon chantilly or ragoût of prawns and salmon with scallop agnolotti are typical examples of the kind of light, unfussy combinations that appear on the set lunch menu. Mains run to more robust numbers, such as roast suckling pork with apple, sage and choucroute tarte fine, but are similarly deft both in terms of execution and presentation. And if you can resist the splendid plate of British and French cheeses, you'll find plenty on the pudding list to tempt you. Modest, knowledgeable staff and a decent, affordable wine list are two more reasons for a return visit.

Gourmet Burger Kitchen ★ ★

44 Northcote Road, SW11 1NZ (020 7228 3309/
www.gbkinfo.co.uk). Clapham Junction rail. **Meals**
served noon-11pm Mon-Fri; 11am-11pm Sat; 11am-
10pm Sun. **Main courses** £4.95-£6.95. **Credit** MC, V.
God bless America! Finally, burgers have grown up.
Yet, hold those preconceptions, for the gourmet
burger concept comes not from over the Pond but
from across the other side of the world: New
Zealand. As soon as you clock that Kiwi fusion
maestro Peter Gordon is behind the menu at GBK
you know you're in for something special. How does
a towering Jamaican take your fancy (100%
Aberdeen Angus beef, mango and ginger sauce)? Or
a zingy chorizo burger (spicy Spanish sausage,
sweet potato, rocket and tomato)? There are also a
number of fine veggie choices, such as a whole
portabella mushroom slapped in a sourdough bun
with sweet red peppers, rocket, red onion and pesto.
The chips are choice and chunky, the decor clean
and sleek, the service swift and smiling. There's also
Steinlager on tap and a small selection of New
Zealand wines. Fast food has never tasted so good.

Lee Fook

76 The Broadway, Tolworth, Surbiton, Surrey KT6
7HR (020 8399 9793). Surbiton rail. **Lunch served**
noon-2.30pm, **dinner served** 5.30-11pm daily. **Main**
courses £4-£6. **Credit** MC, V.
Don't make assumptions based on the 'Hot Buffet
£6' sign. This intimate family-run restaurant boasts
real Chinese food. Chef Ringo Lo led the cooking at
Lee Fook in Queensway (now demolished) to great
acclaim before setting up here and creates dishes
rarely seen on suburban menus (including lobster
with ginger and spring onion, braised belly pork
with Chinese preserved vegetables or crispy belly
pork). But go off menu to be really impressed. Call
a few days before and explain a few favourite foods
and leave the rest to Ringo. Our last meal, ordered
in this way, included a glorious chicken and Chinese
herb broth made with organic, corn-fed chicken.
Other highlights were Chinese sausage wrapped
with beef fillet in a Cantonese sauce and home-made
wind-dried pork stir-fried with Chinese broccoli.

Monsieur Max ★

133 High Street, Hampton Hill, Surrey TW12 1NJ
(020 8979 5546). Kew Gardens tube/rail then R68
bus/Fulwell rail. **Lunch served** noon-2.30pm
Tue-Fri, Sun. **Dinner served** 7-9.30pm daily.
Set lunch (Mon-Fri) £20 2 courses; (Mon-Fri, Sun)
£25 3 courses. **Set dinner** (Tue-Thur) £37.50
3 courses. **Credit** AmEx, DC, MC, V.
Unswayed by fashion, this exemplary restaurant has
been developing its own distinctive branch of 'cuisine
bourgeoise' for years. Chef Alex Bentley weaves a
panoply of elements into challenging, surprising
dishes. It's not for faint hearts, but you'd have to be
an ascetic not to delight in dressed crab and sweet
fennel salad, beignet of baby artichokes and cured
ham, lemon couscous, parsley and olive emulsion;
followed by roasted rack of Welsh lamb, its

sweetbreads and kidneys, smoked aubergine and
lemon caviar, ragoût of haricots blancs and cherry
tomatoes and spiced vinaigrette; rounded off with
rice pudding with Madagascan vanilla, raspberry
fromage frais, roasted apricot and orange tuile. The
setting couldn't be less stuffy – a cosy room
punctuated by coloured glass, old wall tiles and art
deco touches. Factor in the ebullient Gallic staff, who
maintain the perfect balance of chumminess and
professionalism, and you have one fine restaurant.

Numidie

48 Westow Hill, SE19 1RX (020 8766 6166/
www.numidie.co.uk). Gypsy Hill rail. **Lunch served**
noon-4pm Sat, Sun. **Dinner served** 6.30-10.30pm
Tue-Sun. **Main courses** £7.25-£12.50. **Credit** MC, V.
With its narrow, unassuming shopfront entrance,
Numidie is easy to miss, but you'd miss a treat. A
bohemian, 1960s air, inspired by dark-hued, slightly
shabby walls hung with understated artwork,
friendly service and an eclectic selection of good
value North African and southern French dishes –
the owner is a Berber from Marseilles – make for a
winning combination. Dishes range from duck
breast with violet confit and pomegranate juice,
char-grilled baby squid stuffed with garlicky crab,
bouillabaise or red mullet stuffed with garlic and
herbs to more standard tagines and couscous. All
are executed with care and skill. Upstairs North
African music plays discreetly, while those in the
often-packed downstairs wine bar are frequently
entertained by musicians.

Olley's ★

67-69 Norwood Road, SE24 9AA (020 8671 8259/
www.olleys.info). Herne Hill rail/3, 68 bus. **Meals**
served noon-10.30pm Tue-Sat. **Dinner served**
5-10.30pm Mon, Sun. **Main courses** £7.65-£18.25.
Credit AmEx, MC, V.
Lucky indeed are the folk of Herne Hill, having such
a wonderful chippy on their doorstep. Olley's has
won masses of awards, and despite the jokey names
– 'Lord Archer's Experience' (cod and chips, 'tart not
included') – the kitchen is serious about the food.
'Neptune's punchbowl' is a fish soup that could win
prizes of its own, and even humble battered calamari
melts in the mouth. Chips are double-cooked for
crispness and devilishly tasty. Whether fried, grilled
or steamed, Olley's fish is invariably fresh and
cooked to perfection. Even steamed puds and tarts
are worth saving room for. The bare brick, plaster
and wood decor of the converted railway arch may
look like a B-movie Arizona sheriff's office (in the
nicest possible way), but the service and food make
up for any locational shortcomings.

Radha Krishna Bhavan ★

86 Tooting High Street, SW17 0RN (020 8682
0969). Tooting Broadway tube. **Lunch served**
noon-3pm daily. **Dinner served** 6-11pm Mon-Thur,
Sun; 6pm-midnight Fri, Sat. **Main courses** £1.95-
£6.95. **Set thali** (Sun) £5.95-£7.95. **Minimum** £5.
Credit AmEx, DC, MC, V.

Since it opened in 1999, RKB – the house of Krishna and his favourite consort, Radha – has been the undisputed champion of Keralan cooking in Tooting. The interior is humble, yet startlingly kitsch. Don't let this distract you from the 'ever popular specialities', or the even less enticingly described 'dry vegetables'. Take a chance on dishes such as the cabbage thoran (a light and aromatic stir-fry), or kalan (a yoghurt and mango curry). The best dishes are too many to mention, but skip the popadoms and pickles to concentrate on starters of pillow-light idlis, three types of vadai, or main courses such as appam (steamed rice-flour pancakes) and potato curry. With a few exceptions, such as the Kerala fish curry or the kozhi varutha curry, the lamb, chicken and seafood (for which read 'prawn') dishes are much more pedestrian.

Ransome's Dock

35-37 Parkgate Road, SW11 4NP (020 7223 1611). Bus 19, 49, 319, 345. **Brunch served** noon-3.30pm Sun. **Meals served** noon-11pm Mon-Fri; noon-midnight Sat. **Main courses** £10.50-£20. **Set meal** (noon-5pm Mon-Fri) £14.25 2 courses. **Credit** AmEx, DC, MC, V.

Battersea's mellow Ransome's Dock makes the most of its waterside setting with a pretty outside terrace. Other pluses are a friendly, unfussy feel, an enticing 17-page wine list, an enterprising food menu that highlights organic and carefully sourced fish, meats, game and veg, and a family-friendly Sunday brunch. Menus change frequently, but among the near-fixtures are Morecambe Bay potted shrimps and Shorthorn steaks. A typical meal might start with Serrano ham with figs or Caesar salad, followed by a tender Shorthorn hamburger with sweetcorn relish or line-caught cod in beer batter (a Sunday menu fixture), and then finish up with one of the indulgent desserts like lemon panna cotta or summer pudding and cream.

Sarkhel's ★ ★

199 Replingham Road, SW18 5LY (020 8870 1483/ takeaway 8871 0808). Southfields tube. **Lunch served** noon-2.30pm Tue-Sun. **Dinner served** 6-10.30pm Tue-Thur, Sun; 6-11pm Fri, Sat. **Main courses** £6.95-£9.95. **Set lunch** £5 2 courses. **Set thali** £9.95 3 courses. **Credit** AmEx, MC, V.

Sarkhel's exceptional cooking has a deservedly loyal following among the well-to-do folk of Southfields. The best traditional dishes from across India take turns on the menu. Parsi dhansak rice is a dark, sultry concoction, with browned onions and a generous amount of star anise; lamb shank arrives tender and falling off the bone, the gravy subtly spiced. One of the menu's most surprising dishes is from Hyderabad: ringan sambhariya, a thick, coarse paste of fresh grated coconut, ground poppy seed, toasted coriander seed and tamarind, cooked with tiny, slender aubergines. Pudding? Try the bhapa doi, a Bengali dessert that resembles set yoghurt. Quibbles? Tightly packed tables, high noise levels and service that, when stretched, can be tetchy.

Thyme

14 Clapham Park Road, SW4 7BB (020 7627 2468/ www.thymeandspace.com). Clapham Common tube. **Dinner served** 6.30-10.30pm Tue-Sat. **Main courses** £6-£11. **Set meal** £55 5 courses incl 4 glasses of wine. **Credit** AmEx, MC, V.

Thyme's pared-down interior is simple enough, but the cooking's more unusual: every dish is served as a trio of mini-dishes, arranged on a long, rectangular plate. So, you could order a delicate parcel of sole wrapped in cling film, flanked by crunchy roast cockles and scallops. Or garlic roast langoustines, langoustine cannelloni and langoustines velouté, if you're in a langoustine kind of mood. You're meant to order about three dishes, some of which are more suitable as starters (the magnificently thick pea and ham soup is served with bacon slices and ham hock), and some go better as mains (duck confit with foie gras or shin of veal and liver). Not everything works, but the puddings are lovely and were prefaced by a delicious glass of banana froth. If this sounds daunting, it needn't: the staff know their stuff and there's also a choice of set menus (each dish accompanied by a shrewdly selected glass of wine).

Tsunami ★

5-7 Voltaire Road, SW4 6DQ (020 7978 1610). Clapham North tube. **Dinner served** 6-11pm Mon-Fri; noon-11.30pm, Sat. **Main courses** £7.95-£16.50. **Credit** AmEx, MC, V.

Tsunami may be stuck up a side street and look as though it came out of an IKEA flatpack, but this is one of the slickest Japanese restaurants in town (winning the *Time Out* award for Best Japanese for 2002, the year after it opened). Standards are high in general, but the sushi (always served last) is not to be missed. It's tough to choose from the specials, which might include wagyu beef (a hefty £40), sea urchin and shiso leaf tempura, or roast duck, avocado and cucumber roll. Dishes like foie gras and chive roll with eel sauce stray into fusion territory, but the underlying current remains Japanese. Starters like oyster kataifi (an oyster wrapped in thread-thin pastry, deep-fried and served with wasabi sauce) are wonderfully creative and perfectly executed. Eager-to-please staff adeptly guide diners round the menu. Tsunami is highly popular, which leads to its one downside: the noise. Not cheap, but excellent value.

Also in the area

Bar Estilo 44 Broad Street, Teddington, TW11 8QZ (020 8977 6002); **Giraffe** 27 Battersea Rise, SW11 1HG (020 7223 0933); **Giraffe** 30 Hill Street, Richmond, TW9 1TW (020 8332 2646); **Loch Fyne** 175 Hampton Road, Twickenham, TW2 5NG (020 8255 6222); **Strada** 26 Hill Street, Richmond, TW1 1TW (020 7590 4644); **Strada** 11-13 Battersea Rise, SW11 1HG (020 7801 0794); **Strada** 91 High Street, Wimbledon SW19 5EG (020 8946 4363); **Strada** 102-104 Clapham High Street, SW4 7UL (020 7627 4847); **Wagamama** 16-18 High Street, Kingston upon Thames, KT1 1EY (020 8546 1117).

East

Armadillo ★

41 Broadway Market, E8 4PH (020 7249 3633/
www.armadillorestaurant.co.uk). Bethnal Green tube
then 106, 253 bus/26, 48, 55 bus. **Dinner served**
6.30-10.30pm daily. **Main courses** £10-£14.50.
Credit AmEx, DC, JCB, MC, V.
Banish thoughts of stripy rugs and refried beans:
Armadillo brings Latin American eating into the 21st
century. The setting is modern and inviting, much
like the pan-American cooking of Brazilian-born
chef-owner Rogerio David. The shortish menu offers
a unique take on dishes from Peruvian to Colombian.
Starters include a spicy red pepper soup with crème
fraîche and crispy tortillas or a salad of salt cod,
avocado, celery and pomegranate. Stews – chunky
monkfish and crab chupe, duck seco and fried
cassava – feature as mains, along with Argentinian
steak and squash pancakes. Fluffy encanelado –
sponge cake soaked in cinnamon-and-lemon syrup –
with poached pear, plus Mexican coffee, provided a
silky smooth finish. The mainly Latino wine list is
well priced, and service comes with a smile. The back
garden (one table) is a delight. Armadillo was winner
of Best Local Restaurant in the *Time Out* London
Eating & Drinking Awards 2003.

Café Spice Namaste

16 Prescot Street, E1 8AZ (020 7488 9242/www.cafe
spice.co.uk). Tower Hill tube/Tower Gateway DLR.
Lunch served noon-3pm Mon-Fri. **Dinner served**
6.15-10.30pm Mon-Fri; 6.30-10.30pm Sat. **Main
courses** £9.95-£15.95. **Credit** AmEx, DC, MC, V.
Although all Cyrus Todiwala's dishes rely on
traditional techniques to good (or better) effect,
purists may baulk at his use of the unusual (such as
venison tikka and wild boar sausages) alongside
Indian classics. The chutneys and pickles with the
pre-meal popadoms are exemplary. A starter of
seafood samosa encloses crab meat and chopped
prawns cooked in the traditional Keralan manner.
King scallops with ginger and chilli come with garlic
pilau and thin coconut curry. The classic Parsee
shank of lamb dish (masala nu roast gos) is rich but
surprisingly mellow, with a dark brown gravy
oozing ginger and garlic flavours. Service is effective
and friendly. Fellow diners are invariably suited City
types affluent enough (or on expense accounts) to
afford the somewhat high prices.

Cantaloupe

35 Charlotte Road, EC2A 3PD (020 7613 4411/
www.cantaloupegroup.co.uk). Old Street tube/rail.
Lunch served noon-3pm Mon-Fri. **Dinner served**
6-11.30pm Mon-Fri; 7-11.30pm Sat. **Main courses**
£9-£11.75. **Credit** AmEx, DC, JCB, MC, V.

Don't be deterred by the light-industrial, elevated-
pen setting (and hyperactive air-con units). The
short menu at Cantaloupe, at the rear of the bar, is
imaginative and well balanced without being catch-
all eclectic. Vegetarians will be pleased with mains
like potato, feta and coriander cake served with a
top-notch okra casserole. Meat-eaters needn't fret
either, as there are plenty of grilled options. Cumin-
spiced lamb with pomegranate, roast pumpkin and
chickpeas, yoghurt, lemon, honey and tahini sauce
was worth each and every ingredient. After such
nosh (served on rustic earthenware), it might be
necessary to forego desserts like lime mousse and
papaya. Wines by the glass, matching all tastes and
foods, were equally gratifying.

Chandni ★

715 High Road, E11 4RD (020 8539 1700).
Leytonstone tube. **Meals served** 5pm-midnight
Tue-Sun. **Main courses** £2.50-£6. **Set thali** £6.
Credit AmEx, MC, V.
This Gujarati newcomer offers enjoyable home-style
cooking. Vegetable patties and moong kachori burst
with scrumptious flavour. The chilli paneer is
exquisitely spiced, and made of cotton-soft cheese.
Vegetable kofta curry pairs deep-fried mashed
paneer and potato balls – almost meaty in taste and
texture – with a rich, nutty tomato sauce. Rajma
masala (kidney bean curry), an Indian version of
Mexican chilli, is perfect with soft, spongy pooris.
Sweet lassi and falooda are less authentic, but taste
OK. Already popular with locals, this fine restaurant
boasts two chefs – one from Gujarat and the other
from the Neasden Temple (renowned within the
Gujarati community for its food). Service is warm
and hospitable, but the murals are an acquired taste.

Eyre Brothers

70 Leonard Street, EC2A 4QX (020 7613 5346/
www.eyrebrothers.co.uk). Old Street tube/rail.
Lunch served noon-3pm Mon-Fri. **Dinner
served** 6.30-11pm Mon-Sat. **Main courses**
£13-£25. **Set meal** £19 2 courses. **Credit** AmEx,
DC, MC, V.
For an integrated night out, this flash Shoreditch
eaterie is a blast of fresh air. Sit on the elegantly
robust bar stools in the Le Corbusier-style soundbox
of white walls and polished wood and consider the
menu over cocktails at the sleek mahogany bar.
Prices aren't modest, but food combinations look
enticing. Meals can, however, vary sharply. Top-of-
the-range stuffed sardines might be followed by a
stunningly fresh and colourful Portuguese fish stew.
By unaccountable contrast, you could also run into
savourless garlic and ham soup or a salty pork fillet.

Staff deal stylishly with complaints, though. Desserts include a brown bread and ginger ice-cream combination. Look out for the Eyre brothers, one of whom might be prowling about, fittingly for the area, looking like an older Jay Joplin clone.

Fox Dining Room

28 Paul Street, EC2A 4LB (020 7729 5708).
Old Street tube/rail. **Open** noon-11pm Mon-Fri.
Lunch served 12.30-3pm, **dinner served**
6.30-10pm Mon-Fri. **Main courses** £9.25.
Set meals £14 2 courses, £18.75 3 courses.
Credit MC, V.
An old-fashioned boozer that's been tarted up just enough, with a handsome brown bar on the ground floor and a dining room above. Attached to this is a shady terrace decorated with trees in pots and an awning. This is an unexpected pleasure in the mean streets behind Old Street; it looks as though it belongs in the Mediterranean. A short but appealing menu produces the likes of cured sea trout with chicory or an asparagus tart to start, followed by semolina gnocchi with a divinely dressed salad or saddle of rabbit with peas and lettuce. Everything is just so, with the dressings and accompaniments being particularly appealing. There are no extraneous frills and furbelows here, just everything in its rightful place.

Huong-Viet ★

An Viet House, 12-14 Englefield Road, N1 4LS
(020 7249 0877). Bus 67, 149, 236, 242, 243,
243A. **Lunch served** noon-3.30pm Mon-Fri;
noon-4pm Sat. **Dinner served** 5.30-11pm Mon-Sat.
Main courses £4.20-£6.90. **Set lunch** £6 2 courses
incl soft drink. **Credit** JCB, MC, V.
Despite being off the beaten track, Huong-Viet is well worth a visit. Situated inside a Vietnamese cultural centre, it has an atmosphere that belies the sign 'canteen' above the door. The lighting is subtle, framed photographs of Vietnamese scenes line the walls and staff are well turned out and friendly. The place has acquired an alcohol licence, but you can still bring your own booze (corkage is £1.50 per

person). Food, though, is the highlight. The menu is varied (each special is denoted by a box around the number), and staff will recommend their favourite dishes. Vietnamese fish cakes with salad and herbs are moist and bursting with flavour. Fried spicy squid is tender. Vietnamese chicken curry is thick and crunchy with coconut, and spicy Hue noodle soup is tangy and has plenty of prawns. Reassuringly, then, standards haven't slipped.

Mobeen ★

222-226 Green Street, E7 8LE (020 8470 2419).
Upton Park tube/58 bus. **Meals served** 11am-10pm
daily. **Main courses** £2.50-£5.50. **Credit** MC, V.
This marbled Pakistani diner is an institution among local Muslim families. So much so that, at weekends, a complicated multi-row queuing system comes into operation. Service is at a long glass counter, where you can inspect containers of richly spiced concoctions. A couple of cooks battle with flaming karahis to keep up with demand, but most dishes are reheated in the microwave as required. First courses inevitably involve something meaty, cooked in the tandoor. Uncompromisingly spiced seekh kebabs, chicken and lamb tikka don't cost much more than you'd pay in Lahore. Follow them up with meaty lamb karahi, aromatic chicken curry or pungent meat bhuna the colour of dark chocolate. Vegetarians get a minor look-in with a variety of side dishes – most of them, it has to be said, pretty average. Mobeen is run along strict Muslim lines, so smoking and drinking are not allowed.

The Real Greek ★

15 Hoxton Market, N1 6HG (020 7739 8212/
www.therealgreek.co.uk). Old Street tube/rail/26,
48, 55, 149, 243 bus. **Lunch served** noon-3pm,
dinner served 5.30-10.30pm Mon-Sat. **Main**
courses £12.90-£15.90. **Mezedes** £7.90-£8.60.
Set meal (noon-3pm, 5.30-7pm) £10 2 courses,
£13.50 3 courses. **Credit** MC, V.
Offering a unique selection of Greek food and drinks, this place continues to thrive and recently opened a second branch in EC1. Both are decorated in an

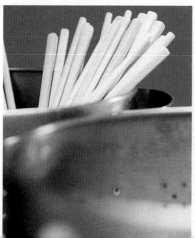

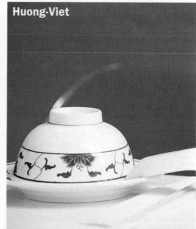

Huong-Viet

interesting fusion of ancient and modern. The menu of mezedes, fagakia (slightly larger dishes) and mains lets you pick and choose. Grilled meats (or souvláki) appear in many guises: in traditional style on a skewer, encased in warm rye sourdough, and with chicken or smoked sausage. Mezedes are equally imaginative. Particularly good are the horta (warm salad of seasonal leaves) with beetroot, htipiti (purée of tangy cheese flavoured with red peppers) and gigandes plaki (giant butter beans baked in a herby tomato sauce). The mains and desserts are usually as good, though there are occasional misses. Food and friendly service are matched by an unsurpassed list of Greek spirits and wines. Next door at No.14 is Mezedopolio (020 7739 8212), a more casual annexe to the restaurant.

Royal China

30 Westferry Circus, E14 8RR (020 7719 0888). Canary Wharf tube/DLR/Westferry DLR. **Meals served** noon-11pm Mon-Thur; noon-11.30pm Fri, Sat; 11am-10pm Sun. **Dim sum** noon-5pm daily. **Main courses** £7-£40, **dim sum** £2.20-£4.50. **Set meal** £28-£36 per person (minimum 2). **Credit** AmEx, DC, MC, V.

On a sunny afternoon you can't do much better than an al fresco lunch here, sitting at a table watching the boats to and fro on the Thames. Even when the weather's poor, the food is ever reliable. On our last visit the steamed scallop dumplings were sublime and the 'turnip paste' (sautéed threads of white radish woven with morsels of meat) achingly tender and comforting. A seasonal treat of translucent, green-speckled dumplings stuffed with juicy prawn and dark wisps of spinach lived up to the standard set by the regular menu. A selection of teas are served in little golden pots, which you can take home if you please: we loved the chance to drink tie guan yin ('Iron Buddha') instead of the ubiquitous jasmine. The atmosphere is chic but laid-back.

Sông Quê ★ ★

134 Kingsland Road, E2 8DY (020 7613 3222). Bus 26, 48, 55, 67, 149, 242, 243. **Lunch served** noon-3pm, **dinner served** 5.30-11pm Mon-Sat. **Meals served** noon-11pm Sun. **Main courses** £4.50-£8.50. **Set meals** £8.50-£14.50 per person (minimum 2). **Credit** MC, V.

Few Vietnamese restaurateurs have succeeded better in bringing the distinctive, sharp, clean flavours of their native cuisine to Londoners than the owners of Sông Quê. Plenty on the 170-plus dish menu would be familiar to anyone with a passing acquaintance with Chinese food, but it's the Vietnamese specialities that really distinguish the place. The national soup dish phô, a meal in itself, comes in an incredible 24 variations, including hardcore versions like 'sliced rare steak, well done flank, tendon and tripe'. Other recommended dishes include grilled beef wrapped in betel leaf (staff will show you how to wrap the tender little parcels) and banh xeo (a crêpe-like pancake packed with flavour-rich chicken and beansprouts). The caff-style dining

room is as authentically Vietnamese as the food. And, best of all, you'll struggle to spend more than £15 a head for a memorable meal.

Viet Hoa ★

70-72 Kingsland Road, E2 8DP (020 7729 8293). Bus 26, 48, 55, 67, 149, 242, 243. **Lunch served** noon-3.30pm Mon-Fri; 12.30-4pm Sat, Sun. **Dinner served** 5.30-11pm Mon-Fri; 5.30-11.30pm Sat, Sun. **Main courses** £3.50-£6.90. **Credit** MC, V.

Viet Hoa has long been a favourite among the Hoxton hip brigade, but judging by the number of suits at recent lunchtimes it's now on the City boys' map as well. Service isn't always as swift as it might be, but staff are friendly and can help to distinguish the Vietnamese from the Chinese menu options. Light, herby summer rolls come with a crunchy satay sauce. Banh xeo, the Vietnamese crispy pancake, can be disappointingly greasy but well filled with chunky pork and prawns. No complaints, though, about the fabulous beef slices in smoked oyster sauce: lean, flavoursome and served with plenty of fresh greens. Chao tom, minced prawns on a stick of sugar cane, is also good, and comes with a generous serving of rice vermicelli and a light fish sauce. It's great to see that despite its ever-growing popularity, Viet Hoa's cooking is as good as ever.

Wapping Food

Wapping Hydraulic Power Station, Wapping Wall, E1W 3ST (020 7680 2080). Wapping tube/Shadwell DLR. Bar **Open** noon-11pm Mon-Sat; noon-6pm Sun. **Main courses** £4.50-£7.50. *Restaurant* **Brunch served** 10am-12.30pm Sat, Sun. **Lunch served** noon-3pm daily. **Dinner served** 6.30-11pm Mon-Fri; 7-11pm Sat. **Main courses** £11-£19. **Credit** AmEx, DC, MC, V.

Once a hydraulic pumping station (which, amazingly, powered curtains in West End theatres until the 1970s), the Wapping Project now combines a leading-edge gallery and performance space with this super-chic restaurant. Much of the original machinery and character have been retained, providing an unusual setting for some impressive cooking. Starters might include, say, creamy roast butternut squash soup, or scallops on risotto nero exquisitely combined with a lemon and thyme dressing. There are two choices each of meaty, fishy and vegetarian mains. Some dishes work well, like wild venison or succulent tuna with black olive crushed new potatoes, roast courgette and salsa verde, though they can be salty. Puds can be dry and a bit of a let-down. However, the all-Australian wine list, is highly drinkable and service is exemplary.

Also in the area

Carluccio's Nash Court, Canary Wharf, London E14 5AJ (020 7719 1749); **Gaucho Grill** 29 Westferry Circus, E14 8RR (020 7987 9494); **Mobeen** 60-62 Green Street, E7 8JG (020 8471 2552); **Mobeen** 725 High Road, E10 5AB (020 8556 0147); **Mobeen** 80-82 Ilford Lane, IG1 2LA (020 8553 9733); **Mobeen** 296-298 Ilford Lane, IG1 2LP (020 8478 2229).

North

L'Aventure

3 Blenheim Terrace, NW8 0EH (020 7624 6232).
St John's Wood tube. **Lunch served** 12.30-2.15pm
Mon-Fri. **Dinner served** 7.30-10.30pm Mon-Sat.
Set lunch £18.50 3 courses incl coffee. **Set dinner**
£31.50 3 courses. **Credit** AmEx, MC, V.
La patronne, le menu, la carte des vins, et le
sommelier are all authentic French. On a balmy
night, with the open (french) doors and the lights
twinkling outside, it's delightful. The set menu gives
excellent choices: chicken sausage with a delicate
taste of foie gras, studded with pistachios; succulent
scallops with basil sauce and an artfully arranged
artichoke; pigeon, served pink, in a pungent
marjoram sauce; veal with sweetbreads and a tian of
luscious lamb – all were perfectly cooked and
beautifully presented. Chocolate gateau with caramel
sauce and an île flottante was gently outshone by two
petites crèmes brûlées of vanilla and pistachio. It's
not cheap, but it is a superior restaurant.

Aviv

87-89 High Street, Edgware, Middx HA8 7DB (020
8952 2484/www.avivrestaurant.com). Edgware tube.
Lunch served noon-2.30pm Mon-Thur, Sun.
Dinner served *Winter* 5.30-11pm Mon-Thur, Sat,
Sun. *Summer* 5.30-11pm Mon-Thur, Sun. **Main
courses** £9.95-£13.95. **Set lunch** (noon-2.30pm
Mon-Thur) £7.95 2 courses. **Set meals** £14.95
2 courses, £18.95 3 courses. **Credit** AmEx, MC, V.
If you're eating for England, this is the place to go –
not only for huge quantities, but for freshness and
well-priced set menus. Mainly Middle Eastern, the
mixed hors d'oeuvres are perfect examples of their
genres: houmous, tahini, aubergine, egg, tomato,
avocado and chopped liver. The charcoal-grilled
specialities include a well-laden skewer of lamb.
Kevas batanur, often a lamb shank, here is more like
an entire leg. Both dishes come garnished with
mountains of excellent chips and salad. All this
comes with a good-value list of French and Israeli
wines, pleasant decor and attentive service. (Kosher
supervised – Beth Din.)

Café Corfu

7 Pratt Street, NW1 0AE (020 7267 8088/
www.cafecorfu.com). Camden Town tube. **Meals
served** noon-10.30pm Tue-Thur, Sun; noon-11.30pm
Fri; 5-11.30pm Sat. **Main courses** £7.95-£12.95. **Set
meals** £16.75 3 courses, £20 4 courses. **Credit** MC, V.
Café Corfu offers a delightfully modern menu, using
superior fresh ingredients (fish and meat are flown
in from Greece) and high standards of presentation.
Starters of sweet, succulent papoutsaki Corfu
(stuffed aubergines) and kalimarakia tiganta
(crisped baby calamares in a pastry basket) are

satisfying. For mains, agnovourno me hylopites
metsouvu (organic wild boar) with tame but tasty
flat noodles is gamey and delicious, and tender
tsipoura (grilled sea bream) smells wonderfully of
the sea. Desserts and drinks (which include
interesting cocktails, organic Greek wines and
dessert wines) are no less impressive. Great service,
too. If only more Greek restaurants were like this.

Café Japan ★

626 Finchley Road, NW11 7RR (020 8455 6854).
Golders Green tube/13, 82 or 139 bus. **Lunch
served** noon-2pm Sat, Sun. **Dinner served** 6-10pm
Wed-Sun. **Main courses** £12-£16.50. **Set lunch**
£6.90 bento box, soup. **Set dinner** £16.50 bento
box, soup. **Credit** MC, V.
The welcoming chorus of 'Irasshaimase' and the
contented buzz from the diners sets a cheerful note
– and the meal could leave you open-mouthed with
amazement. Although unassuming from the outside,
this place serves some of the best sushi in town, in
unheard-of portions and at frankly silly prices. It
isn't only the number of pieces in the £16 special
selection, but the fish-to-rice ratio: about twice as
much as usual, and superbly fresh fish at that. The
spinach side salad in sesame dressing is simple but
effective. With the extra rice and the miso soup, it
takes an effort to finish (not often said of sushi).

Giraffe ★

29-31 Essex Road, N1 2SA (020 7359 5999/
www.giraffe.net). Angel tube. **Meals served** 8am-
11.30pm Mon-Fri; 9am-11.30pm Sat; 9am-10.30pm
Sun. **Main courses** £7-£10. **Credit** AmEx, MC, V.
This seven-strong chain of family-friendly
brasseries never lets you down. Whether you're here
for weekend brunch, a lazy lunch or a casual dinner,
there's something to suit from the eclectic 'global'
(but Asian-slanted) menu, with daily specials.
Typically well-executed dishes include fry-ups,
curries, burgers and stir-fries; desserts are decidedly
comfort food, with highlights such as sticky toffee
and banana pudding. Kids are fussed over and have
their own menu of goodies, such as chicken and
chips or veggie sausages. The drinks lists also
deserve honourable mentions, spanning smoothies,
cocktails, beers, wines and coffees.

Heartstone

*106 Parkway, NW1 7AN (020 7485 7744). Camden
Town tube.* **Meals served** noon-9pm Tue; 10am-
9pm Wed-Sat; 10am-4pm Sun. **Main courses**
£9.50-£15. **Credit** MC, V.
Smoothies on leather banquettes, glowing
minimalist light sculptures next to books on vegan
cooking – this is a good-looking organic café.

Generous portions of spinach salad come with yummy fried cheese cubes. Grilled swordfish is tender and tasty. Earnest desserts are made with 'rapadura sugar' – dried juice of sugar cane grown on sustainable farms in Brazil. Chilled-out staff and a sleek watch-us-cook kitchen create a feeling of being in someone's home. And the addition of a short wine list is welcome news. It's getting a little pricey in its old age, but if you want wholefood without the beads and sandals, the place is still a catch.

The Highgate

79 Highgate Road, NW5 1TL (020 7485 8442).
Kentish Town tube/rail. **Open** noon-11pm Mon-Fri; noon-midnight Sat; noon-10.30pm Sun. **Lunch served** 12.30-3pm Mon-Sat; 12.30-4pm Sun. **Dinner served** 6.30-10.30pm Mon-Sat; 6.30-10pm Sun. **Main courses** £6.50-£9.50 (bar); £8.50-£14 (restaurant). **Credit** AmEx, MC, V.

A giant framed billboard poster leans against one wall of the ground floor of the Highgate, where lively post-work and weekend drinkers tuck into quality dishes such as blue cheese and cherry tomato risotto or fat salmon fish cakes. Downstairs is the restaurant proper, where the cooking takes a more serious turn. Here you may find truffled breast of corn-fed chicken or seared peppered tuna with white beans; and there's a varied wine list to match. Discreet standard lamps provide the lighting, competent, cheerful staff bring the food and a discerning clientele of thirtysomethings pay the bills.

The House ★

63-69 Canonbury Road, N1 2DG (020 7704 7410/ www.inthehouse.biz). Highbury & Islington tube/rail. **Open** 5-11pm Mon; noon-11pm Tue-Sat; noon-10.30pm Sun. **Brunch served** noon-3.30pm Sun. **Lunch served** noon-3.30pm Tue-Fri. **Dinner served** 5.30-10.30pm Tue-Sat; 6.30-9.30pm Sun. **Main courses** £9.50-£14.95. **Set meals** (lunch, 5.30-7pm Tue-Fri) £12.95 2 courses, £14.95 3 courses. **Credit** MC, V.

The staff at the House are utterly professional and the kitchen consistently outstrips competitors. It's an attractive setting for a meal, and one that caters to most requirements. Highlights include the likes of earthy terrine of ham, foie gras and white beans served with fennel slaw and truffle mayonnaise or sublime gnocchi with broad beans and chanterelles. Char-grilled beef rib for two, the priciest of the mains, arrives beautifully pink beneath its shallot crust. Valhrona chocolate pudding is the last word in decadence. There are plenty of wines to choose from and the bar is lively enough to make you want to hang around for a post-dinner drink. Winner of Best Gastropub in the *Time Out* London Eating & Drinking Awards 2003.

Iznik ★

19 Highbury Park, N5 1QJ (020 7354 5697).
Highbury & Islington tube/rail/4, 19, 236 bus. **Meals served** 10am-4pm Mon-Fri. **Dinner served** 6.30pm-midnight daily. **Main courses** £7.50-£9.50. **Credit** MC, V.

To the uninitiated, real Turkish cooking can be revelatory. And there's no better place in London to experience the full range and subtlety of this under-appreciated cuisine than at Highbury's Iznik. Authentic stews and bakes are the speciality here – the likes of karniyarik (aubergines stuffed with minced lamb and baked in tomato sauce) are supplemented with bitingly fresh salads and kisir (cracked wheat with tomatoes, peppers and lemon juice). The food is matched by the friendly service and immensely congenial atmosphere. A gem.

Kovalam ★

12 Willesden Lane, NW6 7SR (020 7625 4761).
Kilburn tube/98 bus. **Lunch served** noon-2.30pm daily. **Dinner served** 6-11.15pm Mon-Thur, Sun; 6-11.45pm Sat, Sun. **Main courses** £2.75-£7.95. **Credit** MC, V.

The House

London

Aficionados of South Indian cuisine should head to this traditional Keralan restaurant. Uzhunnu vadai (savoury lentil doughnuts) delight with their feather-light texture. Breadfruit curry is scrumptious with roasted spices, and a sensational green banana thoran comes with an abundance of grated coconut. Kerala paratha – layered bread – has a crumbly, fluffy texture, and the coconut rice is beautifully aromatic. The tandoori king prawns and kingfish curry are comparable to what you'd find in Mahesh – Bombay's best seafood restaurant. Service is attentive and sweet-natured. This simply decorated restaurant, with its bubbling water feature, antique gramophone and framed pictures of Kovalam beach will have you booking the next flight to Trivandrum.

Lola's

The Mall Building, 359 Upper Street, N1 0PD (020 7359 1932). Angel tube. **Lunch served** noon-2.30pm Mon-Fri; noon-3pm Sat, Sun. **Dinner served** 6-11pm Mon-Sat; 7-10pm Sun. **Main courses** £12.75-£18. **Set lunch/pre-theatre dinner** (6-7pm Mon-Sat) £12.50 2 courses, £17.75 3 courses. **Credit** AmEx, DC, JCB, MC, V.

Lola's, built into the ceiling of a converted tram station, turns out some of the freshest, most surprising taste combinations in N1. New chef Elisha Carter favours bright, distilled flavours. Your introduction to his talents might be an *amuse-bouche* such as chilled tomato consommé with feta. Spectacular starters such as rabbit ravioli in carrot consommé with tarragon sauce heave with flavour. A gutsy main might be gamey veal with spicy sausage and herb gnocchi. A stunning strawbery 'soup' with goat's cheese panna cotta is made unforgettable with a refreshing dusting of lavender powder; sinfully gooey chocolate fondant is livened up with an orange and thyme sorbet.

Mangal Oçakbası ★

10 Arcola Street, E8 2DJ (020 7275 8981/ www.mangal.co.uk). Dalston Kingsland rail. **Meals served** noon-midnight daily. **Main courses** £6.50-£11.50. **No credit cards.**

No menu, just a refrigerated display of raw kebabs (point at what you want), a sizzling oçak grill and a hot table laid with stews and braises – but this simple café has them queuing out the door. Pide and saç breads can accompany a starter of lentil soup. It's a meat-eaters' paradise, but vegetarians will savour the roast aubergine mashed with tomato, hot pepper and green herbs. Kebabs are exemplary and are served over bread with very fresh salad. It's unlicensed, but there's no corkage charge. Still one of the best in this Turkish-dominated part of town.

Mango Room

10 Kentish Town Road, NW1 8NH (020 7482 5065). Camden Town tube. **Lunch served** noon-3pm Tue-Sat. **Dinner served** 6pm-midnight Mon-Sat. **Meals served** noon-11pm Sun. **Main courses** £9-£12. **Set dinner** £18 2 courses, £20 3 courses. **Credit** MC, V.

Mango Room is going from strength to strength. 'Caribbean with a global twist' describes not only the cuisine but the service – distinctly Mediterranean at times. Mains require side orders, which boost the cost, but you can't go wrong with options such as seared salmon fillet with pickled mango sauce. This beautifully flavoured dish could be teamed with rice and peas and fried plantain. Warm ackee and avocado salad is a fine and comfortably large non-meat choice. The enjoyably eclectic decor features raw textures and huge colourful paintings. Ska tunes and ballads from the likes of Ken Boothe and Lord Kitchener add to the laid-back mood.

Mosaica @ the Factory

The Chocolate Factory, Wood Green Business Centre, Clarendon Road, N22 6XJ (020 8889 2400). Wood Green tube. **Open** 10am-9.45pm Tue-Sat; noon-3pm Sun. **Lunch served** noon-2pm Tue-Fri; noon-3pm Sun. **Main courses** £12-£16. **Credit** AmEx, MC, V.

Housed in an ex-factory (now artists' studios), this laid-back restaurant with shabby-chic furniture is spacious and homely. The short menu focuses on the judicious combination of a few ingredients. Starters might include mussels in a garlic and thyme broth, or gallons of creamy (if oily) pea soup. Mains might be grilled swordfish atop a (slightly dull) Caesar salad, or duck breast with mustard mash and red cabbage. Chocolate mousse is scrumptious and big enough for three. Mosaica is a fave with families – there's room to park buggies and let kids roam.

Rasa ★ ★

55 Stoke Newington Church Street, N16 0AR (020 7249 0344/www.rasarestaurants.com). Stoke Newington rail/73 bus. **Lunch served** noon-3pm Sat, Sun. **Dinner served** 6-10.45pm Mon-Thur, Sun; 6-11.30pm Fri, Sat. **Main courses** £3.65-£6.85. **Set meal** £15.50 4 courses. **Credit** AmEx, MC, V.

This small eaterie serves such good Keralan food that booking is essential. The best introduction to the cuisine of the Nair community of south-western India is the Kerala feast, a seemingly endless line of vegetarian dishes. It kicks off with 'pre-meal snacks' of popadoms, achappam (hard flower-shaped rice biscuits), pappadavadai (thin battered popadoms) and murukku (crunchy rice flour sticks flavoured with cumin and sesame), served with pickles and chutneys to die for. Next come the starters proper: probably banana boli (fritters), masala vadai and/or kathrilla (aubergine pakora). Recommended mains include thakkali (tomato and yoghurt curry) and kovakka olathiathu (dry baby cucumbers with cashews and Keralan spices). A fault? Maybe the walls are a tad too pink.

S&M Café

4-6 Essex Road, N1 8LN (020 7359 5361/ www.sandm.cafe.com). Angel tube. **Breakfast served** 8am-noon Mon-Fri; 9am-noon Sat, Sun. **Meals served** noon-11pm daily. **Main courses** £5.95-£6.95. **Credit** DC, MC, V.

Pub crawl: London

Many of the world's best pubs are found in London, but so are the dregs. Conveniently, the worst are in the centre within walking distance of each other, often bearing signs such as 'visitors welcome', 'real London pub' or 'historic old inn'. But there are plenty of good pubs in the middle of town, not least the **Dog & Duck** (18 Bateman Street, W1; 020 7494 0697). Endorsed on TV by Madonna, who can't get enough of their Timothy Taylor Landlord bitter, this smart little Victorian boozer is always packed, but if you jostle your way in, you can marvel at its ceramic wall tiles, mosaics and opulent etched mirrors over a pint.

Those nostalgic for Soho's gloriously seedier days should check out the **Coach & Horses** (29 Greek Street, W1; 020 7437 5920). Still run by legendarily rude landlord Norman Balon (though you now only see him en route to the bank), it's pretty much as it was in its 1960s/1970s salad days, when Jeffrey Bernard held court. It still attracts a scattering of drunks, bores and 'interesting' characters, though sadly none are quite as interesting as their predecessor. Avoid late evenings: the place turns into a hangout for noisy, chain-smoking pre-clubbers.

London's least pretentious historic pubs can be visited in a pub crawl of Holborn and Fleet Street. Begin at the **Cittie of York** (22 High Holborn, WC1; 020 7242 7670), beside Chancery Lane tube station (closed at weekends). Dating from 1430, it all but collapsed in 1923 and was rebuilt in its heyday Victorian neo-Gothic style. Think Tudor barn meets gin palace. This former flagship of the Henekey's wine bar chain boasts the Henekey's Long Bar, which was once

the 'longest in the empire'. The attending lawyers tend to quaff cut-price Samuel Smith beers.

Turning left along High Holborn, you'll soon spot a sign for **Ye Olde Mitre** (1 Ely Court, Ely Place, EC1; 020 7405 4751), a picturesque pub hidden away in Ely Court. Originally the servants' quarters for the Bishop of Ely's palace, it was rebuilt in the late 18th century. The warren of small, low-beamed rooms, accessed by rickety staircases, are reputedly haunted. Heading south-east and climbing up to Holborn Viaduct, you'll soon hit the **Viaduct Tavern** (126 Newgate Street, EC1; 020 7600 1863), built in 1869 in honour of William Heywood's construction. The murals of the viaduct statues are well preserved, as are busts of the 14 hanging judges of the day. The Old Bailey across the road supplies plenty of lawyers, looking very much at home among the carved mahogany and etched glasswork.

Fleet Street has four or five worthy boozers. The **Tipperary** (56 Fleet Street, EC4; 020 7583 6470), London's first Irish pub, was taken over by Dublin brewers SG Mooney in 1700. It's one of London's finest unsung boozers. 'Unsung' is not a word applied to **Ye Olde Cheshire Cheese** (145 Fleet Street, EC4; 020 7353 6170) opposite. Another Sam Smith's heritage pub, it's a multi-bar boozer constructed over cellars that survived the Great Fire. Previous drinkers here have included Dr Johnson, Dickens and Sir Arthur Conan Doyle. The nearby **Seven Stars** (53-54 Carey Street, WC2; 020 7242 8521) is a recent winner of the Best Pub category at the *Time Out* Eating & Drinking Awards. Built in 1602 and named after the naval

---

The formula couldn't be simpler. First you pick your sausages (London traditional rich pork? Lamb and mint? Sun-dried tomato, basil and mozzarella?); then choose your mash (regular with cream and butter? Smoked paprika, leek and cheddar? Bubble and squeak?); and finally decide on your gravy (red onion? Wild mushroom with cream? Wholegrain mustard with chilli?). The result? Comfort food heaven. To leaven the meaty mix there's a handful of salads, plus puddings straight from the nursery. The quality throughout is exemplary, the staff chummy and the vibe buzzy, and the Islington branch of this burgeoning mini-chain has respectfully kept the wonderful 1950s-style melamine, aged wood and burnished metal interior of its caff predecessor.

Sariyer Balik ★

56 Green Lanes, N16 9NH (020 7275 7681).
Bus 141, 341. **Meals served** 5pm-1am daily.
Main courses £6.50-£10. **No credit cards**.
This out-of-the-way place doesn't look much from the outside but you won't get better Turkish fish dishes in London. The menu is entirely fishy (vegetarian options are available on request) and dishes are accompanied by toasted bread rather than pide. Small mixed hot starters (£12 for two) included beautifully tender kalamar soaked in vodka, tasty mussels in beer, and prawns. The mains were simple grilled fish, mackerel and sea bass, perfectly done. Finish with complimentary kemel pashas (small honey-soaked cakes) and good coffee.

London

flag of Holland, this long, thin place rejoices in original low-beamed ceilings, settles and rough plasterwork. Landlady and cookery writer Roxy Beaujolais has injected some much-needed style and the core clientele of lawyers lap up her bistro-style food, real ales and well-chosen wines.

Tucked away in a Borough backstreet, the Victorian two-bar **Royal Oak** (44 Tabard Street, SE1; 020 7357 7173) is Harveys of Lewes's only London boozer. Hence the presence of CAMRA enthusiasts on the razzle. Other essentials on a beer-lover's itinerary include the **White Horse** (1-3 Parsons Green, SW6; 020 7736 2115), a large and comfortable gastropub. Its covered terrace fills up fast in warm weather. Expect half a dozen cask ales, plus a magnificent variety of Belgian beers (including every Trappist brew) and over 120 wines. Then there's the **Wenlock Arms** (26 Wenlock Road, N1; 020 7608 3406) in the industrial wasteland between City Road and Islington. It's an honest local and a real ale addict's paradise. Eight cask ales are sold, as are a decent selection of Belgian beers. They even sell wine.

For riverside drinking our choice is between the stately early Victorian **Duke's Head** (8 Lower Richmond Road, SW15; 020 8788 2552) in Putney – with its Young's beers and spectacular vistas across the Thames – and Wapping's **Town of Ramsgate** (62 Wapping High Street, E1; 020 7481 8000), where Captain Bligh and Fletcher Christian took their bon voyage noggin and Hanging Judge Jeffreys tried to escape to Hamburg disguised as a salty old seadog.

Singapore Garden

83A Fairfax Road, NW6 4DY (020 7624 8233). Swiss Cottage tube. **Lunch served** noon-2.45pm daily. **Dinner served** 6-10.45pm Mon-Thur, Sun; 6-11.15pm Fri, Sat. **Main courses** £6-£15. **Set lunch** (Mon-Fri) £7 2 courses. **Set meal** £25-£32.50 3 courses (minimum 2 people). **Credit** AmEx, DC, JCB, MC, V.
This upmarket restaurant run by a Chinese Singaporean family is an impressively smooth-running affair. The menu is predominantly Chinese, but contains some classic Singaporean dishes. Satay with a lemongrass-fragrant peanut sauce is a good start. Mains, served in generous portions, include a distinctly hot Malay chicken curry; tauhu goreng (fried cubes of tender bean curd covered with a rich,

sweet nutty sauce); moreish kway teow noodles; and a gloriously garlicky oyster omelette studded with fresh oysters. After all that, traditional desserts such as sago gula melaka or cendol might be too much.

Sushi-Say

33B Walm Lane, NW2 5SH (020 8459 2971). Willesden Green tube. **Lunch served** 1-3.30pm Sat, Sun. **Dinner served** 6.30-11pm Tue-Fri; 6-11.30pm Sat; 6-10pm Sun. **Main courses** £6.10-£18.90. **Set dinner** £18.20-£28.60 incl miso soup, rice & pickles, dessert. **Credit** AmEx, JCB, MC, V.
Sushi-Say doesn't look like much from a design point of view. The food, though, is anything but plain. Nigiri of razor clam, sea urchin and bonito are fresh and succulent fish on dainty fingers of rice. Toro sashimi is thick-cut and mouthwateringly tender. Daily specials might include buri daikon (yellowtail and white radish in 'special sauce') or kabocha nitsuke (pumpkin in a 'traditional Japanese' style). Most hit the spot: the sauces are spiky, the fish richly savoury. Some, though, come in tiny portions. But the ice-creams redeem any niggles. The hot-and-cold wasabi version is a sensation not to be missed.

Viet Garden ★

207 Liverpool Road, N1 1LX (020 7700 6040). Angel tube. **Lunch served** noon-3.30pm Mon-Sat. **Dinner served** 5.30-11pm Mon-Thur; 5.30-11.30pm Fri, Sat. **Main courses** £4.50-£6.90. **Set lunch** (Mon-Fri) £5.50 2 courses. **Credit** MC, V.
One block back from restaurant-lined Upper Street, Viet Garden risks going unnoticed, which would be a great shame. Owned by the sisters of the Viet Hoa (*see p66*) founder, this friendly and great-value eaterie offers Vietnamese cooking at its best. Ingredients are fresh, food is piping hot and staff will point diners towards Vietnamese favourites. Starter summer rolls are generously stuffed with prawns, crisp lettuce and light rice noodles. Bun (hot, spicy rice-vermicelli soup) with beef comes with a plate of fresh mint, beansprouts and chillies and packs a tremendous spicy punch. Honeyed, crunchy banana fritters with ice-cream provide a great end.

Also in the area

La Brasserie Trouvaille 353 Upper Street, N1 0PD (020 7704 8323); **Carluccio's** 305-307 Upper Street, N1 2TU (020 7359 8167); **The Gate** 72 Belsize Lane, NW3 5BJ (020 7435 7733); **Gaucho Grill** 64 Heath Street, NW3 1DN (020 7431 8222); **Giraffe** 46 Rosslyn Hill, NW3 1NH (020 7435 0343); **Jashan** 19 Turnpike Lane, N8 0EP (020 8340 9880); **Little Bay** 228 Belsize Road, NW6 4BT (020 7372 4699); **The Living Room** Suncourt House, 18-26 Essex Road, N1 8LN (0870 442 2712); **Loch Fyne** 2 Park Road, N8 8TD (020 8342 7740); **Mangal II** 4 Stoke Newington Road, N16 8BH (020 7254 7888); **Masala Zone** 80 Upper Street, N1 0NP (020 7359 3399); **Rasa Travancore** 56 Stoke Newington Church Street, N10 0AR (020 7249 1340); **Royal China** 68 Queen's Grove, NW8 6ER (020 7586 4280); **Strada** 105-106 Upper Street, N1 1QN (020 7226 9742); **Wagamama** 11 Jamestown Road, NW1 7BW (020 7428 0800).

South East

South East

Hampshire

BISHOP'S WALTHAM

The Restaurant on the Square
Bishop's Waltham, SO32 1AR (01489 891515/ www.therestaurantonthesquare.com). **Lunch served** noon-2pm daily. **Dinner served** 7-9.30pm Mon-Sat. **Main courses** £11.95-£16.95. **Set lunch** £9.95 2 courses, £12.95 3 courses. **Credit** AmEx, DC, MC, V.
Cream walls, wooden floors and white linen bring a serene atmosphere to this Georgian townhouse restaurant. The staff are professional, but friendly with it. Typical dishes include fillet of ostrich poached in cabernet sauvignon or fillet of beef served with blue cheese, duchesse potatoes and wild mushroom compote. The set menu offers excellent value and choice: Caesar salad topped with wafer-thin fried aubergine, and blue cheese and walnut tart with red onion compote were both faultless. Desserts were also very enjoyable, especially the strawberry crème brûlée. Attention to detail can't be faulted here, right down to the descriptive and extensive wine list.

The Wine Bar & Bistro
6-8 High Street, Bishop's Waltham, SO32 1AA (01489 894476/www.thewinebarandbistro.co.uk). **Food served** noon-10pm Mon-Sat; noon-9.30pm Sun. **Main courses** £8.95-£16.95. **Set meals** (Sun) £8.95 1 course, £11.95 2 courses, £14.95 3 courses. **Credit** AmEx, DC, MC, V.
Located in the basement, with a traditional wine bar decor of exposed brickwork, arches, low-level lighting and long bar, this wine bar-bistro offers a mixture of French-style favourites such as confit of duck or cassoulet, along with an oriental influence in the form of teriyaki marinated chicken with spring onion, pink ginger and beansprout salad. Ciabattas and wraps are available too – portions are generous and the accompanying french fries crisp and irresistible. As you'd expect, the wine list is long, varied and competitively priced. The young staff are upbeat and professional and the place is clearly popular with a mixed clientele.

BROCKENHURST

Simply Poussin
The Courtyard, Brookley Road, Brockenhurst, SO42 7RB (01590 623063/www.lepoussin.co.uk). **Lunch served** noon-2pm, **dinner served** 7-9.30pm Tue-Sat. **Main courses** £12.50-£14.50. **Set meals** (Tue-Fri, lunch Sat) £10 2 courses, £15 3 courses. **Credit** AmEx, MC, V.
Simply Poussin can't rely on passing trade, for apart from its name over a nondescript archway there's nothing to indicate its presence. Tucked away behind a parade of shops, however, is a stylish and professionally run restaurant that offers food every bit as good as more pretentious establishments. Beech tables with lines of glasses create an informal yet serious look in the non-smoking restaurant and service is helpful and friendly. The set menu might have soused fillet of mackerel as a starter followed by a duo of pan-fried medallions of pork with stuffed pig's cheek. The à la carte menu features seasonal dishes and suggests different pudding wines by the glass for each of the desserts. The wine list is printed on the back of the à la carte menu and the spelling mistakes which litter the page suggest that a good time was had during its creation.

EAST END

East End Arms ★
Main Road, East End, SO41 5SY (01590 626223/ www.eastendarms.co.uk). **Lunch served** noon-2pm Tue-Sun. **Dinner served** 7-9pm Tue-Sat. **Main courses** £12. **Credit** MC, V.
Well worth beating a path to, this likeable pub tucked down a country lane a few miles from Beaulieu has a tiny garden, a green and white-washed exterior and a cream panelled restaurant at the back. The surroundings are low-key, but the food is simple, fresh and very good value – home-style cooking at its best. Fresh fish is a forte – whether it's sardines grilled with butter and lemon and served with fat chips, scallops with lentils or swordfish flavoured with lapsang souchong. There's ribeye steak and chips, sausage and egg pie, a range of salads and baguettes, plus chocolate tart, bread and butter pudding, rhubarb fool or apple pie to finish. If only more pubs were like this.

EMSWORTH

36 on the Quay ★
47 South Street, Emsworth, PO10 7EG (01243 375592/www.36onthequay.co.uk). **Lunch served** noon-2pm Tue-Fri. **Dinner served** 7-10pm Mon-Sat. **Set lunch** £17.95 2 courses, £21.95 3 courses. **Set dinner** £38.50 3 courses. **Credit** AmEx, DC, MC, V.
With the evening sun shimmering off the water, the Georgian bay window of this stylish, understated establishment has to be one of the best places in Britain to sit on a balmy evening. After drinks in the courtyard (served with smoked almonds, olives and own-made crisps), the quality continued with a pre-starter of leek and potato soup. Next came an impressive ravioli of fresh crab, spiked with mango

and ginger, plus a tian of tomato and courgette. A main course of Scottish scallops on pancetta was subtle and splendid to behold. A pre-dessert, a rhubarb and raspberry fool, would have more than sufficed. But it would have been a sin against gluttony not to experience the pineapple soufflé with coconut coulis. All this, plus own-made petits fours and top-notch service make a meal at 36 on the Quay an absolute must.

ISLE OF WIGHT

Baywatch Beach Restaurant

The Duver, St Helens, PO33 1RP (01983 873259/ www.bay-watch.co.uk). **Breakfast served** 10.30am-noon, **lunch served** noon-3pm, **dinner served** 5.45-9pm daily. **Main courses** £6.90-£12. **Credit** MC, V.

Bembridge Harbour, overlooking St Helens Fort (once a year in August, when the tide is at its lowest, locals walk out across the causeway), is the gorgeous setting for this airy beach restaurant. Starters include crab soup or smoked mackerel and shrimp salad. The menu features moules and chips and lots of fish, as well as pasta, steak and burgers. Fishy specials change daily. A fearsome-looking whole-baked strawberry grouper came with salad (you'll have to ask for dressing) and was moist and delicious, though the promised bed of samphire was a bit stingy; the whole lobster and king prawn salad was huge. Chips or new potatoes and seasonal vegetables are extra. House white is a very drinkable South African Pearl Heights chenin blanc 2002. During the day you can sit outside, otherwise ask for a window table when booking to get the best view of the bay.

The George Hotel

Quay Street, Yarmouth, PO41 0PE (01983 760331/www.thegeorge.co.uk). **Brasserie Breakfast served** 8-10am, **lunch served** noon-3pm, **dinner served** 7-10pm daily. **Main courses** £11.95-£29.95. **Set lunch** (Sun) £19.50 2 courses, £23.50 3 courses. *Restaurant* **Dinner served** 7.15-9pm Tue-Sat. **Set dinner** £45 5 courses incl coffee. **Credit** AmEx, MC, V.

The waterside garden of the George Hotel's brasserie is a beautiful setting for a meal on a summer's day. Inside, the sunshine yellow room with its dressers of china and brassware works less well on a dark evening. The menu lists modern British dishes with French and Californian touches, with lots of fish and locally sourced ingredients. Cod croquettes were fine but the drizzle of tartare sauce was too mean to cut through the blandness of the fish. Sweet pepper tart with goat's cheese was a thick slice of cold cheese atop lukewarm peppers – the flavours didn't meld together at all. However, halibut on a pasta rösti with a mussel and leek sauce was perfectly moist with subtle flavours of coriander and fennel. Warm date and coffee sponge with toffee sauce and vanilla ice-cream was a winner too. There's a large selection of house wines from Europe

and the New World, all very reasonably priced at £12.50 a bottle. Service was friendly and helpful if a little distracted at times.

New Inn

Mill Road, Shalfleet, PO3 4NS (01983 531314/ www.thenew-inn.co.uk). **Lunch served** noon-2.30pm, **dinner served** 6-9.30pm daily. **Main courses** £6.95-£17.95. **Credit** AmEx, DC, MC, V.

This 17th-century inn with oak beams, huge fireplaces and a sunny garden has won a slate of awards and a well-deserved reputation for excellent food, which includes steaks, local crab and lobster and seafood royale (£50 for a platter for two). There is a separate menu for children and those with smaller appetites. The wine list is well chosen and refreshingly informative, with the Domaine de la Mirande – recommended as the 'lip-stinging muscatel of the south' – ideal for the many fish and seafood dishes on the menu. The garden gets very crowded in summer but there are lots of tables inside. A perfect place for lunch if you're exploring the paths around Newtown and Shalfleet Creek.

Red Lion

Church Place, Freshwater, PO40 9BP (01983 754925/www.redlion-wight.co.uk). **Lunch served** noon-2pm daily. **Dinner served** 6.30-9pm Mon-Sat; 7-9pm Sun. **Main courses** £7.50-£12. **Credit** MC, V.

A traditional pub popular with locals, walkers and the dinghy sailors who come down the river from Yarmouth for lunch when the tide is right, this is a good place to stop off if you're cycling or walking along the estuary towards Freshwater. Switch off your mobile phone – if it rings you'll pay a £5 fine to the local lifeboat; the quirky management also fines anyone with the temerity to point out spelling mistakes on the menu, so keep quiet. Daily specials on the blackboard might include herring roes on toast, local pork cutlets with brandy and mushroom sauce or steak and kidney pie. Delicious traditional puddings are also hard to resist. Booking is advisable. While you're here, check out the pretty church next door.

Royal Hotel

Belgrave Road, Ventnor, PO38 1JJ (01983 852186/ www.royalhoteliow.co.uk). *Bar* **Lunch served** noon-2pm daily. *Restaurant* **Dinner served** 7-9.15pm daily. **Set dinner** £29.50 3 courses. **Credit** AmEx, DC, MC, V.

Chef Alan Staley produces reliably classy cooking in this hotel restaurant close to the sea, with dishes such as Mediterranean fish soup flavoured with fennel and served with rouille and toasted garlic croûtes, and mains like medallions of beef fillet with pan-fried potato and horseradish rösti, sauté of wild mushrooms and a truffle-scented jus. For a less formal setting, light lunches such as salads and omelettes are served in the bar and conservatory. Early suppers are also available for children so that parents can dine later in peace.

South East

Seaview Hotel ★

*High Street, Seaview, PO34 5EX (01983
612711/www.seaviewhotel.co.uk).* **Lunch served**
noon-1.30pm daily. **Dinner served** 7.15-9.30pm
Mon-Sat. **Main courses** £13.95-£17.95. **Set lunch**
(Sun) £16.95 3 courses. **Credit** AmEx, DC, MC, V.
One of the best places to eat on the island in one of
the most charming and child-friendly hotels, with
two relaxed and pretty dining rooms (smoking and
non-smoking). The menu uses fresh local produce
wherever possible to serve imaginative modern
cuisine such as starters of sautéed soft herring roes
on brioche with capers, butter and lemon or baked
goat's cheese with rocket and beetroot salad. The
mains make excellent use of local produce with
dishes such as free-range chicken breast with oak-
smoked garlic and rosemary risotto or fillet of local
beef with Perigord hollandaise and fondant potato.
Puddings feature Minghella's ice-cream and English
cheeses with chutney. There are always at least two
vegetarian dishes. If you don't want a full meal, you
can have a superior bar snack such as hot crab
ramekin in one of the two bars, or sitting under the
umbrellas at the front while you watch the world
make its way down to the lovely harbour below.

Sian Elin's

*Quay Street, Yarmouth, PO41 0NT (01983
760054).* **Meals served** 9am-2.30pm, **dinner
served** 6.30-10pm daily. **Main courses** £12.50-
£17.50. **Credit** MC, V.

This large deck overlooking the ferry terminal is a
great place to watch the boats come and go in the
busy harbour. Full English breakfast is served to
hungry sailors between 8am and 10am. The lunch
menu is served until 2.30pm and includes crayfish
Caesar salad, local crab sandwiches, fish cakes and
roasted goat's cheese, as well as steaks and burgers.
In the evening there are changing specials such as
baked whole sea bass and grilled sardines. There's
Stella Artois and Flowers bitter on tap. Coffee and
cakes are available throughout the day.

LOWER WIELD

The Yew Tree

*Lower Wield, SO24 9RX (01256 389224/
www.theyewtreerestaurant.com).* **Lunch served**
noon-2pm daily. **Dinner served** 6.30-9pm
Mon-Fri, Sun; 6.30-9.30pm Sat. **Set lunch** £19.50
1 course, £20 2 courses, £25 3 courses. **Set dinner**
£19.50 1 course, £27 2 courses, £32 3 courses.
Credit MC, V.

This 300-year-old public house, now owned by its
former managers and framed by the ancient yew
tree from which it takes its name, offers wonderful
food in a comfortable interior. The main dishes are
offered with thoughtful accompaniments. The skate
with caper and tomato butter sauce is good and the
melt-in-the-mouth calf's liver with redcurrant sauce
and puréed parsnips is very good. The set menu
represents value-for-money given the quality of the

The George Hotel.
See p77.

food. The dedication poured into this pub shows in the cooking, service and decor. The wine list is extensive; the choice runs from decent house wines right up to a Chateaux Margaux 1982. It adds to the charm of the place that you can simply order a beer and enjoy the ambience. Beware, though, the pub is quite hard to find.

LYMINGTON

The Chequers Inn

Lower Woodside, Lymington, SO41 8AH (01590 673415/www.chequersinn.com). **Lunch served** noon-2.15pm Mon-Fri. **Dinner served** 6.30-9.30pm Mon-Thur; 6.30-10pm Fri. **Meals served** noon-10pm Sat; noon-9pm Sun. **Main courses** £8.25-£13.50. **Credit** MC, V.

This whitewashed pub is absurdly popular. Set on the edge of town, down towards one of Lymington's marinas, the small place gets packed out with sailing types who come to eat the wholesome, above-average grub served in the restaurant and marquee at the back. In summer, tables spill out on to an alfresco bar and courtyard strung with lights, with heaters to keep off the Solent chill. Roast lamb with redcurrant and rosemary, venison steak with a port and stilton sauce or fresh fish of the day are typical, with steak sandwiches, New Forest sausages, beans and chips and Cajun chicken and chips to keep the crowds happy. Book a table in advance, bring a hearty appetite and prepare to tuck in.

MILFORD ON SEA

Westover Hall

Park Lane, Milford on Sea, SO41 0PT (01590 643044/www.westoverhallhotel.com). **Lunch served** noon-2pm, **dinner served** 7-8.45pm daily. **Set lunch** (Sun) £25 3 courses. **Set dinner** £32.50 3 courses. **Credit** AmEx, DC, MC, V.

The bright and sunny restaurant in the Westover Hall Hotel shares the hotel's agreeable, friendly atmosphere. Drop in for mid-morning coffee or afternoon tea, or linger over lunch or dinner to sample the more sophisticated fare produced by the kitchen. There's ham hock and foie gras terrine with pea purée or wild mushroom risotto to start, with brill with mousseline sauce or roasted partridge and root veg to follow. Finish with a plateful of French cheeses served with pickled walnuts and raisin bread, a dark chocolate soufflé or some warm lemon and almond pudding with raspberries. Coffee or tea comes with petits fours, and at £32.50 for three courses at dinner, the price is more than reasonable.

NEW MILTON

Marryat Restaurant at Chewton Glen

Christchurch Road, New Milton, BH25 6QS (01425 275341/www.chewtonglen.com). **Lunch served** 12.30-1.45pm, **dinner served** 7.30-9.15pm daily. **Set dinner** £55 3 courses. **Credit** AmEx, DC, MC, V.

Michael Winner voted this his favourite restaurant. Perhaps it was the conservative air of corporate comfort, the deep pile carpets, heavy drapes and gentleman's club decor that won his vote. Or the serried ranks of unsmiling but efficient staff. Or maybe it was the new swimming pool, the three tennis courts, the croquet lawn and the golf course. Or the helipad. Despite the undeniably no-holds-barred luxury of the place, the well-turned-out classical menu (grilled lemon sole with tomato-infused béarnaise, perfect Sunday roast chicken with bread sauce and buttery vegetables, beef tournedos with horseradish sauce) and the 400-strong wine list, the Marryat appears to lack an essential ingredient – *joie de vivre*. We'd definitely vote to spend our lottery winnings somewhere more fun.

ODIHAM

Grapevine
121 High Street, Odiham, RG29 1LA (01256 701900/www.grapevine-gourmet.com). **Lunch served** noon-2pm Mon-Fri. **Dinner served** 6-10pm Mon-Sat. **Main courses** £9.95-£15.95. **Set dinner** (6-7pm) £14.95 3 courses incl glass of wine. **Credit** AmEx, DC, MC, V.
Bentwood chairs, wooden floors and walls adorned with blackboard menus transform this Georgian property into a classic bistro. The place has Mediterranean aspirations with bottles of infused olive oil, bread and candles on the tables, while the menu and kitchen staff try hard to suit all tastes, offering various combinations including 'veggie', 'early-bird', 'lunchtime quickie' and children's portions, all with a strong Italian influence. The antipasti (for two to share) hold such delights as asparagus with gremolata and char-grilled bruschetta and closely resemble the authentic Italian versions. As a main course, the potato gnocchi served with a choice of sauces is good and comes in generous portions. Desserts maintain the Italian feel, especially the baked pear with Marsala and ice-cream. A popular venue for lunch which offers good value and variety.

PETERSFIELD

JSW
1 Heath Road, Petersfield, GU31 4JE (01730 262030). **Lunch served** noon-1.30pm, **dinner served** 7-9.30pm Tue-Sat. **Set lunch** £17.50 2 courses, £22.50 3 courses. **Set dinner** £27.50 2 courses, £32.50 3 courses. **Credit** MC, V.
So small-scale is JSW and with no external view worth mentioning (despite being in picturesque Petersfield), one was almost wishing for some piped classical music to charge the air. However, once the perfectly petite menu arrived, so too came the energy. Seared scallops with a herb risotto and red wine sauce, and roasted wood pigeon with shallot tarte tatin were much relished, with rich, exquisitely blended flavours. These were followed by wild

salmon with Jersey royals, asparagus and salad, and venison with celeriac purée, broad beans and fresh truffles, both cooked to perfection. Puddings may have sounded like English summer fayre supreme, but they were as French, flouncy and feminine as they come with feuillantine of rhubarb being much more feuillantine than fruit. Service was attentive and helpful. The wine lists rewards investigation.

PORTSMOUTH

American Bar Restaurant
58 White Hart Road, Portsmouth, PO1 2JA (023 9281 1585/www.americanbar.co.uk). **Meals served** noon-10pm Mon-Thur, Sun; noon-10.30pm Fri, Sat. **Main courses** £8.95-£16.50. **Credit** AmEx, MC, V.
The only evidence of America in this garishly painted seafood restaurant is a spiel on the menu purporting that the building was once a prison for convicts en route to the colonies. Besides that, it's a Gallic/Anglo blend right down to the day-trippers from Cherbourg and the traditional fish and chips. Service is lacking in the smiles department, but yellow walls and nautical knick-knacks cheer up the smoky bar with dining off to the side. The place is directly opposite a fish market so no quibbles about freshness. Starters include hot garlic prawns or French fish soup, with hefty fisherman's pie or meltingly tender salmon as choices for mains. A large range of non-fishy dishes also feature, as does a list of more than 135 wines.

Lemon Sole
123 High Street, Portsmouth, PO1 2HW (023 9281 1303/www.lemonsole.co.uk). **Lunch served** noon-2pm, **dinner served** 6-9.45pm Mon-Sat. **Set lunch** £8.95 2 courses. **Credit** AmEx, DC, MC, V.
Choose your fish from the ice cabinet, your wine from the rack and your bread from the basket, then kick back and tuck in. A winning formula for fishophiles features a vast choice: bream, skate, tuna, blue-spotted grouper, anything special caught that day or a medley of each. Fish can be char-grilled, poached, steamed or 'as you like'. Starters include whitebait served in a conch, moules or soup; mains are accompanied by chips, mash or new potatoes. Non-fishy folk are catered for but it's less fun. The decor is clean and simple, with (surprise, surprise!) a fishy theme.

ROMSEY

Prezzos
21 Palmerston Street, Romsey, SO51 8GF (01794 517353). **Meals served** noon-midnight daily. **Main courses** £4.95-£7.50. **Credit** AmEx, DC, MC, V.
Formerly the Old Manor House restaurant, an Italian restaurant group has recently taken over this beautiful beamed building in central Romsey. Its transformation into a contemporary and more affordable eaterie has provided patrons with a

Wykeham Arms. *See p83.*

well-balanced addition to the town. The menu comprises a roster of pizza/pasta predictables but there are various daily specials to liven things up a little. Spaghetti con gamberoni contained a generous helping of tiger prawns; chicken siciliana was less lip-smacking. The small wine list is all Italian and reasonably priced. Splendid cappuccino comes with a little biscotti.

The Three Tuns

58 Middlebridge Street, Romsey, SO51 8HL (01794 512639). **Lunch served** noon-2.30pm Mon-Sat; noon-3pm Sun. **Dinner served** 6.30-9.30pm Mon-Thur; 6.30-10pm Fri, Sat. **Main courses** (lunch Mon-Sat, bar menu) £5-£6.50. **Set dinner** £17 2 courses, £22 3 courses. **Credit** AmEx, MC, V.

A little set back from the centre of town, down a bucolic lane lined with cottages, the Three Tuns has to be sought out, but it's well worth the effort. It's still a cosy local boozer; step through the door and the bar is a few feet ahead of you. But the dining room has been spivved up with a tiled floor and rows of tables, trattoria style. The only downside is the noise – a constant clatter and hubbub magnified by the lack of any textiles. Apart from this caveat, the Three Tuns provides delicious, metropolitan food, full of robust flavours and not too fussy. Black pudding might come with potato purée, poached egg and devilled sauce; whole sole with new potatoes, mangetout and tarragon lemon mayonnaise. Portions are generous and the set price menus make the foie gras options (refreshingly without additional supplement) a steal. The service is friendly rather than well polished.

SHEDFIELD

Wickham Vineyard

Botley Road, Shedfield, SO32 2HL (01329 834042/www.wickhamvineyard.co.uk). **Lunch served** noon-2pm Wed-Sun. **Dinner served** 7-9.30pm Wed-Sat; 6-8.30pm Sun. **Set lunch** (Wed-Sat) £15.50 2 courses, £17.50 3 courses; (Sun) £17.50 2 courses, £19.50 3 courses. **Set dinner** £25.50 2 courses, £31 3 courses. **Credit** MC, V.

This modern barn-style building with large windows overlooking the vineyard has been carefully packaged to create a restful, rural atmosphere. The staff are attentive, professional and unpretentious, yet provide all the trimmings associated with a high-end restaurant. Set menus are available for both lunch and supper, and include such delights as starters of an escabeche of red mullet or a delicate asparagus soup. Main courses include pan-fried turbot with asparagus and crab jus along with a ballotine of chicken on a bed of savoy cabbage with bacon. Both were excellent. Desserts were equally tempting; vanilla pannacotta with five-spice ice-cream is a must-try. Their vineyard-produced house wine is surprisingly good, reasonably priced and accompanied by very little hard sell, while the rest of the wine list is well chosen

if a little hard on the pocket. The clientele is older and the restaurant is clearly very popular as a corporate venue.

STOCKBRIDGE

The Greyhound ★

31 The High Street, Stockbridge, SO20 6EY (01264 810833). **Lunch served** noon-2.30pm daily. **Dinner served** 7-10pm Mon-Sat. **Main courses** £9.50-£19.50. **Credit** MC, V.

Set in an 18th-century inn in a smart Hampshire village, this tasteful gastropub with its solid trestle tables, high-backed leather chairs and black-and-white photos on the walls has an air of urban chic. The food is equally upmarket, focusing exclusively on fresh local produce. Chef Nick Wentworth's signature dish of salmon fish cake served with a perfectly poached egg and chive beurre blanc was faultless; the breast of guinea fowl, pearl barley and sweetcorn velouté was good; better still was roast neck of Hampshire lamb in herb crust. Deserts include clever use of sorbets and an extensive range of cheeses. The short and pricey menu changes weekly, but the wine list is of epic proportions, perfectly chosen and good value. The staff have an air of gap-year student about them; the clientele don't look like they have to worry about the prices.

SWAY

Nurse's Cottage

Station Road, Sway, SO41 6BA (01590 683402/ www.nursescottage.co.uk). **Lunch served** 12.30-2pm Sun. **Dinner served** 6.30-8pm daily. **Set lunch** £15.50 3 courses. **Set dinner** £18.25 2 courses, £20.65 3 courses incl mineral water, coffee, chocolates. **Credit** AmEx, MC, V.

Run by enthusiastic chef-proprietor Tony Barnfield, this tiny white pebble-dashed cottage was once home to Sway's district nurse. Now a restaurant with rooms in the French tradition, the place was recently extensively refurbished and has doubled in size. Decor retains a touch of the clinical in its plainness, but the seasonally changing classic British menu is just what the doctor ordered. Ingredients are locally sourced where possible, some from the cottage's own herb and vegetable garden. Specialities include avocado, orange and prawn salad, breast of guinea fowl flavoured with tarragon and white wine, salmon with Cointreau and, to finish, the gloriously nostalgic flambéed bananas. The wine list contains over 60 choices from around the world, with many half-bottles.

WHITCHURCH

Red House

21 London Street, Whitchurch, RG28 7LH (01256 895558). **Lunch served** noon-2pm daily. **Dinner served** 6.30-9.30pm Mon-Sat; 7-9pm Sun. **Main courses** £9-£16. **Credit** MC, V.

The best Big-hitters

Amaryllis
See p310.

Andrew Fairlie at Gleneagles
See p325.

Auberge du Lac
See p167.

Le Champignon Sauvage
See p159.

Fat Duck
See p150.

Gidleigh Park
See p125.

Gravetye Manor
See p99.

Inverlochy Castle Hotel
See p321.

Le Manoir aux Quat' Saisons
See p169.

Morston Hall
See p193.

Plas Bodegroes
See p335.

Restaurant Martin Wishart
See p306.

Restaurant Michael Deane
See p349.

Shanks
See p347.

Vineyard
See p152.

Waterside Inn
See p151.

Original beams and two large open fireplaces are the main decorative features of this family-friendly eaterie; added touches of church candles, wooden flooring and large mirrors bring a modern balance to the atmosphere. The main dining area is no-smoking with tables well spaced; staff are friendly and attentive. The menu offers good traditional pub food. Sirloin, rump and fillet steaks served with a sauce are a main feature of the menu; a bacon and stilton sauce made a great partner for a perfectly

cooked steak. Interesting vegetarian dishes come in generous portions. The house wine is fairly drinkable and as the pub is a free-house, there's a good selection of beers on tap. A large tiered garden with children's play area has been well thought through and provides a safe environment for toddlers and pre-teens. Barbecue food is available in the summer months.

WINCHESTER

Chesil Rectory ★
1 Chesil Street, Winchester, SO23 0HU (01962 851555). **Lunch served** noon-2pm Sat. **Dinner served** 7-9.30pm Tue-Sat. **Set lunch** £35 3 courses. **Set dinner** £45 6 courses. **Credit** AmEx, DC, MC, V.
If you manage to avoid concussion from one of the antique beams, then expect an evening in this 15th-century building to be a glorious experience. The decor is minimalist – white walls and black beams – and the clientele casual. The six-course menu designed by chef-proprietor Philip Storey spent three months in development. Every course is small enough just to whet the appetite for the next. Pork and black pudding with mustard mash was artistically stacked and drizzled with apple butter sauce. The 'refresher' was a green tea and lime mousse served through a straw; the finale a (very) rich chocolate fondant with peanut butter ice-cream.

Wykeham Arms
75 Kingsgate Street, Winchester, SO23 9PE (01962 853834/www.gales.co.uk). **Lunch served** noon-2.30pm Mon-Sat; noon-1.45pm Sun. **Dinner served** 6.30-8.45pm Mon-Sat. **Main courses** £10.75-£15.50. **Set lunch** £14.50 2 courses, £18.50 3 courses. **Credit** AmEx, DC, MC, V.
The Wykeham Arms is more institution than pub, frequented by the upper echelons of Winchester society – dons from Winchester College, judges and clergy at lunch and anyone lucky enough to get a table for dinner, so popular is the fare and the kooky ambience. Most gather in Nelson's Bar for local ales (Gales), perched at heavily etched school desks and breathing in 200 years of nautical paraphernalia. Dining, which could be in the watchmaker's shop, bishop's bar or V&A dining room, is a contemporary array, changed daily and big on local produce; roasted rack of Hampshire Down lamb with bacon and rosemary new potatoes or char-grilled 10oz ribeye steak on horseradish mash. Fish also features large. The wine menu is vast, the staff are young and laid-back.

Also in the area

Hotel du Vin & Bistro 14 Southgate Street, Winchester, SO23 9EF (01962 841414); **Loch Fyne** 18 Jewry Street, Winchester, SO23 8RZ (01962 872930); **Loch Fyne** Unit 2, Vulcan Building, Gunwharf Quays, Portsmouth, PO1 3BF (023 9277 8060).

Kent

APPLEDORE

Bayleaves ★
33-35 The Street, Appledore, TN26 2BU (01233 758208). **Meals served** 10am-5.30pm Wed-Sun. **Main courses** £7. **No credit cards.**

The impossibly quaint and tiny Bayleaves offers a welcome change from the (admittedly above par) pub grub that's ubiquitous in the Romney Marsh area. It is obviously popular with plummy locals of a certain age who enjoy the banter served with the homely lunches, desserts and cream tea scones. These are all as sumptuous as you'd expect and well priced: smoked haddock and spring onion fish cakes were two inches high and revealed slivers of roasted peppers as they crumbled on our forks. Pork pie came with a tangy pickle and local salad, and strawberry meringue was moist, sticky and irresistible. Children are made welcome.

BIDDENDEN

The West House ★
28 High Street, Biddenden, TN27 8AH (01580 291341). **Lunch served** noon-2pm Tue-Sun. **Dinner served** 7-10pm Tue-Sat. **Set dinner** £24.50 3 courses. **Credit** MC, V.

Under Graham Garrett, who trained with Richard Corrigan, the restaurant is a showcase for superlative modern European cooking. The airy interior is enticing, with beams, wooden floors and candles, and the mood relaxed. The daily-changing menu is inventive – starters include the likes of dab fillets and steamed mussels in Biddenden cider, cream and tarragon or potted mackerel, marinated cucumber and toast. Mains might be a generous portion of monkfish wrapped in Parma ham, sprouting broccoli and smoked anchovy butter or roast spring lamb, new season garlic, verdina beans and basil. Desserts tow the line between comfort food and inventiveness, with a smooth and tangy prune and Armagnac brûlée or strawberry and orange soup with yoghurt pannacotta. The wine list includes plenty of bottles under the £20 mark.

BODSHAM GREEN

Froggies at the Timber Batts ★
School Lane, Bodsham Green, TN25 5JQ (01233 750237). **Lunch served** noon-2.30pm Tue-Sun. **Dinner served** 7-9.30pm Tue-Sat. **Main courses** £12-£19. **Set lunch** (Sun) £14 2 courses, £18 3 courses. **Credit** MC, V.

As country pubs go in this part of the world, the 15th-century Timber Batts presents a pretty typical look, set down corkscrew lanes that require a lot of checking of road signs. It's when you walk inside that you realise this is no ordinary English pub, despite the fairly traditional trappings. A Gallic accent presides, with Joel Gross offering a house wine grown by a cousin in the Loire, some uncompromisingly French cheeses and a chalkboard delivering classics such as onion soup, fantastic stuffed mussels, great confit of duck, fillet of beef with roquefort sauce, profiteroles and tarte tatin. Fish is a strong point, especially in summer, with game from local shoots in the winter.

BRIDGE

The White Horse Inn ★
53 High Street, Bridge, CT4 5LA (01227 830249/ www.kent2do.com/whitehorseinnbridge). Bar **Lunch served** noon-2.30pm daily. **Dinner served** 6.30-9.30pm Tue-Sat. *Restaurant* **Lunch served** noon-2.30pm Wed-Sun. **Dinner served** 6.30-9.30pm Tue-Sat. **Main courses** £11-£19.50. **Set meals** £18.50 3 courses. **Credit** MC, V.

There's more to the White Horse than just going in for a drink. The food is proving an amazing draw – both in the bar and the restaurant. Although the likes of Masterbrew battered cod and chips with tartare sauce, and brown onion soup with French toasts and gruyère, are based on popular pub fare, Ben Walton gives them an extra dimension. He may be an ambitious young chef with a posh kitchen pedigree, but he has great respect for the traditions he's upholding. And there are some pacy, modern British interpretations too. Look out for local fish such as sea bream braised in red wine jus, crushed new potatoes, roasted shallots and salsify.

BROADSTAIRS

Marchesi's
18 Albion Street, Broadstairs, CT10 1LU (01843 862481/www.marchesi.co.uk). **Lunch served** noon-3pm Tue-Sun. **Dinner served** 7-9.30pm Tue-Sat. **Main courses** £8.95-£15.95. **Set lunch** (Sun) £16.50 3 courses. **Credit** MC, V.

Established in 1866, this Broadstairs institution claims to be England's oldest family-owned restaurant, and it's the most popular place in town with locals – so book. The decor is very traditional and not hugely inspiring, but the views of the sea are magnificent and on a warm summer's evening the balcony tables make for a romantic rendezvous. The menu is made up of solid Franco-British fare: starters include salmon gateau topped with smoked salmon and lemon dressing, and Caesar salad with seared chicken breast; mains might feature pan-fried calf's liver with bacon and garlic butter or roast fillet of local cod in a mild curried sauce.

Osteria Posillipo Pizzeria

14 Albion Street, Broadstairs, CT10 1LU (01843 601133/www.osteriaposillipo.co.uk). **Lunch served** *summer* noon-3pm daily; *winter* noon-3pm Mon, Wed-Sun. **Dinner served** *summer* 7-11pm daily; *winter* 7-11pm Mon, Wed-Sun. **Main courses** £7.95-£16.95. **Credit** MC, V.

Sandwiched between Marchesi's (*see p84*) and the Royal Albion is this decent Italian restaurant which specialises, naturally, in seafood, and has an unpretentious rustic feel. Linguine posillipo – with clams, king prawns and mussels in a white wine sauce – is the best bet for a local catch, while the Dover sole in olive oil and lemon is delicate and well cooked. The restaurant is well positioned for a post-dinner stroll too: Viking Bay is just below. Broadstairs used to have a large Italian community and this is one of its remaining outposts.

BOUGHTON LEES

Eastwell Manor

Eastwell Manor Hotel, Eastwell Park, Boughton Lees, TN25 4HR (01233 219955/www.eastwell manor.co.uk). **Lunch served** noon-2pm Mon-Sat; 12.30-2.30pm Sun. **Dinner served** 7-9.30pm daily. **Set dinner** £35 3 courses. **Main courses** £15-£28. **Credit** AmEx, DC, MC, V.

Impeccable service makes eating at Eastwell a delight – the staff are jovial and helpful without being intrusive. With its stucco ceiling, giant stone fireplace and striking brocade, the restaurant is imposing, but the atmosphere is surprisingly relaxed and big windows on to the gardens give it a fresh feel in daylight. Expect a British and French influenced menu, perhaps featuring poached brill with vegetables and lobster jus, morel mushroom risotto with asparagus or guinea fowl with basil, tomato and vegetables. Most produce is sourced locally and while flavours are a little mild on occasion, presentation is faultless.

CANTERBURY

Augustine's

1-2 Longport, Canterbury, CT1 1PE (01227 453063). **Lunch served** noon-1.30pm Tue-Sun. **Dinner served** 6.30-9pm Tue-Sat. **Main courses** £9.50-£15.90. **Set lunch** (Tue-Sat) £10.95, (Sun) £19.50 3 courses. **Credit** AmEx, MC, V.

This family-run restaurant gets everything right, offering one of the finest dining experiences to be found in the city. Friendly and unobtrusive service, culinary expertise and beautifully presented dishes (at reasonable prices) ensure maximum satisfaction. After ordering from the reassuringly short menu in the bar area, you're escorted to your table in the formal yet homely dining area. Moules normande (mussels with Breton cider and cream) was

beautifully fresh, and the delicious juices provided an excellent mopping-up opportunity. Next, pan-fried sea bass with a crisp potato crust came with a tasty tomato fondue and lemon butter sauce, while confit of duck was served on a rich mushroom risotto. Dessert didn't let the side down: the tangy lemon tart (the house speciality) was sublime. Not a place for loud parties; children are welcome at lunch.

The Goods Shed

Station Road West, Canterbury, CT2 8AN (01227 459153). **Lunch served** noon-2.30pm Tue-Fri; noon-3pm Sat, Sun. **Dinner served** 6-9.30pm Tue-Sat. **Main courses** £8-£16. **Credit** MC, V.

A long-disused Victorian engine shed has been renovated to house this restaurant and farmers' market. The high-vaulted ceiling, exposed brickwork and huge cream doors create a harmonious space that reflects the ethos of the place perfectly. Wooden tables overlook the market from a raised platform, while gentle activity from the stalls creates the perfect mood for a leisurely lunch. Fresh, creamy moules marinière and a slightly thin mushroom soup, followed by flavour-packed roast red mullet and a generous vegetable platter – surprisingly the only vegetarian option – made a good meal. A propelling force behind the city's burgeoning food scene.

CRANBROOK

Restaurant 23

23 Stone Street, Cranbrook, TN17 3HF (01580 714666). **Lunch served** noon-2pm Mon-Sat; 12.30-2.30pm Sun. **Dinner served** 7-9.30pm Tue-Sat. **Main courses** £12.50-£17.95.

This restaurant, formerly Soho South, is one to watch. The decor is heavy on beams, dried hops and candles, and the atmosphere is low-key. Service is prone to the occasional lapse, but on the whole the upmarket modern European food compensates. Typical starters from the frequently changing menu include fried goat's cheese with pear and ginger chutney and rocket salad or risotto of seafood and saffron with a lemon dressing. Main courses might be loin of pork with black pudding crust, velouté of peas and broad beans or fillet of local Sussex beef with sun-blush tomato relish, roast provençal vegetables and olive gravy. Desserts, such as apple tarte tatin with vanilla ice-cream, are worth holding out for. The wine list deserves a special mention.

DARGATE

Dove Inn

Plum Pudding Lane, Dargate, ME13 9HB (01227 751360). **Lunch served** noon-1.30pm Tue-Sun. **Dinner served** 7-9pm Wed-Sat. **Main courses** £14.99-£16.75. **Credit** MC, V.

Situated in a tiny village off the Thanet Way, the Dove is now firmly established on the gastropub circuit. The scrubbed pine interior has modernised the Victorian building in some measure, but it still retains a country pub atmosphere. The cooking, too, reflects this balance, with imaginative modern dishes that are still rooted in the classical French tradition. Fresh, well-presented mains of whole plaice with capers, and guinea fowl came with new potatoes and a selection of vibrant vegetables. Moderate-sized servings left us room for cherry clafoutis. Ordering à la carte isn't cheap, although less expensive options are available from the blackboard menu. Still, the quality of the food and wine is high and the owners are welcoming.

DEAL

Dunkerley's

19 Beach Street, Deal, CT14 7AH (01304 375016/ www.dunkerleys.co.uk). **Lunch served** noon-2.30pm Mon-Sat; noon-3pm Sun. **Dinner served** 7-9.30pm Mon-Fri, Sun; 6-10pm Sat. **Main courses** £11.95-£21.95. **Set lunch** £6.95 1 course, £8.95 2 courses, £11.95 3 courses. **Set dinner** £16.95 2 courses. **Credit** AmEx, DC, MC, V.

Dunkerley's is loved along the coastline for its local seafood and inventive decor. Enhanced by music on a grand piano in the bar, the eating experience is intimate with slick, black-tie service. Starters include shrimp pagoda piled high on tiers of melba toast and caramelised scallops with bacon and velouté. Main dishes take in a choice of six fish, including roasted sea bass on saffron mash or plaice fillet seared on banana and sweet potato. There's also fillet of beef on a duxelle croûte. Complimentary palate-cleansers – asparagus soup in an espresso cup and ice-cold Bramley apple stew – were a nice touch.

DOVER

The Arlington

161 Snargate Street, Dover, CT17 9BZ (01304 209444/www.thearlington.co.uk). **Lunch served** noon-2.30pm, **dinner served** 6.30-9.30pm Tue-Sat. **Main courses** £12.95-£16.95. **Credit** MC, V.

Wedged between two angling shops, Kent's tiniest pub, the Arlington, reopened in March 2003 as one of Dover's smallest restaurants, now seating up to 20 people. Brand spankingly new inside, the temptation exists to rough it up a bit, splash colour on the bleak yellow walls, crumple up the white linen. That aside, it's run by a very friendly young couple with an infectious enthusiasm for the place. The menu, quaintly rolled up and tied with ribbon, is highly accessible both in content and price: minute steaks, sausage and mash, followed by crème brûlée or Dutch apple tart with complimentary tea and coffee.

Cullins Yard

New Cullins Yard, 11 Cambridge Road, Dover, CT17 9BY (01304 211666). **Meals served** noon-9.30pm daily. **Main courses** £9.60-£20. **Credit** DC, MC, V.

Not to be missed if dining in Dover. Cullins Yard is a lively, loud fish restaurant on the water's edge at Wellington Dock. Every inch of its deep, wood interior, decked out like a boat, is filled with bric-a-brac up for sale, including giant crabs in glass, masts and sails draped across the ceiling, grandfather clocks and nautical paintings. Every dish takes 30 minutes to prepare, such is the focus on freshness (the live lobsters are on show). Entertaining staff and jazz musicians twice a week fill up the waiting time. Favourites dishes include bouillabaisse, Dover sole and gravadlax, served with the likes of bubble and squeak, chunky chips and white crusty bread.

DUNGENESS

The Pilot

Battery Road, Lydd, Dungeness, TN29 9NJ (01797 320314/www.thepilot.uk.com). **Lunch served** noon-2.30pm, **dinner served** 6-9pm Mon-Fri. **Meals served** *summer* noon-9pm, *winter* noon-2.30pm Sat; noon-8pm Sun. **Main courses** £5.50-£8.70. **Credit** MC, V.

The place to come for fish and chips on Romney Marsh is the Pilot, a seafront pub on the Dungeness promontory serving crisply battered, melting cod nestling on a bed of chips that, while not quite matching the quintessential chip-shop chip, still beat many a restaurant offering. While the huge portions, excellent service and friendly atmosphere of the place doubtless contribute to its popularity, we suspect the glorious traditional seaside puds – towering knickerbocker glories, long banana splits and custard-drowned pies and crumbles – have a lot to do with it too, not to mention good children's meals, a covered veranda and a good range of beers.

HYTHE

Hythe Bay Fish Restaurant & Bar

Marine Parade, Hythe, CT21 6AW (01303 267024). **Lunch served** 12.30-2.15pm Tue-Sat; 12.30-2pm Sun. **Dinner served** 6.30-9.30pm Wed-Sat. **Main courses** £12.50. **Set lunch** (Tue-Fri) £10.95 2 courses. **Credit** AmEx, MC, V.

With the Channel lapping at the door, this is the place to indulge in seafood, whether a dozen oysters and a glass of wine in the bar or osso bucco of cod with garlic and thyme risotto in the restaurant. This unpretentious place has a modestly ambitious streak running through the kitchen, yet still satisfies traditionalists with fish and chips. Plate-glass windows keep the sea firmly in view and the staff are friendly and efficient. The short lunch menu – which featured an intense crab bisque, as well as an unusual fillet of plaice, sag aloo potatoes and minted crème fraîche – offers outstanding value for money.

IVY HATCH

Plough at Ivy Hatch

High Cross Road, Ivy Hatch, TN15 0NL (01732 810268). **Lunch served** noon-2pm Mon-Sat; noon-3pm Sun. **Dinner served** 6.30-10pm Mon-Sat; 6.30-8.30pm Sun. **Main courses** £15. **Credit** MC, V.

A long-standing favourite for seafood in the area, the Plough looks much more like a homely village pub than a restaurant. The extensive and ambitious menu is brimming with marine life in a variety of forms, and while some dishes lack panache, the freshness of the flavours delivers. Mouth-watering Irish oysters, fresh anchovies on bruschetta and a particularly spicy and moreish seafood chowder make good starters, while grilled whole lemon sole and fresh halibut with a mustard and herb crust are decent mains. Desserts are pretty traditional. Service is friendly, and there's a pleasant beer garden.

LANGTON GREEN

The Hare
Langton Road, Langton Green, TN3 0JA (01892 862419/www.hare-tunbridgewells.co.uk). **Meals served** noon-9.30pm Mon-Sat; noon-9pm Sun. **Main courses** £6.95-£15.95. **Credit** MC, V.
The spacious dining rooms of this ever-popular, civilised Edwardian pub pack diners in at all hours for well-executed food. The menu is broken down into little things, bread things, big things and puddings. Delightful little things might include a delicious yet light mushroom and port pâté with toasted brioche and smoked cheese, or a Cajun salmon, mango and rocket filo tart with vanilla dressing. Excellent smoked haddock and salmon fish cakes are only surpassed by a superb grilled halibut with spring vegetables, prawn risotto and salsa verde. The highlight of traditional desserts was a rich ginger sponge pudding with golden syrup and cream. When the weather is fine, dining on the terrace has the added benefit of overlooking a typically English tree-lined green. Food is ordered at the bar, prices are fair and portions generous.

PAINTER'S FORSTAL

Read's
Mackanade's Manor, Canterbury Road, Painter's Forstal, ME13 8XE (01795 535344/ www.reads.com). **Lunch served** noon-2pm, **dinner served** 7-9pm Tue-Sat. **Set lunch** £19.50 3 courses. **Set dinner** £42 3 courses. **Credit** AmEx, DC, MC, V.
The menu at Read's makes good reading. Not only does it offer sumptuous and inventive seasonal dishes, it's interspersed with foodie quotes sure to encourage diners ('Never eat more than you can lift' – Miss Piggy). Run by Michelin-starred chef David Pitchford and his wife Rona, the restaurant has recently moved to a splendid Georgian mansion with an airy drawing room (used for pre-dinner drinks), a dining room that overlooks the garden and a small terrace. Ingredients are locally sourced: fish from Whitstable, lamb from Romney Marsh and vegetables from their own kitchen garden. If you can't choose between hand-rolled gnocchi with asparagus, or brill served with seared scallops, cabbage and sweetcure bacon or roasted Kentish lamb with fondant potatoes, try the imaginative

tasting menu, which offers smaller portions of four dishes. You can also do the same with puddings, which include warm comice pear tart and chocoholics anonymous – four different baby desserts. Presentation is beautiful and the friendly service faultless.

PENSHURST

The Spotted Dog ★
Smarts Hill, Penshurst, TN11 8EP (01892 870253). **Lunch served** noon-2.30pm, **dinner served** 6-9.30pm Mon-Thur. **Meals served** noon-9.30pm Fri, Sat; noon-8pm Sun. **Main courses** £10-£17. **Credit** MC, V.
Behind the panelled bar that dominates this ancient, rambling clapboard pub is a young, professional kitchen producing some very good food. The blackboard menu – short, to the point and changing continually – is based on a repertoire of classic country dishes such as generously portioned local Kentish pork served with red cabbage and apple compote. But there's a modern streak too, with dishes such as grilled fillet of swordfish teamed with stir-fried vegetables, coriander and soy dressing, and brasserie-style favourites of rich chicken liver parfait with red onion compote or fillet of beef with thick-cut chips and garlic herb butter. Sharing equal billing with the food is the sheer friendliness of the place: first and foremost this is a classic local serving real ales to loyal regulars.

PLUCKLEY

Dering Arms
Station Road, Pluckley, TN27 0RR (01233 840371/www.deringarms.com). **Lunch served** noon-2pm, **dinner served** 7-9.30pm daily. **Main courses** £8.45-£20. **Credit** AmEx, MC, V.
Fish and seafood are the mainstays at this wonderfully old and atmospheric former hunting lodge. It's complete with flagstones, wood floors, high ceilings and Dering windows and can be hard to find (it's tucked away by the railway station). At busy times there are lapses in service, but staff are friendly and the food is a cut above. Expect to find starters such as grilled sardines with rosemary butter, garlic king prawns, and mains such as pan-fried scallops with basil spaghetti and saffron sauce or breast of duck with potato and celeriac purée and port sauce. Desserts might include oranges in caramel with Grand Marnier or lemon posset. The wine list features some choice bottles from Down Under – should they prove too tempting, you can stagger upstairs afterwards and stay the night.

RAMSGATE

Surin
30 Harbour Street, Ramsgate, CT11 8HA (01843 592001/www.surinrestaurant.co.uk). **Lunch served** noon-2.30pm Tue-Sat. **Dinner served** 6-11pm

Tue-Sun. **Main courses** £6-£7. **Set lunch** £5.95
2 courses. **Set meals** £20 3 courses incl coffee.
Credit AmEx, DC, MC, V.

The small, simply furnished restaurant near the harbour and seafront is not much to look at, but in a relatively short time, this Ramsgate newcomer has quietly established a local reputation for serving authentic Thai cooking at inexpensive prices. The lengthy menu goes beyond national boundaries to take in dishes from Laos and Cambodia, but delivers long-standing faves such as Thai fish cakes and red and green curries. Waits for food to arrive can seem long, but suggest that everything is freshly prepared. Fish is particularly well handled. Indeed, a blackboard special of Cambodian mixed seafood with tamarind came with delicate plump mussels that had a briny just-out-of-the-sea taste. Standouts here are chicken with basil leaves, and sticky rice steamed with coconut milk.

RINGLESTONE
Ringlestone Inn
Ringlestone Road, Ringlestone, ME17 1NX (01622 859900/www.ringlestone.com). **Lunch served** noon-2pm Mon-Sat; 12.30-2.30pm Sun. **Dinner served** 7-9.30pm daily. **Main courses** £10.50-£15.75. **Credit** AmEx, DC, MC, V.

'No thieves, fakirs, skulking loafers or flee-bitten tramps' are allowed inside the dark and cosy Ringlestone Inn: if you slip under the non-PC wire, you'll be free to sample their speciality pies, fruit wines (cowslip, walnut, elderberry) or imaginative fare (country chicken, pistachio stuffed duck). Built in 1533 as a hospice for monks, the inn became an ale house in 1615 and original flint walls, inglenooks and beams lend a sense of history. The emphasis at Ringlestone is on taking your time, and it's a great place to do just that, particularly in the pub garden.

SANDGATE
Sandgate Hotel Restaurant
8-9 Wellington Terrace, The Esplanade, Sandgate, TT20 3DY (01303 220444/ www.sandgatehotel.com). **Breakfast served** 7-10am Mon-Fri; 7am-noon Sat, Sun. **Lunch served** noon-3pm, **dinner served** 6-10pm daily. **Main courses** £14. **Credit** AmEx, DC, MC, V.

Intimate and simple with beige/cream walls and stained glass doors overlooking the sea, the new restaurant at the Sandgate Hotel (which opened in March 2003 in place of La Terrasse) serves up top-of-the-range modern European fare. Perhaps because it's new or small, the ambience is a tad over-formal – everyone dressed up/on best behaviour – although occasional jocularities from the hotel bar help loosen the mood. Still one or two teething problems: beautifully presented starters took forever to arrive. The tian of Provence vegetables, though a touch bland, was colourfully stacked and dressed with a hazel-nut salad; the fillet of beef was chunky but tender and served with a rich

pesto, chilli, mustard and Swiss chard sauce. Note that at breakfast time the place is also open to all-comers, not just hotel residents.

SANDWICH
Quayside Bar & Brasserie
Bell Lane, The Quay, Sandwich, CT13 9EN (01304 619899/www.quaysidebar.co.uk). **Lunch served** noon-2.30pm Mon-Sat; noon-4pm Sun. **Dinner served** 6-9.30pm Mon-Sat. **Main courses** £6.95-£14.95. **Credit** AmEx, MC, V.

A welcome change from the more historically steeped eateries dotted along the East Kent coast, Quayside is airy, bright and open-plan with light blue and white walls, a long bar and spot-lit columns. Colourful art depicting seaside huts and Miami city scenes fill the walls alongside blackboards detailing cocktails, food specials and upcoming jazz (last Sunday of every month). Service is chatty and casual. Light meals include baguettes and simple tapas – hot chorizo salad, marinated anchovies, nachos with salsa – or, for more hefty dishes, there's calf's liver with crispy bacon, fillet of pork with prune and apricot mousse or a choice of risottos.

SEASALTER
The Sportsman
Faversham Road, Seasalter, CT5 4BP (01227 273370). **Lunch served** noon-1.45pm Tue-Sat; noon-2.30pm Sun. **Dinner served** 7-8.45pm Tue-Sat. **Main courses** £9.95-£17.95. **Credit** MC, V.

It's well worth a detour to this out of the way, quirky coastal pub. The Harris brothers meld contemporary art and a low-key decor with a cooking style that is bang on – modern, light and powerfully flavoured. Ideas are lively and wide-ranging, with dishes not weighed down by fussy presentation. This relative simplicity exposes the kitchen's considerable skills and the quality of the buying (much of it local). It is this combination that turned a sparely described crispy duck, smoked chilli salsa and sour cream into such a memorable dish. Antipasti for two includes exemplary salt cod and oysters with chorizo. Or choose asparagus soup with a duck egg, followed by Thornback ray with balsamic vinaigrette, and a superb rhubarb sorbet and burnt cream.

SISSINGHURST
Rankins
The Street, Sissinghurst (01580 713964/ www.rankinsrestaurant.com). **Lunch served** from 12.30pm Sun. **Dinner served** from 7.30pm Wed-Sat. **Set dinner** £23.50 2 courses, £28.50 3 courses. **Credit** MC, V.

Friendly and self-assured, Hugh and Leonora Rankins' eaterie bucks the trend of the restaurants in the area – the interior won't win any design awards with its step-back-in-time look, but it's good to see such a place stand out against the trendy

The best Vegetarian restaurants

Café @ All Saints
Herefordshire. *See p214.*

Café Paradiso
Cork. *See p356.*

David Bann
Edinburgh. *See p303.*

Demuths
Somerset. *See p141.*

Greens
Manchester. *See p259.*

Quince & Medlar
Cumbria. *See p246.*

Rubicon
York. *See p284.*

Sqeek
Nottinghamshire. *See p228.*

Terre à Terre
Sussex. *See p99.*

Tomlins
Vale of Glamorgan. *See p344.*

newcomers. The menu is short but well executed and local produce features strongly, with lamb from Frittenden and Romney Marsh, and a variety of fish from Rye. Among the signature dishes are a starter of oak-smoked haddock baked in a cheddar-glazed creamy lemon sauce and a dessert of coffee fudge pudding. Prices aren't the lowest, but the wine list has plenty of decent bottles under £20.

THREE CHIMNEYS
Three Chimneys
Three Chimneys, TN27 8LW (01580 291472). **Lunch served** 11.30am-1.50pm Mon-Sat; noon-1.50pm Sun. **Dinner served** 6.30-9.50pm Mon-Sat; 7-9pm Sun. **Main courses** £10.95-£18.95. **Credit** MC, V.
This deservedly popular country pub dates back to 1420 and dried hops and wooden beams set the tone for the decor. The friendly service can be on the slow side and prices are high, but portions are generous and standards impressive. Typical starters include deep-fried brie with Cumberland sauce and crusty bread. Among the mains are fillet of smoked haddock on a bacon, parmesan and spring onion mash with grain mustard butter sauce. Portions are so huge you may well not have room for dessert, though you'll be hard pressed to refuse with the likes of sticky toffee pudding and raspberry and vanilla brûlée to tempt you. Well-kept ales include Adnams, Shepherd Neame and Harveys Best. Booking is advisable (but not possible for Sunday lunch). The garden out back is popular on sunny days.

TUNBRIDGE WELLS
Thackeray's ★
85 London Road, Tunbridge Wells, TN1 1EA (01892 511921/www.thackeraysrestaurant.co.uk). **Lunch served** noon-2.30pm Tue-Sun. **Dinner served** 6.30-10.30pm Tue-Sat. **Main courses** £16-£22.50. **Set lunch** £11.50 2 courses, £12.50 3 courses. **Set dinner** £48 6 courses. **Credit** AmEx, MC, V.

The white timber-fronted former home of novelist and satirist William Thackeray holds one of the best restaurants the area has to offer. Awarded a Michelin star in 2003, young, talented chef Richard Phillips has brought a wealth of experience from London's gastronomic beacons. The charming listed exterior leads into a melting pot of extravagant interiors: two minimalist, stylish and elegant dining rooms on the ground floor contrast with the upstairs gold leaf bar and two private dining rooms. There's even a Japanese-inspired outdoor dining area. The pricey modern French food delivers on all fronts and lives up to the pedigree. Highlights included a starter of duck salad with toasted brioche and a main course of roast monkfish tail, stuffed courgette flower and red wine sauce. A raspberry soufflé with hazel-nut ice-cream and warm raspberry coulis confirmed what a fine kitchen this is. The wine list is extensive; service professional and accommodating.

WEST MALLING
Swan
35 Swan Street, West Malling, ME19 6JU (01732 521910). **Lunch served** noon-2.30pm Mon-Sat; noon-4pm Sun. **Dinner served** 6-10.30pm Mon-Sat; 6-9.30pm Sun. **Main courses** £9-£14. **Credit** AmEx, DC, MC, V.
The makeover of this former town boozer reveals an eye for metropolitan sophistication. Private dining rooms are nothing short of stunning, while the clean lines of the bar and eating areas are as attractive as the food. The menu is lively, reflecting modern ideas and imaginative pairings, and definitely raises the stakes from pub/bar to restaurant with starters of delicately flavoured leek and gruyère tart, as well as a very zippy fresh crab linguine with chilli and basil. Main courses range from classic smoked haddock and chive fish cakes with mustard sauce to roast rump of lamb with roasted root vegetables and rosemary sauce. Desserts are their equal, especially a silky lemon crème brûlée.

The Goods Shed. *See p85.*

WEST PECKHAM

Swan on the Green

The Green, West Peckham, ME18 5JW (01622 812271/www.the-swan-on-the-green.co.uk).
Lunch served 12.30-2pm daily. **Dinner served** 6.30-8pm Mon; 7.30-9pm Tue-Sat. **Main courses** £8.95-£15.50. **Credit** AmEx, MC, V.

Although renovation means the Swan is open-plan, the rural charm of this row of Tudor cottages remains – with beams, bare brickwork and log fires contrasting well with contemporary art, church pews and a gleaming espresso machine. The menu is short but provides a clever balancing act. Go traditional with exemplary British dishes such as intensely cooked oven-baked pork filled with caramelised Bramley apple, or pork and leek sausages with onion gravy. Play them off against modish excursions like char-grilled chicken, black pudding and crispy bacon, or fresh crab meat and shrimp fish cakes with a lime and caperberry crème fraîche and basil couscous. The microbrewery stabled round the back provides the astonishing range of ales on handpump.

WHITSTABLE

Crab & Winkle

South Quay, The Harbour, Whitstable, CT5 1AB (01227 779377/www.crab-winkle.co.uk). **Meals served** 10.30am-9.45pm daily. **Main courses** £7.95-£30. **Credit** MC, V.

The enchanting view from the window tables – overlooking Whitstable harbour – is the best thing about a meal here. On our visit, the quality of the cooking was uneven, and certainly not quite good enough for the prices charged. The seafood is fresh – it would be a sin if it wasn't given the location – and not interfered with too much. Whole plain lemon sole was tender and simply grilled. But the accompanying vegetables were dry and the chunky chips tasted stale. The paella was a better option – generous and with a good assortment of fresh shellfish – although the dish again lacked vibrancy. Service is also variable.

Harbour Street Café ★

48 Harbour Street, Whitstable, CT5 1AQ (01227 772575/www.harbourstreetcafe.co.uk). **Meals served** 9am-4pm Mon-Fri; 9am-5pm Sat; 10am-4pm Sun. **Dinner served** 6.30-10pm Fri, Sat. **Main courses** *day* £3.95-£9.95, *dinner* £9.50-£16.95. **Credit** AmEx, MC, V.

Homespun cooking fits this agreeable, down-to-earth café to a T. It does a roaring trade. A greasy-spoon for the middle classes, beans are either Heinz or own-made, sausages are gluten-free, houmous is organic and mayonnaise is made from free-range eggs. Breakfast includes all the usual suspects (or not if you're having the vegetarian version) plus bubble and squeak. Blackboard specials open with garlic Mediterranean prawns flambéed in Cognac, go on to Singapore crab curry with beansprouts coriander and basil leaves and Thai scented rice, and finish with lemon tart. In between, there could be carrot, coconut and coriander soup, or tofu, lettuce, tomato and mayo sandwiches, or a vegan and gluten-free banana, chocolate and hazel-nut cake.

Hotel Continental

29 Beach Walk, Whitstable, CT5 2BP (01227 280280/www.hotelcontinental.co.uk). **Lunch served** noon-2pm, **dinner served** 7-9pm Mon-Fri. **Meals served** noon-9.30pm Sat; noon-9pm Sun. **Main courses** £6.50-£18.95. **Credit** AmEx, DC, MC, V.

The hotel's split-level brasserie retains the art deco building's upmarket weekend-away atmosphere, with its ochre and maroon walls, parquet flooring, and crisp tablecloths and napkins. So, a good start. However, the smell of stale cooking oil dampened our appetites, and the starter – baked mushrooms and chorizo drowned in oil – didn't do much to reawaken them. Mains were better: Aberdeen fillet of beef with basil sauce and salmon fish cakes were tasty. Vegetable accompaniments weren't at their freshest, however, and the food lacked overall vitality. Granted, it was a busy bank holiday Monday, and staff were trying their best to appease several disgruntled customers, but for the prices charged the quality could be better. Ask for a table with sea views.

Pearson's Crab & Oyster House

Sea Wall, Whitstable, CT5 1BT (01227 272005). **Lunch served** noon-2.30pm Mon-Sat. **Dinner served** 6.30-9pm Mon-Fri; 6-9.30pm Sat. **Meals served** noon-9pm Sun. **Main courses** £8.50-£21.95. **Credit** MC, V.
The first-floor restaurant of this traditional seafront pub has stiff competition. It is right next door to the well-known Whitstable Oyster Fishery Company (*see p92*), but its own take on local seafood is pretty good too, and many locals favour the place for a more intimate meal. The young staff are keen and friendly, and the seafood and fish are superb: a huge seafood platter features the best oysters you could wish for, plus wonderful langoustines, crab, clams, king prawns and cockles, alongside rice and salad. A swordfish steak with salsa (£10.95) was fresh and delicate. The pub itself is fairly uninspiring, but don't be put off by initial appearances: this is a lovely little restaurant.

Tea & Times ★

36A The High Street, Whitstable, CT5 1BQ (01227 262639). **Meals served** 8.30am-5pm Mon-Fri; 9am-6pm Sat; 9am-5pm Sun. **No credit cards**.
Describing itself as a 'sandwich bar and newsagents', Tea & Times is popular with the local arty crowd (and sometimes provides exhibition space to local artists), who come to leaf through the stack of newspapers provided over mugs of freshly ground coffee. The place manages to feel somewhat chaotic and laid-back all at the same time, as demonstrated by the rather erratic service and the messy (crumbs on the tables) but homely interior. Drop in for a quick coffee seated on the wooden bar stools downstairs, or a more leisurely lunch in the spacious upstairs space. There's a good range of appetising sandwiches such as avocado, bacon or brie, as well as tasty own-made cakes and an all-day breakfast for £4.70.

Wheelers Oyster Bar ★

8 High Street, Whitstable, CT5 1BQ (01227 273311/www.whitstable-shellfish.co.uk). **Meals served** 1-7.30pm Mon, Tue, Thur-Sat; 1-7pm Sun. **Main courses** £5-£18. **No credit cards**.
The pink façade is a Whitstable landmark, and Wheelers have been purveyors of the famed native oysters for 150 years. When Mark Stubbs took over the kitchen, locals struggled hard to keep secret his wonderful way with fish. Why? The tiny seafood bar seats four people, while the backroom restaurant has just three tables. Here lobster ravioli with baby leeks, aged parmesan and broad bean cappuccino or pan-fried skate wing, beurre noisette, salsa verde croquettes and steamed vegetables stuffed with mint and basil ratatouille are delivered with a cosmopolitan finesse. No licence (but no corkage)

keeps the bill in line, and if it's fully booked there's consolation in delicate seafood tarts, fish cakes and fresh shellfish to take away.

Whitstable Oyster Fishery Company

The Royal Native Oyster Stores, Horsbridge, Whitstable, CT5 1BU (01227 276856/www.oysterfishery.co.uk). **Lunch served** noon-1.45pm Tue-Sat; noon-2.30pm Sun. **Dinner served** 7-8.45pm Tue-Sat; 6.30-8.15pm Sun. **Main courses** £12.50-£25. **Credit** AmEx, DC, MC, V.
The Oyster Fishery restaurant was the old company headquarters and is now the most atmospheric place in town to sample the local speciality. The restaurant's gastronomic reputation is deserved, but the draw is as much the setting as the food, with a sublime sea view (and often stunning sunsets). And there's the classic yet modern decor – red and white checked tablecloths, exposed brickwork and old photos of local fishermen on the walls. The menu changes regularly. This time around, scallops, for starters, were perfectly cooked in garlic butter. Mains were also good: skate was simply but classically prepared with black butter and capers; organic salmon was char-grilled and accompanied by a flavourful salsa verde. Dessert of chocolate and walnut brownie was generous in terms of flavour, but decidedly stingy in terms of size.

WYE

Wife of Bath

4 Upper Bridge Street, Wye, TN25 5AF (01233 812232/www.wifeofbath.com). **Lunch served** noon-1.30pm, **dinner served** 7-9.30pm Tue-Sat. **Main courses** £15.50-£17. **Set lunch** £12.75 2 courses. **Set dinner** £22.50 3 courses. **Credit** AmEx, MC, V.
For supremely tasty food and a classy yet relaxed environment, the Wife of Bath is a good bet. The restaurant takes up the big, bay-windowed room at the front of the house (there are six bedrooms above), and is staffed by knowledgeable and good-humoured waiters. Intense flavours, local produce and beautiful presentation characterise the dishes, which include pan-fried Kent duckling with honey and cumin or roasted rack of spring lamb. Do try the delicious brown bread ice-cream. It's a very British menu, enlivened by the odd incursion, such as wasabi mayonnaise. Smoking is permitted in the bar, but not in the restaurant.

Also in the area

Carluccio's Caffè The Village, Bluewater Shopping Centre, Greenhithe, DA9 9SE (01322 387276); **Hotel du Vin & Bistro** Crescent Road, Tunbridge Wells, TN1 2LY (01892 526455); **Loch Fyne** 63-65 High Street, Sevenoaks, TN13 1JY (01732 467140).

Surrey

ABINGER COMMON

The Stephan Langton

Friday Street, Abinger Common, RH5 6JR (01306 730775). **Lunch served** 12.30-3pm Tue-Sun. **Dinner served** 7-10pm Tue-Sat. **Main courses** £10.25-£12.50. **Credit** MC, V.
Getting to the Stephan Langton – named after the celebrated 12th-century Archbishop of Canterbury – requires skilful negotiation of what must be the narrowest roads in Surrey. But despite being fairly casual – order at the bar – the food is classy stuff. The choices were few, just three light dishes and eight mains, and included sardines, ham hock, sausage and mash, tuna niçoise and roasts. Here, keeping things simple seems to yield great results. Roast pork came with a tasty mix of peas, diced bacon and fresh Jersey Royals, while char-grilled yellowfin tuna niçoise was tender as can be. Wines are chalked up on a blackboard; about 12 reds and 12 whites, spanning the globe and costing between £11 and £30.

GUILDFORD

Zinfandel

4-5 Chapel Street, Guildford, GU1 3UH (01483 455155/www.zinfandel.org.uk). **Lunch served** noon-3pm Mon-Sat; noon-4pm Sun. **Dinner served** 6-10pm Mon-Sat. **Main courses** £7.95-£13.95. **Credit** AmEx, MC, V.
A discreet alleyway off Guildford's main high street is the location for Zinfandel, a minimalist chrome homage to cuisine from California's Napa Valley. There are salad, pizza, rotisserie and char-grill options. Typical dishes on offer might include calamares 'popcorn' with three salsas: roast garlic aïoli, key-lime guacamole and tomato-chilli jam; or a 10oz char-grilled ribeye with jalapeno slaw. A generously topped pizza of barbecued chicken, smoked gouda and mozzarella went down very nicely indeed. If the golden nashi pear on a stem ginger rice pudding fritter feels like a step too far for pudding, then settle for the fail-safe pecan pie with maple syrup. Unsurprisingly, the decent wine list

stays largely in California. On our visit this place wasn't going to win any awards for atmosphere, but it is child-friendly.

OCKLEY

Bryce's

The Old School House, Stane Street, Ockley, R85 5TH (01306 627430/www.bryces.co.uk). **Lunch served** noon-2pm, **dinner served** 7-9pm daily. **Bar meals served** 11.30am-2.30pm, 6.30-9.30pm daily. **Set lunch** £15.50 2 courses. **Set dinner** £19.50 2 courses, £25 3 courses. **Credit** MC, V.

The Old School House in which Bryce's is situated has been an inn since 1965, and is agreeably located about 200 yards from the large green that's the focal point of this pretty village. This award-winning fish restaurant has been here for ten years. The decor is low-beamed modernised Tudor. To start, we had smoked haddock risotto with pancetta and poached egg which was slightly heavy going, but flavoursome; tender seared tuna with lentil and mango salsa was less demanding. The stand-out main course was Scottish halibut with a saffron, vanilla and balsamic sauce and a prawn and chilli beignet. The specials menu contains plenty of shellfish and also some non-fish options. The interesting wine list includes some bottles from the local vineyard, Denbies.

REIGATE

The Dining Room ★

59A High Street, Reigate, RH2 9AE (01737 226650/www.tonytobinrestaurants.co.uk). **Lunch served** noon-2pm Mon-Fri; 12.30-2.30pm Sun. **Dinner served** 7-10pm Mon-Sat. **Set lunch** (Mon-Fri) £19.50-£22.50 2 courses; (Sun) £28.50 3 courses. **Set dinner** (Mon-Thur) £22.50 2 courses; (Fri, Sat) £28.50 2 courses. **Credit** AmEx, MC, V.

The Dining Room is announced by a first-floor sign and discreet menu by a blink-and-you'll-miss-it door. However, this is a serious restaurant – executive chef Tony Tobin's former years were spent cutting his teeth at Chez Nico and the award-winning South Lodge in Lower Beding. This place is – if you ignore the kangaroo burger – resolutely Modern British. A tender hunk of peppered lamb came with minted pearl barley, braised celery and super-smooth mash. Meanwhile, black pudding was stuffed inside rolls of succulent roast chicken and accompanied by apple chutney and mash. Top marks for presentation and further points for likeable staff and impeccable service.

SHERE

Kingham's

Gomshall Lane, Shere, GU5 9HE (01483 202168/ www.kinghams-restaurant.co.uk). **Lunch served** 12.15-2.15pm Tue-Sun. **Dinner served** 7-9.15pm Tue-Sat. **Main courses** £10.95-£16.95. **Set lunch**

(Tue-Sat) £13.95 2 courses; (Sun) £15.95 2 courses, £19.95 3 courses. **Set dinner** (Tue-Thur) £15.95 2 courses. **Credit** AmEx, DC, MC, V.

This squat, 400-year-old building was once the cottage of the local hangman; it is now, according to a waitress, also home to a resident ghost (a cat). Good use has been made of the cosy, low-lit space, packing in enough (retired) punters to make a convivial atmosphere. The menu is predominantly British, listing dishes such as Gressingham duck, roast partridge and veal escalope. Roast rib of beef with Yorkshire pud, veg and red wine jus proved there's no skimping on portions. Chicken liver, bacon and mushroom in a puff pastry parcel, with a redcurrant and walnut salad, followed by a decently cooked salmon fillet, made for a satisfying meal. Service was charming but not polished. A lengthy wine list spans the globe and includes a good selection of half bottles.

VIRGINIA WATER

Siam Food Gallery

Trumps Green Road, Virginia Water, GU25 4HN (01344 843283). **Lunch served** noon-3pm, **dinner served** 6-11pm daily. **Main courses** £20. **Set lunch** £9.95 2 courses. **Set dinner** £25 2 courses. **Set meal** £35 3 courses. **Credit** AmEx, DC, MC, V.

This former pub has been transformed into a handsome Thai restaurant, with the addition of a conservatory (looking out on to a garden), dark wood furnishings and Thai artefacts. Customers tend to arrive in smart cars, round off the meal with Irish coffees and don't mind the slightly inflated prices. Staff are unfailingly charming and the setting is a soothing one. The wine list has been chosen by Martin Lam of Ransome's Dock (*see p63*). So, with all these pluses, it's a shame that the dishes are mostly Surrey-sanitised versions of the original. Starters of fish cakes and deep-fried minced pork and coriander on bread, both beautifully presented, were the best part of the meal. Punchily flavoured, they outshone the mains – exemplified by slightly rubbery squid stir-fried with chilli, garlic and basil leaves. Still, a very pleasant venue and handy for Wentworth golf course.

Also in the area

Bar Estilo 2 Church Street, Esher, KT10 8QS (01372 468880); **Bar Estilo** 1 Hill Rise, Richmond, TW10 6UQ (020 8940 5013); **Bel & the Dragon** Bridge Street, Godalming, GU7 3DU (01483 527333); **Carluccio's Caffè** Unit 5, Charter Quay, Kingston-upon-Thames, KT1 1HT (020 8549 5898); **Loch Fyne** 5-6 High Street, Egham, TW20 9EA (01784 414890); **Siam Food Gallery** 95-97 High Street, Esher, KT10 9QE (01372 477139); **Wagamama** 24-29 High Street, Guildford, GU1 3DY (01483 457779); **Zinfandel** Bagshot Road, Cobham, GU24 8BP (01276 858 491); **Zinfandel** 44-46 Church Street, Weybridge, KT13 8DP (01932 859779).

MOMMA CHERRI'S SOUL FOOD SHACK...THE ONLY AMERICAN SOUL FOOD RESTAURANT IN BRIGHTON

Small or large groups, family, couples, Shucks you're all welcome!

Family days out at the premier Soul Food Restaurant of the South

"8/10 Giles Coren ..." **The Times**
"Momma Cherri puts the fun back into eating out." **P.P Arnold**
"Come hungry 'cos Momma's serving hefty helpings!" **Atlanta Ga**
"It was just like being back home" **Antonio Fargas (Huggy Bear)**

Rev. Daisy's Southern Fried Chicken, Sweet Potato Pie, Catfish and Red Snapper, Jambalaya (Meat, Fish and Veg), Fabulous Vegetarian selection, Full American Breakfast and Desserts sent from Heaven

Sundays - Gospel Brunch 11am-2pm ,
2-10pm Dinner with a difference
Mon-Thurs 5pm-11pm
Fri-Sat 12pm-midnight

Party time in the Cherri Lounge

Look out for our NEW and ever changing events:
Free seconds on special selected meals, Special deals on combo platters, Regular DJ spots, 2-4-1 cocktails, American microbrews, Sweet soul music, New Orleans funk, and good ol'fashioned classic sounds.

BOOKING HIGHLY RECOMMENDED FULLY LICENSED

11Little East Street, Brighton, BN1 1HT 01273 774545 www.mommacherri.co.uk

Available for OUTSIDE CATERING
**We're on tour serving lunch at selected soulful spots across East Sussex.
Hove by day, Brighton by night, for details call 01273 774545.
Mon.-Thurs. 9am-4pm available for private hire
and lunchtime functions at the shack.**

Sussex

East Sussex

BATTLE

Food Rooms

The Chapel, 55 High Street, Battle, East Sussex
TN33 0EN (01424 775537/www.foodrooms.co.uk).
Meals served 8.30am-5.30pm Mon-Sat; 8.30am-
4.30pm Sun. **Main courses** £7.50-£18.50. **Set lunch**
(Sun) £16.50 2 courses, £19 3 courses. **Credit** MC, V.
The bright and airy entrance is taken up with a
delicatessen-cum-takeaway, with the informal, child-
friendly eating area beyond. Fresh, often organic
produce is provided by known farmers, with even
the coffee roasted locally, and there's always a
decent vegetarian option. But don't let the
earnestness of the operation put you off – the
creative menu is well presented and unbelievably
priced for such great food. The Sunday lunch
(booking is advisable) is a positive bargain: crostini
and olives, followed by a selection of antipasti,
choice of own-made soups, main courses such as
poached salmon with star anise butter or pan-fried
gigot of lamb, and desserts of warm chocolate tart
or baked lemon tart (£16.50 without dessert, £19
with). Service is attentive, informative and friendly
– no wonder the locals can't get enough of this 'eat
in, eat out, eat well' operation.

The Pilgrim ★

1 High Street, Battle, East Sussex TN33 0AE
(01424 772314/www.foodrooms.co.uk). **Lunch**
served noon-3pm Mon-Sat; noon-4pm Sun. **Dinner**
served 7-9.30pm Mon-Sat. **Main courses** £9.80-
£18.50. **Set meal** (Mon-Thur, lunch Fri) £14.75
2 courses, £19.25 3 courses. **Credit** AmEx, MC, V.
Standing on the site of a 12th-century monastic
hospital, in the shadow of Battle Abbey, this sister
restaurant to the Food Rooms (*see above*) is
impressive on many levels – from the beautiful
vaulted hall, period furniture and open fires to the
attentive service and inventive menu. Diners can
enjoy the relaxed atmosphere at a very reasonable
price. £4.50 buys a starter of smoked fish chowder
or garlic cappuccino with shaved truffles; mains
such as pan-fried fillet of whiting with a coriander,
chilli and star anise butter start at £9.80. Those
wishing to push the boat firmly out can try
Brightling venison with field mushrooms, pancetta
and gratin dauphinois or whole Dover sole meunière
(both £18.50). The standard of cooking here is high;
desserts are heavenly – try the chocolate parfait
– while the well-chosen wine list can manage a
decent bottle under £12. Not to be missed. Booking
is essential.

BODIAM

The Curlew

Junction Road, Bodiam, East Sussex TN32 5UY
(01580 861394/www.thecurlewatbodiam.co.uk).
Lunch served noon-2pm, **dinner served** 7-9.30pm
Tue-Sun. **Main courses** £12.95-£19.95. **Credit**
AmEx, MC, V.
In the heart of 1066 country, and a stone's throw
from Bodiam Castle, the local cognoscenti are
treading the well-worn Roman road (aka the A229)
to the Curlew. The pub may look olde worlde, but
the restaurant food is anything but. A cheery
welcome from Aussie front-of-housers is backed
up with good knowledge of the food and wine on
offer. The Roux brothers-trained chef exerts a
Mediterranean influence on the seasonally changing
menu, which might include a spicy Thai soup or
succulent diver-caught scallops. Mains range from
traditional ribeye served with field mushrooms and
fries to a more adventurous teaming of pan-fried red
mullet with green beans, crushed niçoise potatoes,
roasted tomatoes, peppers and chive oil. All were a
complete success. Desserts are moreish, but why opt
for one when the miniature dessert plate gives you
a bite-size portion of each? Bon appetit.

BRIGHTON

Black Chapati

12 Circus Parade, New England Road, Brighton,
East Sussex BN1 4GW (01273 699011). **Meals**
served 7-10pm Tue-Sat. **Main courses** £11.90-
£15.50. **Credit** AmEx, MC, V.
Black Chapati's drab, concrete box exterior and
plainly furnished, café-like interior are at odds with
the quality of pan-Asian cuisine on offer. The short
but well co-ordinated menu features starters such as
fiery Sri Lankan fish patties with fresh chutneys –
deliciously zingy, although the flavour of the fish was
somewhat lost to chilli heat. Mains include grilled
five-spice duck breast; Chinese sausage and potato
cake with rice wine sauce; and delicious succulent
roast cod, dried shrimp and fresh lime salad and rice.
Desserts include a wonderful ginger meringue with
fresh-tasting green tea ice-cream. Palate-pleasing and
imaginative dining, although service can be
disappointing, ranging from inattentive to dour.

Blanch House

Blanch House Hotel, 17 Atlingworth Street,
Brighton, East Sussex BN2 1PL (01273 645755/
www.blanchhouse.co.uk). **Lunch served** noon-3pm
Wed-Sat. **Dinner served** 7-10.30pm Tue-Sat.
Set lunch £15 2 courses, £20 3 courses. **Set dinner**
£27.50 2 courses, £35 3 courses. **Credit** AmEx, MC, V.

Housed in the hotel basement, Blanch House's stylish and classy dining room decor reflects its approach to modern cuisine. Start your meal with a cocktail at the hotel's chic bar; the choices are tempting. The international menu uses locally sourced, mostly organic ingredients. English mackerel fillet and langoustine galette with tomato and lemon may appear alongside a simpler salad of smoked chicken and poached quail's eggs or roast duck breast. Striking vegetarian choices (saffron and almond risotto with cumin aubergine and stuffed courgette flowers) also feature. The cooking is superb, presentation picture-perfect and lengthy wine list impressive; this is undoubtedly a destination dining experience, but service can be slow and a little aloof.

Café Paradiso

Hotel Seattle, Brighton Marina, Brighton, East Sussex BN2 5WA (01273 679799/www.aliashotels.com). **Lunch served** noon-2.30pm Mon-Fri; 12.30-3pm Sat, Sun. **Dinner served** 6-10pm Mon-Fri; 7-10.30pm Sat, Sun. **Main courses** £6.25-£24.95. **Set lunch** £12.95 2 courses. **Credit** AmEx, MC, V.

Hotel Seattle is part of a new development more than two miles from the centre of town, in a soulless marina. The saving grace is the hotel's restaurant, Café Paradiso. The dining room is high-ceilinged, white, light and airy. A big wood-fired pizza oven dominates the room and sets the tone for the menu: mostly Italian/Mediterranean in inspiration, and mid-priced. To start, pan-fried black pudding with chicken liver was rich and hearty. Also good was deep-fried courgette flower stuffed with goat's cheese. But a main course linguine with crab was overcooked, with a gloopy sauce. Duck confit was a generous portion, though some side vegetables or pulses might have been a better accompaniment than the salad garnish. The puds were, like the starters, a high point: rich chocolate tart, smooth-textured ice-creams. Café Paradiso is presumably aimed at both price-conscious, design-aware hotel guests and also the local yachtie folk; as such, it fills a gap perfectly.

The Epicurean

33 Western Street, Brighton, East Sussex BN1 2PG (01273 776618/www.epicurean-brighton.com). **Lunch served** noon-2pm, **dinner served** 7-10pm Tue-Sat. **Main courses** £10.90-£18.90. **Set lunch** £8.50 2 courses, £12.50 3 courses. **Credit** AmEx, MC, V.

Bruno and Theresa Pruvost made a wise choice of location when opening the Epicurean – if perhaps not of venue, a tightly converted fisherman's cottage in Brighton's reasonably fashionable Western Street. Closer to the sea than its nearest competitor in the local gourmet cuisine market, the Gingerman, the Epicurean also benefits from Bruno's experienced welcome and guiding hand. There may only be half a dozen tables filling each of the two floors, but rarely does dining feel uncomfortable. The menu, changed every three months, features

eight starters and nine mains. Although served with grace on stylishly curvy tableware, neither the glazed medley of Dover sole fillet nor the pan-fried king scallops warranted their £18.90 price tag, the modest portions not compensating with maximum flavour. The two-course and three-course lunch deals are excellent, though, and the eight dessert creations are exquisite, by far the best in town.

La Fourchette

105 Western Road, Brighton, East Sussex BN1 2AA (01273 722556). **Lunch served** noon-2.30pm, **dinner served** 7-10.30pm daily. **Set lunch** £8 2 courses, £12 3 courses. **Set dinner** £20 2 courses, £25 3 courses. **Credit** AmEx, MC, V.

The unremarkable pseudo-rustic interior of this popular restaurant belies a menu of beautifully presented, authentic French fare. Heavily fish-oriented (there's a blackboard of 12 daily specials), the main menu also features meaty, saucy dishes such as pheasant terrine, veal fillet and pan-roasted rack of lamb. The token vegetarian options – roast baby vegetable tartelette or croustillant of wild mushrooms and spinach – are surprisingly good. But it's the seafood dishes that really shine – succulent roast monkfish, sea scallops languishing in a buttery sauce, Mediterranean fish soup richly flavoured with gruyère – absolutely wonderful. The largely French wine list has bottles ranging from £9.75 to £25.50.

The Gingerman ★

21A Norfolk Square, Brighton, East Sussex BN1 2PD (01273 326688). **Lunch served** 12.30-2pm, **dinner served** 7-10pm Tue-Sat. **Set lunch** £9.95 1 course, £12.95 2 courses, £14.95 3 courses. **Set dinner** £22 2 courses, £25 3 courses. **Credit** AmEx, DC, MC, V.

This cracking little place has long been a favourite of Brighton foodies. Its buttermilk-and-burnt ochre decor (with incongruous glitterball), modest dimensions (around 30 covers) and out-of-the-way location don't augur culinary fireworks, but there are impressively assured hands at work in the kitchen. The set-price menus are particularly good value at lunch, and display imagination without lapsing into fadism. Start with a peppery mackerel fillet encrusted with a subtle Goan spice mix and served with a cucumber raita, before heading back into more trad territory with a melting fillet of Buchan beef with potato rösti, peas, carrots and spinach. Finish off with an unusual creamy blood orange and grapefruit gratin. Be sure to book.

Nia Café ★

87-88 Trafalgar Street, Brighton, East Sussex BN1 4EB (01273 671371). **Meals served** 9am-10pm Mon-Sat; 9am-6pm Sun. **Main courses** £7.50-£8.25. **Credit** MC, V.

In the heart of Brighton's North Lanes, Nia Café offers a welcome escape from the chaos outside. The simple decor and huge windows give a light, airy feel, even when the place is packed – which it often

South East

The Pilgrim. *See p95.*

is. By day, a menu of crowd-pleasers runs from all-day breakfasts to substantial salads and sandwiches. By night, candlelight gives the place a cosier feel and the menu moves up a notch. Modern bistro dishes like corn-fed chicken with chickpea, chorizo and roast pepper stew focus on robust, simple flavours. A short dessert menu includes beautifully presented classics such as strawberry shortcake served up by friendly staff and accompanied by a short but decent wine list. The laid-back atmosphere and affordable prices ensure Nia Café's enduring appeal.

One Paston Place

1 Paston Place, Brighton, East Sussex BN2 1HA (01273 606933/www.onepastonplace.co.uk). **Lunch served** 12.30-1.45pm, **dinner served** 7.30-9.30pm Tue-Sat. **Main courses** £21-£23. **Set lunch** £16.50 2 courses, £19 3 courses. **Credit** AmEx, DC, MC, V.

In deepest residential Kemptown, this upmarket restaurant has a reputation as one of Brighton's classiest joints. Expect dressy formality, polished service, assured Gallic cooking and high prices – especially if dining from the carte. However, the set lunch menu represents excellent value. Start perhaps with venison salad or roasted scallops with aubergine coulis, then move on to loin of rabbit with roasted garlic mash or Dover sole with mussels, and finish with delectable figs in red wine. Vegetarians should give prior notice so that a meat-free meal can be prepared; butternut squash velouté, goat's cheese and chestnut tortellini proved impressive. The wine list is Franco-centric. Children only welcome at lunch.

Seven Dials

1 Buckingham Place, Brighton, East Sussex BN1 3TD (01273 885555/www.sevendialsrestaurant.co.uk). **Lunch served** noon-3pm Tue-Sat; 12.30-3.30pm

Sun. **Dinner served** 7-10.30pm Tue-Sat; 7-9.30pm Sun. **Set lunch** (Tue-Sat) £10 2 courses, £12.50 3 courses. **Set dinner** £19.50 2 courses, £23.50 3 courses. **Credit** AmEx, MC, V.

Even though the restaurant held a capacity crowd on a Saturday night, the staff at Seven Dials passed every test that the diners threw at them, and even found time to discuss the menu with a small child. Nothing seemed too much trouble. Food-wise, particular praise goes to the foie gras terrine (£2 supplement), although two very different main courses (suckling pig and grilled tuna) and a chocolate fudge pot pudding also proved popular. The site used to be a bank (and still looks very like one from the outside), and benefits from a high ceiling and a dark wood interior enlivened by splashes of colour. One of Brighton's big hitters, but completely without pretence.

Terre à Terre

71 East Street, Brighton, East Sussex BN1 1HQ (01273 729051). **Dinner served** 6-10.30pm Mon. **Meals served** noon-10.30pm Tue-Fri, Sun; noon-11pm Sat. **Main courses** £11.50-£12.50. **Credit** AmEx, DC, MC, V.

Terre à Terre's reputation as one of the country's most celebrated vegetarian restaurants is well deserved, as it ingeniously dispels any notions of vegetarian cookery as a dull, dark art. The innovative menu delivers on interest and presentation, with diners being treated to unusual combinations of ingredients and flavours. Mains might include deep-fried chickpea and sesame socca, drenched in saffron, thyme and orange zest, and served with smoky griddled artichoke, aubergine and peppers. Bricks of minty cracked wheat with pressed sheep's cheese and preserved lemon, with saffron-scented fennel, apricots and tiger nut pesto is another tastebud tickler. Divine desserts include cherry cioccolata churros, doughnut straws with gloopy dipping chocolate and cherries sozzled in organic vodka. Organic wines and beers also feature on the drinks list. Service can be a little slow, but diners are well looked after and this is a nicely unpretentious, laid-back venue for enjoying inventive, gourmet vegetarian food.

DANEHILL

Coach & Horses

Coach & Horses Lane, Danehill, East Sussex RH17 7JF (01825 740369). **Lunch served** noon-2pm Mon-Sat; noon-2.30pm Sun. **Dinner served** 7-9pm Mon-Thur; 7-9.30pm Fri, Sat. **Main courses** £8.50-£12.95. **Credit** MC, V.

It can be a bit tricky to find, but the Coach & Horses is worth the hunt. The splendid front garden is a boon in the summer when locals and rambling tourists scramble for the best spot. There's also more than just pub grub available from the kitchen, with own-made traditional British and Italian-style dishes complementing a brace of pan-Asian offerings such as stir-fried chilli beef. When the weather closes in,

the light and airy main dining area complete with hanging baskets provides most of the shelter, while more intimate evenings can be spent in the cosy, candlelit upstairs room.

DUDDLESWELL

Duddleswell Tea Rooms ★

Duddleswell, East Sussex TN22 3BH (01825 712126). **Open** Feb-Nov 10am-5pm Tue-Sun, bank hols. **Lunch served** noon-2pm. **Main courses** £6.50. **No credit cards.**

There's no finer place to take high tea and scones than at these venerable tearooms. Decorated in true granny style – pink with lace curtains and doilies – you'd be forgiven for thinking that you'd stepped back into the 1950s when entering this twee cottage from its pristine front lawn. It's conveniently situated at the southern end of Ashdown Forest, so ramblers can come here to refuel on the hearty lunches that are now offered. Meanwhile more sedentary customers can walk off the clotted cream in wooded surroundings.

EAST CHILTINGTON

The Jolly Sportsman

Chapel Lane, East Chiltington, East Sussex BN7 3BA (01273 890400/www.thejollysportsman.com). **Lunch served** noon-2pm Tue-Sun. **Dinner served** 6-9pm Tue-Thur; 6-10pm Fri, Sat. **Main courses** £7.50-£16.50. **Set lunch** (Tue-Sat) £11 2 courses, £14.75 3 courses. **Credit** MC, V.

Once a country local, this is now as close as rural Sussex gets to urban gastropub. Forget a pint and dominoes by the fire, the place is all wooden tables, candlelight, pastel shades and Kandinsky-style wall-hangings. It's bye-bye flat caps and talk of compost too, with a crowd that's done well in the City, sold up, moved out and doesn't mind you overhearing all about it. The extensive menu, however, should sate any pangs of nostalgia as local meat and game receive a successful corporate makeover. Sussex lamb spiced with chilli and garlic was beautifully tender and came served with melt-in-the-mouth grilled aubergines. Other positive effects of modernity include a huge wine list, a considered vegetarian menu and attentive service. The back garden, overlooking the Downs, makes the place a delight on summer evenings.

EAST GRINSTEAD

Gravetye Manor ★

Vowels Lane, nr East Grinstead, East Sussex HR19 4LJ (01342 810567/www.gravetyemanor.co.uk). **Lunch served** 12.30-1.45pm, **dinner served** 7-9.30pm daily. **Set lunch** £18 2 courses, £24 3 courses. **Set dinner** £34-£52 3 courses. **Credit** MC, V.

The oak-panelled interior and impeccably trained staff provide the perfect backdrop to a meal in this formal yet unstuffy hotel restaurant. From the canapés you receive while perusing the menu to the coffee and Cognac in the lounge after dining, the whole experience is utterly relaxing. With the bill easily topping £45 per head, you'd expect nothing less. Dishes are often as pleasing on the eye as they are on the stomach and, where possible, use vegetables from Gravetye's own kitchen garden. Ballotine of wild smoked salmon with avocado jus is the pick of the starters. Mains such as fillet of beef with oyster mushrooms in a mild stilton sauce could not be faulted, while the red mullet and seared scallops came with an interestingly piquant olive salsa. The wine cellar boasts around 400 wines and is suitably grand, in keeping with the surroundings – the landscaped gardens making the perfect place to get some air after such a rarefied atmosphere.

FLETCHING

The Griffin Inn

Fletching, Nr Uckfield, East Sussex TN22 3SS (01825 722890/www.thegriffininn.co.uk). **Lunch served** noon-2.30pm daily. **Dinner served** 7-9.30pm Mon-Sat; 7-9pm Sun. **Main courses** £9.50-£18.50. **Set lunch** (Sun) £22.50 3 courses. **Credit** AmEx, DC, MC, V.

If any townies still harboured the idea that country pubs are quiet affairs with only a game of darts or the changing of a barrel offering some excitement, the Griffin Inn should knock them off their stride. It's the focal point for the local young 'uns as well as an older crowd, but they're all united in stoking up a boisterous vibe on long-opening weekend nights. The pub carries a cricket theme throughout – split into a saloon (Pavilion End) and lounge bar (Nursery End) offering Harvey's and Tanglefoot on tap and a bar menu of ciabattas and pastas that's worth a second innings. The restaurant is a more sedate affair and overlooks the sizeable garden, itself a great feature with views stretching towards the Ouse valley. Roasted local venison and sea bass on a vine tomato risotto are just two examples of the confident cooking emanating from the kitchen.

HASTINGS

Bonaparte's

64 Eversfield Place, St Leonards, Hastings, East Sussex TN37 6DB (01424 712218). **Lunch served** noon-1.45pm Tue-Fri. **Dinner served** 7-9.30pm Tue-Fri; 7-10pm Sat. **Main courses** £8.95-£17.95. **Credit** MC, V.

Since the demise of Rösers, Hastings's finest French restaurant, it has fallen to the present incumbents to try and tickle the palates of the locals. The cosy, if twee, dining room is comfortable enough, with banquette seating and a display of porcelain plates (for sale) as decoration. Service is prompt, friendly and informal, and the short menu promises simple, uncomplicated food which clearly appeals to the slightly older clientele. Main courses typically might

include sirloin steak with pâté, or a less successful combination of halibut and anchovies. Desserts include crème caramel and a rather pedestrian cheeseboard. It doesn't achieve the heights of Rösers, but then its prices aren't as keen either.

Maggie's ★ ★

Above the fish market, Rock-a-Nore Road, Hastings, East Sussex TN34 3DW (01424 430205). **Meals served** 5am-3pm Mon-Sat. **Main courses** £3.20-£5.90. **No credit cards.**

Opening at 5am to provide the local fishermen with breakfast (they'll have been out since 2am), Maggie Banford serves the best fish and chips in Hastings, perhaps the world. Locals and fans from further afield crowd into the check-tableclothed café, located in one of the old fishermen's huts, sit beneath grainy black-and-white photos of fishing fleets of yore and look out over the sea. The menu has plenty of 'sausage/spaghetti/pie'-type options, but it would be criminal not to eat the fish which is perfectly cooked in whisper-light batter, accompanied with a heap of hand-cut chips (mushy peas are optional) – an incredible £4.40 standard, £5.90 large. Be warned that 'standard' fills the plate. Kids' meals are available, and drinks might include a glass of wine or a more usual mug of strong tea.

Mermaid ★

2 Rock-a-Nore Road, Hastings, East Sussex TN34 3DW (01424 438100). **Meals served** 6.30am-3pm Mon, Tue; 6.30am-7.30pm Wed-Sun. **Main courses** £4.75-£5.85. **No credit cards.**

Beside the tall black huts where fishermen dry their nets, the Mermaid is a popular venue for fishermen and tourists. Sit inside at wooden tables and chairs, or outside at a table under an umbrella (you'll need to look beyond the car park for a glimpse of the sea) and make your choice from the blackboard menu. Big breakfasts are served early on, giving way to fish and chip lunches (cod, huss and skate), all served with hand-cut chips. Own-made pies, such as steak and onion, are also available, as are children's meals. Traditional desserts feature treacle pudding and spotted dick. It's always busy and there's a ten-minute cooking time for the fish – but it's worth the wait.

HURST GREEN

Eurasia

The Royal George, 54 London Road, Hurst Green, East Sussex TN19 7PN (01580 860200). **Lunch served** noon-2pm Wed-Mon. **Dinner served** 5.30-10.30pm daily. **Main courses** £5.50-£23. **Credit** AmEx, MC, V.

Inauspiciously located on the A21, a Georgian house has been tastefully converted into this local pub/restaurant. The atmosphere is relaxed, service prompt and the cooking of a high standard, with the kitchen making good use of quality ingredients and local produce, including fresh organic vegetables. The extensive menu promises 'east meets west', but in truth the nonya-style cuisine (a fusion of Chinese

Seven Dials. *See p98.*

and Malay cooking) veers closer to Thailand, Vietnam and Japan – but no complaints. Starters include Eurasian prawns cooked in cream and sprinkled with coconut or satay chicken with Eurasia's wonderful sauce. An impossibly long list of mains includes a particularly fine two-ways duck (aromatic duck roasted with Malaysian herbs), nonya mama chicken (fruity) or steamed sea bass. The extensive wine list even includes a dry white from China (£12.80). You can, of course, have a beer at pub prices. Deservedly popular.

LEWES

Circa

145 High Street, Lewes, East Sussex BN7 1XT (01273 471777/www.circacirca.com). **Lunch served** noon-2.30pm Tue-Fri, Sun; noon-2pm Sat. **Dinner served** 6-10pm Tue-Fri, Sun; 7-10pm Sat.

Main courses £16.50. **Set lunch** £11.75 2 courses. **Set dinner** £23 2 courses, £27.50 3 courses. **Credit** AmEx, DC, MC, V.

The space is simple with crowded tables and neutral colours, and for those who prefer to linger over their meal, the restaurant is not short of entertainment. The striking semi-circular frontage, its plate glass windows overlooking the high street, provides plenty of opportunity for people-watching. The menu follows an eclectic agenda. Smoked tangerine tofu, steamed shiitake dumplings, stella butter and yuzu soy is an attractive mosaic of texture and flavour. But pan-fried brill with a parmesan maize crust, young green coconut sambal and Moroccan balls is too complex, demonstrating a fusion-for-the-sake-of-it approach rather than sound culinary judgement. The stand-out here, however, is an indulgent bitter chocolate parfait with salted popcorn cookie dough and passion-fruit lassia.

RYE

The Landgate Bistro

5-6 Landgate, Rye, East Sussex TN31 7LH (01797 222829/www.landgatebistro.co.uk). **Dinner served** 7-9.30pm Tue-Fri; 7-10pm Sat. **Main courses** £10-£13. **Set dinner** (Tue-Thur) £17.90 3 courses incl coffee. **Credit** DC, MC, V.

Ask anyone in Rye for the best restaurant in town and the verdict is unanimous: it's the Landgate Bistro, a small, unprepossessing and thankfully unpretentious place that's as affordable as it is good – and packed out on our visit, so do book ahead. A nicely balanced menu includes a good range of fish dishes and the cooking is refreshingly unfussy, letting the taste of the excellent produce come through with the help of deceptively simple sauces and perfectly cooked vegetables. Desserts look as mouthwatering as they taste: the chocolate truffle loaf was a feast of melt-in-the-mouth heaven that we couldn't quite manage to finish, although that may have had as much to do with the very generous portions as its richness.

Ypres Castle Inn

Gun Gardens, Rye, East Sussex TN31 7HH (01797 223248). **Open** 11.30am-3pm, 6-11.30pm Mon-Fri; 11am-11.30pm Sat; 11am-4pm Sun. **Lunch served** noon-2.30pm daily. **Dinner served** 6.30-9pm Mon-Sat. **Main courses** £11-£13. **Credit** AmEx, MC, V.

Situated at the base of the wonderful 13th-century Ypres Tower, built to protect Rye from marauding French invaders, and just below the even older Church of St Mary, the Ypres Castle Inn serves an eclectic mix of superior pub food at moderate prices. There's the usual mix of locally produced steaks and lamb served with a choice of potatoes, or whole grilled plaice or cod wrapped in prosciutto, for around £13. There are also cheaper starter options as well as a decent range of vegetarian dishes on the menu. Friendly service, nice-looking pub, a great selection of beers. What more could you ask for?

Also in the area

Loch Fyne 95-99 Western Road, Brighton, East Sussex BN1 2LB (01273 716160); **Hotel du Vin & Bistro** Ship Street, Brighton, East Sussex BN1 1AD (01273 718588); **Quod** 160-161 North Street, Brighton, East Sussex (01273 202070).

West Sussex

AMBERLEY

Amberley Castle

Amberley, West Sussex BN18 9ND (01798 831992/ www.amberleycastle.co.uk). **Lunch served** 12.30-2pm, **dinner served** 7-9pm daily. **Set lunch** (Mon-Sat) £15 2 courses; (Sun) £25.50 3 courses. **Set dinner** £38 2 courses, £45 3 courses. **Credit** AmEx, DC, MC, V.

Dine like royalty in the 12th-century Queen's Room, which has thick stone walls, arched doors and windows and a beautiful barrelled ceiling; or the Great Room, with oak floors, suits of armour, tapestries and some nasty-looking weapons. But don't worry, the food is more modern. For starters, if terrine of chicken, baby leek, truffle and wild mushroom wrapped in prosciutto ham with spiced orange reduction sounds a tad too rich, then simple smoked trout mousse with a cucumber salad, pink peppercorn dressing and tossed mixed leaves is also on offer. Next, seared calf's liver, red onion confit, foie gras and mashed potatoes with port and mushroom reduction is counterbalanced by simple roast tuna with sweet and sour vegetables and tomato butter sauce. This is a theatrical experience so dress up. Jacket and tie are essential for male diners, denim – and children under 12 – are frowned upon, and booking is essential.

BURPHAM

George & Dragon

Burpham, West Sussex BN18 9RR (01903 883131). *Bar* **Lunch served** noon-1.45pm Mon-Sat; noon-2.30pm Sun. **Dinner served** 7-9.30pm Mon-Sat. *Restaurant* **Dinner served** 7-9.30pm Tue-Sat. **Main courses** £7.95-£15.95. **Set dinner** £19.95 2 courses, £24.95 3 courses. **Credit** AmEx, MC, V.

This attractive rustic pub is set beside the village cricket pitch in the lovely hamlet of Burpham, just north-east of Arundel. Its gourmet credentials are most in evidence in the restaurant in the evenings, when the dining room is opened for an array of well-cooked dishes such as pavé of sea bass on a bed of leeks, goat's cheese tartlets or baked quail filled with foie gras and cep farci, compote of puy lentils, juniper and game sauce. At lunch it gets packed with walkers, but time it carefully as lunch orders stop at 1.45pm. In the restaurant, booking is recommended.

CHARLTON

The Fox Goes Free

Charlton, West Sussex PO18 0HU (01243 811461). **Lunch served** noon-2.30pm, **dinner served** 6.30-10pm Mon-Fri. **Meals served** noon-10pm Sat, Sun. **Main courses** £7.50-£16.50. **Credit** MC, V.

This traditional 300-year-old country pub, which has been famed for hunting since William III used it as a retreat from London, has a lovely garden with views over surrounding countryside. Inside there are low beams, inglenook fireplaces and a bread oven. Starters include field mushrooms stuffed with garlic and goat's cheese, while mains feature venison steak in port and redcurrant or whole sea bass in lemon and olive oil. Friendly, helpful service (these Aussies get everywhere) and house wines at £10 a bottle (including Concha y Tora merlot from Chile) are further pluses. Real ales on draught include Ballards best, Bass and their own Fox Goes Free bitter, as well as appearances from guest beers.

CHICHESTER

Comme Ça
*67 Broyle Road, Chichester, West Sussex PO19 6BD
(01243 788724/www.commeca.co.uk).* **Lunch
served** noon-2pm, **dinner served** 6-10.30pm
Tue-Sun. **Set meal** (lunch, 6-7.30pm, 10-10.30pm)
£15.25 2 courses, £19.95 3 courses. **Credit** AmEx,
DC, MC, V.

The perfect place for dinner if you're going to
Chichester Theatre or have had your fill of pub
lunches. This converted Georgian inn is an oasis of
French *savoir faire* in this English town. It has just
the right degree of formality plus a canopied and
heated courtyard. Its popularity is down to assured,
unflashy food such as pan-fried local pheasant
breast, baked camembert with avocado and cabernet
sauvignon dressing or Scottish moules. The wine
list includes a decent house wine at under a tenner.
It gets packed out especially on Sunday lunchtimes.
Booking is recommended.

CHILGROVE

White Horse Inn
*1 High Street, Chilgrove, West Sussex PO18 9HX
(01243 535219/www.whitehorsechilgrove.co.uk).*
Open 11am-3pm, 6-11pm Mon-Sat; 11am-3pm Sun.
Lunch served noon-2pm daily. **Dinner served**
7-10pm Mon-Sat. **Main courses** £10.95-£16.95.
Credit AmEx, MC, V.

The White Horse looks traditional enough, but once
inside it is light, airy and surprisingly modern. The
menu in the dining room and the less formal bar
makes good use of local ingredients such as fresh
Selsey crab, pheasant and wild rabbit. Menus
change regularly to reflect availability but might
include starters such as char-grilled pigeon breast
on green lentils or breaded lamb sweetbreads with
a mixed salad. Mains might feature dishes such as
wild rabbit casserole with muscat wine and grape
sauce or braised oxtail off the bone with a pureé of
potatoes. Staff are well informed and friendly.
There's a list of some 600 wines from France and the
New World. The White Horse is just a mile and a
half off the South Downs Way and walkers are
welcome, but are requested to leave their muddy
walking boots outside – padding around in socks is
quite acceptable.

HENLEY

Duke of Cumberland Arms
Henley, West Sussex GU27 3HQ (01428 652280).
Lunch served noon-2.30pm daily. **Dinner served**
7-9.30pm Mon-Sat. **Main courses** £9.95-£15.75.
Credit DC, MC, V.

The tucked-away Duke of Cumberland pub has been
around since the 15th century. The cosy wood-
panelled bar seems barely altered by the ages
(except for the numerous mobile phones nailed to the
walls as a warning to punters not to use them). The
three and a half acres of stepped garden, trout ponds,

streams and view over the Weald to the North
Downs are a dictionary definition of picturesque.
Those trout ponds are also nature's refrigerator; the
food isn't just fresh, it's still alive and the trout are
soon to be joined by mussels. Fish and seafood are
the specialities, but there are plenty of other unfussy
options, such as pepper stuffed with mushroom
risotto. In winter months it's a bit of a squeeze in the
small bar, where pride of place goes to the
impressive log fire. Children – who will love the
garden – are made welcome.

LICKFOLD

Lickfold Inn
Lickfold, West Sussex GU28 9EY (01798 861285).
Lunch served noon-2.30pm, **dinner served**
7-9.30pm daily. **Main courses** £8.50-£17.95.
Credit AmEx, MC, V.

Adjacent to a babbling brook, in a secluded leafy
lane location with a roaring fire in the winter and
capacious garden for the summer, the Lickfold Inn
has it all. Staff make everyone welcome at this wood-
beamed, herringbone brick-built pub and restaurant.
There's always a good selection of local ales at the
bar and a variety of wines. Starters included foie
gras boudin with Madeira jelly and toast, crab soup
or pan-fried chorizo in a spicy sauce. Steak au poivre
needed a sharper knife; better was pan-seared
salmon with sun-blushed tomato sauce and sauté
potatoes, and confit of duck leg with bubble and
squeak. A selection of crispy mangetout, broccoli,
snow peas and an extra dish of fries were polished
off within minutes, barely leaving room for the
dessert: the apple tart was served on a rather burnt
puff pastry base with a delectable honey and
cinnamon ice-cream.

STORRINGTON

Fleur de Sel ★
*Manleys Hill, Storrington, West Sussex RH20 4BT
(01903 742331).* **Lunch served** noon-2pm Tue-Fri,
Sun. **Dinner served** 7-9pm Tue-Sat. **Set lunch**
(Tue-Fri) £15.50 2 courses, £19.50 3 courses.
Set dinner (Tue-Thur) £19.50 2 courses, £23.50
3 courses. **Credit** AmEx, MC, V.

Michelin-starred Michel Perraud's restaurant is a
wonderful combination of classical French with a
contemporary touch and friendly, informed service.
The moment a plate of amuse-bouche magically
appears as you sip aperitifs in the tiny bar, you know
you're in good hands. The quality of the fresh
ingredients is apparent in starters such as a pasta
parcel of Dublin Bay prawns and a poached egg on
a bed of locally grown asparagus. Mains might
include perfectly judged fillets of John Dory in a wild
mushroom and sorrel sauce or breast of
Gressingham duck in a honey and ginger sauce.
Desserts such as carpaccio of mango with orange
sauce and almond ice-cream or coconut milk crème
brûlée display an interesting take on classic dishes.

South West

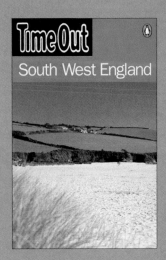

Bristol

Bell's Diner ★

1-3 York Road, BS6 5QB (0117 924 0357/
www.bellsdiner.co.uk). **Lunch served** noon-2pm
Tue-Fri. **Dinner served** 7-10pm Mon-Sat.
Main courses £10.50-£18. **Set meal** £18.50
3 courses. **Credit** AmEx, MC, V.
Bell's Diner is one of Bristol's most acclaimed
restaurants. The intimate dining rooms have
recently been upgraded and extended, but the
superlative cooking and convivial atmosphere
remain the same. A thoroughly modern British
menu combines wild foods with local delicacies and
carefully sourced organic produce. Starters may
include a subtle mussel, saffron and potato
chowder, or beef carpaccio with beetroot sorbet,
parmesan, truffle oil, and pumpkin and hazel-nut
tuille. Among the mains, the tenderest slices of
barbecued Trelough duck breast are perfectly
balanced by the sweet and savoury flavours of fig
compote, baby leeks and rocket, while braised veal
shin is paired with porcini and parmesan baked
custard, turnips and Marsala sauce. To finish, try
the selection of unusual British cheeses or the plate
of deliciously decadent Valrhona chocolate desserts.
The cooking is complemented by a well-chosen
wine list and smiling, unstuffy service. Pay Bell's
Diner a visit.

Bocanova ★

90 Colston Street, BS1 5BB (0117 929 1538).
Open 10am-10.30pm Mon-Thur; 10am-11pm Fri, Sat.
Lunch served noon-2.30pm Mon-Thur; noon-3pm Fri, Sat.
Dinner served 6-10.30pm Mon-Thur; 6-11pm Fri, Sat.
Main courses (lunch) £4.95-£7.95. **Set lunch**
£9.50 2 courses, £12.50 3 courses. **Set dinner**
£19.95 2 courses; £23.50 3 courses. **Credit** MC, V.
Citrus-coloured decor and funky prints provide a
perfect sun-infused setting for a Brazilian and
Mediterranean fusion menu that's occasionally overcomplicated but never boring. Char-grilled meats,
tropical fruit salsas and marinated fish dishes add
an exotic touch to more conventional continental
flavours, and a wicked, freshly prepared Caipirinha
is enough to ensure your meal starts with a sparkle.
Enjoy bossa nova bands on Wednesdays when you
can sample traditional dishes such as fejoada – black
bean, chorizo and smoked ham stew served with
rice, fried cassava and tomato salsa.

Budokan ★

31 Colston Street, BS1 5AP (0117 914 1488/
www.budokan.co.uk). **Lunch served** noon-2.30pm,
dinner served 5.30-11pm Mon-Sat. **Main courses**
£7-£10. **Set meal** (lunch, 5.30-7pm Mon-Sat)
£6.50 3 courses. **Credit** AmEx, DC, MC, V.

An Asian noodle kitchen with a classy aesthetic.
Long windows look in from the street on to a sleek
modern interior bathed in a soft, reddish light. The
raised bar at the entrance is perfect for downing a
Sapporo or two while you wait for a space at the
communal tables in the sunken eating area (no
bookings taken). You'll find plenty to occupy your
chopsticks on the pan-Asian menu. There are the
perennial favourites, of course, like nasi goreng and
Thai green curry, plus a range of hot and sour soups
such as tom yai gai (with chicken and vegetables),
tofu dishes and decent sushi and sashimi. Quality
sometimes falters for the lunchtime and early
evening Rapid Refuel menu, but you can't argue
with the price of £6.50 for a sushi starter, rice or
noodle main and side dish.

Casa Mexicana

29-31 Zetland Road, BS6 7AH (0117 924 3901/
www.casamexicana.co.uk). **Dinner served** 7-10pm
Mon-Sat. **Main courses** £9.95-£10.75. **Credit** MC, V.
The interconnecting, brightly coloured dining rooms
here are just Mexican enough to get you in the mood,
without having to call for the style police, and the
food's the real deal, with recipes sourced by the
owners on regular trips to the Yucatán. Sure, there
are nachos, burritos and some of the best fajitas this
side of the Atlantic, but you'll also find more inventive
dishes such as a citrusy starter of smoked marlin with
mixed leaves and spiced fresh lime olive oil, or a
punchy main course of slowly braised lamb shank
with chorizo and pasilla chilli. Start with a top-notch
Margarita, followed by a bottle from the excellent
wine list featuring choices from Spain, Mexico and
Chile. Great food, plentiful booze and cheerful
surroundings make this a fine place for a party.

Clifton Sausage Bar & Restaurant

7-9 Portland Street, BS8 4JA (0117 973 1192/
0117 970 6511/www.cliftonsausage.co.uk).
Bar **Open** 11am-11pm Tue-Sat; 11am-10.30pm
Sun. *Restaurant* **Lunch served** noon-2.30pm
Mon-Fri; 11am-3pm Sat, Sun. **Dinner served**
6.30-10pm Mon-Fri; 6.30-11pm Sat; 6.30-9pm
Sun. **Main courses** £8.50-£14. **Credit** AmEx,
MC, V.
This relaxed restaurant offers a far more
accomplished menu than its no-nonsense name
might suggest. Sure, there are eight varieties of
beautiful British bangers, all served with mash,
champ or borlotti beans, but you'll also find a host
of other retro classics including some excellent fish
and seafood dishes. Starters might feature a winning
combination of black pudding, potato cake and
seared scallops, or a steaming pot of cockles and
mussels cooked in West Country cider and onions.

Bell's Diner
See p109.

Follow these with steak, toad-in-the-hole or beer-battered cod and chips, accompanied by a gluggable wine from the easygoing list. Finish off with old-fashioned Cambridge cream (a very English crème brûlée) or head to the large, unfussy bar for draught local and continental beers. The pared-down rustic decor encourages a pleasantly informal atmosphere, aided by the smiling efficiency of enthusiastic staff.

Deason's

43 Whiteladies Road, BS8 2LS (0117 973 6230/ www.deasons.co.uk). **Lunch served** noon-2.30pm Mon-Fri; noon-3pm Sun. **Dinner served** 6.30-9.30pm Mon-Fri; 6.30-10.30pm Sat. **Main courses** £12.50-£19.50. **Set lunch** £11.50 2 courses; £14.50 3 courses. **Set dinner** £17.50 2 courses; £21.50 3 courses. **Credit** AmEx, DC, MC, V.
A strangely windowless Georgian basement houses an utterly professional restaurant that combines faultless service with an expertly executed if unexceptional menu. Owner-chef Jason Deason has worked in Switzerland, Sardinia and London, and brings his culinary peregrinations to bear on seasonal dishes that strive to deliver 'a world of taste'. In fact, Modern European is the key note, although you'll also find a sprinkling of Asian fusion dishes, such as an excellent warm oriental salad starter. A la carte choices can be mixed and matched with dishes from the set dinner menu, including a tasty but ponderous twice-baked blue cheese soufflé and a venison main course: rare slivers of meat sautéed with cracked black pepper and blackberry sauce. Presentation is exquisite. Show-stopping desserts echo the room's sculptural flower arrangements: rich chocolate mousse seems to float to the table, topped by a wafer-thin sail of white and dark chocolate. Wine-coloured fabrics and blond wood just about avoid resembling chain hotel decor to create a warm contemporary feel, in keeping with the mellow atmosphere and jazz soundtrack.

Dusk

117-119 St George's Road, BS1 5UW (0117 925 1115). **Dinner served** 5.30-11pm Mon-Sat. **Main courses** £8.95-£22. **Set dinner** £12.95 2 courses. **Credit** MC, V.

Dusk has bravely opted to revisit the 1970s steakhouse formula and reinvent it for today's palates. The menu is upfront about its retro credentials. Starters include the cocktail – king prawns on a bed of lettuce, clams and mussels – and the soup, which may be a large basin of spicy sweet potato and coconut. There are fish, poultry and veggie options among the main courses, but the steaks, sourced from prime Scottish cattle, are the main attraction. Dusk has a piece of meat to suit all appetites, from an obscene 32oz T-bone to a plump 10oz porterhouse, a tender 8oz fillet and even a surf 'n' turf option; what's more, you can opt to have your steak *bleu*. Although there's no quibbling with the star quality of the meat, there's not much entertainment from the supporting cast (dauphinoise potatoes, chunky fries, roast veg or bog-standard mixed leaf salad). Dusk's huge portions, ebullient service and selection of punchy red wines will keep many punters happy, but if you're looking for flair and innovation, eat elsewhere.

Entelia

34 Princess Victoria Street, BS8 4BZ (0117 946 6793). **Lunch served** noon-2.30pm daily. **Dinner served** 6-10.30pm daily. **Main courses** £6.95-£13.95. **Credit** AmEx, MC, V.
If you're looking for a mound of moussaka, followed by a round of drunken plate smashing, you've come to the wrong place. Recently opened in Clifton Village, this Greek restaurant has eschewed the traditional taverna look in favour of an open-plan dining room with minimal millennial decor. But while the surroundings hold little interest, the food is altogether more entertaining, and the lively hubbub of satisfied diners makes up for the occasionally po-faced service. The menu is ambitious in its scope and modern in its presentation. Start with whitebait, mussels or the decadent delights of manidaria yemista – sautéed mushrooms with garlic butter, mascarpone and brie wrapped in filo pastry – before moving on to lamb souvlaki in a garlic, honey and white wine vinegar marinade, or prizzoles: a vast rack of redcurrant-glazed lamb chops served on a pillow of celeriac and thyme mash.

Firehouse Rotisserie

*The Leadworks, Anchor Square, BS1 5DB (0117
915 7323/www.firehouserotisserie.co.uk).* **Meals
served** noon-11pm daily. **Main courses** £10.95-
£14.95. **Credit** AmEx, DC, MC, V.
Reliable, family-friendly US cuisine is served in a
long, spacious dining hall at the heart of Bristol's
regenerated harbourside, with plenty of outdoor
seating when the sun shines. Inside, huge wrought-
iron chandeliers impart a pseudo-medieval look that
is rather at odds with the all-American menu, but
this doesn't seem to bother the tourists tucking into
spit-roasted chicken, gourmet pizzas and
Southwestern specialities. Highlights might include
a starter of fresh and crispy spring rolls with a
zinging chilli dipping sauce, creole-spiced Louisiana
catfish and a delicious side order of coleslaw with
jalapeño peppers. Chirpy service keeps the diners
happy, but the prices aren't quite as friendly as
the casual ambience and accessible food might lead
you to expect.

FishWorks Seafood Café

*128-130 Whiteladies Road, BS8 2RS (0117 974
4433/www.fishworks.co.uk).* **Lunch served**
noon-2.30pm, **dinner served** 6-10pm Tue-Sat.
Main courses £7-£20. **Credit** AmEx, MC, V.
Utter freshness and simple presentation are the
basic keys to the deserved success of this fish
restaurant-cum-fishmonger, whose seafood counter
glitters with all manner of piscine treats caught in
Cornwall and Scotland. The 'classics' menu is truly
mouthwatering in its diversity, offering such
delights as lobster spaghetti with garlic, pine nuts
and basil leaf; roast sea bream delicately flavoured
with a whisper of North African spices; and a huge
vat of steaming Fowey mussels dripping with wine,
garlic and parsley. If that's not enough for you to
choose from, there's also a range of specials that
varies according to the day's catch. A buzzy
atmosphere, well-informed staff and solid, good-
value wine list are the final touches to a winning
formula. Hooked? Then you can also learn how to
cook fish the professional way at the FishWorks
cookery school.

Glasnost

*1 William Street, Totterdown, BS3 4TU (0117 972
0938/www.glasnostrestaurant.co.uk).* **Dinner served**
7-9.30pm Tue-Thur; 6.30-9.45pm Fri-Sat. **Set dinner**
£15.50 2 courses, £18.50 3 courses. **Credit** MC, V.
In one of Bristol's more run-down areas, Glasnost
has managed to make quite an unlikely name for
itself as a must-visit party venue. Light and airy
with stained glass windows, the decor is bright and
fresh, the atmosphere vibrant. The menu is an
almost American-style mix of bar meets bistro.
Goat's cheese, spring onion and spinach tart with a
glaze of balsamic syrup was deliciously cheesy.
Spicy salt and pepper chicken with oriental dip was
a great savoury pick-me-up. Main courses are more
ambitious: mahi mahi en paupiette Hawaiian-style
– steamed in a cooking bag with banana, coconut
and mango – was aromatic, sweet and a risk that
paid off. Mixed bean and lentil burger with tomato,
garlic and onion relish was a good staple. A non-
intimidating wine and beer list, a few house vodkas
and friendly, fast service make this a great place for
a meal with friends.

Lords

*43 Corn Street, BS1 1HT (0117 926 2658/
www.lordsrestaurant.com).* **Lunch served** noon-
2pm Mon-Fri. **Dinner served** 6-9.30pm Mon-Sat.
Main courses £16-£20. **Credit** AmEx, MC, V.
The restaurant formerly known as Markwick's
remains one of the city's most prestigious eating
venues, although the decor does a good job of
convincing you that you've stumbled into a hotel
dining room from the 1970s. The waitresses are
charming despite the humiliation of being dressed
in what look like blue school uniforms, and the staid
business clientele seems untroubled by the uncool
surroundings. The room itself – a former bank vault
– has plenty of original Victorian features, but the
apricot-white paintwork will have style-conscious
diners weeping into their plates. Fortunately, the
menu rises way above its humdrum setting, offering
classic British and European cuisine cooked with
conviction and flair. Among the starters, chilled pea
and ham soup is delicately seasoned with lovage,

Time Out Eating & Drinking in Great Britain & Ireland **111**

while seafood risotto is loaded with crabmeat and topped with two large langoustines. A handful of fish dishes round out the predominantly carnivore-pleasing main courses: try melt-in-the mouth cutlets of rare English lamb served with polenta, roasted garlic and rosemary; or loin of pork with mashed potato, roasted apples, black pudding and Calvados gravy. An extensive wine list is dominated by high-quality French regional wines, and desserts include a delicious, made-to-order tarte tatin, dripping with smoky caramel. Food this good deserves a far classier setting.

Michael Caines at the Bristol Marriott Royal ★

College Green, BS1 5TA (0117 9105309). **Lunch served** noon-2.30pm, **dinner served** 7-10pm Mon-Sat. **Main courses** £19.95-£23.75. **Set lunch** £16.50 2 courses, £19.50 3 courses. **Set dinner** £55 9-course tasting menu. **Credit** AmEx, DC, MC, V.

Bristol may be the birthplace of trip-hop and the erstwhile heart of the British wine trade, but it has never been a centre for great dining. That could be about to change thanks to the arrival of Michael Caines, one of the country's top young chefs, at the Marriott Royal Hotel. The dining room is located in what was once the ballroom. The high ceilings, stone arcading, statuary and paintings of fiercely mustachioed men may not be to everyone's taste, but the cooking makes up for it. It is exquisite. We visited soon after Caines's arrival, when a bargain set-price lunch menu was available. Each dish – from intensely flavoured asparagus soup to salad of honey-spiced duck with soused beetroot or pan-fried sea bass with braised fennel and herb oil – was expertly presented and perfectly timed. Dishes on the à la carte menu are more complex (and pricey). Is this the best food in Bristol? We think so.

Okra ★

6 Chandos Road, BS6 6PE (0117 970 6078/ www.okra-restaurant.com). **Lunch served** noon-2pm Tue-Fri; noon-2.30pm Sat; noon-3pm Sun. **Dinner served** 6-11pm daily. **Main courses** £10.50-£16.95. **Set lunch** £9.95 2 courses. **Set dinner** £12.95 2 courses, £16.95 3 courses. **Credit** MC, V.

This clean-cut restaurant has garnered rave reviews from the local press. The menu combines Spanish, Sicilian, Moorish and Berber influences to create dishes that are paragons of subtle spicing, balanced flavours and beautiful presentation. The kitchen prides itself on a simple approach, using a maximum of four or five ingredients in each dish. Among the starters, you can't go wrong with a faultless Greek salad of feta, figs, olives, cherry tomatoes and lemon oil, or a deliciously sweet and savoury smoked chicken, date and pistachio terrine with quince chutney. Stand-out main courses include a rich lamb, apricot and almond tagine or beautifully aromatic tabil-marinated salmon with saffron pearl barley. Team these dishes with cinnamon couscous, jasmine rice and green herb salad, and a bottle of Moroccan wine from the impressively international list.

Bar crawl: Bristol

Bang in the centre of town, a converted red-brick Victorian wine warehouse shelters the much-loved **Watershed** media centre (1 Canons Road; 0117 925 3845/www.watershed.co.uk), which has an airy bar-cum-café with views over Bristol Docks. Nearby is the **River** (Canons Road; 0117 930 0498), a recent addition to Bristol's harbour scene that has already made its mark thanks to an unfussy, laid-back vibe and a fab sausage-and-mash menu. By Friday evening many of the other bars along this strip are overrun with boob-tubes and shiny shirts swigging back Bacardi Breezers, although the bright red **E-Shed** (Canons Road, 0117 907 4287) is a pleasantly funky hangout at other times.

To preserve your dignity at weekends, you're better off crossing the water to the canteen-style bar at the **Arnolfini** (16 Narrow Quay; 0117 929 9191; closed from Sept 2003 for refurbishment until spring 2005), where the city's arts-based movers and shakers congregate – a local urban myth suggests PJ Harvey once snogged Nick Cave here. Head east to reach the **Mud Dock Café** (40 The Grove; 0117 934 9734), bizarrely situated atop a cycle shop. This is a long-standing Bristol favourite, with a compact south-facing sundeck, a confident Mediterranean menu and an interior decorated with bits of cycling paraphernalia. It's trendy, but without an ounce of pretension. Within staggering distance you'll find **riverstation** (*see p114*) and the **Severnshed** (The Grove, Harbourside; 0117 925 1212/www.severnshed.co.uk), a spacious former boatshed designed by Isambard Kingdom Brunel. Its long waterside terrace is the perfect spot for summer lunch with the glorious spire of St Mary Redcliffe

Olive Shed

Princes Wharf, BS1 4RN (0117 929 1960/ www.therealolivecompany.co.uk). **Meals served** noon-10.30pm Tue-Sat; noon-3pm Sun. **Main courses** £9.50-£12.50. **Credit** MC, V.

The Olive Shed brings a taste of the Mediterranean to the middle of Bristol Docks, with an outside terrace that's just the place to tuck into tapas from the ground-floor delicatessen. Stuffed vine leaves, baba ganoush, salads, panini and an extensive array of olives, prepared on site, are just some of the delicious titbits on offer. As the sun sets, head for the upstairs dining room, a warmly coloured, laid-back venue with large picture windows and art for

South West

looking down on you from the opposite bank. Inside, a sleek mobile bar separates the formal dining room from the ultra-funky drinking area, where stylish staff mix some of the meanest cocktails in the city for a work-and-play crowd. A few streets away, the old-fashioned charms of **Cornubia** (142 Temple Street; 0117 925 4415) remain largely undiscovered, tucked surreptitiously away in a concrete-laden side road. This pub is a CAMRA fave, filled with local workers by day and beer-lovers in the know come sundown. South of the river, meanwhile, the **Tobacco Factory Café & Bar** (corner of Raleigh Road and North Street, Southville; 0117 902 0060) has got warehouse chic down to a T with its airy, industrial-style space, restaurant-standard food and beanbag atmosphere.

In the city centre, you can hang out with the luvvies from the Old Vic theatre at the shabby but friendly **Taverna dell' Artista** (19 and 33 King Street; 0117 929 8291/0117 929 7712), where you'll find all manner of sozzled regulars enjoying Italian red wine and animated conversation into the small hours. Or escape the hordes at **Sukoshi** (Unit 1, Unite House, Frogmore Street; 0117 927 6003), a sleek and chic cocktail and sushi bar that remains inexplicably crowd-free throughout the week. The nearby **Queenshilling** (Frogmore Street; 0117 926 4342) is a stalwart of Bristol's gay scene with a trendy, mirrored interior that attracts a good-looking crowd. Also in this area, though tricky to find, is **Nocturne** (Unity Street; 0117 929 2555), a secretive and über-cool bar-club co-owned by Massive Attack. It's usually members only, but some sharp talking on the door can sometimes work wonders.

Head up the hill from here to the **Park** (37 Triangle West, Clifton; 0117 940 6101), a small, loungy bar with a classy vibe and some quality DJs entertaining the crammed-in clientele, who come here to see and be seen. The latest Bristol hotspot, though, is up the road at **Pam-Pam** (3 Beacon House, Queens Avenue; 0117 973 1249). Currently favoured by dressed-up divas and expense account chancers, this flashy basement bar is too self-conscious to be really cool, but is a good place to inject some glamour into your evening. From Pam-Pam it's a short walk to Whiteladies Road, where bars and restaurants are two-a-penny. One of the most appealing hangouts is **Bar Humbug** (89 Whiteladies Road, Clifton; 0117 904 0061), thanks to an outside terrace, platters of food for sharing, quality cocktails and a hip but relaxed atmosphere. Further up the hill, **ZBar** (96 Whiteladies Road, Clifton; 0117 973 7225) is big, loud and usually full of the young and beautiful. The cocktails are great, the atmosphere's lively and there's decent grub on hand for soaking up that alcohol.

A less brash vibe is on offer in Clifton Village at the **Mall** (66 The Mall; 0117 974 5318), an easygoing pub that is just the place to relax with a coffee, a pint or some very decent bar food after a yomp across the Downs. There's a small beer garden at the back. For a true taste of the West Country, however, head for the **Coronation Tap** (8 Sion Place, Clifton; 0117 973 9617), a near-legendary Bristol cider pub selling (among others) a cider so strong that it's only served by the half pint (ask for Exhibition). The traditional interior is usually full of rustic charm and pissed locals, including the odd celebrity.

sale on the walls. The dinner menu is broadly Mediterranean with seafood and vegetarian highlights, including flaked salt cod with black tagliatelle and walnut, orange, chilli and tarragon oil, or richly loaded bouillabaisse. Fresh, earthy flavours are perfectly complemented by the all-organic European wine list.

One Stop Thali Café ★ ★

12A York Road, BS6 5QE (0117 942 6687).
Lunch served 11am-4pm, **dinner served** 6-11pm Tue-Sat. **Set meal** thali £6.50. **No credit cards**.
This tiny but legendary Bristol restaurant offers up Asian street food in a unique, laid-back environment.

The bohemian-kitsch setting incorporates mannequins in saris, silk cushions, a hotchpotch of furniture and the occasional acoustic musician playing gently funky tunes in the corner. Eating here is a mellow experience: no one suffers agonies of indecision over the menu because there's only one thing on offer – the 'thali' of the day, consisting of six complementary, all-vegetarian dishes served with chapatis on a specially divided steel plate. There's always just-so basmati rice and a fresh salad, plus four beautifully spiced and carefully combined curries. The daytime menus continue the charmingly idiosyncratic and thoroughly tasty Asian theme.

Quartier Vert

85 Whiteladies Road, BS8 2NT (0117 973 4482/ www.quartiervert.co.uk). Bar **Open** 11am-11pm Mon-Sat; 11am-10.30pm Sun. *Restaurant* **Lunch served** noon-3pm daily. **Dinner served** 6-10.30pm Mon-Sat; 6-9pm Sun. **Main courses** £10.50-£18.50. **Set lunch** £14.50 2 courses; £17.50 3 courses. **Credit** MC, V.

One of the most appealing venues on the Whiteladies strip, Quartier Vert offers a provincial Med menu in a simple setting. Freshly made organic dishes are the order of the day. Enjoy tapas – calamares, houmous, anchovies and the like – in the popular bar or order a full meal from the daily-changing menu in the slightly more formal dining room. A la carte choices might include an authentic provençal fish soup; saddle of rabbit with tagliatelle, broad beans, baby leeks, tomato confit and truffle oil; and unfussy grilled tuna with piperade and mixed leaf salad. The wine list is dominated by European wines, but there are also a few carefully selected New World choices, not to mention a notable organic contingent. For dessert, don't miss semi-freddo with lavender shortbread. This place heaves with drinkers and diners at the weekend, but the service manages to remain friendly and unfazed throughout. A cookery school passes on the kitchen's expertise to adults and children on a regular basis.

Red Snapper ★

1-3 Chandos Road, BS6 6PG (0117 973 7999). **Lunch served** noon-2pm Tue-Sat. **Dinner served** 7.30-10pm Mon-Sat. **Main courses** £10.50-£18.50. **Set lunch** £12.50 2 courses. **Credit** AmEx, MC, V.

One of Bristol's most highly regarded restaurants, and rightly so – just don't let the formica tables and dodgy 1980s seating put you off. The fish-dominated menu offers exemplary but unpretentious Modern European cuisine and is constantly evolving. Among the starters, you may find perfectly grilled Cornish pilchards with creamy tartare sauce or a vibrant pigeon and beetroot terrine. Mains might include a generous portion of diver-caught plaice, served with zippy salsa verde and to-die-for chips, or three exquisite Dover soles deliciously partnered with soft mash and richly buttered samphire. Well-informed, enthusiastic staff and a mellow jazz soundtrack contribute to a thoroughly enjoyable dining experience, rounded off nicely by creative desserts and perfect espresso. Highly recommended.

riverstation

The Grove, BS1 4RB (0117 914 4434/www.river station.co.uk). **Lunch served** noon-2.30pm Mon-Fri; noon-3pm Sun. **Dinner served** 6-10.30pm Mon-Fri; 6-11pm Sat; 6-9pm Sun. **Meals served** 10.30am-2.30pm Sat. **Main courses** £10-£16. **Set lunch** £11.50 2 courses, £13.75 3 courses. **Credit** DC, MC, V.

The old headquarters of the city's river police, riverstation remains at the vanguard of Bristol's increasingly hip dining scene due to its bold architecture and creative cuisine. 'Deck one' incorporates a deli and a bar, while the upstairs restaurant caters for an urbane crowd of business lunchers, leisured ladies and trendy twenty-somethings. Expect fresh, cosmopolitan flavours including seared blue-fin tuna with pak choi, plus unusual old-school choices such as fricasee of lambs' sweetbreads. The global wine list has something for all wallets and palates, but you could do a lot worse than the house selections at £11 per bottle. Chill out over brunch on Saturday, or enjoy intimate 'tapas for two' in the evenings.

Sands

95 Queen's Road, BS8 1LW (0117 973 9734). **Lunch served** noon-2.30pm, **dinner served** 6-11pm daily. **Main courses** £7.95-£11.95. **Set lunch** £6.95 1 course, £7.95-£8.95 2 courses. **Set dinner** £14.95 2 courses, £16.50 3 courses. **Credit** AmEx, DC, MC, V.

The basement of a Clifton villa has been converted into an atmospheric, vaulted Lebanese restaurant. Outside, the front garden is perfect for post-work nibbles on summer evenings, and there's also a terrace at the back for more intimate, sultry occasions. Order the special meze for a feast of Middle Eastern flavours, including creamy houmous, smoky baba ganoush, spicy Lebanese sausages and perfumed lamb koftas, accompanied by a bottle of amber-coloured Lebanese wine. Round the meal off with a sweet Arabian coffee, or a puff on a traditional shisha.

Touareg

77 Whiteladies Road, BS8 2NT (0117 904 4488). **Lunch served**, **dinner served** 6-11pm daily. **Main courses** £15.50-£16.95. **Set lunch** £9.95 2 courses. **Set dinner** £9.95 2 courses; £12.95 3 courses. **Credit** AmEx, MC, V.

Carved woodwork, Moroccan lanterns and rich fabrics create an atmospheric Maghreb haven at Bristol's longest-serving North African restaurant. It's a welcome change from the identikit interiors of many of the city's restaurants: subtle lighting and intimate alcoves encourage romantic couples, while a separate dining room decked out as a Bedouin tent provides a striking setting for private parties. Smiling waitresses serve dishes from a confident and wide-ranging menu, which encompasses classic tagines (lamb shank tagine with artichoke, almonds and peas is particularly good) and a choice of meze, as well as less expected dishes such as roast fish of the day with chermoula and basil polenta. Start with crispy duck berbere with harissa and date jam and leave room for must-have desserts such as mocha and cardamom chocolate cake or sticky date pudding.

Also in the area

Brazz 85 Park Street, BS1 5PJ (0117 925 2000); **Budokan Clifton Down** Whiteladies Road, BS8 2PH (08708 377300); **Chez Gerard** 37-39 Corn Street, BS1 1HT (0117 917 0460); **Hotel du Vin** The Sugar House, Narrow Lewins Mead, BS1 2NU (0117 925 5577); **Wagamama** 63 Queen Road, BS8 1QL (0117 922 1188).

Cornwall

CONSTANTINE

Trengilly Wartha

Nancenoy, nr Constantine, TR11 5RP (01326 340332/www.trengilly.co.uk). **Lunch served** noon-2.15pm, **dinner served** *bar* 6.30-9.30pm; *restaurant* 7-9.30pm daily. **Main courses** £6.40-£15.20. **Set dinner** £21 2 courses, £27 3 courses. **Credit** AmEx, DC, MC, V.

There was a time when Trengilly Wartha was simply a pub with rooms which offered a standard menu in its restaurant. That was until wine enthusiast Nigel Logan and chef Michael McGuire took over 15 years ago. Now you can go for a drink (20 wines by the glass), have a meal in the pub, eat in a much more ambitious restaurant or, last but not least, stop off for a bottle or two from its wine merchants. The restaurant feels a little too close to a suburban living room and lacked a sense of occasion. The set menu offers an enticing range of local seafood and game, and a wonderful wine list, but the execution was poor and lacked the quality the bill required. Service was also sloppy. A meal in the bar of this lovely pub may be a better idea.

FALMOUTH

Harbour Lights ★

7-9 Arwenack Street, Falmouth, TR11 3LH (01326 316934). **Meals served** 11am-8pm daily. **Main courses** £3.25-£5. **No credit cards**.

Sitting in the licensed restaurant behind the Harbour Lights fish and chip shop, looking through the picture window at the harbour beyond, it's easy to lose track of time. The atmosphere, like the decor, is light, as is the functional pine furniture. Although the staff are busy, there's plenty of time to enjoy the cod and haddock from Iceland, or plaice – all served skin off and coated in a highly individual batter. Chips are thick-cut Maris Pipers and, along with the fish, they're fried in palm oil. Accompanying the basics are an assortment of pickles, rich own-made mushy peas, a vegetable-based curry sauce and gravy. Cod, chips and peas costs £4.95.

Hunkydory

46 Arwenack Street, Falmouth, TR11 3JH (01326 212997). **Dinner served** 6-10pm daily. **Main courses** £11.75-£16.95. **Credit** MC, V.

Cornwall is certainly not short of good fish restaurants, but Hunkydory's young, lively clientele and stylish, trendy interior make it stand out from the crowd. The front room combines a suave, cruiser-style bar area, while the booths and white wooden panelling of the back room give it a

steamboat feel. Artwork is in regular rotation from the College of Art, with some pieces provided by the chatty, attentive waiting staff. However impressive all this may be, the food is still the crowning glory, with an extensive menu of fresh local fish, prepared in both modern European and classic styles. The signature john dory special was perfect, with the prawn, olive, caper and delicate lemon sauce enhancing rather than masking its superb flavour, while the roast sea bass with a Cornish yarg and basil tart was richer and more adventurous.

Seafood Bar

Lower Quay Street, Falmouth, TR11 3HM (01326 315129). **Dinner served** *July-Oct* 7-10.30pm daily; *Dec-June* 7-10.30pm Mon-Sat. Closed Nov. **Main courses** £11.95-£14.25. **Credit** MC, V.

Down a narrow side street, tucked into its low, dark cellar like an underwater cave, the tiny Seafood Bar is a bastion of tradition in a town where trendy new restaurants are springing up. Forget sun-blush tomatoes, herb crust and cucumber spaghetti; this place serves up enormous seafood platters, super-fresh shellfish and an extensive selection of local fish cooked in simple but exceptionally tasty ways – like the superb turbot with lime, lemon butter and coriander. Prices reflect the quality of the fish, but the rapturous murmurs of cosy fellow diners reassure you they're still good value. A range of quality wines will help wash it all down, while the hearty desserts (apple pie, bread and butter pudding) with heaps of clotted cream show that, properly done, tradition can still weather the storm of change.

Three Mackerel

Swanpool, Falmouth, TR11 5BG (01326 311886). **Open** noon-11pm Mon-Sat; noon-10.30pm Sun. **Lunch served** noon-2.30pm, **dinner served** 6-9.30pm daily. **Main courses** £10.95-£14.50. **Credit** MC, V.

It's true that some Cornish restaurants use their stunning locations as an excuse to serve up shoddy food at over-inflated prices. The award-winning Three Mackerel, however, throws this argument to the wind with its great combination of a superb spot on the cliff – just a mackerel's leap from the ocean – and imaginatively prepared dishes. Oven-baked smoked haddock wrapped in savoy cabbage parcels with butter and white wine was a delicious arrangement of tastes and textures, but the menu also includes a tempting selection of modern European meat and vegetarian dishes – the pork fillet stuffed with apricots and ginger with char-grilled apple and cider sauce comes recommended. A lively crowd flock to the outside wooden deck on sunny days, while the sparsely stylish but slightly Ikea-esque interior is consistently a firm favourite among locals and tourists.

GUNWALLOE

Halzephron Inn

Gunwalloe, TR12 7GB (01326 240406). **Lunch served** noon-2pm, **dinner served** 7-9pm, *July-Aug* 7-9.30pm daily. **Main courses** £8-£17. **Credit** AmEx, MC, V.

This charming pub sits high above the sea on the east side of the Lizard. Tables out the front offer a fresher option, but most visits are best spent in the snug inside. There's a fire-warmed bar, which serves a mean pint of Sharp's Doom Bar (and Special if you're lucky) and an intimate restaurant, as well as more recently added and less charismatic back rooms. You can eat throughout and the food is consistently excellent. Full-flavoured seafood chowder was the pick of the starters, while the imaginative main of john dory with fresh pasta, fennel and asparagus provided a fantastic array of delicate flavours. Desserts are understandably dominated by locally produced Roskilly's ice-cream and each serving, with its generous heaps of clotted cream, provides a deliciously indulgent finale to the meal.

LELANT

Badger Inn Restaurant & Carvery

Fore Street, Lelant, TR26 3JT (01736 752181/ www.badgerinnstives.co.uk). **Open** 11am-11pm daily. **Lunch served** 11am-3pm, **dinner served** 6-11pm daily. **Main courses** £7.95-£36. **Credit** AmEx, MC, V.

A former favourite of Virginia Woolf (she spent childhood summers nearby), this is a classic family country pub in a lovely setting. You can almost smell the sea about five miles away. The eating area is sprawling: from a carvery to a swanky restaurant conservatory, plus traditional pub seating. The decor is old-style pub, the service equally doesn't try too hard. Red pepper and tomato soup was surprisingly sophisticated, scallops from the seafood menu are perfectly cooked and lamb from the carvery is typical Sunday roast fare. Best of all, you can spend as little or as much as you want here (seafood dishes from £10, carvery from £6).

LOOE

Trawlers

The Quay, Looe, PL13 1AH (01503 263593). **Dinner served** 6.30-9.30pm Tue-Sat. **Main courses** £15.50-£17.50. **Credit** MC, V.

Trawlers, now under new management, is literally yards from the harbour's edge and the fish couldn't be fresher. There are some tables outside – great on a good day, although it can be busy with people

enjoying a harbourside walk. Due to its excellent location in this charming fishing village, there is no limit to the number of potential customers, so make sure you book. The previous owners created a name for Trawlers as the best fish restaurant in Looe and the chef has decided to stay on. Timbale of lobster on a crispy salad was excellent, as was the sea bass, although cod and monkfish with spinach and vine tomatoes was disappointingly homogenous.

MAENPORTH

The Cove

Maenporth Beach, Maenporth, TR11 5HN (01326 251136). **Open** *July-Sept* 10.30am-11pm Mon-Sat; noon-10.30pm Sun; *Oct-June* 10.30am-3pm, 6-11pm Mon-Fri; 10.30am-11pm Sat; noon-10.30pm Sun. **Lunch served** noon-3pm, **dinner served** 6-9.30pm daily. **Tapas served** *July-Sept* noon-9.30pm daily; *Oct-June* noon-3pm, 6-9.30pm Mon-Fri; noon-9.30pm Sat, Sun. **Main courses** £10.95-£14.50. **Credit** MC, V.

This one-time family grill and boozer has been recently acquired by the former chef from the Three Mackerel *(see p115)* on the next beach along. Although the varied and well-priced menu echoes its immensely popular neighbour, the location pales in comparison. Set in an ugly building with holiday flats above and the sea view fighting for prominence with the car park out front, the Cove bravely takes these flaws on board and puts in the extra effort to prove itself. To an extent it succeeds – our food was excellent and the service prompt, chatty and helpful. The simple beige decor, subtle lighting and bare stone create a pleasant and relaxed ambience.

MAWGAN

Trelowarren

Mawgan, TR12 6AF (01326 221224/ www.trelowarren.com). **Lunch served** *Easter-Oct* noon-2.15pm daily; *Nov-Mar* noon-2.15pm Thur-Sun. **Dinner served** *Easter-Oct* 7-9.30pm Tue-Sat; *July-Aug* 7-9.30pm daily; *Nov-Mar* 7-9.30pm Thur-Sat. **Main courses** £12-£15. **Set lunch** (Sun) £10 2 courses, £12 3 courses. **Credit** MC, V.

Situated just south of the beautiful Helford river, Trelowarren is a 600-year-old private estate with expansive grounds and lovingly kept gardens. The restaurant opens out on to a cosy yard, with tables ideally placed for summer sunshine. For lunch, most of the food played very safe – a rather bland carrot soup was followed by mackerel salad and chicken with mustard sauce. Baked avocado, brie and crab was one too many rich flavours. The evening menu is more extensive and expensive, with chef Gilles Verin's use of the local catch the highlight.

MEVAGISSEY

The Alvorada

2 Polkirt Hill, Mevagissey, PL26 6UR (01726 842055). **Dinner served** from 6.30pm Mon-Sat. **Main courses** £11.50-£15.50. **Credit** MC, V.

A busy family-run restaurant, the Alvorada packs a lot of the Algarve into a tiny, crowded dining room and has achieved a thoroughly charming ambience. The menu (and for the most part the wine list) is entirely traditional Portuguese, with a good balance of fish and meat dishes and a couple of vegetarian alternatives. As important here as the food, however, is the lively atmosphere, with Sue da Silva, wife of the chef-patron, cheerily fronting the establishment while Antonio cooks, making the occasional foray from his kitchen to deliver a heaped plate to a waiting table. This is a fun place to eat.

MORWENSTOW

Rectory Tea Rooms ★
Morwenstow, EX23 9SR (01288 331251). **Food served** *April-Oct* 11am-5pm, **lunch served** 12.30-2.30pm daily. **Main courses** £4.50-£6.50. **Set lunch** (Sun) £12.50 3 courses. **No credit cards**.
The Rectory Tea Rooms are worth a short excursion down meandering Cornish lanes to savour old-style English cooking at its most unreconstructedly lavish. The lovely old farmhouse on the edge of the coastal path has been in the same family for 50 years. Sit outside at pub tables, surrounded by tubs of flowers, cats and collies; or take one of the few large inside tables for a snug, low-ceilinged meal at high-backed church pews. Either way, you can dine on vast, unfashionable salads, pasties, cod and chips or pies; or not bother and dive straight into one of Cornwall's finest cream teas. Service is matronly.

NEWQUAY

Ed's
The Edwardian Hotel, 3-7 Island Crescent, Newquay, TR7 1DZ (01637 874087/www.edwardian-hotel.com). **Dinner served** 7-9.30pm Wed-Sun. **Main courses** £6.95-£12.50. **Credit** MC, V.
Entry to this sea-fronted venue is tucked away at the side of the Edwardian Hotel. However, Ed's restaurant is worth seeking out for its pleasant, helpful service, relaxed atmosphere and lack of pretensions. The menu offers something for all tastes and appetites. The starter of crisp duck salad with cucumber and mint salsa with vanilla was simple but effective. Main course pumpkin and ricotta lasagne with sage, walnut and amaretto was a light, inventive option, while teriyaki chicken with bok choi, sweet potatoes and fragrant rice was delicious. However, desserts are the real speciality of the house: try chocolate and chilli cake served with banana ice-cream and tequila dressing.

PADSTOW

The Ebb
1A The Strand, Padstow, PL28 8EA (01841 532565). **Dinner served** *July-Oct* 6-10.30pm Mon, Wed-Sun; *Nov-June* 7-10pm Mon, Wed-Sun. **Set dinner** £24 2 courses, £28 3 courses. **Credit** MC, V.

The decor in this trendy, centrally located restaurant is scrubbed, white and minimalist, with beech furniture and stark charcoal sketches of nudes on the walls. The menu offers good use of seasonal local ingredients through an eclectic mix of worldwide cuisines, from the Greek-influenced starter of grilled goat's cheese with honey fig jam, wild rocket and hazel-nut to the main course of Thai vegetable curry. Mouth-watering seared Cornish scallops with sweet chilli dressing, crème fraîche and Padstow herb leaves was a succulent dish. The wine list has plenty of organic options.

Margot's Bistro
11 Duke Street, Padstow, PL28 8AB (01841 533441/www.margots.co.uk). **Lunch served** noon-2pm Wed-Sun. **Dinner served** 7-9pm Mon, Wed-Sun. **Set lunch** £18.50 2 courses, £21.95 3 courses. **Set dinner** £21.95 2 courses, £25.95 3 courses. **Credit** AmEx, MC, V.
Margot's is a tiny little place just a stone's throw from Padstow's harbour. Walls are painted azure blue, tables are packed close and chairs are of the fold-up variety: the feel is casual and unfussy, helped along by friendly, outgoing service. The menu is kept quite short (fish often figures prominently) and the cooking is simple. Dishes are frequently based on classic pairings, such as juicy rack of lamb with a herb crust, potatoes and rosemary jus or a huge portion of ultra-fresh, pearlescent roast cod with anchovies and garlic perched atop herb-flavoured mash. Seasoning isn't always spot-on, but there are certainly more hits than misses. Desserts such as sticky toffee pudding with butterscotch sauce or lemon and lime cheesecake are put together with comfort in mind. Wines are fairly priced.

Pescadou
The Old Charter House Hotel, South Quay, Padstow, PL28 8BL (01841 532359). **Lunch served** noon-2pm, **dinner served** 7-9pm daily. **Main courses** £15.25-£18.75. **Credit** AmEx, MC, V.
This modern, airy restaurant offers a welcome respite from the bustle of the pastie-and-chip crowds of high summer. The lunch menu offers excellent value and all seven main courses include local ingredients, from Cornish yarg cheese in the vine tomato and red onion tart to local rope-grown mussels. Grilled Cornish cod fillet served over crisp fries with minted mushy peas and lemon was more than enough for the biggest of appetites. The cod was light and flaky and the peas fresh, not frozen. The pan-fried pollock fish cakes were light, piping hot and pleasantly fishy. As well as an extensive wine list, there are draught beers and a range of liqueurs. Add attentive and friendly service, and this restaurant can hold its own in Padstein.

The Seafood Restaurant ★
Riverside, Padstow, PL28 8BY (01841 532700/www.rickstein.com). **Lunch served** noon-2pm, **dinner served** 7-10pm daily. **Main courses** £17.50-£39.50. **Set meal** £47 6 courses. **Credit** MC, V.

Porthminster
Beach Café.
See p122.

Situated right across from the water, the Seafood Restaurant dominates Padstow's harbour the way that its owner, TV chef Rick Stein, dominates the town. Stein owns a cookery school, the Middle Street Café (10 Middle Street), the St Petroc's hotel and bistro (4 New Street) and a couple of delicatessens. The Seafood Restaurant, though, is the place that made Stein's name. Bookings are taken months in advance and the place is always full. It's professionally run, but does the food stand up to scrutiny? Overall, yes. The quality of the seafood is divine. A starter-sized plateau de fruits de mer was a thing of beauty: a collection of super-fresh crab, scallops, winkles, oysters and clams served on crushed ice. A thick piece of turbot is served simply, roasted with hollandaise sauce, although other dishes such as monkfish vindaloo are more adventurous. An acrid, burnt-tasting sauce served with skate, black butter and capers was the only bum note. Wines are as well chosen as the ingredients.

PENTEWAN

The Schoolhouse

West End, Pentewan, PL26 6BX (01726 842474/ www.schoolhouserestaurant.co.uk). **Dinner served** from 7pm Tue-Sat. **Main courses** £10.95-£14.95. **Credit** MC, V.

This tall, slightly formal Victorian schoolroom has difficult proportions that may account for a feeling of wasted space, reinforced by high-set windows and the lowering, clenched canvas of a rigid, roof-hung sail. Despite the rather staid atmosphere, however, the patron is jolly enough and the friendly service spot-on, though a touch more ambient noise wouldn't go amiss. The kitchen plays safe and sticks to dishes it has perfected, with a couple of daily specials for the adventurous and no nasty surprises for anyone. Not exactly cutting edge – one would think even the double-baked cheese soufflé may eventually pall – but with starters at around £5 and main courses under £15, the range of (predominantly fish) dishes is unarguably good value.

PENZANCE

The Abbey Restaurant ★

Abbey Street, Penzance, TR18 4AR (01736 330680/ www.theabbeyrestaurantonline.com). **Lunch served** noon-2pm Fri, Sat. **Dinner served** 7-9.30pm Tue-Sat. **Main courses** £12-£25. **Credit** DC, MC, V.

The building used to be a nightclub and the downstairs bar, winding staircases and bright red walls make that a little too easy to imagine. However the main room upstairs is airy, light and relaxed. The food is superb. From a menu with five options for each course, highlights were a sumptuous haddock and leek risotto starter, and a fillet of black bream and turbot main. A sensational chocolate and prune soufflé cake completed a perfect demonstration of why Penzance and its visitors can't get enough of the Abbey Restaurant.

Chapel Street Bistro ★

Chapel House, Chapel Street, Penzance, TR18 4AQ (01736 332555). **Dinner served** 6.30-9.30pm Tue-Thur; 6.30-10.30pm Sat. **Main courses** £9-£13. **Credit** MC, V.

The starched white tablecloths of Passion recently departed, the new Chapel Street Bistro revels gloriously in the lavish bohemian surrounds of the Penzance Arts Club. A colourful mismatch of rugs, curtains, tables and chairs in this cosy basement room give it a relaxed, informal atmosphere that almost feels like dining round a friend's house, while the array of artwork, sculptures and sumptuous nudes on the walls remind you where you are. Monkfish, mussel and prawn curry with coriander and yoghurt was perfectly aromatic, and the tender roast duck breast with asparagus, beetroot, Cornish new potatoes and horseradish crème fraîche showed good use of local organic produce.

Summer House ★

Cornwall Terrace, Penzance, TR18 4HL (01736 363744/www.summerhouse-cornwall.co.uk). **Dinner served** 7.30-9pm Tue-Sat. **Set dinner** £23.50 3 courses. **Credit** MC, V.

Attention to detail has obviously been the key to chef-patron Ciro Zaino's consistent success. His beautiful Summer House is an immaculate, Tuscan-inspired sanctuary, where one can enjoy a peaceful pre-dinner drink with complimentary nibbles in the lovely walled garden before adjourning to the classic formality of the crisp yellow dining room. The short, daily-changing set menu is excellent value, featuring fresh market ingredients expertly prepared in traditional Mediterranean styles. The gregarious Ciro looks after front-of-house, and whether you're staying in one of the rooms upstairs or not, he really makes you feel like his personal house guest.

POLPERRO

The Kitchen

The Coombes, Polperro, PL13 2RQ (01503 272780/ www.kitchenatpolperro.co.uk). **Dinner served** *Apr-Sept* 7-9.30pm Tue-Sun. **Main courses** £11-£15. **Credit** MC, V.
The streets of this ancient Cornish fishing village are steep and extremely narrow. Cars must be left in a car park to the north, but it is an easy and enjoyable walk down. The Kitchen is situated in a converted fisherman's cottage. There are only nine tables and seating is a little cramped. All the cooking is done by the friendly couple who own the restaurant. Emphasis is on spicy Goan and Thai food. Duck with apricot chutney was decidedly limp and uninspiring, but crab in a spicy lime and paprika dressing was excellent. Moroccan lamb tagine was deliciously aromatic, although the portions could have been a little more generous.

PORTHLEVEN

Critchard's

Harbourside, Porthleven, TR13 9JA (01326 562407/ www.critchards.com). **Dinner served** 6.30-9pm Mon-Sat. **Main courses** £11-£18. **Credit** MC, V.
Porthleven is a lovely fishing village. Jo and Steve Critchard's seafood restaurant sits across the road from the inner harbour in an old granary mill. Inside it can feel a little like a 1970s Cornish holiday cottage, but the food is much nearer the mark. The flavour of the deep-fried chopped baby squid came alive with a squeeze of lime and lemon, and ceviche of salmon Russian-style was better still. The fish was daringly cured in fresh lime, vodka, sugar and green peppercorns and served with exhilaratingly hot wasabi and pickled ginger. The pick of the mains was sautéed john dory with vanilla, which combined unlikely flavours to great effect. The menu changes day to day according to availability.

PORTLOE

The Lugger

Portloe, TR2 5RD (01872 501322/www.lugger hotel.com). **Lunch served** noon-2pm, **dinner served** 7-9pm daily. **Set lunch** £15 2 courses,

£20 3 courses. **Set dinner** £35 3 courses, £40.50 4 courses. **Credit** AmEx, DC, MC, V.
If you thought that trouser suits and rugged Cornish fishing villages were incompatible, think again. Nestled in a tiny harbour on the south coast, the Lugger hotel restaurant is doing a good job at mimicking some of London's wealthier quarters, with chinos aplenty and high prices to match. This 17th-century smugglers' inn has been given a classy million-pound makeover, bringing with it crisp white walls, bleached wood and high-backed chairs. The daily fixed menu is the only option but there's enough variation not to make this limiting. Fish, brought in on local boats, features prominently (24 hours' notice for lobster or the seafood platter). Food is adventurous with varying degrees of success – combos such as goat's cheese and beetroot or monkfish and chorizo work well. Cornish ice-cream is a highlight, and there's an extensive wine list.

PORTREATH

Tabb's ★

Tregea Terrace, Portreath, TR16 4LD (01209 842488). **Lunch served** noon-2pm Sun. **Dinner served** 7-9pm Mon, Wed-Sun. **Main courses** £11.50-£19.75. **Set lunch** £15 3 courses. **Set dinner** £18 3 courses. **Credit** MC, V.
If there were ever a case for not judging a book by its cover, this is it. Portreath isn't the prettiest seaside village in Cornwall, and Tabb's looks pretty unexciting on the approach, but it serves some of the best food in the area. Local seasonal ingredients are worked into adventurous yet sturdy dishes by chef Nigel Tabb, and are served by wife Melanie. Dishes are universally well executed, but john dory with chilli and the grilled fillet of gurnard stand out – as do own-made chocolates and sorbets. Presentation is artistic, courses are accurately judged and vegetables are cooked to perfection, to the extent that they almost take centre stage. Service is very discreet – guests are left alone, but not neglected.

ROCK

The Black Pig ★

Rock Road, Rock, PL27 6JS (01208 862622/ www.blackpigrestaurant.co.uk). **Lunch served** 12.30-2pm Mon, Tue, Fri-Sun. **Dinner served** 7-9.30pm Mon, Tue, Thur-Sun. **Main courses** £18. **Set lunch** £14.50 2 courses, £19.50 3 courses. **Set dinner** £27.50 2 courses, £32.50 3 courses. **Credit** AmEx, MC, V.
This gem of a restaurant is a gastronomic experience of the highest order. It's exclusive in all ways, from the elegant white-panelled walls to the best art on loan and, of course, the exquisite and thoughtfully prepared dishes. The menu is small but perfectly formed. Each course offers four choices and each dish is a work of art. The south coast lemon sole with soused vegetables, potato cooked in duck fat and smoked oil emulsion belies its light and delicate

South West

flavours. Mains include Cornish lamb, grilled john dory, roast beef fillet and day-caught turbot, all elegantly executed and with a flair for flavour. Desserts are not to be missed. You can indulge in three courses here, plus enjoy two small specials in between compliments of the chef, and come away feeling exhilarated and spoilt.

St Enodoc Bar & Restaurant ★

St Enodoc Hotel, Rock, PL27 6LA (01208 863394/ www.enodoc-hotel.co.uk). **Lunch served** *summer* 12.30-2pm, *winter* 12.30-1.30pm, **dinner served** 7-9.30pm daily. **Main courses** £17-£23. **Set lunch** (Sun) £21 3 courses. **Credit** AmEx, DC, MC, V.
Rock is a refined town and this smart hotel serves the sort of food its discerning visitors appreciate. The hotel's elevated position provides panoramic views of the Camel estuary. In summer you can dine out on the terrace. Careful thought has gone into creating dishes with panache: smoked haddock brandade with roast red peppers, black olives and crostini or cream of potato, leek, mussel and saffron soup to start. The main course of roast fillet of beef with the trimmings is exemplary. Other winning dishes were roast chicken with chorizo couscous and dill and mint yoghurt alongside pan-fried brill with a warm salad of Cornish ratte potatoes, asparagus, green beans and cockles with rocket pesto dressing. The own-made ice creams are gorgeous. There's a wide selection of wines – do try the the local Camel Valley Brut as an aperitif.

ST IVES

Alba

Old Lifeboat House, Wharf Road, St Ives, TR26 1LF (01736 797222/www.alba-restaurant.co.uk). **Breakfast served** 10.30am-noon, **lunch served** noon-2.15pm, **dinner served** 6-10pm daily. **Main courses** £13.95-£17.50. **Set lunch** £17.50 3 courses. **Set dinner** £21 3 courses. **Credit** AmEx, MC, V.
Perched serenely above the bustling harbour below, Alba is a haven from the pasties and chips culture outside. This stylishly converted old lifeboat house offers a modern European menu that features lots of fresh fish and organic Cornish meat and vegetables. Complimentary 'gifts from the kitchen' such as delicate canapés served with drinks and a portion of lobster bisque before the starter are nice touches that enhance the upmarket appeal of the place; a glance at the special reserve wine list will do the rest. The neutral decor and broad glass window at the front mean spectacular views of the harbour changing in the evening light dominate the show, while the hushed conversations of discerning diners and the quiet but efficient service keep the atmosphere calm but almost a little too subdued.

Blue Fish

Norway Lane, St Ives, TR26 1LZ (01736 794204). **Lunch served** noon-3pm, **dinner served** 6-10.30pm daily. **Main courses** £7.95-£34.95. **Credit** MC, V.

Jersey

GOREY

Suma's

Gorey Hill, Gorey, JE3 6ET (01534 853291). **Lunch served** noon-2.30pm, **dinner served** 6.30-10pm Mon-Sat. **Main courses** £9.75-£18.75. **Set lunch** £14 2 courses, £18 3 courses. **Credit** AmEx, DC, MC, V.
The spectacular views over the impressive castle of Mont Orgueil (which is floodlit at night) mean that the best tables in this elegantly appointed little restaurant are at the window or outside on the diminutive balcony (where heaters and chairs with fleecy rugs keep out the evening chill). But wherever you end up sitting, you're unlikely to be disappointed by the accomplished modern European cooking. Among the starters, plump local scallops are pan-fried with rocket and Serrano ham, while seared yellowfin tuna comes with crab meat and wilted greens. Main-course roast beef fillet is cooked to perfection and partnered with griddled asparagus and sun-blush tomatoes, while fish options include brill, bream, sea bass and lobster fresh from local trawlers. Fruity desserts such as tarte tatin with green apple sorbet or poached pear with pomegranate and Grand Marnier sabayon are definitely worth a punt. Staff do their jobs with efficient, good-natured professionalism.

ST HELIER

Bohemia

Green Street, St Helier, JE2 4UH (01534 880588/www.bohemiajersey.com). **Bar Open** 11am-midnight Mon-Thur; 11am-1am Fri, Sat. **Lunch served** noon-2.30pm Mon-Fri. **Main courses** £3.95-£9.50. *Restaurant* **Lunch served** noon-2.30pm Mon-Fri. **Dinner served** 6.30-10pm daily. **Main courses** £10.50-£19.50. **Set lunch** £14.50 2 courses, £17.50 3 courses. **Credit** AmEx, DC, MC, V.

When it comes to blending great ambience with good food, Blue Fish certainly knows the score. Nestled inside a narrow but stylish net loft conversion, with a large wooden deck looking out over the rooftops and on to the harbour, this excellent fish restaurant is Spanish in flavour and feel. The long menu includes paellas, traditional Spanish fish dishes and a good selection of tapas, as well as lobster (fresh from the Blue Fish tank) and some fine modern European-style seafood delights, all relished by a lively clientele. Zarzuela (Catalan fish stew) came in a large saucepan, with langoustines, mussels, prawns, clams, monkfish and halibut among the flambéed treats in its superb creamy tomato sauce, and was worth every penny

Expect to find slick interior design (funky bar furniture, splashes of modern art, white linen tablecloths) and the kind of clientele who are prepared to pay for it at this much talked-about newcomer to the island's dining scene. The menu, while undoubtedly expensive, is a nonetheless intriguing list of international styles and ingredients. A starter of local scallops is served with a truffle and artichoke salad, while pithivier of shiitake mushrooms comes with sautéed herb gnocchi. Mains are likely to range from turbot with macaroni and smoked salmon to more conventional pairings such as beef rossini with creamed spinach (this latter weighing in at a hefty £19). Desserts are decadent (raspberry and sweet balsamic soufflé with white chocolate fudge ice-cream) and there's a sizeable wine list. The restaurant's bar caters mostly for the cigar and champagne cocktail set but also offers teas, coffees, beer and board games to the others.

Doran's Courtyard Bistro

Kensington Place, St Helier, JE2 3PA (01534 734866). **Dinner served** 6.30-10pm Mon-Sat. **Main courses** £5.25-£12.95. **Credit** AmEx, DC, MC, V.

Conspicuous for its inventive food and quirky 'rustic Hispanic' decor, Doran's stands head and shoulders above the competition on the busy restaurant strip of Kensington Place. Beyond the charming granite façade is a candlelit dining room – which, despite its nautical prints and traditional stone floors, feels more cosy than mawkish – and a heated courtyard with abundant potted greenery. The kitchen makes the most of some excellent local ingredients (from Jersey honey and the inevitable royals to a rich array of seafood) in a variety of what it terms 'New World dishes'. These range from the adventurous (braised beef with pistachio and Moroccan spices; brill fillets with cream cheese

and scallion mash) to the simply delicious (sea bass with asparagus, watercress and lemon crème fraîche; vanilla and lavender pannacotta with polenta cookies). Staff are the right side of attentive and the wine list is both varied and affordable.

ST SAVIOUR

Longueville Manor Hotel ★

Longueville Road, St Saviour, JE2 7WF (01534 725501/www.longuevillemanor.com). **Breakfast served** 7-10am, **lunch served** 12.30-2.30pm, **afternoon tea served** 3-6pm, **dinner served** 7-9.30pm daily. **Main courses** £24.75-£28.25. **Set lunch** £17.50 2 courses, £22.50 3 courses. **Set dinner** £37.50 3 courses incl coffee. **Credit** AmEx, DC, MC, V.

For a long time now, Longueville Manor has been Jersey's only real contender at the fine dining end of the market – and yet, despite this lofty status, it has managed to avoid sinking into complacency. Sure, you can spend a lot of money sipping aperitifs in its landscaped grounds, but you don't have to. Nor are the staff any less charming to those ordering the more modest wines and choosing from the set menu. As for the food itself, risotto of woodland mushrooms with sweet peas and spinach was judged to perfection, while gratin of tiger prawns with wilted greens, spring onion and ginger was a meaty starter subtly infused with vibrant flavours. The half lobster salad was sea-fresh and accompanied by earthy Jersey royals; a second main of grilled sea bass fillet arrived with crispy skin and a pungent sauce vièrge. Huge, ripe strawberries in a mess of meringue shards and cream, followed by coffee and petits fours by the swimming pool, were further highlights. And the total bill for all this? A very affordable £69.50, including four wines chosen from a wide selection available by the glass.

of its £19.50. The tempting cocktail list, slick bar and sociable staff make this a great place to enjoy a long evening Spanish-style. Note that opening times may vary in winter months.

OnShore

The Wharf, St Ives, TR26 1LF (01736 796000/ www.onshorestives.co.uk). **Breakfast served** 9.30-11am, **lunch served** noon-3.30pm, **dinner served** 5.30-10.30pm daily. **Main courses** £5.50-£23.50. **Set lunch** £8.95 pizza and a drink. **Credit** AmEx, MC, V.

This small rectangular space is packed with tables, so be prepared to hear every word of your neighbour's conversation. Excellent wood-fired

pizzas have innovative toppings such as chicken satay with roasted sweet potato and roasted red onions, or crispy duck with hoi sin sauce, cheddar, cucumber and spring onion. Dishes from the main menu need a little more work: although chilli and ginger marinated salmon was tangy and tender, the sesame-crusted tuna loin with braised Chinese greens was smothered by the overpowering, almost Bovril-like taste of its accompanying black bean dressing. OnShore's idyllic position right on the harbour and reasonable prices make it a very popular choice – perhaps to the woe of the friendly but overstretched staff, who often struggled to keep up on our visit.

Porthminster Beach Café ★

Porthminster Beach, St Ives, TR26 2EB (01736 795352/www.porthminstercafe.co.uk). **Lunch served** noon-4pm, **dinner served** 6-10pm daily. Closed Nov-Easter. **Main courses** £14.95-£17.95. **Credit** MC, V.

Porthminster Beach Café takes the best elements of the traditional beachside café and infuses them with a progressive, creative menu, while keeping the prices on track. The café's lovely wooden deck is right above Porthminster's white sands, and the menu reflects the colours of the stunning setting. Seared tiger prawns with green mango salad, roasted cashews, white miso dressing and crispy shallots was fresh and zesty, while vanilla bavarois with sweet tomato sorbet demonstrated the chef's artistic flair. Lunchtimes are bright and bustling, children are welcome and there are colourful windmills in blue beach buckets on the tables. In the evening, the canopy is pulled over the deck, there are candles on the tables, a fuller menu and a more formal atmosphere. Quite rightly the talk of the town, and beyond.

Seafood Café

45 Fore Street, St Ives, TR26 1HE (01736 794004/www.seafoodcafe.co.uk). **Lunch served** noon-3pm, **dinner served** 5.30-11pm daily. **Main courses** £7-£15.95. **Credit** MC, V.

Despite its trendy appearance this is a friendly, local place. Fresh seafood is lavishly displayed next to the bar: you choose what you want and how you want it cooked before you sit down, so ordering is fast and simple. This has its drawbacks: once you get to your table it's not easy to grab the staff to ask for extras, such as side salad or bread. It's hard to go wrong with the food: ingredients are ultra-fresh. Dishes such as seafood kebab with Thai sauce and noodles, and gurnard in a creamy saffron sauce brought smiles all round. A well-priced wine list, young, pleasant staff and a classy selection of desserts make the Seafood Café a worthy player in the St Ives dining scene.

ST KEYNE

The Well House

St Keyne, PL14 4RN (01579 342001). **Dinner served** 7-8.30pm daily. **Set dinner** £32.50 3 courses. **Credit** MC, V.

An austere Victorian building situated in verdant countryside, where diners are ushered into the sitting room for pre-dinner drinks and *amuse-bouches*. (Buster, the Staffordshire bull terrier, was so pleased to see us that he tore a decorative rose off the sandals worn by a junior member of our party.) The dining room is graceful, light and spacious; the service prompt. Carpaccio of tuna and poached haddock in lemon and saffron soup were superb starters, but main courses were disappointing; the lamb too fatty, the pork tenderloin tough and dry. But the puddings lifted our spirits once more.

ST MAWES

Green Lantern

6 Marine Parade, St Mawes, TR2 5DW (01326 270878/www.thegreenlantern.uk.com). **Tea served** summer 3-5pm Mon-Sat. **Dinner served** 7-9.30pm Mon-Sat. Closed 2 wks end Nov; mid Jan-mid Feb. **Credit** MC, V.

This new eaterie boasts an enviable view over St Mawes harbour. The menu offers a descriptive array of choices: the starter of Cornish crab, avocado, mango and cucumber tian, crisp rocket leaves and oven-dried cherry tomatoes with smoked paprika mayonnaise was superb. Samphire was successfully married with asparagus for a vegetarian risotto. However, roast savora mustard-basted monkfish with garlic butter-poached escargot and samphire did not live up to its promise and the roast Gressingham duck breast, overpowered by a Cornish mead jus, also disappointed. The diminutive dessert of scented rice pudding and Earl Grey poached pears provided solace. Note that sluggish service could cause some consternation if you are planning to travel back by the last ferry.

Tresanton Hotel

St Mawes, TR2 5DR (01326 270055/ www.tresanton.com). **Lunch served** 12.30-2.30pm, **dinner served** 7-9.30pm daily. **Set lunch** £20 2 courses, £26 3 courses. **Set dinner** £26 2 courses, £34 3 courses. **Credit** AmEx, DC, MC, V.

The setting counts for a lot at this designer hotel. If the weather is kind, diners can eat on a terrace looking out to sea – and even when it's inclement, there are big windows to gaze out of. Prices are high for cooking that mostly, but not always, hits the heights. A typical meal might feature pan-fried sweetbreads with spinach and girolles, followed by grilled fillet of beef with crispy potatoes, peas and baby onions, finished by dark chocolat fondant with vanilla ice-cream or local cheeses served with celery and grapes. Sink in to one of the sofas in the lounge for coffee. Staff are friendly, the atmosphere urbane.

ST MERRYN

Fryer Tuck's ★

Harlyn Road, St Merryn, PL28 8NG (01841 520724). **Lunch served** noon-2pm Mon-Sat. **Dinner served** 5-9pm daily. **Main courses** £3.99. **No credit cards**.

St Merryn is little more than a sparsely populated dot on the landscape but the activity in Fryer Tuck's indicates that people are coming some distance to sample the fare. Room can be found for 52 inside and 66 outside, assuming the weather is amenable. The fish on offer, mostly from Iceland for reasons of consistency, is cod and plaice. It's portioned by hand, skinned, boned, battered and fried in ground-nut oil, while the chips are cooked separately in vegetable oil. A traditional accompaniment to the meal in this neck of the woods is a pickle, while for dessert there's ice-cream sundae. Fish and chips with a pot of tea and a roll is around £9.50 for two.

Tresanton Hotel

SALTASH

Kelly's of Saltash ★

28 Fore Street, Saltash, PL12 6JL (01752 844000).
Food served 9am-8pm Mon; 9am-9pm Tue-Sat; noon-8pm Sun. **Main courses** £2.60-£5. **No credit cards**.
Light with large windows, Kelly's chip shop-cum-licensed restaurant has a green and white tiled floor, green chairs and beige table tops. Having been together for years, the staff exude an air of competence and cheerful hospitality as they dish up cod, haddock or plaice, skinless and boned. Chips are usually thick-cut Maris Pipers and can be accompanied by a Chinese-style curry sauce, pickles or thick brown gravy. A sweet tooth is usually sated by Langage Farm ice-cream or chocolate pudding with sauce.

TREBURLEY

The Springer Spaniel

Treburley, PL15 9NS (01579 370424). **Lunch** served noon-2pm, **dinner served** 6.30-9pm daily. **Main courses** £6-£15. **Credit** MC, V.
For good pub grub the Springer Spaniel on the A388 between Launceston and Callington is just the ticket. Children and dogs abound. Huge log fires are a welcome respite from the Cornish drizzle. On hot days there are tables in the beer garden, which has the added bonus of a children's play area. Stick to the bar room, as the restaurant is a bit stuffy (you could hear a pin drop). A crab starter needed a spicy pep-up, but a steak and ale pie was impeccable. There's an admirable selection of real ales.

TREGURRIAN

The Beach Hut ★

The beach, Watergate Bay, nr Tregurrian, TR8 4AA (01637 860877). **Open** 10am-late. **Lunch served** noon-4pm, **dinner served** 6-9pm daily. **Main courses** £11.50-£17. **Credit** MC, V.

If you only go to this informal bistro for the spectacular view, your visit will have been worthwhile. On a balmy evening, it's hard to beat watching the sunset over Watergate Bay, especially with an accompanying menu of such high standard. The service is friendly and unobtrusive and the food, full of fresh flavours, is laden with local ingredients. There are surfer dudes here, but the bistro is popular with all ages. A quirky, informative menu offers an interesting choice and helpful rundown of the basics of fish cuisine. The starter of crab and ginger tortellini with fresh tomato sauce was light and impressive, while the main courses boasted inspired fruit accompaniments to fish and poultry standards: cod with kumquat and red onion chutney or pan-fried barbary duck breast with char-grilled pineapple and berry sauce. The generous puds include a hot chocolate fudge cake to die for.

TRURO

Sevens

77 Lemon Street, Truro, TR1 2PN (01872 275767/www.sevenstruro.co.uk). **Dinner served** 6.30-9pm Tue-Sat. **Main courses** £14-£30. **Credit** MC, V.
Kevin Viner is known in Cornwall as the chef who made Pennypots in Blackwater one of the county's finest restaurants. Sevens has seen him move to Truro, a city in need of decent eating options. It opened in early 2003 and we visited during its third week. The menu is trying hard to impress and some dishes, the roast fillet of venison with a prune and Armagnac jus in particular, did just that. No dishes were poor but some, such as grilled fillet of beef with foie gras, morel mushrooms and Madeira jus, were unremarkable. The best moments were the small dishes between courses, including an apple and mint sorbet. But for a £100-plus meal this didn't add up. Service veered between unconfident and forgetful. Let's hope these were teething problems.

Devon

ASHBURTON

Agaric ★
30 North Street, Ashburton, TQ13 7QD (01364 654478/www.agaricrestaurant.co.uk). **Lunch served** noon-2.30pm Wed-Sun. **Dinner served** 7-9.30pm Wed-Sat. **Main courses** £14.95-£17.95. **Set lunch** £11.50 2 courses. **Credit** MC, V.
While its reputation has earned it a loyal clientele, there's more to Agaric than just good food. Chef Nick Coiley and his partner Sophie Crossley have created an epicurean paradise on the edge of Dartmoor where local gastronomes can avail themselves of own-made preserves, made-to-order picnics or even regular cookery demonstrations. Relying heavily on local produce, the varied menu makes for difficult choices – a perfect French-style fish soup resonated flavour, while cured ham with marinated peppers relied on the simplicity of good ingredients prepared with care and attention. Mains like pan-fried venison loin with smoked bacon, parsnip and sorrel purée, roasted squash and local asparagus marry subtle flavours beautifully.

Moorish ★
11 West Street, Ashburton, TQ13 7DT (01364 654011). **Lunch served** noon-2.30pm Tue-Sat; 11am-2pm Sun. **Dinner served** 6-10pm Tue-Sat; 7-9.30pm Sun. **Main courses** £8.50-£14. **Credit** MC, V.
It was a brave step for owners Judy Gordon Jones and Hilary Townsend to open up a North African-themed restaurant among the antique shops of Ashburton, but if the weekend buzz is anything to go by, it has been a resounding success. The two-tiered tapas menu (£3.50 or £4.50 per dish) offers spiced artichoke hearts with olives or carrot and coriander fritters with green yoghurt sauce, while there are usually three main dishes on offer – local spring lamb marinated in lemon, garlic and oregano is a good choice. Puddings like provençal orange tart are exquisite. It's a much-needed hint of spice for local diners – and equally conducive to those who just fancy a drink and a bite.

BIGBURY

Oyster Shack ★
Milburn Orchard Farm, Stakes Hill, Bigbury, TQ7 4BE (01548 810876/www.oystershack.co.uk). **Lunch served** noon-2.30pm Tue-Sun. **Main courses** £6.95-£16.95. **Credit** MC, V.
Plan ahead if you want to visit the Oyster Shack – not only is the road affected by a tidal estuary (it's flooded at high tide) but tables are booked up well in advance, particularly in summer when al fresco

eating at this unconventional little restaurant is one of the most enjoyable ways to spend a lunchtime in the whole county. You'll also need to remember to bring your own wine if you want to avoid the disappointment of having nothing but mineral water to drink with the exceptional seafood. Crab soup, pints of prawns, sardines or smoked salmon – all simply served – could be followed by the 'catch of the day' or the sensational shack hotchpot – a selection of smoked fish and seafood to share.

BOVEY TRACEY

Spice Bazaar
38 Fore Street, Bovey Tracey, TQ13 9AD (01626 833111). **Dinner served** 6-11.30pm daily. **Main courses** £4.70-£11.50. **Credit** MC, V.
With branches in Bovey Tracey and Dartmouth, the Spice Bazaar has something of a hold over lovers of Indian food in Devon. The loyalty of its clientele is unsurprising – there's nowhere else in the county to compete with their encyclopaedic coverage of the sub-continent's gastronomy. Paneer tikka – own-made cheese cooked in tandoori spices – and a scallop masala were miles away from regular curry house fare. The main menu is less of a departure (though accurately cooked) so instead head for the specialities, including dishes from Pakistan, Parsi 'classics' such as chicken patia (a hot, fruity curry with the fragrance of fenugreek leaves) or the Hyderabadi achar gosht (marinated lamb).

BROADHEMBURY

Drewe Arms ★
Broadhembury, EX14 3NF (01404 841267). **Lunch served** noon-2pm daily. **Dinner served** 7-9pm Mon-Fri; 7-9.30pm Sat. **Main courses** £11.50-£16.75. **Credit** MC, V.
Some restaurants seem to require a culinary lexicon to decode the lengthy descriptions on the menu. Not so the Drewe Arms. Over-embellishment is dispensed with both on the blackboard advertising the fare and in the presentation of the meals. Funnily enough, restaurant reviewers can equally dispense with unnecessary adjectives. Instead only two words are really needed: great fish. Top quality catches are served simply and classically in this thatched olde Englande pub: langoustines with garlic mayonnaise, halibut with horseradish, Dover sole with garlic and herb crust, gravadlax. Accompaniments – salad or veg – are kept minimal and puddings are equally straightforward (and no less delicious). A well-matched wine list and local ales fulfil the beverage quotient. Spot on.

Gidleigh Park

BYSTOCK

The Olive Tree

*Queens Court Hotel, 6-8 Bystock Terrace, Bystock,
EX4 4HY (01392 272709/www.queenscourt-
hotel.co.uk).* **Lunch served** noon-2.30pm Mon-Sat.
Dinner served 7-9.30pm daily. **Main courses**
£8.50-£13.50. **Credit** AmEx, MC, V.
Located in a quiet square in the Queens Court Hotel,
the Olive Tree is a haven for lovers of Mediterranean
flavours. The yellow and red colour scheme gives
the requisite sunshine blush to the dining room and
tablecloths bear pictures of the eponymous fruit. A
pre-starter of fresh prawns and mussels set the
direction of the meal, followed by a bouillabaisse –
heaped with more seafood and large chunks of sea
bass and snapper – that conjured up images of the
Côte d'Azur. A hot smoked fillet of brill with saffron
beurre blanc was unusually comforting, while
desserts of orange crème brûlée and French apple
tart put a spin on Gallic favourites. The own-made
chocolates, served with the coffee, were almost
worth the price of the meal alone.

CHAGFORD

Gidleigh Park ★

*Chagford, TQ13 8HH (01647 432367/
www.gidleigh.com).* **Lunch served** 12.30-2pm,
dinner served 7-9pm daily. **Set lunch** (Mon-Thur)

£27 2 courses, £35 3 courses; (Fri-Sun) £33 2 courses,
£41 3 courses. **Set meals** £70 5 courses, £75
7-course tasting menu. **Credit** AmEx, DC, MC, V.
Internationally renowned and justifiably so,
Gidleigh Park showcases the talents of one of
Britain's foremost chefs, Michael Caines, in gorgeous
surroundings. Though the mock Tudor of the main
house itself can be safely ignored, the grounds from
the vantage point of the terrace beckon to be
explored, while the drawing room and oak-panelled
dining rooms possess discreet charm. Caines's food
is heavenly – veal sweetbreads with broad beans
and toasted almonds leaped from the plate, while a
main of guinea fowl leg stuffed with tarragon
mousse and a foie gras velouté inspired paroxysms
of glee. If service was a shade overbearing, then the
desserts – coconut pannacotta with caramelised
pineapple, coconut ice-cream, pineapple and chilli
sorbet or the outrageously hedonistic trio of
chocolate – more than compensated. Superb.

Mill End Hotel

Chagford, TQ13 8JN (01647 432282). **Lunch
served** noon-2pm, **dinner served** 7-9pm daily. **Set
dinner** £35 4 courses. **Credit** AmEx, DC, MC, V.
If you were wondering how the Mill End Hotel got
its name, the working waterwheel visible through
one of the restaurant windows will immediately
assuage any doubt. It also serves as a pleasant
ambient soundtrack to dinner in this neat but faintly

old-fashioned dining room. The service is as quirky as some of the offerings on the menu but, if the coos of neighbouring diners were anything to go by, both are largely successful. A braised ballotine of pig's trotter was a little overpowering, but veal with a globe artichoke and foie gras was both subtle and imaginative. Desserts are more consistent – rhubarb trifle with rhubarb and custard ice-cream was a wholly satisfying conclusion.

22 Mill St

22 Mill Street, Chagford, TQ13 8AW (01647 432244). **Lunch served** 12.30-1.45pm Wed-Sat. **Dinner served** 7.30-8.45pm Mon-Sat. **Set lunch** £19.50 2 courses, £22 3 courses. **Set dinner** £28 2 courses, £32 3 courses. **Credit** MC, V.

Epicureans who are in the vicinity of Gidleigh Park *(see p125)* shouldn't overlook the less ostentatious (and less pricey) culinary offerings of 22 Mill St. Owner, chef and host Duncan Walker has been serving up to residents in Chagford and beyond for six years, winning a loyal clientele and numerous plaudits with a combination of assured service, stylish surroundings, good value for money and a regularly changing menu that offers classic combinations with the occasional well-conceived twist. A set lunch started with fillet of sea bass in a zingy juice of lemongrass, ginger and lime leaves, next a Gressingham duck breast was mouth-wateringly pink. A stupendous crème brûlée finished the meal.

CROYDE

Hobbs

6 Hobbs Hill, Croyde, EX33 1LZ (01271 890256). Mar-Nov **Breakfast served** 9am-noon, **dinner served** from 6.30pm daily. **Main courses** £8.95-£17.95. **Credit** MC, V.

Twenty minutes by car west of Ilfracombe, ten minutes north of Barnstaple, Croyde beach is where surfers head when Woolacombe won't deliver. Hobbs is a very cheerful, bustling bistro on the village's main drag. The Saturday night we dropped in, it was packed to bursting with sun 'n' surf-seekers young and old, all tucking into a menu described as 'English with a Mediterranean twist'. In truth, the food's not particularly special: alongside a reasonable range of pizzas, a basic but acceptable bruschetta and watery salmon proved just about adequate. Also on offer are a range of straightforward wines and beers. But then again it's really the prevailing high spirits and holiday mood that make this cramped, capable restaurant worth a visit.

DARTINGTON

White Hart

Dartington Hall, nr Dartington, TQ9 6EL (01803 847111/www.dartingtonhall.com). **Lunch served** noon-2pm, **dinner served** 6-9pm daily. **Main courses** £6.65-£12.95. **Credit** MC, V.

Tucked away at the corner of the beautiful Dartington Hall, the White Hart is a notch above standard pub fare and a real mainstay for local diners. Service is laid-back, the food unpretentious and great value with mains coming in around £8. Starters of local mussels steamed in white wine and cream or gravadlax with a silky roasted garlic mayo are deliciously moreish; main courses of Italian meatballs with chorizo and smoked paprika or Cornish smoked haddock with spinach and a cheese sauce are homely and satisfying. If you're booking, make sure you request a table in the magnificent dining hall and make time to walk off dinner in the absorbing gardens.

DARTMOUTH

Alf Resco ★

Lower Street, Dartmouth, TQ6 9JB (01803 835880/ www.cafealfresco.co.uk). **Food served** 7am-2.30pm Wed-Sat; 7am-2pm Sun. **Dinner served** *summer* 6.30-9.30pm Fri-Sun. **Main courses** £5. **Set dinner** £18 3 courses. **No credit cards**.

Known far and wide for its permanent buzz, Dartmouth's Alf Resco is a breakfasters' paradise a stone's throw from the waterfront. The varied clientele – from yachtie types in deck shoes to surf dudes with appropriate clothing labels and bleary-eyed parents – gives it a really good-natured feel. Staff are on hand to dish up a typical breakfast menu; try a full English or a bacon sandwich done to a T. While Alf's usually opens from 7am until 2.30pm, there are special evening meals during the summer which continue the party feel (an evening of sea shanties would be typical). The cappuccinos are notable too – even nicer on the terrace outside.

Anzac Street Bistro

2 Anzac Street, Dartmouth, TQ6 9DL (01803 835515). **Dinner served** 6.30-9.30pm Tue-Sat. **Main courses** £10.50-£14.50. **Credit** MC, V.

There's a distinctly Mediterranean air to this lively restaurant that's reflected accurately in the menu – someone's paid careful attention to striking the right balance. It's a consistency that's carried through from the unassuming service to the unpretentious presentation. Eyes widen and mouths water as dishes of smoked salmon with blinis or tiger tail prawns in garlic butter precede fairly laden platters of lamb rump with white bean and rosemary purée or sea bass en papillote. Simplicity, quality and authenticity are key words for this well-balanced menu that's utterly successful in conveying the continental ambience it strives for. Although the bistro is only open in the evenings, it supplies the lunches for its sister establishment, Relish, opposite.

Carved Angel

2 South Embankment, Dartmouth, TQ6 9BH (01803 832465/www.thecarvedangel.com). **Lunch served** 12.30-2pm Tue-Sun. **Dinner served** 7-9.30pm Mon-Sat. **Set lunch** £18.50 2 courses, £23.50 3 courses. **Set dinner** £39.50 4 courses. **Credit** MC, V.

Once renowned as one of the region's finest restaurants, the Carved Angel looks somewhat faded these days – the shabby toilets and backing muzak reminiscent of *Howard's Way* all scream out for a makeover. Mind you, who wants to spend their time looking at the interiors when the place commands such a great view of the Dart Estuary? The atmosphere of museum-like reverence sits a little uncomfortably, but staff seemed attentive and relaxed. If the food lacks the pzazz it once had, it still warrants a visit. Starters such as sautéed gnocchi with morels and broad beans were imaginative and a main of rump of Devon lamb with truffle mash and garlic jus was a particularly heady treat.

Little Admiral ★

27-29 Victoria Road, Dartmouth, TQ6 9RT (01803 832572/www.little-admiral.co.uk). **Food served** 6.30-9.30pm Thur-Sat. **Main courses** £2.20-£10.95. **Credit** MC, V.

Tables fill up pretty quickly at this centrally located restaurant; there's a big demand for their modern take on tapas-style eating and it's only open on Thursday, Friday and Saturday. Consequently, the elegantly minimal dining room tends to throb as the evening wears on and the wine begins to flow. Not only does the Little Admiral appropriate Spanish/North African dishes such as Moorish pork skewers, clams steamed in manzanilla or grilled fresh chorizo, but Iberian ideas of relaxed, extended dining pervade too. There are four price categories with larger 'main' dishes of whole grilled fish or steak on offer for bigger appetites. Fresh seafood such as squid, crevettes or prawns is a highlight.

DODDISCOMBSLEIGH

Nobody Inn

Doddiscombsleigh, EX6 7PS (01647 252394/ www.nobodyinn.co.uk). **Lunch served** noon-2pm, **dinner served** 7-10pm daily. **Main courses** £6.90-£10.50. **Credit** AmEx, MC, V.

Local legend has it that the Nobody Inn got its name when the coffin of a previous landlord was buried without his body being inside. It's that kind of place: redolent with history, neatly thatched and set amid a flurry of flowers. Its reputation keeps this 16th-century tavern busy most nights. Some of the food has an international feel (tiger prawn kebab, gravadlax) but the best dishes are more down-to-earth, like the warming Nobody soup (a house speciality) or a gratifying lamb's liver sautéed with thyme, onion and garlic. The wine list with its extensive range of whiskies is almost encyclopaedic.

EXETER

Cat in the Hat

Magdalen Road, Exeter, EX2 4TA (01392 211700). **Brunch served** 10am-noon, **lunch served** noon-2.30pm Mon-Sat. **Dinner served** 7-9.30pm Tue-Sat. **Main courses** £10.50-£14.25. **Credit** DC, MC, V.

There's obviously been a lot of thought put into this intimate two-tiered restaurant to ensure that every customer goes away satisfied – there's a real attention to detail. A cannellini bean dip arrives unasked for as an introduction to the graceful and unobtrusive service. It's clear that presentation is a key factor to the appeal and every dish is artistically arranged – most notably the precarious tower of crispy polenta or a perfect gleaming roquefort mousse. If some of the flavour combinations are a little wayward, the majority of the dishes are handled with respect and skill. A valuable addition to dining in Exeter.

Michael Caines at the Royal Clarence Hotel

Cathedral Yard, Exeter, EX1 1HD (01392 310031/ www.michaelcaines.com). **Lunch served** 12.30-2.30pm, **dinner served** 7-10pm Mon-Sat. **Main courses** £16.50-£29.75. **Set lunch** £16.50 2 courses, £19.50 3 courses. **Credit** AmEx, DC, MC, V.

'Service with style' is the motto of this centrally located Exeter restaurant – and the experience lives up to it in every way. Waiters are dynamic and knowledgeable, taking an active part in the dining experience rather than just rotating full and empty plates. Set lunches are especially good value featuring, for example, a risotto of baby vegetables with a vegetable nage followed by braised duck leg with spicy savoy cabbage and orange and star anise sauce. Desserts are worth squeezing in too – an exotic couscous with a passion fruit sorbet and basil syrup had a real sense of fun. With its balanced wine list and elegant surroundings, this is without doubt the best Exeter has to offer.

St Olave's

Mary Arches Street, Exeter, EX4 3AZ (01392 217736/www.olaves.co.uk). **Lunch served** noon-1.45pm, **dinner served** 7-8.45pm daily. **Set lunch** £15 2 courses, £19 3 courses incl glass of wine. **Set dinner** £29.50 3 courses. **Credit** MC, V.

Tucked away in a discreet courtyard, St Olave's sits in tranquil seclusion away from the bustle of Exeter city centre, the quietness of the location enhanced by the austere Georgian interiors and reserved service. Spring pea soup was verdant and fresh; main course roast loin of pork was well executed if a little unimaginative. The highlight – a baked chocolate tart with white chocolate ice-cream – was a fantastically well-rounded confection. St Olave's seems to suffer from a case of 'out of sight out of mind' – a lunchtime special of two courses with a glass of wine for £15 seemed extremely reasonable, yet few were there to take up the offer.

GITTISHAM

Combe House Hotel & Restaurant ★

Gittisham, EX14 3AD (01404 540400/ www.thishotel.com). **Lunch served** noon-2pm, **dinner served** 7-9.30pm daily. **Set lunch** £16.50

2 courses, £21-£34 3 courses. **Set dinner** £34
3 courses, £49 7 courses. **Credit** AmEx, DC, MC, V.
The long, winding drive that cuts through the
panoramic parkland belonging to this Elizabethan
manor builds a pleasant anticipation. There's a sense
of magic that's continued in the panelled entrance
hall (complete with stag's head) and in the Augustan
scenes of the mural adorning one of the two dining
rooms. Comfort and relaxation are clearly priorities
– cheery service seems designed to put guests at
ease. Modern British and French collide on the menu:
salad of crab with langoustines and yellow pepper
gazpacho was divine; fillet of local beef had
exceptional flavour even without the foie gras and
morel sauce. It's worth noting that local produce is
loudly – and rightly – trumpeted here, and that the
chef clearly makes the most of the hotel's splendid
kitchen garden.

GOVETON

Buckland Tout Saints Hotel
Goveton, TQ7 2DS (01548 853055/www.tout-
saints.co.uk). **Lunch served** noon-1.45pm, **dinner**
served 7-9pm daily. **Set lunch** £15 2 courses,
£19 3 courses. **Set dinner** £35 3 courses incl coffee.
Credit MC, V.
It requires some serious navigation to find Buckland
Tout Saints Hotel. Perhaps that's why, as the
brochure boasts, it's been the venue for cabinet
meetings in the past. It's certainly worth honing the
map skills: its air of seclusion only enhances the
wonderful romantic feeling that pervades this 17th-
century manor house. A careful balance is
maintained between formality and relaxation here –
there's never any sense that the diner needs to speak
in a whisper, despite the grandeur of the panelled
Queen Anne dining room. The food has a modern
British feel – starters might include terrine of confit
of duck and wood pigeon with black truffle dressing;
mains – such as char-grilled fillet of beef with seared
foie gras – were perfectly conceived. Puddings are
delightful too.

GULWORTHY

The Horn of Plenty ★
Gulworthy, PL19 8JD (01822 832528/
www.thehornofplenty.co.uk). **Lunch served** noon-
2pm Tue-Sun. **Dinner served** 7-9pm daily. **Set**
lunch £18 3 courses. **Set dinner** £25 3 courses.
Credit AmEx, DC, MC, V.
Head chef Peter Gorton's imaginative and precisely
executed culinary creations have put the Horn of
Plenty on the map, attracting swathes of local diners
and gourmands from around the country. He's
picked an enviable location as a backdrop to first-
class dining – this airy, ivy-covered Georgian
country house overlooks the Tamar Valley and
positively oozes charm. There's a welcome lack of
stuffiness, both in the atmosphere of the dining room
and in the staff, who are approachable and sociable.

The modern British/French dishes are unfussy but
intriguing – sautéed scallops with king prawn and
couscous salad in prawn oil might be followed by
roast breast of Gressingham duck with black pepper
and Calvados sauce. Desserts are a must, as are the
wonderful petits fours.

HAYTOR VALE

Rock Inn
Haytor Vale, TQ13 9XP (01364 661305/
www.rock-inn.co.uk). **Lunch served** noon-2pm,
dinner served 6.30-9pm daily. **Main courses**
£8.95-£15.95. **Set dinner** £16.95 2 courses, £19.95
3 courses. **Credit** AmEx, DC, MC, V.
Located in a picturesque village near to one of
Dartmoor's favourite tourist spots, the Rock Inn is
a steadfastly traditional pub which happens to do
good food. The interior decor of horse brasses, dark
oak and laminated place mats gives no concession
to sophistication, aiming more towards mythical
Olde Englande. If the weather is kind enough, the
garden is much more attractive. The food is pleasant
but prices suffer from slight delusions of grandeur.
Starters of pan-fried scallops with roasted hazel-nut
butter and goat's cheese salad with basil oil were
robust; a main course of pan-fried salmon with black
olive and basil butter was more adventurous,
reflecting the inn's largely successful attempt to put
a continental spin on British country cooking.

ILFRACOMBE

Maddy's ★
25 St James's Place, Ilfracombe, EX34 9BJ (01271
863351). **Meals served** noon-10pm daily. **Main**
courses £3.20-£3.50. **No credit cards.**
Ensconced behind a bright shopfront, in one of the
most popular tourist destinations on the north coast
of Devon, is Maddy's fish and chip shop. This 38-
seater is licensed (wine costs about £6 a bottle) and
has solid dark wood furniture consistent with the
wood-panelled walls. The cod, haddock and plaice,
from the Icelandic fleet, arrive via the friendly staff
in generous portions with skin and bones removed.
The chips, leaning towards the thick-cut Maris Piper
school of thought, are cooked in palm oil and dished
up with smooth, own-made mushy peas. Other
alternatives include curry sauce or gravy, unusual
for this part of the world, while for dessert there's a
choice between various gateaux, apple pie or apple
and blackberry pie, both served with custard.

KINGSBRIDGE

Pig Finca ★
The Old Bakery, The Promenade, Kingsbridge, TQ7
1JD (01548 855777). **Food served** 10am-4.30pm,
dinner served 6-9pm Mon-Sat. **Main courses**
£6.95-£9.50. **Credit** MC, V.
A spin-off from the boutique up the road, the Pig
Finca café continues the theme of North Africa meets

Carved Angel.
See p126.

life seen from different angels:

angel fish

guardian angel

angel cake

carved angel

THE CARVED ANGEL

Gaudí meets 1960s kitsch in a maze of distinctive rooms. It's a funky combination that draws a mixed crowd who come as much for the food as the music – soul, world music or chill-out dominates the stereo and bands frequently play. The menu makes the most of a limited selection of ingredients (chorizo, yellowfin tuna, sourdough bread), spinning out tapas-style eating from breakfast through to dinner. The flavours are international with a few dishes, such as mashtuk lamb or the generous meze, standing out. It's so reasonably priced that repeat visits are inevitable, providing you can put up with the haphazard approach to service.

LIFTON

Arundell Arms

Lifton, PL16 0AA (01566 784666). **Lunch served** noon-2pm, **dinner served** 7.30-9.30pm daily. **Set lunch** £19 2 courses, £23.50 3 courses, incl coffee. **Set dinner** £33 2 courses, £39.50 3 courses, incl coffee. **Credit** AmEx, DC, MC, V.

This old coaching inn on the border of Devon and Cornwall, a stone's throw from the A30, is justifiably well known. Quintessentially English, the Arundell attracts not just fly-fishing enthusiasts but those seeking a relaxing break in this stunning and quiet corner of Devon. You can eat a stylish meal based around local produce in the elegant dining room or opt for the bar menu (which can be served outside

in the garden). Hits included chicken liver pâté with apricot chutney, organic smoked salmon, and chargrilled steak (from local beef). However, we did feel slightly short-changed by the fact that an adult's portion was only marginally larger than a child's, at twice the price.

LYDFORD

Dartmoor Inn

Lydford, EX20 4AY (01822 820221). **Lunch served** noon-2.30pm, **dinner served** 6.30-9.30pm Tue-Sun. **Main courses** £12.50-£19. **Set lunch** £10.75 2 courses, £13.95 3 courses. **Credit** AmEx, DC, MC, V.

Situated well away from the A38 corridor, this welcoming gastropub on the dark side of the moor is a real find. The set meals are tremendous value, and the quality of the food puts it on a par with restaurants with much bigger price tags attached. Suppliers of local produce are proudly displayed next to the well-balanced menu, which adds continental twists to a flexibly British focus. Chargrilled scallops with spiced mayonnaise were as pleasing to the eye as the tastebuds, while mains like roast rib of Devon beef showed off excellent ingredients simply and effectively. Busy but not overwhelming, the vibrant atmosphere attests to the inn's deserved popularity. Friendly, engaging service is the cherry on the cake.

LYNMOUTH

Rising Sun Hotel

*Harbourside, Lynmouth, EX35 6EQ (01598
753223/www.risingsunlynmouth.co.uk).* **Lunch
served** noon-2pm, **dinner served** 7-9.30pm
daily. **Main courses** £15.95-£24.95. **Credit**
AmEx, DC, MC, V.

Right on the harbourside in the slightly run-down
resort of Lynmouth, the thatched Rising Sun Hotel
has recently changed hands but continues to provide
some of the most characterful accommodation in the
town. The restaurant is famously ambitious and it's
also expensive, especially given that the low, dark,
olde-worlde ground-floor rooms are only slightly
more comfortable than the bar room next door. The
menu, which features recommended wines, is rich
and flamboyant but also often successful: roulade of
monkfish wrapped in spinach with an oyster and
red mullet broth or sun-kissed tomato risotto
wrapped in smoked courgette, roast fennel and a
cream sauce infused with avocado oil are the kind
of thing to expect and are unlikely to disappoint.

MAIDENCOMBE

Orestone Manor

*Rockhouse Lane, Maidencombe, TQ1 4SX (01803
328098/www.orestone.co.uk).* **Lunch served** noon-
2pm, **dinner served** 7-9pm daily. **Main courses**
£17.50-£23.50. **Set lunch** (Sun) £18.50 3 courses.
Credit AmEx, MC, V.

Seated in the conservatory at Orestone Manor, you
can almost understand why Torbay is known as the
English Riviera. Perched on the hills running down
to Lyme Bay, this Georgian hotel is tucked discreetly
away from Torquay's less salubrious centre; with
its high ceilings, fans and elephant theme there's a
colonial feel, particularly in the bar – an ideal setting
for gin slings. Food at lunch was unimpressive;
dinners offer much more – Start Bay crab consommé
with crab ravioli would be a typical first course,
while steamed breast of guinea fowl flavoured with
lime could follow. Prices are a little inflated, but this
doesn't seem to perturb the tables of happy diners
who clearly enjoy the tranquility of the setting and
the attentiveness of the service.

NORTH BOVEY

Blackaller House

North Bovey, TQ13 8QY (01647 440322). **Dinner
served** 7.30-8pm Thur-Sat by appointment only.
Set dinner £26 4 courses. **No credit cards.**

The small dining room at Blackaller House, a 17th-
century mill house on the banks of the River Bovey,
is only really big enough for hotel guests, so a bit of
advance planning is required if you want to take
advantage of the idyllic location, delectable country
cooking and geniality of the hosts Peter Hunt and
Hazel Phillips. The great-value four-course menu
began with a tangy tomato and thyme tartlet

followed by a well-balanced soup of pea, fresh ginger
and coriander. Honey (from their own hives) is a
speciality and duly appears as a marinade for a
grainy Gressingham duck breast in a tart plum and
port sauce. Coffee in the lounge might be
accompanied by pleas for Peter to play his sitar.

PLYMOUTH

Artillery Tower

*Firestone Bay, Durnford Street, Plymouth, PL1 3QR
(01752 257610/www.artillerytower.co.uk).* **Lunch
served** noon-2pm Tue-Fri. **Dinner served** 7pm-
midnight Tue-Sat. **Set dinner** £26.95 3 courses.
Credit AmEx, MC, V.

Set in a 500-year-old circular gun emplacement,
Artillery Tower is an imposing edifice among the
naval buildings near the Plymouth ferry port
overlooking the pounding surf of the Sound. It's an
interesting, though not entirely settling location –
especially given the proximity of the kitchen to the
dining room. The menu is a little unsettling too –
traditional English favourites such as ribeye with
spring onion mash and rump of lamb wrestle with
grilled tuna and spicy lentils or chicken with
guacamole. There's nothing ground-breaking here
but the portions are generous with flavours to
match, and the staff are attentive and obliging. A
dependable eaterie.

Chez Nous

*13 Frankfort Gate, Plymouth, PL1 1QA (01752
266793).* **Dinner served** 7-10.30pm Tue-Sat. **Set
dinner** £36 3 courses. **Credit** AmEx, DC, MC, V.

It's hard to spot this long-established restaurant
among the more garish frontages in Plymouth's
unsightly pedestrianised shopping precinct, but
once you've tuned into the tricolours you'll know
you've arrived. There's no mistaking the French
influence once inside – art nouveau posters, Gitanes
adverts, and of course the red, white and blue of the
linen. If you were in any doubt as to the authenticity
of the place, chef Jacques Marchal's robust old-
school French cooking will assure you that this is
the real deal – while the well-chosen wine list also
has a strong bias toward the Gallic. Choices from the
set dinner menu might include a game terrine, which
explodes with the flavour of juniper berries and
peppercorns, or mignons de porc aux pruneaux in a
decadently rich sauce.

The Lemon Tree

*Grosvenor Hotel, 9 Elliot Street, The Hoe,
Plymouth, PL1 2PP (01752 265631).* **Dinner
served** 7-10pm Tue-Sat. **Main courses** £12-£18.
Credit AmEx, MC, V.

There's something about basement restaurants that
brings out the romantic – especially one as intimate
as the Lemon Tree. Located in the cellar of the
Grosvenor Hotel on Plymouth Hoe, there's a
secluded, Mediterranean atmosphere to it that's
complemented by the friendly service – a place
utterly conducive to long, lingering meals with

plenty of wine. The menu changes regularly to reflect seasonal produce. Classic French ideas prove to be a solid foundation on which the Lemon Tree builds all sorts of contemporary flavour combinations, from a tangy Caribbean-inspired serving of pan-fried scallops in a jerk seasoning, to a sumptuous, full-bodied pairing of pork tenderloin with mushrooms and black pudding.

Tanners
Prysten House, Finewell Street, Plymouth, PL1 2AE (01752 252001/www.tannersrestaurant.co.uk). **Lunch served** noon-2.15pm Tue-Fri; noon-1.30pm Sat. **Dinner served** 7-9.30pm Tue-Sat. **Set lunch** £12.50 2 courses, £15 3 courses. **Set dinner** £19.95 2 courses, £25 3 courses, £29 5 courses. **Credit** AmEx, MC, V.
Set in one of Plymouth's oldest buildings, Tanners has the feeling of a cloister about it. The medieval surroundings, and in particular the tranquil courtyard, are a welcome relief from the oppressive architecture of the rest of the city. The calmness of the place has obviously rubbed off on the staff, who work with a friendly professionalism that puts the diner at ease. It's a place for long, lazy lunches and leisurely dinners – set menus are good value with an emphasis on West Country produce. Starters might include a subtly flavoured char-grilled rabbit salad, while mains like lemon sole with red wine and butter sauces or steamed turbot with pak choi and soy broth show the range of influences at work. Daily specials are more pricey but definitely worth splashing out on.

Zucca ★
North Quay, Discovery Wharf, Plymouth, PL4 0RB (01752 224225). **Lunch served** 11am-2.30pm Mon-Fri; 11am-6pm Sat, Sun. **Dinner served** 6-10.30pm daily. **Main courses** £8.95-£16. **Credit** MC, V.
Situated almost on the water's edge in an upmarket marina development, Zucca has an international feel to it – vibrant, well designed but lacking idiosyncrasies. That's no bad thing in itself – the plum-coloured interiors, smart waitresses in oriental-style uniforms and comfortable bucket seats emit a cool sense of efficiency and style. Big flavours are the order of the day on this predominantly Italian menu. Pizzas, pastas and grilled fish and meats are enlivened by clever combinations of ingredients and competent preparation. Affordability is another key factor in Zucca's appeal – main courses average out at about £10. Lunch is especially good value, with an appetising selection of dishes such as prosciutto with mustard fruits or roast squash and red pimento ciabatta averaging around £6 each.

ROCKBEARE
Jack in the Green
Rockbeare, EX5 2EE (01404 822240/ www.jackinthegreen.uk.com). **Lunch served** 11.30am-2pm Mon-Fri; 11.30am-2.30pm Sat. **Dinner served** 6-9.30pm Mon-Fri; 6-10pm Sat. **Meals**
served noon-9pm Sun. **Main courses** £3.75-£12.50. **Set meals** £18.50 2 courses, £22.75 3 courses. **Credit** MC, V.
An award-winning roadside pub on the way to Exeter airport, the Jack in the Green is certainly worth stopping at if you're in the vicinity. Head chef Matt Mason has created a well-rounded menu with moments of real inspiration. A celeriac and truffle soup resonated with deep flavours; Whimple lamb (from the next village along) with couscous, yoghurt and mint was superbly cooked; while a dessert of cream tea parfait updated one of the county's traditional afternoon pastimes with real aplomb. If the food is aspirational, it's let down by erratic, disjointed service and a lack of attention to the surroundings – plastic table mats, unattractive furniture and a hotchpotch of repro antiques decorating the walls jarred with the forward-looking vibe of the menu.

SALCOMBE
Catch 55 Bistro
55 Fore Street, Salcombe, TQ8 8JE (01548 842646). **Dinner served** *Mar-Oct* 6.30-10pm Mon-Sat; *July, Aug* 6.30-10pm daily. **Main courses** £6.95-£12.75. **Credit** MC, V.
It was a brave move for the management of Claire's to scrap what for many years has been a winning formula, and yet their new look makes perfect sense. Reopening as Catch 55, the restaurant now offers an alternative to high-end modern British dining. It's closer to an American-style bistro – big portions, lively atmosphere and absolutely unpretentious. Gone are the over-complex dishes, replaced now by more instant choices based around key ingredients. Tuna comes served in four different ways, as do scallops and mussels; there are hand-made burgers and classic pasta dishes (carbonara, bolognese). The accent here is on good eating whatever time it is, from an early evening snack to emergency ballast on the way home from the pub.

Spiritus Sanctus
South Sands, Salcombe, TQ8 8LL (01548 842499/ www.southsands.com). **Lunch served** noon-3pm, **dinner served** 6-10pm daily. **Main courses** £9.95-£15. **Credit** MC, V.
Sitting in the sun on the decked terrace at Spiritus Sanctus, drinking a cappuccino and looking out over the bay at South Sands, it's hard to believe that there's much wrong with the world. It must be blessed with one of the most continental aspects in the South-west with the beach almost coming into the restaurant. It seems that the owners have seen fit to import an entirely Scandinavian workforce who only add to the air of beach bar cool that pervades the premises. The food isn't flashy but it's competently executed – a punchy seafood salad to start, followed by an aromatic saltimbocca of veal – but eating really takes second place to the pleasure of lounging around in this fashionable hangout for all age groups.

South West

STOKE CANON

Barton Cross Hotel

Stoke Canon, EX5 4EJ (01392 841245). **Dinner
served** 7-9.30pm daily. **Set dinner** £22.50
3 courses, £27.50 4 courses. **Credit** AmEx, MC, V.
It's hard to imagine a more traditional-looking
hostelry than this 17th-century pub-cum-hotel
outside Exeter. The thatched building complex
(part-original, part-new) extends around a shady
courtyard, while inside horse brasses, floral print
tablecloths and oak beams set the scene. A friendly
welcome comes with an abundance of pre-dinner
snacks, ideal for trying to pick your way through
the unconventional mix of flavours on the menu.
You could expect ravioli of wild mushrooms with
asparagus and sautéed duck liver, followed by a
midway course of red pepper soup with sweet peas
– both well cooked and distinctive yet somehow the
combinations don't quite work. A main course of
lamb noisettes (deliciously pink) with dauphinoise
potatoes was more successful.

TOPSHAM

Galley Restaurant

*41 Fore Street, Topsham, EX3 0HU (01392
876078/www.galleyrestaurant.co.uk).* **Lunch served**
noon-1.30pm, **dinner served** 7-9.30pm Tue-Sat.
Main courses £16-£23. **Credit** AmEx, DC, MC, V.
More is definitely more at this brooding fish
restaurant in the quaint fishing town of Topsham.
From the proliferation of promotional literature on
offer to the extraordinarily over-the-top garnishes,
the idea here seems to be to subject the diner to
sensory, and possibly gastric, overload. It's a theme
continued in a vast main course like halibut with
mousse de foie gras and seaweed, parsnip and
celeriac mash – a collision of flavours made all the
more intimidating by side helpings of fried potatoes
with tartare and samphire with asparagus – both
impeccable but utterly gratuitous. Despite the
excess, there is some interesting food available here
– perhaps the tapas-style menu is a less
overwhelming introduction.

La Petite Maison ★

*35 Fore Street, Topsham, EX3 0HR (01392
873660).* **Lunch served** 12.30-2pm, **dinner
served** 7-10pm Tue-Sat. **Set lunch** £14.95
2 courses, £17.95 3 courses. **Set dinner** £21.95
2 courses, £25.95 3 courses. **Credit** MC, V.
Word of mouth is often the best way of gauging the
quality of a restaurant. If the number of
recommendations received for this modern
British/French eaterie are anything to go by, then
La Petite Maison's success is almost a foregone
conclusion. It has the kind of informal ambience that
eludes most restaurateurs – the light, airy
surroundings encourage unwinding. The food is
uncluttered too – asparagus, pea and mint soup
married seasonal flavours delicately, while roasted
monkfish with spinach bubble and squeak and chive

and lemon beurre blanc was much more than the
sum of its parts. A startlingly refreshing lime sorbet
was an unexpected highlight, rounding off a
perfectly balanced meal.

TORCROSS

Start Bay Inn

*Torcross, TQ7 2TQ (01548 580553/
www.startbayinn.co.uk).* **Lunch served**
11.30am-2pm Mon-Sat; noon-2.15pm Sun.
Dinner served 6-10pm daily. **Main courses**
£4.70-£12. **Credit** MC, V.
There are no frills here, just a magnificent setting –
the beachfront at Slapton Sands, a sumptuous
pebbly beach that stretches (it seems) across the
whole horizon. What makes the Start Bay Inn even
more worthy of a visit is the fish, landed daily and
served unfussily with the ubiquitous chip – an
obvious attraction to the hordes who descend at
weekends, evenings and any other time the sun
pokes its head out. For the more adventurous,
specials such as crab platter or sea bass are available
and it's possible to top it off with typically English
desserts like spotted dick or treacle tart – just don't
go swimming straight afterwards.

TORQUAY

The Blue Walnut ★

*14 Walnut Road, Torquay, TQ2 6HS (01803
605995/www.thebluewalnut.co.uk). Summer*
Meals served 9.30am-2.30pm daily. *Dinner*
served 6-8.30pm Mon-Sat. *Winter* **Meals served**
11am-2pm daily. **Main courses** £4.95-£10.95.
No credit cards.
If it's top-dollar gourmet meals you're after then
you've come to the wrong place, but as a café there
are few better in Torquay. Fry-ups, omelettes,
sandwiches and great cappuccino all play their part,
but the food isn't the main attraction. The Blue
Walnut is the only fully licensed café with original
nickelodeon in the UK – for non-cinephiles that
translates as a working cinema with seats for 25
people in the back. It's a nostalgic treat and a perfect
antidote to multiplex monotony. Classic films from
the 1940s to the 1960s (think *Casablanca* and
Vertigo) are a speciality – Wednesday matinées
come complete with a cream tea, while weekend
evening shows take in dinner too. A genuine one-off.

Mulberry House

*1 Scarborough Road, Torquay, TQ2 5UJ (01803
213639).* **Lunch served** noon-2pm Fri-Sun.
Dinner served from 7.30pm Wed-Sat. **Main
courses** £9.50-£12.50. **No credit cards**.
You couldn't ask for a more genial host than
Mulberry House owner Lesley Cooper, who attends
to both the cooking and front-of-house duties. At
lunch the dining room has a tearoom feel to it,
transformed by night into a romantic, candlelit space
far from the neon bustle of Torquay centre. Food,

usually a choice of three dishes per course, is set out daily on a blackboard and has a home-cooked, farmhouse feel. Witness our starters of Greek salad with fresh herbs and pungent feta, along with a mutton broth that packed a meaty punch, and mains of roast lamb with a rowan and coriander jelly or a saucy fish pie.

No.7 Fish Bistro

7 Beacon Terrace, Inner Harbour, Torquay, TQ1 2BH (01803 295055). **Lunch served** 12.45-1.45pm Wed-Sat. **Dinner served** *winter* 7-9.45pm Tue-Sat; *summer* 7-9.45pm daily. **Main courses** £9.95-£22. **Credit** AmEx, MC, V.

Overlooking Torquay's harbourside, No.7 Fish Bistro is everything you'd expect from a fish restaurant. Ubiquitous marine-themed objects hang from the walls. Blackboards advertise daily specials including lobster and oysters, a range of freshly landed fish and more exotic delicacies such as tempura. A good selection of white wines is available by the glass as well as the bottle. Daily specials are presented firm and gleaming for selection, then served simply – crab thermidor to start, then lemon sole done in lemon and garlic or a sturdy monkfish fillet. Strawberry ice-cream is advertised as 'the best ever' – you decide. Service is smart and efficient, and the setting warm, hospitable and glowing with an almost cinematic glamour.

TOTNES

Rumour Wine Bar

30 High Street, Totnes, TQ9 5RY (01803 864682). **Lunch served** noon-3pm Mon-Sat. **Dinner served** 6-10pm daily. **Main courses** £9.50-£14.95. **Credit** AmEx, MC, V.

An easygoing Totnes perennial, Rumour is a popular, very often packed wine bar that makes the most of local produce in hearty dishes with a French feel. The menu changes daily but you should expect starters like divine fish soup of sea bass, salmon, brill and mussels finished with tarragon; mains might include roast Gressingham duck breast with oriental spices. This is great informal dining with prices that won't take the breath away. The bar area and restaurant jostle for attention at peak times, which makes for a lively, if a little smoky, atmosphere where the drink is definitely as important as the food. A good wine list is rivalled for quaffability by the selection of Belgian beers – a welcome treat round these parts.

Willow Restaurant ★

87 High Street, Totnes, T29 5PB (01803 862605). **Meals served** 10am-5pm Mon-Sat. **Dinner served** 7-9.30pm Wed, Fri, Sat; Thur during school hols. **Main courses** £5.90-£7.50. **No credit cards**.

If you're in Totnes for the craft shops and crystals, then you'll probably want to dine in Willow. That's not to belittle the place: when on form, they serve some of the area's best vegetarian (GM-free and mainly organic) food. It's self-service from a counter

at lunchtime, but the salads are wonderfully fresh and the various dishes of the day (quiches, pulses, lovely soups, pies) are done with aplomb. Creamy puddings and thick-slabbed cakes complete the scene. All this, along with fruit teas and organic wine and beer, is served in a couple of very pleasant, bright yellow rooms, decorated with local art. Children are lavished with toys, while in the summer the small but lush garden is the perfect spot for a cappuccino. In the evenings, the food's the same, but there's table service: Wednesday night is devoted to Indian cooking; on Fridays you'll be treated to musical performances.

Wills Restaurant

2-3 The Plains, Totnes, TQ9 5DR (0800 056 3006/ www.eladdio.com). **Lunch served** noon-2.30pm Tue-Sun. **Dinner served** 7-9.30pm Tue-Sat. **Main courses** *café* £6.95-£14.95; *restaurant* £14.95-£22. **Credit** MC, V.

Located at the birthplace of 19th-century explorer William Wills, this restaurant is well regarded in the surrounding area. Dining upstairs in this Georgian townhouse has the feel of being present at an exclusive dinner party, with a menu based on a classic French premise but with more exotic ingredients brought into play in dishes like sea bass with a lime leaves cream sauce. The café downstairs is a recent addition, offering more accessible bistro dishes both at lunch and dinner. A typical main course might be poached smoked haddock with a risotto of chorizo, mussels and prawns. Service may be a little more brusque down here but the food is no less appealing.

VIRGINSTOW

Percy's

Coombeshead Estate, Virginstow, EX21 5EA (01409 211236/www.percys.co.uk). **Lunch served** noon-2pm, **dinner served** 7-9pm daily. **Set lunch** £20 2 courses. **Set dinner** £37.50 3 courses. **Credit** AmEx, MC, V.

Percy's is an exclusive, contemporary organic country restaurant with bijou bungalow rooms on a private estate in the middle of Devon. Booking is essential. Tina Bricknell-Webb's cooking concentrates on getting the best out of wholesome local ingredients. Starters might include seared Cornish scallops and squid with a dill, honey and mustard dressing or grilled aubergine, marrow, pepper and goat's cheese. Mains also always feature a vegetarian option, alongside the likes of oven-roast home-reared lamb in a garlic and lavender jus or steamed turbot with spinach tagliatelle, followed by some fine West Country cheeses. The welcome, as we found, isn't necessarily a warm one.

Also in the area

Brazz 10-12 Palace Gate, Exeter, EX1 1JA (01392 252525); **Spice Bazaar** St Saviours Square, Dartmouth, TQ6 9DH (01803 832285).

Dorset

South West

BOURNEMOUTH

Bistro on the Beach

Solent Promenade, Southbourne, Bournemouth, BH6 4BE (01202 431473). **Dinner served** 6.30-10pm Wed-Sat. **Meals served** *June-Sept* 9am-4.30pm daily; *Oct-May* 9am-4pm Sat, Sun. **Main courses** £10.50-£18.95. **Set dinner** £16.95 2 courses, £18.95 3 courses. **Credit** AmEx, MC, V.

The name doesn't lie: this Bournemouth restaurant sits precariously close to the sea – at high tide the waves almost lap at your feet. The interior, fittingly, has been decked out in aquamarine colours and the exquisite blackboard menu is heavy on the fresh fish: a lovely smoked eel dish to start, served with asparagus, pecorino and garlic croustades, or, for the main course, a perfect whole grilled Dover sole with parsley butter. But landlubbers needn't fear – there are plenty of non-piscine treats, such as roasted cherry tomato risotto with parmesan crisps and balsamic dressing. We didn't have room for puddings, which sounded delectable: rhubarb and grenadine crumble with ginger crème anglaise.

CH2

37 Exeter Road, Bournemouth, BH2 5AF (01202 296296/www.customhouse.co.uk). **Lunch served** noon-2.30pm, **dinner served** 6-10.30pm Tue-Sat. **Main courses** £5.50-£18.25. **Credit** AmEx, MC, V.

They say the new Bournemouth is young, hip and happening, and CH2 must have been created with that in mind. The decorators have been studying their style mags: purple formica tables, weird pop art and industrial-chic flourishes abound. The menu is equally up to date, although the food doesn't always live up to expectations. Starters included fanned melon served with Italian cured ham and a pawpaw dressing, and spinach, red onion and ricotta tartlet. Mains ranged from steaks to pasta dishes, but you're best sticking to the thin-crust pizzas, which come with combinations such as goat's cheese, chicken, mango, pine nuts and pesto. Puddings were disappointing, but we're told the menu is being revamped. Custom House (*see p138*) is a branch.

Chef Hong Kong

150-152 Old Christchurch Road, Bournemouth, BH1 1NL (01202 316996). **Lunch served** noon-3.30pm, **dinner served** 6-11.30pm Mon-Sat. **Meals served** noon-11.30pm Sun. **Main courses** £6-£12. **Set meals** £15.50-£23 3 courses. **Credit** AmEx, MC, V.

Oldies go up the road to the posh Mandarin for their Chinese splurge, but this cheeky young upstart is forever crammed with Chinese people – always a good sign. The decor is simple and smart, with wooden floors, cheerful yellow walls and a bit of oriental art. And the Chinese pop music is enjoyably naff. But the main attraction is the dim sum menu, with minced prawn in bean curd pastry, meat croquettes, egg custard tarts and juicy dumplings galore, plus the odd surprise such as grilled turnip paste or Vietnamese pancake rolls. Leave room for the banana toffee sticky balls for dessert.

Chez Fred ★

10 Seamoor Road, Westbourne, Bournemouth, BH4 9AN (01202 761023/www.chezfred.co.uk). **Lunch served** 11.30am-2pm Mon-Fri; 11.30-2.30pm Sat. **Dinner served** 5-10pm Mon-Sat; 5-9.30pm Sun. **Main courses** £4.90-£7.95. **Credit** MC, V.

Chez Fred, a takeaway with adjoining restaurant, aims to be a cut above the average chippie and it succeeds with bells on. An out of season, midweek lunchtime saw the place packed with retired folk, and although no children were there, the 'Sprat Pack' menu suggests they are welcome. Signed celebrity photographs cover the walls and, while fussy, the decor has a cosy feel. Daily specials at £4.75 include tea or coffee and half a baguette. The fish is cooked to order, arriving in a crispy batter, light to the bite and delicious. In a nod to healthy eating, a generous salad (with a choice of three dressings) can be ordered instead of chips; puddings include almond flan, bread and butter pudding, lime and pecan pie. Wine and beer are available and service is efficient.

Coriander ★

22 Richmond Hill, Bournemouth, BH2 6EJ (01202 552202/www.coriander-restaurant.co.uk). **Meals served** noon-10.30pm Mon-Thur, Sun; noon-11pm Fri, Sat. **Main courses** £6.50-£11. **Set lunch** (noon-5pm) £7.50 2 courses, £10 3 courses. **Set dinner** £11.50 2 courses. **Credit** AmEx, MC, V.

This friendly, funky Mexican is a refreshing alternative to Bournemouth's deluge of wannabe style restaurants. Children are made welcome (there are high chairs and children's menus). The interior is rustic and playful, with sombreros and Mexican blankets hanging from the walls, colourful tiles, and cacti in the corner. The food is just as much fun, especially after one or two Margaritas, conveniently served in jugs. Dishes are well-prepared and include enchiladas, quesadillas, burritos and tacos. Puddings – raspberry pavlova, lime cheesecake – don't really stray south of the border.

Westbeach

Pier Approach, Bournemouth, BH2 5AA (01202 587785/www.west-beach.co.uk). **Meals served** 9am-10pm daily. **Main courses** £10-£25. **Set lunch** £13.95 2 courses, £15.95 3 courses. **Set dinner** £19.95 2 courses, £22.95 3 courses. **Credit** AmEx, DC, MC, V.

This modern promenade café/restaurant hosts jazz musicians on Thursday evenings and is a reliable meeting place for a whole range of people throughout the week. Families with very small children enjoy a leisurely lunch; later on trendy young singles come to linger and be seen. Dressed-up fish dishes appear as daily specials but most people opt for the set two or three courses, which might include red onion and celery seed tart, chicken and spring onion risotto or cured salmon with cucumber salsa. Puddings, such as banana tart with coconut ice-cream or Valrhona chocolate crème brûlée, are good, and a selection of farmhouse cheese is also available. Service is friendly and helpful, but it can creak a bit when things are particularly busy.

BRIDPORT

The Riverside

West Bay, Bridport, DT6 4EZ (01308 422011/ www.dorset-seafood-restaurant.co.uk). **Lunch served** *Feb-Dec* noon-2.30pm Tue-Sun. **Dinner served** *Feb-Dec* 6.30-8.30pm Tue-Thur; 6.30-9pm Fri, Sat. **Main courses** £12-£20. **Credit** MC, V.

Overlooking the harbour and more attractive inside than out, this unpretentious, conservatory-like restaurant offers a good choice of fish, plus a few meat dishes. The cheerful service and simple blue and yellow decor create a welcoming impression and the food, while not particularly ambitious, is mostly freshly cooked, honest stuff. Fish soup with hot chilli rouille, brill with crispy spinach and sorrel sauce, and confit of duck with Chinese five spice and honey glaze were all good. The pastry chef's unusual puddings were difficult to choose between – roast rhubarb shortbread with crème pâtissière, lemongrass coeurs à la crème and sticky gingerbread with stem ginger ice-cream were delicious. The Riverside can be very busy, particularly over sunny weekends (children are very welcome), so it is imperative to book.

BURTON BRADSTOCK

The Anchor Inn

Burton Bradstock, DT6 4QF (01308 897228). **Lunch served** noon-2pm, **dinner served** 6.30-9pm daily. **Main courses** £12.95-£28. **Credit** MC, V.

Friendly service and a large choice of fish and shellfish dishes promise much in this popular pub but alas the food, although fresh, is overly fussed with. It is also not cheap (£50 for the shellfish platter for two and £28 for surf & turf – lobster and fillet steak). At these prices you don't expect bottled salad dressings and greasy garlic bread. That said, the menu caters for vegetarians and carnivores as well as for fish fans, and provided the chef is asked to go easy with his deep fat fryer and his Thai sauces, it should be possible to have a meal where the quality of the ingredients speaks for itself. The small wine list is mainly from the New World.

CERNE ABBAS

The Royal Oak

23 Long Street, Cerne Abbas, DT2 7JG (01300 341797). **Lunch served** noon-2pm daily. **Dinner served** 7-9.30pm Mon-Sat; 7-9pm Sun. **Main courses** £7.75-£15.75. **Credit** MC, V.

This child-friendly free house (c1540) is bustling and cosy. Small tables fill the low-ceilinged bar and there is a courtyard with heating for stalwarts. A flagstone passageway and ancient divided seating areas lead into the softly-lit main bar where hundreds of patterned tea cups hang from its beams. Local ingredients are used where possible and additive-free steaks come from accredited UK and Scots herds. Rabbit casserole, trout fillets with creamy basil sauce, steak and blue vinney pie, and spinach-filled baked onion feature as main courses while treacle tart and chocolate fudge cake are among the puddings. The limited wine list includes a Mexican petite sirah at £13.50 and there's a range of real ales. The cooking is unremarkable but the friendly atmosphere and caring service ensures that you leave feeling spoilt.

CHETTLE

Castleman Hotel & Restaurant

Chettle, DT11 8DB (01258 830096/ www.castlemanhotel.co.uk). **Lunch served** noon-2pm Sun. **Dinner served** 7-9.30pm daily. **Main courses** £8.50-£15.50. **Credit** MC, V.

Originally a bailiff's house and then a dower house in the 1730s, this comfortable hotel and restaurant offers a pleasing backdrop for cooking that is deceptively simple yet full of integrity. Meat has a reliable pedigree, being supplied by a renowned local butcher; other local produce, such as Denhay ham, Chettle strawberries and Dorset cheese, makes regular appearances. Prices remain reasonable, however. Starters might include a soup of crab, smoked haddock and saffron, while a grilled veal chop with tarragon butter might feature as a main. There's a good selection of half bottles on the wine list. Conventional middle-aged types outnumber young diners, but the warm welcome and the attentive service make this an increasingly popular haunt, particularly at weekends in the evening.

CORSCOMBE

The Fox Inn

Corscombe, DT2 0NS (01935 891330/ www.fox-inn.co.uk). **Lunch served** noon-2pm daily. **Dinner served** 7-9.30pm Mon-Thur, Sun; 7-9.30pm Fri, Sat. **Main courses** £8.25-£17.95. **Credit** AmEx, MC, V.

This archetypal country pub is serious about food. Fish soup, wild mushroom risotto and gratin of crab are listed among the starters, and fresh fish, loin of lamb and fillet of venison among the main courses; puddings at £3.50 include vanilla cream terrine and rich chocolate torte. Aproned local ladies serve the food cheerfully and in double-quick time, but perhaps too speedily if you want to linger. A sunny conservatory with one huge scrubbed table is set aside for smokers while the bar, with its smooth slate counter and log fire, separates the two non-smoking dining rooms. These three rooms are rather dark so, despite the pictures and memorabilia dotted about, the scene resembles *Babette's Feast*. There's an extensive wine list (plus one for fine wine), and London Pride and Exmoor Ale on hand pump. Look out too for own-made sloe gin and damson vodka.

DONHEAD ST ANDREW

The Forester ★

Lower Street, Donhead St Andrew, SP7 9EE (01747 828038). **Lunch served** noon-2pm daily. **Dinner served** 7-9.30pm Mon-Sat; 7-9pm Sun. **Main courses** £7.95-£15.95. **Credit** MC, V.
This welcoming, busy country pub is worth the detour. A huge blackboard serves as the menu and you make your choice before going through to a comfortable dining room where starched napkins sit on mismatched tables – though if you haven't booked, you're relegated to tables in the bar. An open fire separates the two rooms and the decor is firmly 'Country Pub'. Starters include seared foie gras with black pudding, and smoked pigeon salad, while rabbit rolled in Parma ham, venison steak and mash, and herbed risotto are among the mains. Puddings (£4.25) include apple and prune strudel and chocolate brûlée. Service is efficient, there is a wide-ranging, reasonably-priced wine list and Bass and Adnams are on tap. Food this good, together with a buzzy atmosphere, are rarely found under the same roof in deepest Dorset.

EVERSHOT

The Terrace

Summer Lodge Hotel, Evershot, DR2 0JR (01935 83424/www.summerlodgehotel.com). **Lunch served** noon-1.45pm, **tea served** 4-5.30pm, **dinner served** 7-9pm daily. **Main courses** £22-£28. **Set lunch** £13.50 2 courses, £16.50 3 courses. **Set dinner** £39.50 3 courses. **Credit** AmEx, DC, MC, V.
For an experience, not just a meal, you can do no better than visit Summer Lodge. This large Victorian country house hotel – designed in part by Thomas Hardy – exudes an air of comfortable elegance without being stuffy and although the experience will not come cheap, it is worth it. Meals are ordered from squashy sofas in a flower-filled drawing room – where glorious old-fashioned afternoon teas (£7.50) are taken – and eaten in a room overlooking the gardens. While not overly formal, there is an air of seriousness in the dining room and rightly so, for the food is exceptional. With the emphasis on seasonal ingredients dishes, such as terrine of roasted chicken enriched with foie gras and steamed halibut with mussels in a saffron cream

sauce, burst with flavour. Presentation is innovative yet restrained. As you would expect from a place of this calibre, there is an extensive wine list.

FARNHAM

The Museum Inn

Farnham, DT11 8DE (01725 516261/ www.museuminn.co.uk). Pub **Lunch served** noon-2pm, **dinner served** 7-9.30pm daily. *Restaurant* **Lunch served** noon-2pm Fri-Sun. **Dinner served** 7-9.30pm Fri, Sat. **Main courses** £9-£20. **Credit** DC, MC, V.
Spacious, comfortable and pleasing to look at, the revamped, upmarket Museum Inn is deservedly popular with locals and visitors. You can choose one course alone or have a full-blown meal at one of the small tables in the bar, the conservatory or in the restaurant (the same menu is served throughout), and there is a good choice of wine by the glass or bottle. Dishes might include terrine of quail, risotto of wild rocket or salmon with lobster sauce, while there are puds such as spotted dick with custard and cinnamon, or treacle tart with vanilla ice-cream. Cheerful young girls do their best to keep pace with orders but the demand is sometimes more than they can cope with.

FONTMELL MAGNA

The Crown

Fontmell Magna, SP7 0PA (01747 812222/ 811441). **Lunch served** 11am-3pm Tue-Sat; noon-5pm Sun. **Dinner served** 6-10.30pm Tue, Wed; 6-11pm Thur-Sat. **Main courses** £8.95-£15.95. **Credit** AmEx, MC, V.
The owners of the Old Coach House in Fontmell Magna still run their popular shop with salad bar, but they have now moved their chef and restaurant to the Crown public house across the road. The small bar is warm and welcoming, and the main dining room is light and pleasingly furnished, with country-style touches. The daily specials usually include several choices of fish. The menu proper boasts a locally sourced organic section, as well as vegetarian, fish and meat dishes, and prices include 'appropriate accompaniments' – that is, several vegetables. The good-value wine list, though small, caters for most tastes. You can even stay the night in the B&B.

GILLINGHAM

Stock Hill Country House Hotel

Stock Hill, Gillingham, SP8 5NR (01747 823626/ www.stockhillhouse.co.uk). **Lunch served** 12.30-1.30pm Tue-Fri, Sun. **Dinner served** 7.30-8.45pm daily. **Set lunch** £25 3 courses. **Set dinner** £35 3 courses. **Credit** MC, V.
If you enjoy completely OTT decor and you feel like a fine meal, then Stock Hill House is the place for you. Floor-to-ceiling mirrors reflect the idiosyncratic antiques stuffed into this 1830s country house, and

The Fox Inn. See p135.

the sense that you are in some eccentric prince's Bavarian hideaway is reinforced by the hushed and reverent atmosphere. Young German girls serve drinks and tasty nibbles while you choose from the unusual starters and main courses. The food echoes chef Peter Hauser's Austrian background, and dishes such as sweet dill herring with fennel or locally sourced meat with a spicy dumpling are confidently presented. A perfectionist with flair is clearly the driving force in the kitchen. The wine list contains about 100 predominantly French wines, including the odd half bottle.

MERLEY

Les Bouviers ★

Oakley Hill, Merley, BH21 1RJ (01202 889555/ www.lesbouviers.co.uk). **Lunch served** noon-2pm Tue-Fri, Sun. **Dinner served** 7-10pm Tue-Sat. **Tea served** *May-Sept* 3.30-5.30pm Tue-Fri. **Main courses** £22-£27.50. **Set lunch** £11.95 2 courses, £14.95 3 courses incl coffee. **Set dinner** £25.95 4 courses incl coffee. **Set meal** £29 2 courses, £35 3 courses. **Credit** AmEx, DC, MC, V.

Unpropitiously situated on a main road outside Wimborne, Les Bouviers offers ambitious and accomplished food. The chef trained in France and worked at Le Manoir aux quat' Saisons, which partly explains it, but his own commitment and flair are also evident. Once you have negotiated

the irritatingly complicated menu, you receive perfection on a plate in the form of, say, duck liver parfait so fine it could be foie gras, escalope of salmon with sautéed broad beans and a spring onion and saffron sauce, and warmed spotted dick with amaretto anglaise. All kinds of extras are included: pre-dinner nibbles, a cup of intense vegetable essence, a palate-cleansing sorbet, and petits fours. The 36-page wine list has helpful notes on the vintages for Bordeaux and Burgundy, and a good selection of half bottles. An unsung gem.

POOLE

City Bay Views

The Marina, 23 West Quay Road, Poole, BH15 1HQ (01202 675833). **Lunch served** noon-2pm, **dinner served** 6-11pm daily. **Main courses** £5.75-£27.50. **Set dinner** £19.95-£29.95 4 courses. **Credit** AmEx, DC, MC, V.

This large, first floor Chinese restaurant sits in a business development on the edge of town. It's flash, with statues, concrete fish ponds and canned music. Service is professional, the napiery immaculate and although the food is only just above average, the place is always busy in the evenings. Lucky diners are the ones who bag the tables overlooking the boatyard and harbour, and watch the coastguards' vessels and fishing boats bob while they peruse the menu, which runs to several pages. The more interesting options include salt and crispy squid, and baked fresh crab, and there are four set feasts – lobster, Cantonese, vegetarian and Provincial (Peking and Szechuan dishes). Warm saké is available, alongside wine and beer.

Custom House

Poole Quay, Poole, BH15 1HP (01202 676767/ www.customhouse.co.uk). **Lunch served** 10.30am-2pm, **dinner served** 6.30-9pm daily. **Main courses** £4.50-£12. **Set lunch** £14.75 3 courses. **Set dinner** £19.75 2 courses. **Credit** AmEx, DC, MC, V.

This waterfront Georgian building is featured on all the Poole postcards, and now it houses a restaurant that is just as well known. The minimalist, first-floor space is all blonde wood floors, Rennie Mackintosh-style chairs and Modernist art. By and large, the food lives up to the stylish surroundings. Starters include gravadlax with dill, mustard and horseradish sauce on a salad of beetroot, or steamed local mussels in a Thai curry sauce. Main courses, such as Dorset shank of lamb with caramelised shallots and rosemary jus, or fillet steak with lime butter and prawns, are generous in portion and well prepared. The candlelight and romantic views of Poole Harbour made the meal all the more palatable.

The Mansion House ★

The Mansion House Hotel, Thames Street, Poole, BH15 1JN (01202 685666/www.themansionhouse. co.uk). **Lunch served** noon-2pm Mon-Fri, Sun. **Dinner served** 7-9.30pm Mon-Sat. **Set lunch** £17 2 courses, £19.25 3 courses. **Set dinner** £20.95 2 courses, £26.45 3 courses. **Credit** AmEx, DC, MC, V.

Poole's classiest hotel also houses its best restaurant. The swish main restaurant is a supremely elegant space, with cherrywood panelling, palm trees and a grand piano, while the romantic bistro – open to hotel residents only – is a cosy spot with exposed brickwork and a huge copper hearth. Both share the same kitchen. For starters, celeriac and apple soup was sublime, as was pan-fried crab cake with sunblushed tomato and a mustard butter sauce; main courses included a delicious piece of salmon with sweet onions, mushroom and red wine sauce. A fillet of beef on another table, with a red-wine shallot sauce and horseradish dauphine potato, looked equally mouth-watering. A sinfully good crème brûlée rounded off an excellent meal.

La Roche

The Haven Hotel, Banks Road, Sandbanks, Poole, BH13 7QL (01202 707333/www.havenhotel.co.uk). **Lunch served** *April-Sept* noon-2.30pm daily. *Oct-March* noon-2.30pm Tue-Sat. **Dinner served** 7-9pm Mon-Thur, Sun; 7-9.30pm Fri, Sat. **Main courses** £14.50-£18.50. **Credit** AmEx, DC, MC, V.

Some of the trendier restaurants around here are a case of style over substance: hotel restaurants are often a better bet for a good meal, and the Haven has a sterling reputation. The hotel's main dining room (the Seaview) has won several awards, but it's a bit starchy. For a more stylish experience, try the

adjoining brasserie, a long art deco room with views of Poole Bay. Starters might include own-cured gravadlax served with julienne of pickled cucumber and mint, or scallops on spinach with lime and coriander jus. For mains, pan-fried strips of corn-fed lemon and lime marinated chicken (£13.50) and Pacific halibut pavé topped with goat's cheese, black olives and chorizo (£14.95) are expertly prepared.

Storm

16 High Street, Poole, BH15 1BP (01202 674970/ www.stormfish.co.uk). **Dinner served** 6.30-10pm daily. **Main courses** £12-£20. **Set dinner** £20 2 courses, £26.95 3 courses. **Credit** MC, V.

Poole's newest fish restaurant is a rustic, romantic spot, with rough-hewn wood floors, candlelight and David Gray playing softly in the background. The chef is a fisherman, so everything is freshly caught and simply prepared. Starters include cracked Dorset coast crab with saffron aïoli, and a pleasantly peppery vegetable and fish soup with crème fraîche. For mains, roast cod was cooked with a Welsh rarebit crust on sweet potato mash, and the char-grilled whole royal bream was tender and delicate. By the time we finished wolfing down the wonderful own-made herbed bread – served with olive oil for dipping – we had no room for Cointreau and walnut truffle mousse or rich chocolate pot. We'll be back.

Salterns Waterside Restaurant

Salterns Harbourside Hotel, 38 Salterns Way, Lilliput, Poole, BH14 8JR (01202 707321/ www.salternsharbourside.com). **Lunch served** 1-3pm Sun. **Dinner served** 7.30-9pm daily. **Main courses** £12-£18. **Set lunch** £17.50 3 courses Sun. **Credit** AmEx, DC, MC, V.

This bright restaurant boasts one of Poole's best dining locations and has plenty of outdoor seating in the summer. The cooking is decent, too. You can choose from fresh local seafood – steamed mussels in a white wine and garlic sauce to start, say, or a main course of pan-fried sea bass served with spring vegetables, lemon and vanilla butter and cherry tomatoes . There are also trad meat dishes such as prime fillet steak and pork loin in Somerset cider sauce. For more casual fare – pasta, curries, bangers and mash – try the light, airy bar next door.

SHAFTESBURY

La Fleur de Lys

25 Salisbury Street, Shaftesbury, SP7 8EL (01747 853717/www.lafleurdelys.co.uk). **Lunch served** 12.30-2.30pm Tue-Sun. **Dinner served** 7-10pm Mon-Sat. **Main courses** £16.50-£20. **Set dinner** £21.50 2 courses, £26.50 3 courses. **Credit** AmEx, MC, V.

Good smells greet you as you sip your pre-dinner drinks in the small lobby and choose from the menu before climbing the steep and narrow stairs to the first-floor restaurant. The cooking is ambitious and intricate. The set menu offers seasonal dishes such as roast scallop tart with asparagus and sorrel sauce, while veal sweetbreads, lobster mousse, saddle of roe venison or leek soufflé feature among the à la carte choices. Puddings such as a dark chocolate box filled with almond and amaretto ice-cream are wickedly intense; there's a selection of cheeses too. The wine list has an interesting and comprehensive selection, and there are two pages of half-bottles.

STUDLAND

Shell Bay Seafood Restaurant

Ferry Road, Studland, BH19 3BA (01929 450363). **Lunch served** *Apr-Sept* noon-3pm daily. *Oct-Mar* noon-3pm Sun. **Dinner served** *Apr-Sept* 6-9pm daily. *Oct-Mar* 6-9pm Thur-Sat. **Main courses** £13-£30. **Credit** AmEx, MC, V.

The view from Shell Bay resembles a jigsaw puzzle with cross-Channel ferries, fishing boats, cruisers and yachts passing back and forth. The restaurant, which sits on a spit of sand between Poole Harbour and the open sea, has a few tables outside. There is also an informal bar/bistro in the summer for wet yachtsmen or people with young children (after 8pm, only children over 12 years are allowed). The restaurant menu ranges from oysters and fruits de mer to salt-crusted sea bass or a medley of wild salmon, sea trout, scallops and monkfish in lobster sauce, while the bistro limits itself to five simple dishes, such as feta cheese salad or a pint of prawns and salad, dishes for children and a very small pudding menu. This is a popular haunt for town dwellers a ferry ride away, walkers and yachtsmen.

STURMINSTER NEWTON

Plumber Manor

Sturminster Newton, DT10 2AF (01258 472507/ www.plumbermanor.com). **Lunch served** 1-2pm Sun. **Dinner served** 7.30-9pm daily. **Set lunch** £19.50 3 courses. **Set dinner** £25 3 courses. **Credit** AmEx, DC, MC, V.

A restaurant (with bedrooms) with a decent reputation but a pretty stuffy style. Having said that, there's something comforting about the solid, unchanging restaurant which attracts local farmers and businessmen who seem happy enough, and the 'family measure' gin and tonics before dinner help put aside misgivings about the old-style atmosphere. The food is generally dependable fare, buttered, creamed and generous. The à la carte menu can contain aberrations like crab mousse with lobster and Thai curry sauce or scallops wrapped in bacon served with bubble and squeak, but it generally confines itself to more predictable offerings.

WEYMOUTH

Fish 'n' Fritz ★

9 Market Street, Weymouth, DT4 8DD (01305 766386/www.fishnfritz.co.uk). **Lunch served** noon-2pm Mon-Fri. **Dinner served** 5-9pm Tue-Fri. **Meals served** noon-9pm Sat. **Main courses** £3.35-£4.50. **Credit** MC, V.

On the same street corner for 24 years, this fish and chip shop is flanked, on one side, by a more recent, similarly decorated, licensed restaurant. Cream and green are the colours while the tables and chairs provide the welcome contrast of dark wood. Service is sprightly and polite, as the quality of the food merits. Cod, haddock, plaice, rock and skate wings, from good quality Norwegian, Icelandic and German sources predominate, though these days they're promoting scampi to try and take some of the pressure off the fish stocks. Along with chips there's a choice of pickles or mushy peas and the dessert menu contains sumptuous, additive-free ice-cream, a blackcurrant sorbet and refreshing lemon meringue soufflé. Wine weighs in at about £8 and a fish dinner for two £12.40.

Perry's Restaurant

4 Trinity Road, Weymouth, DT4 8TJ (01305 785799/www.perrysrestaurant.co.uk). **Lunch served** noon-2pm Tue-Fri, Sun. **Dinner served** *May-Aug* 7-9.30pm Tue-Fri, Sun; 7-10pm Sat. *Sept-Apr* 7-9.30pm Tue-Fri; 7-10pm Sat. **Main courses** £10.50-£22.50. **Credit** AmEx, MC, V.

Perry's sits on two floors of a tall Georgian building on Weymouth's old harbour front. The no-smoking front of the restaurant is uncluttered, light and spacious, and service is coolly efficient. Like the decor, the menu is simple and straightforward, and restraint in the cooking allows the flavours of the fresh ingredients to emerge. There's an emphasis on fish, perhaps not unsurprisingly, but spinach and mascarpone cannelloni might also feature, or fillet of beef with dauphinoise potatoes and cep sauce. Pudding fans will not be disappointed with such offerings as brioche bread and butter pudding or passion fruit brûlée.

WIMBORNE ST GILES

Wimborne St Giles Village Hall ★

Wimborne St Giles, BH21 5LX. **Tea served** *Mar-Oct* 3-5pm Sun, bank hol Mon. **No credit cards.**

These old-fashioned teas have become justly popular. They are served by keen local ladies in the village hall of unspoilt Wimborne St Giles; the money goes to charity. Dainty sandwiches and a choice of home-baked cakes (35p-£1.25) are piled on to assorted dining plates and accompanied by pots of tea. If the weather is fine you can sit at tables in the sunny garden, if not, you can eye the cakes from tables set out in the village hall. Enid Blyton and the coronation spring to mind as you sip your tea, reminding you of the days when plaster ducks were the thing and old ladies cycled slowly to evensong.

Also in the area

FishWorks Seafood Café 10 Church Street, Christchurch, BH23 1BW (01202 487000).

Somerset

BARWICK

Little Barwick House ★
Barwick, BA22 9TD (01935 423902/
www.littlebarwickhouse.co.uk). **Lunch served** noon-
2pm Wed-Sat; noon-1.30pm Sun. **Dinner served**
7-9.30pm Tue-Sat. **Main courses** (lunch) £15.75-
£18.50. **Set lunch** (Wed-Sat) £15.50 2 courses, £17.50
3 courses; (Sun) £19.50 3 courses. **Set dinner** £28.50
2 courses, £32.50 3 courses. **Credit** AmEx, MC, V.
Tucked away in the back lanes of Barwick, this
former Georgian dower house is difficult to find but
well worth the effort. A 'restaurant with rooms' is
how it describes itself, and certainly the comfortable
ambience with sofas and books feels more like a
home than a hotel. The food is confident, beautifully
presented and sourced from the West Country – a
terrine of local ham hock with caper mayonnaise
might feature among the starters while Cornish
turbot and sea bass, local beef fillet and pink-roasted
squab pigeon might be main courses. To follow, a
trio of raspberry puddings and iced rhubarb parfait
are seasonal offerings, while a selection of local
cheeses arrives with own-made bread, celery, apples
and grapes. Prices are fair, especially since pre-dinner
nibbles and after-dinner chocolates are included.

BATCOMBE

Three Horseshoes Inn
Batcombe, BA4 6HE (01749 850359/
www.thethreehorseshoesir.com). **Lunch served**
noon-2.30pm daily. **Dinner served** 7-9.30pm
Mon-Thur, Sun; 7-10pm Fri, Sat. **Main courses**
£9.95-£15.95. **Credit** MC, V.
Ostensibly a pub that does great restaurant food,
there are several eating areas here: a quasi-
restaurant, the bit around the bar and – on sunny
days – a sprawling garden (and children's play area).
The restaurant menu, lately revamped by new
ownership, is – perhaps unnecessarily – lavish and
isn't always value for money: calf's liver with bacon
and mash for £13.95 was good but not that good. The
bar menu is more rewarding: a gorgeous, creamy leek
and potato soup worthy of any Parisian brasserie
for an excellent £3.75 and a slightly less exciting
sausages and mash for £8.95. Service is rather
haphazard – more staff are needed at busy times.

BATH

Le Beaujolais
5 Chapel Row, Bath, BA1 1HN (01225 423417/
www.beaujolaisrestaurantbath.co.uk). **Lunch
served** noon-2.30pm Tue-Sat. **Dinner served**

6-10pm Mon-Thur; 6-10.30pm Fri-Sun. **Main
courses** £11.80-£17.80. **Credit** AmEx, DC, MC, V.
The small, burgundy-painted shop front exterior
opens out into a spacious back room with warm
yellow walls and hand-carved wooden lamps of a
naked woman with a giant snail (you might wish to
avoid the escargots). Authentic, flawless French
bistro cuisine predominates (foie gras, coq au vin,
pot au feu and so on), with a fish of the day, and
a somewhat nannyishly healthy dessert menu.
Peopled largely by middle-aged Francophiles and
well-heeled pensioners, it's a great spot to take your
in-laws. The portions can be small, and it's pricey –
you won't get much change out of £20 for a modest-
sized fillet steak with vegetables – but the charming
waiters, who teeter just on the respectable side of
flirtation, rapidly elicit forgiveness.

Bistro Papillon
2 Margaret's Buildings, Brock Street, Bath,
BA1 2LP (01225 310064). **Lunch served**
noon-2.15pm, **dinner served** 6.30-10pm Tue-Sat.
Main courses £9-£13. **Set lunch** £7.50 2 courses.
Credit MC, V.
Miraculously, given the tiny bedsit-sized kitchen
and skeleton staff, this charming Gallic enclave,
which has just celebrated its second birthday, offers
a hard-to-beat night out. Recalling the kind of 'menu-
touristique' vanguards of French catering, there's no
haute cuisine or snooty service here. The friendly,
efficient owner (originally from Limoges) treats his
mixed-bag of diners like guests at an informal dinner
in his own home – and for a great, mid-range
price. French classics from moules-frites to lamb's
liver dominate, the starters particularly strong –
the goat's cheese crostini with prosciutto comes
recommended. But with Edith Piaf on the stereo,
chequered tablecloths, flickering candles and
Normandy cider available by the glass the ambience
is as strong a reason to come as the food.

Café Retro
18 York Street, Bath, BA1 1LN (01225 339347).
Meals served 9am-5pm Mon-Sat; 10am-5pm Sun.
Dinner served 6-10pm Tue-Sat. **Main courses**
£6-£11. **Credit** AmEx, MC, V.
Don't hurry past because you think the crowded
boho coffee joint downstairs looks unsuitable for
serious noshing – upstairs at Café Retro hides a
grown-up, spacious café-restaurant with the soul
of… well, the crowded boho coffee joint downstairs
which shares its menu and staff. Pick and mix from
tapas, snacks like sandwiches and burgers, or
hunker down for the full nine yards, which could
cover smoked salmon and roquefort toasts, steak in
red wine and shallot juice, or apple frangipane.

Vegetarian options are plentiful. Grab a window seat for shoulder-level geraniums and a view towards Parade Gardens, and don't mind the chirpy waiting staff gassing away as though you were a long-lost friend – they're simply as happy to be here as you.

Demuths

2 North Parade Passage, off Abbey Green, Bath, BA1 1NX (01225 446059). **Breakfast served** 10-11.30am, **lunch served** noon-3.30pm, **dinner served** 6-9.30pm daily. **Main courses** £10-£13. **Credit** MC, V.

Demuths has been dedicating itself to innovative vegetarian and vegan food for some 15 years now, and is showing no signs of fatigue. On the contrary, its combination of bold, clashing decor and fresh, vibrant food seems as popular as ever. Inspiration comes from far and wide, with dishes like Lebanese wrap, southern Indian mallung and cajun rice and beans, as well as close to home, with a local Bath soft cheese wrap. The entirely organic wine list is an unusual find. Demuths lets out its culinary secrets with vegetarian cookery courses, each specialising in a different type of cuisine, such as Mexican and Latin American or Mediterranean.

Green Park Brasserie & Bar

Green Park Station, Green Park Road, Bath, BA1 1JB (01225 338565/www.greenparkbrasserie.com). **Lunch served** noon-2.15pm Tue-Sun. **Dinner served** 6-10pm Mon-Sat. **Main courses** £10.95-£15.95. **Set lunch** £8.50 2 courses, £9.50 3 courses. **Set dinner** £13.95 2 courses, £15.95 3 courses. **Credit** AmEx, MC, V.

Located in a disused neo-classical railway station, the Green Park Brasserie has all bases covered – be it a coffee and cake or a three-course lunch. It therefore heaves with a cross-section of the population from clubbers to pensioners. The menu is well-meaningly ambitious for what is essentially a glammed-up Café Rouge-type spot, and scores highly for meals like roast duck breast with sweet orange sauce. However the execution can sometimes flag – the Caesar salad, and some fish dishes, for example, are best avoided. Jazz bands blare merrily out in the evenings from Monday to Saturday, and at Sunday lunchtimes. The front patio gets fumey thanks to the crossroads outside, but the area out back is spacious, and excellent for buggies or restless kids.

The Hole in the Wall

16 George Street, Bath, BA1 2EH (01225 425242). **Lunch served** noon-2pm Mon-Sat. **Dinner served** 6-9.30pm Mon-Thur; 6-10pm Fri, Sat. **Main courses** £13-£17.50. **Set lunch** £12.50 2 courses, £17.25 3 courses. **Credit** AmEx, MC, V.

The Hole in the Wall's stuffy reputation is more to do with its longevity, and the age of the average customer, than its jolly staff or its modern takes on classic Brit cuisine. It makes innovative use of seasonal produce – witness the asparagus, lemon and spinach soup. It also neatly balances delicate and earthy flavours – as in tuna with slow-roasted

tomatoes and artichokes. The vegetarian options are refreshingly imaginative. Rustic, dark varnished tables and Van Gogh chairs are arranged throughout flagstoned, spacious non-smoking and smoking areas, with plaid banquettes pressed up against chocolate and cream paintwork. The two-course lunch at £12.50 is served without the remotest pressure to order extras and service is as sweet as the desserts.

The Hop Pole

7 Albion Buildings, Upper Bristol Road, Bath, BA1 3AR (01225 446327). **Lunch served** noon-2pm Tue-Sat; noon-3pm Sun. **Dinner served** 6-9pm Tue-Sat; 7-9pm Sun. **Main courses** £7.95-£15.95. **Credit** MC, V.

Recent darling of the broadsheets – to rousing hurrahs from its local fan-base – Barry Wallace and Elaine Dennehy's pub-restaurant has long been one of Bath's best-kept secrets. Lunches and dinners are available either in the dark, wood-panelled pub or in the airier, more relaxed basement restaurant and are executed with a gourmand's passion – unfussy, generous and hearty, with a religious zeal for reviving old-fashioned dishes. Go easy on the starters – mouthwatering though the piquillo peppers or crispy whitebait are – if you're aiming for a man-sized main such as the braised oxtail or pigeon breast with haggis, followed by a comfort pudding. The sole downside is the schlep back into town afterwards – although this may prove beneficial, given the portions.

Moody Goose ★

7A Kingsmead Square, Bath, BA1 2BA (01225 466688/www.moody-goose.com). **Lunch served** noon-1.30pm, **dinner served** 6-9.30pm Mon-Sat. **Main courses** £18-£19.50. **Set lunch** £17.50 3 courses. **Set dinner** £25 3 courses. **Credit** AmEx, DC, MC, V.

The modern British fare served in this basement-level restaurant is widely considered to be some of the finest food in Bath. Fresh, locally sourced British ingredients are used to craft aesthetically pleasing dishes, often with a whiff of France, such as Cornish lobster with truffle oil and quails' eggs or rump of lamb with pine kernel crust and ratatouille. Make sure you leave room for tantalising desserts such as vanilla and pear bavarois. The set menus are great value for money, but going à la carte for dinner can leave a sting. Waiting staff are experienced and discreet, and help to create a calm, rather sober, atmosphere. Intimate dining can be had in the small, vaulted area.

The Moon & Sixpence

6a Broad Street, Bath, BA1 5LJ (01225 460962/www.moonandsixpence.co.uk). **Lunch served** noon-2.15pm Mon-Sat; noon-2.45pm Sun. **Dinner served** 5.30-10.15pm Mon-Thur; 5.30-10.45pm Fri, Sat; 6.30-10.15pm Sun. **Main courses** £10-£15. **Set lunches** (Mon-Fri) £7.50 2 courses; (Sun) £8.95 1 course, £11.95 2 courses, £14.95 3 courses. **Set dinners** £20.75-£24.75 3 courses. **Credit** AmEx, MC, V.

The reliable old Moon & Sixpence has for many years smilingly served classic international cooking. Starters like pan-fried scallops lead on to mains such as lamb in tomato and rosemary sauce or beef fillet with wild mushroom ragoût, followed by commonplace but prettily-served desserts of the banoffi pie ilk. It's all delivered with a refusal to pander to fashion and an old-school feel (sliced French bread and butter at your elbow; a tendency to hand the wine list to the male diner). Set menus are a steal. Avoid being seated in the soulless upstairs area en route to the loos. By contrast the ground floor with its green French doors overlooking the courtyard is light, contemporary and bustling.

No 5 Restaurant

5 Argyle Street, Bath, BA2 4BA (01225 444499).
Lunch served noon-2.30pm daily. **Dinner served** 6.30-10pm Mon-Thur, Sun; 6.30-10.30pm Fri; 6.30-11pm Sat. **Main courses** £12.50-£17.
Credit AmEx, MC, V.
The paper tablecloths suggest 'quick bite', but the service and quality of the food implore you to linger over a meal at this classic French bistro. Chef Michel Lemoine trained under the Roux brothers and his delicate brushstrokes are everywhere: the perfectly tossed and dressed curly salad; the vibrant colour and gleam of the sardines stuffed with tomatoes, red onion and lemon in chive butter that suggests a still life painting. The lunch menu is restrictive yet perfect for the smaller appetite (and wallet – with a glass of something it'll come in at around a tenner). The place is popular with business folk and older tourists (due to its location just across Pulteney Bridge), who are no doubt tickled by the discreet, attentive French waiters trilling 'bon appetit'.

The Olive Tree

Queensberry Hotel, Russell Street, Bath, BA1 2QF (01225 447928/www.thequeensberry.co.uk).
Lunch served noon-2pm Tue-Sat; 12.30-2.30pm Sun. **Dinner served** 7-10pm daily. **Main courses** £12.50-£18.95. **Set lunch** (Tue-Sat) £13.50 2 courses, £15.50 3 courses; (Sun) £22.50 3 courses. **Set dinner** (Mon-Fri, Sun) £26 3 courses. **Credit** AmEx, MC, V.
Downstairs from the Queensberry Hotel, but quite independent, the Olive Tree has a deservedly impressive reputation. Elegant but not snooty, this is the place to really spoil your taste buds. Starters might include a Cornish seafood sausage or seared scallops, while mains could offer up a fillet of beef with Parma ham and shallots, or pan-fried john dory. Olive Tree ice-creams take a walk on the wild side, with unusual oat and basil flavours, but in general this is a calm, mature kind of place, where many male diners don a shirt and tie. Informed and friendly staff are on hand to answer any questions.

Pimpernel's

Royal Crescent Hotel, 16 Royal Crescent, Bath, BA1 2LS (01225 823333). **Lunch served** noon-2pm daily. **Dinner served** 7-10pm Mon-Thur, Sun;

7-10.30pm Fri, Sat. **Main courses** £25. **Set lunches** £18 2 courses, £25 3 courses. **Set dinner** £45 3 courses. **Credit** AmEx, DC, MC, V.
Named after the Scarlet Pimpernel, who lived at this address. Head chef Stephen Blake deserves praise for his seasonal menus built around modern British cuisine with global influences, all served on striking Dartington pottery. The bald, unadorned descriptions ('fried cod and dauphinoise potatoes with bacon lardons') are at odds with the fine ingredients, picturesque presentation and lavish explosion of flavours. Hand-painted wallpaper decorates the luxury Regency-style dining room, which is softened by ochre banquettes with puffed-up cushions. Disappointingly, the waiters can verge on the frosty, displaying little knowledge or interest in the menu's offerings. However, for the set lunch deal it's worth suffering some belittlement.

The Priory ★

Weston Road, Bath, BA1 2XT (01225 331922).
Lunch served noon-1.30pm daily. **Dinner served** 7-9.30pm Mon-Sat; 7-9pm Sun. **Set lunch** (Mon-Sat) £20 2 courses, £25 3 courses; (Sun) £30 3 courses. **Set dinner** £47.50 3 courses. **Credit** AmEx, DC, MC, V.
Exceptional in numerous ways, not least the fact that this beautiful country house hotel makes you feel like royalty. Allow a complimentary amuse-bouche to prime the tastebuds for some true event-dining. The menu proper might include ravioli of crab and ginger with langoustine sauce, honey-glazed Gressingham duck breast, or vanilla pannacotta with passion fruit sorbet. Expect to pay a little over £100 for a blowout three-course dinner with wine. The hushed drawing-room style dining room covered in contemporary art overlooks the huge garden – which also supplies vegetables and herbs to the chopping board of chef Robert Clayton (who learnt at the elbow of Nico Ladenis and bagged Michelin stars for The Priory from 1999-2001). It's like a good book you never want to end.

Rajpoot ★

4 Argyle Street, Bath, BA2 4BA (01225 466833).
Lunch served 11am-2.30pm daily. **Dinner served** 6-11pm Mon-Thur, Sun; 6-11.30pm Fri, Sat. **Main courses** £8-£15. **Set dinner** £18-£25 4 courses. **Credit** AmEx, DC, MC, V.
Descending the stairs into Rajpoot is a magical experience. It's like an underground Indian temple – bowing waiters usher you into a low-ceilinged cavern, its dark atmosphere lit by candles and lanterns throwing pretty patterns on to stone walls. Of the three dining rooms, Old India's intimate green booths are always popular with couples sampling the gourmet Bengali cuisine, like lamb rezala and shahi murg mussalam, and the stew-like chicken jaflong. Everything shares a loving attention to detail and a masterful use of herbs and spices. Staff willingly explain dishes and at busy times the beautifully ornate bar area makes waiting a pleasure. More expensive than the average curry house but breathtakingly worth it.

BRUTON

Claire de Lune

2-4 High Street, Bruton, BA10 0AA (01749 813395/www.clairedelune.co.uk). **Lunch served** noon-2pm Thur, Fri, Sun. **Dinner served** 7-9pm Tue-Sat. **Set lunch** £12.95 2 courses, £15.95 3 courses. **Set dinner** £18.95 2 courses, £20.95 3 courses, £23.95 4 courses. **Credit** AmEx, MC, V.

This is a friendly family-run restaurant with occasional surprises on an otherwise traditional menu. The menu combines British, French and Italian dishes and tries very hard: a starter of antipasti Italiano has no less than 12 items on the plate (from cold meats to aubergines). Crottin of foie gras d'oie on a Monbazillac gelatin is lovingly presented. Pavé of kiln roast salmon is fairly plain, but red meats are good here: tournedos of beef is excellent. The wine list isn't at all bad and service is jolly without being fawning.

Truffles ★

95 High Street, Bruton, BA10 0AR (01749 812255/www.trufflesbruton.co.uk). **Dinner served** 7-9.30pm Tue-Sat. **Set dinner** £26 3 courses. **Credit** MC, V.

Run by a husband and wife team, Denise and Martin Bottrill, Truffles has quite a reputation locally and booking is essential. A compact and bijou place with candlelit alcoves, the cream and blue decor is romantic and low-key. The menu is ambitious but brilliantly executed and excellent value. Roasted aubergine mousse with red peppers, asparagus spears and tomato and basil vinaigrette was fresh and spicy. Smoked duck breast with slices of pear and gorgonzola dressing was consummately done. Mains were simpler: fillet of beef with jumbo chips was cooked exactly how it was ordered. Escalope of veal with mint and pea risotto had a perfect mix of flavours, although the meat could have been a little more tender. Desserts here are sublime, especially the house truffle cake: white chocolate cheesecake was addictively good on our visit. Great on details (service is ultra-professional) and with a superb wine list, Truffles also hosts regular lobster, Thai and themed wine nights.

HAMBRIDGE

Café at Brown & Forrest Smokery ★ ★

Bowdens Farm, Hambridge, TA10 0BP (01458 250875/www.smokedeel.co.uk). **Lunch served** noon-2pm Mon-Sat. **Set lunch** £6 1 course, £9.50 2 courses. **Credit** AmEx, MC, V.

Set on the edge of the marsh-like Somerset Levels, the café attached to Brown & Forrest's smokery has become immensely popular. There is nothing pretentious about the light, spacious café but the food is mouthwateringly fresh and well prepared. Produce is mostly sourced locally and there is a sense that high quality, good service and attention to detail are behind its success. As well as light

Café at Brown & Forrest Smokery

lunches, tea, coffee and cakes are available throughout the day. Lunches offer a small range of smoked fish or a soup as starters, while main courses are made up from hot and cold smoked fish or meat served with new potatoes or granary bread, plus a fresh salad. Puddings, such as frozen strawberry and nut crunch, come served with pouring or clotted cream.

MELLS

The Talbot

Mells, BA11 3PN (01373 812254/www.talbotinn.com). **Lunch served** noon-2pm, **dinner served** 7-9pm daily. **Main courses** £11-£15. **Credit** MC, V.

It's not hard to see why people are prepared to travel from Bath and Bristol for a meal at the Talbot. Still the sociable heart of a honeystone village, overlooked by a medieval manor house, this ancient stone-built coaching inn does simple food well. The fish comes fresh from Brixham, they make their own pies, and although some might baulk at paying £14 for main courses in such unreconstructed pub surroundings, the unpretentious and friendly atmosphere wins most people over in the end. There's a large sunny garden with a pétanque pitch beneath old stone walls round the back, and the churchyard next door is worth a look for the grave of Siegfried Sassoon and an unusual equine sculpture by Sir Alfred Munnings in a side chapel.

PORLOCK WEIR

Andrews on the Weir ★
Porlock Weir (01643 863300/www.andrews ontheweir.co.uk). **Lunch served** noon-2.30pm, **dinner served** 7-9.30pm Tue-Sun. **Main courses** £18. **Set lunch** £12.50 2 courses. **Credit** AmEx, MC, V.
Widely regarded for some time as one of the best restaurants on the Exmoor coast, Andrews on the Weir occupies an endearing old guesthouse overlooking the little harbour at Porlock Weir. The decor (except in the dining room) is chintzy and well kept. The front dining room is a different story, with its modish chair covers and bare floorboards, but a comfortable place nonetheless to enjoy a menu that majors expertly on fish, backed up by meat reared in the region. Depending on the season and state of the tide, mains might be local skate or squid, venison or duckling. Fancy puds like caramelised pineapple with coconut sorbet and exemplary British cheeses round off the impression of a delightfully old-fashioned and accomplished restaurant.

SHEPTON MALLET

Blostin's
29-33 Waterloo Road, Shepton Mallet, BA4 5HH (01749 343648/www.blostins.co.uk). **Dinner served** 7-9pm Tue-Sat. **Set dinner** £15.95 2 courses, £17.95 3 courses. **Credit** MC, V.
On the Bristol road out of Shepton Mallet, Blostin's is a long-standing local favourite. From the outside it looks like one of those French wayside places doing authentic country cooking that you always hope to stumble upon but rarely do. This being England, inside it's done up in Navajo orange with bold, colourful artwork on the walls. A very clean and well-run establishment, it serves up locally sourced meats and cheeses in largely traditional combinations (pork with apples, cider brandy and cream or chicken with asparagus and tarragon sauce), as well as offering a more adventurous separate vegetarian menu, all backed up by a serious wine list. At £15.95 for two courses, you might reasonably expect marginally more refined cuisine, but the place has an unhurried charm all of its own.

Mulberry at Charlton House ★
Charlton Road, Shepton Mallet, BA4 4PR (01749 342008/www.charltonhouse.com). **Lunch served** 12.30-3pm, **dinner served** 7.30-9.30pm daily. **Set lunch** £14.50 2 courses, £18.50 3 courses. **Set dinner** £35 2 courses, £45 3 courses. **Credit** AmEx, DC, MC, V.

Owned by Roger and Monty Saul, founders of the Mulberry fashion label, Charlton House is a 'boutique' 17th-century manor house hotel on the edge of Shepton Mallet. The gardens feature lovely sloping lawns beneath a young apple orchard, and the hotel's interior provides a very comfortable showcase for Mulberry products: wine dark reds, stained woods and hunting greens predominate. The menu in the restaurant treats seasonal local ingredients with the respect they deserve: breast of squab pigeon and foie gras in a light juniper berry jus for starters, which also include the likes of succulent seared scallops and a superb duck confit. Mains might be organic salmon in a sweet chilli and red pepper salsa or honey-roast pork belly with mash, black pudding and apple. Good-value lunches make an affordable treat.

STON EASTON

Ston Easton Park
Ston Easton, BA3 4DF (01761 241631/ www.stoneaston.co.uk). **Lunch served** noon-2.30pm, **dinner served** 7-9.30pm daily. **Set lunch** £11 2 courses, £16 3 courses. **Set dinner** £34.50 3 courses, £39.50 3 courses. **Credit** AmEx, DC, MC, V.
Ston Easton Park is a discreet but quite grand stately pile halfway between Bath and Wells, and still something of a local secret despite being part of the expanding Von Essen group, which now includes Cliveden and the Royal Crescent in Bath. It's a Palladian country house hotel with an easy-going atmosphere, elegantly furnished with some genuine antiques and surrounded by gardens featuring water cascades designed by Humphrey Repton. They're overlooked by a dining room that's surprisingly modest in scale, the setting for a limited but luxurious menu of local game specialities and interesting fish dishes. Two-course lunches are good value and the hotel also does full English teas. Walk off the meal in the park accompanied by the house spaniels, Sooty and Sorrel.

TAUNTON

Brazz
Castle Hotel, Castle Green, Taunton, TA1 1NF (01823 252000/www.brazz.co.uk). **Lunch served** noon-3pm, **dinner served** 6-10.30pm daily. **Main courses** £7.50-£15.95. **Credit** AmEx, DC, MC, V.
Annexed but in deliberate contrast to the Castle Hotel restaurant (*see p145*), Brazz is a studiously contemporary brasserie bar. Tropical fish tanks in the walls, funky sounds, Scandi furnishings and designer lighting set a tone that's popular with shoppers and young mothers during the day, students and middle-class youth by night. On a weekly changing menu, the Lunch Express offers hearty staples like spaghetti carbonara or omelette Arnold Bennett at reasonable prices, while mains and the Market Brazz menu in the evening are more ambitious, although still pretty straightforward:

salmon fish cakes with creamed leeks and lemon or seared john dory niçoise. Service on our visit was polite, bright but also alarmingly swift.

Castle Hotel ★

Castle Green, Taunton, TA1 1NF (01823 272671/ www.the-castle-hotel.com). **Lunch served** 12.30-2.15pm, **dinner served** 7-10pm daily. **Set lunch** £18.50 2 courses, £22.50 3 courses. **Set dinner** £35.50 2 courses, £42.50 3 courses. **Credit** AmEx, DC, MC, V.

The smartest restaurant in Taunton is something of a rare breed: a top-notch county hotel dining room. It's the kind of Victorian, classically proportioned, no-nonsense sort of place that once meant a succession of lacklustre meals being served up to maiden aunts and commercial travellers. Nowadays, though, the menu is proud to list the local suppliers of seasonal ingredients handled with confidence by head chef Richard Guest. Starters for dinner could include scrambled duck egg with smoked eel and spiced oil or a refreshing May salad. Mains might be a fillet of wild sea bass with baked garlic, roast saddle of rabbit or pan-fried turbot with slow-cook bacon, tomato compote and mussel sauce. All in all, with superb cheeses like ragstone, elmhirst and montgomery's cheddar to follow, a meal here makes for a very British treat.

Sally Edwards ★ ★

The Crescent, Taunton, TA1 4DN (01823 326793). **Open** 9am-5pm, **lunch served** noon-3pm Tue-Sat. **Main courses** £4-£7. **Credit** MC, V.

A licensed café proclaiming itself 'minimalist at heart', Sally Edwards makes a welcome addition to Taunton's otherwise unimaginative café scene. With white walls, glass-topped tables on black-painted floorboards and all the latest TV chef tie-ins on display, the design makes the most of an unpromising corner site. The tables outside for smokers have a fine view of County Hall and a stream of traffic. Inside, the very good-value daily changing menu features the freshest local and organic produce: warm potato salad with seared hot smoked salmon and asparagus or roast chicken with lemon, rosemary, mascarpone and salad of baby broad beans, green beans and croûtons. Both were delicious and followed by some of the finest coffee in the West Country. There's also a child-friendly playroom at the back.

WELLS

Boxer's Restaurant

1 St Thomas Street, Wells, BA5 2UU (01749 672317/www.fountaininn.co.uk). **Lunch served** noon-2pm daily. **Dinner served** 7-9.30pm Mon-Sat. **Main courses** £8-£13.50. **Set lunch** £7.50 2 courses, £9.95 3 courses. **Credit** AmEx, DC, MC, V.

Situated above the old Fountain Inn, a stone's throw east of the cathedral, Boxer's Restaurant has been winning awards for its superior pub grub since 1981. It's a homely, kitchen-table kind of place, with a wide range of well-garnished and rather dated options on the menu, backed up by some excellent Spanish wines. Expect the likes of smoked duck breast with a fan of melon or fish soup topped with a grilled rouille and parmesan croûte for starters, followed by chocolate chilli-glazed pork on sesame-tossed noodles or oven-baked salmon with a red pepper crust on a medley of citrus-glazed vegetables. Even if they're not the height of culinary fashion, the recipes here are executed with aplomb and served with a smile.

Ritchers

5 Sadler Street, Wells, BA5 2RR (01749 679085/ www.ritchers.co.uk). **Lunch served** noon-2pm, **dinner served** 7-9pm Mon-Sat. **Set lunch** £7.50 1 course, £9.50 2 courses, £11.50 3 courses. **Set dinner** £19.50 2 courses, £23 3 courses. **Credit** MC, V.

Ritchers restaurant is hidden away behind its jolly yellow-painted bistro bar just off the market place and is popular with a mixed crowd of local regulars. The restaurant itself is furnished in an old-fashioned way, something like a 1980s wine bar, but the menu is more ambitious than that might suggest. It features local ingredients given a French or Mediterranean twist. Starters could include caramelised pear and grilled goat's cheese salad or grilled salmon with tarragon cream, followed by slow-cooked lamb or fresh fish of the day. On our visit on a sunny Friday lunchtime, the tiny outdoor courtyard came into its own, a quiet place to enjoy a decent salmon and lobster salad and some succulent sautéed guinea fowl. Service may be a bit shambolic, but there's no doubting the enthusiasm of the friendly staff or the value for money of their lunch offers.

WEST BAGBOROUGH

Rising Sun Inn ★

West Bagborough, TA4 3ES (01823 432575/ www.theriser.co.uk). **Lunch served** noon-2pm, **dinner served** 7-9.30pm Tue-Sun. **Main courses** £9.95-£15.95. **Credit** MC, V.

A mile off the main Taunton to Minehead road, West Bagborough is a charming village on the flanks of the Quantocks. Commanding tremendous views from its upstairs dining room, the thatched 16th-century Rising Sun has been completely renovated inside – using 80 tons of oak, we were told – after a disastrous fire. Now, with its slate bar and solid beams, it makes an unusual and impressive setting for some seriously good seafood: seared cod with welsh rarebit and crispy savoy cabbage, lime-cured salmon with wasabi and soy or a bouillabaisse of seafood with asparagus and saffron, as well as hearty meat dishes like smoked duck salad or fillet steak.

Also in the area

Firehouse Rotisserie 2 John Street, Bath, BA1 2JL (01225 482070); **FishWorks Seafood Café** 6 Green Street, Bath, BA1 2JY (01225 448707); **Loch Fyne** 24 Milsom Street, Bath, BA1 1DG (01225 750120).

South West

Central

Central

Ludlow
Bewdley
Kidderminster
COVENTRY
Rugby
Stourport-on-Severn
Bromsgrove
Kenilworth
Redditch
Royal Leamington Spa
Droitwich
Warwick
Leominster
WARWICKSHIRE
Worcester
WORCESTER-SHIRE
Stratford-upon-Avon
HEREFORD-SHIRE
Great Malvern
Evesham
Shipston on Stour
Banbury
Hereford
Chipping Camden
Adderbury
Kir Su
Ledbury
Paxford
Bloxham
Ross-on-Wye
Tewkesbury
Moreton-in-Marsh
Hook Norton
Deddington
Corse Lawn
Steeple As
Newent
Bishop's Cleeve
Winchcombe
Stow-on-the-Wold
Chipping Norton
Clifford's Mesne
Churchdown
Guiting Power
Oddington
Charlbury
Woott
Mitcheldean
Cheltenham
Upper Slaughter
Shipton-under-Wychwood
Woodstock
Monmouth
Charlton Kings
Bourton-on-the-Water
Long Hanborough
Gloucester
Brockworth
Burford
Witney
Eynsham
Kidling
Cinderford
Arlingham
Ducklington
Wyth
GLOUCESTERSHIRE
MONMOUTH-SHIRE
Bream
Stroud
Coln St Aldwyns
Carterton
Stanton Harcourt
Stonehouse
Frampton Mansell
Barnsley
Bampton
Boars Hill
Sharpness
Chalford
Sapperton
Clanfield
OXFOR
Nailsworth
Cirencester
Fairford
Buckland
Abingdon
Chepstow
Dursley
Minchinhampton
Lechlade
Faringdon
Drayton
Thornbury
Wotton-under-Edge
Tetbury
Cricklade
Highworth
Ardlingt
Caldicot
Crudwell
Stanton Fitzwarren
Watchfield
Shrivenham
Wantage
Frampton Cotterell
Yate
Easton Grey
Malmesbury
Purton
Swindon
West Ilsley
Winterbourne
Wootton Bassett
Wroughton
Lambourn
Chiseldon
Ford
Castle Combe
BRISTOL
Colerne
Chippenham
Marlborough
Ramsbury
Marsh Benham
Kingswood
Lacock
Calne
Hungerford
Kintbury
Keynsham
Whitley
Little Bedwyn
Inkpen
Newbury
BATH
Melksham
Rowde
Holt
Devizes
Pewsey
Marten
Bradford-on-Avon
Great Hinton
Midsomer Norton
Radstock
Trowbridge
WILTSHIRE
Beckington
Westbury
Frome
North Tidworth
Ludgershall
Wells
Larkhill
Andover
Warminster
Shepton Mallet
Amesbury
Glastonbury
HAMF
SOMERSET
Mere
Hindon
Teffont Evais
Wilton
Salisbury
Winchester
Fonthill Gifford
0   30 km
Shaftesbury
© Copyright Time Out Group 2003
0   15 miles
Yeovil
Sherborne
Romsey
Eastleigh
148 Time Out Eating & Drinking in Great Britain & Ireland
Fordingbridge
SOUTHAMPTON
DORSET

Bedfordshire

HOUGHTON CONQUEST

Knife & Cleaver

Houghton Conquest, MK45 3LA (01234 740387/ www.knifeandcleaver.com). **Lunch served** noon-2.30pm Mon-Fri, Sun. **Dinner served** 7-9.30pm Mon-Sat. **Main courses** £10.95-£16.50. **Credit** AmEx, DC, MC, V.

The location of this restaurant is certainly inviting and the delightful 17th-century building almost pulls you through the doors. The atmosphere in the bar where you select your meal is warm and friendly. However, once inside the conservatory-style dining area, much of the ambience is lost. The restaurant specialises in fish and shellfish – grilled fillet of sea bass was outstanding. Rack of Welsh lamb and beef fillet were acceptable, but were let down by the poor standard of the accompanying vegetables. Starters of crab meat thermidor and spiced duck confit cake were passable. The highlight of the meal was perusing the extensive, almost exhaustive, wine list and sampling the sticky toffee pudding.

MILTON ERNEST

The Strawberry Tree

3 Radwell Road, Milton Ernest, MK44 1RY (01234 823633). **Lunch served** noon-2pm Wed-Fri. **Dinner served** 7-8.30pm Wed-Sat. **Main courses** (lunch) £15-£20. **Set dinner** £38 3 courses. **Credit** MC, V.

The food here is excellent. When in season, the vegetables and salads are grown organically in the restaurant's own gardens, while the meats are also either organic or free-range. Starters of vine tomatoes stuffed with goat's cheese and warm asparagus topped with parmesan ice-cream were presented after an appetiser of chilled cucumber soup. Main course of roast best end of Suffolk lamb served with potato dauphinoise, braised lettuce and thyme sauce was cooked to melting pink perfection. Dessert was a simple raspberry pavlova and the cheeseboard (with own-baked biscuits) exceeded expectations. Sadly this old oak-beamed dining area has the atmosphere of an undertaker's parlour, but in the right company this could be overlooked.

Berkshire

BRAY

The Fat Duck ★

High Street, Bray, SL6 2AQ (01628 580333/ www.thefatduck.co.uk). **Lunch served** noon-2pm Mon-Sat; noon-3pm Sun. **Dinner served** 7-9.30pm Tue-Sat. **Set lunch** £27.95 3 courses; £60 8 courses; £75 12-course tasting menu. **Set dinner** £60 8 courses; £75 12-course tasting menu. **Credit** AmEx, DC, MC, V.

The spiky metalwork here has been replaced by a suave collection of softer furnishings, the front of house team have lost their disdainful airs and the food has never been better – it seems the Fat Duck is maturing with the years. Heston Blumenthal is a culinary witch-doctor, ignoring convention and abstractedly combining the mundane and the downright mad to powerful effect. Where previous results were sometimes alarming, creations now have more universal appeal. Concoctions might be cuttlefish and duck cannelloni, layered quail, langoustine and pea mousse, cauliflower and chocolate risotto, slow-cooked lamb and its tongue, chocolate fondant with dried apricot yoghurt and harissa ice-cream. Colours are wild, flavours intricately woven and presentation toe-curlingly good. A posh frock restaurant with serious prices and a satisfying wow factor.

Riverside Brasserie

Bray Marina, Monkey Island Lane, Bray, SL6 2EB (01628 780553/www.riversidebrasserie.co.uk). **Lunch served** noon-3pm Tue-Sun. **Dinner served** 6-10pm Tue-Sat. **Main courses** £13-£16. **Credit** AmEx, DC, MC, V.

Moored inside a forest of masts and sails at Bray Marina, and blessed with a tranquil waterside terrace, the Riverside Brasserie is a nucleus for small and perfectly formed cuisine. Anyone familiar with its landlocked sister restaurant, the Fat Duck (*see above*), should know what to expect from mad scientist Heston Blumenthal's lab: dishes tend to be as bright as they are bold, characterised by strange colours and even stranger combinations. Prices, accordingly, can seem high: a fish soup was flavoursome, but at £8.25 for roughly ten spoonfuls, sadly unsatisfying; peppers stuffed with mackerel (£6.70) were oddly tasteless. Mains were better, if not much bigger: a soft square of pork belly was imaginatively complemented by a sharp celeriac purée, and poached salmon positively leaped off the plate thanks to a textured white bean sauce. Service is intimate and unhurried.

Waterside Inn ★

Ferry Road, Bray, SL6 2AT (01628 620691/ www.waterside-inn.co.uk). **Lunch served** *Feb-Dec* noon-2pm Wed-Sat; noon-2.30pm Sun. **Dinner served** *Feb-May, Sept-Dec* 7-10pm Wed-Sun; *June-Aug* 7-10pm Tue-Sun. **Main courses** £34-£44. **Set lunch** (Mon-Sat) £36 2 courses; (Sun) £52 3 courses. **Set dinner** £78 5 courses. **Credit** AmEx, DC, MC, V.

Outside there's little indication this is hallowed ground for gourmets (the only other place in Great Britain or Ireland to have three Michelin stars is Gordon Ramsay in London); the Waterside resembles the village pub it once was. Within, a small plush lounge leads to a dining room that might be considered dated and gaudy. Mirrors interspersed with wall panels painted with floral scenes are set behind green banquettes. Yet the view, of a stretch of duck-dotted Thames, is glorious and an expanse of French windows show it off to grand effect. Michel Roux and his son Alain's haute French cooking is similarly spectacular, and is enhanced by waiters who flit from nowhere, unveil dishes in synchrony, then dissipate. The seasonal 'menu extraordinaire' enables you to sample five courses taken from the carte: in smaller portions, and without ingredients like sturgeon, foie gras and truffles in such abundance. It will tether the bill to around £100 a head if you opt for one of the half-dozen wines costing under £25 (from a vast French-only list). Choice is limited, but heavenly extras ensure the gamut of gastronomic fireworks is experienced – from *amuse-bouches* such as asparagus quiches, via delectable pre-starters like lobster morsels in a gelée under a creamy fennel mousse topped with sevruga caviar, to luxurious petits fours with coffee. Imagination yet restraint, clarity of flavour and lightness of touch characterise such dishes as an inspiring fish course of steamed salmon fillet flavoured with grapefruit (a successfully bitter counterfoil), served with sliced asparagus, red lentils and an asparagus nage. The only faintly questionable dish was a rose petal sorbet that perfectly captured the floral essence but seemed too sweet a palate-cleanser. Yet rolled loin of lamb with grain mustard, pancetta, soft white beans and girolle mushrooms made a divine, full-flavoured main course, the meat rare and tender. Desserts (try the assiette of three or perhaps a warm raspberry soufflé) are first-class essays in the pudding-maker's art. Paunchy power-brokers dine here, but so do couples celebrating life-shaping events. The view and the food won't let them down.

COOKHAM

Bel & the Dragon

High Street, Cookham, SL6 9SQ (01628 521263/ www.belandthedragon.co.uk). **Lunch served** noon-2.30pm Mon-Sat; noon-3pm Sun. **Dinner served** 7-10pm Mon-Sat; 7-9.30pm Sun. **Main courses** £10.95-£19.95. **Credit** AmEx, MC, V.

Bel & the Dragon looks like a golden oldie from the outside, but inside it opens cavernously in to a red-painted, church-chaired, many-staffed eating hall. Efficiency is the watchword, with orders rapidly taken and thereafter dizzying waves of bread, oil, relishes, olives, wine and other restaurant paraphernalia rushed to table. Bring hordes of hungry friends or a family group – traditional roasts, and sausage and mash through squid tempura and goat's cheese strudel will keep everyone happy. Roast rib of beef, capped by a pudding the size of Yorkshire, while not elegant, was a nice enough dish. Two generous steaks of char-grilled marlin on juicy chickpea salsa suffered from cold side vegetables, but succour came in the form of roast potatoes (handed round to all and sundry). Note that the smoking section is often the more peaceful option.

Manzano's

19-21 Station Hill Parade, Cookham, SL6 9BR (01628 525775). **Lunch served** noon-2pm Mon-Fri. **Dinner served** 7-10pm Mon-Sat. **Set meal** £10 2 courses. **Set meal** £23 2 courses, £28 3 courses. **Credit** AmEx, MC, V.

Manzano is Spanish for apple tree and is also the surname of the young couple who run and own this mid-shop restaurant (previously an Italian). Richard Manzano comes with plenty of experience and, despite the stiff decor and uninspiring location, makes a warmly attentive chef-patron alongside his wife Deena. The food is warm and welcoming too, with paellas aplenty, generous shots of alcohol throughout and a surprisingly good wine list for a 30-seater pad. Mushroom tartlet is intensely flavoured and trickled with a tender sun-dried tomato and sherry-type dressing – a perfect match. Main courses of ribeye beef and ages-cooked lamb stew with peppers are pleasant without moving mountains, and Spanish sherry trifle is superb, with oodles of amaretto-soaked sponge and a creamy cap.

COOKHAM DEAN

The Inn on the Green

The Old Cricket Common, Cookham Dean, SL6 9NZ (01628 482638/ www.theinnonthegreen.com). **Lunch served** noon-2pm Mon-Sat; noon-2.30pm Sun. **Dinner served** 7-9.30pm daily. **Main courses** £14.50-£25.95. **Set meals** (lunch Mon-Sat; dinner Mon-Thur, Sun) £14.95 2 courses, £19.95 3 courses. **Credit** AmEx, MC, V.

Cookham Dean is as verdant and bucolic a spot as any Berkshire can provide – and now one of its three pubs has been turned into a country house hotel, complete with starry London chef (Garry Hollihead).

Central

The setting is something of a problem, for this is not grand country house architecture to go with the grand prices. If you want a drink, you'll have to sit in the foyer-cum-bar where members of staff answer the phones between mixing drinks. The dining room itself is nice enough in a beamed way, but a side room is so dark you might think you've strayed into an Alpine hut. Still, the walled garden is lovely in summer and the cooking is gratifyingly tricksy, with intense flavours and recherché compositions; witness tuna tartare, peashoot salad and deep-fried seaweed or steamed hake, chorizo sausage, buttered curly kale, shellfish liquor and clams.

INKPEN

Swan Inn

Craven Road, Lower Green, Inkpen, RG17 9DX (01488 668326/www.theswaninn-organics.co.uk). **Lunch served** noon-2pm Mon-Fri; noon-2.30pm Sat, Sun. **Dinner served** 7-9pm Mon-Thur, Sun; 7-9.30pm Fri, Sat. **Main courses** £14-£21. **Credit** MC, V.
Allow plenty of time to find the Swan Inn, whose signpost may unhelpfully be pointing in the wrong direction. This is a no-frills pub serving traditional food and local ales such as Berkshire brewed Butts Bitter and Hook Norton Mild (it was CAMRA's West Berks pub of the year in 2002). A sign over the bar reads 'safe food home-made using local organic beef and organic produce wherever possible' and the owners also run an organic farm and farm shop in the village. Wine too is organic. Dishes such as beef stroganoff, leek and bacon gratin or cod in beer batter with excellent chips can be ordered at the bar; for the likes of halibut with sesame seed crust, canon of lamb complete with frenchified sauces and desserts, try the attached Cygnet restaurant.

KINTBURY

Dundas Arms ★

Kintbury, RG17 9UT (01488 658263/www.dundasarms.co.uk). **Open** 11.30am-2.30pm, 6-11pm Mon-Sat; noon-2pm Sun. **Lunch served** 12-2pm Mon-Sat. **Dinner served** 7-9pm Tue-Sat. **Main courses** £13-£14. **Credit** AmEx, MC, V.
Occupying an impossibly lovely garden, flanked by a small river to one side, the Kennet and Avon canal the other and Kintbury lock just across the road, the Dundas Arms could be forgiven for resting on the laurels of its location. Fortunately it doesn't. A crowded bar serves steak and ale pie-type meals while a generously sized, light flooded room looks down on the river Eden and serves more elaborate meals from linen clothed tables. Food combinations are not especially novel but ingredients shine with quality and flavour, forming carefully cooked, well-rounded dishes. Mellow own-made houmous with roast artichokes and red peppers tasted of smoky sunshine; pigeon breasts formed a perfect picture with sweet parsnip purée and piquant fruited sauce. What are you waiting for?

MARSH BENHAM

The Red House

Marsh Benham, RG20 8LY (01635 582017). Bistro & restaurant **Lunch served** noon-2.15pm daily. **Dinner served** 7-10pm Tue-Sat. **Main courses** £13.95-£17.95. **Set lunch** (Sun) £16.95 2 courses, £19.95 3 courses. **Set meal** *bistro* (Mon-Fri) £13.95 2 courses, £16.95 3 courses. **Credit** AmEx, MC, V.
Crisply manicured hedges set the pattern at the Red House. Eating is given more space than drinking in this slick operation, with upmarket bar meals served in the old part of the building and a three-year-old faux-library-cum-restaurant offering food with a French accent. From here tomato and mozzarella tart was a bland assembly with characterless tomatoes, while a nice but diminutive halibut fillet and tomato beurre blanc was surrounded by overpowering brown crabmeat fritters. Desserts read more nicely than they tasted, and the wine list is none too cheap. Still, polished service and a sure-to-impress setting count for a lot in the Shires.

NEWBURY

Vineyard ★

Stock Cross, Newbury, RG20 8JU (01635 528770/www.the-vineyard.co.uk). **Lunch served** noon-2pm, **dinner served** 7-9.30pm daily. **Set lunch** (Mon-Sat) £17 2 courses; (Sun) £26 3 courses. **Set dinner** £45 2 courses, £55 3 courses; (Fri, Sat) £70 8 courses. **Credit** AmEx, DC, MC, V.
As you approach this hotel, restaurant and spa, you could be forgiven for thinking you'd turned into the home of one of James Bond's power-hungry enemies. A valet offers to park your car and efficient staff whisking guests to and fro set you looking for the piranhas and the white cat. Be reassured – all you can expect here is a wonderful meal, conceived and created under the expert eye of chef John Campbell. Starters included roast Anjou squab with black treacle and celeriac, red mullet, fennel and honey purée or ham hock and foie gras terrine with a lentil dressing. From the mains choose corn-fed poussin tarte and truffled eggs, turbot with braised oxtail or saddle of lamb with red cabbage and Venezuelan chocolate – all artistically arranged on the plate and masterpieces for the palate. The wine list extends to two volumes (Californian and international). A chocolate fondant with basil ice-cream to finish capped a memorable meal.

READING

London Street Brasserie

Riverside Oracle, 2-4 London Street, Reading, RG1 4SE (01189 505036/www.londonstbrasserie.co.uk). **Meals served** noon-11pm Mon-Sat; noon-10.30pm Sun. **Main courses** £11-£20. **Set meal** (noon-7pm) £12.95 2 courses. **Credit** AmEx, MC, V.
Reading's rejuvenated riverside Oracle is packed with loud restaurants, bars and the under-25s. A

Al Fassia. *See p154.*

footbridge apart on a little wedge of riverbank, this clean-cut and airy eaterie admits a more multi-generational crowd who swap hooch for champagne and pizza for carpaccio, but maintain a sense of fun while they're at it. Staff are charming. Food reflects skill and interest: roquefort soufflé came on an unusual dandelion, hazel-nut and pear salad, while gratinated onion and goat's cheese tartlet sat well with french beans and teriyaki butter. Main courses are feast-like portions with a Mediterranean or oriental bias, such as pink lamb 'Orvieto' with broad beans, fennel and red wine rosemary jus or crisp sea bass with battered squid rings and char-grilled veg. Don't miss the hot blackberry and Cointreau soufflé.

Despite its convenient proximity to the M4, this old and elegant ex-vicarage is set among verdant striped lawns. Inside, the tall square rooms are divided into a serene modern dining room, a lush plum-coloured bar and two large conservatories, one for eating, one for lounging. Service is crisp and efficient, food delicious. Vegetarian options were limited to one main course across the whole three menus on our visit, and it – cheese soufflé – was off. That aside, marinated fennel and patty pan with pungent goat's cheese, and asparagus with hazel-nuts were light introductions to lovely main courses of salmon with petits pois à la Française, and grilled wood pigeon with watercress purée. Desserts are light, refined and beautifully presented, but ought to be for £16 via the à la carte route. A glamorous venue.

SHINFIELD

L'Ortolan

Church Lane, Shinfield, RG2 9BY (01189 888500/ www.lortolan.com). **Lunch served** noon-2pm daily. **Dinner served** 6.45-9.15pm Mon-Sat. **Main courses** £24-£30. **Set lunch** (Mon-Sat) £27 3 courses; (Sun) £30 3 courses, £40 4 courses. **Set dinner** £49 7 courses. **Set children's meal** £15 3 courses. **Credit** AmEx, DC, MC, V.

SWALLOWFIELD

George & Dragon

Church Road, Swallowfield, RG7 1TJ (01189 884432). **Lunch served** noon-2.30pm, **dinner served** 7-9.30pm daily. **Main courses** £10.95-£15.95. **Credit** AmEx, DC, MC, V.

'Real ale, real wine and serious food' is how this creaky old pub describes its reason for being. Of the former there's Adnams and London Pride, no wine was offered at all (presumably it does exist), and the food fell some way short of serious. Trad horse brasses, dusty red wall sconces, yellow sporting prints and animal traps hanging from beams were not enough to deter locals who crammed in to the point of overspill one Friday lunchtime. Staff offhandedly but fairly efficiently served the likes of lamb with fig jus, roasted garlic and walnut mash, and Portuguese sardines with crispy seaweed and basil oil. From a lighter bar menu, 'dragon' sausages with mustard mash and onion-free onion gravy were poor quality and furiously spicy; more acceptable was a generous stack of lukewarm vegetable slices, polenta and goat's cheese. There are no bargains to be found in a pub that's too busy for its own good.

WEST ILSLEY

The Harrow

West Ilsley, RG20 7AR (01635 281260). **Lunch served** 11am-2pm, **dinner served** 6.30-9pm daily. **Main courses** £10-£15. **Credit** MC, V.

Nestling in the rolling hills just south of the Ridgeway, with a view overlooking the green baize of a village cricket pitch, grazing cattle and errant wild fowl, the Harrow is an unusual find. The pews and country kitchen furniture inside are surrounded by equine art – this is the edge of horse-racing country and the 1989 Derby winner Naswan was trained here – while outside in Laura's Corner, children can enjoy a range of playground treats while their parents are served at tables nearby. The kitchen can be spied through the windows fronting the pub, where the staff are hard at work producing dishes from the select menu. Half a dozen starters and mains include simply grilled langoustines, warm goat's cheese risotto, lamb's liver or Aberdeen Angus steak. The cuts of meat were particularly tender and portions were ample but not excessive. Although service was slow, it was worth the wait.

WINDSOR

Al Fassia ★

27 St Leonards Road, Windsor, SL4 3BP (01753 855370). **Lunch served** noon-2pm, **dinner served** 6.30-10.30pm Mon-Sat. **Main courses** £8.50-£11.95. **Set meal** £15.95 5 courses. **Credit** AmEx, DC, MC, V.

Al Fassia calls itself a 'Restaurant Gastronomique Marocaine' but after that mouthful is a model of unpretentiousness and welcomes you with authentic Moroccan hospitality. The long, slim den of a room is filled with filigree brass lamps, embroidered horse ornaments and well-fed people, and the scent of tagines and mint tea is beguiling. Briwats are deep-fried crunchy filo parcels filled with gently spiced vegetables, minced pork or sardines, while zaalouk – a smoky aubergine and garlic paste – is served at room temperature with warm own-made bread. A

tagine served with featherweight couscous is a must, although long spears of grilled meat and veggie options, such as Sahara-style white bean stew, have dedicated followers. Desserts are of the honeyed pastry and nut sort, while coffee lasts as long into the night as you want it to. Fabulous.

Spice Route

18A Thames Street, Boots Passage, Windsor, SL4 1PL (01753 860720). **Lunch served** noon-2.30pm, **dinner served** 6-11pm daily. **Main courses** £7.95-£14.50. **Set lunch** £5.50 1 course; £7.95 3 courses. **Set dinner** (6-7.30pm) £12.95 2 courses. **Credit** AmEx, MC, V.

Not your usual local Indian restaurant, this, with its noisily stark interior and decent wine list. Proprietoress is Indian cookery writer and Carlton TV chef Mridula Baljekar, a polite and petite woman who can be seen at customers' tables quietly mopping up praise, while the head chef, previously private cook to the Oberoi family, beavers away behind closed doors. Instead of jarringly anglicised versions of nowhere-near-Indian dishes, this team turns out cracklingly authentic food, such as pomegranate and spinach soup, gorgeous venison tikka, clay oven-cooked potatoes and Himalayan wok-cooked chicken. Rice and bread are super-fresh, fragrant and sublime, and you can see the latter as it hits the heat-shimmered tandoor.

YATTENDON

Royal Oak

The Square, Yattendon, RG18 0UG (01635 201325/ www.chorushotel.co.uk). **Lunch served** noon-2pm Mon-Thur; noon-2.30pm Fri-Sun. **Dinner served** 7-9.30pm daily. **Main courses** £13.50-£19.50. **Set lunch** (Sun) £19.50 2 courses, £23.50 3 courses. **Credit** AmEx, DC, MC, V.

There's the smart end and the pub end at this establishment in a well-to-do village outside Newbury. Opt for the smart and you'll end up in a cosy, intimate dining room. Choose the pub end and it's more rustic, more wood than upholstery, but still comfortable. Either way, the food is modern cuisine – don't expect homely country fare – and although our experience has been mixed, the disappointment has never been more than mild. Starters such as watercress soup with bacon pancakes or an artichoke, feta, chicory, pine nut and cherry tomato salad set the tone, followed by roast chicken with wild mushroom risotto and asparagus and leek cream sauce or fillet of beef with wilted greens, topped by seared foie gras and pomme fondant. Service somehow feels better at the smarter end.

Also in the area

Gilbey's 82-83 High Street, Eton, SL4 6AF (01753 854921); **Bel & the Dragon** Thames Street, Windsor, SL4 1PQ (01753 866056); **Loch Fyne** The Maltings, Bear Wharf, Fobney Street, Reading, RG1 6BT (0118 918 5850).

Central

Buckinghamshire

AMERSHAM

Gilbey's

1 Market Square, Amersham, HP7 0DF (01494 727242/www.gilbeygroup.com). **Lunch served** noon-2.15pm, **dinner served** 7-9.30pm daily. **Main courses** £9-£15. **Set lunch** £10.95 2 courses. **Set dinner** £23.50 3 courses (minimum 8). **Credit** AmEx, DC, MC, V.

Old Amersham is a bijou collection of graceful town houses, boutiques, delis and restaurants. The menu and ambience of Gilbey's is far more spirited than at the Kings Arms across the street (*see below*), with a clientele younger by a good 20 years and staff who clearly like food, wine and the business of serving it. Modern French describes the food and the wine list is legendary in these parts – sourced by patron and keen oenophile Michael Gilbey, and offered at very reasonable prices. Loire sauvignon blanc starts at £9.50 and excellent burgundy tops £45. When last here, our starters were pretty though insubstantial in the flavour department, but main courses of char-grilled vegetables with halloumi cheese and grilled steak and rösti were spot on. Raspberry clafoutis with amaretto ice-cream was delectable.

Kings Arms

30 High Street, Amersham, HP7 0DJ (01494 726333/ www.kingsarmsamersham.co.uk). **Lunch served** noon-2pm Tue-Sun. **Dinner served** 7-9.30pm Tue-Sat. **Main courses** £14.50-£16.50. **Set lunch** £12.50 2 courses, £15.50 3 courses. **Set dinner** £19 3 courses incl coffee. **Credit** AmEx, MC, V.

If you get the feeling you've been here before when you clearly haven't, it may be because this creaking, black-beamed pub from the 1450s was portrayed as the Lucky Boatman in *Four Weddings and a Funeral*. Apricot-between-the-beams walls are hung with seedy cartoons, the only corkscrew in the place is tied to a shelf with string and the local brew, Rebellion, comes cold and hoppy in a tankard. The staff can be as quirky as the Olde Englande interior, but nothing dents the Kings Arms' popularity, particularly with those celebrating anniversaries. Such folk enjoy well-rendered dishes like salmon and hollandaise, ragoût of hare and sublime bread and butter pudding. Posher than your average pub, but more appealing when Hugh Grant was here.

CHICHELEY

The Chester Arms

Chicheley, MK16 9JE (01234 391214). **Lunch served** noon-2pm Tue-Sun. **Dinner served** 6.30-9.30pm Tue-Sat. **Main courses** £9-£15. **Credit** AmEx, MC, V.

A number of qualities mark out the Chester Arms. Firstly, its convenient location between Milton Keynes and Bedford; secondly, its exceptionally friendly staff; and thirdly, its simple good value. Sunday lunch costs £10.95 and includes vegetables and spuds two ways, and this makes it a hit with families and older couples who are drawn to traditional fare like roast beef and Yorkshires, chicken chasseur, and grilled cod and chips. On the downside, the Chester Arms has what may well be the smallest tables in the land, a strange windowless pit that you may be unfortunate enough to be seated in, unappealing pictures for sale and an uninspiring line in desserts. Still, this area of the country is the gustatory equivalent of the Gobi dessert, and should you find yourself stranded here you can be sure of a decent hot meal and cheery welcome, courtesy of Greene King.

EASINGTON

The Mole & Chicken

Easington, HP18 9EY (01844 208387/ www.moleandchicken.co.uk). **Lunch served** noon-2pm, **dinner served** 6-9pm Mon-Sat. **Meals served** noon-9pm Sun. **Main courses** £8.95-£15.95. **Credit** AmEx, MC, V.

Easington is no more than a row of farmers' cottages on the very rural frontier of Buckinghamshire and Oxfordshire. Don't expect a road sign before Long Crendon, and from there follow the line of cars from the Angel (*see p157*); the uninitiated and unbooked who will likely be going without lunch at either. Charming without being cutesy, this 19th-century ex-village store has real flames in the hearth, a cracking selection of malt whiskies, multiple snugs and nicely laid tables. The setting is great and so is the food. Bowls of succulent mussels with chilli cream sauce come piled high, beef Wellington is crisp and sumptuous, shoulder of roast lamb is massive, yet oh so tender. The clientele: cyclists, smart folk up from London and locals who wear sensible thornproof clothes but drive Audi Quattros.

GREAT MISSENDEN

Annie Baileys

Chesham Road, Great Missenden, HP16 0QT (01494 865625/www.anniebaileys.com). **Lunch served** noon-2.30pm Mon-Sat. **Dinner served** 7-9.45pm Mon-Sat. **Meals served** noon-8pm Sun. **Main courses** £9.50-£15.95. **Set lunch** £15 2 courses, £18.50 3 courses. **Credit** AmEx, MC, V.

Any restaurant whose front door opens on to rows and rows of Taittinger has its priorities sorted. And

The Mole & Chicken.
See p155.

diners are kept in high spirits from the moment they arrive at this restaurant and bar, bubbling with ambience and charming punters, until the replete moment of departure. David and Heather Berry's Annie Baileys used to be a tiny, successful venture in another tiny Chiltern village (Cuddington), but since September 2002 it has occupied these larger premises in Hyde End, just outside Great Missenden. Expect starters such as baked plum tomatoes on toast with crème fraîche or fresh crab risotto, mains of Gressingham duck with red wine and lentils or fabulous black bream with tomatoes, olives and buttery baked potato slices. Desserts are less predictable than usual, panettone pudding with

cinnamon-baked pears, perhaps. Wine ranges from sensible (although not boring) through to quietly indulgent. Quite a find.

La Petite Auberge

107 High Street, Great Missenden, HP16 0BB (01494 865370). **Dinner served** 7.30-10pm Mon-Sat. **Main courses** £15.60-£16.90. **Credit** MC, V.
This French restaurant is petite even by the bijou standards of Great Missenden. A little menu case and hanging sign mark the spot, shyly hoping to catch your attention and, should you be tempted in off the road, you'll find yourself in granny's front room; spotlessly clean, too much furniture and

pictures from a lost era. Though the menu changes little, the food is seriously good, and the front of house staff, including wife of the chef, Mrs Martel, are crisply efficient, if distant. The locals love this place, so booking is imperative if you want to sample the likes of crab in a courgette flower, scallops and salsify, tender pan-fried venison with cranberries, pinkly roasted lamb and crème brûlée. All are cooked with aplomb. The atmosphere, though, is curiously muted and melancholic.

HADDENHAM

The Green Dragon

8 Churchway, Haddenham, HP17 8AA (01844 291403/www.eatatthedragon.co.uk). **Lunch served** noon-2pm Mon-Sat; noon-2.30pm Sun. **Dinner served** 6.30-9.30pm Mon-Sat. **Main courses** £9.50-£16. **Set lunch** (Sun) £16.95 3 courses. **Set dinner** (Tue, Thur) £10.95 2 courses. **Credit** AmEx, MC, V.

Set in picturesque pub country, a few yards away from the village church and duck pond, once swarming with local Aylesbury ducks (who knows where they ended up), the Green Dragon is a dignified, calm yet inviting set-up, with decent furniture and some striking pottery adorning window ledges. The owners Sue and Peter Moffat and their team of young local waitresses are warm and delighted to serve, taking time to tell the story of the local brewery and serving its liquid labours, CAMRA award-winning Wychert Ale, at just the right speed and temperature. The food is modern, cooked with flair and attractively presented on the biggest plates imaginable: aromatic rosemary griddled vegetables with mozzarella, duck breast with shallot tarte tatin and spiced seville orange sauce, home-made butterscotch and pecan tart with milk chocolate ice-cream, for example.

LONG CRENDON

The Angel ★

47 Bicester Road, Long Crendon, HP18 9EE (01844 208268). **Lunch served** noon-2.30pm daily. **Dinner served** 7-9.30pm Mon-Sat. **Main courses** £12.95-£19.75. **Set lunch** £11.75 1 course, £14.75 2 courses, £17.50 3 courses. **Credit** MC, V.

With leather couches framing the laid-back bar and a conservatory dining room bathed in natural light, the Angel's interior is a treat to behold. It's the food, however, that is genuinely heaven-sent. Starters include such original delights as salad of roast quail, black pudding and pancetta with mustard butter, while mains tend to be rather extravagant but impeccably executed: breast of guinea fowl, for example, comes wrapped in Parma ham and accompanied with a vegetable, saffron and barley broth. Fresh fish arrives daily from Billingsgate market. There are three bedrooms available for those who, quite understandably, refuse to leave.

MARLOW

Marlow Bar & Grill

92-94 High Street, Marlow, SL7 1AQ (01628 488544/www.individualrestaurants.co.uk). **Meals served** noon-11pm daily. **Main courses** £7-£16. **Credit** AmEx, MC, V.

This site seems to have finally found its level with the Marlow Bar and Grill. It panders to Marlow's hip young things with cocktails and champagne around a sleek bar, but doesn't alarm the older set. Beyond the brushed steel bar the fresh dining room measures its considerable length in cherry wood and lapis blue leather, opening to an attractive high-ceilinged conservatory and courtyard garden. The bistro-style food is good value, while the wine list keeps up with the happening vineyards as well as the famous names. Spinach and lentil soup with spiced yoghurt, and roast mushrooms on toast with melted taleggio are gutsy and flavour-packed, while a main course of smoked chicken and artichoke risotto infused with truffle oil is more subtle. A fun place with an interesting menu, and well located to break up a day of shopping or river cruising.

The Vanilla Pod ★

31 West Street, Marlow, SL7 2LS (01628 898101/www.thevanillapod.co.uk). **Lunch served** noon-2pm, **dinner served** 7-10pm Tue-Sat. **Main courses** £16.50. **Set lunch** £16.50 2 courses, £18.50 3 courses. **Set dinner** £30.50 2 courses, £34.50 3 courses, £39.50 7 courses. **Credit** AmEx, MC, V.

Just off Marlow's *très chic* High Street, the Vanilla Pod is a tiny shrine to good food, in which the aforementioned fragrant ingredient crops up frequently in both sweet and savoury dishes. Lots of orangey-red Tuscan colour is packed into the doll's house-sized bar and dining rooms, creating a unique intimacy – most of the folk here know each other anyway. *Amuse-bouche*, pre-dessert and even a mid-meal freebie accompany the three-course menu, which suggests that the seven-course menu gourmand is strictly for those with Desperate Dan-sized appetites. Expect unusual hints of flavour, especially Oriental ones, sneaking into the mainly French-style dishes, such as in a cute cup of tomato consommé speckled with jasmine-scented oil, pork fillet dusted with fennel and spice powder served with tender white beans and sticky rich jus, or in a sexily smooth panna cotta infused with fresh mint and vanilla. All are artfully presented and cooked with a light but assured touch. Worth a trip.

MEDMENHAM

Danesfield House Hotel

Medmenham, SL7 2EY (01628 891010/ www.danesfieldhouse.co.uk). **Lunch served** noon-2pm, **dinner served** 7-9.45pm daily. **Main courses** £9.95-£14. **Credit** AmEx, DC, MC, V.

Danesfield House sits grey and massive on a hill overlooking the whole world. Or that's the way it seems. Below on the Thames tiny boats queue for a lock, while around you stretch undulating lawns, parterres, ponds and statues. On closer inspection things are not so swish. Meals can be taken in the Orangery, an informal, moderately priced sun room with the aforementioned panorama, or the Oak Room, a dark-panelled, white-napieried affair with a library-like calm. From the former a laminated menu suggests the likes of deep-fried goat's cheese with peperonata, roasted dorade with butter and lemon, and vanilla panna cotta with seasonal berries. On our last visit, the quality of the food varied considerably, and service was somewhat hit-and-miss too, with the staff taking our orders while looking over their shoulders. This place looks the part but don't expect culinary fireworks.

NEWTON LONGVILLE
The Crooked Billet
2 Westbrook End, Newton Longville, MK17 0DF (01908 373936/www.thebillet.co.uk). Bar **Lunch served** noon-2pm Tue-Sat. *Restaurant* **Lunch served** 12.30-3pm Sun. **Dinner served** 5.30-11pm Tue-Sat. **Main courses** £11-£20. **Set dinner** £40 8 courses. **Credit** AmEx, MC, V.
The Crooked Billet is a welcome oasis in the gastronomic desert surrounding Milton Keynes. Ex-London chef Emma and sommelier John Gilchrist keep the original pub side of the business going with fruit machines and Greene King ales, while offering a polished restaurant with a serious wine list in two separate dining areas. An astonishing 300-odd wines are available by the glass which, although not the cheapest way to drink, is bliss for anyone wanting to experiment. Food is temptingly described, presented with flair and mostly delicious, although over-reliant upon cream in some cases. Goat's cheese, grilled aubergine and red pepper mousse is one starter, another a gorgeous smoked haddock tart with poached egg. Simply grilled cod, and monkfish with braised beef are good too.

PENN
The Crown Inn
Witheridge Lane, Penn, HP10 8PN (01494 812640). **Meals served** 11am-10pm Mon-Sat; noon-9pm Sun. **Main courses** £5-£15.95. **Credit** AmEx, DC, MC, V.
Situated opposite a picture-perfect country church in the immaculately kept village of Penn, the Crown is just the kind of pub you hope to stumble across on a day-trip to the country. Large and ivy-clad, with a big garden, it has plenty of old-world charm but enough bustle to mark it out as a well-used local resource. You can see why it's popular: as well as the bar area, there are two dining rooms (one reserved for families) and a chalked-up lunch menu that stretches over three densely crammed boards. Service is swift and friendly, the food unpretentious but well executed, ranging from meat-and-veg

staples to classy-sounding fish dishes, and several imaginative vegetarian options. Those tables fill up fast, though, so get there on the early side.

WADDESDON
The Five Arrows
High Street, Waddesdon, SL6 9SQ (01296 651727/ www.waddesdon.org.uk). **Lunch served** noon-2pm Mon-Sat; 12.30-2.30pm Sun. **Dinner served** 7-9pm Mon-Sat; 7.30-8.30pm Sun. **Main courses** £10.75-£19.50. **Credit** AmEx, MC, V.
Residents of Waddesdon probably get tired of having traffic, tourists, Lord Rothschild and his baronial estate on their doorsteps, but the Five Arrows is milking the link for all its worth. Beyond all the horse portraits and Baron de Rothschild wines, though, there's plenty to be cheerful about here, including an exquisite little folly off the main restaurant. The menu proper competes with a bar menu at half the price, both amply passing muster with no discernible difference in either quality or portion size. Mixed mushroom millefeuille with tarragon cream sauce from the former is delicious and surpassed only in presentation by steak and ale pie from the latter. Desserts are miraculously good – make sure you leave space for treacle tart on crisp paper-thin pastry, and caramel and honeycomb ice-cream made on the premises.

WESTLINGTON
La Chouette
Westlington Green, Westlington, Aylesbury, HP17 8UW (01296 747422). **Lunch served** noon-2pm Mon-Fri. **Dinner served** 7-9pm Mon-Sat. **Main courses** £13-£17. **Set lunch** £11 3 courses. **Set dinner** £29.50 4 courses, £36.50 5 courses. **Credit** MC, V.
Labyrinthine lanes winding through fields dotted with country houses are the only landmarks en route to this tucked away Belgian restaurant. Look for a lone faded sign pointing vaguely to Westlington Green and La Chouette (the owl), one of a number of 300-year-old buildings situated in this tiny village. Chef and building have equal character, one typically English, the other typically Belgian, and proud of it. It's not an obvious partnership, but Frederic Desmette knows his onions and can be drawn into arresting conversation on food, wine and wildlife photography when he's not juggling pans in the kitchen and customers in the dining room. Food is hearty but polished and includes Belgian dishes such as asparagus spears with butter and scrambled egg, or roast salmon with crispy onions and lardons. The wine list will capture imaginations with its breadth, if not its insignificant prices. Book ahead as the restaurant doesn't open if it's not busy.

Also in the area
Loch Fyne 70 London End, Old Beaconsfield, HP9 2JD (01494 679960).

Gloucestershire

ARLINGHAM

Old Passage Inn

*Passage Road, Arlingham, GL2 7JR (01452 740547/
www.fishattheoldpassageinn.co.uk).* **Lunch served**
noon-2pm Tue-Sun. **Dinner served** 7-9pm Tue-Sat.
Main courses £10.80-£19. **Credit** AmEx, MC, V.
Were the owl and the pussycat ever to pass by in
their boat, they would feel right at home in this
attractive green painted inn on the edge of the
Severn estuary. The location is remote, on the site
of an ancient ford with views across to the Forest of
Dean, and appropriately it's a mainly fishy menu.
This will come as no surprise to those who have
followed the long and successful career of co-owner
Somerset Moore (he started off as the fish chef at
Prunier's in St James's back in 1966). His son, Raoul,
now does the cooking, and menus are extensive and
imaginative, but always rely on fresh and mostly
Cornish fish and shellfish from sustainable sources.

BARNSLEY

The Village Pub

*High Street, Barnsley, GL7 5EF (01285 740421/
www.thevillagepub.co.uk).* **Lunch served** noon-
2.30pm Mon-Fri; noon-3pm Sat, Sun. **Dinner
served** 7-9.30pm Mon-Thur, Sun; 7-10pm Fri, Sat.
Main courses £9.50-£15.50. **Credit** MC, V.
Deep terracotta and exposed brick line the walls of
one room here, while mahogany bookcases stand
proud against pea-green paint in another. The food
is equally stylish but unpretentious, though portions
could be bigger. Expect dishes such as chicken liver
and foie gras parfait with fig chutney followed by
baked haddock with chive mash, mustard, shallots
and french beans. On our visit desserts (the likes of
coconut tart with lemon curd ice-cream or steamed
apricot pudding with vanilla custard) weren't as
exquisite as the chocolate that came with the coffee.
Given the exclusive feel of the place, the atmosphere
is surprisingly laid-back and welcoming.

CHELTENHAM

The Beehive

*1-3 Montpellier Villas, Cheltenham, GL50 2XE
(01242 579443/www.slack.co.uk).* **Open** noon-11pm
Mon-Sat; noon-10pm Sun. **Lunch served** noon-3pm
Sun. **Dinner served** 7-10pm Mon-Sat; 6-9pm Sun.
Main courses £7.95-£12. **Credit** MC, V.
The Beehive exudes a gloriously thrown-together
charm: newspapers are piled haphazardly on a
dilapidated piano and the large, crowded bar is
cluttered with a random collection of wooden chairs

and occasional chequerboard chess tables. Check the
blackboard, however, and you'll see that this
delightful little boozer is also a brilliant place to eat,
with an upstairs restaurant where starters like
spiced squid salad with caper relish precede
reasonably priced main courses like aubergine and
red onion tart with broccoli and gorgonzola. What
with simultaneously being the best pub in town and
offering some of the finest food, it's no wonder the
Beehive hums sweetly all day long.

Le Champignon Sauvage ★

*24-26 Suffolk Road, Cheltenham, GL50 2AQ (01242
573449/www.lechampignonsauvage.com).* **Lunch
served** noon-1.30pm, **dinner served** 7.30-9pm
Tue-Sat. **Set meal** £35 2 courses, £42 3 courses.
Credit AmEx, DC, MC, V.
Le Champignon looks fairly modest for a temple of
gastronomy (run-of-the-mill Middle England decor
with cheery yellow walls, blue velvet seating, art on
the walls). However, the cooking is pretty flawless.
David Everitt-Matthias is in the kitchen; his wife,
Helen, does front of house with quiet charm. He
makes some brave and bold combinations, but
everything we tried worked – and then some – from
an appetiser of velouté of smoked eel to an
unfeasibly light lemon mousse served with a ball of
melon sorbet and sticks of rhubarb, not to mention
the fabulous petits fours. Further skill was revealed
by a starter of roe deer tortellini matched by the
sharper tang of apple purée and turnip segments
that had been soaked in red wine. A main of cod with
a confit of pig's trotter and tomato was an unlikely
but fine combination. Great own-made bread and a
huge board of English and French cheeses are other
pluses. One quibble: we were late (but still within
the serving times) because, like the other diners, we
were stuck in traffic. Despite having phoned to let
them know, noises from the kitchen made it pretty
clear that we were causing a major inconvenience.
However, such was the sheer seductiveness of the
food, we were won over anyway.

Chelsea Square

*60 St George's Place, Cheltenham, GL50 3PN
(01242 269926).* **Lunch served** noon-2.30pm,
dinner served 6-10.30pm Mon-Sat. **Main courses**
£7.95-£12.95. **Credit** MC, V.
A relatively small front facing on to a quiet street
leads via a smart bar area into a long room where,
during the day, the conservatory roof lets in plenty
of light. This is just as well as the walls are blue and
purple – colours which come into their own at night
when the lights are dimmed. With regular live
entertainment and a fashionably contemporary

menu that's very reasonably priced and changes quarterly, Chelsea Square attracts a trendy local clientele. Grilled goat's cheese on parmesan polenta, overnight slow-cooked lamb with potato and parsnip mash, and hot chocolate moelleux with Madagascan vanilla ice-cream are justifiably some of the most popular choices. There's a great list of cocktails and wines that aren't greedily priced.

The Daffodil

18-20 Suffolk Parade, Cheltenham, GL50 2AE (01242 700055/www.thedaffodil.co.uk). **Lunch served** noon-2.30pm Mon-Sat. **Dinner served** *June-Aug* 6-10pm Mon-Sat; *Sept-May* 6.30-10pm Mon-Sat. **Main courses** £11.75-£19.50. **Set lunch** £10 2 courses, £12.50 3 courses. **Set dinner** (Mon) £15 2 courses; *June-Aug* (Mon-Fri before 7pm) £15 2 courses. **Credit** AmEx, MC, V.

Its name isn't the only thing the Daffodil has retained from its original incarnation as a picture house: seating is staggered across the auditorium, with drinks mixed in the gallery and a kitchen where the silver screen used to be. Food tends to taste as good as it looks: a starter of sea scallops was perfectly soft and presented in glorious technicolour with avocado, chilli and ginger, while loin of lamb en croûte came with a rich feta cheese mash and red wine onions. But it's the interior design that really makes the Daffodil bloom: with low lighting, long-leaf plants and original art deco furnishings, dining here is a cinematic experience from the credits to the final curtain.

Lumiere ★

Clarence Parade, Cheltenham, GL50 3PA (01242 222200). **Dinner served** 7-8.30pm Tue-Sat. **Set dinner** £32 3 courses. **Credit** AmEx, MC, V.

Local epicureans tend to lose their composure when talking about Lumiere, an understated jewel in Cheltenham's culinary crown that they quite reasonably want to keep for themselves. Lin and Geoff Chapman's eclectic modern menu mixes starters such as goat's cheese filo parcels with pan-fried potato and caramelised apple with mains as striking as chicken breast with Thai wild boar stuffing in a red pepper and peanut sauce. Three courses cost £32, and although the menu changes regularly, the atmosphere – bathed in soft white light and as intimate as it is intoxicating – remains a tranquil and strangely tactile place to indulge the senses all year round.

Vanilla

9-10 Cambray Place, Cheltenham, GL50 1JS (01242 228228). **Lunch served** noon-2pm Tue-Fri. **Dinner served** 7-9.30pm Mon-Sat. **Main courses** £9-£16. **Credit** AmEx, MC, V.

This intimate dining space, accessed by an almost unmarked door, is one of Cheltenham's most stylish: candles send shadows dancing over polished wood floors and the whole scene is artfully captured in a large fisheye mirror at one end of the hall. The menu, however, is the real scene-stealer, with regularly changing à la carte starters, such as carpaccio of tuna with horseradish coleslaw, main courses including supreme of salmon, lime and coriander butter sauce and daily specials. It's very busy in the evening, when staff are at their least affable.

CHIPPING CAMPDEN

Hicks Brasserie Bar

Cotswold House Hotel, The Square, Chipping Campden, GL55 6AN (01386 840330/ www.cotswoldhouse.com). **Lunch served** 12-2.30pm, **dinner served** 6-9.45pm daily. **Main courses** £10-£15. **Credit** AmEx, MC, V.

Providing some welcome modern flash to the olde worlde charms of Chipping Campden, Hicks manages to retain a restrained sophistication despite the decor and incongruous background house music. The superb cooking by Michel Roux scholarship-winning chef Alan Dann provides the substance that more than matches the style. Starters of squid with chilli had a pleasing kick, while seared scallops and rhubarb made an interesting counterpoint. Caesar salad with smoked chicken was a simple, well-executed main, as was the more hearty dish of roast guinea fowl and fresh tagliatelle. With a heated terrace and a new menu featuring ten vegetarian dishes, Hicks is setting the standard for classy yet comfortable dining in the Costwolds. The hotel's Garden restaurant is a more formal affair.

CLIFFORD'S MESNE

Yew Tree Inn

Clifford's Mesne, GL18 1JS (01531 820719/ www.theyewtreeinn.co.uk). **Lunch served** noon-3pm Tue-Sun. **Dinner served** 6.30-11pm Tue-Sat. **Main courses** £13.75-£17. **Set dinner** £21.95 2 courses, £27 3 courses, £32 5-course tasting menu. **Credit** MC, V.

This well-maintained former 16th-century cider mill stands in lovely countryside, with panoramic views over the Malvern Hills. Paul Hackett, the owner and chef, trained under Michel Roux at the Waterside Inn, Bray. Menus combine elements of the grand, flamboyant cooking associated with top-rated French restaurants and the simpler, yet still imaginative, food usually associated with English country pubs. A weekday lunch could offer crispy beer-battered Cornish haddock with chips. At other times, the stops are pulled out: lobster cappuccino with Armagnac cream and lobster caviar; breast of Hereford duck with orange, shallots and coriander; roast loin of Gloucester Old Spot pork with prune stuffing and pommery mustard are typical.

COLN ST ALDWYNS

New Inn at Coln

Coln St Aldwyns, GL7 5AN (01285 750651/ www.new-inn.co.uk). **Lunch served** noon-2pm Mon-Sat; noon-2.30pm Sun. **Dinner served** 7-9pm

Old Passage Inn. *See p159.*

Mon-Thur, Sun; 7-9.30pm Fri, Sat. **Set lunch** £21 2 courses, £26 3 courses. **Set dinner** £26 2 courses, £31 3 courses. **Credit** AmEx, MC, V.

The New Inn is the eating element of a market-savvy hotel-pub-restaurant combo selling Cotswold charm and country values to local Land-Rovered devotees and a mixed bunch of hotel guests. It occupies a self-contained courtyard across which the creeper-clad main building and a pleasant raised terrace face off. Dinner is served in the restaurant and matches lighter (though still luxurious) modern starters and richer mains with a fish or meat centrepiece. Presentation and preparation are impressive. At lunch, the bar menu is served in both bar and restaurant, turned into a set two- or three- courser in the latter. Dishes are an appetising update on pub classics, with a brasserie twist. The New Inn's Achilles' heel is vegetarian provision: nothing on the dinner menu and an unpalatable risotto at lunch.

CORSE LAWN

Corse Lawn Hotel

Corse Lawn, GL19 4LZ (01452 780771/ www.corselawnhousehotel.co.uk). **Lunch served** noon-2pm daily. **Dinner served** 7-9.30pm Mon-Sat; 7.30-9.30pm Sun. **Main courses** £12.95-£19.95. **Set lunch** £16.50 2 courses, £18.50 3 courses. **Set dinner** £27.50 3 courses. **Credit** AmEx, DC, MC, V.

Baba and Denis Hine's attractive Queen Anne house is a comfortable and welcoming country retreat. The Hine family (of Cognac fame) have owned it since 1978, and Baba has never ceased serving wholesome, proper food. A few innovations appear from time to time, but essentially this is unfussed-over cooking that relies on quality ingredients, assembled with Baba's natural flair for flavour and composition. Choose from the all-day menu in the bistro or dine in style in the spacious, relaxed dining room. Typical of the French-inspired food are delicious terrine of rabbit with nettle dressing and dandelion leaf salad, tender pan-fried guinea fowl with flageolets, and boudin blanc with tangy lemon tart and lemon ice-cream to finish.

FRAMPTON MANSELL

White Horse

Cirencester Road, Frampton Mansell, GL6 8HZ (01285 760960/www.cotswoldwhitehorse.com). **Lunch served** noon-2pm; noon-3pm Sun. **Dinner served** 7-9.45pm Mon-Sat. **Main courses** £9.95-£14. **Credit** MC, V.

The transformation of a run-down pub is something Emma and Shaun Davis undertook after Shaun's previous experience working at the Feathers at Woodstock and the Marsh Goose in Moreton-in-Marsh. The result is a smartly upbeat, contemporary setting and though the focus is now very much on the food, those still wanting a tipple can relax in a separate area from the diners, perhaps on the large corner settee. Like the decor, the food has moved

with the times, and fish delivered from Cornwall and locally sourced meat are fashioned into imaginative dishes. Start with spicy fish cakes with a sweet chilli sauce, then ribeye steak with a wild mushroom and black pepper sauce, and finally warm plum and frangipane tart and vanilla ice-cream.

GUITING POWER

The Hollow Bottom

Winchcombe Road, Guiting Power, GL54 5UX (01451 850392/www.hollowbottom.com). **Open** 11am-11pm Mon-Sat; noon-10.30pm Sun. **Lunch served** noon-2pm, **dinner served** 6-9pm daily. **Main courses** £8.95-£14. **Credit** MC, V.

Sparsely decorated with racing memorabilia and warmed by a large open fire, the Hollow Bottom is rural beyond mere aesthetics (sport is quietly projected from a TV that may well predate the moon landing, let alone satellite telly), offering locals a quaint and peaceful pub that just happens to be thoroughly welcoming to strangers. Food comes courtesy of Charlie Pettigrew, a former Young Scottish Chef of the Year and advocate of such outlandish delicacies as rattlesnake in a sherry, tomato and mushroom sauce. It's not all kangaroo steaks, wild boar sausages and bison, however: the menu changes daily, and there's always plenty of more traditional grub chalked up on the board, including fresh seafood dishes from around £8 and a delightful range of own-made desserts.

NAILSWORTH

Mad Hatters

3 Cossack Square, Nailsworth, GL6 0DB (01453 832615). **Lunch served** 12.30-2pm Wed-Sat; 1pm Sun by appointment only. **Dinner served** 7.30-9pm Wed-Sat. **Main courses** £14.50-£17.50. **Set lunch** (Sun) £15 3 courses incl coffee. **Credit** AmEx, MC, V.

Mike and Caroline Findlay's passion for honest, wholesome food has resulted in this little peach of a restaurant, where organic and free-range are the bywords. The pretty Georgian bow-fronted exterior hides a delightfully cosy interior: here it's all about being in a relaxed, informal and friendly environment. Good quality produce, mainly from local sources – even their own mini farm – features in the unpretentious dishes. Ingredients are combined to enjoyable effect in a fabulous fish soup, or pork and venison terrine starter, then rabbit dijonnaise or monkfish basquaise. The dinner menu extends the simpler lunchtime choice.

NEWENT

Three Choirs Vineyards Restaurant

Newent, GL18 1LS (01531 890223/ www.threechoirs.com). **Lunch served** noon-2pm Tue-Sun. **Dinner served** 7-9pm daily. **Main courses** £12-£16. **Credit** MC, V.

On a sunny summer's day it would be easy to imagine oneself in deepest French wine country, instead of looking out over the tranquil acres of one of England's leading single-estate vineyards. A vine-covered terrace offers an al fresco lunchtime option, but even the bright, prettily decorated dining room has great views from its large patio windows. Lunch is a simpler affair than dinner, offering the likes of smoked salmon with prawns and lime mayonnaise to begin, followed by a flavoursome grilled chicken breast with basil and pine nut sauce, and a fragrant elderflower crème brûlée for dessert. To accompany the food there's a choice of 14 very reasonably priced own-label wines, including two sparklers.

ODDINGTON
The Fox Inn
Oddington, GL56 0UR (01451 870555/
www.foxinn.net). **Lunch served** noon-2pm daily.
Dinner served 6.30-10pm Mon-Sat; 7-9pm Sun.
Main courses £7.95-£12. **Credit** MC, V.
In a characterful Cotswold village setting, the Fox fits the bill perfectly. Dating way back to the 11th century, its stone exterior is swathed in virginia creeper. Inside there are flagstone floors, beams, open fireplaces, and in summer a plentiful supply of fresh flowers. The dining room, or Red Room as it's known here, has wine as its decorative theme – ancient corkscrews and wine-related curios, as well as an imaginative but uncomplicated modern European menu. With your crusty garlic bread, try carrot, coriander and ginger soup or wilted rocket, olive and parmesan tart, followed by baked sea trout with creamed leeks and saffron or ribeye steak with mustard butter. Sticky chocolate toffee pudding is a lovely rich finale.

PAXFORD
Churchill Arms ★
Paxford, GL55 6XH (01386 594000/
www.thechurchillarms.com). **Lunch served** noon-2pm, **dinner served** 7-9pm daily. **Main courses** £9-£14. **Credit** MC, V.
With the closure of her other project, the Marsh Goose in Moreton-in-Marsh, culinary sorceress Sonya Kidney devotes all her time to producing innovative dishes at this much-feted Paxford pub. Visitors are advised to get in early as the no-booking policy means it's often jam-packed with locals enjoying well-prepared dishes such as black bream with fennel or delicately flavoured lemon sole. Despite the breadth of choice on the chalkboard menu, staff remain busiest serving traditional fare of roast beef or steak and ale pies. Any flair is left to the cooking and the L-shaped interior is happily free of twee, country pub bric-a-brac. It is as conducive to sinking real ales by the bar, as it is to sampling excellent starters such as pan-fried scallops with cucumber and sweet chilli or pigeon breast with roasted red peppers.

SAPPERTON
Bell at Sapperton
Sapperton, GL7 6LE (01285 760298/
www.foodatthebell.co.uk). **Lunch served** noon-2pm, **dinner served** 7-9.30pm daily. **Main courses** £9.50-£16. **Credit** MC, V.
North of the A419, in the heart of the Cotswolds, this 300-year-old village pub is popular with ramblers, horse-riders (a hitching rail is provided), as well as the locals. Renovated in 2000, the stone building retains a civilised country air with natural stone walls, polished flagstones and a mix of wood tables and chairs. You can eat alfresco on the terraces, in the rear courtyard or, when climate dictates, inside by the log fire. The food is varied and imaginative, with fresh fish from Cornwall and a daily changing specials board supplementing the likes of risotto of wild garlic and jumbo prawns or chicken stuffed with bresaola and smoked mozzarella. There are some good wines by the glass, plus a 'fine wine' list.

STOW-ON-THE-WOLD
The Eagle & Child
Digbeth Street, Stow-on-the-Wold, GL54 1BN (01451 830670/www.theroyalist.co.uk). **Lunch served** noon-2.30pm Mon-Sat; noon-3pm Sun. **Dinner served** 6-10pm Mon-Sat; 6-9pm Sun. **Main courses** £9-£14. **Set lunch** £9 2 courses, £12 3 courses. **Credit** AmEx, MC, V.
A gastropub of sorts, the Eagle & Child is in fact part of the Royalist Hotel (England's oldest inn according to the *Guinness Book of Records*). There are two very distinct spaces: a snug, low-ceilinged 17th-century dining room with a log fire or an airy conservatory, somewhat chilly in winter. There's no denying the atmosphere and the waiters are unfailingly friendly, but the menu occasionally promises more than it can deliver: an oxtail faggot with celeriac purée and onion marmalade was insipid, while sea bass with sun-dried tomato and chorizo salsa was wildly over-seasoned as if to compensate. Scallops with herb risotto and apple salad was a happier mix of texture and flavour, however, and there were some imaginative vegetarian options.

Hamiltons Brasserie
Park Street, Stow-on-the-Wold, GL54 1AQ (01451 831700/www.hamiltons.br.com). **Lunch served** noon-2.30pm daily. **Dinner served** 6-9.30pm Mon-Sat. **Main courses** £11.75-£16.50. **Credit** AmEx, MC, V.
It's a sign of the times when a restaurant in a quiet Cotswold town has a modern British menu that wouldn't be out of place at one of London's fashionable hotspots. There's cool, urbane sophistication in the decor too, with its honeyed wood and pale cream walls. Hot and sour chicken and noodle soup is deliciously spiced with ginger, coriander and a kaffir lime infusion, while vanilla makes an appearance with garlic in the white wine

sauce accompanying pan-fried sea bass fillet decorated with ribbons of carrot and leek. Bitter orange tart with Campari and orange posset is just one of several terrific puds. The short wine list is a limited-stop world tour with some good, unusual vintages, all listed by grape variety.

The King's Arms

Market Square, Stow-on-the-Wold, GL54 1AF (01451 830364/www.kingsarms-stowonthe wold.co.uk). **Open** 11am-11pm Mon-Sat; noon-10.30pm Sun. **Lunch served** noon-2pm daily. **Dinner served** 6-9.30pm Mon-Sat; 7-9pm Sun. **Main courses** £8-£15. **Credit** AmEx, MC, V.

Chef Peter Robinson and Louise, his wife, took over this 500-year-old former coaching inn in 2002, after a stint at the Tresanton Hotel, Cornwall. The interior has been quietly refurbished; much of the original character, thankfully, remains. The restaurant is upstairs and shares its thoroughly modern menu with the ground-floor bar. Typical dishes are duck confit cleverly partnered with balsamic figs; spinach and nut salad with feta and sumac, followed by sea bream with salsa rossa or porcini mushroom risotto; then perhaps round off with British cheeses or pannacotta and fresh fruit. The wines are unusually featured, wine merchant style, in racks along a wall, the idea being to browse and choose.

TETBURY

Calcot Manor

On A4135 north-west of Tetbury, GL8 8YJ (01666 890391/www.calcotmanor.co.uk). **Lunch served** noon-2pm, **dinner served** 7-9.30pm daily. **Main courses** £15-£21. **Set lunch** £13.50 2 courses. **Credit** AmEx, MC, V.

This delightful manor house of medieval origins has a choice of dining venues: the elegant Conservatory in the main house, or the separate, smart but very relaxed Gumstool Inn. Food in both tends towards the Mediterranean and portions are divided into ample and generous. At the inn, there's a wide range of moderately priced items like Cornish fish pasties and crispy roast pork belly. These contrast with the more sophisticated cooking of the Conservatory: wonderfully melting griddled scallops with sweet chilli sauce or prime peppered breast of Gressingham duck with creamed spinach and candied shallots. Caramelised banana shortbread with candied pineapple and rum and raisin ice-cream is plate-licking good, as is the Eton mess.

The Close Hotel ★

8 Long Street, Tetbury, GL8 8AQ (01666 502272). **Lunch served** noon-2pm, **dinner served** 7-9.30pm daily. **Set lunch** (Mon-Sat) £12.50 2 courses, £16.50 3 courses; (Sun) £13.50 2 courses, £17.50 3 courses. **Set dinner** £28.50 3 coures. **Credit** AmEx, DC, MC, V.

The setting might be country-house traditional, but the Close Hotel's kitchen is anything but. Inventive starters set the scene. Assiette of smoked salmon starter has the fish in myriad form: tortellini, tartare

and a deliciously moist bundled sausage. From the mains, study of Cotswold lamb – a medley of mini kidney pie, loin, sweetbreads and faggots – worked less well, veering towards the pretentious. Pan-fried cod with seafood foam was a treat though, and the wonderfully witty trio of apple dessert capped everything – you'll never see an apple pie in quite the same way again. Oh, and the selection of British cheeses is not to be sniffed at (literally, in the case of the stinking bishop). Excellent service too, despite the slightly formal surroundings.

Trouble House

Near Tetbury, GL8 8SG (01666 502206/ www.troublehouse.co.uk). **Lunch served** noon-2pm Tue-Sun. **Dinner served** 7-9.30pm Tue-Sat; 7-9pm Sun. **Main courses** £11.75-£14.50. **Credit** AmEx, DC, MC, V.

The whitewashed exterior may not promise much, and even inside the decor has been kept simple and rustic, but chef-proprietor Michael Bedford, who was Gary Rhodes's head chef, offers food that is a cut well above the average. As might be expected, the style is modern British and may include fried smoked haddock dumpling with parsley sauce or cauliflower cheese soufflé to begin, followed by own-made faggots with mash and onion gravy or braised pork belly with sweet and sour red cabbage and spiced fruits. Warm pistachio frangipane with a soft chocolate centre or nougat glacé with pineapple are further fine examples of how sophisticated some pub food has become of late. The wines, like the food, are well balanced and very kindly priced.

UPPER SLAUGHTER

Lords of the Manor

Upper Slaughter, GL54 2JD (01451 820243/ www.lordsofthemanor.com). **Lunch served** noon-2pm, **dinner served** 7-10pm daily. **Main courses** £20-£29. **Set lunch** £16.95 2 courses, £19.95 3 courses; (Sun) £23.50 3 courses incl coffee. **Credit** AmEx, DC, MC, V.

Set in eight acres of parkland and dating back to the 17th century, but with Victorian extensions, this former rectory is quintessentially English. The elegant dining room (smart dress required) looks out on to the walled garden and terrace (available for drinks and al fresco meals). The exceptional carte, liberally studded with luxury items and pricey, is contrasted by a good-value lunch menu whose flavour combinations are well thought out: creamy risotto of spring pea and Parma ham bordered by a frothy mint cappuccino or fillet of royal sea bream accompanied to good effect by onion marmalade, tomato coulis and scallop mousse. A perfect cherry bakewell with mascarpone ice-cream is one of two desserts. Decent wines include several by the glass.

Also in the area

Le Petit Blanc The Promenade, Cheltenham, GL50 1NN (01242 266800).

Hertfordshire

BISHOP'S STORTFORD

Lemon Tree
14-16 Water Lane, Bishop's Stortford, CM23 2LB (01279 757788/www.lemontree.co.uk). **Lunch served** noon-2.30pm Tue-Sat; 1-4pm Sun. **Dinner served** 7-9.30pm Tue-Sat. **Main courses** £10-£16. **Set lunch** (Tue-Sat) £7 1 course, £11 2 courses, £15 3 courses incl glass of wine/soft drink. **Set dinner** £15.50 2 courses, £19.95 3 courses incl half bottle of wine Tue-Thur. **Credit** MC, V.

Like Bishop's Stortford, the Lemon Tree is a quiet, respectable concern with patrons to match. People come here to eat, and with good reason – there can't be anywhere within miles that offers such well-considered, elegant and imaginative cooking. The set lunch menu is flexible and good value. Starters might include a warm poached egg with black pudding, Parma ham and Worcester sauce dressing; or roast red pepper and goat's cheese crostini with tapenade and salad. Next, choose between seared tuna with borlotti beans, fennel and tapenade or oven-roast skate with Puy lentils, savoy cabbage and mustard sauce. Meaty options include confit of duck with thyme-baked new potatoes, black olives and garlic or grilled calf's liver with bacon, caramelised onions and creamed potatoes. Veggies are well catered for too, with dishes such as fricassee of wild mushrooms, parmesan and asparagus. The wine list takes its pick from around the world, with many available by the glass. The restaurant is divided into small rooms, which in theory makes it cosy and welcoming, although on a Saturday lunchtime it was a tad austere. Service started sprightly but tailed off to sluggish.

BUSHEY

St James
30 High Street, Bushey, WD23 3HL (020 8950 2480). **Lunch served** noon-2pm, **dinner served** 6.30-9.30pm Mon-Sat. **Main courses** £10.95-£19.95. **Set meal** £13.95 2 courses. **Credit** MC, V.

Overlooking its namesake church, St James is a smart but relaxed venue where business lunchers sit alongside casual diners. The largely European menu features classic fish and meat dishes, well presented and served by discreet yet attentive staff. Starters might include grilled calamares, mussel and chorizo salad or pan-fried beef fillet patty with quail's egg; for mains, there's sautéed calf's liver with crispy bacon, dauphinoise potato and pea purée or roast pork fillet with pommery mash. Fish dishes include grilled swordfish with Waldorf salad, with seared salmon, spiced Thai green curry and crispy

prawn wun tuns providing an oriental touch. Four vegetarian options (available as either starter or main) include marinated vegetable kebabs with houmous, and couscous with field mushrooms topped with melted goat's cheese and pesto dressing – well executed, if rather unimaginative. Dessert selections, while similarly standard, include a voluptuous lemon posset with fresh berries.

FRITHSDEN

Alford Arms
Frithsden, HP1 3DD (01442 864480). **Lunch served** noon-2.30pm Mon-Sat; noon-3pm Sun. **Dinner served** 7-10pm daily. **Main courses** £9.25-£13. **Credit** AmEx, MC, V.

Set in an absurdly picturesque hamlet, the Alford Arms is one of those secrets that everyone knows about. Inside it's simply decorated, its pale colours and plain wood giving it a rustic but Shaker-ish quality; outside there's a small patio garden that heaves with people on a hot day. Despite the numbers, the staff seem to cope admirably, taking orders at the bar or from the dining area speedily and with good humour. Food is very competently cooked and presented. 'Small plates' such as rustic breads with roast garlic, balsamic vinegar and olive oil or seared scallops on mixed leaves with yellow pepper dressing crank the taste buds into action. The dozen or so main meals incline towards the hearty: roast leg of lamb with redcurrant and rosemary jus; pork, oregano and basil sausages with mash and roast red onion gravy; or Cajun chicken on mash with crushed black pepper sauce. Vegetables or salad cost extra. The Alford is rather a victim of its own popularity, with weekend gastropub fans producing a steady stream of cars that clog up the pretty lanes nearby and make impulsive visits a no-no; book well in advance.

KINGS LANGLEY

La Casetta
18 High Street, Kings Langley, WD4 8BH (01923 263823/www.lacasetta.co.uk). **Lunch served** noon-2.30pm Tue-Fri; 12.30-3pm 1st Sun of mth. **Dinner served** 7-10.30pm Tue-Sat. **Main courses** £10.25-£15.95. **Set lunch** £11.95 2 courses. **Set dinner** £18.95 2 courses, £22.50 3 courses Fri, Sat. **Credit** MC, V.

You have to virtually crawl up the steep, creaky old staircase to the series of tiny olde worlde dining rooms in this former 16th-century cottage, but of course that's part of its appeal to the blazer-and-blouse brigade who habitually dine here. It's an

Sukiyaki

incredibly popular venue – book well ahead – thanks to the combination of rustic charm, extremely diligent service and well-executed modern-ish Italian food. The set menus offer good value. On our visit a pretty standard selection of antipasti was lifted by the inclusion of smoked salmon and spiced mussels; carpaccio of smoked duck breast, redcurrant and port sauce with rocket salad was a successful blend of sweet, peppery and smoky. Roast chicken breast, spinach and roast potatoes with fresh grapes and Vin Santo jus was tasty but unspectacular, while roast salmon with pesto butter crust and niçoise-style vegetables was succulent and flavoursome. The wine list is mainly Italian, but broadened out with a few New World options.

ST ALBANS

Carluccio's Caffé ★

7-8 Christopher Place, St Albans, AL3 5DQ (01727 837681/www.carluccios.com). **Meals served** 8am-11pm Mon-Fri; 10am-11pm Sat; 10am-10pm Sun. **Main courses** £4.95-£10.50. **Credit** AmEx, MC, V.
Bringing its successful recipe of good value, authentic Italian food and family-friendly surroundings to St Albans, this is the first Carluccio's Caffé in the chain to open outside London. Well situated in a pedestrian area off the hectic market street, there's an alfresco dining area out front. Beyond the alimentari indoors, tables are arranged between a coffee bar and banquette seating. At weekends, service can be slow – but comes with a smile, and what's a little wait when the coffee's this good? Salads, antipasti, breads and pastries are all invitingly fresh – try the deep-fried rice balls filled with mozzarella and meat in a red pepper sauce. Larger dishes might be pasta with wild boar ragu, spinach and ricotta ravioli, pan-fried chicken or char-grilled tuna steak with sautéed spinach. We loved their spaghetti alle vongole. To finish, there are lovely mandarin and lemon sorbets, or tiramisu and chocolate truffle pudding for the very sweet-toothed.

The Conservatory

St Michael's Manor Hotel, Fishpool Street, St Albans, AL3 4RY (01727 864444/www.stmichaelsmanor.com). **Lunch served** 12.30-2pm daily. **Dinner served** 7-9.30pm Mon-Sat; 7-9pm Sun. **Set lunch** £21.50 2 courses, £25 3 courses. **Set dinner** £36 3 courses. **Credit** AmEx, DC, MC, V.
The dining room and adjoining conservatory of this stately old ivy-clad hotel are very much in a grand period style – although the exact era is open to debate – with an abundance of gilt mirrors, sombre prints, potted palms, chandeliers and fleur-de-lys wallpaper. During the week it tends to host corporate meetings, with families (children are very welcome), couples and wedding parties heading here more at weekends. The food, mainly available through the set menus, is modern and eclectic, and combines beautiful presentation with an imaginative and light-handed blend of ingredients. Fish is especially good. Starters include langoustine and papaya salad with tamarind dressing or crab and avocado salad with a lemon and orange scented hollandaise. Main courses could be rack of lamb en croute on a bed of celeriac purée; baby aubergines filled with wild mushrooms, topped with basil breadcrumbs and tarragon cream; or carpaccio of beef with rocket, fresh figs and balsamic dressing. Puddings are light and fragrant. The extensive wine list is updated every six months. Sit in the spacious, sunny conservatory if you can – the view over the gardens and lake is lovely.

Sukiyaki

6 Spencer Street, St Albans, AL3 5EG (01727 865009). **Lunch served** noon-2.15pm, **dinner served** 6.30-11.30pm Tue-Sat. **Main courses** £8.50-£17.50. **Set lunch** £7-£9.50 incl miso soup, rice & pickles. **Set dinner** £18.50-£24.50 5 courses. **Credit** AmEx, DC, MC, V.
Sukiyaki's plant-filled interior is clean, bright and simply decorated in light wood with oriental-style tall-backed chairs and framed calligraphy on white

walls; staff are charming and attentive. There are no noodle dishes or sushi (the owners can't find a supplier who can guarantee the necessary freshness). The menu features straightforward, authentic Japanese home cooking – fresh ingredients, delicately and subtly seasoned. The beef shoga set lunch (slices of prime beef cooked in ginger and soy) is served with rice, salad, sharp pickles and a smooth miso soup. For vegetarian diners, replacing king prawns from the Ebi tempura with a selection of vegetables (coated in almost translucent batter) was no problem; a suggested side dish of agedashi dofu – cubes of deliciously crispy deep-fried beancurd and light shoyu sauce – also went down well. Other main courses include the eponymous sukiyaki, tonkatsu and tori tatsuta age (pork and chicken marinated in soy and ginger, and deep-fried in breadcrumbs) and salmon teriyaki. Portions are generous and satisfying, prices fair, the service and surroundings delightful; all in all, an extremely likeable restaurant.

TRING

Fornovivo ★

69 High Street, Tring, HP23 4AB (01442 890005/ www.fornovivo.com). **dinner served** 6-10.30pm Mon-Fri. **Meals served** noon-10.30pm Sat; noon-10pm Sun. **Main courses** £5.75-£10.95. **Credit** MC, V.

Lurking behind Tring's pretty, sedate high street façade is this well-designed, spacious pizzeria, housed in the former post office. The minimalist wood-and-concrete setting looks great, although the acoustics are a challange, especially with naff Italian music playing at full blast. But let's not be churlish; the pizzas (around £5-£8) – slim, crispy and heavily loaded – are cooked in front of you in an enormous stone oven. There are standard but well-presented starters, such as affettati alla forno vivi – a generous platter of cold meats, cheese and char-grilled vegetables – and fairly traditional pasta and meat mains. Service is swift and efficient, the atmosphere

friendly and the whole operation thoroughly spick and span. Kids are welcome and there's a special menu featuring mini portions for £3-£4.

WELWYN

Auberge du Lac ★

Brocket Hall, Welwyn, AL8 7XG (01707 368888/ www.brocket-hall.co.uk). **Lunch served** noon-2.15pm Tue-Sun. **Dinner served** 7-10.30pm Tue-Sat. **Main courses** £14.50-£30. **Set lunch** (Tue-Fri) £28 3 courses; (Sat, Sun) £35 3 courses. **Credit** AmEx, DC, MC, V.

Talented, high-profile chef Jean-Christophe Novelli has risen phoenix-like from the charred remains of his former London venture to set up at Auberge du Lac. A pretty, green-shuttered 18th-century hunting lodge, it overlooks the lake just across from Brocket Hall, an exclusive hotel and golf club. It's furnished in opulent English country house style that just escapes being naff, but the food here is extravagantly French, with no apologies to vegetarians or butter-haters. Main dishes are robust, but are so highly crafted that you're never in danger of overkill. Favourites include braised pig's trotter or 'selection of the day butcher plate', one stuffed and the other chosen 'according to Jean-Christophe's versatile mood'. Lighter concoctions include a crab, avocado and Norwegian prawn salad with lemon, poached quail's egg, caviar and anchovy dressing, exquisitely flavoured and assembled. Desserts revolve around fresh fruit, cream and spirals of spun sugar; the wine list, as you'd expect, is extensive, and with a strong French presence. Guests are well looked after by enthusiastic staff and you may well be graced with a visit from the great man himself.

Also in the area

Loch Fyne 12 Hadley Highstone, Barnet, EN5 4PU (020 8449 3674); **Wagamama** Unit 6, Christopher Place, St Albans, AL3 5DQ.

Oxfordshire

ARDINGTON

The Boar's Head

Church Street, Ardington, OX12 8QA (01235 833254). **Lunch served** noon-2pm Tue-Sat; noon-2.30pm Sun. **Dinner served** 7-9pm Mon-Thur; 7-10pm Fri, Sat. **Main courses** £13.95-£16.95. **Credit** AmEx, MC, V.

Ardington is a pretty estate village sitting below the Ridgeway just outside Wantage. The Boar's Head is situated next to a large flintstone church, and is believed to have been an inn since the 18th century. The eating area is beyond the bar, in a couple of rooms opened up and lightened with the strategic use of simple blocks of colour. The mod Brit food is equally bright and breezy. A terrine of foie gras came with a drizzle of quince syrup and balsamic jelly, while roast tomato tatin was filled out with melted goat's cheese and a rather anonymous avocado salsa. Indeed the salsa was the weakest link in a fine selection of flavoured sauces – breast of duck came with a flighty elderflower sauce; steamed turbot with scallop mousse was sweetened by a rich chive butter sauce; and Dover sole with a truffle hollandaise. While the Boar's Head is not premier league, we've never left disappointed.

BUCKLAND

The Lamb at Buckland

Lamb Lane, Buckland, SN7 8QN (01367 870484/ www.thelambatbuckland.co.uk). **Lunch served** noon-2pm Tue-Sat; noon-3pm Sun. **Dinner served** 6.30-9pm Tue-Fri; 6.30-10pm Sat. **Main courses** £10.95-£21.95. **Set meals** *bar* (Tue-Thur) £7.95 2 courses, £11.95 3 courses. **Credit** MC, V.

Buckland is a small village on the edge of the Cotswolds, with pleasant stone cottages. The Lamb is also a hotel, and the old building has the almost obligatory ugly dining extension. However the beamed bar area is more prepossessing; here an open fire roars below a blackboard listing a wide range of dishes. A creamy goat's cheese came with a chutney and red pepper tomato sauce, while fresh asparagus with melted butter and parmesan was a generous portion of rather bland but hefty stalks. Steak and kidney pie swam in a rich dark sauce below a pastry lid, while spiced chicken, bacon and avocado was plentiful. Unfortunately service was very slow (the bread arrived half an hour after the butter), but this may have been on account of the rugby club dinner that slowly formed a noisy grunting scrum in the bar, although the quality of the cooking remained unaffected.

The Trout

Tadpole Bridge, Buckland Marsh, Buckland, SN7 8RF (01367 870382/www.trout-inn.co.uk). **Lunch served** noon-2pm daily. **Dinner served** 7-9pm Mon-Sat. **Main courses** £7.95-£15.95. **Credit** MC, V.

Set in an isolated spot near the Cotswold villages of Bampton and Buckland, the Trout can cater for both the hearty local drinker at the long bar at the front, or for large parties of diners at the tables round the side and in the substantial garden. Formalities are kept to a minimum – on our visit the maitre d' (far too grand a title) wore shorts, while the lively bar is a constant reminder that there is no point standing on ceremony. The menu is original and imaginative: a pork terrine starter comes with a prune compote and a poached pear; the trout gravadlax with marinated cucumber and drop scones. Mains are equally inspiring. Try roast rack of lamb with haggis sauce, almond-crusted roast loin of venison with vanilla risotto and chocolate sauce or pan-fried loin of pork with apple tatin and black pudding. On the whole the combinations are very successful (the venison's risotto and chocolate sauce was appropriately subtle, although the duck – with sweet potato rösti – was too pink), and reflect a refreshing appetite for experimentation in the kitchen.

BURFORD

Jonathan's at the Angel

14 Witney Street, Burford, OX18 4SN (01993 822714/www.theangeluk.com). **Lunch served** noon-2pm Tue-Sun. **Dinner served** 7-9.30pm Tue-Sat. **Main courses** £13.95-£18.50. **Set lunch** £14.50 2 courses, £18.50 3 courses. **Credit** MC, V.

This country-kitchen brasserie, housed in a 16th-century coaching inn in one of the Cotswolds' most beautiful towns, comes as something of a relief after all the formal pub dining rooms in the area. It has a mellow, welcoming feel and unmistakeably personal tone – for all that it's part of a hotel it feels far from institutional, perhaps because chef-patron Jonathan Lewis is very hands-on. His blackboard menu is likely to include five or six starters plus an 'interesting' soup such as chilled smoked salmon and watercress, and the same number of mains. Dishes are modern British/European, more complex than the brasserie setting might suggest: try monkfish roasted in smoked bacon with a citrus salsa, followed by fig and frangipane tart with pecan and maple syrup ice-cream. There's often game too. In summer there's the back terrace, with awning, if the very pine-heavy dining room, candlelit at night, doesn't appeal.

Central

Lamb Inn & Restaurant

Sheep Street, Burford, OX18 4LR (01993 823155).
Bar **Lunch served** noon-2.30pm, **dinner served**
7-9pm daily. *Restaurant* **Lunch served** noon-2pm,
dinner served 7-9.30pm daily. **Main courses**
£14.95-£19.50. **Set lunch** (Sun) £15 2 courses,
£22.50 3 courses. **Credit** MC, V.

Burford is turning into a bit of a restaurant mecca
with the arrival of Jonathan's at the Angel (*see p168*),
but the Lamb still more than holds its own. An
upmarket pub that's kept its wooden bar settles and
a proper drinking area (admittedly gentrified), it has
a lovely dining room and candlelit courtyard terrace,
all smartly kept and staffed. The restaurant is
formal without being oppressive: simple white
nappery and paintwork, botanical prints, rich
curtains and, a nice detail, well-designed modern
cutlery. The menu is short (perhaps a little too short;
on our visit one alternative ran out) and uses luxury
and seasonal ingredients in dishes firmly in the
modern vernacular. Cooking varied from the good
(pancetta-wrapped monkfish with sesame seed rice)
to the excellent (foie gras and guinea fowl ravioli),
though we're not sure where on that continuum to
place a strawberry cake whose tired fruit was
unsubtly overlaid with fresh cream.

CHINNOR

Sir Charles Napier

*Spriggs Alley, nr Chinnor, OX39 4BX (01494
483011/www.sircharlesnapier.co.uk).* **Lunch served**
noon-2.30pm Tue-Sat; 12.30-3.30pm Sun. **Dinner
served** 7-9.30pm Tue-Sat; 7-10pm Sun. **Main
courses** £11.50-£17.50. **Set meal** (Tue-Fri) £16.50
2 courses. **Credit** AmEx, MC, V.

There's something simultaneously formal and
unfussy about the Napier: throughout the building,
ornate mirrors and artful, modern furnishings
compete for space with a glorious jumble of wicker
baskets and raffia placemats, but there's nothing
haphazard about the menu, which is subtle and
superb from the first. A starter of tomato risotto with
squid and parmesan was a masterpiece of
complementary colours and flavours, and we were
equally pleased by a main of baked red mullet with
orange ratatouille. Finally, a sublime chocolate
fondant with pistachio ice-cream was the last word
in indulgence. In the winter there might be pumpkin
and garlic soup followed by roast woodcock, braised
endive and rösti; and on Sundays the comfort of
roast Oxfordshire pork with crackling and apple.

GORING

The Leatherne Bottel

*The Bridleway, Goring-on-Thames, RG8 0HS (01491
872667/www.leathernebottel.co.uk).* **Lunch served**
noon-2pm Mon-Fri; noon-2.30pm Sat; noon-3.30pm
Sun. **Dinner served** 7-9pm Mon-Thur; 7-9.30pm
Fri, Sat. **Main courses** £17-£20. **Set dinner**
(Mon-Fri) £23.50 3 courses. **Credit** AmEx, MC, V.

If you can't decide on a setting of river or
countryside, this is for you. Pick a sunny day, relax
and drink in the peace and champers – there's plenty
of both and the first one is free. The two-part
sunshine yellow dining room is decorated with sleek
bronze nudes and jolly oil paintings of Cuba (both
for sale). Cigars, caviar and fine wines advertise their
presence rather pompously and the menu isn't
exactly a bargain, with vegetarian main courses
running at £18, but you can have a piece of riverside
paradise for as long as you like once you've ordered.
Garden crosses into kitchen often, such as in an own-
grown herb salad with at least a dozen different
leaves, and in an elderflower and lemon meringue
roulade. Otherwise, roast vegetable and goat's
cheese lasagne was light and punchily flavoured,
and Thai fish curry another extrovert dish. Children
are not encouraged.

GREAT MILTON

Le Manoir aux Quat' Saisons

*Church Road, Great Milton, OX44 7PD (01844
278881/www.manoir.com).* **Lunch served** 11.15am-
2.45pm, **dinner served** 6.45-9.30pm daily. **Main
courses** £36-£38. **Set lunch** (Mon-Fri) £45
3 courses. **Set meal** £95 7 courses. **Credit** AmEx,
DC, MC, V.

It's hard to imagine having a better meal anywhere.
Raymond Blanc's winning formula is simple: you
pay serious money for seriously good food in a
beautiful setting. Expect lunch to cost upwards of
£80 a head, with dinner rising into the hundreds.
While the house and gardens are beautifully
maintained, they're comfortable rather than
pretentious and although most people do dress up,
a few souls can be seen in casual garb. In fact, while
the Manoir is undoubtedly smart and expensive, it
really isn't stuffy. You'll be waited on hand and foot
by a young, all-smiling, all-French assortment of
staff as you enjoy drinks and a plate of appetisers
(mini soufflés, smoked salmon blinis, tapenade on
toastlets) in the drawing room, and from there it's to
your table and a *bonne-bouche* (in our case a tiny cup
of gazpacho) and a wonderful choice of ten or so
breads. Hors d'oeuvres include pan-seared scallops
and langoustines, braised fennel with a lemon confit
or baby garden vegetable risotto, Sicilian tomatoes
and mascarpone cream. Then on to roast breast of
Trelough duck, gratin dauphinois and foie gras
sauce or pan-fried veal kidneys, Burgundy snails,
red wine jus with green chartreuse and purée of
shallots (or at least one vegetarian and three fish
dishes). Puddings such as raspberry soufflé and its
own sorbet and crème brûlée with Tahiti vanilla
make a fine finish. For a little bit of everything try
the menu gourmand. You'll need to book four to six
weeks in advance to be sure of a table. If you haven't
had to foot the bill, you can buy a selection of
Raymond Blanc's cookery books and merchandise
in the foyer; if you are the paymaster, then you might
want a consoling wander round the gardens.

Central (vertical tab)

KING'S SUTTON

White Horse

The Square, King's Sutton, OX17 3RF (01295 810843). **Lunch served** noon-2pm Mon-Sat; noon-4pm Sun. **Dinner served** 6-9pm Mon-Sat. **Main courses** £6.95-£14.95. **Credit** AmEx, MC, V.

A refurb has turned this sports bar into a chic local dining destination. The look is stripped pine, mismatched chairs and tables, softened with warm tones on the walls, pillar candles and arty lamps. Starters are under a fiver and include such delicacies as black pudding salad with lardons and a poached egg. Next, beer-battered cod was a chunky piece of fish with a crisp batter and came with hand-cut chips. Coffee crème brûlée was good too, with a perfect not-too-thick-not-too-thin caramel crust. The dark chocolate tart, though, was tired and the chocolate measly. At Sunday lunch roast lamb (£7.95) comes piled high with spuds and vegetables.

MIDDLE ASSENDON

Rainbow Inn

Middle Assendon, RG9 6AU (01491 574879). **Lunch served** noon-2pm, **dinner served** 7-9pm daily. **Main courses** £7.50-£12.95. **Credit** MC, V.

The Rainbow is a pretty, no-frills 17th-century pub, with a sweet garden set in a charming village. Enter the dining area, and the simple tables and basic settings suggest that there's no room for airs and graces here. The disarmingly friendly landlord and the familiar banter from the next door bar confirm that this is still very much the village pub, popular with the locals and untarnished by the justifiably fine reputation of its kitchen. The menu has something for everyone, with starters ranging from brie wedges to herrings marinated in sherry to an excellent bruschetta of tomatoes, onions, garlic and pesto. The mains will also satisfy a wide range of tastes – there's Thai chicken curry, own-made chicken and mushroom pie or salmon fish cakes with a slick cream and lemon sauce. The Rainbow isn't a grand affair, but it is all the better for that, and you can be guaranteed a hearty welcome and a fine meal.

MOULSFORD

The Beetle & Wedge

Ferry Lane, Moulsford, OX10 9JF (01491 651381/ www.beetleandwedge.co.uk). Brasserie **Lunch served** noon-2pm, **dinner served** 7-10pm daily. **Main courses** £12-£20. *Restaurant* **Lunch served** noon-2pm Sun. **Dinner served** 7-10pm Thur-Sat. **Main courses** £15-£21.50. **Set lunch** £37.50 3 courses incl coffee. **Credit** AmEx, DC, MC, V.

This is the place to bring your parents for that special meal, or for a romantic getaway from the city, although best to come in a Range Rover if you don't want to feel out of place. The Beetle & Wedge is both

Chiang Mai Kitchen. *See p172.*

Central

a hotel and a restaurant, and has a delightful riverside setting. The impeccably decorated dining room feels more like a sumptuous drawing room, and a grand conservatory overlooks the Thames as it glides idly by. The old boat house offers a large, more down-to-earth dining area. Whichever you choose, expect an enticing menu (vegetarians excepted). The dining room begins with an emphasis on fish – avocado and Cornish crab salad, gravadlax, smoked salmon and Mediterranean prawns with blinis, or saffron risotto with parmesan shavings, asparagus, mussels, tiger prawns and langoustines. Monkfish or Dover sole are also available for mains, but this is when the meat muscles in – Gressingham duck, saddle of venison with chestnuts, beef with shallots or veal cutlets and liver. The cuts are tender and juicy, and the sauces sweet and subtle, and all the mains come with a creamy gratin dauphinois. If you choose to eat in the boat house, there's a wider choice, including a selection of fish and meats from the charcoal grill, but it's not much cheaper. All in all, though, it's well worth a mooring fee.

NETTLEBED

The White Hart
High Street, Nettlebed, RG9 5DD (01491 641245/ www.whiteheartnettlebed.com). Bistro **Lunch served** noon-2.30pm, **dinner served** 6-10pm daily. **Main courses** £9-£16. **Set meals** £10 2 courses, £15 3 courses. *Restaurant* **Lunch served** noon-2.30pm, **dinner served** 6-10pm Tue-Sat. **Set meals** £25 2 courses, £35 3 courses, £50 8 courses. **Credit** MC, V.

You could be seated just a pavement's width from the main road in this hotel restaurant, but you wouldn't know it. A Scandinavian-inspired modern interior and a centuries-old building make for an arresting setting: whitewashed beams are set against clean pine and chrome lines and sharp bright pictures sit on irregular walls. Ignore the MOR numbers churning in the background and attend to the artful, good-value menu. From around half a dozen starters and mains, spinach, broccoli and feta tart with a rocket salad and a creamy sweet cauliflower soup made a great beginning. Ribeye steak and fish cakes were sound but unspectacular, though they came with fab chips and glazed french beans. Service was unassuming and efficient. In short, one to return to.

OXFORD

Bar Meze ★
146 London Road, Headington, Oxford, OX3 9ED (01865 761106/www.bar.meze.co.uk). **Lunch served** 11.30am-5pm, **dinner served** 5-10.30pm daily. **Main courses** £10-£14. **Set lunch** £6 2 mezes incl drink. **Credit** AmEx, MC, V.

A success on a previously jinxed site, this modish Turkish meze joint has quickly become Headington's prime dining spot. Keen prices and a long list of hot and cold snacks are the draw. Feta salad comes with sun-dried tomatoes and olives; marinated squid comes with chickpeas; and lahmacun pizzas arrive sprinkled with tasty minced lamb. Main courses shouldn't be ignored, incik lamb stew featuring alongside a selection of more workaday kebabs. The long dining room is decorated with rag-rolled yellow walls, leather armchairs, wooden flooring and bronze artefacts. At the rear a skylight brightens lunchtime proceedings. Staff are competent if not always chirpy. Musicians play on Mondays.

Branca ★

111 Walton Street, Oxford, OX2 6AJ (01865 556111/www.branca-restaurants.com). **Meals served** noon-11pm Mon-Thur, Sun; noon-11.30pm Fri, Sat. **Main courses** £8.25-£16.95. **Set lunch** (noon-5pm Mon-Fri) £5 1 course incl drink. **Set dinner** (5-7pm Mon-Fri) £10 2 courses incl drink. **Credit** AmEx, MC, V.

The three-year-old Branca is bright, confident and bustling. This large trend-conscious bar-brasserie offers a well-sourced collection of modern Italian dishes: char-grilled squid salad or a creamy, parsley-speckled smoked haddock risotto topped with a perfect poached egg. The menu also has room for stone-baked pizzas (featuring goat's cheese, roast peppers and so on), a clutch of pastas and more substantial mains, such as roast monkfish with smoked Italian ham and braised lentils. Breezy young women in white tops and jeans provide the service. Cocktails, an interesting Italian wine choice and a well thought out children's menu also augur well. The £5 lunch deal (pizza, antipasti, salad or risotto, plus glass of wine or beer) is an excellent one, especially when accompanied by the complimentary bread and olive oil.

Brookes

Oxford Brookes University, Gipsy Lane, Headington, Oxford, OX3 0BP (01865 483803/ www.brookes.ac.uk/restaurant). **Lunch served** noon-2pm Mon-Fri. **Dinner served** 6-8.30pm Fri. **Main courses** £9-£14. **Set lunch** £10.95 3 courses. **Credit** MC, V.

Run by the university's department of hospitality, Brookes is worth knowing about. Food is well-executed modern European, inexpensive and expertly presented; the setting (despite a drab campus exterior) is light and stylish. Well-dressed academics and their business accomplices lunch in the plusher rear section; more informal meals are served at the front. You needn't book for the 'quick lunch' (featuring light dishes such as salmon with leek and dill purée), but then you might miss the likes of marinated mushrooms on red chard, sage croûtons and gorgonzola vinaigrette, followed by guinea fowl with lemon and coriander couscous on cumin velouté. Ingredients tend to be seasonal and local; vegetarians are well cared for. Staff are professional, though it's a pity students aren't given more of a role – to sample their skills, book for an evening theme night (see the website for details).

Cherwell Boat House

Bardwell Road, Oxford, OX2 6SR (01865 552746/ www.cherwellboathouse.co.uk). **Lunch served** noon-2pm, **dinner served** 6.30-9pm daily. **Set lunch** (Mon-Fri) £12.50 2 courses, £15.50 3 courses (express), £19.50 3 courses; (Sat, Sun) £20.50 3 courses. **Set dinner** £22.50 3 courses. **Credit** AmEx, MC, V.

A verdant, unspoilt stretch of the River Cherwell makes a tranquil setting for lunches at the Boat House. By night, the place gets packed with Oxford's haute bourgeoisie; birdsong and bucolic views are replaced by braying and blazers. The oft-changing set-price modern European menu might kick off with own-cured gravadlax (though for 'coriander and lemon coleslaw' read 'coleslaw and a wedge of lemon'). Next, pink and perfect barbary duck breast could be teamed with a too-sweet ensemble of roast pear, red cabbage and blackcurrant jus. Creamy, tart lemon posset was the star of a recent meal. A refit has rendered the interior light and modern, though in fine weather an outside seat by the water remains the hot ticket. The wine list is notable (the proprietor is a wine merchant) and, like the occasionally off-hand but competent staff, is mostly French.

Chiang Mai Kitchen

Kemp Hall Passage, 130A High Street, Oxford, OX1 4DH (01865 202233/www.chiangmaikitchen.co.uk). **Lunch served** noon-2.30pm daily. **Dinner served** 6-10.15pm Mon-Thur; 6-10.30pm Fri, Sat; 6-10pm Sun. **Main courses** £7-£10. **Credit** AmEx, DC, MC, V.

Like much of Oxford, it is the surroundings that make this popular, upmarket Thai so memorable. The beautiful 14th-century building that houses the restaurant is to be found in a dinky side-street off the High Street opposite the market. The main dining room upstairs is more reminiscent of a gentlemen's smoking club than a modern Thai. A starter of rice dumplings stuffed with pork has delightful little nuggets of water chestnut hidden in the mix. The stir-fried beef with garlic was a tad chewy, but all fish dishes proved successful and satisfying. There is a high turnover of customers here, for proof of that look no further than the paper tablecloths. Service is very attentive, but the setting's the thing.

Edamame ★

15 Holywell Street, Oxford, OX1 3SA (01865 246916/www.edamame.co.uk). **Lunch served** 11.30-2.30pm Tue-Sat; noon-4pm Sun. **Dinner served** 5-8.30pm Thur-Sat. **Main courses** £6.50-£14. **Credit** (dinner) MC, V.

A tiny Japanese refuelling stop on one of Oxford's most beautiful streets, Edamame frequently has queues erupting from its doors. Don't worry if you're at the back – no one lingers, despite the pleasant, simple interior. You'll usually have to share a table (with post-exam Japanese students in subfusc on our trip). Pay the pleasant staff as soon as you order. There are eight meal-in-one choices for lunch plus a few side dishes, the odd special (piquant Korean pickles, perhaps, or refreshing seaweed salad), and drinks such as calpis, Asahi beer and saké. Chicken karaage teishoku (deep-fried breast chunks with rice and miso soup) was going down a treat opposite, and we liked the miso ramen: a vast bowlful of noodles in nourishing stock. Dinner on Friday and Saturday has a little more choice, while there's sushi on Thursday evenings.

The Flame

1 The Parade, Windmill Road, Headington, Oxford, OX3 7BL (01865 760309). **Lunch served** noon-1.30pm Mon, Wed-Sun. **Dinner served** 6-11pm Mon, Wed-Sat; 6-10pm Sun. **Main courses** £6.50-£11. **Credit** AmEx, DC, MC, V.

The frontage and bar betray signs of the building's curry house ancestry, but to the rear is a roomy, light, twinkling Persian restaurant. Hubble-bubble pipes (£5 a puff), terracotta flooring and vibrant artefacts create a space that's alluringly exotic. Food, ditto. Start with dips – perhaps the tasty sludge of aubergine, butter bean and lamb (halim bademjan) – with feather-light Persian bread. Kebabs are well seared and juicy, judging from the minced lamb version (there's a vegetable option); stews feature long-simmered chicken or lamb in rich, often fruity, rarely chilli-hot sauces. Rice is Persian perfect. A pot of sumac spice (on the table) and dough yoghurt drink (on the menu) add welcome sour notes. Service is warmth itself, if forgetful; wine is well priced. The Flame deserves more custom.

Gee's

61A Banbury Road, Oxford, OX2 6PE (01865 553540/www.gees-restaurant.co.uk). **Lunch served** noon-2.30pm Mon-Sat; noon-3.30pm Sun. **Dinner served** 6-10.30pm Mon-Thur, Sun; 6-11pm Fri, Sat. **Main courses** £10.50-£18.95. **Set lunch** (Mon-Fri) £12.50 2 courses, £16 3 courses. **Set dinner** £24.95 3 courses. **Credit** AmEx, MC, V.

A capacious Victorian conservatory with wrought-iron candelabras and bamboo chairs makes an impressive dining venue. Popular with business lunchers, Gee's offers a varied wine list (eight choices by the glass), smart service and a menu suffused with Mediterranean modishness plus seasonal 'star dishes' (pan-fried sea bass with tagliatelle and samphire). A set lunch began with cheesy risotto peppered with aromatic home-grown herbs. Next, a well-marinated pork T-bone steak had to be sent back for extra cooking, and though the accompanying black pud and tart apple slices were apt, a willy-nilly drizzling of olive oil was not, giving the dish a fry-up sheen. Standards soared with a warm, moist apricot and almond tart with blueberry compote. So, a patchy meal, but Gee's is well liked by Oxford's cognoscenti. Run by the folk behind the Old Parsonage (*see p174*).

Kazbar ★

25-27 Cowley Road, Oxford, OX4 1HP (01865 202920). **Lunch served** noon-5pm Fri-Sun. **Dinner served** 5-11pm daily. **Tapas** £3-£4.50. **Set lunch** £5.50 2 tapas incl drink. **Credit** MC, V.

A tapas bar with North African leanings, Kazbar is popular with office workers by day and a funkier mix of students and tourists by night (when the music is loud). An ancient Spanish bar has been recreated by dint of heavy wooden doors, wrought-iron grilles, soaring ceilings (in the glass-roofed bar), adobe-hued walls and a display of vast vases in the rear dining area. Moorish snacks such as chicken tagine are joined on the menu by Spanish standards (flavour-suffused patatas con chorizo), daily specials such as asparagus with chilli butter and 'sweet tapas' (baklava). Stews are best as most food is microwaved, though the bocata bread is warm and fresh. Staff are alert. The lunchtime two-tapas-plus-drink deal for £5.50 is worth pursuing.

Liaison ★

29 Castle Street, Oxford, OX1 1LJ (01865 242944/251481). **Dinner served** 6.30-11.30pm Mon-Thur; 6.30pm-12.30am Fri, Sat; 7-11pm Sun. **Main courses** £1.80-£28. **Set dinners** £14.95-£18 3 courses. **Credit** AmEx, MC, V.

To find Liaison in a quaint building in Oxford is astonishing, for this is a real Chinese restaurant attracting real Chinese diners. Come at lunchtime for dim sum that's on a par with many served in Chinatown in London (if occasionally of rather indelicate construction). A mountain of gelatinous pig's skin paired with tender squid tentacles is a textural treat for just £2.80; grilled pork dumplings are nicely scorched; king prawn cheung fun features slithery-fresh pasta. Fill up on one of many noodle dishes. The full menu, too, contains food rarely seen outside Chinatowns: hot-pots such as belly pork with preserved vegetables and textural juxtapositions such as fried aubergine with minced prawns. The windowless interior can seem cramped when full, though spotlights, faux windows and mustard-hued walls leaven the mix. Service is efficient and friendly.

Mario ★

103 Cowley Road, Oxford, OX4 1HU (01865 722955). **Meals served** 6-11pm Mon-Sat; 6-10.30pm Sun. **Main courses** £5.80-£7.90. **Credit** MC, V.

Cherished as much for its cheery Italian service as its pizza and pasta, Mario's soon fills with a mix of students, ex-students and hangers-on. Enter past the takeaway counter-cum-kitchen and ascend the few stairs at the back into the dining area, simply furnished with bright pictures on yellowing walls. When this gets full, a lower-ground area comes into play. Songs from back home play. Mario's pizzas have chewy bases and nicely scorched bottoms (too burnt on occasion). There's nothing outlandish about the toppings: spicy sausage, artichokes, ham, olives and anchovies being the bung-it-all-in option. Tortellini with chopped ham and salami, fresh tomatoes and cream was a fairish rendition, though mixed salad was dull. Specials like whitebait or calzone broaden the choice. Come for a convivial chat over a bottle of red.

Central

The Old Parsonage

*1 Banbury Road, Oxford, OX2 6NN (01865
310210/www.oxford-hotels-restaurants.co.uk).*
Breakfast served 9-10.30am, **lunch served**
noon-2.30pm, **dinner served** 6-10.30pm daily.
Tea served 3-5pm Mon-Sat; 3.30-5pm Sun. **Main
courses** £10-£15. **Credit** AmEx, DC, MC, V.
For a fairly posh hotel in the centre of Oxford, the
main dining space of the Old Parsonage is
wonderfully informal. It's more like a pub lounge than
a restaurant, with comfy armchairs to sit in, low tables
and walls that are plastered with Oxford-themed
prints and photographs. Food is MOR modern
European: salmon and dill fish cakes with green salad
and lemon mayo; rump of Welsh lamb with roast
peppers and rosemary jus. An excellent twice-baked
spinach and parmesan soufflé hinted at heights the
kitchen can hit. There is a pretty, sunken front garden
to eat in on sunny days and the restaurant is also open
for breakfast, lunch and highly recommended scone
and cream-crammed afternoon teas.

Quod

*92-94 High Street, Oxford, OX1 4BN (01865
202505).* **Meals served** noon-11pm daily. **Main
courses** £8-£17. **Set lunch** (noon-3pm Mon-Fri)
£8.75 2 courses. **Credit** AmEx, MC, V.
Like its London counterparts, this branch of Quod
is huge, occupying a former bank on a prime site in
the High Street. Bag a window seat and crane your
head upwards for a view of dreaming spires.
Alternatively lounge on a banquette, perch on a bar
stool or grab a chair on the back terrace. Keen,
youthful, corporately trained staff dressed in blue
flit hither and thither. Tourists and locals flock here.
The modern Italian-leaning menu has a forte in
cured meats. The good-value 'express lunch' began
with a stringy broccoli and asparagus soup. Next,
char-grilled chicken breast rested on two thick slices
of supposedly marinated aubergine and nicely fried
leeks. Pizzas, pastas, main courses such as slow-
roasted lamb shank and fish specials are
alternatives. Vanilla panna cotta is among the
puddings. The wine list includes over a dozen
choices by the (small or large) glass.

ROTHERFIELD PEPPARD

The Greyhound

*Gallowstree Lane, Rotherfield Peppard, RG9 5HT
(01189 722227).* **Lunch served** noon-3pm,
dinner served 7-9.30pm daily. **Main courses**
£12-£16. **Credit** AmEx, DC, MC, V.
This charming period building is a local favourite,
drawing well-heeled inhabitants from their leafy
retreats in and around Henley. The main bar area
certainly dates back centuries, but the huge vaulted
dining room is not quite as Elizabethan as its
impressive beamed interior suggests; it is, in point
of fact, only about 20 years old. Nevertheless, with
portraits and grand oil paintings gracing the walls,
the Greyhound succeeds in presenting an aged
image. The menu, however, is anything but old. A

creamy smooth haddock and mushy pea fish cake
was a beautifully presented blend of flavours, and
two generous slices of calf's liver on a bed of mash
was sweetened by a red wine jus and caramelised
onion. Gruyère cheese and spinach soufflé, and fillet
steak in a rich peppercorn and garlic sauce were
equally successful, and although service was a tad
too quick, the kitchens at the Greyhound are doing
justice to the grand extension.

SHIPTON-UNDER-WYCHWOOD

Lamb Inn

*Simons Lane, Shipton-under-Wychwood, OX7 6DQ
(01993 830465/www.traditionalvillageinn.co.uk).*
Lunch served noon-2.45pm, **dinner served**
6.30-9.45pm daily. **Main courses** £8-£15.
Credit AmEx, MC, V.
This lovely Cotswold stone inn dates back to the 16th
century but its current tenants have given both menu
and interior design a sleek 21st-century update: it's
charming, but not chocolate-box. Sit in the tiny
restaurant area, the larger low-lit bar or on tree-
shaded or sunny terraces, drink a glass of ale and
choose boldly flavoured (if occasionally oversalted)
dishes from an internationally influenced menu:
perhaps grilled scallops with cucumber noodles and
tomato and herb consommé; a herb-suffused
haddock and saffron risotto; or a fine sirloin steak
with chorizo and garlic jus. Seasonal fruit dishes
aside, puddings know little restraint (just try the
banana tarte tatin) and the Bailey's bottle rather
well. The young staff are friendly and professional.

STADHAMPTON

Crazy Bear Hotel

*Bear Lane, Stadhampton, OX44 7UR (01865
890714/www.crazybearhotel.co.uk). English
restaurant* **Lunch served** noon-3pm, **dinner
served** 7-10pm daily. **Main courses** £16.50-£17.50.
Set meal (lunch Mon-Sat; dinner Mon-Thur) £12.50
2 courses, £15 3 courses. *Thai brasserie* **Lunch
served** noon-3pm Mon-Sat. **Dinner served** 7-10pm
Mon-Sat; 4-10pm Sun. **Main courses** £8.50-£18.50.
Credit AmEx, DC, MC, V.
Tucked away in a village just outside Oxford, the
Crazy Bear isn't what you might expect from a 16th-
century country inn. There are no horse brasses
here, instead the decor – all pink leather upholstery
and Grecian busts – is decidedly more urban chic.
The food and service match the glam interiors, and
waiting staff wear shirt and tie. There is a rather
bewildering range of menus on offer. The set menu
and all-day menu represent the best value, with more
expensive choices available from the à la carte
English and Thai menus. Classics like kedgeree are
served alongside more quirky choices, such as
sautéed frogs' legs. Dishes are tasty and elegantly
presented. The Crazy Bear is definitely not the place
to stop for a pie and a pint, and if Le Manoir is out
of your price range, it's a novel alternative.

STEEPLE ASTON

Red Lion

South Side, Steeple Aston, OX25 4RY (01869 340225/www.leorufus.co.uk). **Lunch served** noon-2pm Tue-Sun. **Dinner served** 7-9pm Tue-Sat. **Main courses** £7.50-£14.95. **Set lunch** (Sun) £12.95 2 courses, £14.95 3 courses. **Credit** MC, V.

Not to be confused with the White Lion in the village, the red version is a small, handsome country pub with jovial bar staff. The tiny, wonky-walled dining room makes you realise how Alice in Wonderland felt when she took that magic pill. Don't be put off by the predictable menu – it's the way they cook 'em that counts. Pâté-stuffed mushrooms are nothing to write home about, but chicken liver terrine is. The local steak is dry-aged and has a gamey tang, and beef bourguignon is a rich, sticky mass. Chocolate truffle torte is a perfect cylinder of wickedness and its crowning white chocolate truffle is the booziest we've tasted. Even the house wines are good.

STOKE ROW

Crooked Billet

Newland Lane, Stoke Row, RG9 5PU (01491 681048/ www.thecrookedbillet.co.uk). **Lunch served** noon-2.30pm, **dinner served** 7-10pm Mon-Fri. **Meals served** noon-10pm Sat, Sun. **Main courses** £10.75-£19.50. **Set lunch** (Mon-Sat) £11.95 2 courses, £14.95 3 courses; (Sun) £16.95 3 courses. **Credit** MC, V.

Tucked away down a winding lane, the Crooked Billet is a hidden gem. Although it calls itself a pub and has regular jazz and folk concerts, it is in reality more of a restaurant, with a busy sideline in weddings. Ironically perhaps for an institution so keen to launch couples into wedded bliss, children are not so welcome – a notice on the door demands that they behave themselves. As a result, even the small front garden, which slowly loses its charm as the car park fills up and the purring BMWs park alongside, is a relatively child-free zone. The food is excellent: grilled local asparagus and hollandaise was just the right side of al dente; and moreish ham hock came with crisp salad and a puy lentil vinaigrette. The mains included four different fish – haddock, halibut, sea bass and monkfish – but we opted for a moist chicken breast and goat's cheese and a hefty roast rump of lamb with Tuscan country vegetables. Service was quick and efficient, and it capped a low-key but stylish meal.

TETSWORTH

The Swan

High Street, Tetsworth, OX9 7AB (01844 281182/www.theswan.co.uk). **Lunch served** noon-2.15pm Mon-Sat; noon-1.30pm & 3-3.45pm Sun. **Dinner served** 7-9.30pm Tue-Sat. **Main courses** £10.50-£16.75. **Credit** MC, V.

The Swan is a much-loved local institution in Tetsworth, and has been refreshing travellers for over 500 years. In the late 1980s, however, it fell into

disrepair and a fire saw it close entirely. However, in 1995 it reopened as the novel pairing of restaurant and antiques centre; the latter is huge, and represents 80 dealers in a warren of 40 rooms. It was presumably the source for many of the collectable furnishings within the small and delightfully rickety restaurant. Despite the lofty gaze cast by its large, unframed huntsman's portrait, the Swan's atmosphere is anything but stuffy. Staff are young and unassuming, and the first-class menu offers unpretentious, well-prepared food, such as scallop and bacon salad, crispy duck salad with red pepper and chilli dressing, sea bass fillets with citrus vanilla vinaigrette or calf's liver and colcannon imaginatively paired with lime and sage oil. Note that on Sunday there are two sittings for lunch.

THAME

The Old Trout

29-30 Lower High Street, Thame, OX9 2AA (01844 212146/www.theoldtrouthotel.co.uk). **Lunch served** noon-2.30pm, **dinner served** 6.30-9.30pm daily. **Main courses** £9.50-£16.95. **Set lunch** (Mon-Sat) £12 2 courses; (Sun) £16 3 courses. **Credit** AmEx, DC, MC, V.

Opposite the old forge on the High Street in the pretty market town of Thame is the Old Trout, one of a number of 16th-century buildings lining this charming street. The interior is low-ceilinged and beamed (except for a brighter, airier room at the back), with snugs, flagstones and inglenook fireplaces. The menu, like the bulk of the clientele, is upmarket, and the generous portions are best worked off by a gentle saunter around the shops or down to the nearby church. There's a choice of ten starters and ten mains. Pick from a roast beetroot salad, fritto calamares with citrus, stilton and walnut cheesecake or slow-braised pork ribs in a teriyaki sauce. Move on to a halibut fillet en papillote, shellfish paella, pan-fried red bream or porcini-scented risotto – in short, a fair mix of fish and meat with a vegetarian option thrown in. There's a smaller lunch menu, but this is more of an evening out venue.

TURVILLE

The Bull & Butcher

Turville, RG9 6QU (01491 638283/ www.bullandbutcher.com). **Lunch served** noon-2.30pm, **dinner served** 7-9.45pm Mon-Sat. **Meals served** noon-4pm Sun. **Main courses** £10-£16. **Credit** MC, V.

One of those pubs that has everything going for it. At the foot of the Chilterns and set in a chocolate-box village, it is extremely well run, and even on the busiest of summer Sundays, service is timely and courteous. The menu has something for everyone: king prawns with garlic mayonnaise or mozzarella with figs and balsamic vinegar to start, lightly poached salmon or smoked bacon and pepper tagliatelle for mains, with own-made ice-cream for pudding. There is ample seating inside and out, and you can even eat your food off a glass-topped table covering an old, disused well in the main dining room. The Bull & Butcher is popular with walkers doing the Chiltern trail, families and, above all, the locals. Note that at the time of writing, the current manager is planning to relocate to Devon. We can only hope that the new management retains this winning formula.

WANTAGE

Thyme & Plaice

8 Newbury Street, Wantage, OX12 8BS (01235 760568). **Lunch served** noon-2pm Tue-Fri. **Dinner served** 7-9pm Tue-Sat. **Main courses** £15. **Set lunch** £10 2 courses. **Set dinner** (Tue-Thur) £18.50 3 courses. **Credit** AmEx, MC, V.
This 18th-century townhouse is just off the market square in King Alfred's birthplace of Wantage, and has been earning a healthy local reputation since it opened a year ago. There are two rooms set either side of the hallway, with high red-backed chairs adding colour to an otherwise light and simple decor. A small bar fronts the kitchen, where the owner Duncan conjures up a choice selection of modern British fare. Begin with a castle of crab with sweet and sour cucumber and mango salsa, or a smoked duck, pepper and mango salad, and move on to a lamb leg steak on braised lettuce, shallots and minted peas with lemon thyme rösti or a pavé of lightly smoked salmon steak on warm pasta. Mains also include the likes of barbary duck, roast pork fillet and grilled sea bass, but vegetarians are only catered for by request.

WITNEY

The Fleece

11 Church Green, Witney, OX28 4AZ (01993 892270/www.peachpubs.com). **Open** 7.30am-11pm Mon-Sat; 8am-10.30pm Sun. **Breakfast served** 7.30-11am Mon-Sat; 8-10.30am Sun. **Lunch served** noon-2.30pm Mon-Sat; noon-3pm Sun. **Dinner served** 6.30-10pm Mon-Sat; 6.30-9.30pm Sun. **Main courses** £7-£14. **Credit** DC, MC, V.
The Fleece hotel and restaurant has recently been taken over. The new owners have worked hard to provide a comfortable, light and spacious interior: large mirrors hang on the brown and cream walls, and sofas are interspersed among chairs and tables on the wooden floor. Elvis provided the soundtrack on our visit, and an open fire and a selection of the day's papers allow you to enjoy a drink here and dip into the snacks that they also offer – sandwiches, salads, soups and a healthy selection of dips and nibbles from the 'deli board'. You can also sit outside overlooking the green, although the occasional car might spoil the idyll. There was a long wait for the food to arrive, and when it did it was fine, but not exactly memorable: bland roast chicken with leek

and bacon dauphinoise potato in red wine sauce; unremarkable ribeye steak with chips and peppercorn sauce. Perhaps vegetarian options of mozzarella and basil Wellington or Thai green vegetable curry with saffron would have had more zip. Crème brûlée was good. A modern haunt with a metropolitan vibe.

WOODSTOCK

Feathers Hotel

Market Street, Woodstock, OX20 1SX (01993 812291/www.feathers.co.uk). **Lunch served** 12.30-2.30pm, **dinner served** 6.30-9.30pm daily. **Main courses** £16-£22. **Set lunch** £15.50 2 courses, £19.50 3 courses; (Sun) £23.95 3 courses. **Set dinner** £22 2 courses, £28 3 courses. **Credit** AmEx, DC, MC, V.
The Feathers Hotel is the other Woodstock landmark (after Blenheim Palace). It's a handsome beast full of country charm and urbane efficiency. The bar area, with historical accents and otherwise tasteful modern decor, and the prize-winning garden are lovely settings; the restaurant is a dining room of two halves. The oak panelling works better than the creamy paint job, though the tasteful food-related art and impeccable table settings run throughout. You can eat from an informal menu in the bar and garden, and you possibly should unless you're comfortable with formal done the proper *haut* way even at Sunday lunch: grave service, tasting menu, *amuse-bouche*, petits fours, fancy presentation and dishes announced as they arrive. The menu matches (as, naturally, does the wine list). It's serious, French-influenced stuff, very nicely turned out: follow chicken liver parfait with roast rump of lamb, pomme purée and asparagus, and finish with almond panna cotta and peaches.

WOOTTON

King's Head ★

Chapel Hill, Wootton, OX20 1DX (01993 811340/ www.kings-head.co.uk). **Lunch served** noon-2pm daily. **Dinner served** 7-8.30pm Mon-Sat. **Main courses** £9.95-£16.50. **Credit** MC, V.
An unpretentious and very personal pub-restaurant highly thought of by local foodies, and with good reason. A meal here is like being cooked for by severely talented, somewhat genteel friends and attended to in their own dining room: though the decor may not appeal (a few too many Jocasta Innes wall splashes and flowery sofas, perhaps), it's comfortable, low-lit and a relaxing step away from the fashion mainstream. And it's what's on the plate that counts: quality ingredients exquisitely prepared and elaborately presented. Very good on our visit were an olive pâté with artichoke hearts and bramble dressing, pork medallions with onion confit and plump juniper berries, and a warm fish salad with fir apple potatoes, the latter from a blackboard

menu changed according to availability that comprises maybe half of the main courses. Special mention should also go to a lovingly made sticky toffee pudding. The wine list is well put together, by taste category.

WYTHAM

The Whyte Hart

Wytham, OX2 8QA (01865 244372). **Lunch served** noon-2.30pm daily. **Dinner served** 7-10pm Mon-Sat. **Main courses** £10.95-£18.50. **Credit** MC, V.
This country pub and restaurant has got a lot going for it. The Whyte Hrt's setting is idyllic, but it's just a short drive across the Thames from Oxford. The menu in the rustic-elegant dining room is confident and sophisticated, with specials like red snapper

with celeriac mash, and an array of irresistible puddings, including a wonderfully light update of bread and butter pudding. The wine list is varied and the service friendly. And then there's the large flag-stoned bar and conservatory, which serves appetising family lunches – ideal after a brisk walk in the beautiful surrounding countryside (some owned by the university and used for environmental experiments) – and is very popular at weekends.

Also in the area

Livebait 16 Turl Street, Oxford, OX1 3DH (01865 324930); **Loch Fyne** 55 Walton Street, Oxford, OX2 6AE (01865 292510); **Loch Fyne** 20 Market Place, Henley-on-Thames, RG9 2AH (01491 845780); **Le Petit Blanc** 71-72 Walton Street, Oxford, OX2 6AG (01865 510999).

The Whyte Hart

Wiltshire

BECKINGTON

Woolpack

*Warminster Road, Beckington, BA11 6SP (01373
831244/www.beckington.org).* **Lunch served** noon-
2.30pm daily. **Dinner served** 6.30-9.30pm Mon-Sat;
6.30-9pm Sun. **Main courses** £10.45-£16.95. **Credit**
AmEx, MC, V.
While under private ownership this 16th-century
coaching inn established a strong local reputation
for excellent cooking and attentive service, and little
has changed now it is part of the Old English Inns
chain. The airy bar area with its flagstone floor and
large open fireplace is a good place for lunch, when
dishes run from warm roast beef baguette with
horseradish cream to own-made chicken, ham and
leek pie with mash. In the evening try the more
formal surroundings of the restaurant or the garden
room. By this time, the menu has moved on to the
likes of Thai spiced crab cakes with sweet chilli and
coriander sauce, followed by roast rump of lamb on
courgette and tomato galette with rösti.

BRADFORD-ON-AVON

Woolley Grange Restaurant

*Woolley Grange Hotel, Woolley Green,
Bradford-on-Avon, BA15 1TX (01225 864705/
www.woolleygrange.com).* **Lunch served**
noon-2pm, **dinner served** 7-9.15pm daily. **Main
courses** £18.50. **Set lunch** £15.50 2 courses,
£20 3 courses. **Set dinner** £34.50 3 courses.
Credit AmEx, DC, MC, V.
The restaurant at Woolley Grange serves the best
of country house cooking in an appropriately grand
setting. The internal dining area is split into two
rooms, plus an adjoining conservatory with a more
casual tone. All serve the same menu, consisting of
dishes such as veal with ceps, oxtail dumplings and
shallot and port sauce, or roasted guinea fowl with
prunes, brandy and pancetta. Aside from the set
lunches, the place is unsurprisingly pricey, with
main courses going on for £20. Ingredients are as
local as possible (including vegetables from the
hotel's own garden). The wine list is extensive and
the selection of desserts and cheeses sumptuous.
The hotel is part of the Luxury Family Hotels group,
and so children are well looked after.

CASTLE COMBE

Bybrook Restaurant

*Manor House Hotel, Castle Combe, SN14 7HR
(01249 782206/www.exclusivehotels.co.uk).* **Lunch
served** noon-2pm, **dinner served** 7-9.30pm daily.

Set lunch £16.95 2 courses, £18.95 3 courses. **Set
dinner** £35-£45 3 courses. **Credit** AmEx, DC, MC, V.
The River Bybrook passes through the 26 acres of
gardens and parkland that surround this part 14th-
century manor house, and lends its name to the
baronial, L-shaped formal dining room. Long-serving
chef Mark Taylor's fashionable Mediterranean food
hits the mark, with Franco Campioni ensuring front
of house is a very professional set-up. Roulade of
guinea fowl and foie gras with pear chutney might
be followed by new season lamb with turnip
dauphinoise, balsamic and garlic jus. There are some
decent vegetarian options too, such as samosa of wild
mushrooms with young spinach and morels. For
dessert, try iced strawberry parfait, shortcake,
warmed strawberries and basil syrup. Prime British
cheeses are a good savoury alternative. Afternoon
teas and excellent bar snacks are also available. The
wine list is fairly encyclopaedic and could incite
lengthy study.

COLERNE

Lucknam Park Hotel

*Lucknam Park, Colerne, SN14 8AZ (01225 742777/
www.lucknampark.co.uk).* **Lunch served** 12.30-
2.30pm Mon-Sat; noon-2pm Sun. **Dinner served**
6.30-10pm daily. **Main courses** £18-£27. **Credit**
AmEx, DC, MC, V.
The Lucknam Park experience starts with the mile-
long, tree-lined drive from the gates to the door of
this Palladian mansion. Grand, certainly, but it only
gets grander. You'll be ushered into an imposing
drawing room, plied with *amuse-gueles* and handed
Robin Zavou's menu, an appealing take on
traditional English cooking with a few more
adventurous dishes to boot. Starters may include a
slightly overcomplicated tian of crab, smoked
salmon and avocado; mains might run to
immaculate Dover sole with wild mushroom and
truffle oil sauce or tender venison in a red wine sauce
served with a deliciously poached pear. All in all
very good, but at these prices so it should be; for two
people, each having a pre-dinner drink, three courses
and coffee, and sharing a mid-priced bottle of wine,
the bill came to £180, a tip – service, the sniffy
sommelier excepted, was faultless – sending it over
the £100-a-head mark.

CRUDWELL

The Old Rectory ★

*Crudwell, SN16 9EP (01666 577194/
www.oldrectorycrudwell.co.uk).* **Lunch served**
noon-2pm daily. **Dinner served** 7-9.30pm Mon-Sat;

7-9pm Sun. **Set lunch** (Mon-Sat) £15.95 2 courses, £18.95 3 courses; (Sun) £13.95 2 courses, £16.95 3 courses. **Set dinner** (Mon-Sat) £26.50 3 courses. **Credit** AmEx, DC, MC, V.

Chef Peter Fairclough has earned this excellent hotel restaurant much acclaim with a modern British style that places considerable emphasis on fresh seasonal ingredients, organic wherever possible. It's a lovely dining area, informal but smart and looking out to an impeccable garden. A cappuccino of wild mushroom appetiser set the tone, followed by lovely roast chump of lamb with dauphinoise potato, spinach and rosemary and baby caper jus. There's a good cheeseboard to follow but make sure you leave room for dessert (the iced banana parfait with glazed banana and dark chocolate sauce is a must). Take heart that when owners Derek and Karen Woods do the rounds asking if you're satisfied, you won't be telling any porkies.

DEVIZES

The Healthy Life
4 Little Brittox, Devizes, SN10 1AR (01380 725558). Café **Meals served** 10am-4pm Mon-Sat. **Main courses** £3.95-£6. *Bistro* **Dinner served** 7-11pm Tue-Sat. **Set dinner** £14.95 2 courses, £19.95 3 courses. **Credit** AmEx, MC, V.
Peter Vaughan offers what he terms 'body-friendly' foods in his natural food shop and first-floor café-cum-bistro, located in the pedestrianised town centre. A good proportion of the ethically sourced, organic and bio-dynamic ingredients used in the food preparation are from within the county, while others are of fair trade origin. Peter's experience in five-star hotel restaurants ensures dishes possess a commendable degree of sophistication and innovation (and no trace of the crankiness once associated with healthfood establishments). The set-price three-course menu could kick off with fricassée of chicken livers and apple with Somerset apple brandy flambé, followed by boiled Bromham ham with lovage and parsley broth and mashed potatoes. Ricotta and lemon cheesecake or local cheeses might round things off.

EASTON GREY

The Dining Room & Le Mazot at Whatley Manor
Easton Grey, SN16 0RB (01666 822888/ www.whatleymanor.com). Le Mazot **Lunch served** noon-2pm, **dinner served** 7-10pm daily. **Main courses** £11.50-£14. *The Dining Room* **Dinner served** 7-10pm daily. **Set dinner** £60 3 courses, £75 7-course tasting menu. **Credit** AmEx, DC, MC, V.
Opened in July 2003, this Swiss family-owned Cotswold stone manor house is the latest hotel geared almost exclusively at those with money and time on their hands. Abounding in understated luxury and with exceptional standards of service,

this place turns out to be more beautiful private home than rigidly formal hotel. Martin Burge heads the kitchens and his time with the likes of John Burton-Race and Raymond Blanc has enabled him to introduce a menu of very appealing modern, classically based dishes. In the elegant Dining Room the carte is supplemented by a gourmand menu. The food is simpler, but no less enjoyable, in the brasserie-style Le Mazot, named and themed in the style of an original wooden Swiss chalet. Here, chicken liver parfait with a walnut salad and crusty bread might be followed by sea bream steamed with cockles and mussels, served with fresh pasta and a lightly creamed sauce.

FONTHILL GIFFORD

The Beckford Arms
Fonthill Gifford, SP3 6PX (01747 870385). **Lunch served** noon-2pm, **dinner served** 7-9pm daily. **Main courses** £8.90-£15.95. **Credit** MC, V.
Situated on the edge of the Fonthill estate that once belonged to the eccentric William Beckford, this charming 18th-century inn operates as both a B&B and a very pleasant pub/restaurant. Wooden floors, rustic tables, an open fire and an airy garden room with a high-pitched ceiling provide a casual setting for some fine mod Euro food served by friendly young staff. Starters include the likes of oak-smoked salmon with rocket or goat's cheese, red pepper and oregano tart; some are also available as mains. Inventive meat, fish and pasta dishes – say, beef with balsamic roast onions, butterfish with prawn and caper salsa or Thai vegetable curry – make up the mains. Superior baguettes (pesto chicken and black olive tapenade) are also offered at lunchtime. Well-kept beers come from Hop Back, Greene King and Timothy Taylor.

GREAT HINTON

Linnet
Great Hinton, BA14 6BU (01380 870354). **Lunch served** noon-2pm Tue-Sun. **Dinner served** 6.30-9.30pm Tue-Sat; 7-9pm Sun. **Main courses** £10.25-£15.95. **Set lunch** £10.25 2 courses, £12.95 3 courses. **Credit** AmEx, MC, V.
Whether it's a Sunday lunch of traditional roast beef, preceded by an enjoyable haddock and spinach tart, and finished with a sweetly rich Baileys bread and butter pudding with white chocolate ice-cream, or a romantic candlelit dinner in the restaurant, the food at this appealing old pub offers a wealth of variety. Unusual combinations abound – as in a starter of smoked chicken and sesame seed cake with guacamole, and a main of salmon fillet with pea and dill crust on caper hollandaise. The light lunch menu includes warm focaccia with smoked salmon and lemon mayonnaise or peppered beef and wild mushroom salad. The bread, pasta and ice-creams are all made on the premises. Enthusiasm and dedication is much in evidence.

HINDON

Angel Inn

Angel Lane, Hindon, SP3 6BJ (01747 820696/ www.theangelhindon.fslife.co.uk). **Lunch served** noon-2pm daily. **Dinner served** 7-9pm Mon-Sat. **Main courses** £9.95-£14. **Credit** MC, V.

At the heart of an unspoilt Georgian village, the Angel's classic exterior is contrasted by a smart, modern interior. The two bars have pine furniture, wine-red walls and a blackboard menu of the daily-changing carte. The restaurant towards the rear is light and airy: tables with candles and flowers, photographs of local scenes on the pale walls and a look-in on the open-plan kitchen. The same menu applies throughout and is an imaginative mix: crispy fish cake with remoulade sauce; smoked ham, chips and two duck eggs; sausages, mash and onion gravy; slow-roast lamb shank with bubble and squeak and Madeira jus. To finish, try panettone bread and butter pudding or pineapple tarte tatin with coconut ice-cream.

HOLT

Tollgate Inn

Ham Green, Holt, BA14 6PX (01225 782326/ www.tollgateholt.co.uk). **Lunch served** noon-2pm Tue-Sun. **Dinner served** 7-9pm Tue-Sat. **Main courses** £10.50-£16.50. **Set lunch** £9.95 2 courses, £11.95 3 courses. **Credit** MC, V.

The colourful first-floor restaurant at this large part-painted roadside stone inn was once a chapel for the weavers, who worked below in what is now a warmly decorated, cosy bar. To the rear is a well-

established garden. The menu has a light, modern Mediterranean touch with ingredients of traceable local provenance used in the preparation of confit of duck with raspberry dressing or pan-fried red gurnard and grey mullet with bouillabaisse sauce. There are good English farmhouse cheeses and desserts feature their own ice-creams such as lavender with honey and summer rose petal. Lunchtime sees bargain set-price deals, and a tempting light-bite menu that includes a truly delicious omelette Arnold Bennett made with natural smoked haddock.

LACOCK

At the Sign of the Angel

6 Church Street, Lacock, SN15 2LB (01249 730230/ www.lacock.co.uk). **Lunch served** 1-2pm Tue-Sun. **Dinner served** 7-9pm daily. **Main courses** £8.95-£16.25. **Credit** AmEx, DC, MC, V.

This year sees the Levis family celebrating 50 years at this 15th-century former wool merchant's house in a National Trust village that's without TV aerials, yellow lines or overhead cables to spoil the picturesque views. Inside it's all as characterful as the ancient-looking half-timbered gabled exterior would lead you to expect: log fires, dark oak panelling, low beams, creaking floorboards and a warm, welcoming ambience. In the three very cosy candlelit dining rooms the menu of simply prepared, enjoyable, mainly English food includes Cornish crab soup, medallions of pork with sage and honey mustard, and treacle and walnut tart with clotted cream. Lunch specials and the evening carte are somewhat more ambitious – perhaps fillet of lamb

Luknam Park Hotel. *See p178.*

£15.50-£18.95. **Set lunch** £15.95 2 courses, £19.95 3 courses. **Set dinner** (Tue-Thur) £19.95 2 courses. **Credit** MC, V.

Named after the windmill that's a mile northwards, this isolated restaurant stands alongside the A338. The quiet location and the conservative dining room with its gilt-framed mirrors, polished mahogany tables and plum walls and upholstery are contrasted by a menu that's bang up to date and hits all the right notes. Prepared using organic and locally sourced ingredients, the combinations are well thought out, and while limited to six choices per course, there's ample variety. Ham hock terrine with red cabbage and beetroot cream is a terrific starter, while champagne and saffron sauce works well with pan-fried monkfish and spiced leeks. Passion-fruit pannacotta and sorbet is further evidence of the kitchen's easy confidence with flavours.

ROWDE
George & Dragon
High Street, Rowde, SN10 2PN (01380 723053). **Lunch served** noon-3pm, **dinner served** 7-10pm Tue-Sat. **Main courses** £8.50-£16. **Set lunch** £10 2 courses, £12.50 3 courses. **Credit** MC, V.

Both name and decor imply this is a pub, but don't be fooled: despite well-kept ales, drinking at Helen and Tim Withers's welcoming operation comes second to the food. The list of starters is a guaranteed appetite-whetter, taking in the likes of rich boudin of chicken and duck with apple sauce, enjoyably simple asparagus and ham pancakes, and oak-smoked salmon tart. But the restaurant has built its reputation on the fresh fish, brought in from Cornwall. The dishes change daily, the list chalked up above the bar. When we visited, this included a notably meaty skate with capers and black butter, and fillet of John Dory with a perfectly balanced crab sauce. If you're lucky, desserts on offer will include delicious marmalade sponge pudding with whisky sauce and custard.

SALISBURY
Bernières Tea Room ★
The Wardrobe, 58 Cathedral Close, Salisbury, SP1 2EX (01722 413666/www.thewardrobe.org.uk). **Meals served** 10am-5pm, **lunch served** noon-2pm daily. **Main courses** £6.50. **No credit cards**.

This green and pink tearoom in a converted coach house in front of the local regimental museum is a handy spot for a cream tea (£3.95) after touring the cathedral. There are also a couple of tables outside. Tuck into old-fashioned cakes or a selection of sandwiches (£3.75) while eavesdropping on the gossip of local matrons. Home-cooked lunches offer the likes of steak and kidney pie or roast beef. A railway station sign from the Normandy village of Bernières hangs above the window; it was presented to British troops by the village's grateful mayor after the D-Day landings.

in puff pastry with rosemary and onion gravy, with chocolate St Emilion for pud. There is a decent wine list and service is helpful.

LITTLE BEDWYN
Harrow
Little Bedwyn, SN8 3JP (01672 870871/ www.harrowinn.co.uk). **Lunch served** noon-2pm Wed-Sun. **Dinner served** 7-9pm Wed-Sat. **Main courses** £18-£24. **Set lunch** £15 2 courses, £17.50 3 courses, £50 7-course tasting menu. **Credit** MC, V.

This once-dilapidated Victorian pub is now a thriving and successful restaurant. The terrace is ideal for al fresco dining. Otherwise it's the series of interconnected dining rooms – with colourful curtains, large prints of wine and seafood on the deep red walls, and crisp white linen on the tables – that's the setting for a classy menu which is big on seafood. Seared king scallops come with chorizo; grilled line-caught turbot with lobster risotto. There are meat dishes too, although the precise time and date that the named, pure-bred Aberdeen Angus steer was killed is perhaps more than we need to know. Each dish on the seafood tasting menu is matched by wines from the amazing 500-strong wine list. There are Spanish provisions and wines for retail sale.

MARTEN
Windmill
Salisbury Road, Marten, SN8 3SH (01264 731372). **Lunch served** noon-2pm Tue-Sun. **Dinner served** 7-9pm Tue-Thur; 7-9.30pm Fri, Sat. **Main courses**

Haunch of Venison

1-5 Minster Street, Salisbury, SP1 1TB (01722 322024). **Lunch served** noon-3pm Mon-Sat. **Dinner served** 6-9pm Mon-Thur; 6-10.30pm Fri, Sat. **Main courses** £5-£15. **Set meal** (noon-1pm, 6-7pm) £5 1 course incl glass of wine. **Credit** MC, V.

As you might expect from the name, venison is the speciality at this original Dickensian chop-house, with black-timbered walls and floors every bit as crooked as Fagin. If you don't fancy venison sausages with mash and red onion marmalade or the Haunch Platter (a selection of venison dishes plus beer or wine, £8.75), fish and chicken dishes also put in an appearance. Homely puds include apple tart with vanilla ice-cream and a delicious mini summer pudding. Cooking is hearty rather than sophisticated, but the setting is marvellous. Alternatively, you can just have a pint in one of Britain's two remaining pewter bars in the tiny nobs' snug halfway up the cramped staircase.

STANTON FITZWARREN

The Rosemary Restaurant ★

Stanton House Hotel, The Avenue, Stanton Fitzwarren, SN6 7SD (01793 861777/ www.stantonhouse.co.uk). **Lunch served** noon-2pm daily. **Dinner served** 6-10pm Mon-Sat; 6-9.30pm Sun. **Main courses** £5-£24. **Credit** AmEx, DC, MC, V.

The nearby Honda car plant is the main reason why this elegant Cotswold stone mansion contains one of the few Japanese restaurants outside London. Apart from a few low wooden screens, the decor owes more to British tradition than the sleek simplicity of most that comes out of Japan. A well-laid out authentic carte offers a full and wide choice, plus reasonably priced set meals. Deep-fried tofu in hot soba soup, tuna sashimi or stir-fried pork with onions in ginger and garlic sauce are typical of the choices. Such is the quality of the food and the dedication and professionalism of the staff that there's a loyal following of native diners too. There's a sushi bar on Sunday lunchtimes.

TEFFONT EVIAS

Howard's House ★

Teffont Evias, SP3 5RJ (01722 716392). **Lunch served** noon-2pm Mon-Thur, Sat, Sun. **Dinner served** 7.30-9pm daily. **Main courses** £13.95-£23.95. **Set meal** £23.95 3 courses. **Credit** AmEx, DC, MC, V.

Built in 1623, but with an unusual Swiss-style roof added in Victorian times, this former dower house stands in a particularly pretty village of medieval origins. Standards of comfort are high and the food, served in a beautifully appointed dining room with French windows leading out on to a sunny terrace and garden, is both sophisticated and modern. Flavours are distinct and complementary, as in a

starter from the imaginative carte of pan-fried fillet of red mullet which comes with a warm niçoise salad and fresh basil oil, or a main of loin of Wiltshire venison with red cabbage, honey fondant potato, foie gras pithiviers and juniper jus. For dessert, hot Grand Marnier soufflé is perfectly contrasted by a tangerine glaze and marmalade ice-cream. This is a gem of a hotel.

WARMINSTER

Mulberry Restaurant

Bishopstrow House, Warminster, BA12 9HH (01985 212312/www.bishopstrow.co.uk). **Lunch served** 12.15-2pm, **dinner served** 7.30-9pm daily. **Main courses** £6.50-£17. **Set dinner** £38 4 courses. **Credit** AmEx, DC, MC, V.

Situated on the B3414 south-east of the town centre, this stately late Georgian house stands in 28 acres of grounds. Public rooms are formal and very elegant, and the restaurant which overlooks the garden and heated outdoor pool (there's a magnificent indoor pool as well) has comfortable, well-spaced and smartly appointed tables. For lunch or a light bite in the bar, there's an eclectic menu of flavoursome dishes, while the fixed-price dinner menu is no less imaginative: seared tiger prawns with chorizo and rocket; crispy duck confit with colcannon, wild mushrooms and peppercorn sauce; toffee and cappuccino tartlet with vanilla ice-cream. Simple but enjoyable snacks are served in the lounge, or out in the garden in fine weather, between 2pm and 6pm.

WHITLEY

Pear Tree ★

Top Lane, Whitley, SN12 8QX (01225 709131). **Lunch served** noon-2pm daily. **Dinner served** 6.30-9.30pm Mon-Thur, Sun; 6.30-10pm Fri, Sat. **Main courses** £8.50-£18. **Set lunch** (Mon-Sat) £11.50 2 courses, £14 3 courses; (Sun) £12.50 2 courses, £14.95 3 courses. **Credit** MC, V.

This former farmhouse has been very tastefully updated, maintaining the original character of what is now a well-managed country pub. At the front is a comfortable bar where locals gather for a pint or two. This opens out into a spacious rear dining area with low beamed ceiling and a converted barn addition with oak beams and conservatory doors opening on to a patio and lovely split-level garden. Mark Nacchia's menu is long and varied, traditional options (a simple but impeccable plum tomato and celery soup; a perfectly tender piece of roast beef served with spuds and a Yorkshire pud) balanced by more playful concoctions (a starter of warm wood pigeon salad was deceptively rich, a main of baked cod in Parma ham flavourful). It's almost worth making the journey just to sample the wonderful sticky apricot and walnut pudding in toffee sauce, which we rounded off with. Great, solid wine list. Terrific, all told.

East Anglia

East Anglia

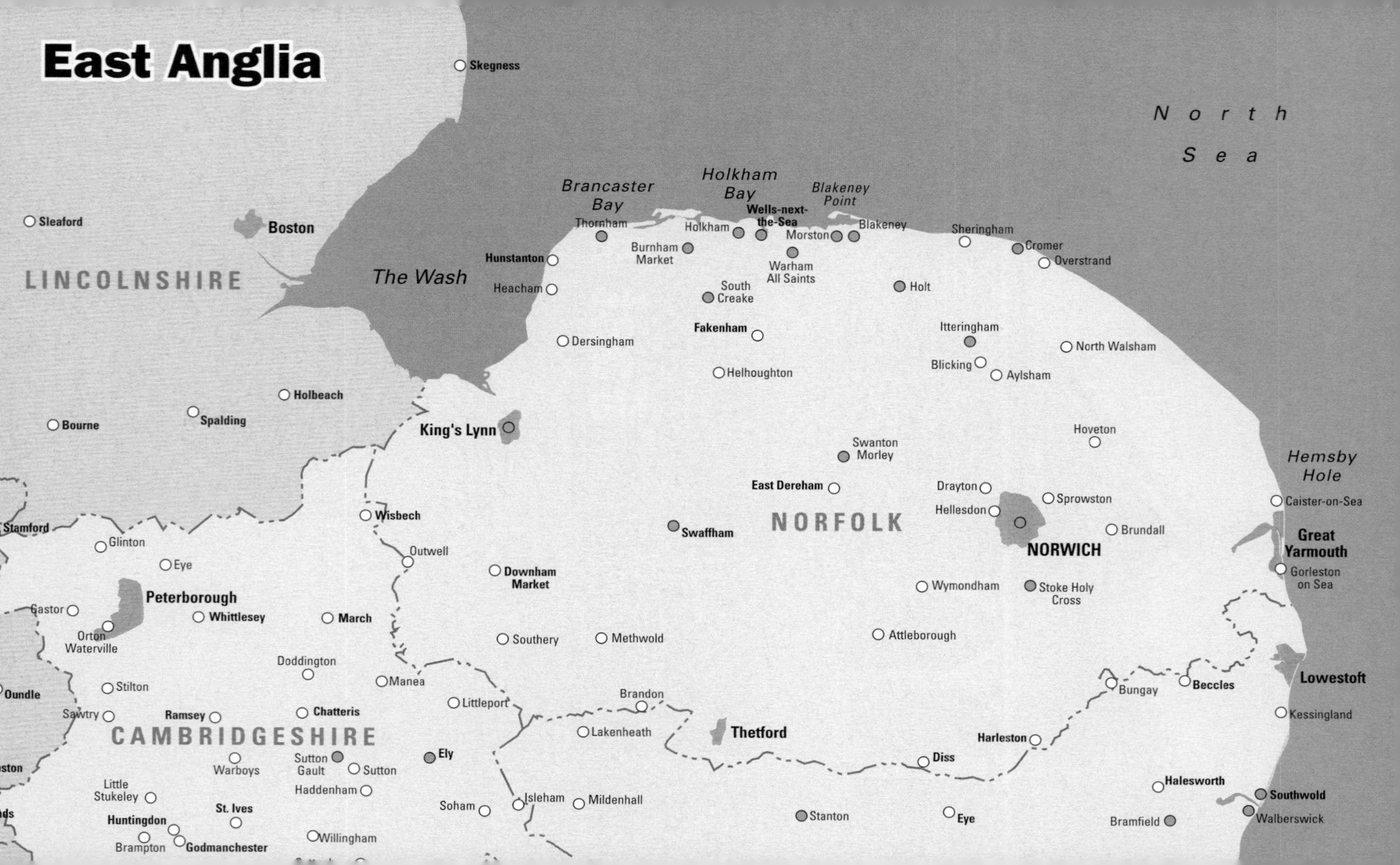

North Sea

Skegness

Boston

The Wash

Holbeach

Spalding

Bourne

Sleaford

LINCOLNSHIRE

Brancaster Bay

Holkham Bay

Blakeney Point

Hemsby
Hole

Caister-on-Sea

Great Yarmouth

Gorleston
on Sea

Lowestoft

Kessingland

Southwold

Walberswick

Halesworth

Bramfield

Beccles

Bungay

Brundall

Hoveton

North Walsham

Sprowston

NORWICH

Stoke Holy
Cross

Harleston

Diss

Eye

Overstrand

Cromer

Sheringham

Aylsham

Blicking

Itteringham

Drayton

Hellesdon

Wymondham

Attleborough

Stanton

Holt

Blakeney

Morston

Wells-next-the-Sea

Warham
All Saints

Swanton
Morley

East Dereham

NORFOLK

Thetford

South
Creake

Fakenham

Helhoughton

Swaffham

Holkham

Burnham
Market

Thornham

Hunstanton

Heacham

Dersingham

Methwold

Brandon

Lakenheath

Mildenhall

Isleham

Southery

Downham
Market

Littleport

Soham

Ely

King's Lynn

Outwell

Wisbech

Manea

March

Doddington

Chatteris

Sutton
Gault

Sutton

Haddenham

Willingham

Holbeach

Whittlesey

Peterborough

Eye

Glinton

Stilton

Ramsey

Warboys

St. Ives

Godmanchester

Brampton

Huntington

Little
Stukeley

CAMBRIDGESHIRE

Bourne

Castor

Orton
Waterville

Sawtry

Stilton

Stamford

Oundle

Thrapston

Raunds

184 Time Out Eating & Drinking in Great Britain & Ireland

Cambridgeshire

East Anglia

CAMBRIDGE

Michel's

21-24 Northampton Street, Cambridge, CB3 0AD
(01223 353110). **Lunch served** noon-2.30pm
Mon-Sat; noon-3.30pm Sun. **Dinner served** 6-10pm
Mon-Sat. **Main courses** £12.50-£18. **Set lunch**
(Mon-Sat) £9.45 2 courses, £11.95 3 courses.
Credit AmEx, DC, MC, V.
The menu is short at this cosy restaurant – six
starters and six mains – but the choices are
interesting and generally successful. Combinations
of textures and flavours include pan-fried scallops
with haggis and a whisky beurre blanc or Jerusalem
artichoke salad with pancetta, ceps and parmesan.
Mains are a little more haphazard. Pumpkin risotto
with truffles and hazel-nuts was bland, while beef
fillet with girolles and glazed shallots was well
flavoured, but a tad overcooked. Booking is essential
at weekends. The restaurant is non-smoking, though
you can nip up to the wine bar if you're desperate.

Midsummer House ★

Midsummer Common, Cambridge, CB4 1HA
(01223 369299/www.midsummerhouse.co.uk).
Lunch served noon-2pm, **dinner served** 7-10pm
Tue-Sat. **Set lunch** £20 2 courses; £26 3 courses.
Set dinner £45 3 courses. **Credit** AmEx, MC, V.
With one Michelin star under his belt, Daniel
Clifford, chef-patron of Midsummer House, is after
another. The 'House' offers two floors and a
conservatory of high-quality French dining. Service
is formal and informative, as it needs to be with a
32-page wine list. Food is impeccably presented,
perfectly cooked and often marries unusual
ingredients and flavours. Starters include seared
scallops with celeriac purée and truffle, and quail
ravioli that looks more impressive than it tastes.
Slow-cooked fillet of beef on creamed spinach with
cep mousse was exceptionally tender, while firm-
fleshed sea bass on white beans with chilli cream
was a fine combo. Desserts, such as pineapple
parfait, are beautifully crafted. Supplements of £8.50
for a cheeseboard, £5 for the slow-cooked beef and
£4 for a coffee are rather less appealing, but it's still
a memorable place to celebrate. No smoking.

Venue on the Roof

Cambridge Arts Theatre, 3rd floor, 6 St Edward's
Passage, Cambridge, CB2 3PJ (01223 367333/
www.venuerestaurant.com). **Meals served** 11am-
11pm Mon-Sat. **Main courses** £10-£17. **Set meal**
(11am-7.30pm) £10 2 courses. **Set dinner** £13.95
2 courses. **Credit** AmEx, MC, V.
This petite restaurant – recently relocated from
Regent Street to the first floor of the Arts Theatre –

is a haven of quality contemporary food and crisp
modern decor (orange Arne Jacobsen chairs, white
piano). The regularly changing menu lists a handful
of well-chosen and artistically presented dishes that
draw on international influences. Mains might
include melt-in-the-mouth beef fillet, lemon and
tarragon roasted chicken or Moroccan lamb, while
desserts range from vanilla bean crème brûlée to
raspberry and sweet cheese chimichanga. A
medium-sized wine list covers all bases, with a
heavy nod to the New World. Classy without being
stuffy and with fair prices to boot.

ELY

The Old Fire Engine

25 St Mary's Street, Ely, CB7 4ER (01353
662582/www.theoldfireenginehouse.co.uk). **Lunch**
served 12.15-2pm daily. **Dinner served** 7.15-9pm
daily. **Main courses** £13-£16.40. **Credit** MC, V.
Two minutes' walk from Ely's magnificent cathedral
– 'the ship of the fens' – is a splendid rustic eaterie
concentrating on traditional British food. Before
settling down to dine, take time to enjoy some
Suffolk ale in the snug bar and soak up the
atmosphere. Above the grate is a photograph of the
original fire crew. The airy restaurant seats 26 and
is easy to manage; as a result the service is sprightly.
Treats on the reasonably priced menu include
locally smoked eel, pickled herring with yoghurt,
pigeon casserole with bacon, black olives and
asparagus sauce or beef shallots braised in Guinness
and port. The wine list rewards study. After a stroll
round the garden, enjoy a simple refreshing dessert.

GRANTCHESTER

The Red Lion

High Street, Grantchester, CB3 9NF (01223
840121). **Lunch served** noon-2.30pm. **Dinner**
served 6-9.30pm Mon-Thur. **Meals served** noon-
9.30pm Fri, Sat; noon-8.30pm Sun. **Main courses**
£7.25-£15.25. **Credit** AmEx, MC, V.
Newly refurbished, this pub has a lively atmosphere.
It's worth a visit for its huge, leafy garden alone.
Traditional pub fare with a twist included own-
made tomato soup packed with fresh basil and
thyme, and garlicky stuffed mushroom with
breadcrumbs, feta and vegetables. Scampi with
chips was top pub food, served with a lavish salad
and fresh tartare sauce. Beef stroganoff was less
successful: bland and lacking in spices, it was at
least generous and came with a plateful of rice and
vegetables. The kitchen is trying hard – the menu
needs more time to develop, but shows promise.

MADINGLEY

The Three Horseshoes ★

High Street, Madingley, CB3 8AB (01954 210221).
Lunch served noon-2pm Mon-Sat; noon-2.30pm
Sun. **Dinner served** 6-9.30pm Mon-Sat. **Main
courses** £9.50-£23. **Credit** AmEx, DC, MC, V.
Location-wise, the Three Horseshoes has it made:
it's in a very pretty thatched-cottage village just
outside Cambridge and has a garden backing on to
the village cricket pitch. There is a smart-ish
restaurant menu and a cheaper bar-grill menu. We
sat in the spacious conservatory and, hopping
between the two, customised a very pleasing lunch.
Portland crab salad with grilled baby leeks, saffron
aïoli and lemon was startlingly yellow but delicious
(if a bit short on crab), and Parma ham with melon,
radish and coriander cress was an equally good,
more generous serving. Next came succulent
monkfish roasted with garlic and rosemary, made
special by the accompanying potato, cheese and
onion cake; and an amazingly good tagliatelle with
garlic, spring greens and pecorino from the bar
menu, served with an equally first-class salad. For
dessert, poached peaches with sherry ice-cream was
a triumph. Not cheap – but worth it. Part of the same
group as the Falcon in Northamptonshire (*see p224*).

MELBOURN

The Pink Geranium

*Station Road, Melbourn, SG8 6DX (01763 260215/
www.pinkgeranium.co.uk).* **Lunch served** noon-
2.30pm Tue-Sun. **Dinner served** 7-9.30pm Tue-Sat.
Main courses £17.50-£26.50. **Set lunch** £15
2 courses, £19 3 courses. **Set dinner** £23 3 courses.
Credit AmEx, MC, V.
Residing in beautifully kept gardens set back from
the road, the Pink Geranium is an award-winning,
conservative, chintzy restaurant. It also happens to
be very pink. Inside everything is crisp, mannered
and a little awkward, though the service is attentive

The Three Horseshoes

East Anglia

and the excellent wine list extensive. The food is unadventurous with plain dishes unenlivened by sauces. Strips of beef, fondant potato, buttered spinach and grain mustard jus failed to impress, but desserts turned out to be a rich, indulgent high point. This is the sort of place to bring your granny, not a hot date.

Sheene Mill Hotel & Restaurant ★

Station Road, Melbourn, SG8 6DX. (01763 261393/ www.sheenmill.com). **Lunch served** noon-2.30pm daily. **Dinner served** 7-10.30pm Mon-Sat. **Main courses** £8 (lunch), £17 (dinner). **Set lunch** £18.50 3 courses. **Set dinner** £30 3 courses. **Credit** AmEx, MC, V.

Run by a master chef, author and TV presenter – recognisable as 'that chef off *Ready Steady Cook*' – Steven Saunders's Sheene Mill is at the forefront of organic cookery in Britain. The old mill lake makes the perfect backdrop to a sumptuous restaurant appealing to eyes and ears, as well as tastebuds. Influences from all over the world are evident on the menu, including Thai fish cakes with a sweet chilli dipping sauce, pan-fried marlin and a super-smooth duck liver pâté balanced by onion chutney. The local organic goat's cheese hits the flavour bell, as does wild mushroom tortellini. It's easy to get caught up in the enthusiasm generated by such vibrant food; in fact it's irresistible.

SUTTON GAULT

Anchor Inn

Bury Lane, Sutton Gault, CB6 2BD (01353 778537/ www.anchor-inn-restaurant.co.uk). **Lunch served** noon-2pm daily. **Dinner served** 7-9pm Sun-Fri; 6.30-9.30pm Sat. **Main courses** £11.50-£15. **Set lunch** (Sun) £19.95 3 courses. **Credit** AmEx, MC, V.

On the western edge of the Isle of Ely, Sutton Gault is home to the cosy pale-cream Anchor Inn, which huddles beside the New Bedford river. Tiled floors and low beams set the tone inside with darkwood tables arranged around the various nooks and crannies adding to the cosseted air. A good selection of wines, all reasonably priced, balances the eclectic offerings from the menu and various blackboards. The primary culinary drive is towards comforting food, with inventive ingredient combinations and sauces. Particular favourites are the smoked haddock fish cakes, char-grilled calf's liver with bacon and mushroom mash and creamy onion sauce, and the pannetone bread and butter pudding.

Also in the area

Chez Gérard 27-28 Bridge Street, Cambridge, CB2 1UJ (01223 448620); **Loch Fyne** The Old Dairy, Elton, Peterborough, PE8 6SH (01832 280298); **Loch Fyne** The Little Rose, 37 Trumpington Street, Cambridge, CB2 1QY (01223 362433).

Essex

BLACKMORE

The Leather Bottle

The Green, Blackmore, CM4 0RL (01277 823538). **Lunch served** noon-2pm Mon-Sat; noon-4pm Sun. **Dinner served** 7-9pm Mon-Sat. **Main courses** £6.95-£12.95. **Set lunch** (Mon-Sat) £7.99 2 courses; (Sun) £12.50 2 courses, £14.95 3 courses. **Credit** MC, V.

Midway between Ongar and Brentwood, Blackmore is a harmonious blend of old and new – and so is Gary Witchalls's approach at this small pub near the village green. There are plenty of traditional dishes – smoked salmon, steak, crème brûlée – but bolder options such as pan-seared scallops with leek tagliatelle or spicy lamb keftede with tomato jam betray his origins as a one-time deputy director of the Butler's Wharf Chef School. One bar is set aside for drinkers, while tables are laid out in the other and in the large, airy conservatory, which opens on to a pleasant garden. All mains are accompanied by a hefty vegetable selection. Chocolate orange mousse

and sticky toffee pudding will bring any meal to a comforting and calorific end. The wine list is short, but the well-kept real ale merits attention.

CLAVERING

The Cricketers

Wicken Road, Clavering, CB11 4QT (01799 550442/ www.thecricketers.co.uk). **Lunch served** noon-2pm, **dinner served** 7-10pm daily. **Main courses** £11-£18. **Set dinner** £26 3 courses. **Credit** AmEx, MC, V.

The family home of celebrity chef Jamie Oliver offers top-notch food at affordable prices. His mum and dad own and run this busy pub-restaurant with Oliver Senior acting as maître d'. The starter of salmon nori roll with tempura batter in a sesame seed, soya and truffle oil dressing looks and tastes great; the main of grilled darne of halibut served on fresh runner beans and cherry tomatoes is delicious. For dessert, banana baked with rum, muscovado sugar and vanilla, served with a rich toffee sauce and rum 'n' raisin ice-cream, deserves special

The Company Shed. See p190.

mention. Service is provided by a group of friendly ladies who buzz enthusiastically around the place. Sunday lunch is good here – a wide range of dishes includes a traditional roast.

COLCHESTER

The Lemon Tree

48 St John's Street, Colchester, CO2 7AD (01206 767337/www.the-lemon-tree.com). **Meals served** noon-10pm Mon-Sat. **Main courses** £7.95-£16.95. **Set lunch** (Mon-Fri) £5.95 1 course, £7.95 2 courses, £9.95 3 courses. **Set dinner** (Mon-Thur) £6.95 1 course, £9.95 2 courses, £12.95 3 courses. **Credit** AmEx, DC, MC, V.

This zesty restaurant has a cavern-like Roman cellar, an airy ground floor and courtyard seating overlooking the street. Furniture is practical, but the ambience is stylish, with cool jazz to accompany the meal. Dishes include tangy deep-fried brie on red onion marmalade, pan-fried fillet steak with chorizo mash, and banana and Baileys cheesecake. Prices are not outlandish and the wine list offers a varied selection under £20. It's advisable to book because this popular venue hosts various events, including wine tastings, jazz nights and gourmet evenings.

DEDHAM

Fountain House

Dedham Hall, Brook Street, Dedham, CO7 6AD (01206 323027/www.dedhamhall.demon.co.uk). **Dinner served** 7-9.30pm Tue-Sat. **Set dinner** £24.50 3 courses. **Credit** MC, V.

In this cosy 15th-century farmhouse you can watch owner and chef Wendy Sarton prepare her upmarket version of home cooking. The fixed price dinner menu offers a choice of seven starters including wild mushroom tart and king prawns with chilli mayonnaise. Nine main courses are proffered with the roast duck breast, pan-fried lemon sole and lamb's kidneys with mushrooms and Madeira the pick of the bunch. A broad selection of wines at reasonable prices caters to most palates.

Milsoms

Stratford Road, Dedham, CO7 6HW (01206 322795). **Lunch served** noon-2.15pm daily. **Dinner served** 6-9.30pm Mon-Thur, Sun; 6-10pm Fri, Sat. **Main courses** £8.95-£14.95. **Credit** AmEx, DC, MC, V.

This groovy 80-seater restaurant-bar with outdoor eating area is busy seven days a week. It has a Mediterranean/New World vibe and first-come first-served policy. Perched on farmhouse tables are menus and order sheets – customers complete them and leave them at the bar – while a specials blackboard sports excellent-value alternatives. Food is inventive, bistro-style and accompanied by either new potatoes, fat chips, seasonal veggies, mustard mash or tossed salad (extra side dishes cost £2.50). Starters include Asian duck tacos and hoi sin sauce, while mains range from shepherd's pie to baked field mushrooms with ratatouille and appenzeller cheese. For dessert choose from peppered pineapple tart with vanilla pod ice-cream or lemon pannacotta with stewed fruits, both delicious.

Le Talbooth ★

Gun Hill, Dedham, CO7 6HP (01206 323150/ www.talbooth.com). **Lunch served** noon-2pm daily. **Dinner served** 7-9.30pm Mon-Sat. **Main courses** £15.50-£24.95. **Set lunch** £21.50 2 courses, £24 3 courses. **Credit** AmEx, DC, MC, V.

This much-refurbished, picturesque 16th-century house, overlooking a pretty section of the river, provides an extraordinary dining experience with exceptional food. The Talbooth propounds the virtues of low-lit, high-priced, high-class, luxurious dining with hovering 'stealth' waiters, dressed all in black, to fulfil every request, spoken or not. The menu reads like a who's who of classic dishes with a few surprises – fricassee of monkfish and lobster with broad beans, herbs and tomato vermouth sauce or basmati rice and seared gnocchi with gateau of vegetables and goat's cheese – and the wine list accommodates some truly wonderful vintages.

GREAT DUNMOW

The Starr

Market Place, Great Dunmow, CM6 1AX (01371 874321/www.the-starr.co.uk). **Lunch served** noon-2pm daily. **Dinner served** 7-9.30pm Mon-Sat. **Set lunch** £12.50-£22.50 2 courses, £27.50 3 courses. **Set dinner** £27.50-£37.50 3 courses. **Credit** AmEx, DC, MC, V.

If you're looking for an old-school restaurant, this could be the place for you. The Starr is subtly lit and tables are comfortably placed to allow you to chat about your day without the neighbours chipping in. Although no dress code is advertised, most of the male clientele don a jacket, and often a tie. The menu includes country classics with a twist – crispy Scottish salmon with gazpacho and crayfish tails or fillet of beef with herby brioche – plus some more up-to-date treats. The tomato soup is particularly special, as is the rosemary-encrusted rack of new season lamb with baby veg and redcurrant jus. The wine list is dominated by New World vintages and service is friendly. The bill can sting (roughly £100 for two), as you'd be hard-pushed to describe the food, though good, as sensational.

HARWICH

Harbourside Restaurant

The Pier Hotel, The Quay, Harwich, CO12 3HH (01255 241212/www.pier@harwich.com). **Lunch served** noon-2pm, **dinner served** 6-9.30pm daily. **Main courses** £9.95-£30. **Set lunch** £16 2 courses, £19 3 courses. **Credit** AmEx, DC, MC, V.

A comfortable first-floor eaterie with stunning views over the harbour. A ship's wheel and brass compass stand give an inkling of the intended theme, confirmed by the toll of a ship's bell whenever a vessel passes. For the best harbour backdrop ask for tables one to four. Main courses include fish and chips, grilled lobster or (more adventurously) delicious poached halibut fillet with bubble and squeak, and an all-encompassing 'Chef's Pic' of cod, salmon, prawns, scampi and scallops in a saffron and white wine sauce. Non-fish options and one vegetarian choice, in this case a sauté of assorted wild mushrooms, are available, while a flotilla of reasonably priced wines awaits.

MANNINGTREE

Stour Bay Café

39-43 High Street, Manningtree, CO11 1AH (01206 396687/www.stourbaycafe.com). **Lunch served** 12.30-2pm, **dinner served** 7-9.30pm Wed-Sun. **Main courses** £10-£16. **Credit** MC, V.

Intimate, atmospheric and busy, the Stour Bay Café offers a mouthwatering combination of local ingredients (including basketloads of excellent fish) enhanced with Mediterranean flair. Grilled sardines with basil butter and a tapas of fishy bits top the starters menu, while the cataplana – lobster, crab, langoustines, mussels, haddock and mullet in a tomato fondue – is a culinary event. For those not enamoured of fish, the fillet of Scotch beef and braised lamb shank will suffice; vegetarians should check with the helpful staff. House wines £12 to £14.

SAFFRON WALDEN

The Restaurant

2 Church Street, Saffron Walden, CB11 4LT (01799 526444/www.the-restaurantweb.com). **Food served** 7.30-10pm Tue-Sat; 12.30-3pm Sun. **Set dinner** (Tue-Thur) £9.95 2 courses, £13.95 3 courses. **Main courses** £9.95-£17.95. **Credit** MC, V.

This basement space is divided into smoking and no-smoking rooms, with bare brick walls framed by clean colours and lines. The minimalist decor is matched by a concise menu (about six starters and mains), which includes dishes such as pan-fried pigeon breasts in a fruit jus served with green beans and garlic roasted potatoes, or grilled fillet of beef in a wild mushroom sauce with sautéed potatoes, shallots and caramelised garlic. Produce is organic wherever possible and the wine cellar offers a reasonable range. Service is almost too relaxed.

WEST MERSEA

The Company Shed ★ ★

129 Coast Road, West Mersea, CO5 8TA (01206 382700). **Meals served** 9am-4pm Tue-Sat; 10am-4pm Sun. **Main courses** £8-£30. **No credit cards**.

Among the fishing boats and pleasure craft is a wooden shed overlooking the water, while inside the cool interior live lobsters and crabs scuttle about in special trays and ice-covered fish eye customers from the counter. The place is nearly always full and there's no booking, so turn up and queue. The only food comes on platters overflowing with lobster, green-lipped mussels, roll-mop herring, tiger prawns, peeled prawns, cockles, smoked salmon and smoked mackerel. Extras include whole lobsters, crabs, oysters and whelks. In terms of wine and bread it's BYO – all you get is seafood, condiments and a couple of slices of lemon. It's heaven.

Also in the area

Loch Fyne 280-282 High Road, Loughton, Essex IG10 1RB (020 8532 5140).

Norfolk

BLAKENEY

White Horse

White Horse Hotel, 4 High Street, Blakeney, NR25 7AL (01263 740574/www.blakeneywhitehorse.co.uk). **Bar Lunch served** noon-2.30pm, **dinner served** 6-9pm daily. *Restaurant* **Dinner served** 7-9pm Tue-Sun. **Main courses** £10-£17. **Credit** AmEx, MC, V.

Set on the narrow high street a furlong from Blakeney's wild waterfront, the White Horse makes a fine refuge from the Norfolk breezes. The much-extended pub features a cosy bar, bright conservatory and (at night) an enclosed little restaurant where chef Chris Hydem operates. Local produce dominates the lunch menu; the likes of thick cockle chowder are augmented by such blackboard specials as intensely flavoured warmed smoked sprats in a honey and mustard dressing, followed by (less than tender) braised pork with pepper, olive and haricot casserole. The restaurant cuisine is of a different, more exalted, order. Here, warm three-cheese tartlet might precede roast rack of lamb on lentil casserole with crispy leeks, or grilled fillet of sea bass with roast cherry tomatoes and rocket salad. Woodeforde's and Adnams provide the ales and nine wines come by the glass. Puddings are often traditional British fatteners. The young staff are friendly if a touch dippy.

BURNHAM MARKET

Fishes ★

Market Place, Burnham Market, PE31 8HE (01328 739588). **Lunch served** noon-2pm Tue-Sun. **Dinner served** 7-9.30pm Tue-Sat. **Main courses** £13. **Set lunch** £15.50 3 courses. **Set dinner** £25 3 courses. **Credit** MC, V.

Looking out through old shop-front windows on to Burnham Market's comely, if car-jammed green, Fishes attracts the area's weekenders with its bright, unfussy interior (one room crimson, the other white; cork flooring, wicker chairs, pine tables). Marine life dominates the fixed-price, regularly changing menu: often locally caught, usually expertly cooked in Mediterranean or British style. A marvellous bowlful of plump Stiffkey cockles might be matched with chilli, ginger, garlic, parsley, lemon and olive oil. To follow, meaty mixed fish kebab comes with houmous, tsatsiki, own-made pitta (a classy touch) and chilli sauce. Deep-fried goujons of brilliant-white plaice arrive with big chips and chunky tartare sauce. Puddings such as dark chocolate fondant with rhubarb sorbet further demonstrate culinary flair. The wine list is enticing and the black-clad staff polite, if a trifle slow on occasion.

The Hoste Arms

The Green, Burnham Market, PE31 8HD (01328 738777/www.hostearms.co.uk). **Lunch served** noon-2pm, **dinner served** 7-9pm daily. **Main courses** £8.95-£16.50. **Credit** MC, V.

The canary yellow stucco of the Hoste stands out from its surroundings in one of Norfolk's prettiest villages. Inside, a large flagstoned bar caters to the locals, while a sophisticated restaurant across three rooms feeds weekend guests and Norfolk diners in search of reasonably priced, imaginative food served in delightful surroundings. In fact, the menu is

The best Afternoon teas

Bonnet's
Half-café, half-chocolate shop in Scarborough. *See p289.*

Duddleswell Tea Rooms
Venerable tearooms near Ashdown Forest. *See p99.*

Gilpin Lodge
A Lakeland stunner where teatime is taken seriously. *See p249.*

Rampsbeck Country House Hotel
Take tea on the terrace at this Ullswater gem. *See p248.*

Rothay Manor
A splendid buffet selection of sweet and savoury Cumbrian treats. *See p245.*

Sharrow Bay
Classy teas at Cumbria's most famous country house hotel. *See p247.*

The Terrace
Gloriously old-fashioned afternoon teas in deepest Dorset. *See p136.*

Tickle Manor Tearooms
Cream teas are a speciality in Lavenham, Suffolk. *See p199.*

Wimborne St Giles Village Hall
Only in Dorset. This time the cakes really are home-baked. *See p139.*

East Anglia

Walpole Arms

perhaps overambitious – on one visit two of the starters, including local Burnham Creek oysters, were unavailable. That said, what we did have – brochette of scallops, followed by best end of English lamb in a herb crust – was very good, and the sorbets are sensational. There are plenty of wines by the glass, and coffee can be taken in the sink-in leather sofas and armchairs spread around the ground floor. All highly satisfactory.

CROMER

Mary Jane's Fish Bar ★
27-29 Garden Street, Cromer, NR27 9PL (01263 511208). **Meals served** 11.30am-9pm Mon-Thur; 11.30am-10.30pm Fri, Sat; noon-9pm Sun. **Main courses** £3-£5. **No credit cards**.
Housed within a pale blue building, on a corner of one of the narrow Cromer streets, is this 64-seater licensed fish and chip restaurant decorated in grey, blue and candyfloss pink. It may not look appetising, but shield your eyes and wait for a treat. Quality fish predominates on the menu with a choice of cod, haddock, plaice, rock and skate, all served skin-on unless otherwise requested. Breaking open the batter creates a puff of steam and reveals fresh white flesh, in contrast to the golden chips and vibrant green mushy peas soaked overnight in bicarbonate of soda. A bottle of the house wine costs around £8 and cod, chips and mushy peas stings the wallet to the tune of £5.65.

HOLKHAM

The Victoria
Park Road, Holkham, NR23 1RG (01328 711008/ www.victoriaatholkham.co.uk). **Lunch served** noon-2.30pm, **dinner served** 7-9.30pm daily. **Main courses** £11-£16.90. **Credit** MC, V.
No wonder the 'Vic' is a magnet for urban sophisticates. The old hotel-cum-gastropub is the centrepiece in a perfectly preserved Victorian village set back from Norfolk's most famous beach by a field or two of the Holkham Estate. Outside, a walled orchard and stable block make lovely beer gardens; inside, the spacious bar, sitting and dining rooms (got up in country house-meets-Rajasthan style) are peopled with smart holidaymakers and workmen in wellies. Children's menus are an absolute steal: £5.50 for mini fish and chips, spaghetti with meatballs and so on, followed by ice-cream. Adults don't do too badly either: fish is sparklingly fresh and fried in tempura batter, while burgers are made with Holkham Estate beef. More complex dishes betray a lack of flair (risotto of prawns and calamares was bland), but desserts are brilliant, rising to such giddy heights as rhubarb jelly with ginger ice-cream. A lovely reward after a walk in the bracing winds.

HOLT

Yetman's
37 Norwich Road, Holt, NR25 6SA (01263 713320/ www.yetmans.net). **Lunch served** 12.30-2pm Sun. **Dinner served** 7-9.30pm Wed-Sat (Sun during Aug & bank hols). **Set meal** £26.50 2 courses, £32 3 courses, £36.75 4 courses. **Credit** AmEx, MC, V.
With his wild hair and casual clothes, Peter Yetman looks like a throwback to 1960s hippiedom. But there's nothing scruffy about his restaurant – two converted cottages painted primrose yellow – which is as bright and clean as a new pin. While his wife labours in the kitchen, he wanders between tables chatting to diners, most of whom seem to be regulars. You can see why. Although a bit pricey by local standards, the food is excellent. The menu, which changes daily, offers a good selection of dishes made from fresh local ingredients. Scallops came with a delicious garlic and brown butter sauce; asparagus and gruyère tart was light and simple. To follow we could have had sea trout, brill or spinach gnocchi but opted for succulent roast fillet

of beef with a subtle tarragon and orange hollandaise sauce, and tender char-grilled duck breast marinated in muscat, its flavour offset by the tang of spiced figs. With its walnut pastry and subtle sauce, the pear and chocolate tart was a hit.

ITTERINGHAM

Walpole Arms ★
The Common, Itteringham, NR11 7AR (01263 587258). **Lunch served** noon-2pm daily. **Dinner served** 7-9pm Mon-Sat. **Main courses** £8.95-£16. **Credit** MC, V.
Since a wine merchant and a producer of *Masterchef* took over this idyllic pub in 2001, awards and customers have followed. Inside is a log fire, beams, chunky tables and a stalk of a restaurant annexe with linen tablecloths. Good-value weekend brunches bring in urbane families. Big portions of eggs baked in a terracotta bowl with sublime mushroom purée and (slightly tough) lardons of bacon arrive with sourdough toast. To follow there's bratwurst with lyonnaise potatoes, crunchy and tangy red cabbage and outstanding gravy. The pricier full menu has a rustic Mediterranean feel – witness baked hake and puttanesca potatoes with paprika and garlic oil. Poached rhubarb with marzipan parfait, clued-up staff, ten wines by the glass (and Adnams and Woodeforde's ales by the pint) all underline the Walpole's laid-back class.

KING'S LYNN

Riverside
27 King Street, King's Lynn, PE30 1HA (01553 773134/www.riversiderestaurant.com). **Lunch served** noon-2pm, **dinner served** 6.30-9.30pm Mon-Sat. **Set dinner** £20 2 courses, £25 3 courses. **Credit** AmEx, MC, V.
Come here at high tide on a sunny day, taking with you a slice of irony, and you'll likely enjoy yourself.

The Riverside is set in a venerable yet barely tarted-up part of Lynn. You'll have to traverse an unbecoming yard before reaching a beautiful old garden, the barn-like restaurant and a terrace (with plastic furniture) looking over the vast River Great Ouse. The decor is pastel-shaded beneath glorious old beams: prissy 1970s posh. At a weekend lunch, elderly well-bred customers were tucking in, and service was exceedingly polite. (Yes, sir.) Food, though scarcely cutting-edge, is not of the prawn cocktail era, even running to roast vegetable and goat's cheese tart. Prices are high, but there's a clutch of better-value dishes, including the 'light lunch' (lamb and apricot casserole, say). We began with pungent, creamed Arbroath smokies, followed by uncommonly light salmon and coriander fish cakes, then rhubarb, orange and ginger crumble. Not bad, considering.

MORSTON

Morston Hall ★
Morston Hall Hotel, The Street, Morston, NR25 7AA (01263 741041/www.morstonhall.com). **Lunch served** 12.30-1pm Sun. **Dinner served** 7.30-8pm daily. **Set lunch** £24 3 courses. **Set dinner** £38 4 courses. **Credit** AmEx, MC, V.
Probably Norfolk's finest rural restaurant, Morston Hall is a 17th-century house-turned-hotel, yet its style is more comfortable than designer. The attraction is Galton Blackiston's cooking, which continues to entertain scores of eager gourmets at four-course, no-choice dinners. Since these are served in one sitting, the experience feels nicely communal. You might not have ordered warm egg yolk in pan-fried brioche with sautéed wild mushrooms, but it turns out to be delicious. Ingredients are carefully chosen and sometimes surprise with their simplicity, like Morston lobster served with lime mayonnaise or Norfolk asparagus with new potatoes and hollandaise. But for the most

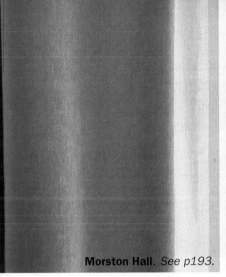

Morston Hall. *See p193*.

part, preparations are complex, verging on the exquisite – which is, after all, what most of us want from a meal costing £38 without the impressive accompanying wines.

NORWICH

Adlard's

79 Upper St Giles Street, Norwich, NR2 1AB (01603 633522/www.adlards.co.uk). **Lunch served** 12.30-1.45pm Tue-Sat. **Dinner served** 7.30-10.30pm Mon-Sat. **Main courses** £16-£19.50. **Set lunch** £19 3 courses. **Set dinner** £25 3 courses. **Credit** AmEx, DC, MC, V.

Unfazed by our early arrival, the friendly staff brought us a complimentary appetiser – a scallop on a bed of delicious caramelised carrot. The place was full, but the calming decor and baskets of wholemeal bread enhanced our mood of pleasant expectation. The menu offers a limited choice – four items in each section – but descriptions are enticing. We were disappointed, though. Tian of Cromer crab and confit of lentils and avocado was a strange mixture of tastes and textures, while warm goat's cheese, wilted spinach and red pepper syrup was a bland cylinder of cheese cased in tasteless leaves. In the mains, beautiful arrangements did not make up for tiny portions. Perched on a minuscule circle of pommes fondant, surrounded by a tasty jus and slithers of carrot, the loin of lamb was rather tough. Three mouthfuls of roasted halibut rested on a disc of mashed potato. The desserts that came past were no larger than a mouthful, so we decided to skip further disappointment and expense. Let's hope this was an off-night, as Adlard's has a good reputation.

By Appointment

25-29 St Georges Street, Norwich, NR3 1AB (01603 630730). **Dinner served** 7.30-9pm Tue-Sat. **Main courses** £16.95. **Credit** MC, V.

Go through a side entrance into a pretty courtyard – with tables for alfresco dining – and then into the kitchen. You'll be greeted like long-lost friends and led to a high-camp dining room. The menu is recited (the blackboard is indecipherable) – the waiter enjoyed this more than we did and we could have done without the telling-off when one of our party asked about vegetarian dishes (apparently we should have given advance warning). That said, a vegetarian menu was quickly produced. Twice-baked cheese soufflé and potato dauphinoise tartlet were fine starters, but the crown went to a delectable hot fish soup with an ice-cold garlic mayonnaise. Next, spiced mushroom risotto and lamb shank slow-cooked with a berry sauce proved more interesting than a tender steak. Puds – crème brûlée, sweet lemon tart – are worth ordering. Service is attentive, but the courses arrived a little too close together. This place makes for an intimate if slightly fussy night out.

Tatlers

21 Tombland, Norwich, NR3 1RF (01603 766670/ www.tatlers.com). **Lunch served** noon-2pm, **dinner served** 6.30-10pm Mon-Sat. **Main courses** £12-£16. **Set lunch** £14 2 courses, £17 3 courses. **Credit** AmEx, MC, V.

Nicely positioned near the cathedral, Tatlers is a handsome restaurant on two floors of an old house. Stripped floorboards and bare wooden tables are offset by shining cutlery and glasses, and by lots of paintings (all for sale). Staff are welcoming and efficient, and add to the easygoing atmosphere. Food is less casual, although there's always something simple such as wild mushroom risotto or bruschetta with goat's cheese and tomato on the menu. And they're not above providing tomato ketchup for young diners (the thin-cut chips are fabulous, with or without the sauce). More typical are dishes such as spiced crab cake with curried velouté, followed by

roast chump of Norfolk lamb with a warm broad bean, spinach and molasses-cured bacon salad and a café au lait sauce. Quality food in a convivial setting.

SOUTH CREAKE

The Ostrich Inn

1 Fakenham Road, South Creake, NR20 9PB (01328 823320/www.ostrichinn.co.uk). **Lunch served** noon-2.15pm, **dinner served** 7-9.15pm Mon, Wed-Sun. **Main courses** £7.50-£13.95. **Credit** MC, V.

They've built holiday flats behind this pleasant village pub and in summer and at weekends it's wise to book, since things get very busy. That doesn't stop the atmosphere being very friendly and the service good. Chalked up on a board is a varied menu which includes own-made pies, several types of fish – salmon steaks, monkfish and sea bass – ostrich steaks and a small choice of vegetarian dishes such as ratatouille and mushroom fricassée. For starters, whitebait was delicious and stilton mushrooms tasty. A crispy choux pastry towered over the chicken and leek pie, which was a bit bland compared with the deliciously rich steak and kidney pie. A Barnsley chop came in a fruity red sauce and was huge, tender and succulent. After enormous portions washed down with draught cider and Adnams ale, it was hard to find room for spotted dick or Devon toffee pudding but, between us, we tackled a jam suet pudding which brought memories of childhood flooding back.

STOKE HOLY CROSS

The Wildebeest Arms ★

82-86 Norwich Road, Stoke Holy Cross, NR14 8QJ (01508 492497). **Lunch served** noon-2pm, **dinner served** 7-9pm daily. **Main courses** £9.95-£18.50. **Set lunch** £9.95 2 courses, £12.95 3 courses. **Set dinner** £15 2 courses, £18.50 3 courses. **Credit** AmEx, DC, MC, V.

The Wildebeest Arms, a restaurant where you can drink (rather than a pub), was quiet on the Sunday night we chose, but on Friday and Saturday nights it's hard to get a table. You can see why. Starter of confit of duck was a crispy leg on a bed of rocket sprinkled with pomegranate seeds – a classy combination; char-grilled scallops were fresh, springy and sensible in number. Mains included pan-fried salmon and sea bass, but we opted for red meat. Chump of lamb came with fondant potatoes and slices of courgette and red peppers in a delicious caper jus. Sitting on layers of spinach and fondant potatoes, succulent Aberdeen Angus steak sprouted an Afro frizz of sweet onion curls. We still had room for desserts, though. The mango rice pudding and lemon sorbet was a bit bland, but crème brûlée was splendidly offset by a rhubarb sorbet. We'd driven quite a long way to catch the Wildebeest; it was worth every mile.

SWAFFHAM

Strattons

4 Ash Close, Swaffham, PE37 7NH (01760 723845/ www.strattonshotel.com). **Dinner served** 7pm Mon-Sat by appointment. **Set dinner** £35 4 courses. **Credit** AmEx, MC, V.

Hidden down a lane off the market square, Strattons occupies the ground floor of a Palladian mansion. You'll first be ushered upstairs to a flamboyantly attired drawing room to choose from Vanessa Scott's set-price modern European menu (where local and organic ingredients hold sway), and a long, elaborately annotated wine list. Thence down to the cool grey, seagrass-floored restaurant, looking on to the lawns. Creamy timbale of Cromer crab with radicchio might start a meal, perhaps followed by the more daring but equally accomplished plum tomato tart with monkfish, lemon mash and stilton sauce. Roast chicken pudding, sage gravy and mushroom mash was a flavour-packed triumph of a main course. After this, then English cheeses, puddings can be a mite heavy, though there's no denying the allures of apricot and nut steamed pudding, or of Strattons as a whole: a country-house hotel with liberal, metropolitan nous. Like-minded lucred-up Londoners love it.

SWANTON MORLEY

Darby's Free House

1-2 Elsing Road, Swanton Morley, NR20 4NY (01362 637647). **Lunch served** noon-2.15pm, **dinner served** 6.30-9.30pm Mon-Fri. **Meals served** noon-9.45pm Sat; noon-9pm Sun. **Main courses** £5-£13. **Credit** MC, V.

Formed by two houses recently converted into a long bar and restaurant, this pub manages to look pleasingly old and has a relaxed atmosphere that attracts a lot of locals. Perch on seats belonging to old ploughs, sample a wide variety of local ales – Adnams, Tanglefoot, Marstons Pedigree and Old Peculiar – and eat the same food served in the restaurant. This is quite small, so do book. Bypassing super-size barbecue spare ribs we sampled Cromer crab and brie and salmon salads: crisp and fresh, but fridge-cold. Next, steak and mushroom pudding was rich, tender and juicy inside, though the suet pastry wasn't quite right. Baked sea bass was very fresh with a subtle flavour enhanced by watercress. We could have chosen toffee profiteroles or banoffi pie, but plumped for French apple tart – spoiled by that pub standby, squirted cream.

THORNHAM

The Lifeboat Inn

Ship Lane, Thornham, PE36 6LT (01485 512236/ www.lifeboatinn.co.uk). **Lunch served** noon-2.30pm, **dinner served** 6.30-9.30pm daily. **Main courses** £8.50-£15.95. **Set dinner** £25 3 courses. **Credit** MC, V.

You can sit on old pews and wooden settles at this rambling 16th-century smugglers' inn, drink local ales and eat decent bar food such as courgette, broccoli and brie soup, followed by steak and kidney pudding or baked salmon fillet and pesto noodles. We booked a table in the restaurant – which, by comparison, is a bit po-faced. Tian of smoked salmon, prawns and avocado was an interesting combination and the fresh Cromer crab came with a top-notch dill mayonnaise. Portions are small, though. Juicy scallops seemed more like a starter than a main, with only five arranged round a small mound of peppery noodles. Roast monkfish was exceptional but similarly modest in size. Still, it meant we had plenty of space for the delights of chocolate and Guinness sponge, and date and ginger pudding with toffee sauce. The Lifeboat overlooks the salt marshes, where you can wander for miles.

WARHAM ALL SAINTS

Three Horseshoes ★ ★

Bridge Street, Warham All Saints, NR23 1NL (01328 710547). **Lunch served** noon-1.45pm, **dinner served** 6-8.30pm daily. **Main courses** £5.80-£8.20. **No credit cards**.

The Three Horseshoes is just about the perfect village pub and, not surprisingly, it gets chock-a-block. From the bar, which is little more than a hole in the wall, you can order local ales, cider and own-made lemonade; if you're bored with chardonnay or cabernet sauvignon you can try wines made from gooseberries, rhubarb, plums, rose petals or silver birch. Chalked up on the board are dishes that vary according to the day's catch, individual pies and, for vegetarians, a rather pedestrian cottage garden bake. Substantial pies – steak and stilton, steak and kidney, game and wine, Norfolk beef – are topped with flaky choux pastry, while the steak and kidney pudding comes wrapped in suet. Desserts such as blackberry and apple tart, mixed fruit crumble or bread and butter pudding exemplify traditional British cooking at its very best.

WELLS-NEXT-THE-SEA

The Crown ★

The Crown Hotel, The Buttlands, Wells-next-the-Sea, NR23 1EX (01328 710209/ www.thecrownhotelwells.co.uk). **Dinner served** 7-9.30pm daily. **Set dinner** £24.95 2 courses, £29.95 3 courses incl coffee. **Credit** AmEx, MC, V.

Chef Nick Anderson (of Rococo fame) has gone, but many of his staff remain and the Crown still sparkles. A stately old hotel on Wells' handsome green, it has been updated for the town's new bourgeoisie. The bar (Adnams beers, Aspall's ciders, gastropub menu served lunch and evening) has armchairs, pine flooring and an outdoor terrace, while the separate, stylish restaurant sports mustard-hued walls, bright paintings, crisp white table linen and a fixed-price menu (many choices, no supplements) of exquisitely presented modern European food. After tantalising *amuse-bouches* came a pre-starter of rich, intense lobster bisque, before we embarked on a sweetbread and lamb shank terrine that needed a more tart accompaniment than date chutney. No complaints, though, about the main course of perfect pink duck breast topped by a barely cooked scallop and resting on crushed new potatoes, its phenomenal gravy forming a heavenly duck-scallop nexus. Puddings (order the assiette taster of four, if you can) surpass even this with creations such as unthinkably delicate sticky toffee pudding with honey ice-cream. Assured service and an enticing wine list add extra polish to the lustrous Crown.

Also in the area

Loch Fyne 30-32 St Giles Street, Norwich NR2 1LL (01603 723450).

Suffolk

ALDEBURGH

The Golden Galleon ★
137 High Street, Aldeburgh, IP15 5AR (01728 454685). **Meals served** noon-2pm, 5-8pm Mon-Thur; noon-2.30pm, 4-8pm Fri, Sat; noon-6pm Sun. **Main courses** £3-£4.30. **No credit cards**.
Since 1967 the Aldeburgh Fish & Chip Shop (226 High Street; 01728 452250) has been legendary. The Golden Galleon, just up the road, is the highly efficient, first-floor, sit-down-and-eat, 32-seater, BYO off-shoot, run by the same folk. Overlooking the high street, it is decorated with pale yellow walls, paintings of sea-going galleons and solid, light oak furniture. Service is friendly and there's a choice of cod, haddock, skate wing or plaice as well as a variety of burgers, pizzas, pies and desserts, including ice-cream, treacle pudding and tangy lemon sponge.

The Lighthouse
77 High Street, Aldeburgh, IP15 5AU (01728 453377/www.thelighthouserestaurant.co.uk). **Breakfast served** 10.30am-noon, **lunch served** noon-2pm, **dinner served** 6.30-8pm daily. **Main courses** (lunch) £6.75-£9.50. **Set dinner** £14.25 2 courses, £17.50 3 courses. **Credit** AmEx, MC, V.
The menu at this bright and airy Aldeburgh bistro changes according to the daily catch. Cod or skate are bought fresh from beachside suppliers and crab, asparagus and smoked fish are sourced locally. Dinner is a very reasonably-priced £14.25 for two courses or £17.50 for three courses, and at lunch there's a seasonally changing menu with eight or ten choices in each course. Don't miss the potted Norfolk shrimps, hot smoked salmon with new potatoes or freshly dressed Cromer crab with herb mayonnaise. But you don't have to stick to fish: there's also creamy duck liver parfait with pickled figs and toast, juicy fillet steak with chunky chips or calf's liver and mash if you prefer.

Regatta
171 High Street, Aldeburgh, IP15 5AN (01728 452011). **Lunch served** noon-2pm, **dinner served** 6-10pm daily. **Main courses** £8-£14. **Set dinner** £9 2 courses, £12 3 courses. **Credit** AmEx, DC, MC, V.
A long-standing favourite, Regatta offers a flexible menu in laid-back, sunny surroundings in a prime position on Aldeburgh's high street. Run by Robert Mabey and his wife Johanna, it opened in 1992 and has been going great guns ever since. Regatta's strengths include local game and produce, and there's a particular emphasis on fresh fish and shellfish in the spring and summer months. The place is pleasantly family-friendly during the day and also runs a series of popular gourmet evenings devoted to themes like game or wild mushrooms. The place is popular, so book.

BRAMFIELD

Queen's Head
The Street, Bramfield, IP19 9HT (01986 784214/ www.queensheadbramfield.co.uk). **Lunch served** noon-2pm daily. **Dinner served** 6.30-10pm Mon-Sat; 7-9pm Sun. **Main courses** £5.95-£14.95. **Credit** AmEx, MC, V.
Set beside the church in a small village, this hugely likeable pub is an unpretentious place with exposed brick walls, blue and white check tablecloths and a pleasant garden for sunny afternoons. The appealing menu emphasises organic and locally sourced ingredients. These include juicy slabs of 'River Farm Smokery' salmon, aromatic chickpea and leek soup, filo pastry with goat's cheese and sea bass with a garnish of caper berries and olives. Plentiful but unadventurous vegetables arrived in a side dish. Puddings feature an array of home-made ice-creams, well cared for British cheeses and a sumptuous lemon cheesecake with Jersey cream. Service is ineffably friendly and the odd blip in the cooking can easily be forgiven. Children are well catered for with high chairs, toys and books.

BURY ST EDMUNDS

Maison Bleue at Mortimer's
30-31 Churchgate Street, Bury St Edmunds, IP33 1RG (01284 760623/www.maisonbleue.co.uk). **Lunch served** noon-2.30pm Tue-Fri; noon-2pm Sat. **Dinner served** 7-9.30pm Tue-Thur; 6.30-10pm Fri, Sat. **Set lunches** £9.95-£12.95 2 courses, £14.95 3 courses. **Set dinner** £19.95 3 courses. **Credit** AmEx, MC, V.
If you only go to one restaurant in Bury, make it this one. Almost all the fish is locally caught and each dish is exquisitely put together – that means taste as well as presentation. The stylish blue interior is cosy and intimate, while the French waiting staff know how to be attentive without becoming obsequious. Marinated king scallops with salmon, lime and coriander in filo pastry were equally matched by the black tiger gambas in a tangy tomato salsa. Oven-baked dorado à la provençale and whole grilled Dover sole didn't disappoint either. One tip – save some room for the grand board of well-kept cheeses. Eating à la carte costs around £35 per head at dinner (with wine) and it's worth every single penny.

IPSWICH

The Galley

25 St Nicholas Street, Ipswich, IP1 1TW (01473 281131/www.galley.uk.com). **Lunch served** noon-2pm Mon-Sat. **Dinner served** 6.30-10pm Mon-Thur; 6.30-11pm Fri, Sat. **Main courses** £13.95-£16.95. **Credit** AmEx, MC, V.

Decorated pink and aquamarine, this leaning Elizabethan building conceals one of the best restaurants in the area. Upstairs the little rooms are open between the wall beams to create light while sloping floors add charm. Service is quick and to the point, though the owner will talk the hind legs off a donkey if asked about the food. Lobster, fresh fish and seasonal vegetables are often the order of the day and nearly all the ingredients are local. That's why the Gressingham duck liver pâté, Capel St Mary flat mushrooms and Tuddenham Hall asparagus really hit the spot. Sauces are inventive, prices are not disheartening and the wine list is idiosyncratic but fun (down to the owner), with a very good selection around £20.

LAVENHAM

The Angel

Market Place, Lavenham, CO10 9QZ (01787 247388/www.lavenham.co.uk/angel). **Lunch served** noon-2.15pm, **dinner served** 6.45-9.15pm daily. **Main courses** £8.50-£14.95. **Credit** AmEx, MC, V.

Licensed premises since 1420, the Angel offers solid, rural food with occasional inspired additions from around the world – steak and ale pie; glazed duck with spring greens and sweet and sour sauce; grilled halibut with anchovies, capers and white wine sauce – and is aimed squarely at the upper end of the pub grub spectrum. The dark-beamed pub is full of atmosphere and quaffing locals, the dining room quieter and more roomy, while the tables outside overlooking Market Square provide the ideal spot to watch the massed tourists rubber-necking historic buildings. Three courses will lighten the wallet by £20 or more and also curtail the ability to walk. Booking is essential.

Great House ★

Market Place, Lavenham, CO10 9QZ (01787 247431/www.greathouse.co.uk). **Lunch served** noon-2.30pm Tue-Sun. **Dinner served** 7-9.30pm Tue-Sat. **Main courses** £10.95-£18. **Set lunch** £9.95 2 courses, £15.95 3 courses. **Set dinner** £21.95 3 courses. **Credit** AmEx, MC, V.

This was once Stephen Spender's house; now it's an elegant, formal, relaxed French restaurant with accommodation, run with Gallic verve and style by Régis and Martine Crépy. Fresh white tablecloths decorate the simple tables, and contrast with the golden wood floors. The menu, undoubtedly one of the best and most fairly priced in Suffolk, derives its strength from the use of subtle flavours, including pan-fried John Dory with watercress coulis, fillet of prime beef with fresh duck foie gras or cassolette of

sautéed wild mushrooms and asparagus finished with garlic and cream parsley. Among the starters the carpaccio of marinated beef with coriander dressing on a parmesan rocket salad takes some beating; and if dessert tempts, go for the creamy lime and lemon tart which leaves the tastebuds zinging. Children are welcome, particularly for Sunday lunch.

Tickle Manor Tearooms

17 High Street, Lavenham, CO10 9PT (01787 248438). **Meals served** 10.30am-5pm daily. **Main courses** £3-£5.95. **No credit cards**.

It's easy to miss this traditional, askew little Elizabethan teahouse. It has a modest sign by the door and embodies many comforting virtues. The rooms, both upstairs and down, are small but the assortment of tables are a decent arm's length apart. The service is swift and the food is simple, consisting of sandwiches, toasties, baguettes and salads, all reasonably priced, well presented and filling. For devout tea drinkers there's a broad selection to choose from and cream teas are a speciality. There's coffee and a refreshing elderflower pressé too. The scones and cakes, particularly the apple cromwell and the Suffolk honey cake, are worth writing home about.

LIDGATE

Star Inn

The Street, Lidgate, CB8 9PP (01638 500275). **Lunch served** noon-2pm Mon-Fri; noon-2.30pm Sat, Sun. **Dinner served** 7-9.30pm Mon-Thur; 7-10pm Fri, Sat. **Set lunch** (Sun) £14.50 3 courses. **Credit** AmEx, MC, V.

The Catalan menu in this 16th-century inn has proved so popular that the Lidgate Star (as it's known locally) has become more of a restaurant than a pub these days – although it still serves some fine ales from the bar. Indeed, on a Friday and Saturday evening, there are likely to be so many people dining on fall-apart, slow-cooked Spanish lamb, tasty chorizo and bean soup and oven-baked fish that there's barely enough elbow room to use the bar billiards table. Spanish landlady Teresa is never too busy to talk people through the extensive blackboard menu and her staff are as friendly as they can be.

LONG MELFORD

Black Lion

Church Walk, The Green, Long Melford, CO10 9DN (01787 312356/www.blacklionhotel.co.uk). **Food served** *Wine bar* noon-2pm, 7-9.30pm daily; *Restaurant* 7-9.30pm daily. **Set meal** £25.95 2 courses, £29.95 3 courses. **Set lunch** (Sun) £18.95 3 courses. **Credit** AmEx, MC, V.

With a comforting and comfortable interior, bar dining from a blackboard menu and (for more formal occasions) a plush restaurant, the Black Lion straddles two stools. Staple dishes on the restaurant menu are traditional, including grilled loin of lamb with cabbage and rich mint jus, dried smoked haddock and potato with beef tomatoes or red pepper and butter bean cakes. The blackboard offers a few more hearty options, such as sausage, mash and black bacon and onion gravy or crispy battered cod with chips. Desserts such as hazel-nut tart with local honey and crème fraîche tend to be light but tasty and the house wines provide enough variation to keep you clear of the otherwise expensive restaurant wine list.

Scutchers of Long Melford

Westgate Street, Long Melford, CO10 9DP (01787 310200/www.scutchers.com). **Lunch served** noon-2pm, **dinner served** 7-9.30pm Tue-Sat. **Main courses** £12-£18. **Credit** AmEx, MC, V.
Within this unspectacular grade II listed Georgian building is what looks like a neat, informal little restaurant, but in fact it's much more than that. Vying for attention on the menu are deep-fried tiger prawns in a tempura batter, seared scallops with crab and chive mash, pan-fried halibut on tomatoes and chilli, calf's liver and bacon in a rich gravy or fillet of beef with creamy herb and shallot sauce. Veggies have to make do with a puff pastry case full of spinach, caramelised onions, mushrooms, poached egg and red pepper sauce. Poor devils. There's a broad wine list with an equally varied price range.

MARLESFORD

Farmcafe ★ ★

Main Road (A12), Marlesford, IP13 0AG (01728 747717/www.farmcafe.co.uk). **Breakfast served** 7am-noon, **lunch served** noon-5pm. **Main courses** £5-£8. **Credit** MC, V.
If only all roadside cafés were like this. Run by a group of local residents, the Farmcafe offers a range of daily specials and excellent staples, such as all-day Suffolk brunch, proper own-made burgers, bangers and mash or fresh local fish. Most of the food is sourced from the area, including excellent bacon and prize-winning sausages. As well as the airy restaurant space, there is a pleasant covered veranda and garden area at the back. Local produce and plants are available from the adjacent food market. A great place to refresh yourself on your way to or from the Suffolk coast.

NAYLAND

White Hart Inn

11 High Street, Nayland, CO6 4JF (01206 263382/ www.whitehart-nayland.co.uk). **Lunch served** noon-2.30pm Tue-Sat. **Dinner served** 6.30-9.30pm Tue-Fri; 6.30-10pm Sat; 6.30-9pm Sun. **Main courses** £9.90-£16. **Set lunch** £12.95 3 courses. **Set dinner** £21.50 3 courses. **Credit** AmEx, DC, MC, V.
The plaster has been removed from some of the walls, and the whole of the former pub area is now incorporated into a restaurant and small bar section.

Service is impeccable and friendly; the quality of the traditional French cookery is high. Chilled Andalucian gazpacho and cucumber sorbet made a lively and refreshing start, while roast rolled loin of suckling pig with Calvados sauce melted in the mouth. Desserts include a warm pancake filled with fresh strawberries and dreamy own-made vanilla ice-cream. There's also a selection of French farmhouse cheeses. House wines are a very reasonable £11 a bottle.

ORFORD

The Butley-Orford Oysterage ★

Market Hill, Orford, IP12 2LH (01394 450277). **Lunch served** noon-2.15pm daily. **Dinner served** *Apr-Oct* 6.30-9pm Mon-Fri, Sun; 6-9pm Sat. *Nov-Mar* 6.30-9pm Fri; 6-9pm Sat. **Main courses** £6.90-£12.50. **Credit** MC, V.
Bill Pinney not only has his own fishing fleet and oyster beds, but runs a small but flourishing smokehouse as well. The family-run oysterage is small but perfectly formed, with stripped down café surroundings and motherly service. Specials are chalked up daily on a blackboard, including fresh skate, sole, cod, herring or sprats, served with new potatoes and a simple side salad. Otherwise, choose from a mouthwatering array of own-smoked salmon, eel, trout, haddock or prawns, with a variety of accompaniments. Freshness and simplicity are the order of the day and the place is hugely, deservedly popular as a result.

The Trinity ★

Crown & Castle Hotel, Orford, IP12 2LJ (01394 450205/www.crownandcastle.co.uk). **Lunch served** noon-2pm daily. **Dinner served** *Apr-Oct* 7-9pm daily; *Nov-Mar* 7-9pm Mon-Sat. **Main courses** £9.50-£18. **Credit** MC, V.
Well worth the necessary advanced booking, a meal at the Crown & Castle's polished bistro is always a pleasure. The short but flexible menu offers a range of modern European dishes such as pan-fried local skate with french beans and new potatoes, grilled salmon with pea and tarragon purée and crispy pancetta or own-potted shrimps with farmhouse toast. There's also a savvy wine list. Staff are pleasant and professional and the atmosphere invariably convivial. After Trinity tiramisu or warm pecan nut and bourbon tart (with proper custard), climb to the top of the splendid castle for unmissable views over Orford Ness.

POLSTEAD

The Cock

The Green, Polstead, CO6 5AL (01206 263150/ www.geocities.com). **Lunch served** 11am-2.30pm, **dinner served** 6-9.30pm Tue-Sun. **Main courses** £6.95-£12.50. **Credit** MC, V.
In an appealing annexe attached to the pub overlooking the village green, the Cock is a popular black-beamed restaurant with bare brick walls

East Anglia

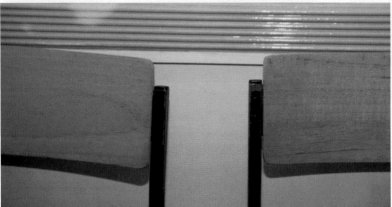

The Butley-Orford Oysterage

seating 40-plus diners. Alongside the extensive menu and specials board are a range of Suffolk Huffers – large soft white rolls peculiar to the area, with various fillings. The wine list offers palatable vintages between £10 and £20, and an eye-catching array of malt whiskies awaits the discerning. The menu includes traditional meat pudding (sitting on a hotchpotch of vegetables and surrounded by new potatoes), lamb's liver and bacon or salmon fish cakes, plus vegetarian choices such as wild mushroom stroganoff and creamy pesto vegetables topped with puff pastry. For dessert try the apple and blackberry crumble or marmalade bread and butter pudding.

SAXMUNDHAM

The Bell Hotel ★

31 High Street, Saxmundham, IP17 1AF (01728 602331). **Lunch served** noon-2pm Tue-Sun. **Dinner served** 6-9pm Tue-Sat. **Main courses** £8-£15. **Set lunch** £10.50 2 courses, £13.50 3 courses. **Set dinner** £16 3 courses. **Credit** MC, V.
The restaurant at this small hotel is a pleasant surprise, offering excellent food in tranquil surroundings. The dining room is an oasis of sage green and crisp white linen, enlivened by some tasteful splashes of chintz. Starters include a tasty terrine of vegetables, an excellent gazpacho and tiger prawns and juicy scallops on slightly-too-salty saffron risotto. Next, succulent corn-fed chicken served with peas, broad beans and asparagus was easily matched by a robust pan-fried fillet of beef with Parma ham. An intense chocolate and Amaretto mousse, panna cotta with strawberries and a plate of farmhouse cheeses made a fine finish. Ingredients are sourced locally where possible and the overall quality of the dishes is high. Service is unhurried and friendly (and nice to children).

Harrison's

Main Road (A12 opposite the Kelsale turning), nr Saxmundham, IP17 2RF (01728 604444). **Lunch served** noon-2.30pm, **dinner served** from 7pm Tue-Sat. **Main courses** £10.50-£18. **Set lunch** (Tue-Fri) £11.50 2 courses, £13.50 3 courses. **Credit** MC, V.
An Elizabethan hall ambience is accentuated by the uneven brick floors, open fireplaces and exposed beams, while the almost stark decor implies a monastic concentration on good food. The seating is comfortable, the darkwood tables well spaced and there is almost no noise from the busy main road. Gloucester Old Spot terrine with pickles and toast; boiled ox tongue, swede and brussels tops; crisp-coated Aylesbury duck with rösti potato and red wine sauce; and local roast cod, asparagus and Parma ham salad suggest that tradition is important here, but it's not allowed to get in the way of a good time. Service is polite and knowledgeable and an almost daunting array of wines beckons from around £12 to £30.

SOUTHWOLD

Crown Hotel

90 High Street, Southwold, IP18 6DP (01502 722275). **Breakfast served** 8-10am, **lunch served** noon-2pm, **dinner served** 6-8.45pm daily. **Set lunch** £18.50 2 courses, £21.50 3 courses. **Set dinner** £24 2 courses, £29 3 courses. **Credit** MC, V.
One of busy Southwold's most popular eating options, the Adnams-run Crown has a formal front room restaurant and a buzzing bar area. Despite the overcrowding, we'd recommend opting for the more flexible, better-value menu offered at the front or back bar, where the atmosphere's more jolly and service slicker. Choices in the bar include smoked haddock and mussel chowder or roast salmon with potatoes and snake beans. We fared badly in the restaurant, with a soup-like ragoût of broad beans, new potatoes and ceps, a passable duck with spinach and pommes dauphinés and a leaden pannacotta to finish. At £24 for two courses, this didn't feel like good value. *See also* the Swan, *p203*.

The Harbour Inn ★

The Harbour Inn, Southwold, IP18 6TA (01502 722381). **Open** 11am-11pm Mon-Sat; noon-10.30pm Sun. **Lunch served** noon-2.30pm, **dinner served** 6-9pm daily. **Main courses** £8-£11. **Credit** MC, V.
Perfectly perched on the Southwold side of the River Blyth, the Harbour Inn has long been a haunt of locals and visitors alike. It has views over the harbour, a big ramshackle garden leading on to the marshes, snug rooms with roaring fires in winter, good beer, a hearty menu and fabulous fish and chips. A mound of locally caught crunchy sprats, pork and garlic bangers with lashings of mash, and flaky haddock in Adnams beer batter were all dishes to savour. A delicious, predictably mountainous apple crumble and custard finished the feast. The kitchens are understandably busy at peak times, but the quality of food is consistently good. This mecca of comfort food is best approached after a long day in the fresh air.

Mark's Fish Shop ★

32 High Street, Southwold, IP18 6AE (01502 723585). **Lunch served** 11.45am-2pm Mon-Sat; noon-2.30pm Sun. **Dinner served** 5-8pm Mon-Thur; 5-8.30pm Fri, Sat. 5-7.30pm Sun. **Main courses** £3.40-£4.20. **No credit cards**.
A five-minute walk from the Adnams brewery is Mark's – an unpretentious, licensed fish and chip restaurant where friendly service, good value and lovely food are the order of the day. Space, at the fixed seats and formica tables, can be found for 32 people among dangling fish nets, local paintings and historic photos. Pride of place on the menu goes to cod, plaice, skate and haddock, but it's worth checking the specials board to see if Southwold rock/huss is available. All the fish is served skin on, fried in beef dripping and accompanied by chips, mushy peas or curry sauce. Try it with a pint of Adnams Suffolk Strong.

Leaping Hare

Swan Hotel ★

Market Place, Southwold, IP18 6EG (01502 722186). **Lunch served** noon-2pm daily. **Dinner served** 7-9pm Mon-Thur, Sun; 7-10pm Fri, Sat. **Set lunch** £18 2 courses, £22 3 courses. **Set dinner** £23.50 2 courses, £28.50 3 courses. **Credit** MC, V.

The more grown-up of the two Adnams pub-hotels in Southwold (*see p202* the Crown), the Swan's civilised dining room has a country-house feel and big windows overlooking the busy high street. Service is friendly and efficient, while dishes on the modern European menu are slickly produced. Begin with a powerful Bloody Mary in the bar (made the traditional way with a dash of sherry), while you choose from the likes of cream of celeriac soup with truffle oil, charcuterie, pan-fried sea bass with new potatoes or risotto with mushrooms and broad beans. There's a lengthy wine list and a nicely priced Adnams selection.

STANTON

Leaping Hare

Wyken Hall, Stanton, IP31 2DW (01359 250287). *Café* **Meals served** 10am-6pm daily. *Restaurant* **Lunch served** noon-2pm daily. **Dinner served** 7-9pm Fri, Sat. **Main courses** £14.95-£16.95. **Credit** MC, V.

Attractively housed in a vast 400-year-old barn, the Leaping Hare restaurant is just part of the attraction of coming to Wyken Hall – so head this way for lunch rather than dinner. As well as the food, there are also gardens, a woodland walk, a farmers' market and a shop selling classy gifts to explore. Local produce features heavily on the modern British menu, and the Wyken Vineyards wine makes a refreshing change from the usual pinot grigio or shiraz. Locally, the Leaping Hare's reputation is held in high esteem but, although focaccia and olive oil and a starter of Suffolk asparagus couldn't be faulted, on our visit the main courses didn't taste quite as good as they sounded on the menu. The sauces were slightly overpowering and the wild sea bass tasted like it hadn't had a swim for a while.

STOKE-BY-NAYLAND

Angel Inn

Polstead Street, Stoke-by-Nayland, CO6 4SA (01206 263245/www.horizoninns.co.uk/ theangel.html). **Lunch served** noon-2pm Mon-Sat; noon-5pm Sun. **Dinner served** 6.30-9.30pm Mon-Sat; 5.30-9.30pm Sun. **Main courses** £9.95-£14.50. **Credit** MC, V.

The best

Fish & chips

Carlo's
Northumberland's finest. *See p281.*

Ernie Beckett's
An island of calm amid the bright lights of Cleethorpes. *See p221.*

Fish 'n' Fritz
Twenty-four years on the same street corner in Weymouth. They must be doing something right. *See p139.*

Golden Galleon
Aldeburgh may be posh, but the GG will see you right. *See p197.*

Harbour Lights
Lose yourself in the view of Falmouth harbour and the thick-cut Maris Pipers. *See p115.*

Kristian
The wet fish shop and busy restaurant are perfect quayside partners on the Tyne. *See p282.*

Les's
Bluff northern chippie where fish reigns supreme. *See p243.*

Maddy's
Gravy, curry sauce and custard. It's the extras that count in Ilfracombe. *See p128.*

St Anne's
Lytham St Anne's stalwart with a very special batter. *See p252.*

Seniors
Come to Blackpool for a splendid variety of fish. *See p250.*

At the Angel Inn you can eat in the Well Room (it boasts a 52ft well) or at a table for two on a lovebird balcony looking down on the barn-like room. Alternatively, you can eat in one of a number of timbered rooms in the pub or, in summer, outside in the sunshine in the handsome bricked courtyard. A wide-ranging menu offers choices such as black bacon and portobello mushroom salad, griddled sardines, char-grilled teriyaki ribeye steak or seared mackerel fillets, while vegetarians have the likes of pepper, potato and aubergine moussaka to pick from. An interesting wine list ranges in price from £9 to £40 a bottle. This is a pleasant, atmospheric spot with good service, and lots of people seem to know about it – so make sure you book well in advance at weekends.

WALBERSWICK

Bell Inn
Ferry Road, Walberswick, IP18 6TN (01502 723109/www.blythweb.co.uk/bellinn). **Lunch served** noon-2pm Mon-Sat; noon-2.30pm Sun. **Dinner served** 7-9pm Mon-Thur, Sun; 6-9pm Fri, Sat. **Main courses** £6.95-£11.25. **Credit** MC, V.
This 600-year-old inn with rooms in coastal Walberswick is owned by Adnams, but has none of the corporate blandness that this might lead you to fear. Huge, rambling and flagstoned, the place is reputedly haunted, though the atmosphere is jolly rather than spooky. Crowds pack the place at the weekends for the better than average food, including fresh and crispy fish and chips, lamb tagines, Cumberland sausages, fish cakes, Suffolk smokies and fresh-cut sandwiches. Obviously there's a full range of Adnams ales, plus a good choice of wine.

WICKHAM MARKET

Eat Inn ★
73 High Street, Wickham Market, IP13 0RA (01728 746361). **Lunch served** 11.30am-1.45pm. **Dinner served** 4.30-10pm Mon-Sat. **Main courses** £2.80-£3.80. **No credit cards**.
A family-run fish and chip shop and licensed restaurant since 1967, the Eat Inn is squeezed into a couple of brightly decorated rooms with low ceilings, dark beams and sturdy, light-coloured wooden furniture. Staff are up for the job and the fish, more often than not, comes fresh from Lowestoft. Cod, haddock, rock/huss and locally caught skate (in season) are most frequently requested, served skin on, boned – with large pieces weighing 10oz – and lightly coated with batter before being fried in sizzling palm oil. By way of accompaniment try medium-cut chips, mushy peas and chilli sauce.

WOODBRIDGE

Captain's Table
3 Quay Street, Woodbridge, IP12 1BX (01394 383145/www.captainstable.co.uk) **Lunch served** noon-2pm Tue-Sun. **Dinner served** 6.30-9.30pm Tue-Thur; 6.30-10pm Fri, Sat. **Main courses** £6.95-£15.50. **Credit** MC, V.
A bit close to a busy road for comfort, this whitewashed wayside restaurant nevertheless has a pleasant, stencilled interior and is close to the pretty Woodbridge estuary. The menu shows eclectic influences, with lamb kleftiko or tiger prawns with a Thai curry dip alongside spaghetti bolognese, but allows room for popular classics such as char-grilled ribeye or duck leg confit with lentils and red wine. There is also a specials board which changes daily and makes good use of locally sourced ingredients, particularly fresh fish – perhaps classic skate wing with black butter and capers, dressed crab and lobster, or locally smoked prawns. In summer, there are tables outside on a gravel terrace.

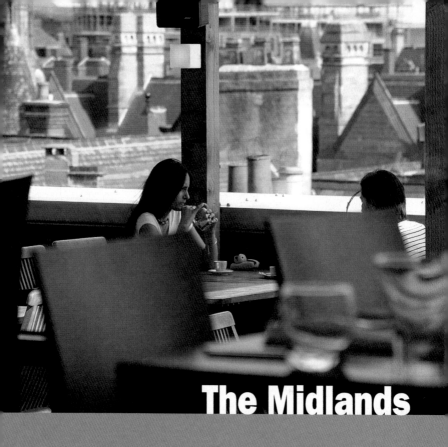

The Midlands

Midlands

Birmingham

Adil's Balti ★

148-150 Stoney Lane, Sparkhill, B12 8AJ (0121 449 0335). **Meals served** noon-midnight daily. **Main courses** £4.39-£7. **Set lunch** (noon-4pm) £5.95 4 courses. **Credit** AmEx, MC, V.

Birmingham's most famous balti house lies in one of the city's less salubrious suburbs. Nevertheless Adil's attracts a variety of diners, from students looking to stretch their loan a little further to tourists on a pilgrimage to the 'Balti Triangle'. There are no frills, but at these prices you shouldn't expect any. Starters are a little uninspired; main courses – a wide range of meat and vegetarian balti dishes served with naan bread – are a better bet. Groups should try the great value 'table naan'. Adil's is unlicensed, but bottles from the off-licence next door help to contribute to the lively atmosphere, which, coupled with the friendly service, keeps them coming back.

Bank Restaurant & Bar ★

4 Brindleyplace, B1 2JB (0121 633 4466/ www.bankrestaurants.com). **Breakfast served** 7.30-10am Mon-Fri. **Lunch served** noon-2.45pm Mon-Fri; 11.30am-3pm Sat, Sun. **Dinner served** 5.30-11pm Mon-Sat; 5-9.30pm Sun. **Main courses** £9.50-£18. **Set meals** (lunch, 5.30-7pm daily; 10-11pm Mon-Sat) £11.50 2 courses, £14 3 courses. **Credit** AmEx, DC, MC, V.

Where Bank led, others followed. Dishes such as fish and chips or seared tuna grace menus everywhere but, as far as Brum's concerned, it all started in this massive modern restaurant. Bank is a slick operation that pays close attention to detail, whether it's the service – attentive without being intrusive – or the thoroughly modern food. The fish and chips are still there, so is sausage and mash, but there's also the likes of osso bucco of venison or chicken crostini thrown into the mix. In all, Bank offers a good range of traditional and contemporary flavours to suit most budgets. Children are made very welcome; there's a separate menu and high chairs.

Bar Epernay

The Mailbox, 172-173 Wharfside, B1 1RL (0121 632 1430). **Meals served** noon-9pm Mon-Thur; noon-10pm Fri, Sat; noon-8pm Sun. **Main courses** £11.75-£14.50. **Credit** AmEx, MC, V.

The aspirational side of the giant shopping and entertainment complex the Mailbox is summed up neatly by this stylish bar-restaurant named after the capital of the Champagne region. Here you can sample some of the finest fizzes on offer, many by the glass, along with straightforward yet high-quality brasserie food. Choices may include lemon sole, Morecambe Bay potted shrimps, Aberdeenshire

beef tournedos or lobster salad. Just the thing to go with a bottle of Cristal as you gaze out over the sparkling canals listening to classy music from the rotating grand piano. But this is not a stuffy, snobby place. Its water walls, stylish decor and comfortable chairs make for feel-good dining.

Bar Estilo

The Mailbox, 110-114 Wharfside Street, B1 1RF (0121 643 3443). **Meals served** noon-11pm Mon-Sat; noon-10.30pm Sun. **Main courses** £7.50-£11.95. **Credit** AmEx, MC, V.

Everyone loves Bar Estilo, making it one of the most popular places in the Mailbox, Birmingham's prestigious temple to the designer label. Even when the rest of the centre is quiet, Bar Estilo is usually hopping. Families particularly love it – the relaxed atmosphere is child-friendly and the lengthy menu is a crowd pleaser. There are tapas, tostadas and paellas for those who want to stick to the Spanish theme and burgers, lamb shank and ribeye steaks for the rest. OK, so it's not particularly authentic but with the fancy ironwork and huge ornate lamps, it's close enough for most. Service is young and can sometimes be a little too laid-back.

Café Ikon

1 Oozells Square, Brindleyplace, B1 2HS (0121 248 3226). **Lunch served** noon-3pm Tue-Sun. **Dinner served** 5-10pm Tue-Sat. **Main courses** £4-£12.50. **Credit** AmEx, MC, V.

You don't have to be pierced to work here but it helps. Café Ikon's staff are as young, cool and trendy as the place itself, housed in Birmingham's major modern art gallery and featuring glass laboratory-style tanks filled with veg à la Damien Hirst. Decor aside, the range of tapas and raciones is the most appealing in the city. This is solid, hearty stuff, from tasty habas à la Montanesa (baby broad beans and artichokes with thyme and goat's cheese) to fried cod with lentils and tomato. Fill up on two or three of these (average £4-£5) or pick a paella. You may have to wait 50 minutes for the paella but it's worth it.

Café Lazeez

The Mailbox, 116 Wharfside Street, B1 1RF (0121 643 7979). **Meals served** noon-midnight Mon-Sat; noon-10.30pm Sun. **Main courses** £6.95-£16.60. **Set meals** £17.95-£24.95 5 courses. **Credit** AmEx, DC, MC, V.

The 1960s were never so stylish as they are in their reincarnated version at Café Lazeez. Against this colourful, funky backdrop, the food pulls off a similar trick in giving traditional elements a contemporary and deliciously sparky twist. The number of chefs hard at work in the open-plan kitchen is impressive

Bar crawl: Birmingham

The bar scene has truly taken off in Birmingham, with new additions popping up at every turn and seemingly every week. Among the most recent venues, the lounge bar **Red** (Temple Street, 0121 643 0194) is becoming a must-visit haunt, especially for immaculately groomed lunching ladies who arrive weighed down with designer carrier bags. Trendy but unintimidating, **One Ten** (0121 236 1110) in nearby Colmore Row is fantastically stylish, with a marble-lined bar and brown leather sofas, and is perfectly placed for thirsty office workers, as are **Metro Bar & Grill** (*see p211*) and **Primitivo** (Barwick Street, 0121 236 6866). Those who want to drink a little later should try the late-night bar **Digress** in neighbouring Edmund Street (0121 200 0980).

Elsewhere, the smart set like **Apres** (0121 212 1661) in the Summerrow development, a bar which goes for a ski-lodge look, with wall-mounted wood-burning stoves and lots of vibrant red. **Zinc Bar & Grill** (0121 200 0620) over the way at Regency Wharf on Broad Street is Sir Terence Conran's Birmingham presence, with a wonderful zinc-lined bar, impressive spiral staircase and great waterfront spot. **Bar Estilo** (*see p208*) and **Bar Epernay** (*see p208*), in the Mailbox, offer tapas and champagne. No-nonsense **Bar Room Bar** (0121 632 1199) keeps things simpler. The bar at the **Malmaison** hotel (*see p211*) is wow-level good-looking, though the **Hotel du Vin** bar (*see p210*) runs a close second.

Laid-back lounge is what you get at the **Living Room** on Broad Street (0870 442 2539), along with some decent food and music from the grand piano (it makes for a

feel-good Sunday brunch). If live music does it for you, check out the brilliant **Jamhouse** on St Paul's Square in Hockley (0121 200 3030), a Jools Holland-backed bar-restaurant-cum-performance venue.

Tarnished Halo in nearby Ludgate Hill (0121 236 7562) is yet another devilishly chi-chi haunt, very friendly too, with good food. **Café Couture** on Hall Street (0121 212 2979) is equally chic and very relaxed with it.

The Arcadian Centre off Hurst Street is well blessed with drinking spots, but they all get swamped with a young crowd, especially at weekends. **Poppy Red** (0121 687 1200) is snazzy, hopping and offers some basic but good quality dishes too. Trendy little **Sobar** (0121 693 5084) has a winning combination of beer and good noodles (perfect stomach-lining grub for drinkers). **Barocco** (0121 246 7862) comes over all Moroccan in looks (nice lanterns), though the food sticks to the tried-and-tested pasta and fish cakes range.

If your mood is more bohemian, the **Green Room** café-bar on Hurst Street (0121 605 4343) could well be more your Gauloise-smoking bag, especially if you fancy rubbing shoulders with luvvies and dancers from the Hippodrome theatre across the street.

Broad Street is another bar and club mecca and **Bar Risa** (0121 632 4936), attached to the Jongleurs comedy club, is one of the best. This sizeable development features a club, restaurant and several bars, all with the sort of good-humoured atmosphere you'd have every right to expect.

and so are the dishes they produce. Cumin-crusted sea bass, lamb seekh gilafi and almond-spiked tilapia perfectly illustrate the Café Lazeez mix of old and new. It's not a cheap place by any means, but food this fresh and inventive deserves something of a premium. This is one to dress up for.

Café Soya ★

Unit B106, Cathay Street, Arcadian Centre, B5 4TD (0121 683 8350). **Main courses** £2.80-£7.90. **Set meals** (noon-5pm) £5.45 2 courses; (5-10pm) £10.95 3 courses. **No credit cards.**
Ignore the unappealing façade, the weird orange walls and the fact that the kitchen is just one screened-off corner of the room, Café Soya is an absolute gem, and one of the best budget restaurants around. All the

dishes on the laminated fold-out menu hover around the £3 to £4 mark and they're good quality. It's mostly Chinese fare but there are Thai and Vietnamese touches too. The Vietnamese steamed prawn pancake rolls, for instance, are packed with juicy prawns. Beef spicy rice is a whopping bowlful of fresh flavours and the veggie fare, such as tofu and peppers in satay sauce, is delicious. Café Soya gets packed and noisy but will do your street cred no end of good.

China Red

193-194 Broad Street, B15 1AY (0121 632 6688). **Lunch served** noon-2.30pm daily. **Dinner served** 6-11.30pm Mon-Thur, Sun; 6pm-midnight Fri, Sat. **Main courses** £8.50-£12.50. **Set lunch** £8.50 2 courses. **Set dinner** £16-£28 2 courses. **Credit** AmEx, MC, V.

Chinese food goes upmarket at China Red, one of the latest recruits to busy Broad Street. A big, light, spacious place, it really looks the designer part, with an army of chic, young but very solicitous waiting staff and some stunning features – the yellow Perspex chairs in the front section, for instance, and the wooden panelling punctuated with tiny portholes of light. The food is straightforward traditional Cantonese but is very well executed. Get messy with deliciously gloopy spare ribs or pig out on richly savoury pork and prawn dumplings to start with, then move on to duck with ginger and spring onions or premiership league chicken satay. A strong contender for the best Chinese food in the city centre.

Denial Bar & Restaurant

The Mailbox, 120-122 Wharfside Street,
B1 1RQ (0121 632 1232). **Meals served**
noon-10pm Mon-Fri; 10am-10.30pm Sat;
10am-5pm Sun. **Main courses** £12.75-£15.75.
Set meals (noon-3pm, 5-7pm Mon-Fri) £11.95
2 courses, £13.95 3 courses. **Credit** AmEx,
MC, V.
Denial has had something of a relaunch since it first arrived in the Mailbox world, proud – and rightly so – of its independent status. The ownership has changed (bringing with it tablecloths and a refurb) but this canalside venue is still hip enough to keep the bar busy, although the restaurant can be rather quiet. And that's a shame because the food can be very good indeed, with great soups, well-handled fish dishes, such as roast cod with pea purée, and – a gratifying sign of attention to detail – some delicious side orders, such as olive oil and parsley mash. Expect to pay about £30 a head.

Fino ★

The Mailbox, 27-29 Wharfside Street, B1 1RD
(0121 632 1323). **Meals served** 11am-5pm
Mon-Sat; 11am-4pm Sun. **Main courses** £3-£8.95.
Credit MC, V.
Birmingham city centre seemed unable to hang on to a good modern Italian restaurant in the past but fingers crossed Fino will be an exception to the rule. This is just the sort of place the city has been crying out for – authentic and delicious Italian food in matey but good-looking surroundings, and at sensible prices. The antipasti are delicious – try the fabulous char-grilled artichokes, the thyme-fragrant aubergine or the combo of speck and tasty bread. There are also risottos, pastas, salads and bruschetta. There's even a deli at the front – a bit limited but decent enough. It's a shame you can't buy the artichoke antipasto though, and that Fino is only open during the day.

Hotel du Vin & Bistro ★

25 Church Street, B3 2NR (0121 200 0600/
www.hotelduvin.com). **Lunch served** noon-2pm,
dinner served 6-10pm daily. **Main courses**
£14.50-£18. **Set lunch** (Sun) £22 3 courses.
Credit AmEx, DC, MC, V.

If you've eaten in one Hotel du Vin bistro, you've eaten in them all. And that's a compliment. Whichever one you find yourself in, you'll be surrounded by the same warm blend of wood and candlelight, distressed walls, cobwebby wine bottles and contented locals. The Birmingham site's two linked rooms (within an old eye hospital) are an immensely congenial space in which to enjoy bistro food that rarely disappoints (if rarely excites). Crayfish and pepper risotto or ham hock terrine with home-made piccalilli are no-quibble starters, while mains range from the proudly proletarian corned beef hash, fried egg and HP sauce to buffed-up bourgeois confit duck leg, pommes lyonnaise, wilted spinach and port jus. Finish with a classic crème brûlée or mixed berry pavlova. Service is smilingly Gallic, and, as you'd expect, the wine list is a treat.

Indi ★

The Arcadian Centre, Hurst Street, B5 4ST (0121
622 4858). **Meals served** noon-2am Mon-Sat; noon-
12.30pm Sun. **Main courses** £3-£4.95. **Credit** MC, V.
Indi is a remarkable place in a little centre of bars and eateries near the club and theatre quarter. The area is more closely connected with the dance scene than family days out but Indi is child-friendly enough, though its arty whiteness, minimalism and sunken seating are a world away from most kid-pleasing joints. The curious focus here is 'Asian tapas' – predominantly Indian food given a surprising Mediterranean twist. Prepare yourself for goshi brocheta, patatas de kofta and pakora verduras, among others. A bit odd maybe but it's moreish and generally well-cooked. A good place if you're visiting the cinema or Hippodrome theatre nearby, or if you're fuelling up before a night out.

Kempsons

37 Bennetts Hill, B2 5SN (0121 200 3115). **Lunch**
served noon-3pm, **tapas served** 5.30-8pm Mon-Fri.
Main courses £4.50-£11. **Credit** AmEx, MC, V.
Office workers just love Kempsons in the commercial district. It's snazzy and buzzing, with a lively bar to ease those lunchtime or post-work worries and a lovely little atrium dining room to give the taste buds a good workout. The menu keeps things short and simple. Lunchers can stay low-key with chunky sandwiches, nachos, salads and soups but there are also excellent pastas, risottos, roast chicken, steak and chips and perfect puddings to take your mind off the in-tray – this is comfort food for the overworked or overshopped. Kempsons is friendly and reliable, and its prices won't do too much damage.

Lasan Restaurant & Bar

3-4 Dakota Buildings, James Street, St Paul's
Square, B3 1SD (0121 212 3664/www.lasan.co.uk).
Dinner served 6-11pm Mon-Sat. **Main courses**
£4.50-£12. **Credit** AmEx, MC, V.
Lasan is one of the new breed of Indian restaurants shunning flock wallpaper and cloying curry sauces. The interior is sleek without being stark, and well-

Metro Bar & Grill

spaced tables and friendly service keep things relaxed even on busy Saturday nights. The menu mixes old favourites with more unusual choices, all of which are given a modern makeover. From the starters, the trio of samosas is light and flaky and crammed with delicately spiced fish, lamb and mushroom. Mains include lamb rogan josh alongside the more inventive braised sea bass in sour mango sauce. Puddings strike an odd note: dishes such as peach and almond crumble seem incongruous. The very reasonable prices and great location in the hip St Paul's Square area mean Lasan is justifiably popular with the city's cool crowd.

Malmaison

The Mailbox, Royal Mail Street, B1 1XL (0121 246 5000/www.birmingham@malmaison.com). Bar **Open** 11am-midnight daily. *Restaurant* **Lunch served** noon-2.30pm Mon-Sat. **Dinner served** 6-11.30pm daily. **Main courses** £10.50-£14.50. **Credit** AmEx, DC, MC, V.

Malmaison hotel spells style, and the restaurant is no exception, with its posh lighting, swish seating and cool staff. You can even buy the CD of the background music. Happily, the food manages to keep its end up. It's straightforward brasserie fare but is well turned out. Modern classics such as chicken liver parfait, beef carpaccio, fish cakes and clafoutis are all likely to feature on the reassuringly short and French-dominated menu. Starters come in at about £6 and mains about £12-£13 – not bad for this kind of setting. Perfect for when you're trying to impress someone with your impeccably good taste.

Mechu

45 Summerrow, B3 1JJ (0121 212 1661/ www.summerrow.com). Bar **Open** noon-midnight Mon-Wed, Sun; noon-2am Thur-Sat. *Restaurant* **Meals served** noon-10.30pm Mon-Thur; 10am-1am Fri, Sat; noon-4pm Sun. **Main courses** £10.95-£14.25. **Credit** AmEx, MC, V.

At last one of Birmingham's newer developments has devoted itself to a rather neglected sector – the over-25s. Mechu has memory lane music (not too loud to disrupt conversation, of course), a disco ball in the bar and a swish, modern Japanese-style dining area that should hit the spot for everyone. And if that fails, the food should do it. The emphasis is on fish and seafood, with oceanloads of lobster, crab, mussels, prawns and oysters in every taste variation. Then there's the usual roll-call of ribeye steaks, seared tuna, Thai fish cakes and so on. It's all generous, populist and competently cooked, and tots up to about £30 a head. Mechu (pronounced meet-you) is well placed for the Rep theatre and Symphony Hall. Children are welcome during the day, when there's a £7.95 three-course menu aimed at them.

Metro Bar & Grill

73 Cornwall Street, B3 2DF (0121 200 1911/ www.themetrobar.co.uk). **Lunch served** noon-2.30pm Mon-Fri. **Dinner served** 6.30-9.30pm Mon-Fri; 6.30-10pm Sat. **Main courses** £9-£17. **Set dinner** (Mon-Fri) £12 2 courses; £15 3 courses. **Credit** AmEx, MC, V.

Right in the middle of the business quarter and a second home for an awful lot of the city's wheelers and dealers, the Metro Bar & Grill is as professional and slick as its clientele. The interior – with its curved mirrored walls and glass roof – is strikingly modern and the food easily lives up to the surroundings. A rotisserie and plenty of daily fish specials add to the appealingly imaginative choices, whether it's corn-fed chicken supreme stuffed with goat's cheese and served with broad bean pesto and lemon tagliatelle, or a tart of chorizo, aubergine, tapenade and mozzarella with rocket oil. Even the side orders, such as new potatoes with pancetta and mint, are innovative.

Naked Pepper

55-59 Newhall Street, B3 3RB (0121 212 2511). **Lunch served** noon-3pm Mon-Fri. **Dinner served** 5-10pm Tue-Fri; 6-11pm Sat. **Main courses** £5.95-£12.50. **Credit** AmEx, MC, V.

Midlands

Naked Pepper is not held back visually by its location in the staid old commercial sector. Colour matters here, with flamboyant purples and pinks all over the shop (though looking far more tasteful than that might lead you to expect). The food is vibrant too – mainly pizzas and pastas with the emphasis on top-quality ingredients. So dishes sound simple, but it all tastes great. Naked Pepper deserves a place on anyone's list of regular haunts: it's friendly and totally unpretentious. The bar at the front is a comfy, laid-back kind of place too.

Shimla Pinks

214 Broad Street, B15 1AY (0121 633 0366/ www.shimlapinks.com). **Lunch served** noon-2.30pm Mon-Fri. **Dinner served** 6-11pm daily. **Main courses** £10.95-£14.95. **Set Lunch** £7.95 3 courses. **Set dinner** £19.95-£24.95 3 courses, £34.95 4 courses, £44.95 5 courses. **Credit** AmEx, MC, V.

There are several pretenders to the throne these days but Shimla Pinks led the way when it came to knockout contemporary surroundings for Indian food. These days, the look at the cavernous Broad Street restaurant is defiantly retro – psychedelic lights and groovy fittings are more Austin Powers than days of the Raj but who cares? The food doesn't offer too many surprises and it's more expensive than your local Indian, but it's generally good quality and you're paying for the surroundings too. This is a long-standing favourite. But be warned: tables are packed in and the place can get very noisy.

Thai Edge

7 Oozells Square, Brindleyplace, B1 2HL (0121 643 3993). **Lunch served** noon-2pm Mon-Sat; (buffet) noon-3pm Sun. **Dinner served** 5.30-11pm Mon-Sat; 6-10.30pm Sun. **Main courses** £10-£28. **Set lunch** £9.90 2 courses. **Set dinner** £19.80-£29.80 3 courses. **Credit** AmEx, DC, MC, V.

The gorgeous looking and elegantly friendly Thai Edge was one of the first oriental eateries in Brum to go for broke on aesthetics. Forget standard OTT decor, this is beautifully white with lots of clever touches, such as pretty wicker screens and a row of feathers behind glass making a lovely frieze. There is the odd piece of Thai sculpture here and there to remind you of where your food is coming from, and good food it is too. There's a massive choice of fantastic soups, salads and traditional curries (rated for chilli heat). With this sort of quality, it will come as no surprise that this place ain't cheap, nor is it quiet. There's a branch called Thai Meat Ranch at 41-43 Hurst Street (0121 622 2287).

La Toque d'Or ★

27 Warstone Lane, Hockley, B18 6JQ (0121 233 3655/www.latoquedor.co.uk). **Lunch served** 12.30-1.30pm Tue-Fri. **Dinner served** 7-9.30pm Tue-Sat. **Set lunch** £15.50 2 courses, £18.50 3 courses. **Set dinner** £24.50 3 courses. **Credit** AmEx, MC, V.

The best food in Birmingham. There, we've said it. La Toque d'Or is famously known as the gem in the jewellery quarter and although this bijou little place

is hidden away down an alley, it's more than worth seeking out. The food, by French chef-patron Didier Philipot, is modern Gallic and highly accomplished without being overly complicated, or overpriced. The only moan – heard on occasion – is that beautifully proportioned though the food is, we could do with more veg. But don't let that put you off – reserve a table and indulge yourself at one of the city's few small independents without breaking la banque.

West 12

Marriott Hotel, 12 Hagley Road, Five Ways, B16 8SJ (0121 452 1144/www.marriotthotels.com/bhxbh). **Bar Open** 11am-11pm Mon-Sat; 11am-10.30pm Sun. *Restaurant* **Lunch served** noon-2.30pm Mon-Sat; 12.30-3pm Sun. **Dinner served** 6-11pm daily. **Main courses** £9-£19. **Credit** AmEx, DC, MC, V.

Just out of the city centre at a mega traffic island called Five Ways (for obvious reasons), the impressive Marriott Hotel keeps a sedate and regal watch. Within its elegant portals is the restaurant West 12, a smart yet relaxed eaterie that replaced the old formal fine dining restaurant, the Sir Edward Elgar. This is altogether more modern and urbane, with its smart bar and oversized banquettes. The spaciousness is much appreciated, particularly by the business fraternity who don't care for tables close enough to allow for eavesdropping. Service is keen and attentive, while the food covers bistro basics and keeps the choices to a sensible number. Prices are a bit expensive, though the children's menu is a wallet-friendly £7.50 for three courses.

Wing Wah

278 Thimble Mill Lane, Nechells, B7 5HD (0121 327 7879). **Meals served** 11am-11pm daily. **Main courses** £6.80-£16. **Set meals** £12.50-£22 per person (minimum 2). **Credit** AmEx, MC, V.

A little bit of Chinatown in inner city Nechells, Wing Wah sits resplendent beside the equally flamboyant Wing Yip supermarket, bringing a vivid splash of colour to one of the city's less exciting areas. This big and rather functional restaurant offers fantastic value if all-you-can-eat buffets (at lunch) are your thing. And if you go à la carte, you'll sample some of the best Chinese food in Birmingham. The fish and seafood are particularly good, whether it's salt-crusted squid or succulent sea bass. Wing Wah is one of those places that you promise yourself you'll return to so you can explore more of the tome-like menu. It's not high on atmosphere or friendliness but it's so busy it's great for people-watching.

Also in the area

Budokan The Mailbox, 128-130 Wharfside Street, B1 1RQ (08708 377300); **The Living Room** Unit 4, Regency Wharf, 2 Broad Street, B1 2JZ (0870 442 2539); **Loch Fyne** The Bank House, High Street, Knowle, B93 0JU (01564 732750); **Petit Blanc Brasserie** 9 Brindleyplace, B1 2HS (0121 633 7333); **Wing Wah** 188 Causeway Green Road, Olbury, B68 8LQ (0121 552 0041).

Derbyshire

ASHFORD-IN-THE-WATER

Riverside House ★

Riverside House Hotel, Fennel Street, Ashford-in-the-Water, DE45 1QF (01629 814275/www.riverside househotel.co.uk). **Lunch served** noon-2pm, **dinner served** 7-9pm daily. **Set lunch** (Mon-Sat) £18.95 2 courses, £26.95 3 courses; (Sun) £28.95 3 courses. **Set dinner** £39.95 3 courses incl coffee. **Credit** DC, MC, V.

This delightful country house hotel takes great pride in its fine, and rather fancy, restaurant. Chef John Whelan has succeeded in creating an eaterie of consistency and character. Dishes are perfectly presented (or over-presented) and ready for their close-up. Close your eyes, though, and the effect is equally successful. Pan-seared Cornish scallops and braised organic pork belly makes a winning combination, as does roast pigeon with foie gras and wild mushroom risotto – the punchy and the delicate each finding their space on your palate without too much of a fight. Perfect puddings include rose petal pannacotta with iced orange curd yoghurt, but the cheeseboard is also worth saving space for.

BAKEWELL

Renaissance

Bath Street, Bakewell, DE45 1BX (01629 812687/ www.renaissance-restaurant.com). **Lunch served** noon-1.30pm Tue-Sat; 1st 2 Sun of mth. **Dinner served** 7-9.30pm Tue-Sat. **Set dinner** (Tue-Thur) £14.95 3 courses incl coffee. **Set meal** £20.45 2 courses, £23.95 3 courses. **Credit** AmEx, MC, V.

Eating options in tourist towns like Bakewell don't have to try too hard. That some try, and succeed, is cause for celebration. Such is the case at the Renaissance, Bakewell's best restaurant by far. It offers an unambitious bistro-style range of decent food. But it's always delightful, and service is never without a smile. You could enjoy venison sausage with mushroom sauce, ham hock with a light parsley sauce or a fluffy omelette. Whatever you have, you'll wish there were more places like this offering good, no-nonsense food at similarly sensible prices.

BASLOW

The Gallery ★

Cavendish Hotel, Baslow, DE45 1SP (01246 582311/www.cavendish-hotel.net). **Lunch served** 12.30-2pm, **dinner served** 6.30-10pm daily. **Main courses** £16.50-£19.95. **Credit** AmEx, DC, MC, V.

The quiet Peakland village of Baslow is the perfect setting for the Cavendish Hotel and its justifiably

popular restaurant, the Gallery. Looking out over the Peak District, you can enjoy puréed sweet pepper soup with char-grilled monkfish, followed by oven-roast fillet of Derbyshire beef and peppercorn jus, with perky veg. If the view and the main course haven't sated your appetite, you could finish with a glorious pink grapefruit and orange terrine. The wine list is approachable, with a decent Sancerre coming in at under £15. Save up and stay the night!

BIRCH VALE

The Waltzing Weasel ★

New Mills Road, Birch Vale, SK22 1BT (01663 743402/www.w-weasel.co.uk). **Lunch served** noon-2pm, **dinner served** 7-9pm daily. **Main courses** (lunch) £6.95-£12.50. **Set dinner** £23.50 2 courses, £27.50 3 courses. **Credit** AmEx, MC, V.

This Peak pub is a real find. Trouble is, it has already been found. So make a booking to guarantee some of the most thoughtful food on offer in the Peak National Park. Food is honest, fresh and filling. Yet there's a sophistication here that comes as a welcome surprise, too. The aim is to provide an exciting mix of real English cuisine, rich Italian flavours and tempting vegetarian options. This translates into menus featuring Italian beef casserole, roast game or tarte provençal – layered with aubergine, peppers and tomato, and topped with a cream, garlic and cheese sauce. Well worth ferreting out.

DERBY

Darleys

Darley Abbey Mills, Darley Abbey, Derby, DE22 1DZ (01332 364987/www.darleys.com). **Lunch served** noon-2pm Mon-Sat; noon-3pm Sun. **Dinner served** 6.30-9pm Mon-Thur; 6.30-9.30pm Fri, Sat. **Main courses** £16.50-£18.50. **Set lunch** £13.50 2 courses, £15.50 3 courses. **Set dinner** (Mon-Thur) £22.50 3 courses. **Credit** AmEx, DC, MC, V.

Refurbished in May 2002, Derby's top restaurant bizarrely claims that its interior 'echoes the calm influences of both Zen and colonialism'. And if that smacks of a restaurant trying a little too hard, eating here can leave you with a similar impression. Because while the top-end modern European cuisine is undeniably decent, the decor stylish and the location in an old mill alongside the River Derwent impressively picturesque, you can't help feeling they're so busy aspiring to be a top restaurant that they forget eating out is meant to be fun. Still, the locals seem to lap it up. But a little less old-school formality and a little more friendliness would go a long way at Darleys.

FROGGATT

The Chequers Inn

Froggatt, S32 3ZJ (01433 630231/www.chequers-froggatt.com). **Lunch served** noon-2pm, **dinner served** 6-9.30pm Mon-Fri. **Meals served** noon-9.30pm Sat; noon-9pm Sun. **Main courses** £7.75-£15.50. **Credit** AmEx, MC, V.

The Chequers Inn has no need to add swags and tassels to its simple interior. It has been a popular roadside halt for 500 years, so why hire the designers to add trimmings to this winning recipe? Food is similarly straightforward. Starters may include glazed goat's cheese with roasted vegetables and mustard dressing, or tiger prawns in garlic butter. Simple. Mains use local produce such as trout with an almond and herb butter, or loin of venison with mash and Madeira jus. Delicious. There's a super garden to the rear, where you can enjoy honest food, great views and a traditional ale or two (or wine).

HATHERSAGE

The Plough Inn

Leadmill Bridge, Hathersage, S32 1BA (01433 650319/www.theploughinn-hathersage.com). **Lunch served** 11.30am-2.30pm, **dinner served** 6.30-9.30pm Mon-Fri. **Meals served** 11.30am-9.30pm Sat; noon-9pm Sun. **Main courses** £8.95-£15.95. **Credit** MC, V.

Hathersage is the birthplace of Robin Hood's mate Little John who, we all know, was a rather big chap with, doubtless, an appetite to match. The Plough Inn, a sturdy roadside inn with rooms, is just the sort of place to refuel after you've done all that stealing-from-the-rich stuff. The menu is scarily all-encompassing, but we didn't find any duds: starters of fettuccine of leek, red onion and gorgonzola with pine nuts and parmesan or wild boar terrine were as good as they get. There's an excellent vegetarian section, but the local meat and poultry dishes are justifiably favourite.

WEST HALLAM

The Bottle Kiln ★

High Lane West, West Hallam, DE7 6HP (0115 932 9442). **Open** 10am-4.45pm Tue-Sun. **Lunch served** noon-2pm Tue-Sun. **Main courses** £3.35-£6.90. **Credit** AmEx, MC, V.

Lunchtime queues at this delightful gallery/café are testament to meticulous quality control. Yes, the menu's brief; yes, it's straightforward. But by 'eck it's good. Rediscover the joys of a jacket potato, scrummy salads and own-made meat pies. Enjoy a rhubarb crumble while checking out some bold canvasses by local artists displayed all around you, and remind yourself that eating out doesn't have to be a fashion parade – it can be fun.

Herefordshire

BRIMFIELD

Roebuck Inn

Brimfield, SY8 4NE (01584 711230/www.theroebuckinn.com). **Lunch served** noon-2.30pm Mon-Sat; noon-3pm Sun. **Dinner served** 7-9.30pm daily. **Main courses** £8.95-£16.95. **Credit** MC, V.

No shortage of history here: the black-and-white Roebuck dates back to the 15th century. The inn is set in the charming little village of Brimfield, and its dining facilities include two lounge bars and a non-smoking dining room. Most of the ingredients in the food are sourced locally, but the dishes themselves range far and wide. The menu changes to follow the seasons and offers a temptingly broad choice of fare: risotto of wild mushrooms, Thai spiced chicken boudin or grilled goat's cheese salad to start; their 'famous' fish pie (containing salmon, cod and prawns), roast rump of lamb or the fillet Roebuck (fillet steak stuffed with stilton and served with a rich Madeira sauce) as mains. The specials board

typically features plenty of fish, with sybaritic options like lobster grilled with garlic and shallot butter. The wine list is creditably lengthy and well drawn up, the Château Montaiguillon St-Emilion being one of the highlights.

HEREFORD

Café @ All Saints ★

High Street, Hereford, HR4 9AA (01432 370415/www.cafeatallsaints.co.uk). **Food served** 8.30am-5.30pm, **lunch served** 11.30am-3pm Mon-Sat. **Main courses** £5.50-£6. **Credit** MC, V.

A money-making concern inside a still-operational place of worship? Theologically dubious, surely? Owner Bill Sewell's other gastrochurch venture, the Place Below in London (*see p46*), occupies a crypt; here, your table is just a bun's throw from the altar. Still, as an architectural insert, this popular lunch and coffee venue has been rightly hymned, its sleek, curvy steel-and-wood balcony making a dramatic contrast to the medieval fabric of its host. Food (veggie) and drink (tea, coffee, juices – but no fizzy pop) are had at the counter, and you can sit on the ground floor with the rotating art exhibitions or – a better bet – on the upper level with the stained glass. Grub is of the 'good, but no hosanna' variety: the daily lunch menu typically runs to soup and quiche, a hot special (potato, onion and gruyère gratin on our visit) and salads, one with – the quaintest item – WI chutney. Outside the lunch hour, there are home-style sarnies, cheesecakes and so on. Service is in Latin (just kidding).

La Rive at Castle House

Castle Street, Hereford, HR1 2NW (01432 356321/ www.castlehse.co.uk). **Lunch served** 12.30-2pm, **dinner served** 7-9pm daily. **Set lunch** £18.95 3 courses. **Set dinner** £36.95 3 courses, £47.95 7 courses. **Credit** AmEx, DC, MC, V.
Fill your lungs before you order: 'I'll start with the pressing of poussin and foie gras with shallot and lime pickle, gewürztraminer jelly and bacon biscuit, followed by the' – and breathe! This hotel restaurant certainly takes its, ahem, sophistication seriously: reference the seven-course chef's special menu, dubbed (in incorrect French) 'La Surprise du Marches' – and, from the dessert menu, the 'Study in blackberries' (or 'citrus', or 'banana'). Assuming you have the stomach for such richesse, there's no quibbling with the quality of the ingredients – including Gloucester Old Spot pork, Hereford beef, organic eggs, poultry and vegetables, all sourced from La Rive's own farm – or the care that goes into the presentation. Though the mention of an 'executive chef' (Stuart McLeod) on the menu didn't raise our spirits any, the poached loin of lamb forestière with its encyclopedia of trimmings was tasty enough. Meanwhile, everything else in the yellow dining room, from its dark wood to the crisp table linen, murmured 'you are having a sophisticated dining experience'.

KINGTON

Penrhos Court

Kington, HR5 3LH (01544 230720/www.pen rhos.co.uk). **Dinner served** 7.30-8.45pm by arrangement only. **Set dinner** £32.50 4 courses. **Credit** MC, V.
This gorgeous converted 700-year-old farm, all black-and-white façades and ancient stonework, serves great organic food. Proof that brevity can be a blessing (or at least, not a handicap), the succinct daily menu leads in with soup, following on with an interim course of, say, nettle ravioli, a choice of three mains – fillet of sea trout with marsh samphire or beetroot risotto with blue cheese and sage – and four desserts. There's nothing excessively fancy in the selection of grub – it's all just well made, flavourful and nourishing fare: the dessert list, featuring dishes such as blackcurrant and vanilla ice-cream or apricot and almond tart, epitomises the kitchen's approach. Winner of various organic awards – from the Soil Association et al – and with physical features as

attractive as the fantastic 13th-century crook hall and impressive main courtyard (to say nothing of the surrounding history-rich countryside), this is a lovely setting for a country meal.

LUNTLEY

The Cider House Restaurant at Dunkertons

Luntley, HR6 9ED (01544 388161). **Open** *summer* 10am-5pm, **lunch served** noon-2.30pm Mon-Sat. **Credit** MC, V.
Bloody Turk, Sheep's Nose, Foxwhelp, Knotted Kernel, Strawberry Norman: just a few of the more resonant apple varieties that get turned into superior cider by this well-established mill. Apples and cider also feature prominently on the menu in the adjoining barn-cum-restaurant. The surrounding countryside is truly lovely, and in a perfectly timed display of rural authenticity, two sparrows flitted in and out of the beamed dining room all through our summer luncheon. From the short seasonal menu, we opted for the onion and tarragon soup with parsley dumplings (light and pleasant if a trifle bland), then the satisfying cottage pie made with Hereford beef, marjoram and (natch) cider, and served with red onion relish and assorted vegetables. We skipped dessert, though the choice runs to own-made ice-cream, rum and treacle tart with vanilla custard, and a local cheese selection; there's also at least one vegetarian starter and main course. Staff will happily show visitors round the mill (for a small fee), while the excellent organic cider and perry can be bought from the shop or had on draught at the bar; their apple juice is pretty good too.

ROSS-ON-WYE

Pheasant at Ross

52 Edde Cross Street, Ross-on-Wye, HR9 7BZ (01989 565751). **Dinner served** 7-10pm Thur-Sat; also by appointment. **Main courses** £14.90. **Credit** AmEx, DC, MC, V.
The serial award-winner's namesake and his hen (both stuffed) lord it over a large herd of novelty hippos in the washroom: that's the Pheasant in a nutshell. On the one hand, its proud commitment to culinary excellence; on the other, a sense of fun that sends airs and graces out the window. The Pheasant's other double act – chef Eileen Brunnarius and Kiwi wine expert Adrian Wells – formed in the early 1990s, with the genial Wells presiding over the wood-beamed, 20-seat dining room and shaping the superb, globe-trotting wine list – which comes in three volumes! The fruits of his '30 years of dedicated boozing experience' are here, and his suggestions are spot on – a light sémillon to go with the goat's cheese fritters, perhaps, or a symphonic Californian zinfandel to partner the rich, succulent old English duck pie. Almost all of the menu's produce is sourced locally – varietal apple juices? can do – and there's an emphasis on rare breed

Midlands

Lough Pool Inn

livestock; all of which makes this the very model of the imaginative English country restaurant: small but perfectly farmed.

SELLACK

Lough Pool Inn

Sellack, HR9 6LX (01989 730236). **Lunch served** noon-2pm daily. **Dinner served** 7-9.30pm Mon-Sat; 7-9pm Sun. **Main courses** £9.50-£14. **Credit** MC, V.
This pretty 16th-century black-and-white timbered inn has a pleasant cottage feel – beams, low ceilings, knick-knacks – and three rooms for dining, including the cosy bar area. Chef-proprietor Stephen Bull is a firm convert to the country life (he swapped advertising for the restaurant trade in London, and then moved here), but he's not averse to foreign influence: you might find the menu globe-trotting from Scotland (haggis fritters with beetroot relish) to the Middle East (falafel with baba ganoush) and back via Italy (linguine). Happily, the sort of solidly English fare which seems so essential to such a setting is also available – dishes like Goodrich Longhorn beef and Hereford ale stew with herb and mustard dumplings. The dessert menu features the much-lauded whole orange cake with maple syrup and clotted cream, as well as Eton mess with local raspberries. Prices are not especially skimpy, but as culinary package holidays go this one offers a long list of destinations.

TITLEY

Stagg Inn ★

Titley, HR5 3RL (01544 230221/www.thestagg.co.uk). **Lunch served** noon-2pm Tue-Sun. **Dinner served** 6-9pm Tue-Sat. **Main courses** £11.50-£16.50. **Set lunch** (Sun) £13.50 3 courses. **Credit** MC, V.
To the obvious question – what are the connotations of the extra 'g'? – no one here can supply an answer ('though', says their leaflet, 'past landlords have had their stories'). Never mind: the extraneous consonant provides this much written-about country inn with a mild air of mystery, which can only be good for the appetite. Set in prime walking territory, the spot has pulled in peckish wayfarers since medieval times, and never more so – awards oblige – than recently. Three old guns hang in the narrow corridor

to the salmon-coloured dining room, and though we wished one would go off and put some speed into the service, the food lived right up to our expectations: exquisite goat's cheese and caramelised shallot tart; succulent saddle of venison; and summer fruits with a champagne sabayon. The extensive wine list is interesting and international – a heady Gigondas was a tasty treat – and there's a good number of spirits and ports on offer. Gavroche-trained chef Steve Reynolds is a Herefordian himself and sources his meat, game and (often organic) fruit and veg from local farms; the cheese selection is excellent. Diners come here from far and wide: advance booking is essential.

ULLINGSWICK

Three Crowns Inn ★

Bleak Acre, Ullingswick, HR1 3JQ (01432 820279/ www.threecrownsinn.com). **Lunch served** noon-2pm, **dinner served** 7-9.30pm Tue-Sun. Closed 2 wks from 24 Dec. **Main courses** £13.75. **Set lunch** (Tue-Sat) £10.50 2 courses, £12.50 3 courses. **Credit** MC, V.

This begonged gastropub is off the beaten track and then some, but its food is worth several wrong turns and a gallon or two burned doubling back. The Three Crowns won the (now defunct) Flavours of Herefordshire award scheme in 2000 and 2001, with its alluring combination of locally sourced organic produce, rare breed livestock and home-made cheeses. 'Simple sophistication' is its watchword, translated into real dishes by chef Brent Castle. Simplicity also applies to the prices – identical within each category (starters, mains and desserts are £5.75, £13.75 and £4.25 respectively) – and the friendly, efficient service. On a weekend lunch visit, the meal opened with a lovely blue cheese soufflé with spiced pear and walnut dressing, followed by tender roast rump of Buccleuch beef with airy Yorkshire pud and a generous side serving of veg. The menu has touches of exoticism – we loved the hibiscus flower and red berry soup with basil ice-cream – and the cheese course serves up such flavourful local examples as Mrs Bells Blue. A glass of the eminently smooth Hereford cider brandy makes a sophisticated endpoint to a meal here – unless, of course, you're navigating.

Leicestershire

HINCKLEY

Watergate

Trinity Marinas Complex, Wharf Farm, Coventry Road, Hinckley, LE10 0NB (01455 896827/ www.trinitymarinas.co.uk). **Open** 11am-11pm Mon-Sat; noon-10.30pm Sun. *Bar* **Meals served** 11am-8.30pm daily. *Restaurant* **Lunch served** 11am-2.30pm, **dinner served** 6-10pm daily. **Main courses** £10-£15. **Credit** DC, MC, V.

They call Hinckley the cradle of the hosiery trade and with the Watergate, the area has finally got itself a glamorous silk stocking of a restaurant. A modern, spacious place, it makes the most of its scenic canalside spot with great floor-to-ceiling windows. Designer-ish tables and chairs in pale wood win full marks for style, as do lofty angled rooflines and a smart tiled floor. If the weather's up to it, grab a table outside on the decking or in the garden. The upmarket fodder includes the likes of slow-roasted belly pork with fruit farci, choucroute and lentil jus, or brill with a cumin crust and clams, braised veg and coriander – all in generous portions and non-scary prices. Only the service can sometimes let the suave side down: young staff don't always have as much polish as the glassware.

KIBWORTH BEAUCHAMP

Firenze

9 Station Street, Kibworth Beauchamp, LE8 0LN (0116 279 6260/www.firenze.co.uk). **Lunch served** noon-2pm Tue-Fri. **Dinner served** 7-10pm Tue-Sat. **Main courses** £7-£17. **Credit** MC, V.

The reputation of the small, family-run Firenze is spreading like wildfire from its chi-chi village setting. The Italian menu is sensibly small and simple; ingredients are top quality. Frittata with vegetables, taleggio cheese and tomato 'jam' was a cracker, while chickpea bruschetta with squid, rocket and chilli was another starter that will linger in the memory. Substantial mains include red mullet with crushed potatoes and basil or grilled lamb cutlets with roast vegetable tart, but we continued with a moreish trenette al pesto alla Genovese. Positively delinquent puddings ('chocolate, chocolate and more chocolate') add to the pleasure.

LEICESTER

Bobby's ★ ★

154-156 Belgrave Road, LE4 5AT (0116 266 0106/ www.eatatbobbys.co.uk). **Meals served** 11am-10pm Tue-Fri; 11am-10.30pm Sat, Sun. **Main courses** £3.99-£4.75. **Set thali** £6.49-£7.99. **Credit** MC, V.

Leicester's abundance of Indian restaurants splits into two general categories – one side of the city is Indian, both Gujarati and Punjabi, while the other side is mostly Bangladeshi with a sprinkling of Indian. The legendary Bobby's, on the restaurant 'golden mile', is vegetarian Gujarati (like Sharmilee and Sayonara Thali, *p219*). Its popularity – this is one of the city's all-time faves – may be partly down to its retro-chic decor, but is mostly due to decent food at decent prices. To start, there's a varied choice of farsan and chaat snacks; a selection of Bobby's special chaat is unmissable at £4.50. After that, it's a choice between an array of sweetish Gujarati curries (undhyu, vegetables and rice dumplings in a rich sauce), thalis or house specialities such as uthappam (a rice flour pancake with tomato and peppers, with dahl sambhar and coconut chutney). And who is Bobby? Actually, it's the nickname of owner Atul Lakhani and comes from a 1970s Bollywood film.

The Case Restaurant & Champagne Bar

4-6 Hotel Street, LE1 5AW (0116 251 7675/ www.thecase.co.uk). **Open** 11am-10.30pm Mon-Sat. **Lunch served** noon-2.30pm Mon-Fri; noon-3pm Sat. **Dinner served** 7-10.30pm Mon-Thur; 6.30-10.30pm Fri, Sat. **Main courses** £6-£19. **Credit** AmEx, DC, MC, V.

A favourite of bright young things keen to enjoy a little high living, the Case has a champagne bar downstairs (where evening 'bites' include mini hot dogs with ketchup and mustard) and a bright, spacious, thoroughly modern restaurant with bar area above it. Occasional jazz combos suit the refined yet unstuffy atmosphere perfectly. Staff are unobtrusively friendly. Foodwise, dishes run from a richly flavoursome ravioli of shiitake mushroom and spinach with smoked cheese and tarragon sauce to a nicely gamey smoked venison with honey-crumbed brie. Alternatively, there's roast Cajun monkfish with bubble and squeak or a top-notch roast duck breast on hoi sin veg and noodles with orange and cucumber dressing.

The Curry Fever ★

139 Belgrave Road, LE4 6AS (0116 266 2941). **Lunch served** noon-2pm Tue-Sat. **Dinner served** 6-11.30pm Tue-Sun. **Main courses** £4.90-£13.90. **Credit** AmEx, MC, V.

This Punjabi eaterie is traditional in the best sense of the word. The decor has plentiful greenery breaking up the pinks and peaches of the walls, while crisp white cloths are dotted with shining glassware. There's a sense of genuine pride in what this down-to-earth and amiable place – run by Anila and Sunil Anand – has to offer. The Curry Fever's menu springs no surprises, but it attracts a lot of repeat custom.

Friends Tandoori ★

41-45 Belgrave Road, LE4 6AR (0116 266 8809). **Lunch served** noon-2pm, **dinner served** 6-11.30pm Mon-Sat. **Main courses** £6-£11.50. **Credit** AmEx, MC, V.

This place was called Friends long before the American sitcom arrived, so don't accuse it of jumping on any bandwagons. With dining rooms on two floors, it can pack in more than 100 hungry diners and still manage to look after everyone serviceably well. The place is decked out with lots of mahogany, exotically colourful pictures and pastel walls. The north Indian, Punjabi-style dishes are cooked with care and at sensible prices. Tawa and tandoori dishes are popular.

Jones's Café Bistro

93 Queens Road, LE2 1TT (0116 270 8830). **Lunch served** 10am-2pm daily. **Dinner served** 6.30-9.30pm Mon-Thur; 6.30-10pm Fri, Sat. **Main courses** £7.95-£13. **Credit** MC, V.

Informal, relaxed and pretty, Jones's Café Bistro is the sort of easy-eating, neighbourhood restaurant that everyone would love to have down their street. It's only small – just 35 covers – so booking is essential. Warm and friendly staff serve dishes such as a great seafood risotto packed with prawns, mussels, swordfish and salmon, and comfort food like sausage and mash or fillet steak on rösti. There's a great choice for vegetarians too and prices are sensible.

The Opera House

10-12 Guildhall Lane, LE1 5FQ (0116 223 6666). **Lunch served** noon-2pm, **dinner served** 7-10pm Mon-Sat. **Main courses** £15-£19.50. **Set lunch** £7.75 1 course, £11.75 2 courses, £13.50 3 courses. **Credit** MC, V.

Set in a Grade II listed building and originally part of St George's Hall, the Opera House offers rather self-consciously fine dining and regularly wins accolades as 'best restaurant in Leicestershire'. An intimate place (perfect if you're out to impress on a big date) and with ultra-smooth service, this is special occasion food. Roasted goat's cheese with poached pear and a hazel-nut vinaigrette was a satisfying mix of sweet and savoury flavours, while braised shank of lamb fell succulently and beautifully off the bone. For this, it's worth enduring occasional instances of 'menuspeak' and over-use of the indefinite article ('a collection of fish', 'a brace of quail' and 'a wild mushroom timbale').

Sayonara Thali ★

49 Belgrave Road, LE4 6AR (0116 266 5888). **Meals served** noon-9.30pm Mon-Fri, Sun; noon-10pm Sat. **Main courses** £1.95-£4.95. **Set meals** £6.50-£7.50 3 courses, £12.50 4 courses. **Credit** AmEx, MC, V.

In an area embarrassingly well off for Indian vegetarian eateries, this is a real stalwart. Sayonara Thali, a smart 63-cover place, has been dishing up quality fare for more than 30 years. The masala dosa is a classic, as is the thali special. How about uthappam or idli sambhar or mogo chips? 'And would sir like a falooda perhaps to help it go down?' Friendly, bustling and down-to-earth, and it won't break the bank – most main courses here don't go over £4.50.

Sharmilee ★

71-73 Belgrave Road, LE4 6AS (0116 261 0503/ www.sharmilee.co.uk). **Lunch served** noon-2.30pm, **dinner served** 6-9pm Tue-Fri. **Meals served** noon-9.30pm Sat; noon-9pm Sun. **Main courses** £3.90-£4.95. **Set thali** £6.90-£8.95. **Credit** AmEx, DC, MC, V.

If piped sitar music drives you crazy, Sharmilee may well be right up your street. The interior manages a mix of modern and traditional (here, the latter is

Barnstaple Pannier Market

Market Street, Barnstaple, Devon
(www.northdevon.gov.uk/recreation/
market/index.shtml). **Open** (for food)
9am-4pm Tue, Fri, Sat.
An ornate Victorian market hall holding
a harvest festival of fruit and vegetables,
much of it locally sourced, augmented
by nearby 'Butcher's Row'.

Birmingham Market

The Bullring, Edgbaston Street,
Birmingham (www.bullring.co.uk/
the_markets.htm). **Open** 9am-5.30pm
Mon-Sat.
Moving into a new indoor hall a couple of
years ago, this huge market is fabulous for
meat and fish. Watch out for faggots and
pork scratchings.

Bury Market

Market Street, Bury, Lancashire
(www.burymarkettraders.co.uk/
food.htm). **Open** *Outdoor market*
9am-4pm Wed, Fri, Sat; *market hall*
9am-5pm Mon, Wed-Sat.
There's a wealth of North-western produce
here: you'll find Chadwick's famous black
puddings (served hot from a steamer),
'pot herbs' for Lancashire hot-pots, Eccles
cakes and crumbly Lancashire cheese.

Skipton Market

High Street, Skipton, North Yorkshire
(www.skiptonmarkets.co.uk). **Open** 9am-
5pm Mon, Wed, Fri, Sat.
Over 100 types of cheese from the Dales
and beyond at the Lawson family's stall,
part of a market that takes over the town
centre four days a week. Fish and meat also
make an appearance.

Swaffham Market

Market Place, Swaffham, Norfolk
(www.aboutswaffham.co.uk/Market.html).
Open 9am-4.30pm Sat.
A highly traditional weekly shindig which
attracts farmers and villagers from a wide
radius. Seasonal fruit and vegetables,
Cromer crabs, Brancaster mussels,
Feltwell cheeses and samphire are the
local highlights.

Thame Market

Upper High Street, Thame, Oxfordshire
(www.thame.net/markets.asp). **Open** 9am-
4pm Tue. *Farmers' market* 9am-1pm 2nd
Tue of month.
A major weekly event, Thame market gets
still bigger once a month when it (unusually
and successfully) incorporates a farmers'
market. Pork and trout are fortes there, but
weekly attractions include the Women's
Institute's cakes, flans and preserves, and
plenty of fruit and vegetables.

---

provided by the wood carvings dotted prettily
around). As a mainly Gujarati/southern Indian place,
the food is reliably meat-free, mostly well-cooked
and fantastically cheap (starters about £2, mains
mostly £5). Try the slow-cooked 'handi' dishes such
as the Haidrabadi biriani.

The Tiffin

1 De Montfort Street, LE1 7GE (0116 247 0420/
www.the-tiffin.co.uk). **Lunch served** 11am-2pm
Mon-Fri. **Dinner served** 6-11pm Mon-Sat. **Main
courses** £7-£12. **Credit** AmEx, MC, V.
Slightly higher than average prices suggest that the
Tiffin considers itself a cut above the local
competition. Certainly the dishes here are good
quality, with well-balanced spicing, served in
surroundings that include two dining areas (one a
conservatory with statutory frilly blinds). Yet there
is little that is remarkable on the menu. A roll-call of
much-loved curry-house dishes runs from starters
such as chicken chaat and prawn puri, to mains
including radam pasanda (lamb with almonds) and
fish bhuna. Try the spicy, dry tawa chicken,

chopped and fried on the tawa griddle. The Tiffin
has two bars and can get very busy. On occasion,
staff could do with a stint at charm school.

WYMONDHAM

Berkeley Arms

59 Main Street, Wymondham, LE14 2AG (01572
787587). **Lunch served** noon-2.30pm Tue-Sun.
Dinner served 7-9pm Tue-Thur; 7-9.30pm Fri, Sat.
Main courses £8-£13. **Credit** MC, V.
This is a village pub and it looks the part too, but
there's also a fair bit of culinary ambition on show
at the Berkeley Arms. Chef-landlord Nick McGeown
claims Raymond Blanc (who he worked with for four
years) and Nico Ladenis as his guiding lights but
worry not, the food here doesn't overreach itself. We
followed an oozingly delicious deep-fried goat's
cheese with pesto dressing and grilled Med
vegetables with a spot-on roast salmon fillet in a
prawn and dill sauce. Prices are reasonable for the
quality; service is warm and capable.

Midlands

Lincolnshire

CLEETHORPES

Ernie Beckett's ★
21 Market Street, Market Place Corner, Cleethorpes, DN35 8LY (01472 691234). **Meals served** 11.30am-9pm Mon-Sat; 11.30am-6pm Sun. **Main courses** £3.10-£5.70. **No credit cards.**
An award-winning local institution and island of calm among the bright lights of Cleethorpes, Ernie Beckett's is a traditional fish and chip shop, with a cosy 38-seater restaurant. The functional decor reflects the exterior, in that it's predominantly blue, with wood panelling beneath the dado rail. All in all it provides an agreeable setting in which to sit and munch tasty haddock, fresh from nearby Grimsby. The fish is cooked in beef dripping, served skin-on and coated in crunchy batter, made from a secret recipe. Also on offer are verdant green mushy peas, gravy or curry sauce. A slap-up sit-down feast of fish, chips, mushy peas, bread and butter and a pot of tea costs £10.60 for two.

GREAT GONERBY

Harry's Place ★
17 High Street, Great Gonerby, NG31 8JS (01476 561780). **Lunch served** 12.30-2pm, **dinner served** 7-9.30pm Tue-Sat by appointment only. **Main courses** £30. **Credit** MC, V.
Despite its unprepossessing exterior and lacklustre location on a busy road opposite the village social club, there's nothing ordinary about the food or wine in this tiny three-table Michelin-starred restaurant, the home and business of husband and wife Harry and Caroline Hallam. With Harry cooking and competent Caroline front of house, the couple serve immaculately prepared produce, such as North Esk wild salmon, Scottish scallops and French chicken, in the cheerfully rustic dining room. The menu is short and the ingredients painstakingly sourced, though inevitably there's a price to pay for quality (£30 for a main course). Puddings such as apple and Calvados soufflé or cherry brandy jelly are intensely flavoured and expertly done. If you like busy, buzzy restaurants this isn't for you, but for an intimate experience, where food and wine are taken very seriously indeed, it's somewhere to linger.

GRIMSTHORPE

The Black Horse
Grimsthorpe, PE10 OLY (01778 591247). **Lunch served** noon-2pm Tue-Sun. **Dinner served** 7-9pm Tue-Sat. **Main courses** £12. **Credit** AmEx, MC, V.
Here's an unchanged corner of rural England with characterful regulars chewing over issues of the day at the bar, a log fire crackling in the grate and overcooked vegetables on the menu. This is unreconstructed English cookery with enormous portions of partridge, pheasant, pigeon, lamb and fish served with complicated calorie-busting sauces. In every sense, it's all a bit too much. Sweets such as lemon tart with mandarin sorbet are good, but also over-generously portioned. It's more relaxing to eat in the bar at lunchtime and it has a lower-priced menu than the beamed restaurant, at around £20 for two courses. Service couldn't be friendlier and when it comes to wine, traditional ales and malt whiskies, the patron knows his stuff.

HORNCASTLE

Magpies
71-75 East Street, Horncastle, LN9 6AA (01507 527004). **Dinner served** 7.30-9pm Wed-Sat. **Set dinner** £24 3 courses. **Credit** MC, V.
A quaint restaurant, situated on the main road through this little town. Service is very welcoming and efficient. The set-price menu changes daily, but might feature a warm salad of Toulouse sausage, puy lentils and balsamic vinegar or a ragoût of wild mushrooms on toasted brioche to start. Mains are the likes of supreme of Gressingham duck with apple compote and cider sauce or rack of lamb with provençal vegetables and a rosemary and Madeira jus. Finish with cheese or white chocolate mousse with raspberry vodka milkshake. Coffee comes with chocolates and the mood is relaxed. A super neighbourhood joint.

LINCOLN

Brown's Pie Shop
33 Steep Hill, Lincoln, LN2 1LU (01522 527330). **Lunch served** 11.45am-3pm, **dinner served** 5-10pm Mon-Fri. **Meals served** 10am-10pm Sat, Sun. **Main courses** £7.95-£16. **Set lunch** £6.50 2 courses. **Credit** AmEx, MC, V.
Don't be misled by the name of this place – it's a bona fide restaurant and a good venue for an evening meal as well as lunch. Modestly decorated but well lit, its upstairs room is lined with tables that are spaced to allow a relative amount of privacy. Young couples, families and groups of visiting businesspeople tuck into an extensive menu that offers steaks and dishes such as seared sea bass or Cumberland sausages alongside a full range of pies. These, however, deserve to be tried: choices include local rabbit with Dorset scrumpy, steak and kidney,

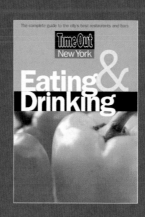
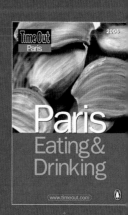

a three cheese veggie option and a game one. It's a price -concious place – there's a beat-the-clock dinner menu and daily specials too.

The Cheese Society ★

1 St Martins Lane, Lincoln, LN2 1HY (01522 511003/www.thecheesesociety.co.uk). **Meals served** 10am-4.30pm Mon-Sat. **Main courses** £4.95-£8.95. **Set lunch** £7.95 2 courses, £9.95 3 courses. **Credit** AmEx, MC, V.

This is a real find in a city not overwhelmed with truly good places to eat. Handily situated just off the tourist drag of Steep Hill, it's a little shop (the website is worth checking out) and café. Dishes – many of which have cheese as the star turn – run from salads (feta, couscous and roast veg), sandwiches (Swiss cheese with grapes and mayo or roast ham with beetroot and horseradish relish) and melts (blue cheese and bacon) to more sizeable offerings. You could order sirloin steak with frites, but melted raclette over hot new potatoes or fondue (for two) are hard to resist. Save room for the yellow belly tart (lemon curd) with ice-cream. Booking is advisable for lunch; at other times it's easy to pop in for one of the many varieties of tea and a slice of Lincolnshire plum bread. Service is charming.

Elite Fish & Chip Shop ★

Moorland Shopping & Industrial Complex, Tritton Road, Lincoln, LN6 7JW (01522 509505). **Meals served** 11.30am-7.30pm Mon, Sun; 11.30am-9.30pm Tue-Sat. **Main courses** £3-£5. **No credit cards**.

A modern, purpose-built chippy and licensed restaurant in unprepossessing surroundings may not sound appealing, but the Elite produces the best fish and chips for miles around. In keeping with its single-storey, brick bungalow shell, the interior is anodyne, combining piped music, 104 light oak chairs surrounding matching tables and pale pink walls. Sprightly service and good food make up for it, with a choice of haddock, cod, plaice, rock salmon, huss or skate (from Hull), coated in a family-recipe batter and served with thick-cut Maris Piper chips, all cooked in traditional beef dripping. The unenhanced mushy peas are as green as Ireland and a bottle of wine costs just £6.50. Expect to pay no more than £8 for dinner with dessert.

The Jews House

15 The Strait, Lincoln, LN2 1JD (01522 524851). **Lunch served** 11.30am-2.30pm, **dinner served** 6.30-9.30pm Tue-Sat. **Main courses** £12.75-£18.95. **Set lunch** £12.95 2 courses, £14.95 3 courses. **Credit** DC, MC, V.

Possibly the oldest inhabited house in the country (it dates back to 1190), the Jews House plays host to the most upmarket restaurant in Lincoln. It may ask you to pay for the privilege but offers immaculate service and modern European food of a decent calibre in return. A small, peaceful room overlooking the street on Steep Hill, it typically attracts smartly-dressed older couples enjoying muted conversation and background classical music. A typical meal here

might be baked figs with goat's cheese and a watercress and dill salad, followed by braised pork belly and seared loin of pork with steamed pak choi and coriander foam. Finish with glazed lemon tart with lime muffin or white chocolate and passion fruit mousse with chocolate shortbread. Staff are pleasant.

Wig & Mitre

30 Steep Hill, Lincoln, LN2 1TL (01522 535190/www.wigandmitre.com). **Meals served** 8am-11pm Mon-Sat; 8am-10.30pm Sun. **Main courses** £9.50-£16.50. **Set meals** (noon-6pm daily) £9.50 1 course, £11 2 courses, £13.95 3 courses. **Credit** AmEx, DC, MC, V.

If you're after somewhere for a leisurely Sunday lunch with the newspapers then look no further than the Wig and Mitre, whose several floors host real ales, an impressive wine list and very acceptable food. Breakfast options include a wonderfully creamy porridge; sandwiches run from cheddar and red onion to pan-fried fillet steak with mushrooms and caramelised onions; more substantial offerings might be roast Lincolnshire sausage with garlic and black pudding mash and apple cream sauce or roast tomato and basil risotto with aged balsamic and parmesan crackling. This music-free venue offers a variety of seating arrangements from pub trestle tables to more formal table service dining. Prices are slightly high, but are on the whole justified. There's nowhere else like this (relaxed, civilised, open all day) in the city. One gripe – after a number of visits, we're wondering when they'll ever stock the fresh orange juice advertised on the menu.

STAMFORD

The George

71 St Martins, Stamford, PE9 2LB (01780 750750/www.georgehotelofstamford.com). **Bistro Meals served** noon-11pm daily. *Restaurant* **Lunch served** noon-2.30pm, **dinner served** 7-10pm daily. **Main courses** £15.50-£24. **Set lunch** (Mon-Sat) £17.50 2 courses. **Credit** AmEx, DC, MC, V.

From the outsized silver dome covering the vast side of roast beef to the cartwheel of cheddar on the cheese trolley and the piled platters of seafood on ice, everything at this 17th-century coaching inn is slightly theatrical – including the sardonic maître d'. Choose from the less formal, cheaper and open-all-hours garden room (or, in fine weather, the cobbled courtyard) serving tasty own-made pasta, superior fish and chips and a salad buffet, or opt for an indulgent experience in the panelled dining room where efficient waiters whisk out comfortable chairs and flourish napkins, and men must be booted and suited to get in. Trad dishes (around £17) are the menu mainstays, including hearty portions of rack of lamb, good roast beef with strong horseradish and Norfolk duck. Puddings are blowsy, bland versions of lemon meringue, strawberry millefeuille and a crème caramel big enough to feed a family for a week. There's an adventurous wine list, which changes four times a year.

Northamptonshire

FOTHERINGHAY

The Falcon ★
Fotheringhay, PE8 5HZ (01832 226254/
www.huntsbridge.com). **Lunch served** noon-2.15pm
daily. **Dinner served** 6.30-9.30pm Mon-Sat; 7-9pm
Sun. **Main courses** £9.75-£19.50. **Set lunch** £11
2 courses, £14.75 3 courses Mon-Sat. **Credit** AmEx,
DC, MC, V.
The newest of four exceptional pub-restaurants (the
others are the Pheasant, Keyston – 01832 710241;
Three Horseshoes, Madingley – *see p187*; Old
Bridge Hotel, Huntingdon – 01480 424300). Like the
rest in the group, the Falcon functions at different
levels. There's the 'local' atmosphere of the tap bar
with its well-kept ales and darts team. Then there's
the blackboard menu of snacks and the smart, no-
smoking dining room and conservatory. The buzz
about this place is its informality – you eat what you
like where you like. So tempting is the menu that
choosing between the featured fashionable modern
European dishes, which have vibrant flavours
aplenty, is almost impossible. To accompany, there's
a terrific wine list at sensible prices compiled by John
Hoskins, who's a Master of Wine.

KING'S CLIFFE

King's Cliffe House
*31 West Street, King's Cliffe, PE8 6XB (01780
470172).* **Dinner served** 7-9.15pm Wed-Sat.
Main courses £11-£16.50. **No credit cards**.
Andrew Wilshaw and his partner Emma Jessop
have a touch of the *Good Life* here: the 1.75-acre
walled garden of their part 17th-century family
home provides the seasonal vegetables, fruit and
herbs used in the House's flower-bedecked
restaurant. They do their own hot smoking,
charcuterie and salting, and there are wonderful
local supplies of additive-free meat, chicken and
duck. Even the pastor does his bit, supplying
organic vegetables. With just the two of them to do
everything, dinner is a gentle, relaxed affair. The
cooking is skilled and flavours well balanced, with
a surprisingly imaginative choice on the short menu:
Southorpe asparagus in tempura batter with sorrel
hollandaise; guinea fowl with muscat and Parma
ham sauce; rhubarb in honey saffron custard.

NORTHAMPTON

Academy Coffee Haus ★
1 College Street Mews, NN1 2QF (01604 232111).
Meals served 9.30am-5pm Mon-Sat. **Main
courses** £2.10-£3.95. **No credit cards**.

The best Places for...

Cider
The Nantyffin Cider Mill Inn, Wales.
See p340.

Fruit wines
The Three Horseshoes, Norfolk (*see
p196*) and the Ringlestone Inn, Kent
(*see p88*).

Microbrews
The Swan on the Green, Kent. *See p90.*

Local artists get the opportunity to exhibit their work
in this cheerful, funky café with its cool green and
white decor. The location – down a mews in the town
centre – provides an ideal setting where pavement
tables are the draw in fine weather. When it first
opened, students made up most of the customers. But
now it attracts shoppers and townsfolk of all ages,
who come for the very wide selection of sandwiches,
filled jacket potatoes or wraps, salads and toasties.
There's even a tortilla special, plus a few pasta
dishes. Plain or orange hot chocolate, cafetière and
espresso coffees, as well as milkshakes and
smoothies provide suitable liquid refreshment.

ROADE

Roade House
*16 High Street, Roade, NN7 2NW (01604 863372/
www.roadehousehotel.co.uk).* **Lunch served** noon-
2pm Tue-Fri, Sun. **Dinner served** 7-10pm Mon-Sat.
Main courses £15-£20. **Set lunch** £16 2 courses,
£19 3 courses Tue-Fri; £21 3 courses Sun. **Credit**
AmEx, MC, V.
Minutes from J15 of the M1, what was once the local
ale house is now an updated but still pretty beamed
restaurant with rooms. Lunchtime sees a short,
fixed-price two- or three-course menu based on the
evening carte. Variety is the key, with an eclectic
mix of imaginative and well-prepared items, ranging
from broad bean soup or pan-fried lamb patty with
couscous and mint yoghurt to Parma ham-wrapped
chicken breast stuffed with chorizo on sauerkraut,
or roast duck with a Chinese-style sauce. Puddings
are more traditional, though still given a subtle twist:
apple crumble with sultanas and Calvados and
cinnamon ice-cream or chocolate cake perked up
with ginger and served with hazel-nut cream.

Midlands

Nottinghamshire

CAUNTON

Caunton Beck

Caunton, NG23 6AB (01636 636793). **Meals served** 8am-10pm Mon-Sat; noon-9.30pm Sun. **Main courses** £9.50-£14. **Set menu** (Mon-Fri) £10 2 courses; £12.95 3 courses. **Credit** AmEx, DC, MC, V.

Located in a quiet village near Newark, the Caunton Beck has forged a strong reputation for its cooking and draws customers from significant distances. Its sister establishment is the Wig and Mitre in Lincoln (*see p223*). The menu is the star attraction and sparkles with possibilities: Thai mussel curry, roast skate wing, shoulder of Welsh lamb, marinated duck breast with bok choi. However, vegetarians aren't well served – zucchini frittata was the only option on our visit – and if you're not careful, wine can prove expensive (a 175ml glass of pinot noir at £7.90). Nevertheless, the food more than justifies a drive out and a stroll along the riverside is a quintessential English countryside experience.

COLSTON BASSETT

Martin's Arms ★

School Lane, Colston Bassett, NG12 3FD (01949 81361). **Bar Open** noon-3pm, 6-11pm Mon-Sat; noon-3pm, 6.30-10.30pm Sun. **Lunch served** noon-2pm, **dinner served** 6-10pm Mon-Sat; 6.30-10pm Sun. **Main courses** £5-£7.95. *Restaurant* **Lunch served** noon-1.30pm daily. **Dinner served** Mon-Sat; 6.30-9pm Sun. **Main courses** £9.50-£19. **Credit** AmEx, MC, V.

This place is every inch the picturesque country pub. Traditional and cosy inside, the Martin's Arms also boasts a huge garden – a perfect spot to enjoy a pint of ale. Renowned among Nottinghamshire's discerning diners, this gourmet pub is consistently in demand for dishes such as sea bass with crab mashed potatoes and sweet sorrel cream, or pork chop with grilled apple and black pudding tartlet. Service is excellent – personified by the exchange of a potato cake with cheddar for the ordered version with stilton (Colston Bassett is famous for its stilton, so it's a must). Not only was the dish changed without fuss, it was also taken off the bill. Class.

NEWARK

Café Bleu

14 Castlegate, Newark, NG24 1BG (01636 610141/ www.cafebleu.co.uk). **Lunch served** noon-2.30pm Mon-Sat; noon-3pm Sun. **Dinner served** 7-9.30pm Mon-Fri; 6.30-10pm Sat. **Main courses** £9.50-£14.95. **Credit** MC, V.

This is the best food you'll find in Newark. And don't they know it. The slight smugness of this gourmet outpost near the regenerated Riverside is understandable, given the high-quality cooking – contemporary cuisine with a Mediterranean influence. There are innovative combinations – from pan-fried black pudding with parsley potatoes to grilled sardines with roast aubergine, and Cropwell Bishop stilton with parma ham. Above all, this is serious food at fairly serious prices – main courses are rarely less than a tenner. With regular jazz and flamenco and some 'lively' artwork, Café Bleu certainly tries hard. One caveat: they really pack in the smartly attired punters – it can be hard to extricate yourself from the tight tables.

NOTTINGHAM

Chino Latino ★

41 Maid Marion Way, Nottingham, NG1 6GD (0115 947 7444/www.chinolatino.co.uk). **Meals served** noon-11pm Mon-Sat; 1-10pm Sun. **Main courses** £13-£16. **Set lunch** £12 2 courses. **Credit** AmEx, DC, MC, V.

It's no surprise to hear that the chef at this high-concept venue also worked at London's legendary Nobu. In fact, there are striking similarities in both the cutting-edge interior design and the equally innovative Japanese-South American fusion food. Where else in Nottingham would you find green tea soba noodles, breaded lobster and jalapeños with coconut rice and lotus seeds, or grilled shrimp served with Peruvian pesto potato? Although there are more familiar sashimi and sushi options, Chino Latino is an opportunity to experiment with texture and flavour. Best experienced at night when the lighting is subdued, there's a slick metropolitan buzz here. Of course, it's all a bit pretentious – a Sherwood Dragon cocktail is described as a 'lime-infused nijisaki built with lillet blanc and topped with Canada Dry' – but great fun. A restaurant guaranteed to impress.

4550 miles from Delhi

41 Mount Street, Nottingham, NG1 6HE (0115 947 5111). **Lunch served** noon-2.30pm Mon-Fri. **Dinner served** 5.30-11pm Mon-Sat; 5.30-10pm Sun. **Main courses** £6.95-£11.95. **Credit** AmEx, MC, V.

Right from the off, 4550 miles from Delhi attempts to distinguish itself from the usual Nottingham curry house – huge windows, minimalist design, cool lighting and funky jazz rather than the obligatory sitar soundtrack. Not to mention the Indian rickshaw, sawn in half, that's attached to the side of the building. Yes, this is a destination restaurant with the food being only part of the deal. The menu isn't particularly daring or overly pricey, especially compared to the restaurant's aesthetic. The usual Indian favourites are spiced up by a few interesting dishes including salmon tikka, tandoori chaat, Kerala fish curry, masala chilli wings, and deep-fried stuffed green chillies. Service is speedy if a little erratic, particularly if orders are shouted above the din of a raucous Saturday night crowd.

Hart's ★

Standard Court, Park Row, Nottingham, NG1 6GN (0115 911 0666/www.hartsnottingham.co.uk). **Lunch served** noon-2pm daily. **Dinner served** 7-10.30pm Mon-Sat; 7-9pm Sun. **Main courses** £11.50-£18.50. **Set lunch** (Mon-Sat) £11 2 courses, £14.95 3 courses; (Sun) £18 3 courses. **Set dinner** (Sun) £14.95 3 courses. **Credit** MC, V.

Hart's has earned its place in the affections of Nottingham's cognoscenti over the past six years. Housed, rather bizarrely, in the old A&E department of the former Nottingham General Hospital, the discreet and efficient service, contemporary-yet-formal interiors and modern British cuisine have ensured a loyal clientele of lunching solicitors and affluent diners. The menu – from chump of lamb to Gressingham duck breast and grilled sea bass – isn't particularly extensive and doesn't seem to change very regularly. But the quality of dishes is beyond reproach. All this doesn't come cheap, of course – a meal for two can easily top £100 with cocktails and

wines from a wonderful drinks menu. But, with the opening of an adjacent hotel in April 2003, Hart's continues to set the standard.

Merchants

29-31 High Pavement, Nottingham, NG1 1HE (0115 852 3200/www.lacemarkethotel.co.uk). **Lunch served** noon-2.30pm Mon-Fri, Sun. **Dinner served** 7-10pm Mon-Sat. **Main courses** £10-£15.50. **Credit** AmEx, MC, V.

Merchants is a contemporary brasserie trading on its location within the voguish Lace Market Hotel – Nottingham designer chic. Bumping into visiting celebrities is a distinct possibility and it's certainly a place to be seen in. However, we'd been mixed reviews of the food, soon confirmed by our experience. While the salad of marinated wild mushrooms was fine, the main courses – salmon with fresh asparagus and new potatoes; provençal vegetable tart with rocket – were distinctly uninspiring. Banana crème brûlée with rum and raisin ice-cream retrieved the situation slightly but, overall, the meal didn't quite deliver, despite friendly service. Nevertheless, Merchants seems consistently busy – either due to the hotel's ongoing success or the willingness of its well-heeled clientele to accept style over substance.

Saltwater

The Cornerhouse, Forman Street, Nottingham, NG1 4AA (0115 924 2664/www.saltwater-restaurant.com). **Lunch served** noon-2.30pm

---

Bar crawl: Nottingham

Nottingham has always known how to have a good time and, in recent years, the emergence of a buzzing late-night bar scene has begun to eclipse its renowned club culture. Most of the action happens within the rejuvenated Lace Market/ Hockley area where dozens of fashionable bars have sprung up among the loft conversions, boutiques and ad agency offices. **Bluu** (5 Broadway; 0115 950 5359) is typical – a minimalist, industrial interior with a basement DJ bar where Nottingham's cognoscenti hang out on huge leather sofas.

Other bars of note in the area include the tiny **Brass Monkey** (11 High Pavement; 0115 840 4101) for innovative cocktails, the recently renovated **Brownes** (17-19 Goosegate; 0115 958 0188), now a local institution, the ski-chalet interiors of **Eleven** (23 Goosegate; 0115 959 8831) and the ever-popular **Dogma** (9 Byard Lane; 0115 988 6833) whose basement bar is thunderingly loud at weekends. Broad Street is also a good bet – particularly for the café-bar at the

Broadway Cinema (Broad Street; 0115 952 6611), the local arthouse, which attracts a suitably arty crowd for its impressive European beer menu and video installations.

Nearby **Cabaret** (22 Fletcher Gate; 0115 941 3111), on the site of the famous Old Vic, hosts contemporary comedy. For cutting-edge music, meanwhile, head to the **Social** (23 Pelham Street; 0115 950 5078) – the northern outpost of London's Heavenly Social – which has showcased bands like the Strokes and Starsailor.

Two good retreats from the masses are the **Loft** (217 Mansfield Road; 0115 924 0213), a groovy space on the bohemian Mansfield Road, and **Moog** (Newdigate Street, off Alfreton Road; 0115 841 3830), one of the few worthwhile venues outside the city centre. After a quiet start, the secret is finally out on this unpretentious-yet-hip Radford bar. Moog's acclaimed hip hop nights have helped to make it one of Nottingham's truly funky haunts.

Saltwater

Mon-Fri; noon-5pm Sat, Sun. **Dinner served**
6-10pm Mon-Thur; 6-10.30pm Fri, Sat; 6-9pm Sun.
Main courses £11-£16. **Set lunch** (Mon-Sat) £9
2 courses, £12 3 courses; (Sun) £12 2 courses, £15
3 courses. **Set dinner** (6-7pm Mon-Sat) £9 2 courses,
£12 3 courses. **Credit** AmEx, MC, V.
The rumoured £800,000 investment in Saltwater,
one of the final additions to Nottingham's thriving
Cornerhouse entertainment complex, is surely
money well spent. The roof terrace overlooking the
city is a great draw, especially in summer. The
whole vibe of the restaurant, inside and out, is
organic chic – stark woods and cactus interiors,
and a volcano-style char-grill. The Pacific Rim-
influenced menu is conceptual: choose from 20 meat
or fish options, match your choice with a sauce
(anything from roast red chilli and red pepper to
peppercorn and brandy cream) and add either frites,
wasabi mash or jasmine rice. It's fun and fashionable,
though not a bargain given the small portions.

Sat Bains ★
Old Lenton Lane, Nottingham, NG7 2SA
(0115 986 6566/www.hoteldesclos.com).
Lunch served noon-2pm Tue-Fri. **Dinner**
served 7-9.30pm Tue-Sat. **Set lunch** £17.95
2 courses, £21.95 3 courses. **Set dinner** £45
tasting menu, £65 surprise menu. **Credit** AmEx,
DC, MC, V.
Mr Sat Bains is Nottingham's culinary superstar,
earning the restaurant at Hotel des Clos the city's
first – and only – Michelin star. After working with
Raymond Blanc and the Roux brothers, this young
chef's reputation for classics with a twist has helped
put this small hotel, housed in Victorian farm
buildings, on the map. And you'll certainly need a
map to find it – within the semi-industrial maze of
business parks around the A52 flyover. This
location is the worst of both worlds, devoid of either
rural charm or metropolitan buzz. Concentrate
instead on the inventive cooking – the tasting menu
includes roast scallop with Indian spices, Anjou

pigeon, ballotine of foie gras and Balmoral Estate
venison. This is serious food, confidently served
to affluent local epicureans and visiting business
types. If you enjoy ordering off-menu, Sat would
undoubtedly relish the chance to impress.

Shaw's
20-22 Broad Street, Hockley, Nottingham, NG1 3AL
(0115 950 0009/www.shawsrestaurant.co.uk).
Meals served 10am-11pm Mon-Sat. **Main**
courses £9-£13. **Credit** AmEx, DC, MC, V.
Despite being located next door to the buzzy
Broadway cinema, Shaw's still feels like a real find.
Housed over two floors in a beautiful old industrial
building, there's no indication of the interesting
interior – antique shop fittings, red lamps, wicker
chairs and sofas seemingly thrown together – until
you enter. There is genuine warmth, character and
charm here. Luckily, the food – from a daily handwritten menu – lives up to expectations. The fish
soup with gruyère croûtons was sensational, as were
the huge portions of salmon and caper berry fish
cakes, and the wild mushroom gnocchi. With a meal
for two coming in at around £50 with drinks, this
bohemian bolt-hole retains the feel of a well-kept
neighbourhood secret. Just don't tell everyone…

Skinny Sumo ★
11-13 Carlton Street, Hockley, Nottingham, NG1
1NL (0115 952 0188). **Meals served** noon-3pm,
6-11pm Mon-Fri; noon-11pm Sat; noon-3pm, 6-10pm
Sun. **Sushi** £1.50-£3.50. **Set meals** £7 9 pieces, £12
17 pieces. **Credit** AmEx, DC, MC, V.
Nottingham's first – and only – restaurant with a
rotating sushi conveyor has proved a great addition
to Hockley's main drag. The revolving colour-coded
sushi plates are dwarfed by the 'China boat' which,
for £7, features a meal-sized medley of seaweed-
wrapped faves. But it's not all about raw fish.
Sensibly, Skinny Sumo also features other Japanese
dishes (teriyaki, tempura and udon noodles) and

Midlands

Far-Eastern culinary classics – including Thai curries, pad Thai and spicy tom yum soup. And, since Wagamama arrived in town, Skinny Sumo has upped its game by offering excellent-value weekday lunch deals – like 'Noodle Wednesday' for a bargain £3.50. So, despite its authentic feel, this isn't Japanese food for the purist. Rather, it's a fairly cheap and usually cheerful oriental treasure.

Sonny's

3 Carlton Street, Hockley, Nottingham, NG1 1NL (0115 947 3041). **Lunch served** noon-2.30pm Mon-Sat; noon-3pm Sun. **Dinner served** 7-10.30pm Mon-Thur, Sun; 7-11pm Fri, Sat. **Main courses** £11.50-£16.50. **Set lunch** (Mon-Fri, Sun) £12.95 2 courses, £15 3 courses. **Set dinner** (Wed-Sun) £15 2 courses, £19.50 3 courses. **Credit** AmEx, MC, V.
Over the past decade, Sonny's has become something of a Nottingham institution. This chic restaurant came to prominence in 1993 when Quentin Tarantino made it his HQ during the nearby Broadway cinema's crime film festival. Now that it faces more intense competition, Sonny's isn't the landmark restaurant it once was and its airy, white look with slanted blinds seems ever-so-slightly dated. Still, the food remains a genuine attraction – the modern European menu features dishes like pigeon breast with herb polenta and chorizo, and butternut squash risotto. Sonny's is a favourite pit-stop during weekday shopping trips and, on Sundays, there is an admirably cheap (£3.50) children's menu.

Squeek

23-25 Heathcote Street, Nottingham, NG1 3AG (0115 955 5560). **Dinner served** 6-10pm Mon-Sat. **Main courses** £9.95. **Set dinner** £11.95 2 courses; £13.95 3 courses. **Credit** AmEx, MC, V.
Billing itself as Nottingham's only exclusively vegetarian restaurant, Squeek is more hip than hippie. This smart, slightly bohemian outpost attracts a word-of-mouth clientele. However, it has to be said that its prices aren't quite as enlightened. At £4.25 for starters and £9.50 for main courses, the portions could be more generous. That said, the monthly menu is consistently inventive – featuring, on our visit, fresh rosemary and apple sausages with chunky parsnip and fresh berry gravy, fragrant tofu stir-fried spring rolls or tomato, feta and olive tartlets. With smiley service and the relaxed vibe of like-minded souls, it's a restaurant that you'll want to love – but those prices could test your fidelity.

World Service ★

Newdigate House, Castlegate, Nottingham, NG1 6AF (0115 847 5587/www.worldservicerestaurant.com). **Lunch served** noon-2.15pm Mon-Sat; noon-3pm Sun. **Dinner served** 7-10pm Mon-Sat, 7-9pm Sun. **Main courses** £11.50-£19. **Set lunch** £10.50 2 courses, £14 3 courses. **Credit** AmEx, MC, V.
Discreetly housed in a historic 17th-century building, an arrow's flight from Nottingham Castle, World Service has spearheaded Nottingham's drive towards voguish dining. From the Japanese walled garden to the clean lines, muted colours and eclectic collection of Far Eastern art and artefacts, there is a Zen-like atmosphere of contemporary cool helped along by an ambient soundtrack. Dishes include lobster and parmesan risotto flavoured with vanilla and baked halibut with pea risotto and a red pepper jam. But, best of all, the comprehensive wine list and cocktail selection is the most fabulous in town and the vast range of sakés is pure showmanship.

PLUMTREE

Perkins

The Old Station, Station Road, Plumtree, NG12 5NA (0115 937 3695 /www.perkinsrestaurant.co.uk). **Lunch served** noon-2pm Tue-Sat; noon-2.30pm Sun. **Dinner served** 6.45-9.30pm Tue-Sat. **Main courses** £9-£14. **Set lunch** (Tue-Sat) £9.75 2 courses. **Set dinner** (Tue-Thur) £16.95 3 courses. **Credit** AmEx, MC, V.
Housed in a converted 19th-century railway station in the sleepy village of Plumtree, Perkins is a good stop for a gourmet country pub experience. There's an intimate feel to this homely place that attracts a generally mature crowd. Our mains of roast chicken with celery and grape, and spinach and feta cheese roulade with beansprouts (the only vegetarian option) were excellent. On a summer's evening, it's great to chill out at the outside tables adjacent to the now-abandoned railway line. Plaudits also to the laid-back staff who let us linger over the chardonnay well past closing time.

SOUTHWELL

Saracen's Head

Market Place, Southwell, NG25 0HE (01636 812701). **Meals served** noon-9.30pm Mon-Sat; noon-3pm; 6-9pm Sun. **Set lunch** £12.50 3 courses. **Set dinner** £18.50 3 courses. **Credit** AmEx, MC, V
Providing an excellent excuse to visit Southwell, one of Nottinghamshire's most beautiful small towns, the Saracen's Head dates back to the 12th century and is steeped in history. Most famously, Charles I spent his last night of freedom here in 1649. Today this charming inn has benefited from some loving restoration and an updated modern menu in the Lord Byron (a former Southwell resident) restaurant. The three-course set menu is decent value with imaginative dishes like tiger prawns in garlic and dry cider, pork medallions on apple rösti with stilton sauce, and asparagus and parmesan lasagne. A venue with wonderful character.

Also in the area

The Living Room 7 High Pavement, The Lace Market, Nottingham, NG1 1HF (0870 442 2716); **Loch Fyne** 17 King Street, Nottingham, NG1 2AY (0115 988 6840); **Shimla Pinks** 38-46 Goose Gate, Nottingham, NG1 1FF (0115 958 9899); **Wagamama** The Courthouse, Burton Street, Nottingham, NG1 4DB (0115 924 1797).

Midlands

Rutland

CLIPSHAM

The Olive Branch

Main Street, Clipsham, LE15 7SH (01780 410355).
Lunch served noon-2pm Mon-Sat; noon-3pm Sun.
Dinner served 7-9.30pm Mon-Sat. **Main courses**
£8.25-£17. **Set lunch** (Mon-Sat) £10.50 2 courses,
£12.50 3 courses; (Sun) £15 3 courses. **Credit** MC, V.
Gastropubs are still a rarity around here, but this
place isn't just a welcome relief from the warm-pint-
and-microwave alternatives. From the shabby chic
interior to its location in a gorgeously pretty stone
village, with friendly young service and a menu that
makes the most of local ingredients, the Olive
Branch hits all the right notes. Char-grilled fish and
meat feature strongly on the menu, with appetising
accompaniments such as sage mash or crispy sweet
potatoes and a good choice of real ales (some locally
brewed). Puddings, including chocolate Eton mess
and treacle tart with yoghurt ice-cream, are
unmissable. The well-heeled clientele in their crisp
casuals clearly don't need a bargain, but the three-
course set lunch is a steal.

UPPER HAMBLETON

Finch's Arms

*Oakham Road, Upper Hambleton, LE15 8TL
(01572 756575/www.finchsarms.co.uk).* **Lunch
served** noon-2.30pm, **dinner served** 6.30-9.30pm
Mon-Sat. **Meals served** noon-9.30pm Sun. **Main
courses** £8.95-£13.50. **Set lunch** (Mon-Fri) £9.95
2 courses, £11.95 3 courses. **Credit** MC, V.
A textbook example of how to maintain an old pub
while moving seamlessly into the 21st century. The
Finch's Arms is a pub, though in name alone: the
decor is a tasteful, slyly modish set-up with a
restaurant attached at the back giving views over
Rutland Water (you can also eat from the same menu
in the pub bit). Beers come from Grainstore, and the
food from an inventive chef: grilled mackerel with
stir-fried vegetables, shark steak with sushi rice or
a divine chicken breast salad. The welcome is warm
and the ambience a delight. A winning enterprise.

Hambleton Hall ★

*Upper Hambleton, LE15 8TH (01572 756991/
www.hambletonhall.com).* **Lunch served** noon-
1.30pm, **dinner served** 7-9.30pm daily. **Main
courses** £25-£39. **Set meal** £35 3 courses.
Credit AmEx, DC, MC, V.
Imperiously overlooking Rutland Water from its
own landscaped grounds on the central peninsula,
Hambleton Hall is an English country hotel par
excellence. 'Do as you please' is the order of the day
emblazoned over the entrance, a throwback to wild

Georgian party scenes – and, in keeping, Tim and
Stefa Hart manage to uphold an atmosphere of
relaxation amid the sumptuous chintz and Regency
stripes. This really is a temple to food – from the
minute you walk into the place you're plied with
irresistible offerings. Monsieur Michelin was
mightily impressed, and it's easy to taste why. Any
notion of stuffiness drops away as soon as the
gourmet treats arrive: sweetmeats and veal or
intimate cuts of the newest baby lamb drizzled with
semi-precious jus and chef Aaron Patterson's secret
alchemical sauces, all exploding with layer upon
layer of sensation so surprising you'll want to giggle
and share. Service is expert, unobtrusive and friendly.

WING

King's Arms

*13 Top Street, Wing, LE15 8SE (01572 737634/
www.thekingsarms-wing.co.uk).* **Lunch served** noon-
3pm, **dinner served** 6.30-9pm daily. **Main courses**
£6.95-£15.50. **Credit** MC, V.
Wing is best known for its unusual turf maze, but a
recent makeover at the 17th-century King's Arms
has given another reason to visit this small village
near Rutland Water. An airy lightness now infuses
the once dreary dining room, and the menu under
head chef Simon Richards reflects the transformation.
Locally sourced fish and meat are presented simply
– such as a main course fillet of salmon on crushed
new potates with a zesty lemon and prawn
hollandaise, or fillet of pork with a roast red pepper
and foie gras terrine as a colourful and flavour-
packed starter. You'll also find exotica like crocodile
and ostrich alongside imaginative vegetarian
options. Desserts might include a warm chocolate
fondant with Turkish delight ice-cream, the wine list
is short but well thought-out and there are ales from
Grainstore. Service is friendly and prompt.

The best Whisky lists

Haldane's
Enjoy single malts in a very Scottish
setting. *See p303.*

Manor House Inn
Home to over 50 whiskies. *See p272.*

Nobody Inn
Drink whisky in a thatched inn. *See p127.*

Midlands

Shropshire

BROMFIELD

The Cookhouse

Bromfield, SY8 2JR (01584 856565/
www.thecookhouse.org.uk). **Open** 11am-11pm
Mon-Sat; noon-10.30pm Sun. **Lunch served**
noon-2.30pm, **dinner served** 6.30-9pm daily.
Main courses £12.95-£15.95. **Set lunch** £15.75
3 courses. **Credit** AmEx, DC, MC, V.

With all the traditional eateries in these parts, the
Cookhouse makes a refreshing change. Just a couple
of miles outside the gastropolis which is Ludlow,
this stately redbrick building is the rather surprising
roadside home to a modernist 'café bistro', as well
as a more genteel and sedate restaurant. Anywhere
else in the country would have a Little Chef. Here it's
all pretty informal, wherever you choose a table, and
it's decent quality too. There are some very good
house salads (try the Cajun chicken with avocado
and orange and honey dressing), but they also do a
lovely Cookhouse terrine – as well as deeply
comforting sweet and sour chicken with stir-fried
veg and egg-fried rice. Fairly simple stuff but
homely and done well.

DORRINGTON

Country Friends

Dorrington, SY5 7JD (01743 718707). **Lunch**
served noon-2pm, **dinner served** 7-9pm Wed-Sat.
Set meals £29.50 2 courses, £31.90 3 courses.
Credit MC, V.

Country Friends is a perfect name for this
comfortable old black-and-white timbered haunt just
outside Shrewsbury. The decor is unexciting, but
the food packs in more flavour than is decent –
although at these prices that's as it should be. There
is plenty here for the sturdy yeoman. A starter of
carpaccio of beef with wasabi is not for the faint-
hearted but is worth ordering. Goat's cheese-stuffed
chicken breast with roasted beetroot and red onion
is a treat for the eyes as much as the taste sensors,
closely followed in popularity by fillet steak with
Welsh rarebit and onion marmalade. Service is
mumsy and caring.

LLANFAIR WATERDINE

The Waterdine ★

Llanfair Waterdine, LD7 1TU (01547 528214/
www.the-waterdine.co.uk). **Lunch served** noon-2pm
Tue-Sun. **Dinner served** 7-9.30pm Tue-Sat.
Main courses £10.50-£16.50. **Set lunch**
(Sun) £15 3 courses. **Set dinner** (Sat) £26.50
3 courses. **Credit** MC, V.

The best | Designer hotels

Arthouse
So smart it has an indoor waterfall.
See p310.

Hotel du Vin
The friendly face of modern hotels.
See p210.

Malmaison
Dressed to impress but within most
budgets. *See p211.*

Seaham Hall
Ultra-cool destination for those with deep
pockets. *See p272.*

Whatley Manor
Luxurious newcomer deep in the country.
See p179.

Hidden away down a narrow country lane, the
Waterdine takes some seeking out but it's a joy to
come across for the hungry and weary traveller. The
ancient longhouse is home and workplace for chef
Ken Adams – the man who opened the first decent
restaurant in Ludlow (Oaks, now Hibiscus). There
are pretty rooms available in this friendly, colourful
place and you'll want to take advantage of them, for
this is a gorgeous riverside spot with wonderful
views across to a tree-dotted hill. The perfect
backdrop for some fantastic feasting, whether fried
calf's liver on a fig and onion flan with reduced
vinegar sauce (sublime) or maybe an open ravioli of
spinach, quail's egg and parmesan with truffle oil
(gorgeous). Prices hover around the £14 mark for
main courses.

LUDLOW

Hibiscus ★

17 Corve Street, Ludlow, SY8 1DA (01584 872325).
Lunch served 12.15-1.30pm Wed-Sat. **Dinner**
served 7-10pm Tue-Sat. **Set lunch** £19.50
2 courses, £25 3 courses. **Set dinner** £35 3 courses,
£42.50 7 courses, £50 9 courses. **Credit** MC, V.

Shaun Hill may be king of Ludlow but there's a
pretender to the throne – young Frenchman Claude
Bosi, who runs Hibiscus with wife Claire. This is an
extraordinary place – not in decor, though that's all
very tasteful with pale modern hues and warm oak

panelling, but in food. Gourmets will be in seventh heaven. Dishes may look deceptively simple – roast local asparagus scented with citrus perhaps or rack of veal with young carrot – but don't be fooled. Superb ingredients are treated with technical wizardry and incredible talent to create dishes that are exquisite. The three-course menu also includes appetisers and between-course nibbles but is so well designed that it's all delightfully manageable.

Koo

17 Old Street, Ludlow, SY8 1NU (01584 878462). **Lunch served** noon-2pm, **dinner served** 7-10pm Tue-Sat. **Set lunch** £10.95 2 courses. **Set dinner** (Tue, Wed) £16.95 3 courses; (Thur-Sat) £22.50 4 courses. **Credit** MC, V.

A Japanese restaurant in Ludlow? It seems rather odd in this historic setting, but it's a welcome arrival all the same. With decent prices and surprisingly good food on the set menus, this elegant little place seems to be doing well. Sushi and sashimi are spot on and there are other tempting treats when you're in the mood for clean-tasting, healthy oriental food full of lively flavours. Try the delicious yaki sakana (poached sea bass with saké and ginger) or the equally tasty buta tomato sakana – stir-fried pork with spinach and tomatoes. If you want to up the heat factor, gyu karani – spicy stir-fried beef with peppers and chilli – is a must. Dead friendly too – you may even get a visit from the resident cat and dog.

Les Marches

Overton Grange Hotel, Old Hereford Road, Ludlow, SY8 4AD (01584 873500/www.overtongrange hotel.co.uk). **Dinner served** 7-9pm daily. **Main courses** £18. **Set dinner** £35 3 courses. **Credit** MC, V.

Overton Grange didn't give up and die when its star chef Claude Bosi moved into Ludlow town centre to set up his own place. The genteel hotel dusted itself down and got on with the business of providing quality fare in its Les Marches restaurant. It's still

very French (thanks to chef Olivier Bossut) and beautifully done. The Edwardian panelled dining room is a formal place and everything is just so, from the repertoire of seasonal, innovative dishes to the sparkling table settings. And they're so proud of their wine list here that they'll even show you around the cellar if you're interested. The hotel is a couple of miles outside Ludlow and although the building isn't much to write home about architecturally, the grounds are impressive.

The Merchant House ★

62 Lower Corve Street, Ludlow, SY8 1DU (01584 85438/www.merchanthouse.co.uk). **Lunch served** 12.30-2pm Fri, Sat. **Dinner served** 7-9pm Tue-Sat. **Set meal** £33 3 courses. **Credit** MC, V.

Its legendary status hasn't given the Merchant House any airs and graces; it remains down-to-earth, straightforward and utterly reliable. This is quite simply one of the top restaurants around. It's only small and its understated interior is scarcely sumptuous (the chairs win no points for comfort), but this is the place to be for perfect food. Shaun Hill's cooking is exemplary and he manages the rare feat of making it all appear effortless. His light hand is brilliant with fish – monkfish with mustard and cucumber sauce, for instance, is a classic. But the man can do no wrong with meat and vegetarian dishes either (the latter should be requested in advance). A landmark venue.

Mr Underhills ★

Dinham Weir, Ludlow, SY8 1EH (01584 874431/ www.mr-underhills.co.uk). **Dinner served** 7.30-8.15pm Mon, Wed-Sun. **Set meals** £32 3 courses, £36 4 courses. **Credit** MC, V.

Of all the really great places to eat in Ludlow, Mr Underhills enjoys the best position. It sits below the castle walls by the crashing waters of the weir, a wonderful spot for wildlife as well as fabulous food. A pretty garden makes the most of the surroundings but the serious eating is done inside,

The Merchant House

where chef-patron Chris Bradley's set menu offers a 'wow' factor with every course. All the dishes are packed with fantastic flavours, whether it's a stunning risotto primavera or a paradisical coffee parfait. The wine list is also wonderful thanks to the expert choices of Judy Bradley, who also oversees the front of house proceedings.

MAESBURY MARSH

Warehouse Restaurant at the Navigation Inn
Maesbury Marsh, SY10 8JB (01691 672958). **Lunch served** *bistro* noon-2pm Wed-Sat, *restaurant* noon-2pm Sun. **Dinner served** 7-9pm Wed-Sat. **Set lunch** (Sun) £11.95 2 courses, £13.95 3 courses. **Set dinner** (Wed-Fri) £17.95 2 courses, £19.95 3 courses; (Sat) £19.95 3 courses. **Credit** AmEx, MC, V.
The Navigation Inn dates back to 1824 and the Warehouse restaurant building is even older. Inside, as you might expect, all is oak beams and trad decor, with seating provided by 18th-century church choir stalls and canal boat decorations adding to the waterside feel. Both food and drink are more than up to the mark. There are real ales, good ciders and wines from the renowned Tanner's in Shrewsbury. Dishes in the popular Warehouse restaurant are good, solid quality; excellent ingredients include local organic meat. A melting and succulent beef

Wellington and duck with caramelised apricots were both winners. Chef-owner Eric Bruce used to head the kitchen team at the prestigious Belfry golf venue so there's a good culinary pedigree in the kitchen.

SHREWSBURY

Drapers Restaurant & Brasserie
Drapers Hall, 10 St Mary's Place, Shrewsbury, SY1 1DZ (01743 344679). **Lunch served** 10.30am-3pm, **dinner served** 7-9.30pm Mon-Sat. **Meals served** noon-9.30pm Sun. **Main courses** £12.50-£20. **Set meals** (Mon-Fri, Sun; lunch Sat) £12.50 2 courses, £14.50 3 courses. **Credit** AmEx, DC, MC, V.
Dining at Drapers Hall is as grand as it sounds. The building is elegantly Elizabethan and surrounded by equally impressive historic buildings. It's all very baronial in the restaurant, with crisply draped tables, enormous chandeliers and fireplaces that a family of four could live in. Not that it's stuffily formal; there may be jazz playing in the background, the staff are pleasant and the food is upmarket but not too fussy. Fillet of red mullet comes with fresh lobster and Mediterranean vegetables, while escalope of salmon has crayfish and Cognac sauce. For more relaxed eating, try the Yellow Room (the lounge bar where brasserie dishes are on offer). The menu is created by head chef Nigel Huxley, a bit of a local star whose credits include the Savoy.

Staffordshire

ALREWAS

The Old Boat
Kings Bromley Road, Alrewas, DE13 7DB (01283 791468/www.theoldboat.co.uk). **Lunch served** noon-2.30pm Tue-Sun. **Dinner served** 6.30-9.30pm Tue-Sat. **Main courses** £7.95-£19.95. **Credit** AmEx, MC, V.
The canalside location is a real boon for this cosy, thoroughly pubby place. But even if the weather means that sitting outside isn't an option, it's still no hardship to eat in the comfortable restaurant or bar – especially when the food on offer is as good as it is here. Seafood is a particular treat and kept sensibly simple; whole sea bass with lemon oil or monkfish with noodles and lime being two very successful examples. Otherwise, it's good standard basics – shank of lamb with mustard mash and redcurrant gravy or seared duck breast, here served with plum mash and port wine gravy. Attractive prices – £10 for mains on the whole – only add to the satisfaction.

LICHFIELD

Chandlers Grande Brasserie
Corn Exchange Building, Conduit Street, Lichfield, WS13 6JU (01543 416688/www.chandlersrestaurant.co.uk). **Lunch served** noon-2pm, **dinner served** 6-10pm daily. **Main courses** £8.50-£12.95. **Set lunch** £5.75 1 course, £8.75 2 courses. **Set dinner** £11.75 2 courses, £15 3 courses. **Credit** AmEx, MC, V.
Its home may be an impressive listed building but Chandlers is no stuffy, formal eaterie. The galleried interior is stylish, the service is matey and the atmosphere is buzzing. A long list offers food that's equally lively; the modern European and British dishes include lots of fresh fish and seafood. The plat du jour menus are good deals, but going à la carte won't break the bank, with starters about £4 and mains about £9. Expect hearty brasserie flavours such as rabbit confit; white bean, sausage and grain mustard casserole, or linguine with crayfish, pimento and rose harissa.

Warwickshire

BISHOP'S TACHBROOK

Mallory Court ★

*Harbury Lane, Bishop's Tachbrook, CV33 9QB
(01926 330214/www.mallory.co.uk).* **Lunch served**
noon-1.45pm, **dinner served** 7-9.30pm daily. **Main
courses** £16-£26. **Set lunch** (Mon-Sat) £19.50
2 courses, £25 3 courses; (Sun) £29.50 3 courses. **Set
dinner** £37.50 3 courses. **Credit** AmEx, DC, MC, V.
Save up all your pocket money for a trip to Mallory
Court, a country house hotel in rural splendour just
outside Leamington. If you want all-you-can-eat-for-
a-fiver places, go elsewhere. Michelin-starred chef
Simon Haigh provides food that is perfect for this
elegant-yet-easy venue. The excellence of the
ingredients is beyond doubt and allowed to shine
through. Canon of lamb with confit tomato and a red
wine jus is top notch, as is grilled Dover sole with
parsley butter. There's a stunning terrace where you
can lunch when the weather's warm. Have no
worries about an intimidating atmosphere – staff
are warm and genuinely friendly.

GREAT WOLFORD

Fox & Hounds Inn

Great Wolford, CV36 5NQ (01608 674220).
Lunch served noon-2pm Tue-Sat; noon-2.30pm
Sun. **Dinner served** 7-9pm Tue-Sat. **Main courses**
£9.50-£13.50. **Credit** MC, V.
A pair of beady foxy eyes watch your approach to
this wisteria-clad 16th-century pub. The bar, with
nearly 200 bottles of alphabetically arranged malt
whiskies, is a lovely place to linger. Modern British
dishes made with quality produce are well executed
and beautifully presented. Creamy chicken liver
parfait came with crisp toasted brioche and
contrasted well with a citrus sauce. The delicately
smoked haddock was grilled to perfection, retaining
its moist, yielding texture. It was paired with sautéed
potatoes and a sassy bacon and chorizo combo.
Puddings, such as bread and butter or sticky toffee
(both £4.25), are belt looseners. Booking is essential.

HENLEY-IN-ARDEN

Edmunds ★

*64 High Street, Henley-in-Arden, B95 5BX (01564
795666).* **Lunch served** noon-2pm Tue-Fri. **Dinner
served** 7-9.45pm Tue-Sat. **Set lunch** £10 2 courses,
£15 3 courses, £24.50 3 courses. **Set dinner** £24.50
3 courses. **Credit** MC, V.
One of the prettiest villages around Birmingham's
commuter belt, Henley-in-Arden isn't short of places
to eat. But Edmunds easily, unobtrusively stands

out from the crowd. Chef-owner Andy Waters now
has a Michelin star, but anyone expecting an august
atmosphere will be nicely surprised. In a fine old
house with low beams, the dining room feels a bit
like a cosy country pub; the young staff are
charmingly attentive and welcoming. It's also quite
exceptional value. A starter of feuilletage of girolles
and pleurottes with an asparagus quenelle, from the
main menu, combined richly flavoured mushrooms
with deliciously crisp pastry; chump of lamb with
mint couscous was a variation on an English roast.
Desserts kept up the enjoyment level: a strawberry
shortbread with rosewater cream arrived with a
superb sorbet. The wine list shows the same
combination of generosity and savvy as the menu.

ILMINGTON

Howard Arms

*Lower Green, Ilmington, CV36 4LT (01608 682226/
www.howardarms.com).* **Lunch served** noon-2pm
Mon-Sat; noon-2.30pm Sun. **Dinner served** 7-9pm
Mon-Thur; 7-9.30pm Fri, Sat; 6.30-8.30pm Sun. **Main
courses** £9-£15. **Set lunch** £17.50 3 courses Sun.
Credit MC, V.
The vibe is definitely pub at the Howard Arms –
although there's a separate dining room, you choose
from the chalked-up menu and order from the bar.
The weekly changing menu incorporates seasonal
produce and dishes are imaginative but not
overfussy: a sauté of lambs' kidneys, spinach, grain
mustard and cream to start; a prime lamb steak with
roast garlic sauce and aubergine purée, or char-
grilled tuna, garlic and thyme potato cake with
anchovy cream sauce to follow. There's a good
choice of cask ales and keg beers, including
Everard's Tiger and North Cotswold Brewery's
Genesis. If you've overdone it, repair to one of the
cosy bedrooms upstairs (doubles £74-£84), look out
on to the village green and dream of moving to the
country (children aren't encouraged after 7.30pm).

KENILWORTH

Restaurant Bosquet

*97A Warwick Road, Kenilworth, CV8 1HP (01926
852463).* **Dinner served** 7-9.30pm Tue-Sat. **Main
courses** £17-£18.50. **Set dinner** £27.50 3 courses.
Credit AmEx, MC, V.
One of the smaller venues on Kenilworth's gourmet
row, the Bosquet has a snug, house-sized dining
room decorated in traditional style with just a few
modern touches. Chef-owner Bernard Lignier and
his wife Jane present refined modern French cuisine
at fairly refined prices. Some of the French

restaurant niceties are kept up, although tiny pizza appetisers didn't seem all that French. The highlight was a starter of mousse of roquefort with quince and sweet wine. Mains tended to be very rich, and not so impressive: saddle of lamb en croute with black pudding and sage sauce was overpowering, while a fillet of beef with mustard sauce lacked flavour. Desserts are, again, rich – as in an over-egged crème brûlée. The wine list offers a substantial French range. One gripe – very long gaps between courses.

Simpson's ★
101-103 Warwick Road, Kenilworth, CV8 1HL (01926 864567/www.simpsonsrestaurant.co.uk). **Lunch served** 12.30-1.45pm, **dinner served** 7-9.30pm Tue-Sat. **Main courses** £9.95-£13.25. **Set meal** £30 3 courses, £45 5 courses. **Credit** AmEx, DC, MC, V.
Contrasting with its less-than-glamorous location on the traffic-heavy Warwick Road, Simpson's is an arresting sight – perfectly manicured miniature trees outside, blonde wood and crisp linen tablecloths inside. House specialities include a starting torte of Salcombe crab, Loch Fyne smoked salmon and creamed guacamole, followed by honey-glazed shank of lamb with Swiss chard and chickpea gremolata. Andreas Antona's place is deservedly Michelin-starred, and accordingly pricey – but the three-course £30 deal represents real value.

LAPWORTH

The Boot Inn ★
Old Warwick Road, Lapworth, B94 6JU (01564 782464/www.thebootatlapworth.co.uk). **Open** noon-11pm Mon-Sat; noon-10.30pm Sun. **Lunch served** noon-2pm, **dinner served** noon-10.30pm daily. **Main courses** £8.95-£16.95. **Credit** AmEx, MC, V.

The Boot at Lapworth was one of the original gastro-pubs around these parts and as famous for the flash motors in the car park as it was for great food. It's as successful today as always and is now one of a chain of pubs owned by Paul Salisbury. All feature the same winning formula – fantastically stylish interiors (great blends of new and old), young, gorgeous staff and exciting, clever menus. There's a deceptive, tantalising simplicity and sense of innovation about such dishes as seared Moroccan spiced salmon with skordalia and tomato onion salad or gammon pavé with mash, parsley sauce and truffle oil. If you enjoy the Boot, try the Crabmill at Preston Bagot (01926 843342) – trendy yet homely. Alternatively, head to the Orange Tree at Chadwick End (01564 785364) – especially if you're a pizza/pasta fan.

LEAMINGTON SPA

King Baba ★
58 Bath Street, Leamington Spa, CV31 3AE (01926 888869). **Food served** 6pm-midnight Tue-Thur, Sun; 6pm-2.30am Fri-Sat. **Main courses** £4.75-£6.50. **Credit** AmEx, MC, V.
Leamington is close enough to Birmingham to claim a share of the second city's glory as home of the balti dish. If you've never had the pleasure, prepare for a sizzling iron skillet of fresh-cooked, mix-and-match ingredients. For example, you might go for a balti chicken, sag and chana, cooked madras-hot with sizzling tomatoes and onions, or a coconutty lamb korma balti, all mopped up with a large, sweet, buttery tandoori nan. Balti options are all around £6, plus rice and bread and side dishes. King Baba's local reputation is second to none among the seven or eight old-town options on Bath Street alone. Staff are smart, helpful, child-doting and chatty.

The Bell. *See p236.*

Love's ★

*15 Dormer Place, Leamington Spa, CV32 5AA
(01926 315522)*. **Lunch served** noon-2pm,
dinner served 7-9.30pm Tue-Sat. **Set lunch**
(menu rapide) £13.50 3 courses. **Set dinner** £23.50
2 courses, £27.50 3 courses; £25 3 courses Tue-Thur;
£37.50 6 courses. **Credit** MC, V.

After studying under the Roux brothers and Alain
Ducasse in Paris, local chef Steve Love set up shop
independently at the end of 2001. His menus offer
notably intricate dishes. A starter of beetroot
risotto with goat's cheese crêpinette and garlic
broth had a smooth, satisfying mix of flavours. To
follow, an assiette de viandes was a bravura
demonstration of Love's skill with meats, featuring
a pork and black pudding crêpinette, pan-fried pork
fillet and braised shoulder of lamb. Dessert was
another opulent combination, a 'trio of lemon' with
glazed tartlet, a sorbet and a deliciously fresh
mousse. Almost as memorable were the many
complementary niceties that punctuated a leisurely
meal: appetisers of braised lentils, Toulouse
sausages and cumin broth, a black cherry sorbet
between firsts and mains, a 'pre-dessert' of rhubarb
jelly with cinnamon cream. Prices, moreover,
remain extremely reasonable, and there's an
intelligently chosen wine list to match.

PRIORS HARDWICK

The Butcher's Arms

*Church End, Priors Hardwick, CV47 7SN (01327
260504/www.thebutchersarms.com)*. **Lunch served**
noon-2pm Mon-Fri; noon-3pm Sun. **Dinner served**
7-9.30pm Mon-Sat. **Main courses** £12-£20. **Set
lunch** (Mon-Fri) £17 3 courses, (Sun) £26.50 3
courses. **Credit** AmEx, DC, MC, V.

This 14th-century inn has been in Portuguese hands
for the last 30 years. Aperitifs, served either in the
capacious garden or the cosy bar (replete with oak
beams, flagstone floor and inglenook fireplace), give
you a chance to peruse the menu before you're led
upstairs into the buzzing restaurant area. Ignore the
copper plates and chintzy furniture and instead
focus on starters of very fresh scampi meunière,
shellfish in brandy sauce or rich lobster soup. Meaty
mains such as perfectly tender roast saddle of
spring lamb and wild boar with sautéed porcini
mushrooms dominate, but there are own-made fish
cakes with a superb grain mustard sauce too. The
heavenly dessert trolley, laden down with
everything from bread and butter pudding to
caramelised oranges, is a sight to behold. The 200-
strong wine list ranges from house wines at £11.50
up to Chateau Petrus Grand Vin de Pomerol 1992
at £495. We plumped for owner Lino Pires's
favourite, a Ribamar 1994 Reserva Particular Paulo
de Silva (£18.25).

STRATFORD-UPON-AVON

Callands Restaurant

*13-14 Meer Street, Stratford-upon-Avon, CV37
6QB (01789 269304)*. **Lunch served** noon-2pm
Tue-Sun. **Dinner served** 6-9.30pm Tue-Sat.
Set lunch £5.95 2 courses, £7.95 3 courses.
Set dinner £19.95 2 courses, £23.95 3 courses
Credit AmEx, MC, V.

Set above the deli of the same name, the original
features of the 16th-century building, including the
wooden beams, are effectively combined with
contemporary bright colours. The menu is short and,
although eclectic, the dishes stop short of being over-
elaborate. The quality of the cooking is indisputably

high, likewise the standards of presentation – as in the excellent pheasant which comes roasted in its own juices with honey glazed parsnips, pickled red cabbage and game chips. A three-course deal even includes the priceless warm coconut and rum tart with mango ice-cream. Service is friendly and agreeably unhurried – let's not say slow.

Fox & Goose Inn

Armscote, off A3400 Stratford-upon-Avon, CV37 8DD (01608 682293/www.aboveaverage.co.uk). **Lunch served** noon-2.30pm, **dinner served** 7-9.30pm daily. **Main courses** £8.95-£14.95. **Credit** AmEx, MC, V.

The interior of the reinvented, renovated Fox & Goose is inviting and rather sumptuous – dark red walls and velvet cushions. The inventive food from the daily changing menu board is one of its major attractions. A warm salad starter of black pudding, bacon, chorizo, sausage and sesame works alchemical magic, likewise the pumpkin and chilli soup. Then on to seared razor clams and linguine and own-made cep mushroom and goat's cheese tagliatelle. The wine list is also first class, with champagne available by the glass. Beers include the pub's own Fox & Goose Bitter by Brakespeare. The self-described 'slightly eccentric' Cluedo-themed bedrooms are true to their name, but are nonetheless very luxurious. Diners can also sit out on the deck in the lovely garden (where barbecues are held during the summer).

Lamb's of Sheep Street

12 Sheep Street, Stratford-upon-Avon, CV37 6EF (01789 292554/www.lambsrestaurant.co.uk). **Lunch served** noon-1.45pm Mon-Sat; noon-3pm Sun. **Dinner served** 5-9.30pm Mon-Fri; 5-10pm Sat. **Main courses** £7.25-£15.95. **Set meals** (lunch, 5-7pm) £11.50 2 courses, £14 3 courses. **Credit** MC, V.

Olde-worlde is overplayed in Stratford, but Lamb's of Sheep Street – which really was here when the Bard was a boy – combines a fresh, modern feel with its ancient oak beams. The menu offers a bistro-style selection. One of the day's specials, seared tuna with spinach and shiitake mushrooms, was exceptional and a more traditional platter of devilled whitebait featured lots of juicy fish. Of mains, roast cod with chorizo cassoulet was a fine mix, but pork escalopes pan-fried with sage, Italian ham, spinach and mash wasn't quite so impressive. Desserts brought invention – panna cotta with an espresso poured over it. Our solitary grouch would be the practice of charging for absolutely everything (including chocolate truffles with coffee). Staff are young, bright and several notches above the norm.

Restaurant Margaux

6 Union Street, Stratford-upon-Avon, CV37 6QT (01789 269106/www.restaurantmargaux.co.uk). **Lunch served** noon-2pm, **dinner served** 6-10pm Tue-Sat. **Main courses** £11.95-£18. **Credit** AmEx, MC, V.

It's only right that in a town like Stratford-upon-Avon a restaurant should offer a sense of theatre – and that's the case at Restaurant Margaux. Owner Maggie is a one-woman floorshow with the energy of ten whirling dervishes. She knows when you want to be left alone. But if you're up for some banter, you've come to the right place. The food is great – as zippy and lively as the woman herself and with real quality behind those global mix-and-match flavours. Start with seared scallops with lemon, cinnamon and sauce vierge or roast red mullet with langoustines, herb salad and truffle vinaigrette. For mains there's Scottish beef fillet with oxtail dumpling or braised collar of pork with mustard sauce. It's a good-looking place too, user-friendly rustic with modern colours, and speedy enough in delivery to make a brilliant pre-theatre spot.

TANWORTH IN ARDEN

The Bell

The Green, Tanworth in Arden, B94 5AL (01564 742212). **Open** noon-3pm, 6-11pm Mon-Fri; noon-11pm Sat; noon-10.30pm Sun. **Lunch served** noon-2pm Mon-Sat; noon-3pm Sun. **Dinner served** 6.30-9pm Mon-Sat. **Main courses** £8.95-£13.95. **Credit** AmEx, MC, V.

New owners have given this elegant pub in a chocolate-box village a new lease of life. Kitted out with a trendy new interior (all brown leather), it's good-looking but very comfortable with it. Service is friendly to an almost back-slapping degree, while the food is a belt-busting, satisfying round-up of the usual suspects – Cumberland sausage and mash, lamb shank, pasta – with some surprises thrown in. It's pretty rare round these parts to see Arabic meze with Egyptian bread (three tasty dips and delicious, flaky flatbread). Ditto roast fillet of Nile perch or Moroccan chicken with raita and Arabic couscous. But they're here and they're great. Prices are very reasonable, especially given the quantities involved.

WARWICK

Findon's

7 Old Square, Warwick, CV34 4RA (01926 411755/ www.findons-restaurant.co.uk). **Dinner served** 6.30-9.30pm Mon-Sat. **Main courses** £12.95-£18.95. **Credit** MC, V.

Occupying an early Georgian townhouse and serving rich French-influenced food amid swish curtains and chandeliers, there's no denying the pedigree of the modern cooking at Findon's. Main courses might include pavé of new season lamb with a herb crust, light fresh pea and roasted shallot sauce. Or, if meat isn't your thing, then go for one of the imaginative vegetarian dishes, such as warm salad of goat's cheese, portobello mushrooms, rocket, basil and walnut pesto with spiced polenta cake. Prices are high at Findon's, but they reflect the standard of cooking. Note that only children over eight years old are welcome.

Worcestershire

BOURNHEATH

Nailers Arms
62 Doctors Hill, Bournheath, B61 9JE (01527 873045/www.thenailersarms.com). Bar **Lunch served** noon-3pm Mon-Sat; noon-4pm Sun. **Dinner served** 6-9pm Mon-Thur; 6-9.30pm Fri, Sat. *Restaurant* **Dinner served** 6-9pm Mon-Thur; 6-9.30pm Fri, Sat. **Main courses** £10.50-£15.50. **Credit** MC, V.

With its amazingly modern restaurant, this country pub in a chintzy little village near Bromsgrove makes its culinary aspirations perfectly plain. This is not your average chicken-in-a-basket sort of place – it's pub grub to the power of ten. Mussels may be Thai spiced, fillet steak may be coated in herb polenta and salmon dusted with cumin. It's designed to impress and it does, with skills that are up to the challenge of combining bright, contemporary flavours. Staff are friendly, if on the young side, and can be a little too relaxed and unhurried but this place deserves its growing gastro reputation.

BROMSGROVE

Grafton Manor
Grafton Lane, Bromsgrove, B61 7HA (01527 579007). **Lunch served** noon-1.30pm Mon-Fri, Sun. **Dinner served** 7.30-9.30pm Mon-Sat. **Set lunch** (Mon-Fri) £20.50 3 courses; (Sun) £18.50 3 courses. **Set dinner** £27.85 3 courses, £32.75 4 courses. **Credit** AmEx, DC, MC, V.

An impressive country seat with lovely grounds, Grafton Manor has 'wedding venue' written all over it. But on a weekend when it hasn't been pre-booked by lovestruck couples, try out the restaurant – especially if you feel like pushing the boat out. This is a special occasion place. Pre-dinner drinks are taken in a room decorated in suitable baronial style. Down in the cosier, yet still formal, dining room, the service is young and watchful and the food excellent. The chef Simon Morris (son of the owners) is an expert on Indian food but only touches of it turn up here. You're more likely to enjoy beautifully cooked roast leg of Worcestershire lamb, crisp-skinned succulent duck confit or the renowned Lord Grafton's whisky pudding. All menus are set, and there's a separate one for vegetarians.

CHADDESLEY CORBETT

Brockencote Hall
Chaddesley Corbett, DY10 4PY (01562 777876/www.brockencotehall.com). **Lunch served** noon-1.30pm Mon-Fri, Sun. **Dinner served** 7-9.30pm daily.

Main courses £19.50-£22.50. **Set lunch** (Mon-Fri) £13 2 courses, £17 3 courses; (Sun) £22.50 3 courses. **Set dinner** £27.50 3 courses incl coffee, £46.50 5 courses incl coffee. **Credit** AmEx, DC, MC, V.

Driving up the elegant, long drive to this superb country house hotel may make you wonder if you haven't been miraculously beamed over to France. The lovely building is very Gallic-looking and, quite appropriately, the owner is French. France also dominates the cuisine (courtesy of French chef Jerome Barbancon). This is serious cooking, concentrating on getting the best flavours out of good ingredients – a pressed terrine of Cornish lamb with scallions and red onion marmalade, or crépinette of beef blade with cabbage mash, or scallops with a medley of asparagus. Prices are largely what you'd expect in a place with 70 acres of grounds and a 300-year history, but the lunch menus are a steal.

CUTNALL GREEN

The Chequers
Kidderminster Road, Cutnall Green, WR9 0PJ (01299 851292). **Lunch served** noon-3pm daily. **Dinner served** 6-11pm Mon-Sat; 7-10.30pm Sun. **Main courses** £10-£12. **Credit** MC, V.

This big roadside pub may seem rather out of the way in this tiny village but the food is more than worth the journey. And so it should be, for the chef-patron is Roger Narbett, who is also chef to the England football team. In the spacious, vibrantly coloured interior (a great blend of pale ancient beams and modern touches), expect excellent and hearty gastropub fare; from ribeye steaks to delicious pastas (rotolo packed with spinach and pine nuts was particularly memorable). The Narbetts also run the Bell and Cross at Clent (01562 730319), another top pub in more typical olde worlde surroundings.

GREAT MALVERN

La Boucherie
23 Abbey Road, Great Malvern, WR14 3ES (01684 562676). **Dinner served** 6-9pm Fri, Sat. **Set dinner** £21 2 courses, £25.75 3 courses. **Credit** AmEx, MC, V.

Malvern is the most genteel of Worcestershire towns and well deserves the sort of relaxed, quality cooking that's available at La Boucherie. It's a small, ancient place next to the grand Abbey Hotel and was a butcher's shop in a previous life (La Boucherie sounds so much better than the Butcher's). The pretty interior, complete with stunning black-and-white tiled original floor, is a good backdrop for beautifully executed dishes (from chef-patron

La Boucherie.
See p237.

Andrew Gotting) attentively served. Try the sea bass fillet with ravioli of shiitake mushrooms and ginger, confit potato and oriental basil jus; or the rack of lamb with dauphinoise potato, confit shallots, white bean and rosemary jus. Booking is essential, and note the restricted opening times

OMBERSLEY

Venture In ★

Main Road, Ombersley, WR9 0EW (01905 620552). **Lunch served** noon-2pm Tue-Sun. **Dinner served** 7-9.30pm Tue-Sat. **Set lunch** (Tue-Sat) £16.95 2 courses, £19.95 3 courses; (Sun) £19.95 3 courses. **Set dinner** £30.50 3 courses. **Credit** MC, V.

If quaint old villages are your thing, Ombersley is a must-see. A lovely place close to Worcester, it has more than its fair share of places to eat but the black-and-white timbered Venture In is by far the best. Under chef-patron Toby Fletcher, the food is hale, hearty and totally delicious. Beware the trencherman portions – it's best not to eat the day you go to spare yourself the misery of having to leave anything on the plate. Big flavours feature in everything from roast breast of Gressingham duck with sweet pickled red cabbage and port and sage sauce to a mixed mushroom and asparagus risotto headily scented with truffle oil. Friendly service and reasonable prices complete the picture.

STOURBRIDGE

French Connection

3 Coventry Street, Stourbridge, DY8 1EP (01384 390940). **Brunch served** 9.30am-noon, **lunch served** noon-4pm Tue-Sat. **Dinner served**

7-9.30pm Wed-Sat. **Main courses** £10-£20. **Set lunch** £9.50 3 courses. **Set dinner** (7-7.45pm Wed, Thur) £9.95 3 courses. **Credit** AmEx, MC, V.

Bustling Stourbridge provides plenty of custom for this unpretentious French-style café. It's tucked away down a side street and regulars pile in to grab a cramped gingham-topped table under the whirring ceiling fans and get their culinary fix. This could be garlicky mussels (bib provided), the potage du jour, chunky country-style pâtés, pastas, salads, or more substantial meat or fishes dishes, much of which is supplied by the next-door deli. Though more of a lunchtime place, when it opens for dinner things move a little more upmarket. If the weather's fine you might like to sit outside at a pavement table. La vie en rose hits Stourbridge.

WORCESTER

Browns

24 Quay Street, WR1 2JJ (01905 26263). **Lunch served** noon-2.30pm Tue-Fri, Sun. **Dinner served** 7-9.45pm Tue-Sat. **Set lunch** £20.50 3 courses. **Set dinner** £38.50 4 courses. **Credit** AmEx, MC, V.

For a taste of the high life, smart, eternally elegant Browns cannot be beaten. A converted cornmill, its painted brick interior is a study in serene pastels and there is a beautiful view over the River Severn. Go for a greenery-fringed window table if possible, so you can gaze down on the swans as you eat. Dishes, such as confit leg with roast duck, or herb-crusted baked cod, may be described as modern British but they tend towards the classic and are confidently put together. Staff are slick, attentive and utterly professional. Take your best credit card and try not to think about the bill.

North West

North West

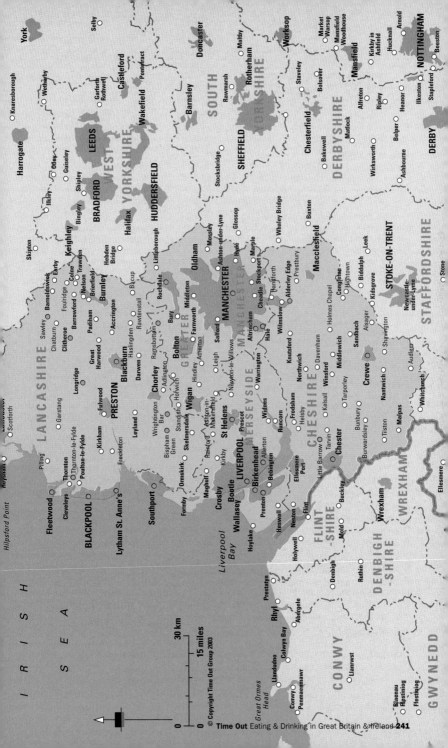

Cheshire

ALDERLEY EDGE

The Wizzard
Macclesfield Road, Alderley Edge, SK10 4UB
(01625 584000). **Lunch served** noon-2pm Tue-Sun.
Dinner served 7-9.30pm Tue-Sat. **Main courses**
£9-£16. **Set lunch** (Tue-Sat) £13.50 2 courses,
£16.50 3 courses; (Sun) £12.95 1 course, £15.95
2 courses, £18.95 3 courses. **Credit** AmEx, MC, V.
The Wizzard's 'modern British food in a traditional
setting' is exactly that. Simple lunches are deservedly
popular, with dishes such as salad of smoked duck,
spinach, celery and grapes. But come at night, when
the menu is more daring. Starters include grilled black
pudding on mashed potato with poached egg. Many
can be super-sized into mains, but why restrict
yourself when the second course might be grilled fillet
of baby halibut on asparagus or devilishly succulent
char-grilled fillet steak with truffled mash and ceps?
Surroundings are warm, relaxed and kick-your-shoes-
off comfortable. Wines are well priced too.

ALTRINCHAM

Juniper
21 The Downs, Altrincham, WA14 2QD (0161 929
4008). **Lunch served** noon-2.15pm Tue-Fri. **Dinner**
served 7-9.30pm Tue-Sat. **Main courses** £19-£23.
Set lunch £17.50 2 courses, £21.50 3 courses. **Set**
dinner £32.50 3 courses. **Credit** AmEx, MC, V.
Imaginative, sparky and occasionally downright
batty cooking ensures Juniper's place among the very
best eating experiences in the North. But be prepared
to be challenged and delighted in equal measure.
There's no doubt that Juniper deserves its reputation
as a top-flight gastronomic restaurant, but it manages
to inject excitement with unusual sauces (cod with
liquorice sauce or scallops with fruitcake sauce) and
out-there combinations of flavours. Hidden among the
hoopla are some memorable tastes: for example,
saddle of rabbit fillet with assiette of smoked salmon
mayonnaise, smoked mackerel glaze, globe artichoke,
carrot julienne, hazel-nuts, black olive tile, lemon,
sautéed scallop and courgette lasagne? (That's one
course, by the way, not a banquet.) Wines are pricey,
but the list is long and there's a comprehensive
selection of half bottles.

BIRKENHEAD

Capitol
24 Argyle Street, Birkenhead, CH41 6AE (0151 647
9212/www.capitol-restaurant.co.uk). **Lunch served**
11.30am-2pm Mon-Fri. **Dinner served** 6-11.30pm
Mon-Sat; 4-11pm Sun. **Main courses** £7-£13. **Set**

lunch £7.95 3 courses. **Set dinner** £16.95 7 courses;
(6-7pm Mon-Thur, 4-7pm Sun) £11.95 5 courses.
Credit AmEx, DC, MC, V.
Easily the best Chinese restaurant across the water,
Steve Tam's place is popular with local connoisseurs
and visiting Chinese bigwigs – and has scooped up
several honours over nearly 40 years of business. At
first glance, the menu looks just a notch above classic
– black bean sauce, satay rolls, Szechuan ribs, cashew
nuts – but the preparation eschews gloop and gunge.
Light, healthy meals are standard here – as are fresh,
seasonal ingredients. There are some nice surprises,
like steamed pork bun, lobster tail, deep-fried lychee
and even pig's ear. If you know your Cantonese
cuisine, they can make it here – and if you don't, scan
the chef's choices and enjoy. Capitol is located in a
Grade II listed building on Hamilton Square, meaning
the surroundings are as elegant as the food.

Station Restaurant
24-8 Hamilton Street, Birkenhead, CH41 1AL
(0151 647 1047). **Open** 8am-4pm Mon, Tue; 8am-
9pm Wed; 8am-9.30pm Thur, Fri; 9am-9.30pm Sat.
Lunch served 11.30am-2.30pm Mon-Sat. **Dinner**
served 5.30-9pm Wed; 5.30-9.30pm Thur-Sat. **Main**
courses £8-£14.50. **Credit** AmEx, DC, MC, V.
Just two blocks from the ferry port and a block from
the elegance of Hamilton Square, this bright and
breezy diner caters to the needs of those who work in
the civic and legal buildings of the posher parts of
Birkenhead. At weekends it's quieter. On the menu
are fruity crab, mango and coriander fish cakes, Cajun
cod loin fresh enough to have got back into the
Mersey and salmon gravadlax on Irish soda bread;
starter-sized pastas and cakes keep the kids smiling.
Almost all the main dishes are a tenner or less and
the European house wines, served by the glass, are
great value. There's a shop on site selling organic
pastas, pulses, olive oils and breads.

CHESTER

Albion Inn ★
4 Park Street, Chester, CH1 1RN (01244 340345/
www.albioninnchester.co.uk). **Lunch served**
noon-2pm daily. **Dinner served** 5-8pm Mon-Fri;
6-8.30pm Sat; 7-8pm Sun. **Main courses** £3.50-
£6.70. **No credit cards**.
We were unlucky here, being turned away on our
first visit due to a party and arriving a second time
to find it was the cook's day off. Out of the only three
dishes on offer, a chicken and bacon stew set a
standard that friendly locals assured us is usual
(although it was microwaved to near boiling point).
It was hearty and delicious, and accompanied by
cabbage, carrots and creamy mash. The 'Trench

Rations' menu offers British fare: liver, bacon and onions in cider gravy; Staffordshire oatcakes; haggis, tatties and neeps; doorstep sandwiches. Union Jack bunting and ancient adverts decorate the busy pinky-red wallpaper. The little restaurant is bedecked with World War I memorabilia and the room is lit with candles and red-fringed lampshades. It's cosy and seems geared towards a generation nostalgic for the good old days when standards were standards. They are apparently 'family hostile'.

The Arkle ★

Chester Grosvenor Hotel, Eastgate, Chester, CH1 1LT (01244 324024 /www.chestergrosvenor.co.uk). **Lunch served** noon-2.30pm Tue-Sun. **Dinner served** 7-9.30pm Tue-Sat. **Set lunch** £30 3 courses. **Set dinner** £45 2 courses, £52 3 courses, £60 5 courses. **Credit** AmEx, MC, V.

This elegant hotel restaurant is a delight, and worth that coveted Michelin star. The horse-racing theme may suggest stuffy old gentlemen, but cool marble is warmed by richer mahogany tones and natural light filters through a skylight, enhancing an atmosphere that is sophisticated, modern and welcoming. A three-course meal is complemented by a selection of a dozen breads and rounded off with coffee and sweetmeats in the library lounge. Hits include hot tea-smoked salmon with puy lentils on warm tomato and onion, followed by roast monkfish and stuffed morels, and a selection of pork cuts served with glazed apple, grilled onion, and parsnip and cabbage purée. The rhubarb crumble soufflé served with rhubarb fool, sorbet and caramelised ginger is worth every second of its 20-minute cooking time.

Brasserie 10/16

10-16 Brookdale Place, Chester, CH1 3DY (01244 322288/www.brasserie1016.com). **Main courses** £6.95-£17.95. **Set meals** (noon-10pm Mon-Thur, Sun; noon-7pm Fri, Sat) £8.80 2 courses. **Credit** AmEx, DC, MC, V.

An unprepossessing exterior, busy roundabout and garish bingo hall next door hardly suggest Brasserie 10/16 would be the pleasurable eating experience it is. The calming interior ensures you leave your cares outside; wines served in large glasses helps too. Cream walls, light wood fittings and midnight blue oil burners gently lighting each table set the scene for indulgence. Upstairs you can lounge on sumptuous red sofas. Portions are large and highlights included a cool, light torte of juicy prawns in red Thai mayonnaise or succulent roast cod on onion mash with a deliciously peppery red jam. The dessert plate for two aroused envy from fellow diners. Miniature raspberry ripple cheesecake, brownie, sticky toffee pudding, white chocolate tart and ice-cream comprise this pudding paradise.

Tonic Bar & Grill

2 Abbey Green, Chester, CH1 2JA (01244 329932). **Lunch served** noon-3pm daily. **Dinner served** 6-10.30pm Mon-Sat; 6-10pm Sun. **Main courses** £7-£16. **Credit** MC, V.

The highlight here is the small deck out the back, surrounded by trees. Great food is served speedily inside and out, on quirky crockery. Down a little dark corridor you'll find an intimate restaurant, with browns, beiges and gentle lighting. Golden fish cakes or spinach and spring onion frittata with chunky chips and bright crunchy salad set the standard for a very reasonable lunch. In the evening prices and choice are upped. The daily changing menu centres around modern British fare. Puddings are the likes of apple and blackberry crumble.

CREWE

Les's Fish Bar ★

49-51 Victoria Street, Crewe, CW1 2JG (01270 257581). **Meals served** 11am-5pm Mon-Sat. **Main courses** £3.15-£3.60. **No credit cards.**

Large, bright, airy and spotlessly clean, this award-winning restaurant is decorated with brightly coloured tiles bearing fishy motifs, while Les's logo adorns the carpet. An air of bluff northern friendliness characterises the service and the trad fish and chips are distributed with zeal. Although the main focus is on cod and haddock, served with the skin off, there's also plaice, skate and rock, or a selection of dishes including fresh baked pies and steak puddings. A dinner of cod or haddock, chips, mushy peas, bread and butter and a pot of tea is just £5.05.

HALE

Amba

106-108 Ashley Road, Hale, WA14 2UN (0161 928 2343/www.amba.uk.com). **Lunch served** noon-2.30pm, **dinner served** 6-10.30pm, **tapas served** noon-6pm daily. **Main courses** £7.95-£14.95. **Tapas** £1.75-£3.95. **Set meals** (noon-5pm Sun, 6-7pm daily) £11.95 2 courses, £14.95 3 courses. **Credit** AmEx, MC, V.

A confident addition to this slice of Cheshire's ebullient restaurant scene, Amba is doing everything right. A comfortable lounge bar area draped in rich amber and earthy fabrics leads to a bright, unfussy dining room. The Mediterranean-leaning menu has a separate tapas section, though this seems rather tacked on, despite Amba initially being known as a tapas bar. Try feisty modern dishes such as pan-fried mozzarella cakes with aubergine or smoked haddock Welsh rarebit for starters, and teriyaki salmon tagliatelle or Mexican chicken with calf's liver for mains. Top of the desserts list is banana tarte tatin with Cheshire farmhouse ice-cream. It's worth a journey for this alone. Service is warm and chatty, if a bit haphazard.

LITTLE BARROW

The Foxcote Arms

Little Barrow, CH3 7JN (01244 301343/ www.thefoxcote.com). **Lunch served** noon-2.30pm, **dinner served** 6-10pm Tue-Sat. **Meals served** noon-4pm Sun. **Main courses** £11-£18. **Set meals** (6-7pm Tue-Thur) £12 2 courses, £15 3 courses. **Credit** MC, V.

More gastro than pub, and definitely more surf than turf, this unremarkable-looking roadside inn has been steadily hauling in praise from local diners and national press for its consistently deft treatment of fresh local fish. The interior is an awkward, rather soulless hotchpotch of pub fittings and restaurant ambitions. But hold your nerve, for the collection of blackboard menus hold a treasure trove of fabulous dishes. Fish with a twist is favourite. Eastern spices and crispy spring rolls may be combined with halibut; simpler treatments may include hunks of hake with horseradish mash, smoked salmon and a brie beurre blanc. There's a well chosen list of great, crisp white wines to accompany. Or red, should you dare ask for steak (which you can when the ribeye's this good).

PRENTON

Villa Jazz

7-9 Rose Mount, Oxton Village, Prenton, CH43 5SG (0151 653 7733/www.villajazz.co.uk). **Lunch served** noon-3.45pm Sun. **Dinner served** 5.30-10pm Mon-Sat; 5.30-9.30pm Sun. **Main courses** £12.95. **Set dinner** (5.30-6.45pm Wed-Sat) £9.95 2 courses, £14.45 3 courses;

(6.45-10pm Wed-Sat) £16.95 2 courses, £21.45 3 courses; (dinner Mon, Tue, Sun) beat the 24hr clock (eg £17.30 for 2 at 5.30pm). **Credit** AmEx, MC, V.

With plenty of stiff competition from several serious restaurants in upscale Oxton Village, Villa Jazz is funkier to look at and more fun to eat in than most. Chef Ged Smith's kitchen is eclectic, experimental and sometimes plain eccentric, ranging over cream of sweetcorn and chilli soup with a dash of coconut, through to Tuscan mushrooms on toast and a wonderful liver with lentils. Prize for top pudding goes to the unpromising-sounding tapioca with lemon curd. Sometimes the menu ideas, which change regularly, are a tad too wacky to be taken seriously (Rolf's kangaroo sausages with Vegemite gravy sounds like a student's last supper), but the sourcing is reliable. Given the extras of jazz musicians, a decent wine list and lively company, this is an attractive option in one of the posher parts of the Wirral.

Also in the area

Les's Fish Bar 172 Widnes Road, Widnes, WA8 6BL (0151 424 2444); **Les's Fish Bar** 15 Dingle Walk, Winsford, CW7 1BA (01606 556425); **Les's Fish Bar** 57 Bridge Street, Warrington, WA1 2QW (01925 444554); **Piccolino Knutsford** 95 King Street, Knutsford, WA16 6EQ (01565 751402).

Cumbria

AMBLESIDE

Drunken Duck Inn

Barngates, Ambleside, LA22 0NG (015394 36347/ www.drunkenduckinn.co.uk). **Lunch served** noon-2.30pm, **dinner served** 6-8.45pm daily. **Main courses** £9.95-£16.95. **Credit** AmEx, MC, V.

An unlikely mix of leather-clad bikers, tourists and ramblers mingles comfortably at this 400-year-old inn, and is catered to by friendly, if sometimes harried, staff. Welcoming oak settles, dark wood furniture and walls crammed with prints, paintings and local knick-knacks set the informal scene for supping local ales. The restaurant is divided between two spacious and homely rooms and serves robust, reasonably priced British meals. Desserts are star attractions – a hefty helping of orange and hazel-nut sponge pud, topped with marmalade ice-cream and lashed with whisky syrup is truly scrumptious. On our visit, the roast chicken was a tad dry but a mound of garlicky mashed spuds and meltingly soft caramelised red onions on the side made up for any shortcomings.

Glass House

Rydal Road, Ambleside, LA22 9AN (015394 32137). **Lunch served** noon-5pm daily. **Dinner served** 6.30-9.30pm Mon-Fri, Sun; 6.30-10pm Sat. **Main courses** £11.75-£27. **Set dinner** £15 2 courses, £18 3 courses. **Credit** MC. V.

Originally a fulling mill, then a saw mill, now this 15th-century glass-fronted grade II listed building caters for the tastes of 21st-century diners. The interior is open-plan, spread over four floors and features lots of oak beamwork. Open throughout the year, it's busiest at weekends when specials appear alongside the regularly changing carte. Lakeland confit duck leg with potato salad and chilli jam is a good starter; an alternative is the vegetarian-based house soup, perhaps roast cherry tomato. Local Herdwick braised lamb shank never leaves the menu, it's so popular. For dessert look out for Baileys bread and butter pudding with white chocolate. Belgian beer is supplied on draught and the flavoured vodkas will have you dancing like a Cossack in no time.

Lucy's on a Plate

Church Street, Ambleside, LA22 0BU (015394 31191). **Meals served** 10am-9pm daily. **Main courses** £9-£19. **Credit** MC, V.
It may not be Lucy in the sky with diamonds but a visit here is still a trip. Lucy Nicholson opened the deli in 1989, then seven years later the restaurant-cum-café, followed now with a conservatory and garden. Breakfast kicks off proceedings, followed by an all-day menu of snacks and light meals – notably crostini and DIY baguettes (plenty for veggies). While the dinner menu lists dishes with names like Jemima's hotlegs (duck confit), chilli fishy dishy (fish cakes with chilli dip) and, wait for it, thyme for Bambi (pan-fried venison with juniper and thyme gravy), the food is taken seriously and all dishes are carefully prepared on the premises. There's a long list of great traditional puds (no fancy names) to finish. If you love Lucy, then visit Lucy Four across the road (2 St Mary's Lane, 015394 34666) for tapas-style bites.

Rothay Manor

Rothay Bridge, Ambleside, LA22 0EH (015394 33605/www.rothaymanor.co.uk). **Lunch served** 12.30-2pm Mon-Sat; 12.45-1.30pm Sun. **Dinner served** 7.30-9pm daily. **Set lunch** £16 3 courses. **Set dinner** £30 3 courses, £34 5 courses. **Credit** AmEx, DC, MC, V.
Nostalgia and homeliness abound at the Nixons' elegant country house hotel. Dinner can be three or five courses – at only a few pounds extra most should opt for the latter, but they tend not to. The cooking is safely traditional, with just the tiniest nod towards modernity: lemon and coriander butter with asparagus; avocado, tomato and basil salsa with the sea bream and sea bass. Most dishes are a success, though the kitchen can over elaborate. Fight for a place in one of the comfortable lounges for the terrific afternoon teas. Unusually, it's a buffet with a selection of teas delivered beforehand. The choice of food, both savoury and sweet, is phenomenal and incredibly good value. After that, a five-course dinner might just be out of the question.

Zeffirelli's ★

Compston Road, Ambleside, LA22 9AD (015394 33845/www.zeffirellis.co.uk). **Meals served** 10am-9.30pm daily. **Main courses** £5.95-£7.85. **Credit** MC, V.
A useful complex that includes a daytime café, which at night becomes a restaurant serving the building's cinema. Though popcorn is at hand, cinema-goers can dine before the main feature, or on certain evenings watch an early performance before sitting down to a choice of vegetarian Italian-style dishes. These include pizzas – all with wholemeal flour bases, and with toppings like sun-blushed tomatoes, courgettes, black olives, cheddar and mozzarella – drizzled with rosemary-infused oil. Spinach and ricotta cannelloni, porcini mushroom ravioli, and tagliatelle with stilton and mushroom sauce are other options. For dessert, choose from soft frozen yoghurts, locally produced ices and great sundaes.

APPLETHWAITE

Underscar Manor

Applethwaite, nr Keswick, CA12 4PH (01768 775000). **Lunch served** noon-1pm, **dinner served** 7-8.30pm daily. **Main courses** £19-£21. **Set lunch** £28 3 courses. **Set dinner** £38 5 courses. **Credit** AmEx, MC, V.
The Italianate house overlooking Derwentwater has a very ritzy conservatory dining room that's all rich drapes, chandeliers, lacy cloths and French-style dining chairs. Smart dress for the menfolk is stipulated at dinner, when the menus include some complex creations. Scottish scampi in crispy batter with herb risotto, sweet and sour sauce and deep-fried cabbage is a typical starter; followed by herb-crusted roast rack of lamb with a lamb hot-pot gateau, beans in filo pastry, Puy lentil and red pepper gateau, roast garlic and a grain mustard sauce. For dessert, a hot individual rhubarb crumble tart comes with an orange sorbet and vanilla custard. The set lunch is good value, as is the wine list that's strong on champagne but has only token offerings from other areas.

BOWNESS-ON-WINDERMERE

Linthwaite House

Crook Road, Bowness-on-Windermere, LA23 3JA (015394 88600/www.linthwaite.com). **Lunch served** 12.30-1.30pm daily. **Dinner served** 7.15-9pm daily. **Main courses** (lunch Mon-Fri) £5.95-£14.95. **Set lunch** (Sun) £17.95 3 courses. **Set dinner** £42 4 courses. **Credit** AmEx, DC, MC, V.
Andy Nicholson's been the chef here for two years and his modern style of cooking is well-balanced and enjoyable. The warm, intimate, candlelit dining room with its polished mahogany tables is a fine setting for the dinner menu (canapés, four courses, coffee, petits fours). House-cured salmon, cucumber, crème fraîche, caviar, quail's egg, dill and shallot dressing is one choice from four to begin, with cauliflower soup as a set intermediate course. Again from four, the main could be Goosnargh duck with beetroot gratin, spinach, foie gras, apple compote, roast baby onions and a thyme sauce, with egg custard tart or fresh strawberries with strawberry ice-cream for dessert. Instead of, or in addition to, the latter, the all-British cheeses are outstanding.

Porthole Eating House

3 Ash Street, Bowness-on-Windermere, LA9 3EB (015394 42793/www.porthole.fsworld.co.uk). **Lunch served** noon-2pm Thur, Fri, Sun. **Dinner served** 6.30-10.30pm Mon, Wed-Sun. **Main courses** £11-£19. **Credit** AmEx, DC, MC, V.
Lakeland quaintness abounds at Gianni and Judy Berton's pretty 17th-century cottage down a narrow pedestrianised street in the town centre. For more than 30 years Gianni, originally from near Venice, has offered a menu of familiar Anglo-Italian classics tempered with a few from France. Spaghetti alla bolognese, chicken saltimbocca, veal escalope

viennoise and Dover sole meunière show the style, but there's also Thai chicken stir-fry and a few veggie options. Raspberry pavlova, tiramisu and the Porthole rum topf are among the desserts, which Judy prepares. She also bakes the bread. It's a friendly, family-run concern with an Italian-style rear patio that's ideal for summer dining.

CARTMEL

L'Enclume

Cavendish Street, Cartmel, LA11 6PZ (015395 36362/www.lenclume.co.uk). **Lunch served** noon-1.45pm, **dinner served** 7-9.30pm Tue-Sun. **Main courses** £18-£26. **Set lunch** £19.50 3 courses. **Set dinner** £65 8 courses, £90 8 courses incl wine, £90 16 courses. **Credit** AmEx, DC, MC, V.
Opened in 2002, this reworked village smithy, sited next to Cartmel Priory, has forged a new identity as a gastronomic French restaurant. Stone-flagged flooring, rough white walls and original features retained from its previous life provide a stylishly rustic backdrop for L'Enclume's ambitious menu and extensive wine selection. Innovative little numbers such as hot cherry soufflé, served drizzled with black pepper and rosemary tea, work wonders with an explosion of fruitily spiced bites. Prawns encased in retro-tasting, rather bland aspic didn't fare quite as well, and came with an underwhelming potato salad. Chef-patron Simon Rogan plays with other unusual combos too – black bream served on a bed of lamb's tongue combines intense flavours with the delicacy of fish. Service is on-the-ball and well in tune with the needs of L'Enclume's well-heeled customers.

Uplands

Haggs Lane, Cartmel, LA11 6HD (015395 36248/www.uplands.uk.com). **Lunch served** 12.30-1pm Fri-Sun. **Dinner served** 7.30-8pm Tue-Sun. **Set lunch** £16 3 courses. **Set dinner** £29.50 4 courses. **Credit** AmEx, MC, V.
You get wonderful views down to distant Morecambe Bay, though it's not just the location that's the draw here. After aperitifs in the homely lounge, the meal begins with a freshly baked loaf served on a board with a bread knife. Lunch in style on fresh dressed crab mayonnaise on an avocado salad with langoustines, or a tureen of tomato, apple and celery soup, then a choice of two main courses. These could be baked fillet of lemon sole with a cucumber, dill and lemon sauce or pan-fried venison medallions with a blackcurrant and juniper sauce. The accompanying vegetables, including grated beetroot with lime, and carrots with mint, deserve equal billing. Chocolate Grand Marnier mousse, sticky toffee date pudding or fresh figs in Pernod will round things off nicely.

COCKERMOUTH

Quince & Medlar ★

13 Castlegate, Cockermouth, CA13 9EU (01900 823579). **Dinner served** 7-9.30pm Tue-Sat. **Main courses** £11.65. **Credit** MC, V.

Long gone, thankfully, are the indigestible nut roasts of the earliest vegetarian restaurants. Standing next to the castle, this wood-panelled, intimate candlelit restaurant in a listed Georgian building is one of the new breed. Colin Le Voi offers a short menu that's full of interest. Starters could include baked Allerdale goat's cheese and rocket soufflé or French onion tart, while mains might take in spiced Lebanese pancakes or Thai lentil strudel, all served with a side plate of seasonal vegetables. For dessert there's iced apricot amaretti, lemon cheesecake with raspberry sauce or a hot pudding like date and pecan nut with toffee sauce. All wines are organic.

CROSTHWAITE

Punch Bowl Inn ★

Crosthwaite, LA8 8HR (015395 68237/www.punchbowl.fsnet.co.uk). **Lunch served** noon-2pm Tue-Sun. **Dinner served** 6-9pm Tue-Sat. **Main courses** £8.95-£14.75. **Set lunch** (Tue-Sat) £9.95 2 courses, £11.95 3 courses; (Sun) £13.95 2 courses, £15.95 3 courses. **Set dinner** (6-7pm) £15.95 2 courses, £17.95 3 courses. **Credit** MC, V.
Steven Doherty, former head chef at Le Gavroche in London, caused a bit of a stir when he upped sticks and settled in Cumbria. The dishes on offer in the low-ceilinged, beamed dining room reflect aspects of his classical training. The food may be haute when compared to the competition, but it isn't haughty, and prices are reasonable for the quality. A starter of smooth chicken liver parfait comes with warm button onions, sultanas, toasted pine kernels, damson balsamic glaze and brioche toast, while a main of roasted chump of Cumbrian Fell-bred lamb is sliced on grain mustard mash with a rich red wine, thyme and lamb sauce. Desserts like warm chocolate nemesis and glace amandine are exquisite.

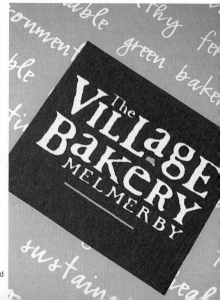

North West

GRASMERE

White Moss House

Rydal Water, Grasmere, LA22 9SE (015394 35295/ www.whitemoss.com). **Dinner served** 7.30-8pm Mon-Sat. **Set dinner** £34.50 5 courses. **Credit** MC, V.

Built in 1730 and occupied by Wordsworth's descendants until the 1930s, comforting White Moss is one of the English Lakelands' most favoured places to stay and dine. Peter and Sue Dixon may have been hosts in residence for more than 30 years but in the pretty dining room, with its polished mahogany tables, Peter's cooking style moves with the times. His five-course menus change daily, but there isn't a choice until dessert. A typical dinner will begin with fennel and apple soup, move on to Esthwaite Water wild trout on salad leaves, then to maize-fed Lakeland guinea fowl braised in cider on Puy lentils. Before a selection of British cheeses there'll be guardsman's pudding – sticky chocolate hazel-nut cream slice with chocolate sauce or mango sorbet.

MELMERBY

The Village Bakery ★

Melmerby, CA10 1HE (01768 881811). **Meals served** *Apr-Nov* 8.30am-5pm Mon-Sat; 9am-5pm Sun. *Dec-Mar* 8.30am-4.30pm Mon-Sat; 9am-4.30pm Sun. **Main courses** £4.50-£8. **Credit** MC, V.

This light, airy modern barn conversion is home to an upbeat café and an organically inspired shop. Arrays of bread, all baked in wood-fired ovens, are notable features on the restaurant menu – varieties include gluten-, wheat- and yeast-free. Hearty soups, sandwiches, pasties and fruit pies provide comforting and homely sustenance, and are popular dishes with lunching young families and hungry cyclists. With most of the attention lavished on

bread, the salad accompaniments were a neglected lot, let down by limp leaves and uninspiring vegetables. Despite gripes, eating here is a satisfying experience and the puddings are fab. Service becomes a trifle frenetic when the place gets busy, but waitresses cope well and their smiles don't slip for a second.

PENRITH

Scott's ★

34 Burrowgate, Sandgate, Penrith, CA11 7TA (01768 866961). **Lunch served** 11.30am-2pm, **dinner served** 4.30-8pm Tue-Sat. **Main courses** £3.50-£7.95. **No credit cards**.

Air-cooled, relaxing and licensed, this fifty-seater fish and chipper, decorated in magnolia with a dado rail and dark wood furniture, offers anything from chip butties to salmon steak. In Scott's what you see is what you get – simple, inexpensive, very tasty food and a bottle of vino, for anything from £8 to £12. Desserts are all £2.50 and range from ice-cream and ginger balls to banana splits, while the main courses include cod, plaice, haddock (predominantly), halibut, hake and skate wings. The haddock is fresh from Aberdeen and most of the cod comes from the Norwegian fleet. Both are generously portioned in the shop and served skinless and boned. Chips are thick and the own-made mushy peas have a touch of mint, making them 'posh'.

POOLEY BRIDGE

Sharrow Bay ★

Pooley Bridge, CA10 2LZ (01768 486301/ www.sharrow-bay.com). **Lunch served** 1-1.45pm, **dinner served** 8-8.45pm daily. Closed mid Dec-

North West

The Village Bakery

end Feb. **Set lunch** £38.25 4 courses incl coffee. **Set dinner** £49.25 5 courses incl coffee. **Credit** AmEx, MC, V.

Stone-fronted Sharrow Bay is one of Britain's best-known country house hotels and has breathtaking views across Ullswater. More Italian villa than Cumbrian in outward appearance, Sharrow Bay's interiors are seasoned with antiques, flower arrangements and expensive-looking upholstery. Sophisticated modern British cooking delivers the goods with style, but meals here don't come cheap and children under the age of 13 are discouraged. Even the steak and kidney pudding uses Scottish fillet steak and gets the roasted shallots and burgundy sauce treatment. Special (some may say precious) though the lunch and dinner menus are, locals looking for a treat swear by the superb afternoon teas – and with very good reason. Hot buttered toast, own-made biscuits, finger sandwiches and a selection of heavenly pâtisseries whisper tearoom indulgence with every last bite. An attentive yet unobtrusive service team pours out a classy cuppa with highly elegant restraint.

TIRRIL

Queens Head Inn

Tirril, CA10 2JF (01768 863219/www.queenshead inn.co.uk). **Lunch served** noon-2pm daily. **Dinner served** 6-9.30pm Mon-Sat; 7-9pm Sun. **Main courses** £8.50-£13.95. **Credit** MC, V.

Right in the village centre and dating from 1719, the whitewashed Queens Head is as traditional as they come, and features 2ft-thick walls that keep things cool in summer and hold the heat of the inglenook fireplace in winter. In 1999, landlord Chris Tomlinson opened the Tirril brewery on the premises and now offers three house real ales – John Bewsher's Best, Thomas Slee's Academy and Charles Gough's Old Faithful, each named after a local character. The food, whether a simple bar snack or a more substantial meal in the restaurant, is enjoyable, prepared where possible from locally sourced ingredients: brewer's pudding is a steamed suet pudding with steak and Tirril ale; braised Lakeland lamb comes with redcurrant gravy.

TROUTBECK

Queens Head

Townhead, Troutbeck, LA23 1PW (015394 32174/ www.queensheadhotel.com). **Lunch served** noon-2.30pm, **dinner served** 6.30-9pm daily. **Main courses** £7.25-£14.25. **Set dinner** £15.50 3 courses. **Credit** MC, V.

The views over to Garburn Pass add to the appeal of this ancient coaching inn. Inside are slate floors, low-beamed ceilings, a bar counter made from an Elizabethan four-poster bed and a roaring inglenook fire to ward off chills. Up on the first floor the Mayor's Parlour has a great carved oak chair and is the setting for the village's mayor-making ceremony,

as well as being the pub dining room. The menu lists a varied choice of imaginative-sounding modern dishes that sometimes lose the plot flavour-wise. A starter of pan-fried boudin of game layered with chillied red onion marmalade and edged with raspberry and soy dressing, or pork tenderloin wrapped in pancetta on black pudding and apricot mash with Calvados jus, are typical.

ULVERSTON

Bay Horse

Canal Foot, Ulverston, LA12 9EL (01229 583972/ www.furness.co.uk/bayhorse). **Lunch served** noon-1.30pm Tue-Sun. **Dinner served** 7.30pm for 8pm daily. **Main courses** £22.50-£23.50. **Set lunch** £17.95 3 courses. **Set dinner** £27.50 3 courses. **Credit** AmEx, MC, V.

From Ulverston, follow signs for Canal Foot to find this old pub with an intimate conservatory dining room overlooking the Leven estuary. Chef Robert Lyons offers a short, well-balanced menu of dishes that taste as good as they read. Among the starters are local brown shrimp and avocado salad with lemon and tarragon mayonnaise; or chicken, York ham and apricot terrine with salad leaves and Cumberland sauce. Mains range from lightly poached natural smoked haddock fillet with leeks, prawns and water chestnuts in a white wine and herb cream sauce, to pan-fried Barbary duck breast with grilled pancetta and caramelised red onions. Profiteroles filled with banana cream and served with hot chocolate sauce or strawberries poached with green peppercorns, Cointreau and fresh mint are among the moreish desserts.

WATERMILLOCK

Rampsbeck Country House Hotel ★

Watermillock, CA11 0LP (01768 486442). **Lunch served** noon-2pm daily by appointment only. **Dinner served** 7-8.30pm daily. **Set lunch** £26 3 courses. **Set dinner** £36 3 courses, £42.50 4 courses incl coffee. **Credit** MC, V.

Tom and Marion Gibb's 18th-century country house has 18 acres of grounds on Ullswater. The candlelit dining room commands excellent lake views and Andrew McGeorge offers superb four-course dinner menus. There's pan-fried red mullet with baby fennel, tomato, olives and fennel cream or roast quail lasagne with wild mushrooms and fried quails' eggs to begin. Next a soup, either jerusalem artichoke or fresh pea with smoked bacon and foie gras. Then a main, perhaps roast beef fillet with veal sweetbreads wrapped in Cumbrian air-dried ham with seared foie gras and Madeira sauce, or braised organic pig's cheek with roast root vegetables and truffled potatoes. For dessert, hot prune and Armagnac pudding with prune and Armagnac ice-cream is to-die-for. Further pluses are light lunches and terrific afternoon teas in the bar or on the terrace.

WINDERMERE

Gilpin Lodge ★

*Crook Road, Windermere, LA23 3NE (015394
88818/www.gilpinlodge.com).* **Coffee served** 9am-
noon, **lunch served** noon-2.30pm, **tea served**
3-5.30pm, **dinner served** 7-9.15pm daily.
Main courses (lunch) £4.75-£8. **Set lunch** £14.95
2 courses, £19.50 3 courses. **Set dinner** £38.50
5 courses. **Credit** AmEx, DC, MC, V.
Built in 1901, the lodge was originally a private
home and retains its cosy air of comfort and
tranquillity. There are several small, beautifully
appointed dining rooms, including a bright
conservatory, all imbued with quiet, formal
elegance. Mark Jordan is the new head chef and he
brings a touch of urbane sophistication to the usual
Lakeland five-course dinner menu. A spring menu
delivered ravioli of north coast crab with wilted
spinach and parsnip broth, followed by a cappuccino
of red mullet with lobster oil. Then came lemon and
thyme sorbet and, for the main course, roasted
chump of Holker Hall lamb with boulangère
potatoes and a roast pepper sauce. For dessert,
raspberry pavlova with raspberry sorbet typifies the
studied simplicity of the cooking. Coffee and petits
fours are served in the lounges, and are extra. Also
worth sampling is their afternoon tea.

Holbeck Ghyll ★

*Holbeck Lane, Windermere, LA23 1LU (015394
32375/www.holbeckghyll.com).* **Lunch served**
noon-2pm, **dinner served** 7-9.30pm daily.
Set lunch £25 4 courses. **Set dinner** £42.50
6 courses. **Credit** AmEx, DC, MC, V.
Once owned by Lord Lonsdale, the 'Yellow Earl', this
19th-century former hunting lodge commands a
majestic view over Lake Windermere. Sharing the
memorable scenery are the impressive oak-panelled
dining room and terrace restaurant. The cooking
here is very accomplished, and the style modern
British, with French influences. The daily-changing
menu typically includes an amuse-bouche such
as watercress velouté with poached quail's egg,
then roasted scallops with celeriac and truffle, and
a main course of breast of guinea fowl with pommes
purées and crisp pancetta. Date pudding with vanilla
ice-cream and caramel sauce is the description of
that Lakeland favourite – sticky toffee pudding.
There are some good vintages and a decent number
of half bottles, but not many bargains on the varied
wine list. Children over the age of eight years
old are welcome.

Jerichos ★

*Birch Street, Windermere, LA23 1EG (015394
42522).* **Dinner served** 6.45-9.30pm Tue-Sun.
Main courses £13.50-£16.95. **Credit** MC, V.
When head chef Chris Blaydes left Miller Howe (*see
below*) following John Tovey's retirement five years
ago, he moved into the town centre and converted
a local chippie into an upmarket little restaurant,
which he now runs with his wife, Jo. The short,

imaginative menu lists a selection of mouth-
watering dishes that live up to all expectations.
Crème fraîche and toasted pine kernels add even
more interest to cream of parsnip, cumin and celeriac
soup, while ragoût of chicken breast comes with wild
mushroom and tarragon glazed noodles, buttered
spinach, roast plum tomatoes and a red wine sauce.
Finally, for dessert, twice-baked chocolate fudge
cake with orange sauce and home-made ice-cream
should set the seal on a truly enjoyable experience.
Note that the under-12s are not encouraged.

Miller Howe ★

*Rayrigg Road, Windermere, LA23 1EY (015394
42536/www.millerhowe.com).* **Lunch served**
12.30-2pm, **dinner served** 8pm daily. **Set lunch**
(Mon-Sat) £17.50 3 courses. (Sun) £19.95 4 courses.
Set dinner £39.50 6 courses. **Service** 10%.
Credit AmEx, MC, V.
John Tovey's creation high above Lake Windermere
continues to be a major draw, even though he has
retired to South Africa. Now owned by former
newspaper editor Charles Garside (Tovey remains
a consultant), the hotel has been lovingly
refurbished throughout yet retains touches of its
former camp eccentricity. Lunches have been
introduced (to which children are welcome), but
dinner is still the main event – one sitting and the
lights are dimmed. The six-course menu is as
inventive as ever, so be prepared for unusual
combinations. A spring dinner featured smoked
duck breast with cassoulet of haricot beans and
beetroot jus; mackerel fillet with rhubarb and
vegetable escabeche; strawberry and pink
champagne sorbet; loin of venison with candied red
cabbage; and, finally, sticky toffee pudding. The
New World is well represented on the wine list.

Samling

*Ambleside Road, Windermere, LA23 1LR (015394
31922/www.thesamling.com).* **Lunch served** Sun
by appointment only. **Dinner served** daily by
appointment only. **Set lunch** £27.50 3 courses
Sun. **Set dinner** £45 4 courses, £60 9 courses.
Credit AmEx, MC, V.
Exclusive and very chic, this all-suite hotel (sister
establishment to Seaham Hall, *see p272*) stands up
a very steep drive in 67 acres overlooking Lake
Windermere. There's no bar or reception, but
unsurpassed standards of service cater for every
need. The understated elegance of the interior, from
the wood-panelled drawing room with its deeply
comfortable seating to the unfussily appointed
dining room, is matched by well thought out,
uncomplicated menus. The Gourmand menu has
eight beautifully balanced courses, but the carte is
no less enticing, with a choice of five dishes per
course. The latter might include a starter of pan-fried
hand-dived scallops with pea purée and ventrèche
bacon; a main of herb-encrusted best end of
Herdwick lamb with basil pommes purées, roast
artichoke and confit tomato; then, for dessert,
savarin of roast pineapple and Szechuan pepper.

North West

Lancashire

BISPHAM GREEN

Eagle & Child
Maltkiln Lane, Bispham Green, L40 3SG (01257 462297). **Lunch served** noon-2pm Mon-Sat. **Dinner served** 6-8.30pm Mon-Thur; 6-9pm Fri, Sat. **Meals served** noon-8.30pm Sun. **Main courses** £8-£11. **Credit** MC, V.
This whitewashed, 16th-century inn, complete with bowling green outside and flagstone floors within, is a real hub for the local community. Eat here and you might see a game of bowls on a summer's evening, or be caroused by a local folk group. Whatever else is going on, though, you can be sure of some serious food. The regular menu doesn't steer too far from the traditional with the likes of sausage and mash, cod fillet and co vying for your attention. Our advice? Head for the specials menu, the cool, ambient alternative to the regular menu's finger-in-ear folk. Try the pressed terrine of salmon, sea bass and spinach with rémoulade for starters and continue with, say, local pigeon breasts with champ potato and port jus. The wine list is good value, if lacking in surprises.

BLACKBURN

Northcote Manor ★
Northcote Road, Langho, Blackburn, BB6 8BE (01254 240555/www.northcotemanor.com). **Lunch served** noon-1.30pm Mon-Fri; noon-2pm Sun. **Dinner served** 7-9pm Mon-Thur, Sun; 7-9.30pm Fri; 7-10pm Sat. **Main courses** £18.50-£24.50. **Set lunch** (Mon-Fri) £17.50 3 courses incl coffee; (Sun) £20 3 courses. **Set dinner** £50 5 courses incl coffee. **Credit** AmEx, MC, V.
In the heart of the Ribble Valley, the Manor's dining room has stunning views across the countryside. The decor is modern and rather stark but at night the place still manages to feel romantic. Menus are spectacularly elaborate, frequently change and more than live up to the place's gourmet reputation. Treacle-cured salmon and Cornish crab with oyster cream was meltingly delicious and was only just topped by a ridiculously tender loin of Bowland lamb with artichokes, spinach and tomatoes. Desserts are also a strong point: delice of double Valrhona chocolate, white chocolate and raspberry ice-cream was fabulous. Look out for the degustation menus (dishes served with matching wines) for around £50 a person. You are so thoroughly spoilt (with champagne, canapés, amuse-bouches and petits fours all the way) that it's extraordinarily good value. The hotel rooms and lounges are cosy, relaxing and just as stunning as the food.

BLACKPOOL

Kwizeen
47-49 King Street, Blackpool, FY1 3EJ (01253 290045/www.kwizeen.co.uk). **Lunch served** noon-1.30pm Mon-Fri. **Dinner served** 6-9.30pm Mon-Sat. **Main courses** £10. **Credit** MC, V.
Restaurants with ambitions to rise above the chip papers and greasy spoons of Blackpool come and go. This area of Lancashire has always been more funfair than fine fare. Kwizeen aims high – and, on the whole, succeeds. OK, the interior is a little dated, with the sort of 'modern' furniture you found in Sunday supplements about five years ago (that goes for the achingly bad restaurant name too). But we're being churlish, as the food is refreshingly good and the service is never less than cheerful. Seafood features strongly in starters, such as own-smoked salmon with potato and chive salad. Mains are eclectic and feature a jaunty combination of flavours. Cantonese-flavoured chicken breast with braised leeks and noodles just about pulls it off, while the roasted loin of veal, chestnut and Marsala sauce is an out-and-out winner. Excellent value too.

Seniors ★ ★
106 Normoss Road, Blackpool, FY3 8QP (01253 393529/www.seniorsfishexperience.com). **Lunch served** 11.30am-2pm. **Dinner served** 4.30-8pm Mon-Sat. **Main courses** £3-£7. **No credit cards**.
Of late there's been something of a revolution at Seniors, turning it into one of the best licensed fish and chip restaurants in the country. It's now bright blue and yellow, has a 72-seat capacity, ash furniture, a highly motivated staff and a display cabinet to show off all its awards. A glass of house wine costs £1.75, a bottle of Moet & Chandon £27.50, and in between is reasonable plonk at £7. Best of all is the fresh fish, including all the usual suspects plus any one from halibut, hake, whiting, john dory, skate, monkfish, black bream, red snapper, sea bass and salmon. Also on the menu are excellent fish cakes and an exclusive range of locally produced ice-cream.

CLITHEROE

Inn at Whitewell ★
Dunsop Road, Whitewell, Clitheroe, BB7 3AT (01200 448222). **Lunch served** noon-2pm, **dinner served** 7.30-9.30pm daily. **Main courses** £12.50-£22. **Credit** MC, V.
This beautiful old coaching inn sits in the Forest of Bowland, still a largely ignored area of real charm near enough to the M6 to flee to when it all gets too

North West

much. And you could chose no better bolt-hole. The à la carte is a trim selection featuring the very best local produce thoughtfully transformed into mouth-watering creations. Locally reared beef is fantastic, as is the (ubiquitous) plump, juicy Goosnargh chicken. Bar snacks are equally top-notch; even the grilled Norfolk kipper doesn't seem out of place. The Inn shares its premises with a wine wholesaler so the list is commendably broad, with a refreshing tilt towards notable New World producers. Order another bottle and make a night of it, staying in one of the characterful bedrooms overlooking the ancient hunting grounds of Bowland.

FLEETWOOD

New Granada Bar ★

5 North Alberts Street, Fleetwood, FY7 6AA (01253 776674). **Meals served** 11.30am-9pm Mon-Sat. **Main courses** £3-£4.15. **No credit cards**.

Fleetwood, home of the fish market, combines many of the best elements of Blackpool's rock-and-floss culture but it's quieter and easier on the nerves. Close to the rattle of passing trams is Christopher Day's fish and chip shop and restaurant, which is intimate, clean and comfortable. Service, like the decor, is unfussy and efficient. Icelandic cod, haddock and

Spread Eagle. *See p253.*

North West

plaice top the menu and are generously portioned, boned and skinned in house. When the fish emerges from pure vegetable oil, its coating is crisp and the flesh moist and white. Beside it are firm Maris Piper chips and a dollop of satisfying mushy peas. A meal for two will hardly dent the wallet.

LONGRIDGE

Longridge Restaurant ★
104-106 Higher Road, Longridge, PR3 3SY (01772 784969/www.heathcotes.co.uk) **Lunch served** noon-2.30pm Tue-Fri. **Dinner served** 6-10pm Tue-Fri; 5-10pm Sat. **Meals served** noon-9pm Sun. **Main courses** £12-£22. **Set lunch** £14 2 courses, £17 3 courses. **Credit** AmEx, DC, MC, V.
The unremarkable village of Longridge is an unlikely setting for one of northern England's finest dining spots. For more than a decade Paul Heathcote's signature restaurant has been delivering the goods and now, with a revamp and a new name, the work continues. Sharply executed dishes display a contemporary sensibility. The Goosnargh duck and chicken are of the highest standard. Black pudding always makes at least one appearance on the menu – perhaps paired, daringly, with fillet of brill and served with an apple hash brown and bay leaf butter. In addition to the carte, there is a good spread of daily specials – for instance, grilled goat's cheese with tiny apple fritters, or mussels with crab meat and a saffron broth. The dining space stretches through a series of comfortably decorated connected rooms.

Thyme
1-3 Inglewhite Road, Longridge, PR3 3JR (01772 786888). **Lunch served** noon-2.30pm, **dinner served** 6-9.30pm Tue-Sat. **Meals served** 1-8pm Sun. **Main courses** £11.95-£16.95. **Set lunch** (Tue-Sat) £6.95 2 courses, £7.95 3 courses; (Sun) £9.95 2 courses, £11.95 3 courses. **Credit** AmEx, DC, MC, V.
Quirky, idiosyncratic Thyme knows that, above all, eating out should be fun. Still giving Longridge's other eaterie a run for its money, Thyme is regularly praised for its repertoire of great ingredients, its international flavours and its inspired cooking. Starters might include Bury black pudding with Lancashire cheese rarebit (£4.45) and mains, roast rack of Bowland lamb, Guinness shallots, parsnip purée and redcurrant jus. That you'll be treated well, enjoy great wines and see more puns of the word 'thyme' than you thought possible must also add to the draw. It's an immensely pleasurable experience, rounded off with some of the freshest Lancashire-produced cheeses (or, for more indulgence, perhaps a strawberry and vanilla crème brûlée).

LYTHAM ST ANNE'S

St Anne's ★
41 St Andrew's Road South, Lytham St Anne's, SY8 1PT (01253 723311). **Lunch served** 11.45am-1.30pm, **dinner served** 5-8pm Mon-Sat. **Main courses** £3.80-£4.80. **No credit cards.**

Hiding behind the compact façade of a chip shop is this comfortable, licensed 62-seater restaurant, which, rather like Dr Who's Tardis, is bigger than it looks from the outside. A wooden ceiling and furniture are lightened by creamy walls, making the decor gentle on the eye. Service is fast and efficient and the fish, all fresh, is from Scotland via Fleetwood. Alternatives to haddock and cod are hake, halibut and plaice, all skinless and boned. Batter is made to order by a little-known Blackburn firm, ensuring a dry and crisp finish, and everything's fried in vegetable oil. Adventurous souls can try the vegetable-based curry sauce and hungry ones might opt for the sponge pudding or pineapple fritters for afters. Wine costs about £7.50 a bottle.

RAMSBOTTOM

Ramsons
18 Market Place, Ramsbottom, BL0 9HT (01706 825070). **Lunch served** noon-2.30pm Tue-Sat; 1-3.30pm Sun. **Dinner served** 6-10pm Tue-Sat. **Main courses** £8.50-£16.50. **Set lunch** (Sun) £16 2 courses, £18 3 courses, £20 4 courses. **Set meal** £11 2 courses, £14.50 3 courses, £17 4 courses, £37.50 8 courses (taster menu). **Credit** MC, V.
Without fuss or fanfare, Ramsons has been providing the good folk of Ramsbottom with great, family-cooked food for over 20 years. There's a new chef at the helm, but it's still very much business as usual. Oh, that's Ramsbottom, Umbria, by the way. For it's authentic Italian flavours you'll be tasting. Owner Chris Johnson is a man with a passion – and

The best Oysters

Butley-Orford Oysterage
Suffolk-based, family-run café. *See p200.*

Café Royal Oyster Bar
A stately Edinburgh old-timer. *See p301.*

Kishorn Seafood Bar
Basic, brilliant and surrounded by amazing scenery. *See p323.*

Loch Fyne Oyster Bar
The original, and the best in the chain. *See p319.*

Oyster Shack
Check the tides, bring a bottle and the Shack will do the rest. *See p124.*

Silver Darling Seafood Restaurant
Aberdeen's best restaurant boasts a new oyster bar. *See p318.*

North West

it's boot-shaped. Quality ingredients are used in inspiring and unusual Italian dishes. Have it Chris's way and have a plate of vegetables before the main course so you can really enjoy the intensity of the skillfully prepared meats, pastas and sauces. We loved the beef casserole with mustard mash, but couldn't leave without tasting the fab pasta and asparagus rosette with roast cherry tomatoes. A refreshingly unreconstructed Italian in the heart of Lancashire. Fantastico!

ROCHDALE

Nutters ★

Edenfield Road, Norden, Rochdale, OL12 7TY (01706 650167). **Lunch served** noon-2pm Mon, Wed-Sat; noon-4pm Sun. **Dinner served** 6.30-9.30pm Mon, Wed-Sat; 6.30-9pm Sun. **Main courses** £14.80-£16.95. **Set lunch** (Sun) £19.95 3 courses. **Set dinner** £32 6 courses (gourmet menu). **Credit** AmEx, MC, V.

TV-chef restaurants should be approached with caution. Chances are the closest you'll get to the celeb is the name over the door. Not so Andrew Nutter's homely, moorland outpost. Nutter's exuberant on-screen persona isn't a sham – there's a real sense of fun here, but there's also a skill that's more *Master Chef* than madman. The menus alter frequently and boast top-notch local ingredients. The gourmet menu is a fail-safe (and good value) way to enjoy six wonderfully eclectic courses. But you won't know what they are until they arrive. You may sample crispy duck fritters with a caramelised shallot confit for starters and roast cod drizzled with lemongrass oil accompanied by smoked haddock fritters to follow, both worth the price of the gourmet menu alone. But the fillet of beef with melting rocket pesto is, if anything, even better. Wines are well chosen, and puddings divine. Vegetarians are well catered for too. All in all, a great find.

SAWLEY

Spread Eagle ★

Sawley, BB7 4NH (01200 441202/ www.the-spreadeagle.co.uk). **Lunch served** noon-2pm Tue-Sun. **Dinner served** 6-8.45pm Tue-Sat. **Main courses** £5.25-£10.50. **Set lunch** (Tue-Fri) £8.50 2 courses, £11.45 3 courses. **Set dinner** £8.75 2 courses, £11.70 3 courses. **Credit** AmEx, DC, MC, V.

Originally a 17th-century coaching inn, the Spread Eagle is one of the nicest places to eat in Lancashire. The setting, deep in the folds of the Ribble Valley, is knockout, and the restaurant's cool, calm interior takes your stress levels down a notch or two before you've even sampled chef Greg Barnes's restrained, satisfying dishes. Starters may include an effortlessly simple trio of lobster, spinach and chicken with a citrus dressing or a more robust medallion of black pudding with crushed potatoes and braised lentils. Ingredients, on the whole, hold few surprises, but that's not what the Spread Eagle's

about. Nor should it be when the raw material's this good. Main courses are comfortably mainstream: flash-roasted venison haunch steak, or pan-roasted fillet of pork, both with squeakily fresh vegetables. Desserts are pure nostalgia. Our vote goes to the bread and butter pudding with apricot purée.

THORNTON-LE-FYLDE

River House

Skippool Creek, Thornton-le-Fylde, FY5 5LF (01253 883497/www.theriverhouse.org.uk). **Dinner served** 7.30-9.30pm Mon-Sat. **Main courses** £16-£20. **Set dinner** £25 4 courses incl coffee. **Credit** MC, V.

The Fylde Coast isn't over-endowed with dependable eating places, so when you stumble across one as good as this it's tempting to keep it to yourself. Located on the delightfully named Skippool Creek, the River House is a quiet Victorian country house hotel, with a superb restaurant open to non-residents (just as well, there are only four bedrooms). Food is a straightforward selection of freshly caught seafood, locally reared meats and market fresh veg. And with basic ingredients this good, there's little need to fiddle. So you may enjoy a sauté of chicken livers in a marjoram cream sauce to start and continue with eye of loin lamb roasted with rosemary. Back-to-basics has never tasted better. Puddings are more elaborate, such as dark chocolate mousse with Grand Marnier and orange shortbread biscuits. Children under seven years are not encouraged.

WRIGHTINGTON BAR

Mulberry Tree

9 Wood Lane, Wrightington Bar, WN6 9SE (01257 451400). **Lunch served** noon-2pm Mon-Sat; noon-2.30pm Sun. **Dinner served** 6-9pm Mon-Thur, Sun; 6-10pm Fri, Sat. **Main courses** £9.50-£17.95. **Set lunch** (Sun) £17.95 3 courses. **Credit** MC, V.

This relative newcomer is already pressing the right buttons and winning over foodie fans for its confident modern British cooking and its genuinely warm welcome. Chef Mark Prescott knows a thing or two. He's trained with the best (including Albert Roux at le Gavroche) and travelled extensively. So he has brought some eclectic twists to the Mulberry's home-grown, Lancashire-friendly menu. Seafood dominates the starting line. Gravadlax of salmon on a warm carrot and beetroot rösti with crème fraîche are colours you'd never mix on your walls but on the tongue they're a treat. Mains include sinfully good, slow-roasted belly pork with savoy cabbage and roast breast of chicken with ribollita and Morteau sausage. There could be more choice for vegetarians, however.

Also in the area

Simply Heathcotes 23 Winckley Square, Preston, PR1 3JJ (01772 252732); **Thyme at the Sirloin Inn** Station Road, Hoghton, PR5 0DD (01254 852293).

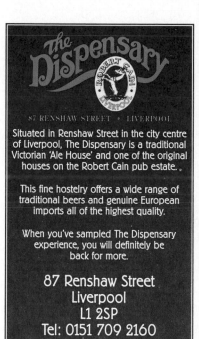

Liverpool & Merseyside

LIVERPOOL

Baltic Fleet

33A Wapping, Liverpool L1 8DQ (0151 709 3116).
Open noon-11.30pm Mon-Thur; 11.30am-11.30pm Fri,
Sat; noon-11pm Sun. **Lunch served** noon-2.30pm
Mon-Fri; noon-3pm Sat; noon-4pm Sun. **Dinner
served** 6-8.30pm Wed, Thur; 5.30-9.30pm Fri; 6.30-
9.30pm Sat. **Main courses** £6.25-£11. **Credit** MC, V.
A rare bit of old real estate near souped-up, shiny
Albert Dock, this tug-shaped pub moored next to a
chandler's and flagmaker's warehouse is easily
bypassed. Only those aware of its regular real ale
prizes and unusually artful pub food stop by, taking
a pew-type seat at one of the few tables and tucking
into the likes of chicken liver with thyme pâté, pork
sausages in leek mash, and more Mediterranean
options, such as grilled sardines, tuna and feta fish
cakes or suffed filo parcels. The sauces are packed
with herbs and spices. The small menu changes
regularly. The friendly atmosphere and cosy,
nostalgia-rich maritime decor makes the Baltic Fleet
a nice place to be marooned all afternoon.

Chung Ku

*Columbus Quay, Riverside Drive, Liverpool L3 4DB
(0151 726 8191/www.chungkurestaurant.co.uk).*
Meals served noon-11.30pm Mon-Thur; noon-
midnight Fri, Sat; noon-10pm Sun. **Main courses**
£8.70-£12. **Set meals** £18-£35 per person
(minimum 2). **Credit** AmEx, MC, V.
Often booked to the rafters, the attractions here
include an impressive vista over the river and
cutting-edge architecture. Shirking Chinatown and
the usual decor of red, gold and Chinese characters,
the interior is ultra-modern. The menu is
unremarkable, but the sauces and standards of
chicken, pork, beef and vegetables are above average.
Dim sum is excellent as a lunch option and there's a
handsome seafood platter for larger groups. Popular
with big groups, Chung Ku is part of the city's
movement back towards the river and keeps the
Chinese community and its cuisine in the front line.

Don Pepe Restaurant & Tapas Bar ★

*Union House, 19-21 Victoria Street, Liverpool L1
6BD (0151 227 4265).* **Lunch served** noon-3pm,
dinner served 5.30-10.30pm Mon-Sat. **Main
courses** £11-£14. **Tapas** £1.95-£6.50. **Set meal**
(lunch, 5.30-7pm) £7.50 3 courses. **Set tapas** £11.95
6 tapas, £13.95 7 tapas (per person, minimum 2).
Credit AmEx, MC, V.
As the commercial core gets brightened up with
terrace caffs and bars, old-style Iberian cellar
restaurante Don Pepe has more competition for

passing trade. The authenticity, range and sheer
quality of its tapas – all made fresh and on site –
ensure its continuing success: white anchovies in
vinaigrette, spicy potatoes and monkfish in bacon
were outstanding. Trout and hake are popular
mains, though the liver with sage and sherry was a
fine, richly flavoured alternative. Daily specials at
around £5 are incredible value. The dark, wood-
lined interior is a moody refuge from the glazing and
glitz of the regenerated central business district and
nicer than many of the newer themed joints.

Everyman Bistro ★

*5-9 Hope Street, Liverpool L1 9BH (0151 708
9545/www.everyman.co.uk).* **Meals served**
noon-midnight Mon-Wed; noon-1am Thur;
noon-2am Fri, Sat. **Main courses** £4.90-£7.50.
Credit MC, V.
Over 30 years, the basement bar-restaurant of 'the
Ev' has proven as much of a draw as the theatre, not
least as a pre-club drinking den. The lights go down
at 8pm and the pub atmosphere kicks in – and food
can run out too. But eating is not an afterthought
with a menu that changes twice daily and ranges,
somewhat randomly, over Italian and Greek
standards, through beef in ale and Middle Eastern
spiced lamb. The underground setting means
echoing noise and no light, but takes nothing away
from the lively buzz. One warning: though this is a
chef-controlled bistro, food is prepared, laid out,
selected and then microwaved, so some dishes, such
as fish and pasta, suffer.

Gulshan

*544-8 Aigburth Road, Liverpool L19 3QG (0151
427 2273/www.gulshan-liverpool.com).* **Dinner
served** 5-11pm daily. **Main courses** £6.95-£12.
Set thali £16.95 per person (minimum 2); £16.45
per person (mimimum 3); £14.80 per person
(vegetarian). **Credit** AmEx, DC, MC, V.
Enjoying near legendary status, this is Liverpool's
challenge to the top curry houses of Bradford and
Birmingham. Out of the centre in the Sefton Park
area, it's a bit of a trek but it may be the
neighbourhood setting that has allowed – or forced
– Gulshan to keep standards high and not bow to
passing fads. Not that this is crusty old Indian
cuisine – the idea is rather to offer top-notch
standards like pasandas and thalis, alongside more
novel recipes such as trout kofta or the Gulshan
Special – king prawns, chicken tikka, tomatoes,
coconut, mushrooms, all in a cream and wine sauce
and topped with cheese and egg soufflé (all for
£7.65). Faded and lived-in, Gulshan is definitely
worth a car ride through the Dingle and into the
leafier 'burbs of Aigburth Road.

North West

Left Bank

*1 Church Road, Wavertree, Allerton, Liverpool
L15 9EA (0151 734 5040/www.theleftbank
restaurant.co.uk).* **Lunch served** noon-3pm Tue-Sat;
noon-4pm Sun. **Dinner served** 5-10pm Tue-Sat.
Main courses £12-£16. **Set lunch** £7.95 3 courses.
Set dinner (5-7pm) £11.50 2 courses, £15 3 courses.
Credit AmEx, MC, V.

This lovely little French bistro is the pride of the
increasingly trendy Wavertree/Penny Lane area.
Half the menu is faithful to France (onion soup,
snails, duck, great steaks and filet mignon) – though
there's also room for black pudding, fish cakes and
beetroot soup. The chef seems to have a soft spot for
seafood and it is always good here; we've had less
success with certain meat dishes. Service is top
grade and extremely friendly. Furnishings – wood
floors and bare brick – are quietly chic. The wine list
is long and nicely priced.

The Living Room

*15 Victoria Street, Liverpool L2 5QS (0870 442
2535/www.thelivingroom.co.uk).* **Meals served** noon-
10.30pm Mon; noon-11pm Tue, Wed; noon-11.30pm
Thur; noon-midnight Fri, Sat; noon-10pm Sun.
Main courses £7.95-£15.95. **Credit** AmEx, MC, V.

Modelled on a colonial hotel lobby, with palms, sofas
and lots of light, this is a refined R&R place for all-
comers. The unpretentious mix of clients is typical
of Liverpool. Now a chain, the Living Room is
known across Merseyside for kick-starting the
regeneration of Victoria Street and the business
district – and it keeps up the standards. A dizzyingly
long menu runs from bites and salads to substantial
dishes such as vegetable tart, risotto with dolcelatte
and some decent meatballs and spaghetti. Polenta

cake comes with a range of toppings, including an
interesting salmon and poached egg number. Coffee
can be accompanied by waffles, pecan pies and some
very British puddings. The place also operates as a
cocktail bar and pre-clubbing hangout.

Lower Place

*Manweb Suite, Philharmonic Hall, Hope Street,
Liverpool L1 9BP (0151 210 1955/www.liverpool
phil.com).* **Lunch served** noon-2pm daily. **Dinner
served** 4-10pm Mon-Fri; 5-10pm Sat, Sun. **Main
courses** £11-£17. **Set dinner** £16.50 2 courses,
£20 3 courses; (when RPO plays) £12.50 2 courses,
£15 3 courses. **Credit** AmEx, DC, MC, V.

In the basement of the Liverpool Philharmonic's
smart art deco block, this is your classic pre-concert
restaurant (and opening times fluctuate according
to the programme of events). Attracting an older
audience than most of the other eateries on Hope
Street, the idea behind chef Paul Askew's menu is
to offer modern and classic dishes to please regulars
and pull in new punters. It just about does this,
though there is a slightly stuffy, formal air here
when the place is quiet and you can hear the stiff
linen crack. The three-course fixed menu is
appetising stuff, featuring oven-roasted Bury black
pudding, toasted cheese brioche and butternut
squash risotto. There are spectacular tarts and raw
milk cheeses to finish. How fitting this is before three
hours of Wagner is doubtful, but it's sumptuous fare.

The Other Place Bistro

*29A Hope Street, Liverpool L1 9BQ (0151 707
7888).* **Lunch served** 11.30am-2.30pm Tue-Fri.
Dinner served 6-10pm Tue-Sat. **Main courses**
£9.50-£15. **Set dinner** (6-7pm) £13.25 3 courses.
Credit MC, V.

60 Hope Street

ultra-private snugs, waltzer-style sofas and acres of space in the gorgeous split-level warehouse building, this is about as cool as you get. Fantastic cocktails are a further plus. It's no wonder TV and football celebs come here to relax, eat well and be ignored. Albert Dock has never quite decided what it is – heritage site or lonely satellite – but the Panam is its sharpest outlet to date.

Pod

137-9 Allerton Road, Mossley Hill, Liverpool L18 2DD (0151 724 2255). Bar **Open** noon-11pm Mon-Sat; 6-10.30pm Sun. *Restaurant* **Lunch served** noon-3pm Mon-Sat. **Dinner served** 6-9.30pm daily. **Tapas** £3-£4.95. **Credit** AmEx, MC.

As canny and cool as the up-and-coming corner of Liverpool it feeds, Pod's penchant is small, sexy tapas picked at while you listen to the strains of blues and jazz. An enterprising bar-restaurant project hatched at Liverpool's Hope University, it does have the feel of a mild cultural conspiracy: you get the distressed walls and school desks and, on the menu, tabouleh, fish cakes, mussels, something Lebanese, something with lime in it. It's all supra-familiar, but that doesn't mean it's dull or merely decorative. It's fresh and tasty enough, and gleefully global, while delightful desserts and decent wines prove that restaurant wins over bar – at least till 9pm or so. Weekend nights are rowdyish and a tad too noisy for dining.

Simply Heathcotes ★

Beetham Plaza, 25 The Strand, Liverpool L2 0XL (0151 236 3536/www.heathcotes.co.uk). **Lunch served** noon-2.30pm daily. **Dinner served** 6-10pm Mon-Fri; 6-11pm Sat; 6-9.30pm Sun. **Main courses** £8.75-£15.50. **Set meal** (lunch, 6-7pm) £13.50 2 courses, £15.50 3 courses. **Credit** AmEx, MC, V.

Despite the slightly twee name, this is a cutting-edge building grafted on to a block of offices behind one of the famous Three Graces port edifices. The Heathcote in question is Paul Heathcote, famed throughout the north-west for his unprovincial performances in kitchens and on screen, and both lunch and evening menus are lavish with clever reworkings of familiar themes. For example, a starter of black pudding with poached egg and devilled sauce is a must-have dish. The suited regulars and the deadzone setting should put no one off indulging, as the prices are ultra-competitive.

60 Hope Street ★

60 Hope Street, Liverpool L1 9BZ (0151 707 6060/ www.60hopestreet.com). Café & Bar **Open** 11.30am-10.30pm Mon-Sat. *Restaurant* **Lunch served** noon-2.30pm Mon-Fri. **Dinner served** 7-10.30pm Mon-Sat. **Main courses** £13.50-£18.50. **Credit** MC, V.

Located in a gorgeous Grade II listed mansion near the Anglican cathedral, 60 Hope Street is gaining a reputation as one of the best places to eat in the north of England. Tasteful and tranquil, the emphasis is on classy, creative cooking in a discreet, arty but

60 Hope Street

The 'other' comes from this elegant bistro's bid to win pre-concert and pre-theatre diners from its neighbours the Everyman and Lower Place. It seems to be succeeding, and then some. The dinner menu changes every other week and is kept short but luxurious – roast cod with noodles, roast skate wing with a caper beurre, a lavish game mixed grill of rabbit, pheasant and pigeon. The shorter lunch menu (changing every three months) is lighter – North African-seasoned chicken with couscous, for example. Own-made puddings and sandwiches are nice enough to pull a separate tea and coffee crowd, but this is an intimate hangout – in the pared-down parlour of a fine Georgian townhouse – for drinking good wines and lounging in style.

The Panamerican Club

Unit 22, Britannia Pavillion, Albert Dock, Liverpool L3 4AD (0151 709 7097/www.lyceumgroup.co.uk/ panamerican). Deli **Meals served** noon-10.30pm Mon-Thur, Sun; noon-11.45pm Fri, Sat. **Lunch served** noon-2.30pm daily. **Dinner served** 6-10.30pm Mon-Thur, Sun; 6-11.45pm Fri, Sat. **Main courses** £8-£15. **Set dinner** £25 3 courses. **Credit** AmEx, MC, V.

With the Blue Bar well-established for twenty-something drinks and dining, Liverpudlian entrepreneur Rob Gutmann has now decked out another large unit on the dockside – formerly the Richard and Judy *This Morning* studios – with a stylish space for a slightly older crowd. Chef John MacGloughlin toured the US and came up with a regional menu that mixes Tex-Mex, Pacific Rim, NY Deli and other stateside genres, all delivered with flair and easy elegance by staff dressed like air hostesses. With Japanese tables on the mezzanine,

North West

unstuffy setting. The Manning family serve a Modern European menu with nods to country cooking and Asian food. From the outside, the place looks severe, but they serve a deep-fried jam sandwich and give you an Uncle Joe's mint ball from Wigan as you leave. The family-friendly basement café, open for Saturday lunch, offers a good selection of sandwiches and an impressive meze.

Tabac Ltd ★

126 Bold Street, Liverpool L1 4JA (0151 707 9795). **Meals served** 8.30am-11pm Mon-Fri; 9am-11pm Sat; 10am-11pm Sun. **Main courses** £7-£7.50. **Set dinner** (5-11pm) £10 2 courses. **Credit** MC, V.
Always popular with Bold Street's younger shopping crowd, this cosy café-restaurant was revamped in 2001 and now does a lively trade in sandwiches, salads, beers and breakfasts. Inside and out are a stylish teak-look brown, with leather banquettes and some self-promo nonsense about being 'a place of beauty' to fulfil the highly marketable *Wallpaper** ideal. But leek and mushroom cottage pie, pork loin and other mains are top-of-the-range comfort cuisine and it's easy to see why this is one of the most popular existential angst arenas – OK, coffee shops – for Liverpool's burgeoning student population.

Yuet Ben

1 Upper Duke Street, Liverpool L1 9DU (0151 709 5772/www.yuetben.co.uk). **Dinner served** 5-11pm Tue-Sun. **Main courses** £5.80-£8.50. **Set meals** £12.50-£17 per person (minimum 2). **Credit** AmEx, DC, MC, V.
Facing Chinatown's ostentatious entrance arch, this lofty terrace is home to the area's oldest Peking-style restaurant, where Shandong flavours have been tailored to western tastes. Grand as it sounds, it is a buzzing, youngish meeting place. Waiters frantically dash round to dish up the popular house special of Yuet Ben dried barbecued ribs, piled up high on platters. Sometimes dishes lean towards takeaway standards – the tomato sauce on one prawn dish was only a noodle's width away from sweet-and-sour goo – but this is still one of the best old-style Chinese eateries in town. Accompany your meal with Chinese lagers and finish with a banana fritter.

ST HELENS

Colours

St Helens College, Water Street, St Helens, WA10 1PZ (01744 623295). **Lunch served** noon-1pm Tue-Fri; noon-2pm Sun. **Dinner served** 6.30-8pm Wed, Thur; 6.30-8.30pm Fri; 6-9pm Sat. **Main courses** £9.25. **Set lunch** (Tue-Fri) £6.50 2 courses, £8 3 courses; (Sun) £9.50 3 courses. **Set dinner** (Sat) £19.50 5 courses. **Credit** MC, V.
St Helens is in raptures over this discreet but quietly daring culinary venture attached to the local college – creatively as well as physically. Except for the duty maître d' and head chef, Colours' cooks and front of house staff are culled from the cooking programme and every meal you get is the outcome

of courses on sauces, baking, mixing, serving. The Saturday £19.50 five-course deal is exceptional, ranging over exquisitely prepared fritters and salads for starters through subtle pastas, lusty steaks and stuffed chicken. The wine list is short, and extremely good value. With its new bar and club scene, this one-time mining town is going through a style overhaul, and Colours is in the vanguard.

SOUTHPORT

Dolphin

30-34 Scarisbrick Avenue, Southport, PR8 1NW (01704 538251). **Meals served** 11.30am-6.30pm daily. **Main courses** £3.95-£4.65. **No credit cards**.
In between the imposing Georgian and Victorian edifices of Southport's main road are narrow pedestrian alleys leading to the promenade and in one such is Dolphin, a famous fish and chip shop and restaurant – and the public face of a fish-frying dynasty dating back to World War II. The restaurant has the look of a typical traditional seaside eaterie. Tradition also dictates that the menu concentrate on cod, haddock and plaice (from Scotland via Fleetwood), which are boned and skinned before being fried in vegetable oil. Chips are thick and mushy peas are gloopy. Other extras include gravy and bread and butter. Service is attentive.

Warehouse Brasserie

30 West Street, Southport, PR8 1QN (01704 544662/www.warehouse-brasserie.co.uk). **Lunch served** noon-2pm, **dinner served** 5.30-10pm Mon-Sat. **Main courses** £7.95-£15.50. **Set lunch** £7.95 2 courses, £9.95 3 courses. **Set dinner** (5.30-7pm Mon-Thur) £10.95 2 courses, £13.95 3 courses. **Credit** AmEx, MC, V.
The Victorian resort of Southport is a conservative kind of place, where new ideas are kept at bay – even the sea stays away – but the Warehouse has livened things up. Owner Paul Adams and chef Marc Verite have come up with a Euro-Asian menu which juxtaposes Southport shrimp and Moroccan meatballs – both wonderful – with the eccentric Jack Daniels glazed baby back ribs. Baked Alaska dessert was a treat and the wine list is decent if a bit dear. A cross between a diner and a cocktail bar, the Warehouse feels a bit like it's part of a chain, but the staff are strong on personal skills and quick service. Established eateries on nearby Lord Street are already raising their hackles – standards to follow soon – and for the moment this is where to stop in Merseyside's most genteel and geriatric town. Look out for soap stars and the odd footballer.

Also in the area

Chung Ku East Lancashire Road, Carr Mill, St Helens, WA11 9TL (01744 609868); **The Other Place Restaurant** 141-143 Allerton Road, Liverpool L18 2DD (0151 724 1234); **Tai Pan** WH Lung Building, Great Howard Street, Liverpool L5 9TZ (0151 207 3888).

Manchester

Choice Bar & Restaurant

Castle Quay Building, off Deansgate, Castlefield, M15 4NT (0161 833 3400/www.choicemcr.co.uk).
Meals served 11am-11pm daily. **Main courses** £12.95-£14.95. **Set lunch** (noon-4pm) £12.50 2 courses. **Credit** AmEx, MC, V.

Right on the waterside, in the Castlefield district of the city, Choice offers a restrained and relaxed dining experience, with crisp, unfussy surroundings. The cool interior is divided in two, restaurant and bar, with a grand piano occasionally providing a light jazzy soundtrack. A compact menu confidently mixes the best local produce with some international flavours, while never overreaching itself. You could try Cheshire cheese scones topped with seared king scallops and served in a light saffron sauce for starters. Following the delicious local cheese theme, move on to slow-roasted ham shank served with pease pudding and smoked Lancashire cheese sauce. Children are made welcome too.

Croma ★

1 Clarence Street, M2 4DE (0161 237 9799/ www.cromamanchester.co.uk). **Meals served** noon-11pm Mon-Sat; noon-10pm Sun. **Main courses** £4.25-£6.95. **Credit** AmEx, MC, V.

Not surprisingly for a restaurant run by a team who previously held the franchise for a local Pizza Express, Croma aims to serve good-value gourmet pizzas in a modern setting to a trendy(ish) crowd. But Croma's menu is more ambitious. Here, alongside the usual americanas and funghis, you'll find the anatra (a Peking duck pizza with hoi sin sauce instead of tomato), the tandoori chicken, the chicken Caesar salad and the inglese (topped with sausage, bacon and egg). Although the hoi sin makes the anatra a choice only for those with a sweet tooth, the quality of Croma's light, crispy pizzas easily lives up to the imagination of the toppings. That, and the friendly, unpretentious vibe, explains why it's always bustling with hungry, young Mancs (expect queues at weekends).

East

52-54 Faulkner Street, M1 4SH (0161 236 1188).
Meals served noon-midnight Mon-Thur, Sun; noon-3.30am Fri, Sat. **Main courses** £4.50-£8.50. **Set lunch** (noon-2pm Mon-Fri) £4.50. **Set meals** £14.50 3 courses. **Credit** AmEx, MC, V.

The latest offering from Chinatown impresario Raymond Wong, East is a fresh, stylish new Chinese restaurant occupying the first floor of a fabulously bright and clean Victorian office conversion in the heart of the city. The interior is conventional to a point, although there are some subtle, contemporary touches – cool blue lighting and modular brown leather sofas set the scene. The bulky menu, too, doesn't veer too far from standard Chinese fare. But there's nothing workaday about the ingredients or the way they're handled. Signature dishes include sautéed monkfish with mangetout – uncomplicated and delicious. Or the succulent sliced lamb fillet with aromatic sauce. A good choice of well-priced wines helps to refresh the somewhat dry atmosphere.

The French Restaurant

The Crowne Plaza Midland Hotel, Peter Street, M60 2DS (0161 236 3333). **Dinner served** 7-10.30pm Mon-Thur; 7-11pm Fri, Sat. **Main courses** £24.95-£29.95. **Set dinner** (Mon-Thur) £22 2 courses, £29 3 courses. **Credit** AmEx, DC, MC, V.

One of several first-class Manchester hotel restaurants, the French Restaurant is perhaps the most ebullient, and certainly the most long-standing. If you're looking for a touch of drama to accompany your evening, the Midland Hotel won't short-change you. It's difficult not to be dazzled by the gilt, the ornate plaster and the hushed reverence of the French's loyal diners. But beneath the rococo flourishes you can enjoy some competent, even memorable meals. Certainly, the steamed sea bass with parmesan, rocket mash and cappuccino of caviar is an experience you're unlikely to forget in a hurry. Equally elaborate is the smoked venison with a steamed pudding of pancetta, young onions, field mushrooms and thyme gravy. Good-value set dinners bring this place within budget for many.

Greens ★

43 Lapwing Lane, West Didsbury, M20 2NT (0161 434 4259). **Lunch served** noon-2pm Tue-Fri; 12.30-3.30pm Sun. **Dinner served** 5.30-10.30pm daily. **Main courses** £10.25. **Set lunch** (Tue-Fri) £5.95 1 course, £7.50 2 courses, £10 3 courses; (Sun) £12.50 3 courses. **Set dinner** (Mon, Sun; 5.30-7pm Tue-Sat) £12.50 3 courses. **Credit** MC, V.

A stalwart of the south Manchester dining scene, Greens has consistently challenged preconceptions of what a vegetarian restaurant can offer the serious foodie. With half the menu being vegan, no alcohol licence and an out-of-town location, it's fair to say that Greens has its work cut out. That it thrives is testament to its commitment to bring exciting, spicy and diverse flavours from around the world and combine them in a constantly evolving range of dishes. It's a noisy, unpretentious place and service is informal. But there's a real buzz here. Try the red Thai curry or the baked goat's cheese rolled in honey, sesame seeds, chilli and mint served on a mango coulis, but leave room for their delicious organically brewed presses. Alternatively, take your own wine.

Koh Samui

*16 Princes Street, M1 4NB (0161 237 9511/
www.kohsamuirestaurant.co.uk).* **Lunch served**
noon-3pm Mon-Fri. **Dinner served** 5.30-11.30pm
daily. **Main courses** £6-£10. **Set lunch** £7
2 courses. **Credit** AmEx, DC, MC, V.
This blink-and-you'll-miss-it basement restaurant,
just outside the precincts of Chinatown, has quickly
established itself as one of the city's most
dependable Thai restaurants, although its decor is
uninspiring. Fortunately, the weighty (and rather
daunting) menu adds the bells and whistles the
decorators left out. Options are vast, but steer
towards the seafood and you won't be disappointed:
the fish red curry with sea bass or bream is simply
gorgeous. That said, you'll be hard-pressed to fault
the zingy Thai fried noodles with pork or the
imaginative set meals either. These, perhaps, offer
the best way to introduce yourself to Koh Samui's
efficient, no-nonsense and consistently above
average Thai cuisine.

Koreana

40A King Street West, M3 2WY (0161 832 4330).
Lunch served noon-2.30pm Mon-Fri. **Dinner
served** 6.30-10.30pm Mon-Thur; 6.30-11pm Fri;
5.30-11pm Sat. **Main courses** £6.50-£13.50.
Set lunches £5.50-£7.50 2 courses. **Credit**
AmEx, MC, V.
Tucked down a flight of stairs on King Street West
is this delightful, family-run restaurant. There are
some rather self-conscious Korean souvenirs dotted
around, but for real authenticity look no further than
the booklet-thick menu. Here, enticing descriptions of
what lies in store start the juices flowing long before
the food arrives. Service is friendly and instructive,
and staff are ready to steer you towards making the
right choices: such as dining Korean style, where
everything comes as one course for you to work your
way through at will. To go traditional, try one of the
Koreana specials – seafood hotpot, beef flat rib, soya
bean, pork, noodle, tofu and tempura. Fabulous,
especially the crisp, clean cod and courgette tempura.

The Lime Tree ★

*8 Lapwing Lane, West Didsbury, M20 8WS (0161
445 1217/www.thelimetreerestaurant.com).* **Lunch
served** noon-2.15pm Tue-Sun. **Dinner served**
6-10.15pm daily. **Main courses** £10.50-£14.50.
Set meal (lunch, 6-6.45pm daily) £10.95 2 courses,
£14.95 3 courses incl coffee. **Credit** AmEx, MC, V.
Perma-busy and almost without peer in Manchester,
the Lime Tree has been quietly increasing its loyal
army of followers for well over a decade. A
consistent all-rounder, this bijou West Didsbury
haunt has recently been spruced up (still no car
parking spaces) and has lost none of its buzzy bistro
atmosphere. But while this compact gem is
somewhat off the beaten track, its kitchen can knock
out competent cooking of the highest order, and
certainly gives some of the swankier, centre-of-town
operations a run for their monkfish. Booking is
essential if you want to enjoy lemon sole fillet with

smoked salmon and spinach, organic pork chops
with mustard mash and desserts of the sticky toffee
pudding variety. And even if you're not a familiar
face, you'll be welcomed just as warmly. A treat.

The Lincoln

*1 Lincoln Square, M2 5LN (0161 834 9000/
www.thelincolnrestaurant.com).* **Lunch served**
noon-2.30pm Mon-Fri; noon-4pm Sun. **Dinner
served** 5.30-10.30pm Mon-Fri; 5.30-11pm Sat.
Main courses £9.95-£15.95. **Set meal** (lunch,
5.30-7pm Mon-Sat) £12.50 2 courses, £14.50
3 courses. **Credit** AmEx, MC, V.
The Lincoln has been somewhat overshadowed in
recent years, as newer, brasher places have come
(and gone) in and around Albert Square. But it's still
here and still very much in business. OK, so it's not
the most scintillating of places and its stuffiness can
sometimes kill conversation. But the Lincoln's
modern British cuisine can easily do all the talking.
That's modern British cuisine with a well-thumbed
passport, by the way. For the menu oscillates wildly
from beer battered fish and chips to Korean honey-
marinated duck breast with plum and chilli sauce.
Puddings are celebratory, so leave plenty of room.
Service is prompt and efficient, and you'd be advised
to dress up. Everyone else seems to.

Little Yang Sing

*17 George Street, M1 4HE (0161 228 7722/
www.littleyangsing.co.uk).* **Meals served** noon-
midnight Mon-Fri; noon-12.30am Sat; noon-10.45pm
Sun. **Main courses** £5.50-£10.25. **Set meals**
(noon-6pm Mon-Fri, Sun; noon-5.30pm Sat) £7.50
2 courses, £9.50 3 courses. **Set dinner** £19.50-£26
4 courses. **Credit** AmEx, MC, V.
A little more self-consciously contemporary since its
Changing Rooms-esque makeover, this baby brother
to the mighty Yang Sing has grown – and there's
really nothing little about this basement favourite
these days. Despite the revamp, there's no change in
the kitchen. The LYS can still impress with its well-
chosen carte of Cantonese favourites. The menu is
less bulky than many of its neighbours, but it still
manages to pack quite a punch. Don't leave without
sampling the excellent dim sum – as the fortune
cookie might say, good things come in little
packages. Try chicken roll in black pepper sauce, or
one of many well chosen vegetarian options, such as
steamed spicy nut dumpling. There's a reasonably
priced wine list, and service is brisk and efficient, if
never exactly effusive.

Lounge 10

*10 Tib Lane, M2 4JB (0161 834 1331/www.lounge
10manchester.com).* **Lunch served** noon-6pm Fri-
Sun. **Dinner served** 6-11pm Mon-Sat; 6-10pm Sun.
Main courses £8-£25. **Credit** AmEx, MC, V.
With red material covering its windows and explicit
paintings of cavorting couples hanging from its
walls, this top-end restaurant has the feel of a
Turkish bordello. But it's the quality of the food and
cooking that really sets Lounge 10 apart. Here, the
beauty is in the detail. Perfectly cooked mains are

accompanied by, say, a mouthwatering lemon and rosemary risotto or a serving of glorious saffron potatoes. Meanwhile their superb puddings arrive with bizarrely flavoured ice-creams (black pepper or balsamic vinegar) that, while odd on their own, cleverly complement the desserts' flavours. Where Lounge 10 lets itself down, though, is in its slightly pushy staff (the sort that offer you more drinks every couple of minutes) and – at the time of our visit – a lunch menu that confused us into ordering three courses for what seemed to be a set price, whereas the puddings were almost £6 apiece extra. We left with a slightly bad taste in our mouths.

Love Saves the Day ★

Unit G18, Smithfields Buildings, Tib Street, M4 1LA (0161 832 0777/www.lovesavestheday.co.uk).
Lunch served noon-3pm Mon-Fri; noon-4pm Sat.
Main courses £4.95-£6.95. **Credit** AmEx, MC, V.
In an area of town known as much for its 'adult' shops as its alternative ones, Love Saves the Day's cheeky, blinking neon sign advertising 'Sexy Food' is spot-on – although there's nothing seedy about this delightful family-run deli. Call in for a coffee and try the macchiato. As with the Italian-roasted coffees, food is tilted towards the land of pasta and pesto, with the Middle East getting a healthy second billing. Primary ingredients, however, are sourced locally where possible, resulting in favourite treats such as Cheshire smoked salmon with asparagus custard or niçoise salad with tuna loin and bottarga. The best niçoise in Manchester, they say. And they're probably right. Desserts change daily, but are always a highlight. Perhaps the walnut and orange cake with vanilla and whisky sauce might make an appearance. They really love their wines here and will help you choose just the right bottle to go with your meal.

The Market Restaurant

104 High Street, Northern Quarter, M4 1HQ (0161 834 3743/www.market-restaurant.com).
Dinner served 6.30-9.30pm Fri, Sat. **Main courses** £12.95-£15.95. **Credit** AmEx, MC, V.
Because the couple who run the Market Restaurant have day jobs, their small bistro only opens on Friday and Saturday nights (although this may be changing – check the website for details), and has the definite feel of a place operated for love not profit. Not that it's particularly cheap – main courses hover around the £15 mark – but everything from the warm welcome to the restaurant's newsletter *The Marketeer* points to the enjoyment they get from it. The monthly-changing menu of six mains and six starters has a French bistro flavour, with a nod to world cuisine (at the time of writing it included a Lebanese salad starter and a sautéed aubergine kebab main). With ingredients sourced from local markets, the standard of the food is high, although portions aren't massive. Still, the Market takes its puddings seriously (they run Sweet Meets, a monthly pudding club) so at least you'll have room to try one.

Mr Thomas's Chop House

52 Cross Street, M2 7AR (0161 832 2245).
Lunch served noon-3pm daily. **Main courses** £8.95-£14.95. **Credit** AmEx, DC, MC, V.
With its original iron fittings and tiles covering the floor and walls, the interior of this evocative city centre Victorian pub hasn't changed much since it opened in 1870. The menu, too, concentrates on quality versions of British classics such as fish pie, steak and kidney pudding and doorstop sandwiches with a choice of own-made chutneys. There are, though, some nods to modern fashions that old Mrs Beeton would probably have never heard of: one of the starters is a tasty, if somewhat pricey dim sum selection which includes a steak and kidney samosa and a mushy pea bhajia, while the hearty corned beef hash comes with sautéed potatoes and creamed onions. Still, Mrs B would probably be pleased to know that, alongside a lengthy wine list, the pub offers a range of real ales. A branch, Sam's Chop House, can be found at Backpool Fold, Chapel Walks; 0161 834 3210.

Moss Nook

Ringway Road, Moss Nook, M22 5WD (0161 437 4778). **Lunch served** noon-1.30pm Tue-Fri.
Dinner served 7-9.30pm Tue-Sat. **Main courses** £19.50-£22.50. **Set lunch** £19.50 5 courses.
Set dinner £36.50 7 courses. **Credit** AmEx, MC, V.
Maybe it's the setting close to Manchester airport that fails to inspire, but the Moss Nook looks like your typical out-of-town, unexceptional but reliable family restaurant. However, it's been wowing locals and travellers alike with its solid, dependable and confident French cooking for over 30 years. The dining room is just this side of sumptuous, with stained glass, gleaming silver platters and squishy chairs, but there's a lightness of touch which makes the Moss Nook more relaxed than restrained. Food is simply treated, and the first-class ingredients are given real space to shine. A soufflé of Swiss cheese with chives served with apple and walnuts is lighter than air, while the pan-fried escalope of veal on buttered spinach leaves is a textbook lesson in less is more.

New Emperor

52-56 George Street, M1 4HF (0161 228 2883/ www.newemperor.co.uk). **Meals served** noon-midnight daily. **Main courses** £7.50-£9.50.
Set meals £15.50 3 courses (minimum 2).
Credit AmEx, DC, MC, V.
Another stalwart in the heart of Chinatown, the New Emperor is anything but subtle. It's always busy, noisy and frenetic – and with 250 covers, this can add up to quite a full-on eating experience. Steel your nerves, though, as the New Emperor offers food that's often surprising, sometimes intriguing, but always rewarding. For surprising, you could try a simple brisket casserole, which is melt-in-the-mouth delicious. Want some intrigue? How about one of the New Emperor's crossover dishes, such as Spanish fried rice. Traditionalists won't be disappointed,

Bar crawl: Manchester

We're not saying that 21st-century Manchester is a modern-day pleasure dome devoted to hedonism and excess but, with every new building given over to luxury urban apartments, swanky lounge bars and Sainsbury's Locals, it's not far off. You'll have to go a long way to find a warm pint of Boddies and a smoky snug these days. But should you hanker after a Belgian cherry beer and a bruschetta, come on in.

The Northern Quarter still retains a gritty, student-friendly buzz, with bars such as **Dry** (28 Oldham Street, 0161 236 9840), **Cord** (Dorsey Street, 0161 832 9494) and **Centro** (74 Tib Street, 0161 835 2863). All three are always full of hustle and bustle. Some say the best days of Dry are behind it, but its reputation couldn't have been better served than when it was featured in the gun-toting scene of *24 Hour Party People*. Of the Northern Quarter's many haunts, Centro is perhaps the most vibrant, with its regular art exhibitions and new media vibe.

Deansgate Locks is a string of pretty bars attracting the tanned and the trim, over the road from the new Hacienda apartments (with the ingenious tagline: 'Now the party's over, you can come home'). **Loaf** (0161 819 5858) is, well, brown. More wholemeal than Mighty White, it also manages to be cavernous yet intimate (work that one out). **Sugar Lounge** (0161 839 5511) is more funky than trendy, and **Fat Cat** (0161 839 8242) has a bizarre, boat-shaped mezzanine level. All have separate floors for dancing – usually to Justin Timberlake and Jamiroquai. Who'd have thought so many sexy bars would find a place next to the Rochdale Canal?

Since being lionised in *Queer as Folk*, Canal Street is now something of a day-trippers' attraction. Bars are a mixed bunch, many still suffering from a bitchiness and attitude overdose, but **Velvet** (2 Canal Street, 0161 236 9003) is cool and friendly (TVs showing QVC in the toilets are an inspired touch). Meanwhile, **Spirit** (10 Canal Street, 0161 237 9725) has a fab teak-and-swirly-carpets interior, like a Pan Am first-class lounge circa 1975.

For Manchester's ultimate low-slung and funky lounge bar, head further out of the Gay Village, towards UMIST, for **Tribeca** (50 Sackville Street, 0161 236 8300). In fact, end your bar crawl here, as Tribeca obligingly has beds to really chill you out.

Loaf

North West

with dishes such as king prawn with Szechuan sauce in bird's nest, complete with the plumpest prawns. Service is welcoming, which comes in handy when much of the menu is in Cantonese.

The Ox

71 Liverpool Road, Castlefield, M3 4NQ (0161 839 7740). **Lunch served** noon-2.45pm Mon-Wed; noon-5.45pm Sun. **Dinner served** 5-10.30pm Mon-Wed. **Meals served** noon-11pm Thur-Sat. **Main courses** £9.25-£16.95. **Credit** MC, V.

If any pub in Manchester could be said to be the antithesis of the Rovers Return, this is it. The Ox is a traditional pub on a traditional street in Castlefield. It serves great beer and has a loyal local crowd. But there's more to this hostelry than hot-pot. Much more. For a start, this pub is splendidly overdressed, almost brothel-like, with rich fabrics and snug booths. The Ox's extensive menu might harbour fears of an overambitious kitchen. Not a bit of it. Their Pacific Rim-inspired creations are almost always a success. Try the spicy Thai fish cakes – just fish and flavour, and absolutely perfect. Vegetarians are warmly received too. Sautéed forest mushrooms with melting gruyère may not be the most ambitious of duos, but when they complement each other this well, who cares? Oh, and why not try a hand-pulled guest ale with your meal instead of the chardonnay? You may be pleasantly surprised.

Pacific

58-60 George Street, M1 4HF (0161 228 6668/ www.pacific-restaurant-manchester.co.uk). Thailand **Lunch served** noon-3pm Mon-Fri, Sun. **Dinner served** 6-11.30pm Mon-Fri, Sun. **Meals served** noon-11.30pm Sat. **Main courses** £7.90-£12.90. **Set lunch** (buffet) £6.95. **Set dinner** £25-£38 3 courses (minimum 2). China **Meals served** noon-11.30pm daily. **Main courses** £7.50-£16.

Set lunch (Mon-Fri) £5.50-£7.50 2 courses, £9.50 3 courses. **Set dinner** £20 3 courses, £35 4 courses (minimum 2). **Credit** AmEx, MC, V.

Pacific is innovative without being gimmicky. Two floors offer Pacific Chinese and Pacific Thai cooking. Each floor has its own team of chefs, so there's no cross-contamination of cultures. Attentive staff on both levels are keen to help you make the most of your time here. Eat in China and you can feast on a refreshingly restrained selection of dishes, such as stir-fried shredded dried scallop with egg, crab meat and silver beansprouts. Alternatively, banquets are imaginative and good value. Thailand offers sautéed mixed seafood with dry yellow curry, or maybe roast pork spare ribs Pacific Thai-style. Flavours are balanced and clean. Again, banquets are a wise choice if you want a high-level view of it all. Feng shui-ed interiors are calming and simple, a welcome interlude from the rattle and hum of Chinatown.

Le Petit Blanc Brasserie ★

55 King Street, M2 4LQ (0161 832 1000/ www.petitblanc.co.uk). **Lunch served** noon-3pm, **dinner served** 5.30-11pm Mon-Sat. **Meals served** noon-10pm Sun. **Main courses** £8.45-£17.25. **Set meals** (noon-3pm, 5.30-7pm, 10-11pm Mon-Sat) £13.50 2 courses, £16 3 courses. **Credit** AmEx, DC, MC, V.

Raymond Blanc's brasserie takes some finding, but it's worth the effort. The surroundings – black wooden tables, curved banquettes, giant amaryllis in blue glass vases – are as smart as the clientele, but staff are laid-back, welcoming children with special menus that come with crayons and origami 2CVs. Starters of deep-fried goat's cheese in crispy pastry with tomato chutney and Mediterranean fish soup with gruyère croûtons were superb, neither too rich nor too voluminous, so that a wild mushroom risotto with autumn vegetables and beef bourguignon, mousseline potatoes and french beans

Yang Sing. *See p266.*

could be enjoyed. Crème brûlée was twice the normal diameter yet so good it was polished off in half the time. A gloopy, overly nutty rhubarb and almond crumble was less successful. The 44 items on the wine list show an expected French bias, but there's plenty of variety. Service was outstandingly good.

Piccolino ★

8 Clarence Street, M2 4DW (0161 835 9860).
Meals served 8am-11pm Mon-Fri; 10am-11pm Sat; 11am-10pm Sun. **Main courses** £10.50-£20. **Credit** AmEx, MC, V.

Like a scene from *Casino* or *Goodfellas*, Piccolino is awash with New York Italian atmosphere. Maybe we're just suckers for this kind of thing, but we think it adds a real buzz – especially when the attention to detail is this good. Grab a booth, order a jug of Bud and soak it all in. Oh, and don't forget to eat. This is, after all, a serious restaurant. Not to upset budding Donnie Brascos, portions are huge. Antipasti starters are big enough for two, with juicy salami, artichokes and mozzarella. Pasta is well represented on the menu, but specials are tempting too. Chicken with rosemary was full of flavour. Service is first-rate.

Restaurant Bar & Grill

14 John Dalton Street, M2 6JR (0161 839 1999).
Bar **Open** noon-11pm Mon-Thur, Sun; noon-midnight Fri, Sat. **Meals served** noon-6pm Mon-Sat; noon-5pm Sun. **Main courses** £3.95-£8.25. *Restaurant* **Lunch served** noon-3pm, **dinner served** 6-10.30pm Mon-Fri. **Meals served** noon-10.30pm Sat, Sun. **Main courses** £5.25-£15.50. **Credit** AmEx, MC, V.

Achingly trendy and looking for all the world like a *Wallpaper* double-page spread, Restaurant Bar and Grill never takes its eye off the ball. Everything is here for a reason, from the glass water wall to the floor-to-ceiling windows forcing diners to see and be seen. Cooking, too, is transparent. There are few

surprises and few flourishes. Mediterranean and fusion recipes feature strongly. And dishes arrive looking like they've just been styled. Crab cakes with lime dipping sauce are a meaty treat, and the skewered lamb fillets with cumin and garlic have a pleasing, smoky bite. Wines are good value and service is smiley.

The River Room

The Lowry Hotel, 50 Dearmans Place, Chapel Wharf, Salford, M3 5LH (0161 827 4000/ www.thelowryhotel.com). **Lunch served** noon-2.30pm Mon-Sat; 12.30-4.30pm Sun. **Dinner served** 6.30-10pm Mon-Thur; 6-10.30pm Fri, Sat; 7-10pm Sun. **Main courses** £13.50-£18.95. **Set lunch** (Mon-Sat) £15 2 courses, £18 3 courses; (Sun) £17.75 3 courses. **Credit** AmEx, DC, MC, V.

Cool, crisp and confident, Marco Pierre White's River Room at the Lowry holds few surprises. Yes, you could cut your fingers on the creases in the linen; yes, service is surgically efficient; and yes, there are at least three things on the menu that you thought were names of French philosophers. That said, for modern British cooking with flair, theatre and finesse, you can't really go wrong here. Overlooking a section of the Manchester canal, you can sample five-star food such as an omelette of lobster with sauce americain or a pig's trotter with black pudding. Mains are classic, the flavours are clean. The red mullet with olive couscous is one of the more simple dishes. Suckling pig with baby vegetables is too good for words. Prices are steep but fair.

Shimla Pinks

Dolefield, off Bridge Street, M3 3EN (0161 831 7099). **Lunch served** noon-3pm Mon-Fri. **Dinner served** 6-11pm Mon-Thur, Sun; 6-11.30pm Fri, Sat. **Main courses** £8-£14. **Set meals** £15 2 courses, £20 3 courses. **Credit** AmEx, MC, V.

North West

Shimla Pinks opened with ambitions to become the best Indian restaurant in the city. It's never quite reached these heights, but there's a lot to be said for this bright, modern restaurant. And after a shaky start, food is now consistently good, though service borders on truculent at busy times. Buffets are a great introduction to the Shimla Pinks experience. The lamb karahi is fabulously rich and moreish, as is the murgh malai tikka. Thankfully, while flock is out and stripped wood is in, the menu isn't overly shocking. New twists to old favourites seem to be the order of the day and the boisterous crowd lap it up, along with the lager.

Simply Heathcote's

Jacksons Row, M2 5WD (0161 835 3536/ www.heathcotes.co.uk). **Lunch served** noon-2.30pm daily. **Dinner served** 5.30-10pm Mon-Fri; 5.30-11pm Sat; 6-9.30pm Sun. **Main courses** £10-£15. **Set meals** (lunch, 5.30-7pm Mon-Sat, 6-9.30pm Sun) £13.50 2 courses; £15.50 3 courses. **Credit** AmEx, DC, MC, V.

This Manchester satellite of local-boy-done-good Paul Heathcote's chain is always OK. Never fantastic, never terrible. A recent revamp has injected a little more warmth and soul into the place, but little things still let it down. On our last visit, we had to practically beg to see the wine list and plates arrived with sloppy smears around the rim. Gripes aside, the ingredients (many locally produced) are first-rate and cooking is never less than competent. Best dishes this time around were starters of artichoke and leek tart, and smoked haddock, celeriac and poached egg.

Stock ★

4 Norfolk Street, M2 1DW (0161 839 6644/ www.stockrestaurant.co.uk). **Lunch served** noon-3.30pm, **dinner served** 6-10pm daily. **Main courses** £14.65-£17.10. **Credit** MC, V.

Stock has taken up lodgings in the former stock exchange in the commercial heart of the city and sets its sights on southern Italian specialities. But if your Italian geography lets you down, don't despair as classic Italian cooking from top to toe of the boot of Italy is well represented. Simple starters such as rocket salad with wild mushrooms, prawns and parmesan in herb vinaigrette are sensible choices for the intense flavours to come. Fish, a staple of southern Italian diets, makes a good showing. The sea bass baked in foil with tagliolini pasta, tomatoes, herbs and garlic is divine. The wine list is top-notch.

Tai Pan ★

81-97 Upper Brook Street, Ardwick, M13 9TX (0161 273 2798). **Meals served** noon-11.30pm Mon-Sat; noon-9.30pm Sun. **Main courses** £5.60-£11. **Set lunch** (Mon-Fri) £5.45 2 courses, £9.45 3 courses. **Set dinner** £15 3 courses, £30 4 courses. **Credit** MC, V.

Part Chinese supermarket and wholesaler (and fascinating to visit for these alone), part spacious dining hall, Tai Pan is a real treat for lovers of no-nonsense, traditional Chinese cooking. And despite being somewhat out of the centre, towards the university, this cavernous restaurant is always bustling with an eclectic range of diners, from chatty Chinese families to stern-faced businessmen. They come for the fabulous dim sum, the cuttlefish cakes – a delight if you like that sort of thing – and the rest of the wonderfully fresh dishes.

Tampopo ★

16 Albert Square, M2 5PF (0161 819 1966). **Meals served** noon-11pm Mon-Sat; noon-10pm Sun. **Main courses** £5.95-£7.95. **Set lunch** £6.95 2 courses, £13.95 3 courses. **Set dinner** £15.95 3 courses. **Credit** AmEx, MC, V.

In spite of competition from national chains, local boy Dave Fox's original noodle house still retains premier position, especially with those seeking a broader range of South-east Asian dishes. Malay, Thai, Japanese and Indonesian ingredients are all brought to the fore here, creating a greatest hits of eastern cuisine. The Japanese gyoza (delicate parcels of veg or pork served with a soy dip) are almost too good. Order two portions. Chicken ramen – egg noodles floating on a chicken stock, with chicken breast and teriyaki marinade – is just sublime. Meals look effortless and the dining area is stripped down. There's another branch in the city at 126 The Orient, The Trafford Centre; 0161 747 8878.

Yang Sing ★

34 Princess Street, M1 4JY (0161 236 2200/ www.yang-sing.com). **Meals served** noon-11.30pm Mon-Thur; noon-midnight Fri, Sat; noon-10.30pm Sun. **Set meals** £15-£40. **Credit** AmEx, MC, V.

For over a quarter of a century, Yang Sing has been at the sharp end of the UK's Cantonese cooking revival, constantly delivering world-class dishes. It's not without competition, yet Yang Sing still maintains pole position in Manchester's vibrant Chinatown. Discreet service, laundry-fresh table settings and gleaming mirrors all push the comfort factor skywards. Oh, and there's a waterfall too. Dim sum is the highlight of a menu that, frankly, you could throw darts at and still come away a winner. Steamed chopped ribs with plum sauce is a lively alternative to classics such as shredded chicken with bamboo shoots in oyster sauce. Fish dishes are sublime, and vegetarians can revel in a well thought-out selection of meat-free alternatives.

Also in the area

Chez Gerard 43A Brown Street, M2 2JJ (0161 214 1120); **Livebait** 22 Lloyd Street, M2 5WA (0161 817 4110); **The Living Room** 80 Deansgate, M3 2ER (0870 442 2537); **Malmaison** Piccadilly, M1 3AQ (0161 278 1000); **Nawaab** 1008 Stockport Road, M19 3WN (0161 224 6969); **Nawaab** 47 Rochdale Road, M4 4HT (0161 839 0601); **Second Floor Restaurant, Bar & Brasserie** Harvey Nichols, 21 New Cathedral Street, M1 1AD (0161 828 8898); **Wagamama** 1 The Pineworks, Corporation Street, M4 4DG (0161 839 5916).

North East

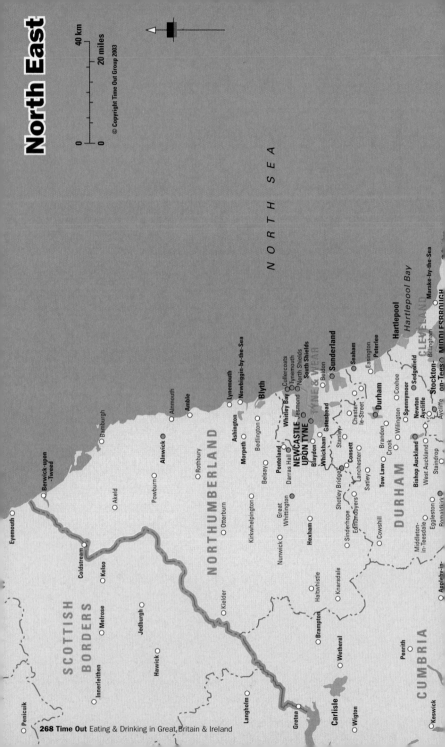

North East

40 km
20 miles

0   0

© Copyright Time Out Group 2003

NORTH SEA

SCOTTISH BORDERS

NORTHUMBERLAND

DURHAM

CUMBRIA

TYNE & WEAR

CLEVELAND

Hartlepool Bay

Penicuik
Eyemouth
Innerleithen
Melrose
Jedburgh
Hawick
Coldstream
Kelso
Berwick-upon-Tweed
Akeld
Powburn
Langholm
Gretna
Kielder
Brampton
Haltwhistle
Knarsdale
Wetheral
Carlisle
Wigton
Penrith
Keswick
Appleby-in-

Bamburgh
Alnmouth
Amble
Newbiggin-by-the-Sea
Lynemouth
Blyth
Ashington
Morpeth
Bedlington
Alnwick
Rothbury
Belsay
Otterburn
Kirkwhelpington
Great Whittington
Nunwick
Hexham
Sinderhope
Edmundbyers
Cowshill
Middleton-in-Teesdale
Eggleston
Romaldkirk

Cullercoats
Whitley Bay
Tynemouth
North Shields
South Shields
Jesmond
NEWCASTLE UPON TYNE
Ponteland
Darras Hall
Gateshead
Blaydon
Whickham
Stanley
Consent
Consett
Shotley Bridge
Lanchester
Satley
Tow Law
Brandon
Crook
Willington
Chester-le-Street
Durham
Coxhoe
Spennymoor
Bishop Auckland
West Auckland
Staindrop
Aycliffe
Newton Aycliffe
Sunderland
Boldon
Seaham
Easington
Peterlee
Sedgefield
Stockton-on-Tees
Billingham
Hartlepool
Marske-by-the-Sea
MIDDLESBROUGH

County Durham

AYCLIFFE

The County

13 The Green, Aycliffe, DL5 6LX (01325 312273/
www.the-county.co.uk). **Lunch served** noon-2pm
Mon-Sat; noon-2.45pm Sun. **Dinner served**
5.30-9.15pm Mon-Sat. **Main courses** £10.95-£16.95.
Credit AmEx, MC, V.
After winning Raymond Blanc's first scholarship in
1995, Andrew Brown set off on a working tour of
top restaurants before settling down in this village
pub overlooking a pretty green. His experience
working with the likes of Gary Rhodes in London,
David Wilson at Peat Inn, and Georges Blanc at
Vonnas in France has evolved into a style of modern
British cooking that suits the informal setting. Ham
and honey mustard terrine with pease pudding is a
good starter; pan-fried Deben duck breast with
sweet potato purée, cranberry and port sauce a
flavoursome main. Raspberry cranachan enriched
with whisky should see you on your way in good
spirits. Service is very agreeable.

BISHOP AUCKLAND

Morley's ★

12 Fore Bondgate, Bishop Auckland, DL14 7PF
(01388 606239). **Lunch served** 11am-1.30pm
Mon-Wed; 11am-2pm Thur, Fri; 11am-2.30pm Sat.
Main courses £2.90-£5.50. **No credit cards**.
An unpretentious town centre shop and restaurant
in the main pedestrianised thoroughfare just a short
walk from the market square. Morley's epitomises
the traditional fish and chip restaurant with bright
but essentially functional decor and furniture.
Service, like the shop and restaurant, is cheery, busy
and efficient with a raft of locals, from far and wide,
chatting in between munching on large portions of
cod or haddock from the Faroe Islands. Fish is
filleted and portioned on the premises, fried in
vegetable oil, served skin off and coated in a light
batter. Chips, thick-cut, are pre-fried and finished off
by a hot flash fry, while the own-made mushy peas
have a better reputation than the local council and
are considerably easier on the pocket.

DURHAM

The Almshouses Café ★

Palace Green, Durham, DH1 3RL (0191 386 1054).
Meals served *Sept-May* 9am-5pm daily. *June-Aug* 9am-8pm daily. **Main courses** £4.95-£6.20. **Credit** AmEx, MC, V.

Well-known for its puddings and cakes, this café has been thriving for 20 years. The location close to the cathedral helps of course, but it's the quality of the baking that draws everyone in. The lunch menu changes daily. Typically the selection could include: saffron fish soup; salad bowl with almond and pesto dressing; Craster crab pâté with cream cheese and chives; lemon and basil risotto; lamb and barley casserole with Black Sheep ale. Then, maybe, double chocolate bread and butter pudding. Filled rolls, scones with jam and cream, and chocolate fudge cake help satisfy appetites the rest of the day.

Bistro 21 ★

Aykley Heads House, Aykley Heads, Durham DH1 5TS (0191 384 4354). **Lunch served** noon-2pm Mon-Sat. **Dinner served** 7-10.30pm Mon-Fri; 6-10.30pm Sat. **Main courses** £10.50-£16.50. **Set lunch** £12 2 courses, £14.50 3 courses. **Service** 10% for parties of 10 or more. **Credit** AmEx, DC, MC, V.

The third of chef-proprietor Terry Laybourne's acclaimed ventures in the North East (*see p278 & p281*), Bistro 21 is the city's best serious-eating

place. It occupies the kitchen of a restored 17th-century hall in a suburb that's a cab ride from the centre. In keeping with a rustic theme, the bar is in a vaulted stone-built cellar. The dining area too is full of quaint nooks and crannies, and has romantic candlelit tables with elegant place settings. There's also a courtyard, lovely when the sun shines. The food is modern: pressed ham knuckle and parsley terrine, one of Terry's signature dishes, is always worth ordering. As are the aromatic shank of lamb with soft lemon polenta, and jam roly-poly with bay leaf custard.

Hide Café Bar & Grill ★

39 Saddler Street, Durham, DH1 3NU (0191 384 1999/www.hidebar.com). **Breakfast served** 9.30am-noon Mon-Sat; noon-3pm Sun. **Dinner served** 6-10pm Mon-Thur; 6-10.30pm Fri, Sat. **Main courses** £8-£16. **Service** 10% for parties of 6 or more. **Credit** MC, V.

Students from the Bailey find the laid-back ambience of this smart café-bar and grill close to the cathedral a big attraction. In addition, the drinks list has some great cocktails, beginning with shooters for £2.50. At 9.30am the all-day menu kicks off with breakfast – Red Bull is an alternative to coffee with your bacon sarnie. The rest of the day sees an eclectic mix of above-average burgers, pastas and pizzas. The choice becomes a little more

Seaham Hall. *See p272.*

North East

sophisticated in the evening (when booking is required) with pan-fried sea bass with Milanese risotto, and confit vine tomatoes consorts with char-grilled ribeye with fries, béarnaise or pepper sauce.

ROMALDKIRK
Rose & Crown
Romaldkirk, DL12 9EB (01833 650213/www.rose-and-crown.co.uk). **Lunch served** noon-2pm Mon-Sat; noon-1.30pm Sun. **Dinner served** *Bar* 6.30-9.30pm Mon-Sat. *Restaurant* 7.30-9pm Mon-Sat. **Set lunch** £14.95 3 courses. **Set dinner** £26 4 courses. **Credit** MC, V.

Built in 1733, the former coaching inn stands out in this remote Teesdale village. Whether it's a meal served in the bar, or in the elegant part-panelled dining room, there's tons of variety foodwise. It's mostly traditional British stuff. Bar meals include dishes such as own-made corned beef with pickled red cabbage, Welsh rarebit or steak, kidney and mushroom pie with Theakston's ale gravy. The four-course fixed-price dinner in the restaurant is more sophisticated, offering the likes of a fine fillet of turbot with fennel and tomato broth, and roast duck with fruit chutney and port wine sauce.

SEAHAM
Seaham Hall ★
Lord Byron's Walk, Seaham, SR7 7AG (0191 516 1400/www.seaham-hall.com). **Lunch served** noon-2.30pm, **dinner served** 6.30-9.30pm daily. **Main courses** £27-£28. **Set lunch** £15.75 2 courses; £19.75 3 courses. **Set dinner** £34 3 courses. **Credit** AmEx, MC, V.

Like its sister, the Samling in Windermere (*see p249*), this is an ultra-cool all-suite hotel, only here the location is a few hundred yards from the sea. The poet Byron was married here in 1815 and were he alive today he'd probably recognise only the classic elegance of the exterior. Inside it's decked out in a stylishly contemporary fashion. The food is artily crafted and the kitchen, under chef John Connell, performs with great aplomb. The short carte (say, roast scallops with sauce vierge, followed by breast of Goosenargh duck, foie gras and gratin potatoes) is supplemented by an equally desirable three-course fixed-price menu of the day. Service is pleasantly low-key and the wine list well-chosen.

SEDGEFIELD
Dun Cow
43 Front Street, Sedgefield, TS21 3AT (01740 620894). **Lunch served** noon-2pm daily. **Dinner served** *Bar* 6-9.30pm Mon-Sat; 7-9pm Sun. *Restaurant* 7-9.30pm Mon-Sat; 7-9pm Sun. **Main courses** £7.95-£14. **Credit** AmEx, MC, V.

Just under three miles from J60 of the A1(M), Sedgefield was once a market town, but since the markets departed it's now classed as a village. At its heart stands this old white-painted inn with rooms where, after securing a candlelit table in either the back bar dining area or the pretty restaurant, you can choose from a specials board groaning with locally supplied seafood. Mussels in a light curry sauce are popular – as is cheese-topped Finnan haddock, or lemon sole. The rest of the food's traditional and familiar: prawn cocktail, Loch Fyne smoked salmon, steak and kidney pie and steaks from the grill. Sunday lunch is a three-course affair, with three classic roasts and all the usual trimmings.

SHOTLEY BRIDGE
Manor House Inn
nr Shotley Bridge, DH8 9LX (01207 255268). **Lunch served** noon-2pm, **dinner served** 7-9.30pm Mon-Thur. **Meals served** noon-9.30pm Fri, Sat; noon-9pm Sun. **Main courses** £10.95-£15.95. **Credit** AmEx, MC, V.

High up on the A68 close to the Derwent Reservoir, the former Bolbec Manor House was once part of an estate with a history dating back to Norman times. Nowadays, one of the most popular snacks in the refurbished bar and lounge is spicy chicken with salsa and sour cream on ciabatta. The candlelit restaurant, located in converted 200-year-old stables, features a something-for-everyone menu, with fish from North Shields and meat from Corbridge. Sausage and black pudding with bubble and squeak, and locally smoked kippers are among a few northern specialities sitting alongside more up-to-date offerings. Vegetarians aren't forgotten, and there are puds such as sticky toffee. What's more, as well as real ales, there are more than 50 malt whiskies.

STOCKTON-ON-TEES
Moby Grape ★
Calverts Lane, Stockton-on-Tees, TS18 1SW (01642 611311). **Meals served** 11am-10pm Mon-Thur; 11am-8.30pm Fri, Sat; noon-6pm Sun. **Main courses** £3-£10. **Credit** MC, V.

Is this the coolest place in town? Probably. Located at the back of the town centre, the smart café-bar has wooden floors and tables and large windows with fantastic river views. It is *the* spot for local office lunches. Food takes precedence in the day and early evening; after that the cellar bar takes over, with DJs, and sometimes musicians till the early hours (the club here goes on until 2am Wed-Sat). A selection of sandwiches and wraps, filled jacket potatoes, burgers and combination salads are offered as well as bowls of steaming hot egg noodles with toppings such as fresh mussels in Thai green sauce, and stir-fried beef with basil. From 5-7pm there are pasta and risotto specials, after 7pm it's tapas all round.

Also in the area
Bimbi's 29 Neville Street, Durham, DH1 4EY (0191 384 5303); **Bimbi's** 11 Market Place, Durham, DH1 3NE (0191 384 8974).

Leeds

Arts Café Bar ★
24 Call Lane, LS1 6DT (0113 243 8243/
www.artscafebar.co.uk). **Open** 11am-11pm Mon-Sat;
11am-10.30pm Sun. **Meals served** noon-10pm Mon-
Thur; noon-10.30pm Fri, Sat; noon-9.30pm Sun. **Main
courses** £7.50-£14.50. **Credit** AmEx, DC, MC, V.
The Calls district overflows with café-bars but Arts
was always the first, least pretentious and best. Its
new owner has retained the rough-hewn wood and
notice-board feel and wisely kept to the founding
principles of exhibiting good art and good food. Put
a canal outside and you could be in Amsterdam.
Well, almost. Go for fried halloumi with lime and
caper vinaigrette; follow with pot-roast chicken with
wholegrain mustard, carrots and a creamy leek and
fennel sauce. Best value are the one-course lunch
plates: typically chorizo, potatoes, smoked salmon,
feta, vegetable couscous and exemplary bread. All
that for a fiver? An unbeatable deal.

Brasserie 44 ★
44 The Calls, LS2 7EW (0113 234 3232/
www.brasserie44.com). **Lunch served** noon-2pm
Mon-Fri. **Dinner served** 6-10.30pm Mon-Thur;
6-11pm Fri, Sat. **Main courses** £10-£16. **Set meals**
(lunch, 6-7.15pm) £11 2 courses, £14 3 courses.
Credit DC, MC, V.
Brasserie 44 opened in a converted warehouse in
1991 and kick-started a new and adventurous
reputation for Leeds. Chef Jeff Baker has been here
from the start, cooking simultaneously for the highly
upmarket Pool Court (*see p277*) next door, so you can
expect Michelin skills at brasserie prices. Invariably
excellent, dishes come as 'large plates' or 'small
plates'. A small plate of mussel risotto with pimento
and leeks could be followed by a large plate of oxtail
casserole with butter beans and prunes. There's
steak, tuna and venison from the char-grill; smoked
salmon, cod and feta from a Whitby smokehouse.
Blackboard specials and great puddings – try the
chocolate fondue – round things off.

Brio
*40 Great George Street, LS1 3DL (0113 246
5225/www.brios.co.uk).* **Lunch served** noon-
2.30pm, **dinner served** 6-10.30pm Mon-Sat. **Main
courses** £5.75-£14.50. **Credit** AmEx, DC, MC, V.
There are plenty of Italian restaurants in Leeds but
Brio is currently the best. It's traditional in its veal,
steak and chicken dishes; in its staff, kind to your
kids and charming to your granny; in its bustle and,
yes, brio. But where it cuts above the rest is in its
sharp styling and the zest of the dishes. Begin with
a hefty sausage casserole and chickpeas or a lighter
dish of roast pear salad with dolcelatte, walnuts and

roast beetroot. Follow with linguine and bottarga or
a fab combination of farfalline and fagioli beans with
bacon. There's another Brio in Harrogate.

Bryan's ★ ★
*9 Weetwood Lane, Headingley, LS16 5LT (0113 278
5679).* **Meals served** noon-9pm Mon; noon-9.30pm
Tue-Thur; noon-10pm Sat; 12.30-7pm Sun. **Main
courses** £6.80-£12.50. **No credit cards.**
Throughout the county Bryan's is mentioned in the
same breath as Headingley and Yorkshire bitter. Set
beside an old stone cottage that houses the busy
takeaway is a 1960s extension containing the 136-
seater, licensed restaurant. Pride is taken in friendly,
quick service and the quality of the fish and chips.
Haddock from Iceland, boned and skin on, dominates
the menu, but there's also space for fresh plaice, hake,
halibut, lemon sole and mussels. Keep an eye on the
specials boards because they sometimes offer skate,
cod, potato scallops and grilled sardines – all in
generous portions. Everything is fried in beef
dripping, the chips are chunky and the mushy peas
are steeped overnight and cooked fresh each day.

Casa Mia Grande
*33-35 Harrogate Road, Chapel Allerton, LS7 3PD
(0113 239 2555/www.casa-mia.co.uk).* **Lunch
served** noon-2.30pm Mon-Sat. **Dinner served**
5.30-10.30pm Mon-Thur; 5.30-11pm Fri, Sat. **Meals
served** 12.30-9.30pm Sun. **Main courses** £6.95-£15.
Set lunch (Sun) £15.95 3 courses incl coffee. **Set
dinner** (5.30-7.30pm) £10 2 courses. **Credit** MC, V.
Casa Mia is in danger of taking over Chapel Allerton.
It began as a little deli that heated up a few of its
dishes and squeezed in a table or two for fun. Then
it broke in next door to become a so-so bistro. Then
it spawned the bigger and far more expensive Casa
Mia Grande over the road. There's worthy meat,
poultry, vegetables and salad, but fish with Italian
verve catches the eye. A giant ice-filled counter
brims with everything from scallops, prawns and
salmon to sea bass, zander and Arctic char. They're
deftly grilled on charcoal, fulsomely flavoured with
masses of garlic and herbs. No contest really.

The Flying Pizza
*60 Street Lane, Rondhay, LS8 2DQ (0113 266
6501/www.theflyingpizza.co.uk).* **Lunch served**
noon-2.30pm Mon-Sat; 12.30-3pm Sun. **Dinner
served** 6-11pm Mon-Wed, Sun; 6-11.30pm Thur-Sat.
Main courses £6-£17. **Credit** MC, V.
If they'd set *Footballers' Wives* in Leeds, this is
where the fur, Ferraris and Frascati would be flying.
Everyone should try it once on a Friday or Saturday
night to gawp at nouveau Yorkshire. The food is
more prosaic, rarely straying far from a familiar

Italian mainstream: tuna and bean salad, avocado and prawns, beef stroganoff and veal saltimbocca. Fish blackboard specials ring the changes. Pizza and pasta are dependable. With swift service and friendly waiters, no one is complaining. After 29 crowded years it's never going to set the pace, but in its way it's never gone out of fashion either.

Fourth Floor Café & Bar

Harvey Nichols, 107-111 Briggate, LS1 5AZ (0113 204 8000). **Meals served** 10am-6pm Mon-Wed; 10am-10pm Thur, Fri; 9am-10pm Sat; noon-5pm Sun. **Set meals** £10.95 2 courses, £14 3 courses. **Credit** AmEx, DC, MC, V.

It may be pricey but the top-floor location is hard to beat. Formica-topped tables set the retro chic tone. Linguine with crab, chilli and flatbread or watermelon, feta and toasted pine nut salad with citrus dressing are typical starters. There's halibut in Parma ham or calf's liver with haricot beans for mains. The quality is admirable, although drinks and extras bump up the bill: fries and aïoli cost £2.75, rocket and parmesan salad is £3. Check out their special events for a fun gourmet evening.

Fuji Hiro ★

45 Wade Lane, Merrion Centre, LS2 8NJ (0113 243 9184). **Meals served** noon-10pm Mon-Thur, Sun; noon-11pm Fri, Sat. **Main courses** £5.50-£6.95. **Set meal** £9.95 vegetarian, £10.50. **No credit cards**.

Fuji Hiro is more like a station waiting room than a restaurant. But this is worth far more than a brief encounter. There's no better quality, or better value refuelling in Leeds. For under a tenner you can have a set meal of noodles, dumplings and a bottle of beer. Try the chilli beef ramen: a clear broth thick with ramen noodles, steak, chilli, shallots, spring onion, mint and coriander. And it's hardly splashing out to go for tasty extras like prawn dumplings or teriyaki chicken. With no additives or MSG, Fuji Hiro is not just good for the purse, it's good for the soul.

Hansa's ★

72-74 North Street, LS2 7PN (0113 244 4408). **Lunch served** noon-2pm Sun. **Dinner served** 5-10.30pm Mon-Fri; 6-11pm Sat. **Main courses** £3.95-£6.25. **Set thali** £7.75, £9.95. **Credit** MC, V.

Created by Hansa Dabhi, this is the city's most original and atmospheric Indian restaurant. Staffed by women, it serves vegetarian Gujarati food. Typical dishes include kachori, a dahl and pea mixture wrapped in pastry, and vadhu, sprouted mung beans, chickpeas and vaal bean curry. Friendly staff will navigate you through the specials of chickpea and potato curry with creamed coconut sauce or fluffy rice dumplings in dahl. Play safe with the thali, a complete meal with curries, breads, rice, pudding and lassi. Whatever you order, you're in for a charming meal in a warm, homely setting.

Leodis

Victoria Mill, Sovereign Street, LS1 4BJ (0113 242 1010/www.leodis.co.uk). **Lunch served** noon-2pm Mon-Fri. **Dinner served** 6-10pm Mon-Sat. **Main**

courses £8-£14. **Set meal** (lunch, dinner Mon-Fri; lunch, 6-7.15pm Sat) £16.95 3 courses. **Credit** AmEx, DC, MC, V.

The brasserie that did so much to raise the standards of Leeds restaurants when it was most needed. Now sometimes overlooked beside some starrier neighbours on the canalside, this airy mill conversion with an easygoing vibe is still a good choice for modern brasserie food in a modish setting. Fish dishes have always been a sure bet: market specials, moules marinière, oysters, seared squid, grilled sea bass, roast cod with tapenade. Meat dishes (steak, venison, calf's liver, duck breast) and desserts (brûlées, sticky toffee pudding and ice-creams) hold fewer surprises.

Livebait

11-15 Wharf Street, Shears Yard, The Calls, LS2 7EY (0113 244 4144/www.santeonline.co.uk/ livebait). **Lunch served** noon-3pm Mon-Sat. **Dinner served** 5.45-10pm Mon-Wed; 5.45-11pm Thur-Sat. **Main courses** £7.95-£29.75. **Set meals** (lunch, dinner Mon-Fri; lunch, 5.45-7pm Sat) £10.95 2 courses, £13.95 3 courses. **Credit** AmEx, DC, MC, V.

This former ship chandler's provides a nautical setting for this chain fish restaurant in the Calls. It looks great, the cooking's OK but it *is* a chain and the experience is ultimately formulaic. There's fish and chips, and even whelks and cockles. There's monkfish and scallop skewers or whole sea bass. Or there's the Livebait platter (a blow-out £49.50 for two) complete with Dorset crab, whole lobster, Madagascan crevettes, Atlantic prawns and Saudi white crevettes. Global sourcing is Livebait's claim. But hang on. Has anyone at HQ heard about 'food miles'? Or checked out the excellent crab, lobster, turbot and white fish landed at Yorkshire ports?

Lucky Dragon ★

Templar Lane, LS2 7LN (0113 245 0520). **Meals served** noon-midnight daily. **Main courses** £3.30-£10.50. **Set meal** £17.50 4 courses (per person, minimum 2). **Credit** AmEx, MC, V.

This cellar in a defiantly unmade-over fringe of the city represents the best of Leeds's moribund Chinese restaurant scene. None of them has changed in years. Not the decor, not the service, much less anything new in the kitchen. Here are pages of the usual Cantonese offerings, reliable dim sum and sizzling platters. The best endorsement is the wave of Chinese families who fill the place for Sunday lunch before stocking up at the Chinese supermarket next door. Follow them off the *gweilo* menu and go for duck web and chicken feet, or tripe with ginger, or whatever they're having. Oh for a Chinese newcomer with the imagination to break the mould.

No.3 York Place

3 York Place, LS1 2DR (0113 245 9922/ www.no3yorkplace.co.uk). **Lunch served** noon-2pm Mon-Fri. **Dinner served** 6.30-9.45pm Mon-Sat. **Main courses** £12.95-£19.95. **Set meals** (lunch, 630-7.30pm) £14.50 2 courses, £18.50 3 courses. **Set dinner** £45 6 courses. **Credit** AmEx, MC, V.

Bar crawl: Leeds

Not so long ago nobody drank at night in Leeds city centre unless they were waiting for a bus or a fight. The pubs were invariably old, dingy and male-dominated. The notion of food was laughable. Chucking out time was chucking up time. These days, on Friday nights the students pour down the hill from Hyde Park and Headingley, City station disgorges crowds of revellers, the young suits step out of their riverside offices and apartments, and the weekend party begins.

The biggest concentration of activity is around the Corn Exchange/Calls Quarter. Start on Call Lane at a bar with no name and a big plate glass window. This is **Norman** (No.36; 0113 234 3988), whose funky plastic decor came to symbolise the Leeds renaissance in the 1990s. It's still popular, and has a good noodle bar with sensible prices. Opposite is **Oporto** (Nos.32-33; 0113 243 4008), which maintains a high standard of drinks, food and a commendably relaxed ambience under pressure.

In Assembly Street is **Townhouse** (0113 219 4004), probably Leeds' best-known bar for a slightly more sassy, well-heeled customer. It's big, noisy, stylish and fun, with drinkers spilling on to the street with their cocktails. Back in Call Lane, **brb** (No.37; 0113 243 0315) and **Mook** (0113 245 9967), round the corner in Hirst's Yard, are chains, but they manage to disguise it pretty well.

Now the arguments begin. Overcrowded and overrated or cool and trendy? One man's pose is another man's poison, but at least the choice is there. Highest on the coolometer is probably still the urban chic cavern of **Oslo** (No.174; 0113 245 7768) on Lower Briggate. But is it chilled or just plain cold? Around another corner, **Elbow Room** (64 Call Lane; 0113 245 7011) has a warmer heart, in a barn that ranges over two floors with pool, music

and booze. It's a great venue for a mixed crowd. **Dr Wu's** (35 Call Lane; 0113 242 7629) is another popular bar along the strip. **Milo** (10-12 Call Lane; 0113 245 7101) has a hard core of regulars who enjoy its laid-back, friendly atmosphere and its mix of soul, funk and rare groove. Tucked away at the top of the town, on Merrion Street, is loud **Mojo's** (No.18; 0113 244 6387) and our favourite, **Isis** (Nos.12-14; 0113 242 9020). It's small, it's sane, it's got impeccable taste in music and it makes the best fresh fruit cocktails in town.

The coolest of the gay bars are centered around Lower Briggate – **Fibre** (No.168; 0870 120 0888), **Queen's Court** (No.167; 0113 245 9449) and the purple plush and chandeliered **Velvet** (11-13 Hirst's Yard; 0113 242 5079).

Head east for the burgeoning dance, music and theatre district and **Wardrobe** in St Peter's Building (No.6; 0113 383 8800) – an unpretentious bar/restaurant with jazz, blues, funk and soul musicians in the basement. Go west for beer and indie bands at **Joseph's Well** (Chorley Lane, off Hanover Walk; 0113 203 1861). Traipse north for traditional student dives at **The Faversham** (1-5 Springfield Mount; 0113 243 1481) and **Dry Dock** (Woodhouse Lane; 0113 203 1841), bizarrely a barge marooned on a traffic island.

And when you want to swap your esoteric import Estonian lager for a cheap hand-pulled pint of Yorkshire's best, real ale abounds. For top traditional settings try the art deco **Guilford** (115 The Headrow; 0113 244 9204) or the elegant **Victoria Commercial Hotel** (28 Great George; 0113 245 1386), but above all, slip along an easily missable Briggate tunnel for the jewel in Leeds' crown since time immemorial: the marble, brass and bevelled glass of **Whitelock's** (Turks Head Yard; 0113 245 3950).

A stylish, stellar restaurant in the heart of the business district that's a docu-soap waiting to happen with all its financial and kitchen ructions. Out goes mercurial Michelin-starred chef/proprietor Simon Gueller. In comes his former tyro, Martel Smith, licking wounds from the demise of his own ambitious venture out of town. On the surface it's still a swan, all tan leather banquettes, mirrored booths and suave service. If there's less foie gras and truffles, the Gueller signature largely remains, including his spectacular pig's trotter stuffed with

ham hock and black pudding. The three-course lunch and early evening menu du jour is good value.

The Old Police Station

106 Harrogate Road, Chapel Allerton, LS7 4LZ (0113 266 8999). **Open** noon-11pm Mon-Thur; noon-midnight Fri, Sat; noon-10.30pm Sun. **Lunch served** noon-2pm, **dinner served** 6-10pm Mon-Sat. **Meals served** noon-8pm Sun. **Main courses** £9-£16. **Set meals** (lunch, 6-7pm) £13.50 2 courses, £15 3 courses. **Credit** AmEx, MC, V.

This was Chapel Allerton's classic Victorian nick before the police decamped to a compound up the hill. In their place the community has gained a stylish new bar-restaurant. Happily free of any helmet and truncheon references, the owners have retained one original feature: an old cell complete with steel door and peephole (bookable for private parties). The menu has ten starters and mains fairly priced at around £5 and £12 respectively. Grilled asparagus with poached egg and hollandaise was a good spring starter, followed by a pleasing salmon and smoked salmon risotto. Syrup pudding and custard are among a selection of homely puds.

Pool Court at 42 ★

42 The Calls, LS2 7EW (0113 234 3232/ www.poolcourt.com). **Lunch served** noon-2pm Mon-Fri. **Dinner served** 7-10pm Mon-Thur; 7-10.30pm Fri; 7-8.30pm Sat. **Set meals** £30 3 courses, £44 3 courses, £55 6 courses. **Credit** MC, V.

Suave and sophisticated, Pool Court has the aura of an exclusive private club. But don't be intimidated by this upstairs neighbour of Brasserie 44 (*see p273*). Jeff Baker's top-end £55 menu delivers six finely executed and exquisite courses: you could have a heady consommé and truffle, then smoked halibut with blinis and Oscietra caviar, then goose foie gras and poached rhubarb, then fillet steak with a Hermitage wine sauce, then the cheese course, then pudding and coffee and handmade chocolates. It's every bit as high end as it sounds. The à la carte is a pared down version with three courses for £44 and the daily menu is almost a bargain at £30.

Raja's ★ ★

186 Roundhay Road, LS8 5PL (0113 274 0411). **Lunch served** 11-2pm, **dinner served** 5-10.30pm Mon-Fri. **Meals served** 3.30-10.30pm Sat, Sun. **Main courses** £5.25-£7.95. **Credit** MC, V.

Curry connoisseurs can argue like beer bores, but there's usually common ground that this is the pick of the plethora of Indians that line Roundhay Road, and maybe all Leeds. It reliably delivers cheap, exemplary curries where the spices really sing out. The best of BP Singh's dishes come from his clay tandoor oven – inches thick and packed with sand for insulation, it burns night and day. Try the mixed tandoor or the special makhan chicken, cooked in the oven and then simmered in cream. Bread is slapped on the side of the tandoor to be delivered deliciously blistered to your table.

Room

Bond House, The Bourse Courtyard, Boar Lane, LS1 5DE (0113 242 6161/www.roomleeds.com). **Open** 11am-11pm Mon-Wed; 11am-2am Thur-Sat. **Lunch served** noon-2.30pm, **dinner served** 6-10.30pm Mon-Sat. **Main courses** £12.50. **Set meals** (lunch, dinner Mon-Fri) £12.95 2 courses, £15.95 3 courses. **Credit** AmEx, DC, MC, V.

Room is a very slick operation. The staff are immaculately smooth. The plum upholstery and suave design is still new and unmarked. The menu knowingly reworks any number of corny standards – prawn and avocado cocktail, salade niçoise, coronation chicken, salmon teriyaki, steak and onion rings, yes, even duck à l'orange – and does it well. It's all very witty and self-confident, if perhaps a little pleased with itself. Room is a welcome and accomplished addition to the city centre but the real test will come when its clientele start to ask whether there's enough warmth and soul in the room, the service and the food to keep them coming back. Leeds doesn't often go for highly detached cool.

Salvo's

115 Otley Road, Headingley, LS6 3PX (0113 275 5017/www.salvos.co.uk). **Lunch served** noon-2pm Mon-Sat. **Dinner served** 6-10.45pm Mon-Thur; 5.30-11pm Fri, Sat. **Main courses** £9.95-£15.95. **Set lunch** £5 2 courses. **Set dinner** (6-7pm Mon-Thur; 5.30-7pm Fri) £10 2 courses, £12.95 3 courses. **Credit** AmEx, DC, MC, V.

A legendary neighbourhood restaurant. Salvo's has been serving good food in improbable portions at square prices via successive generations of the Dammone family since 1975. There have been various makeovers of decor down the years, and the menu has gradually gone upmarket, but the constants of pizza and pasta are the bedrock – pizza margharita and penne arrabiata are just about unbeatable locally. More expensively, there are rich veal dishes, steaks and fish specials, all competently done if with more gusto than grace. The infamous weekend queues and rousing atmosphere have calmed down since it expanded next door. But you still need to have a hard heart not to fall for Salvo's.

Sous le Nez en Ville

The Basement, Quebec House, Quebec Street, LS1 2HA (0113 244 0108). **Lunch served** noon-2.30pm Mon-Sat. **Dinner served** 6-10pm Mon-Fri; 6-11pm Sat. **Main courses** £8.95-£17.50. **Set meal** (lunch Sat; 6-7.30pm Mon-Sat) £12.95 3 courses incl half bottle wine. **Credit** DC, MC, V.

This subterranean wine bar and restaurant is an honourable fixture in the business district. Wine buffs appreciate a cellar that holds bottles several cuts above the usual suspects without excessive sting. Vegetarians are blessed with half a dozen non-meat starters, such as risotto of leeks or warm asparagus salad, as well as main course choices. Otherwise there's Toulouse sausage with red cabbage or black pudding tarte tatin for starters; braised pork shank with haggis or whole partridge and sage jus for mains. Lighter fish fare includes moules marinière or sea bass with herb risotto.

Also in the area

The Living Room 7 Greek Street, LS1 5RW (01565 631234); **Malmaison** Sovereign Key, LS1 1DQ (0113 398 1000); **Simply Heathcote's** Canal Wharf, Water Lane, LS11 5PS (0113 244 0736). **Tampopo** 15 South Parade, LS1 5PQ (0113 245 1816); **Thai Edge** New Portland Place, 7 Calverley Street, LS1 3DY (0113 243 6333).

North East

Newcastle

Barluga

35 Grey Street, NE1 6EE (0191 230 2306). **Lunch served** noon-4pm Mon-Sat; noon-5pm Sun. **Dinner served** 6-10pm Mon-Thur. **Main courses** £8-£11. **Credit** AmEx, DC, MC, V.

Behind the austere, classic façade stands what a few years ago would have been anathema to most Geordies: a sophisticated champagne and caviar bar. Such is the pace of change in this up-and-coming city that now it's the favoured destination of aspiring and well-heeled locals. Built on two levels, the focus is primarily on the bar and lounge. The dining area is on the ground floor and deals in light snacks and trendy sandwiches: mixed tempura vegetables; Irish oysters with Japanese salsas; egg mayonnaise and rocket; goat's cheese crostini. An imaginative carte is available too. There's a good choice of wines, with tasting notes. The all-day brunch on Sunday comes with a Bloody Mary, jazz and newspapers.

Billabong Bistro & Bar

Caledonian Hotel, Osborne Road, Jesmond, NE2 2AT (0191 281 7881). **Main courses** £8-£13. **Credit** AmEx, DC, MC, V.

The Caledonian, one of many hotels in this area, distinguishes itself further by having an attractive bright, modern bistro as part of its facilities. The menu offers a wide selection, which includes duck tortilla wraps, nachos with guacamole, tiger prawn kebab salad, linguine with spiced sausage and mushrooms, Moroccan chicken tagine, char-grilled steaks, summer pudding and hot fudge sundae. The choice of accompanying drinks, from draught and bottled beers to pichets of wine, and pitchers of cocktails (check out the 'billabong' bowls for four) are perfectly matched to the food and surroundings.

Bimbi's ★

Sidgate Bistro, 12 Eldon Square, NE1 7XF (0191 230 2640/www.bimbis.co.uk). **Meals served** 9am-5.30pm Mon-Wed, Fri; 9am-8pm Thur; 9am-6pm Sat. **Main courses** £3-£5. **No credit cards.**

Good old cod and chips are the mainstay of this 90-seater licensed bistro-style self-service restaurant in the city centre. The 5oz portions of fish are coated in a crisp, secret recipe batter and fried in vegetable oil. The spuds, which are usually Maris Piper and come from north of the border or down in Lincolnshire, are hand-cut daily at the Neville Street branch in Durham (the only branch, incidentally, using traditional beef dripping – *see p272*). Haddock and scampi are on the menu too, as are standards like burgers, meat and pork pies, salads, sandwiches, even lasagne and a few Indian dishes.

Café Royal

8 Nelson Street, NE1 5AW (0191 231 3000). **Meals served** 11.30am-6pm Mon, Tue; 11.30am-8pm Wed-Sat; 10am-4pm Sun. **Main courses** £6.50-£11.50. **Credit** AmEx, MC, V.

A former public house within a listed building has been extensively refurbished, creating an elegantly contemporary setting for a short, modern Mediterranean-style menu: seared tuna niçoise salad; char-grilled chicken, salsa rossa and saffron tagliatelle; salmon fish cakes, wilted greens and garlic cream; leek, parmesan, tomato and thyme tart. A stainless steel staircase with oak treads leads to the first-floor restaurant for waitress service. Downstairs, the busy coffee shop ambience has a faster turnover. The menu's the same throughout. From their own bakery comes a changing selection of great flavoured breads, quiches and pastries, plus they do a nice line in smoothies and juices. No bookings are taken on Fridays and Saturdays.

Café 21 ★

19-21 Queen Street, Princes Wharf, Quayside, NE1 3UG (0191 222 0755). **Lunch served** noon-2pm Mon-Sat. **Dinner served** 6-10pm Mon-Sat. **Main courses** £15-£20. **Credit** AmEx, DC, MC, V.

The name and decor may have changed, more tables added and the menu simplified, but Terry Laybourne's original restaurant still wows with the high quality of the cooking. The menu reads so well that making a choice is agonisingly difficult. This is food on a par with London's best. It's uncomplicated, yet imaginative, and the results on the plate are sensational. You'll eat handsomely, whether you follow an outstanding crispy pork terrine and sauce gribiche with smoked haddock fish cake on buttered spinach with soft poached egg and hollandaise sauce, or chicken breast with morels, tarragon and potato pancakes. Then, there's apple crumble soufflé, or rosewater parfait with chilled rhubarb soup. Café Live (27 Broad Chare, Quayside; 0191 232 1331) is Terry's clever riposte to McCoys at the Baltic across the river (*see p280*).

The Cluny ★

36 Lime Street, Ouseburn, NE1 2PQ (0191 230 4474). **Meals served** noon-9pm Mon-Sat; noon-5pm Sun. **Main courses** £4-£6. **Credit** AmEx, MC, V.

Were it not for the tall bridges spanning the Ouseburn valley one could easily imagine oneself in some pretty country location rather than less than a mile from Newcastle city centre. The former Cluny whisky warehouse is now a thriving local arts centre. It's in the bar, where there's also an art gallery and nightly musical performances, that some enjoyable, simple food is on offer. Blackboards list a short, daily-changing selection – chicken and leek soup, or carrot and coriander, an all-day breakfast, steak and mushroom pie, and jacket potato with smoked salmon and rocket cream. Equally good is the even simpler fare like hot bacon or sausage sarnies. There's a decent choice for vegetarians too.

Fisherman's Lodge ★

Jesmond Dene, Jesmond, NE7 7BQ (0191 281 3281/ www.fishermanslodge.co.uk). **Lunch served** noon-2pm, **dinner served** 7-10.30pm Mon-Sat. **Main courses** £21-£23.90. **Set lunch** £19.50 3 courses. **Credit** AmEx, MC, V.

Part of a small group that includes the Samling (*see p249*), Seaham Hall (*p272*), and Treacle Moon (*p280*), the Lodge is at the top of the tree as far as deluxe dining in this city is concerned. So it's best bib and tucker for the house speciality: seafood, much of it from North Shields. There are a couple of meat options, all on a menu that's thoroughly modern French, and though the prices may appear a little steep, it's quality all the way, from the cooking and presentation, to the efficient service. The three-course set lunch is good value, and if the weather's fine book to eat alfresco on the lawn.

King Neptune

34 Stowell Street, NE1 4XQ (0191 261 6657). **Lunch served** noon-1.45pm daily. **Dinner served** 6-10.45pm Mon-Fri; 6-11.30pm Sat; 6-10.30pm Sun. **Set lunch** £8 4 courses. **Set dinners** £13-£30.80. **Credit** AmEx, MC, V.

The Mak brothers, who in 1986 originally set up King Neptune in the heart of Newcastle's Chinatown, have sold their share of the business, but Yen Mak, one of the two siblings, remains manager. Thankfully, the change of ownership has altered little, so it's still wise to book, such is the restaurant's enduring popularity. There are plentiful meat, and some vegetarian options, with the spicier cooking of Szechuan well represented too. Hot and sour soup, Peking spare ribs and crispy duck are good, but seafood is really the house speciality. Choose from a dozen prawn dishes, as well as squid, not forgetting the excellent Northumbrian crab, steamed scallops, and stir-fried lobster in chilli sauce.

Leela's ★

20 Dean Street, NE1 1PG (0191 230 1261). **Dinner served** 6-11pm daily. **Main courses** £7.95-£12.95. **Credit** AmEx, DC, MC, V.

A homely South Indian restaurant where front of house is run by hospitable and charming Leela Paul, while husband Kuriakose does the cooking. This place is streets ahead of some of the local competition, both in terms of food and ambience, so don't go expecting a curry in a hurry washed down by pints of lager. The menu lists a good selection of authentic vegetarian dishes that sit alongside well-prepared meat and fish dishes. Specialities include good crisp paper dosas (made from rice and lentil flour), dhahi vada (soft lentil balls in a spicy yoghurt dressing), then move on to a filling vegetarian thali, king prawns in a creamy tamarind sauce, or lamb fillet marinated with almonds and coconut milk.

McCoys at the Baltic.
See p280.

North East

McCoys at the Baltic ★

South Shore Road, Gateshead, NE8 3BA (0191 440 4949). **Lunch served** *Riverside* noon-2pm, *Rooftop* noon-1.45pm daily. **Dinner served** *Riverside* 6-9.30pm, *Rooftop* 7-9.30pm Mon-Sat. **Set lunch** £16.95 2 courses, £19.95 3 courses. **Set dinner** £27 2 courses, £32 3 courses. **Credit** MC, V.

Hot on the heels of the Angel of the North, the Baltic, one of the largest art spaces in Europe, is an even more potent symbol of the rebirth of the North East. With a stunning Rooftop restaurant as well as a smart Riverside brasserie and café-bar, it offers good quality food to suit virtually all tastes and pockets. The McCoy brothers, of Tontine at Staddlebridge fame, have been charged with providing the catering and their style here is definitely populist modern European. The colourful, well thought-out dishes have exciting flavours: goat's cheese and rosemary bruschetta; lamb with apricot and almond couscous and merguez sausage; and warm plum pizza with red plum coulis and lemon mascarpone.

Pani's ★

61 High Bridge, NE1 6BX (0191 232 4366). **Meals served** 10am-10pm Mon-Sat. **Main courses** £5-£10. **Credit** MC, V.

A genuine Italian restaurant that's also a pizza-free zone: a rarity. In this simple city-centre bistro you'll find authentic Sardinian cooking, hence the virtually unpronounceable names of some dishes. Typical are: 'malloredus'e su cuccureddu' (delicious, quite firm small pasta twists with strips of beef, Parma ham and tomato sauce), and 'caserecc' é s'ortu' (home-style pasta with artichokes, sun-dried tomatoes, spinach and garlic). Luckily, there are plenty of familiar-sounding dishes, too, from minestrone to meat or vegetable lasagne, and a great choice of flavoursome ways with chicken breasts – pollo montevecchio, with bacon, mushrooms, garlic, chilli and white wine is excellent. The daytime menu is mostly ciabatta sandwiches, plus bruschette and toasties. Very amiable service is a further plus.

Paradiso ★

1 Market Lane, NE1 6QQ (0191 221 1240). **Meals served** 11am-11pm daily. **Main courses** £6-£14. **Set lunch** £6.95 2 courses, £8.95 3 courses. **Credit** MC, V.

A successful attempt at creating a semblance of European café culture in what was once an old printing works. The place is tucked away down a side street and its cool contemporary decor, and good, inexpensive Mediterranean food is an irresistible combination for a lively mix of young suits and students. Popolo, the bar on the ground floor, is generally heaving and is where, alongside the drinks, a range of well-prepared light bites are available. Imaginative sandwiches include roast salmon, masala chicken, and lamb kebab. The first floor has a few stylish booths, while the second shares a no-smoking section with the open-plan kitchen. On fine days the balcony really comes into its own.

Treacle Moon

5-7 The Side, Quayside, NE1 3JE (0191 232 5537/www.treaclemoonrestaurant.com). **Dinner served** 5.30-10pm Mon-Sat. **Main courses** £15-£20. **Credit** AmEx, MC, V.

Lord Byron married at Seaham Hall (under the same ownership, *see p272*) and thought his honeymoon so sweet he called it a 'treacle-moon'. The Side can't be considered a fairytale location, but the upmarket bistro's interior creates a sensual setting for a short menu of modern European dishes. A starter of hot, house-smoked salmon comes with beetroot and crème fraîche given a pleasant kick by wasabi. Roast lamb rump has a leek and shallot mash, some baby vegetables and a blueberry sauce, while a shared sticky treacle date pudding with butterscotch sauce might lead to a night of blissful stargazing. *See also* the Samling (*p249*) and Fisherman's Lodge (*p279*).

Valley Junction 397

Old Jesmond Station, Archbold Terrace, Jesmond, NE2 1DB (0191 281 6397). **Lunch served** noon-2pm Tue-Sat. **Dinner served** 6-11.30pm Tue-Sun. **Main courses** £6.95-£14.50. **Set meal** £25-£27.50 per person (minimum 2). **Credit** AmEx, MC, V.

A railway carriage built in 1912 and Jesmond station's former signal box make for one of the country's more unusual Indian restaurants. Brightly refurbished, the smart interior feels more like a long, narrow regular dining room than anything that once trundled on rails. There's authenticity and plenty of variety on a menu that runs from simple but enjoyable onion bhajias and tender lamb tikka, to duck breast in a mildly spiced coconut sauce. All the usual tandoori and biriani items are here, too, as well as a selection of the hotter curries. Vegetarians have a decent range: anaj vuj is their version of a thali. Pleasant, efficient service adds to the appeal.

Vujon ★

29 Queen Street, Princes Wharf, Quayside, NE1 3UG (0191 221 0601/www.vujon.demon.co.uk). **Lunch served** noon-2.30pm Mon-Sat. **Dinner served** 6-11.30pm daily. **Main courses** £6.90-£14.90. **Set meal** £20-£27.50. **Credit** AmEx, DC, MC, V.

On Newcastle's quayside, Vujon has to be the smartest Indian restaurant in the North East. Waiters wear dazzling waistcoats and there's an amazing trompe l'oeil. The food is exceptional, fitting the location perfectly with its nouvelle cuisine style and arty presentation. The menu steers clear of familiar 'hot' curries, focusing instead on a wide choice of regional specialities distinguished by delicate spicing. Kathi kebab, a starter of buttered chapati wrapped around tender tandoori lamb, is terrific, as is a main of roast duck breast cooked with spiced honey. Vhandaris Surprise, a ten-course banquet, is a well-balanced intro to the cooking here.

Also in the area

The Hide Bar The Gate, Newgate Street, NE1 5RF (0191 243 5558); **Malmaison** The Keyside, NE1 3DX (0191 245 5000).

Northumberland

ALNWICK

Carlo's ★

7-9 Market Street, Alnwick, NE66 1SS (01665 602787). **Meals served** 11.30am-2.30pm, 4.30-10.30pm Mon-Fri; 11.30am-10.30pm Sat. **Main courses** £3.05-£3.25. **No credit cards.**

Carlo's fish and chip restaurant and takeaway – run by Laura and Carlo Biagiomi for the last 12 years – has a fast and efficient air, but customers are never rushed. The main attraction is cod from Norway and Iceland, followed by haddock and plaice. Fish is generously portioned, boned on the premises and served without skin. Meals come with thick chips, and mushy peas soaked overnight to make them vibrant green with a pleasing gloopy consistency. Fish and chips for two costs £9.

DARRAS HALL

Café 21

33-35 The Broadway, Darras Hall, NE20 9PW (01661 820357). **Lunch served** noon-2pm Sat. **Dinner served** 5.30-10pm Mon-Sat. **Main courses** £9-£20. **Credit** MC, V.

Terry Laybourne opened his second restaurant (*see p271* Bistro 21) some way out of the city centre in a parade of shops that's part of a large residential estate. It's dinner only (apart from Saturday) in the simply appointed bistro, and while it's all friendly enough and well run, it can get busy as there's nothing in the way of local competition. The menu features enjoyable modern European cooking, and is supplemented by a blackboard of specials. Cheddar and spinach soufflé, seared scallops and duck confit are a few of the highlights.

GREAT WHITTINGTON

Queen's Head

Great Whittington, NE19 2HP (01434 672267). **Lunch served** noon-2pm Tue-Sun. **Dinner served** 6.30-9pm Tue-Sat. **Main courses** £10-£17. **Set lunch** (Tue-Sat) £9.95 2 courses; (Sun) £14.95 3 courses. **Credit** MC, V.

In a quiet village just north of Hadrian's Wall is this simple stone pub. It dates back to the 17th century, and retains a characterful beamed interior. There's a selection of good beers, including its own Queen's Head bitter, but the emphasis now is very much on the food. The restaurant, candlelit at night, has a homely, cottagey look. There's plenty of choice on the menu, which is ambitious without over-reaching itself. The short wine list, mostly priced under £20, has a fairly even mix from the Old and New Worlds. Children are welcomed at lunch only.

Real ale & food

Buckinghamshire
Green Dragon Haddenham. *See p157.*

Cumbria
Queens Head Inn Tirril. *See p248.*

Dorset
Royal Oak Cerne Abbas. *See p135.*

Hampshire
Red House Whitchurch. *See p82.*

Kent
Swan on the Green West Peckham (*see p90*); **Three Chimneys** Three Chimneys (*see p89*); **Spotted Dog** Penshurst (*see p87*).

Manchester
Mr Thomas's Chop House. *See p262.*

Norfolk
The Crown Wells-next-the-Sea (*see p196*); **Darby's Free House** Swanton Morley (*see p196*); **Lifeboat Inn** Thornham (*see p196*); **Walpole Arms** Itteringham (*see p193*); **White Horse** Blakeney (*see p191*).

Nottinghamshire
Martin's Arms Colston Bassett. *See p225.*

Rutland
Olive Branch Clipsham. *See p229.*

Sussex
The Fox Goes Free Charlton. *See p102.*

Wales
Nant Ddu Lodge Hotel Nant-ddu (*see p342*); **The Nantyffin Cider Mill Inn** Crickhowell (*see p340*); **Old Black Lion** Hay-on-Wye (*see p341*).

North East

Tyne & Wear

CULLERCOATS

Bill's Fish Bar ★
4a Victoria Crescent, Cullercoats, North Shields,
NE30 4PN (0191 253 5003). **Meals served**
11.30am-9.30pm daily. **Main courses** £3-£3.50.
No credit cards.
With a spectacular view of the sea front, Bill's first-
floor restaurant, over the chip shop of the same
name, is a relaxing and comfortable place. From
dark wood seats you can watch boats slip by
silhouetted against the horizon, while nearer at hand
local fishermen pick up their crab pots. Service is
friendly and quick, and most of the fish is caught
locally. The menu concentrates on cod and haddock,
served skin on, in a modulated batter mix – added
vinegar subtly enhances the flavour of the fish.
Portions are generous and accompanied by thick-cut
(Maris Piper) chips, and own-made mushy peas,
dark gravy or curry sauce.

NORTH SHIELDS

Kristian Fish Company ★
3-6 Union Quay, North Sheilds Fish Quay, North
Shields, NE30 1HJ (0191 258 5155). **Meals served**
11am-9pm Mon-Sat; 11am-4pm Sun. **Main courses**
£3.20-£3.70. **No credit cards**.
Situated on a redeveloped fish quay on the Tyne is
a bustling takeaway, wet fish shop and stylish
restaurant. At times the 44 wooden seats around the
marble-topped tables don't seem enough, as this
place is so popular, but the hustle and bustle of
customers and staff add to the dockside
atmosphere. Portions of cod and haddock are
gigantic – explaining the lack of a dessert menu –
and fish is served skinless and boneless in a golden
batter. Although not on the menu, a large number
of fish varieties are available; do ask, if it's in the
wet fish shop they'll cook it for you. Kingsize
haddock with chips, bread and butter and a pot of
tea costs £4.70.

SUNDERLAND

11 Tavistock Place
11 Tavistock Place, Sunderland, SR1 1PB (0191 514
5000). **Lunch served** noon-2pm, **dinner served**
6-10pm Mon-Sat. **Main courses** £10-£16. **Set meal**
(lunch; 6-9pm Mon-Thur; 6-7pm Fri) £10.50
2 courses, £13.25 3 courses. **Credit** AmEx, MC, V.
The plain and unprepossessing exterior next to a
multi-storey car park leads down to a smart
basement with part red brick walls hung with
modern art. Metal pillars support the arched ceiling,

and floors are polished wood. It adds up to one of
the city's trendiest dining venues. The menu, which
leans towards the Mediterranean, with a few
oriental-inspired items, is uncomplicated but has
ample choice. Crisp and meaty tempura king prawns
are accompanied by a zingy Thai dipping sauce;
char-grilled ribeye steak comes with flavoursome
field mushrooms, slow-roasted tomatoes and garlic
and rosemary potatoes. There's a good selection of
wines under £20 from France and the New World.

Throwingstones
National Glass Centre, Liberty Way, Sunderland,
SR6 0GL (0191 565 3939). **Open** 10am-5pm,
meals served noon-5pm daily. **Main courses**
£7. **Set lunch** £8.60 2 courses, £12.50 3 courses.
Credit MC, V.
Well signposted from major roads, the National
Glass Centre is an award-winning building on the
River Wear. The spacious high-tech restaurant on
the ground floor has great views from its all-glass
frontage and good value lunch menus. Changing
weekly, these might include smoked salmon and
caramelised onion flatbread followed by lamb
cutlets on roast potato with cranberries and
mozzarella, with toffee-apple crumble with cream for
dessert. The chips are excellent. From 10am till
closing time at 5pm snacks – smoked ham, pease
pudding, honey and mustard tortilla, grilled goat's
cheese and red pepper sandwich, and pepperoni,
tomato and chilli penne pasta – are served.

TYNEMOUTH

Sidney's
3-5 Percy Park Road, Tynemouth, NE30 4LZ
(0191 257 8500). **Lunch served** noon-2.30pm
Mon-Sat. **Dinner served** 6-9.45pm Mon-Sat.
Main courses £10-£16. **Set lunch** £8.50
2 courses, £10.95 3 courses. **Set dinner** (6-7pm
Mon-Sat) £9.95 2 courses, £12.95 3 courses.
Credit AmEx, MC, V.
A stylish, modern bistro with two dining areas, just
off Tynemouth's busy Front Street. The ground
floor space has high ceilings, large windows,
striking crimson and purple walls, polished wood
floors, beech tables and chairs, and a stainless steel
bar counter. The lower level room is quieter. The
short menu is imaginative and each dish is
accompanied by a wine recommendation. Thus a
shot of manzanilla sherry made a fine companion to
an excellent anchovy and roquefort tartlet with lime
crème fraîche, and a glass of viognier was perfect
with honey and lavender duck breast. Almost all
bottles on the short list are priced below £20.

York

Bengal Brasserie
York Business Park, Millfield Lane, Poppleton, YO26 6PQ (01904 788808/www.bengal-brasserie.com). **Lunch served** 12.30-2pm Sat. **Dinner served** 5.30-10.30pm Mon-Sat. **Meals served** 12.30-11pm Sun. **Main courses** £6.95-£10.95. **Set thali** £10.95. **Credit** AmEx, MC, V.

You'd never guess from its stylish interior, but Bengal Brasserie is housed in a characterless business park off York's ring road. The restaurant's main attraction is the quality and authenticity of its Bengali cuisine. As well as their takes on usual curry standards, the Brasserie offers a 'connoisseur's choice' menu for those 'with a discerning palate'. Each arrives with rice, naan, a delicately flavoured vegetable curry and tarka dahl. One of these – the impressive murg (chicken) Bengal spice – deservedly propelled chef Mohan Miah to the finals of the National Curry Chef 2002 competition. With each 'choice' costing under a tenner you can understand why the Brasserie's friendly waiters are on first-name terms with many of the customers.

Bettys Café Tea Rooms
6-8 St Helens Square, YO1 8QP (01904 659142/www.bettysbypost.com). **Meals served** 9am-9pm daily. **Main courses** £6.75-£9.50. **Credit** MC, V.

No trip to York would be complete without a scone and a cuppa in these revered surroundings. But the world's most famous tearoom is overpriced and under-serviced – and oh so very touristy. With the big, sun-lit windows and the waitresses in 1940s-era outfits, Americans come here so they can experience a British tearoom as they've always imagined it and Brits come here to relive a sugar-coated memory of family trips at half-term. But nobody comes here for the rather ordinary cakes or to pay 35p extra for a tiny dish of jam to go with a £2.95 scone. This could be one of the best tearooms in the world. Instead, it's just one of the most famous. Let's hope for better things in other branches.

The Blue Bicycle ★
34 Fossgate, YO1 9TA (01904 673990/www.bluebicyclerestaurant.com). **Lunch served** noon-2.30pm daily. **Dinner served** 6-10pm Mon-Sat; 6-9pm Sun. **Main courses** £12.80-£19.80. **Credit** MC, V.

Ask just about anybody in town and they'll tell you this is York's most exciting young restaurant. With a colourful, vibrant atmosphere, excellent food, personable staff and an attention to detail that would please even the most savvy urban diner, it satisfies on every level. Candlelit with wood floors and a posh bistro feel, the menu changes seasonally, and even simple dishes like prawn cocktail are given new

twists. For mains, a thick Aberdeen Angus fillet with chorizo cream all but filled the plate, cooked precisely to order, while creamy prawn and monkfish chowder was really more of a stew, with large prawns and big chunks of fish in a hearty sauce. Puddings are just as exceptional – the delicate blueberry and lemon crème will haunt you forever.

Café Concerto
21 High Petergate, TO1 7EN (01904 610478). **Meals served** 10am-10pm daily. **Main courses** £9.95-£15. **Credit** MC, V.

This sweet, sunny restaurant-coffee shop has a laid-back attitude and an eclectic menu. The walls are papered with yellowed sheet music (we sat next to *Six Selections of Mandolin Solos*). Starters tend towards fusion, with items like oriental chicken breast salad in spicy sesame dressing, though there are traditional items too. The house special is the daily gratin dauphinoise, a kind of affected shepherd's pie whose filling changes daily – on our visit it was tuna. If that scares you, just find something simple like the grilled salmon. Desserts are similar fusions: we ordered the luscious-looking strawberry cheesecake with chocolate mint.

The Ivy
The Grange Hotel, 1 Clifton, YO30 6AA (01904 644744/www.grangehotel.co.uk). **Lunch served** noon-2pm Sun. **Dinner served** 7-10pm Mon-Sat. **Main courses** £13-£21. **Set lunch** £9.95 2 courses, £12.95 3 courses. **Set dinner** £28 3 courses incl coffee. **Credit** AmEx, DC, MC, V.

One of York's poshest restaurants, the Ivy – inside the swanky Grange Hotel – is the sort of place people take their grandparents for a very nice dinner. It's also popular with honeymooning couples splashing out on starters like seared scallops with Parma ham and parmesan crisp, or quail and watercress ravioli. Mains are of the heavy and trad variety with elegant twists: duo of Gressingham duck with white bean and truffle purée. Puddings are especially gorgeous. The iced rum and raisin timbale with banana fritters and an adorable little jug of butterscotch sauce was almost too pretty (and too rich) to eat. Service is exceptional. Make a booking for Sunday lunch.

Melton's Too
25 Walmgate, YO1 9TX (01904 629222/www.meltonstoo.co.uk). **Meals served** 10.30am-10.30pm Mon-Sat; 10.30am-9.30pm Sun. **Main courses** £6.90-£11.90. **Credit** MC, V.

This is one of those cases of the child overshadowing the parent. Owned by the same people who run the older, and widely respected, Melton's restaurant further from the city centre (7 Scarcroft Road; 01904

634341) this junior version has quickly taken the upper hand. A younger crowd than the one at the other operation can be found in the ground-floor café-bar of the lovely, historic building. Upstairs, the pleasantly casual bistro-style dining space is often packed. Starters include a constantly changing slate of tapas, as well as choices like pasta with rocket, red pepper and parmesan. Mains include hearty portions of grilled steak with red wine and shallot sauce, cassoulet of duck and Toulouse sausage or corn-fed chicken with garlic and seasonal vegetables. Desserts are specialities (including hazelnuts and chocolate on liqueur-soaked sponge cake) and service is so friendly you'll never want to leave.

Middlethorpe Hall

Bishopthorpe Road, YO23 2GB (01904 641241/ www.middlethorpe.com). **Lunch served** 12.30-1.45pm, **dinner served** 7-9.30pm daily. **Set lunch** £16.95 2 courses, £19.50 3 courses. **Set dinner** £37.95 3 courses. **Credit** MC, V.

If you enjoy jacket-and-tie dining, this may be the place for you. Set inside a hotel that was once a country house, the vast gardens are overlooked by this classic restaurant with wood panelling and white linen. The menu changes regularly, but features starters like civet of rabbit with mustard, bacon and lettuce, and mains such as roast corn-fed chicken with cep custard, roast garlic and parsley or loin of veal with sweetbread tortellini and hazel-nut butter. There are always good fish dishes on the menu, and there's a short vegetarian menu. Puddings include aniseed parfait with roast pears and blueberries, or passionfruit jelly with lime ice-cream and poppyseed tuille. Service is as formal as the building.

19 Grape Lane

19 Grape Lane, YO1 7HU (01904 636366). **Lunch served** noon-2pm Thur-Sat. **Dinner served** 6-10pm Tue-Sat. **Main courses** £12.50-£17. **Credit** MC, V.

Tucked away on one of the charming, winding medieval lanes, this is a romantic, quiet restaurant in a historic building. The building itself is lovely – a medieval structure with low-beamed ceilings and many original fittings. At night, with candles lit on the tables, it's beautiful, if small and a bit cramped. The food veers from traditional to contemporary, with well-produced mains like entrecôte steak or trout stuffed with crab meat. Starters similarly offer the mundane – chicken and grape salad – and the unusual: prawn cocktail with banana and pineapple. The menu changes constantly. It is understandably popular, so booking is a good idea at weekends.

Rubicon ★

5 Little Stonegate, YO1 8AX (01904 676076/ www.rubiconrestaurant.co.uk). **Meals served** 11.30am-10pm daily. **Main courses** £6-£9. **Set meal** (11.30am-6.30pm) £8.50 2 courses, £11.50 3 courses; (6.30-10pm) £17 2 courses, £18 3 courses. **Credit** AmEx, MC, V.

This isn't your typical vegetarian restaurant and you'll only notice the lack of meat if you examine the menu. Rubicon is modern, elegant and cool, attracting a cross-section of locals and tourists. They linger over starters like the divine rapini (roasted aubergine, garlic, ricotta cheese and mushrooms) or the diabolically good stilton pâté (a blend of stilton, cream cheese, walnuts and port). Mains such as a roasted Mediterranean vegetable tart, veggie lasagne and a Turkish stuffed aubergine continue the hearty theme. We tried the latter – all subtle spices and excellent flavours – before moving on to a lovely, gooey carrot cake.

St William's College Restaurant

5 College Street, YO1 7JF (01904 634830). **Lunch served** noon-2.30pm, **dinner served** 6-10pm daily. **Main courses** £10-£15. **Credit** AmEx, DC, MC, V.

Directly across the street from the soaring cathedral, this restaurant sits in one of the city's most impressive medieval timber-framed buildings, built in 1462. The name harks back to the structure's original purpose as a school for Minster priests; today it's a popular tourist restaurant serving British cuisine with modern touches. The interior is a disappointment, with simple pine tables and little decoration. The food has its moments though – we enjoyed starters such as cured salmon and dill frittata with honey mustard dressing, and mains like roast loin of lamb with sweet potato sauté and aubergine confit. Puddings include marsala-poached peaches with vanilla mascarpone, and strawberry and elderflower jelly with lavender biscuits. Staff are efficient and the view is extraordinary.

The Tasting Room

13 Swinegate Court East, YO1 8AJ (01904 627879/ www.thetastingroom.co.uk). **Lunch served** 11.30am-3.30pm daily. **Dinner served** 6-10pm Tue-Sun. **Main courses** £9-£15.25. **Set dinner** (order before 7pm, leave by 8pm) £12.95, 6-8pm £18 2 courses. **Credit** DC, MC, V.

Tucked away among the winding snickelways not far from the Minster, this breezy, cheery restaurant has as many tables outdoors as in, and makes a lovely spot for a lazy summer lunch or dinner. The menu features a wide array of salads and sandwiches for lunch (including a tuna and spiced herb oil sandwich and a sun dried tomato, crispy bacon and parmesan salad), while dinner sees the likes of pork fillet in tomato and cider sauce served with roast garlic and crispy parsnips. It can get overcrowded on warm days and staff can be overstretched, causing long waits. But if you've got nothing else to do, it's nice to linger.

Also in the area

Bengal Brasserie 21 Goodramgate, YO1 7LW (01904 613131); **Bengal Brasserie** 4 High Street, Market Weighton, YO43 3AH (01430 876767); **Little Bettys York** 46 Stonegate, YO1 8AS (01904 622865); **Miller's Famous Fish & Chips** 77 Main Street, Fulford, YO10 4PN (01904 637301).

Yorkshire

East Riding

BRIDLINGTON

Audrey's ★
*2 Queen Street, Bridlington, East Riding YO15 2SF
(01262 671920)*. **Meals served** 11.30am-6pm daily.
Main courses £3-£4.25. **No credit cards**.
Best among the plethora of fish and chip shops and
restaurants in Bridlington is Audrey's. It's a simple
little takeaway, bright yellow on the outside with a
predominantly magnolia 50-seater restaurant on the
floor above. Tables are formica-topped and chairs
tubular steel, but it's comfortable with good views
of the energetic town – and the service is fast and
cheery. Specialities are (mostly) cod and haddock,
fresh from the local docks, and plaice from further
afield. The fish, boned but with the skin on, is coated
in a batter made from a secret family recipe that
produces a light, crisp finish and is dished up with
thickish chips, mushy peas, gravy or curry sauce.

North Yorkshire

ARNCLIFFE

Amerdale House Hotel
*Arncliffe, North Yorkshire BD23 5QE (01756
770250)*. **Dinner served** 7.30-9pm daily. **Set
meal** £34.50 4 courses. **Credit** MC, V.
Guests at this large Victorian manor usually dine,
and diners usually stay over in one of 11 elegantly
furnished bedrooms – by dint of the fact that
Arncliffe (population 100) is miles from anywhere.
The short, handwritten four-course dinner menu
reveals an impressive dedication to local lines of
supply with Swaledale lamb, perhaps simply
roasted with garlic and rosemary, followed by a
selection of Dales cheeses. Although the kitchen
doesn't stretch too far or take too many chances, the
cooking is sound, displaying careful technique.
Garden-grown vegetables appear in season and
there's always a choice of fish dishes.

ASENBY

Crab & Lobster
*Dishforth Road, Asenby, North Yorkshire YO7 3QL
(01845 577286/www.crabandlobster.com)*. **Lunch
served** noon-2.15pm daily. **Dinner served**
7-9.30pm Mon-Fri, Sun; 6.30-9.30pm Sat. **Main
courses** £12.50-£25. **Set meal** (Mon-Sat) £11.50
2 courses, £14.50 3 courses; (Sun) £14.50 2 courses,
£16.50 3 courses. **Credit** AmEx, MC, V.

The inside of this rambling pub-restaurant
resembles the aftermath of a riot in an antiques
warehouse. Bric-a-brac litters every surface. David
Barnard, the man who created this engaging
mayhem, has moved on to other ventures, but his
eccentric vision remains. Fortunately, so does his
head chef. Figures of a crab and a lobster dominate
the thatched roof, so it's no surprise that seafood
dominates a long, intelligent menu. A chunk of cod
encrusted with parmesan, topped with a little
celeriac remoulade and moated with a subtle pea
cream sauce is typical of the bright ideas. The
atmosphere is laid-back, but loosely choreographed
service can turn a meal into a marathon.

BOLTON ABBEY

Burlington
*Devonshire Arms Hotel, Bolton Abbey,
North Yorkshire BD23 6AJ (01756 710441/
www.devonshirehotels.co.uk)*. **Dinner served**
7-9pm daily. **Set meal** £55 5 courses. **Credit**
AmEx, DC, MC, V.
This is country house dining deluxe at the Duke and
Duchess of Devonshire's showpiece Dales hotel.
Flunkies are everywhere amid the gun cases and
green waders. They've recently collected a Michelin
star so expect a show for your dinner. Dainty and
delicious trimmings pop up at every turn: amuse-
gueles, pre-pudding pudding, eight varieties of petits
fours. Assiette of duck sets the tone with morsels
sliced and layered in pâté and foie gras. But there
are cracks. Ravioli of crab with buttered lettuce and
ceps had less of a wow factor. The best part of a dish
of sea bream on mashed peas was an exquisite purée
of globe artichoke. The chef was spot-on with an
intense pot of smoked haddock soup and a main
course of boned quail layered with mushroom and
celeriac. A shot of blood orange jelly and blood
orange sorbet was a superb between-course taster.
Who needs chocolate fondant and milk ice-cream or
a feuillantine of vanilla cassonade with poached
pear? If highfalutin' food and service is your bag
then you get it here with highly polished knobs on.

Devonshire Brasserie & Bar ★
*Devonshire Arms Hotel, Bolton Abbey,
North Yorkshire BD23 6AJ (01756 710710/
www.devonshirehotels.co.uk)*. **Lunch served**
noon-2.30pm Mon-Sat; noon-3pm Sun. **Dinner
served** 6.30-10pm Mon-Sat; 6.30-9pm Sun. **Main
courses** £9.75-£16.95. **Credit** AmEx, MC, V.
Quite a shock after the polished oak and silver
service of the Burlington at the other end of the
Devonshire Arms Hotel (*see above*). Here is a rare

blast of modernity in timeless Upper Wharfedale. The bistro's contemporary makeover in bright blue and white has been a resounding success. The menu handily offers a dozen dishes that can be taken as either a starter or a main course. Wild mushroom risotto, salmon fish cakes, Caesar salad or pigeon breast with horseradish mash indicate the range. It's decent brasserie fare complete with steaks, and a children's menu if needed. Follow up with treacle sponge, mulled fruit and ice-cream or cheeses.

BOROUGHBRIDGE

The Dining Room ★

20 St James's Square, Boroughbridge, North Yorkshire YO51 9AR (01423 326426). **Lunch served** noon-2.30pm Sun. **Dinner served** 7-9.30pm Tue-Sat. **Main courses** (Sun) £15. **Set meals** £19.95 2 courses, £23.50 3 courses. **Credit** MC, V.

The ornate fountain in St James's Square was the main source of Boroughbridge's water in Victorian times. Today's diners sipping Perrier have a fine view of it from the windows of a restaurant where the immaculate tables, neutral walls and contemporary pictures whisper chic elegance. Chef-proprietor Christopher Astley's modern British menu echoes these attributes in dishes that are not frightened of simplicity: salad of Cornish crab, melon with elderflower sorbet, seared salmon with pea and mint sauce. But he's equally capable of producing a punchy main course of guinea fowl with wild mushrooms, Bury black pudding and a tarragon sauce. Strong technique also produces a sensuous warm chocolate mousse with a liquid chocolate centre and a white chocolate sorbet. Lisa Astley runs the front of house with quiet style.

BURNSALL

Devonshire Fell Hotel & Restaurant

Burnsall, North Yorkshire BD23 6BT (01756 729000/www.devonshirehotels.co.uk). **Lunch served** 11.30am-2.30pm daily. **Dinner served** 6.30-10pm Mon-Sat; 6.30-9pm Sun. **Main courses** £10.50-£15. **Set meals** £15.95 2 courses, £19.95 3 courses. **Credit** AmEx, DC, MC, V.

Beautifully situated in the Wharfedale village of Burnsall, the sturdy old Fell Hotel has been given the same high chic makeover as its sister restaurant, the Devonshire Brasserie (*see p285*). It's all done out in vibrant greens and blues, furniture is contemporary and the informal menu is reasonably priced. Begin with a tapas selection: chicken tikka, skewered anchovies or lamb kofta. Or go straight for what the menu calls 'considerable' like whole pigeon wrapped in Parma ham or smoked haddock and new potatoes. Food conservatives and kids can shift down the scale to ham, eggs, chips and pineapple, or even beans on toast. Get a window seat at the front to gaze at the Dales.

CRAYKE

The Durham Ox

Westway, Crayke, North Yorkshire YO61 4TE (01347 821506/www.thedurhamox.com). **Lunch served** noon-2.30pm Mon-Sat; noon-3pm Sun. **Dinner served** 6-9.30pm Mon-Fri; 6-10pm Sat; 6-8.30pm Sun. **Main courses** £8.95-£14.50. **Set lunch** (Sun) £14.95 2 courses, £16.95 3 courses. **Set meals** (6-7pm Mon-Fri, 6-8.30pm Sun) £9.95 2 courses, £13.50 3 courses. **Credit** AmEx, MC, V.

Halfway up the hill made famous by the Grand Old Duke of York, in one of the area's prettiest villages, is pub food to restore 10,000 men. Its dining room has dramatic blue walls and matching blue chargers but the rough pine tables of the bar assert an easy charm. Blackboard menus above the enormous inglenook fireplace confirm the Ox's robust English qualities: steak and kidney pie, fish pie and an assured tomato, onion and goat's cheese tart. For a flourish, order mussels with chorizo; an enormous puffed-up foil pillow that, once punctured, wafts heavenly aromas of wine, garlic, seafood and cream.

FERRENSBY

General Tarleton

Boroughbridge Road, Ferrensby, North Yorkshire HG5 0PZ (01423 340284/www.general tarleton.co.uk). Brasserie **Lunch served** noon-2.15pm, **dinner served** 6-9.15pm daily. **Main courses** £11-£17. *Restaurant* **Lunch served** noon-2.15pm Sun. **Dinner served** 6-9.15pm daily. **Main courses** £14-£19. **Set lunch** (Mon-Sat) £9.95 2 courses; (Sun) £17.50 3 courses. **Set dinner** £14.95 2 courses, £17.95 3 courses. **Credit** AmEx, MC, V.

The unremarkable exterior of this sprawling roadhouse in the Vale of York flatlands hides a commendable restaurant. The stamp of quality is in the breeding, sired by the much-loved Angel at Hetton (*see p287*). Some of the Angel's best features are faithfully reproduced: the log fires, the mismatched furniture, the formal dining room, the seafood moneybags, the provençal fish soup and a choice wine cellar. The General can march to its own drum, too. There are pleasing small dishes like wild mushroom and truffle pasta or Thai crab cakes. More substantial dishes star sea bass and tomato tart or duck breast with ginger and maple syrup. Puddings are familiar, but still tempting.

HAROME

The Star Inn ★

Harome, North Yorkshire YO62 5JE (01439 770397/www.thestaratharome.co.uk). **Lunch served** 11.30am-2pm Tue-Sat; noon-6pm Sun. **Dinner served** 6.30-9.30pm Tue-Sat. **Main courses** £9-£17. **Credit** MC, V.

Andrew and Jacquie Pern have taken the pleasantly sleepy village of Harome and the wider gastropub world by storm with their stunning transformation of the local inn, producing a Michelin star, a gourmet corner shop, boutique lodgings and, above all, fantastic food sourced from village farms and local producers. The menu's the same in the cosy thatched bar or the formal dining room. Feast on roast suckling pig with apple and black pudding or steak with blue wensleydale, a daily blackboard of fish and shellfish from Grimsby or Whitby, the best of British cheeses and if you can't choose between desserts like caramelised lemon tart, rich dark chocolate cake or a truly salivating bread and butter pudding, then have the lot in miniature. The Star is a cast-iron recommendation for a special meal out.

HARROGATE

Drum & Monkey
5 Montpellier Gardens, Harrogate, North Yorkshire HG1 2TF (01423 502650). **Lunch served** noon-2.30pm Mon-Sat. **Dinner served** 6.30-10.15pm Mon-Sat. **Main courses** £7.85-£19.55. **Credit** MC, V.
Seafood has been passed across the marble-topped bar here since 1979. The menu, largely unchanged, offers such period classics as sole mornay (stuffed with spinach with a rich cheese sauce) or bonne femme (stuffed with crab and mushrooms with a hollandaise sauce). But if these dishes are stuck in a timewarp, the Drum's enduringly popular formula revolves around doing the simplest dishes very well: mussels, crab, lobster, smoked salmon or half a dozen Pacific oysters with a glass of steely white wine can be just about perfect. There's an upstairs dining room, but bag an early seat at the more atmospheric bar downstairs. Here gathers the 'Harrogate-shire' establishment in full fig and cry.

Sasso
8-10 Princes Square, Harrogate, North Yorkshire HG1 1LX (01423 508838). **Lunch served** noon-2pm Tue-Sat. **Dinner served** 6.30pm-midnight Mon-Sat. **Main courses** £6.95-£16. **Set lunch** £6.95 2 courses. **Credit** MC, V.
This discreet basement Italian makes little noise in a town chock-full of restaurants touting for passing trade. But it's a little gem. Chef-proprietor Stefano Lancellotti makes all his own pasta and the pay-offs include his blissful ravioli with spinach and ricotta in a porcini mushroom and truffle sauce or fusilli with crisp pancetta and baby broad beans and pecorino. There are simple salads, tip-top bruschetta and a spicy Tuscan soup. Main dishes feature beef fillet in a wild mushroom and foie gras sauce or classic lamb cutlets with rosemary. Puddings are panna cotta with crème anglaise, semi-freddo with caramelised walnuts and white chocolate or tiramisu.

Villu Toots
Franklin Mount, Harrogate, North Yorkshire HG1 5EJ (01423 705805/www.villutoots.co.uk). **Lunch served** noon-2pm Mon-Fri, Sun. **Dinner served** 7-9.45pm Mon-Fri, Sun; 6-9.45pm Sat. **Main courses** £8.50-£16.50. **Set lunch** £8 2 courses. **Set dinner** £20 3 courses. **Credit** AmEx, MC, V.

Villu Toots is the chic, contemporary dining room of the deeply traditional and suburban Balmoral Hotel. A refreshing surprise when it was created, it has survived a change of chef and ownership with flying colours. A modern British menu features roast rack of lamb in a red wine broth or monkfish tail wrapped in Parma ham. For best value, go for the two-course lunch. A three-cheese salad was followed by a seafood tart with scallops and prawns; another sharply dressed lardon salad was followed by chicken breast moistened by a ringing tarragon sauce. The wine list is clever, the desserts sophisticated and the service smooth. Off the beaten track but well worth seeking out.

Wild Ginger ★
5 Station Parade, Harrogate, North Yorkshire HG1 1UF (01423 566122/www.wild-ginger.co.uk). **Meals served** 10am-3.30pm Mon-Thur; 10am-8pm Fri, Sat. **Main courses** £4.50-£6.50. **Credit** MC, V.
Behind Green's wholefood shop amid the tat of Station Parade, this wholesome vegetarian café is welcoming in a homespun, veggie way with its deep orange walls, little lamps and piles of newspapers and old magazines. There's a regular menu of salads, potato wedges, pastas and pancakes. Specials chalked up daily liven up the range with the likes of apple and parsnip soup or a hot-pot of spiced vegetables and chickpeas. For dessert, try apple compote topped with a crumble of nuts, seeds and oats, served with custard or ice-cream.

HAXBY

Miller's Famous Fish & Chips ★
55 The Village, Haxby, North Yorkshire YO32 2JE (01904 769169). **Lunch served** 11.30am-1.30pm Tue-Sat. **Dinner served** 4.30-10.30pm Mon; 4.30-11.30pm Tue-Thur; 4.30-11pm Fri, Sat. **Main courses** £3-£3.25. **No credit cards.**
A basic restaurant with tables in front and to one side of a large serving counter, the decor is predominantly light and minimalist. Miller's is a family-run business with a chef trained on the QE2 who cooks cod fresh from the Faroe Isles and haddock fresh from Scotland. Everything is generously portioned, skinned and boned on the premises before being dunked in home-made batter and fried in beef dripping. They use thick-cut Maris Pipers to make chips, but have a penchant for French potatoes when the spuds don't measure up. Mushy peas are cooked fresh daily.

HETTON

The Angel at Hetton ★
Hetton, North Yorkshire BD23 6LT (01756 730263). **Lunch served** *Bar* noon-2.15pm daily. **Dinner served** *Bar & restaurant* 6-9.30pm Mon-Sat; 6-9pm Sun. **Main courses** £12-£15. **Set lunch** (Mon-Sat) £8.77 2 courses. **Set dinner** (6-7pm Mon-Fri) £19.25 3 courses incl glass of wine. **Credit** AmEx, MC, V.

The Magpie Café. *See p291.*

It was 1983 when Denis Watkins began serving angelic food in this lovely Dales pub. It was Yorkshire's prototype gastropub long before the concept existed. There is a dining room, but everyone normally dashes for the bar with its old settles and roaring fires. Current prizes are braised belly of pork and black pudding topped with foie gras; a fabulous fish soup served with gruyère, rouille and aïoli croûtons; as well as duck breast with cabbage and creamy potatoes. Moneybags – a seafood trio in pastry – is the all-time house favourite. Yorkshire rhubarb crème brûlée is the pick of the stickies and there's a true wine lover's wine list.

INGLEBY ARNCLIFFE

McCoy's Bistro ★
The Cleveland Tontine, Staddlebridge, nr Ingleby Arncliffe, North Yorkshire DL6 3JB (01609 882671/ www.mccoysatthetontine.co.uk). **Bistro Lunch served** noon-2pm daily. **Dinner served** 7-9.30pm Mon-Thur, Sun; 7-10pm Fri, Sat. **Main courses** £17-£20. **Set lunch** (Mon-Sat) £12.95 2 courses, £14.95 3 courses; (Sun) £17.95 3 courses. **Set dinner** (7-8pm Mon-Thur, Sun) £16.95 2 courses, £19.95 3 courses. *Restaurant* **Dinner served** 7-10pm Sat. **Set dinner** £30 3 courses. **Credit** AmEx, DC, MC, V.
Two McCoy brothers – the third, Peter, runs the nearby Golden Lion at Osmotherley (*see p289*) – have been deserved fixtures in food guides for the past 25 years. This is a large stone house on a busy intersection of the A19, but you soon forget the traffic in the atmospheric basement bistro where candlelight plays on dark oak. First-rate cooking delivers risotto, terrine, fresh mussels, half a dozen oysters, sea bass, halibut, lamb confit, braised pork hock and steak any way you like. The upstairs

restaurant – in an eclectically decorated room which first put McCoy's on the map – now opens for its superior £30 dinner on Saturday night only.

MARTON

The Appletree Country Inn ★
Marton, North Yorkshire YO62 6RD (01751 431457/www.appletreeinn.co.uk). **Lunch served** noon-2pm, **dinner served** 6.30-9.30pm Mon, Wed-Sun. **Main courses** £10-£16.90. **Credit** MC, V.
Fast making a name for itself as a country gastropub well worth the mileage, chef Trajan Drew (TJ) and his partner Melanie Thornton took over this village inn in 2001. There is a menu of striking modern British dishes consummately cooked. Lemon sole stuffed with salmon on pickled samphire or deep-fried squid on a seaweed salad to start can be followed by roast suckling pig on black pudding with glazed apple and Calvados or local Marton lamb wrapped in puff pastry with tapenade, olives and rosemary jus. Leave room for one of TJ's stunning puddings: milk chocolate pyramid filled with black forest chocolate mousse is the house special.

MOULTON

Black Bull
Moulton, North Yorkshire DL10 6QJ (01325 377289). **Lunch served** noon-2pm Mon-Fri. **Dinner served** 6.30-10.15pm Mon-Sat. **Main courses** £15-£21. **Set lunch** £16.50 3 courses. **Credit** AmEx, MC, V.
The very essence of an English village pub with a menu that goes straight to the heart of traditional British cooking – with some snappy updating. It's a large, rambling place, where a snack lunch in the beamy bar brings Welsh rarebit and bacon, steak

North East

THE MAGPIE CAFE

Main courses £15-£18.50. **Set meal** (tasting menu) £45 7 courses. **Credit** AmEx, DC, MC, V.
As good as it gets in the Dales: a picture-perfect setting in a former shooting lodge on the village green in Upper Nidderdale and Frances Atkins's fabulous Michelin-starred food. The menu, a seven-course celebration of the finest Yorkshire produce, begins with Yorkshire potted beef and ham hock terrine, goes on to lobster ravioli, roast turbot, Nidderdale lamb pie, braised Dales hare, beignet of yorkshire blue cheese and a selection of chocolate puds. But don't be intimidated. Walkers can still leave boots in the porch and if the ham and eggs no longer features, two superior courses from the à la carte should set you up.

RIPLEY

Boar's Head Hotel

Ripley Castle Estate, Ripley, North Yorkshire HG3 3AY (01423 771888/www.boarsheadripley.co.uk). **Lunch served** noon-2pm, **dinner served** 7-9.30pm daily. **Set lunch** £11 2 courses, £15 3 courses. **Set dinner** £18.50-£30 3 courses. **Credit** AmEx, DC, MC, V.
Ancestral portraits gaze down from ochre walls at tables cloaked in white damask. Antiques, polished silver and fresh flowers complete the picture in this estate village. But while the dining room is pretty formal, it's not stiff. Sir Thomas (who compiles the wine list) and Lady Ingilby (who helps plan the menus) are foodies and run the place with an engagingly light touch. Although the restaurant can attract suits and blue rinses, its atmosphere seems to draw all types. And Jason Main's spirited menu brings a modern edge to old stagers, hence duck breast and assorted berries on a chocolate and orange jus and a winning twice-baked yorkshire blue cheese soufflé. For shallower pockets, there's a pub bistro next door.

SCARBOROUGH

Bonnet's ★

38-40 Huntriss Row, Scarborough, North Yorkshire YO11 2EF (01723 361033). **Meals served** 9am-5pm Mon-Sat; 10.30am-4.30pm Sun. **Main courses** £3-£8. **Set lunch** (Sun) £7.95 2 courses, £9.95 3 courses. **Credit** MC, V.
A smart, well-run café-cum-tea shop, the other half of a hand-made chocolate shop, that's boldly upholding classic traditions. This is the place to go for a pot of Earl Grey and cherry and walnut scone, or decent Welsh rarebit. That said, the cooking is enthusiastic and the kitchen makes an effort to include fresh, modern ideas. As well as a broad range of delicious-looking cakes, the kitchen delivers light lunches of omelettes, baked potatoes, pasta, and salads. Blackboards offer daily specials – perhaps Cornish king scallops with crispy bacon, new potatoes and garlic butter or mushroom risotto with fresh pesto, and gooseberry crumble and custard.

and Meaux mustard baguette, or queen scallops in garlic with wensleydale and thyme crumb. At dinner fish is a strong point, delivering fillets of lemon sole with prawns, creamed leeks and white wine glazing sauce, or poached salmon, asparagus and hollandaise sauce. And it's all served in the conservatory restaurant or the Brighton Belle – an original 1930s pullman carriage.

OSMOTHERLEY

Golden Lion ★

6 West End, Osmotherley, North Yorkshire DL6 3AA (01609 883526). **Lunch served** noon-2pm, **dinner served** 6-9pm daily. **Main courses** £6.50-£11.95. **Credit** MC, V.
The McCoy brothers have long been the leading restaurateurs around the far fringes of the North York Moors, and now Peter McCoy has downsized to pull off a near-perfect village pub with food. His unchanging menu is deceptively simple: mussels in white wine; spaghetti vongole; grilled sardines; salmon fish cakes; charcoal-grilled poussin dripping in butter, rosemary and garlic; lemon risotto deliciously topped with caramelised onions. Vegetables are rarely more than chips and frozen peas and it all combines robustly like really confident home cooking. The decor exudes the same deceptively simple ethos: white walls, dark wood, peat fires, brass candlesticks and fresh flowers.

RAMSGILL

Yorke Arms Country Inn ★

Ramsgill, North Yorkshire HG3 5RL (01423 755243/www.yorke-arms.co.uk). **Lunch served** noon-2pm daily. **Dinner served** 7-9pm Mon-Sat.

Golden Grid ★

*4 Sandside, Scarborough, North Yorkshire YO11
1PE (01723 360922/www.goldengrid.co.uk).* **Meals
served** *Feb-Oct* 10am-10pm daily. *Nov-Jan* 10am-
7pm Mon-Thur; 10am-10pm Fri-Sun. **Main courses**
£3.99-£10.95. **Credit** MC, V.

Scarborough's oldest seafood restaurant has been
serving up the freshest of fish since the 1890s. Daily
deliveries bring skate, whole lemon sole, Atlantic
cod, haddock and more, offered as exemplary fish
and chips with optional mushy peas and a choice of
three sizes. The nautical theme reinforces the old-
fashioned seaside restaurant look and the upper
floors have unrivalled views across to Flamborough
Head. Breakfasts, teas, roast beef with Yorkshire
pudding, grills and steak and kidney pies are
proudly served. Crabs and lobsters are a speciality.

Marmalades Restaurant

*Beiderbeckes Hotel, 1-3 The Crescent, Scarborough,
North Yorkshire YO11 2PW (01723 365766/
www.beiderbeckes.com).* **Lunch served** noon-2.30pm
Mon-Sat. **Dinner served** 6.30-10pm Mon-Sat; 7-8pm
Sun. **Main courses** £10.95-£14.95. **Credit** MC, V.

Marmalade's was a New Orleans jazz dive and Bix
Beiderbecke was a 1920s cornet player who drank
himself into a young grave on prohibition liquor.
(The owner of this dark old Scarborough hotel is a
jazz fan.) The decor and branding is almost as dated
as the music, but on a more upbeat note there's tasty
smoked haddock fish cakes or an oriental duck salad
with hoi sin dressing and sesame toasts. Mains
sensibly exploit pheasant from the North York
Moors, Ryedale lamb and locally landed halibut and
lemon sole. Desserts are competently produced. Very
good by Scarborough's humdrum standards.

Restaurant at the Stephen
Joseph Theatre

*Westborough, Scarborough, North Yorkshire
YO11 1JW (01723 370541).* **Lunch served**
noon-2.30pm Mon-Fri. **Dinner served** 5.30-8pm
Mon-Thur; 5.30-10pm Fri. **Meals served** 10am-
10pm Sat. **No credit cards**.

The grand Odeon Cinema has metamorphosed into
a theatre. A broad staircase leads to a second-floor
restaurant that's flooded with light from a huge oval
sweep of glass, but both bar and eating area bear
the hallmarks of a tight furnishing budget. As a
place to eat it is good value, with lunch bringing a
menu of salads, filled baked potatoes, pasta dishes
and sandwiches. However, potted salmon with
country bread or pan-fried liver, black pudding,
caramelised onion and bacon mash deliver more
substantial fare. The short set evening menu is more
focused: shellfish chowder, braised shank of lamb,
and rhubarb and yoghurt tartlets.

Tuscany

*29 St Nicholas Street, Scarborough, North Yorkshire
YO11 2HF (01723 372100).* **Dinner served**
6-11pm Mon-Thur, Sun; 6-11.30pm Fri, Sat. **Main
courses** £6.25-£14.95. **Credit** MC, V.

The interior here is cheerful in a simple, pseudo-
Mediterranean sort of way, summed up by the life-
sized statue of David in the entrance. The menu may
be trad, but the ingredients are of a decent quality,
cooked to a sound standard and, as lamb chops with
onions, red wine, rosemary and garlic proved, served
in generous portions. Linguine with chopped cherry
tomatoes, crab and prawns, pizzas, wild mushroom
risotto and classics such as involtini di pollo alla
piemontese are firm favourites. Staff are welcoming
and go out of their way to be helpful.

SKIPTON

Bizzie Lizzie's ★

*36 Swadford Street, Skipton, North Yorkshire BD23
1QY (01756 793189).* **Meals served** 11.30am-
11.15pm Mon, Sun; 11.30am-11.30pm Tue-Thur;
11.30am-midnight Fri, Sat. **Main courses** £2.75-
£3.20. **No credit cards**.

Overlooking the canal and the higgledy-piggledy
charm of the houses lining it, Bizzie Lizzie's fish and
chip restaurant is alongside and above the takeaway
– with extra seating in the conservatory. The air-
conditioned cream and blue (licensed) restaurant has
swift, polite staff. If you're ravenous, start with a
prawn cocktail. Cod from Iceland, served skinless
and boned, is the most popular item on the menu,
but haddock, plaice and scampi are also available.
After the fish is battered, it's fried in beef dripping
and emerges with a light, crunchy finish. Have it
with neon-green mushy peas and flash-fried chips.

Le Caveau

*86 High Street, Skipton, North Yorkshire BD23 1JJ
(01756 794274).* **Lunch served** noon-2pm, **dinner
served** 7-9.30pm Tue-Sat. **Main courses** £9.75-
£16.95. **Credit** AmEx, MC, V.

Felons and sheep rustlers once gathered in this
barrel-vaulted cellar, which was a prison in darker
times. Today, even if the location is down to earth
and a touch cramped, the inmates are classier and
the food aims high. Richard Barker's menu inclines
towards the classics, but oldies are brought to life
with a deft touch. Melon is still decorously fanned,
but it is given a brunoise of tropical fruit and a
passion-fruit syrup. Chicken is stuffed – but with a
mousse of roasted garlic and thyme. Value is
reasonable at dinner; keener at lunchtime.

STAITHES

Endeavour

*1 High Street, Staithes, North Yorkshire TS13 5BH
(01947 840825/www.endeavour-restaurant.co.uk).*
Dinner served 7-9.30pm Tue-Sat. **Main courses**
£10-£15. **Credit** AmEx, DC, MC, V.

The best restaurant on this coast. Crab and lobster,
turbot, cod, lemon sole and halibut all go daily direct
from quay to kitchen. By evening they're
transformed into prime crab cocktail, grilled lobster
in hazel-nut butter, halibut in red wine sauce and a
cassoulet of squid, ling, cod and prawn. Meat, game

The Weaver's Shed. *See p295.*

and vegetarian dishes reinforce the house policy of best local sourcing and, among a selection of accomplished puddings and regional cheeses, the luscious slick of crème brûlée with raspberries stands out. There's an enticing atmosphere to the two compact dining rooms. The seashell and candlelight is just about right for an old smuggling harbour and most leave with a salty glow.

WATH

Sportsman's Arms

Wath, North Yorkshire HG3 5PP (01423 711306). Bar **Lunch served** noon-2pm daily. **Dinner served** 7-9pm Mon-Sat; 7-8pm Sun. *Restaurant* **Dinner served** 7-9pm Mon-Sat. **Main courses** £11.50-£12. **Set lunch** (Sun) £20 3 courses. **Credit** MC, V.

This 17th-century inn has been run by the same family since 1978. It is reached via a packhorse bridge and it's no surprise to find that calm, cosseting, old-style comfort is the hallmark. Food fads have made little impact on a kitchen that derives much of its produce from Yorkshire and many of its ideas from France. The dining room has a down-home elegance that finds an echo in the menu. It's impressively strong on fish. Expect roasted halibut with immaculate hollandaise or ling with a potent basil, tomato and garlic sauce. Trout is pulled from the River Nidd outside, and served with almonds and capers, while the surrounding moors provide excellent lamb and grouse.

WEST TANFIELD

Bruce Arms

Main Street, West Tanfield, North Yorkshire HG4 5JJ (01677 470325/www.brucearms.com). **Lunch served** noon-2pm Sun. **Dinner served** 6.30-9.30pm Wed-Sun. **Main courses** £10-£16. **Credit** MC, V.

A courtyard and stables give a settled look to this ivy-clad Georgian inn and the sense of calm continues in the bar, with its plain colour-washed walls and assortment of candle-topped wooden tables. Once a country local, it now styles itself as 'a bistro with rooms'. Large blackboards offer better-than-average pub food which might include a pleasingly savoury twice-baked wensleydale soufflé or a chunk of cod on creamy herb risotto with roasted red pepper sauce. The wine list is an enthusiast's compilation. Service is eager, though at busy times not always brisk.

WHITBY

Greens of Whitby

13 Bridge Street, Whitby, North Yorkshire YO22 4BG (01947 600284/www.greensofwhitby.com). **Food served** noon-10pm daily. **Dinner served** 6-10pm Mon-Sat; 6-9pm Sun. **Main courses** £11-£17. **Credit** MC, V.

Greens of Whitby is a welcome sanctuary from the tourist hordes. Naturally, fresh seafood features prominently. Look out for potted Whitby crab, Dover sole, sea bass and blackboard specials. Beyond fish, the emphasis remains on good local ingredients like braised daube of Yorkshire beef or fried Grosmont goat's cheese on a fig and hazel-nut salad with truffle oil. The mains are up around the £15 mark but the cooking is strong and the portions are hefty. Pancakes with soft fruits and ice-cream lead a choice of homely puddings; there are excellent English, if not Yorkshire, cheeses. All this in a charming, informal dining room and bar: nice place, nice people.

The Magpie Café ★ ★

14 Pier Road, Whitby, North Yorkshire YO21 3PU (01947 602058/www.magpiecafe.co.uk). **Meals served** 11.30am-9pm daily. **Main courses** £7.95-£17.95. **Credit** MC, V.

North East

The queues outside this family-run café opposite Whitby harbour are the stuff of legend. Once inside, the reasons for the crowds are clear – fish and chips don't get much better than this. The fish is always fresh and usually local, the batter is crisp and light, the chips are thick and perfectly cooked, the prices are reasonable and the portions are enormous. Their wide range of other seafood mains, like salmon with lime crème fraîche or skate in black butter, are equally impressive in terms of quality and quantity. No wonder the Magpie's been packing them in since 1937.

Sanders Yard ★
95 Church Street, Whitby, North Yorkshire YO22 4BH (01947 825010/www.sandersyard.co.uk). Café **Meals served** noon-6pm daily. *Restaurant* **Dinner served** 6-9pm daily. **Main courses** £9.95-£11.95. **Credit** AmEx, DC, MC, V.
Buried at the back of this crammed wholefood outlet, gift shop and B&B is an estimable café. Edge past the cheeses, the dried fruits and the real liquorice sticks, past kaftans and beeswax candles, to a colourful room of rough pine tables and mismatched chairs. At an invariably busy counter, young Whitby girls dispense teas and tisanes, fruit cups and coffee, sandwiches, wholesome soups, baked potatoes and own-made cakes. If you have children there is another room where they can stretch out on the floor and play with the toys – and leave you in blessed peace to sink into a sofa and read the paper.

White Horse & Griffin
Church Street, Whitby, North Yorkshire YO22 4BH (01947 604857/www.whitehorseandgriffin.co.uk). **Breakfast served** 8.30-10.30am, **lunch served** noon-3pm, **dinner served** 5-9pm daily. **Main courses** £6.95-£15.95. **Credit** MC, V.
This lovely old 17th-century coaching inn sports narrow passageways, stone-flagged floors and antique paraphernalia. If you don't get in the mood for Whitby's colourful history here, you never will. Amid the candles and the firelight, there is a carte offering steak, roast duck, steamed monkfish with mussels, wild mushroom cassoulet, a fast-track lunch and even a 'power' breakfast which includes sirloin steak and two fried eggs. Sadly, recent meals here have seen a dip in quality. More skill at the stove, more restraint with the cream jug could restore this Whitby treasure.

YARM

Chadwick's
104B High Street, Yarm, North Yorkshire TS15 9AU (01642 788558). **Meals served** 10am-5pm Mon-Sat. **Dinner served** 5.30-9.30pm Mon-Thur; 5.30-10pm Fri, Sat. **Main courses** £11.95-£16.50. **Credit** MC, V.
This popular town-centre bistro has attractive, inviting decor – the cosy ambience enhanced by lots of greenery, pine tables and a colour scheme that's shades of red, pink and taupe. Friendly staff in smart black and white uniforms serve a daytime menu

that's mostly Italian: ricotta ravioli, penne with pancetta and various pizzas, as well as specials like chicken satay and Chaddies Big Breakfast – a proper fry-up. Evenings see the weekly-changing menus step up a gear and broaden their horizons to include a short but eclectic selection: seared rare tuna with lime and ginger butter; king prawn and monkfish curry; grilled salmon with wok vegetables. Desserts return to the sweet haven of comfort puds.

Also in the area

Aagrah York Road, Steeton, Tadcaster, North Yorkshire LS24 8EG (01937 530888); **Aagrah** Unicorn House, Devonshire Place, Keighley Road, Skipton, North Yorkshire BD23 2LR (01756 790807); **Bettys Café Tea Rooms** 1 Parliament Square, Harrogate, North Yorkshire HG1 2QU (01423 502746); **Bettys Café Tea Rooms** 188 High Street, Northallerton, North Yorkshire DL7 8LF (01609 775154); **Bizzie Lizzie's** Albion Yard, Otley Street, Skipton, North Yorkshire BD23 1ED (01756 793785); **Brio** 44 Commercial Street, Harrogate, North Yorkshire HG1 1TZ (01423 529933); **The Hide Bar** 32 High Street, Yarm, North Yorkshire TS15 9AG (01642 355 558); **Hotel du Vin & Bistro** Prospect Place, Harrogate, North Yorkshire HG1 1LB (01423 856800); **McCoy's in Yarm** Strickland & Holt, 44 High Street, Yarm, North Yorkshire TS15 9AE (01642 791234).

South Yorkshire

SHEFFIELD

Blue Moon Brasserie
798 Chesterfield Road, Sheffield, South Yorkshire S8 0SF (0114 255 2004). **Dinner served** 6-9.45pm Mon-Thur, Sun; 6-10.30pm Fri, Sat. **Main courses** £8.95-£15.95. **Set dinner** (6-7pm) £14.95 3 courses. **Credit** MC, V.
An unlikely location on a busy road on the outskirts and an unprepossessing exterior hide a relaxed and satisfying dining experience. There is a large lounge bar area, that gets lively when busy, and a spacious pillared dining area. The food is a combination of traditional British dishes – calf's liver and black pudding tower on spinach and mash – and oriental sizzlers. Desserts such as chocolate and nut brownie with honey ice-cream are real crowd pleasers. Service varies from efficient to friendly.

Carriages
289 Abbeydale Road South, Sheffield, South Yorkshire S17 3LB (0114 235 0101/www.carriagesrestaurant. co.uk). **Lunch served** noon-2.30pm Sun. **Dinner served** 7-10pm Wed-Sat. **Main courses** £10-£16. **Set lunch** £14.95 2 courses, £18.95 3 courses. **Set dinner** £17 2 courses, £22 3 courses. **Credit** MC, V.
This popular restaurant would benefit from a makeover. Occupying a converted shop, the place lacks atmosphere. There is a small waiting area in the restaurant itself and the tables are closely set. The food is modern British with oriental touches: for example, Thai-spiced salmon comes with sweet chilli

jam, rocket and crème fraîche, but could be followed by a dish as trad as noisette of beef fillet with a steak and kidney pudding. Dishes look beautiful, but on our last visit, didn't quite deliver. Consolation may come in the form of roast vanilla peach tart with Sauternes custard or a selection of cheese.

Curator's House Restaurant & Tea Rooms ★

Botanical Gardens, Clarkehouse Road, Sheffield, South Yorkshire S10 2LN (0114 268 7788). **Lunch served** 11.30am-2.30pm daily. **Dinner served** 7-9.30pm Tue-Sat. **Main courses** £12.50-£15. **Credit** AmEx, MC, V.

In the botanical gardens and overlooking the newly restored palm houses, this place offers inventive café food by day and Sheffield's finest dining by night. The building is part-converted house and part-modern extension. Dishes are modern stuff, perfectly cooked. Starters may include sweet potato with chilli jam and crème fraîche (a favourite) or smoked duck with salsa verde; mains might be pork chop with apple and black pudding tart or seared red sea bream with spiced potato and raita. Try the crème brûlée (flavours change nightly), or stick with coffee and delicious petits fours. Service is confident and low-key, and there is a helpful, descriptive wine list.

Kashmir Curry Centre ★

121-125 Spital Hill, Sheffield, South Yorkshire S4 7LD (0114 272 6253). **Dinner served** 5pm-midnight Mon-Sat. **Main courses** £3.80-£6. **Set dinner** £8-£10 3 courses. **No credit cards**.

A Sheffield institution, offering freshly cooked curries in an unassuming café-style restaurant. There's no licence but a mutually beneficial relationship with the Eastwood pub opposite means jugs of lager and hand-pulled bitter can be brought across if the fruit lassi doesn't appeal. But this is not a curry-after-the-pub experience. The choice of main courses is almost infinite, involving meat, fish and unusual vegetables (try the pumpkin and blackbean karai). Service is prompt and friendly, the breads are excellent and the kulfi is compulsory.

Maso

33 Surrey Street, Sheffield, South Yorkshire S1 2LG (0114 272 1080). **Lunch served** 11.30am-3pm, **dinner served** 5.30-11pm Mon-Sat. **Main courses** £6.90-£15.60. **Set buffet** (11.30am-3pm, 5.30-7pm Tue-Sat) £5. **Credit** MC, V.

This city centre Italian-run restaurant is great value for money, offering Italian food that some say rivals Nonna's (*see below*) for quality and authenticity. Go à la carte and choose between pastas (say conchiglie with spinach, pine nuts, fresh tomatoes and ricotta), fish dishes (perhaps a Mediterranean fish and shellfish stew) and meaty mains (grilled lamb cutlets with a red wine, garlic and rosemary sauce). The buffet is very good value at £5 (it includes soup, salad and two hot dishes). Service is helpful, and this restaurant deserves to be more widely known.

Nonna's

537-541 Ecclesall Road, Sheffield, South Yorkshire S11 8PR (0114 268 6166/ www.nonnas.co.uk). **Lunch served** noon-3.30pm Mon-Thur; noon-4pm Fri, Sat; noon-5pm Sun. **Dinner served** 6-9.45pm daily. **Main courses** £7.95-£13.95. **Credit** MC, V.

This much-loved Italian has blossomed over the years to become a café-restaurant-antipasti bar. The place has a real Mediterranean vibe, helped by the largely Italian staff. Antipasti (£1.50-£1.95) range from marinated olives to squash, dolcelatte and red onion crostini. You could order a panini, but more substantial dishes at lunch include a fabulously tasty salad of courgette, mozzarella, mint, chilli, almonds and tomato or a slightly heavy grappa-cured salmon, smoked salmon and mascarpone terrine. To follow, chicken breast with salted lemons, couscous and pepper salad was more of a hit than penne, courgette and feta. In the evening the menu is extended to include the likes of a fish platter.

Rafters ★

220 Oakbrook Road, Nether Green, Sheffield, South Yorkshire S11 7ED (0114 230 4819). **Dinner served** 7-9.30pm Mon, Wed-Sat. **Set dinner** £24.95 3 courses. **Credit** AmEx, MC, V.

Once you're past the slightly unprepossessing entrance, things start to look up. The pleasantly decorated first-floor dining room is very restful; but there's no hushed reverence, even though the food is taken very seriously. Impressive starters include steamed asparagus with toasted brioche, truffle oil and lemon herb hollandaise, and locally reared smoked venison with Asian salad. Next char-grilled fillet of Angus beef with a rarebit glaze was served with frittata of wild mushrooms, baby spinach and shiraz wine sauce. This was beaten – just – in the taste stakes by rosemary-roasted cannon of Derbyshire lamb rolled in herbs and served with a tart of puréed parsnips and spring baby veg. Alluring puddings include trifle of mango, grapes and Muscat wine jelly with mascarpone cream and almond tuilles. An impressive operation in an unlikely setting.

Slammers

625-627 Ecclesall Road, Sheffield, South Yorkshire S11 8PT (0114 268 0999/ www.slammersseafood.co.uk). **Lunch served** noon-2.30pm Tue-Sat. **Dinner served** 6.30-10pm Mon-Sat. **Main courses** £11-£14. **Credit** MC, V.

This specialist fish restarant has expanded into the next-door shop since opening 18 months ago. The trademark dish is the slammer – six or 12 shot glasses of individual fish dishes, which are tasty if a little cold – but the menu is flexible, with many dishes being offered in small or large sizes. Non-shot options include Thai crab fish cakes, roast sea bass with tiger prawn and spinach curry and a seafood platter. The cooking could be a just little more inventive, but this is a popular restaurant which is busy throughout the week. Bring your own wine from Monday to Thursday (£2.50 corkage).

Thyme ★

*32-34 Sandygate, Crosspool, Sheffield, South
Yorkshire S10 5RY (0114 266 6096/
www.thymeforfood.co.uk).* **Lunch served** noon-
2.30pm daily. **Dinner served** 6-9.30pm Mon-Sat.
Main courses £10-£20. **Set lunch** (Mon-Sat)
£15 3 courses; (Sun) £20 3 courses. **Set dinner**
£22.50 3 courses. **Credit** AmEx, MC, V.

Chef-proprietor Richard Smith is a man with a
mission: to bring high-class cooking to the citizens
of Sheffield. In general, he succeeds. The light and
bright dining room is appealing, all blond wood and
white walls with eccentrically high-backed chairs.
The set Sunday lunch offered some upmarket takes
on British classics: Yorkshire pudding as a starter,
roast beef or pork loin with all the trimmings as
mains. Other main courses included tomato,
courgette and pesto risotto or roast Whitby cod with
Moroccan couscous, aubergines and yoghurt.
There's a slightly precious air to the proceedings and
the rigid booking policy staggers dining times,
meaning the restaurant was half-empty on our visit.

Also in the area

Aagrah Great North Road, Woodlands, Doncaster,
South Yorkshire DN6 7RA (01302 728888);
The Hide Bar 3 Wood Street, Doncaster,
South Yorkshire DN1 3LH (01302 760777).

West Yorkshire

ADDINGHAM

The Fleece

*152-154 Main Street, Addingham, West Yorkshire
LS29 0LY (01943 830491).* **Lunch served** noon-
2.15pm, **dinner served** 6-9.15pm Mon-Sat. **Meals
served** noon-8pm Sun. **Main courses** £5.75-£13.
Credit MC, V.

Chris Monkman transformed this village pub in
2002. Rough wood tables, odd chairs and a
blackboard menu are the setting for lamb hot-pot,
Whitby fish pie, roast belly of pork with a honey
glaze, omelettes, sandwiches stuffed with rare roast
beef and a worthy Ploughmans. Specials feature fish
such as Whitby crab, clams in garlic, grilled
sardines, seared tuna and seared scallops on a fennel
and tarragon risotto. Praise, too, for a superior kids'
menu of moules marinière or sausage and mash.
Among desserts, check out a silky St Clements
cheesecake with warm caramel sauce. Jazz nights
and outdoor eating in summer are further attractions.

BRADFORD

Karachi ★

*15 Neal Street, Bradford, West Yorkshire BD5 0BX
(01274 732015).* **Meals served** 11am-1am daily.
Main courses £3.30-£4.50. **No credit cards.**

Arguably the first curry house in Bradford,
probably still the cheapest, and never quite finished.

With chipped formica tables, tubular chairs and bare
walls, for years it supplied neither a menu nor
anything more than a chapati to scoop up the food.
Karachi regulars travel miles for their spicy fix.
Onion bhajias are 50p, two samosas cost £1 and the
dahl lentil curry is £2.90. More pertinently, the food
emerging from the rough-hewn open kitchen is as
good as it's ever been.

Mumtaz Paan House ★

*286-300 Great Horton Road, Bradford,
West Yorkshire BD7 3HS (01274 571861/
www.mumtaz.co.uk).* **Meals served** 11am-midnight
daily. **Main courses** £5.99-£9.50. **Set meals**
£12.50-£22.50 3 courses. **Credit** AmEx, DC, MC, V.

An old stone cottage and a modern conservatory
house one of Bradford's most successful and
fashionable Indian restaurants. Start with samosas,
pakoras or paneer rolls, lovely filo-style pastries
stuffed with cheese. Often fiery but singing with
flavour, the lamb, chicken, fish and vegetable karahi
dishes are sold by weight: 220g or 440g. Karahi
chana is a chickpea dish in rich curry sauce served
with rice or roti. Marinated cod needed yoghurt to
quell the heat. The milder karahi paneer shahi has
cheese, tomato, mustard seed and chestnut cream.
Mumtaz is strictly no alcohol. Have a fruit juice or a
jug of sweet or salted lassi and enjoy Bradford's
smartest young Asian blades strutting their stuff.

Nawaab ★

*32 Manor Road, Bradford, West Yorkshire BD1
4QE (01274 720371/www.nawaab.com).* **Lunch
served** noon-2pm Mon-Fri. **Dinner served** 5.30-
11.30pm Mon-Thur; 5.30-12.30am Fri, Sat; 4-11pm
Sun. **Main courses** £5-£11. **Set lunch** £7.95
3 courses. **Set dinner** £10-£22 3 courses. **Credit**
AmEx, DC, MC, V.

Nawaab has been just about at the top of the
Bradford tree for 15 years, and in a city with some
150 Indian restaurants that's some achievement.
There are now Nawaabs in Manchester and
Huddersfield, in Benidorm and Majorca. Housed in
the former NatWest bank, Nawaab's menu has some
200 dishes. Happily they are invariably cooked with
consummate professionalism and skill. Dishes are
rich, aromatic and subtly spiced, if a little too subtle
for some die-hards. Butter chicken is as succulent and
rich as it sounds; lamb haandi is a beautiful slow-
cooked Punjabi dish soaring with flavours. Service
veers from smooth and friendly to slow and surly.

CLECKHEATON

Aakash ★

*Providence Place, Bradford Road, Cleckheaton, West
Yorkshire BD19 3PN (01274 878866/870011/
www.aakash.co.uk).* **Dinner served** 6-11pm daily.
Main courses £7.50-£8.50. **Credit** AmEx, MC, V.

Spectacular. It claims to be the biggest Indian
restaurant in the world and with 900 covers it might
even be true. Arrive after dark to see the massive
Victorian Congregational chapel floodlit like a latter-

day Parthenon. Inside the balconied and pillared hangar is a neon-lit bar and a sky mural on the ceiling, all done up in dazzling gold, blue and white. There is an à la carte menu, but staple business centres on the Friday and Saturday buffets – and at £15 a head (£8 children aged ten or younger), it's a record price for these parts. There are eight different curries, as well as familiar pakoras, samosas, Indian breads, rice and salads. Of course, the quality can't live up to the setting but that's hardly the point.

ELLAND

La Cachette

31 Huddersfield Road, Elland, West Yorkshire HX5 9AW (01422 378833). **Lunch served** noon-2.30pm Mon-Sat. **Dinner served** 6-9.30pm Mon-Thur; 6-10pm Fri, Sat. **Main courses** £8.95-£15.95. **Set lunch** £8.95 2 courses. **Set dinner** (Mon-Thur; 6-7pm Fri, Sat) £15.95 3 courses incl half bottle wine. **Credit** MC, V.
Modernism meets Edwardiana in this genial, clubbable restaurant. While candlelit corners are calculated to promote intimacy, dining booths extending from the central bar offer a more sociable approach. The menu opens with 'starter size dishes', which might include honey-roasted ham with poached pear and stilton mousse, before heading off down various pathways: salads, pastas, risottos, eggs, fish, seafood, meat, poultry and grills. Bistro

classics like beef bourguignon exemplify the gutsy cooking. If the menu reaches Old Testament lengths, it's nothing compared to the stunning wine list.

GOLCAR

The Weaver's Shed ★

Acre Mill, Knowl Road, Golcar, West Yorkshire HD7 4AN (01484 654284). **Lunch served** noon-2pm Tue-Sun. **Dinner served** 7-9pm Tue-Fri; 7-10pm Sat. **Main courses** £13.95-£18.95. **Set lunch** (Tue-Fri) £9.95 2 courses, £12.95 3 courses. **Credit** DC, MC, V.
One of Yorkshire's best restaurants back in the dark ages of the 1970s, this high Pennine sanctuary has peaked under Stephen Jackson. Real precision and skill in the cooking is witnessed in roast loin of rare breed pork with pig's trotter or 24-hour apple confit terrine with gingerbread ice-cream. But the keynote is his commitment to local ingredients. Best of all is the produce from their gardens and orchard. Wild garlic goes into butter, nasturtiums and marigold into salads, meadowsweet into ice-cream. Even the Pimms gets salad burnet and borage flowers.

HAWORTH

Weaver's

15 West Lane, Haworth, West Yorkshire BD22 8DU (01535 643822/www.weaversmallhotel.co.uk). **Lunch served** noon-2pm Sun. **Dinner served** 6.30-9pm

Salts Diner. See p297.

Tue-Sat. **Main courses** £8.95-£16.95. **Set meals** (6.30-7.30pm Tue-Thur, 6.30-7pm Fri, noon-2pm Sun) £12.50 2 courses. **Credit** AmEx, DC, MC, V.

The Rishworth family has run this place for 25 years and continuity expresses itself in consistency of food and service. The owner's son is now at the stove, cooking a menu whose strong regional thread comes from respect for local produce, particularly game in season. Modernism gets a look-in, but the house style is seen to best advantage in a shoulder of local lamb slowly braised to melting stickiness. And puddings are worth a trek across these desolate moors. Service by local young people is immensely friendly. An educated wine list is fairly priced.

HEBDEN BRIDGE

Laughing Gravy

The Birchcliffe Centre, Birchcliffe Road, Hebden Bridge, West Yorkshire HX7 8DG (01422 844425/ www.laughinggravy.co.uk). **Dinner served** 7.30-8pm Thur-Sat; 4.30-5pm Sun. **Set meal** £15.75 12 dishes. **Credit** MC, V.

While the Birchcliffe residential conference centre (in a reclaimed hillside chapel) runs the life-enhancing courses, Laughing Gravy does the vegetarian catering and on Friday and Saturday evenings it opens its informal basement restaurant to the public. On the menu are four starters, four mains and four puddings – and you get the lot, as a sort of veggie meze. Delicious food and high value. It might be butterbean pâté, tomatoes stuffed with wild rice, dulce and saké, or kidney bean croquettes filled with melting garlic butter.

HONLEY

Mustard & Punch

6 Westgate, Honley, West Yorkshire HD9 6AA (01484 662066). **Lunch served** noon-2pm Tue-Fri. **Dinner served** 7-10pm Tue-Thur; 6-10pm Fri, Sat. **Main courses** £9.95-£15.95. **Set lunch** £10.50 2 courses, £13.50 3 courses. **Set dinner** £17.95 2 courses, £21.95 3 courses. **Credit** AmEx, DC, MC, V.

Wall-mounted jars of Colman's provide the mustard while two chef brothers supply the punch at this elegant Pennine village bistro. Classicism informs, but rarely stifles an ever-questing menu. It might run from smoked eel and foie gras terrine with jus Parisien and granny smith apples, to pigeon with purple fig tart, spiced lentils and morel-scented gnocchi. The ground floor dining room is the best place to enjoy all this, though the basement is not without atmosphere. A resourceful wine list pursues some interesting byways. Service is the only variable.

ILKLEY

Box Tree

37 Church Street, Ilkley, West Yorkshire LS29 9DR (01943 608484/www.theboxtree.co.uk). **Lunch served** noon-2.30pm Tue-Sun. **Dinner served**

7-9.30pm Tue-Sat. **Main courses** £12.50-£22. **Set meals** £19.50 2 courses. **Credit** AmEx, DC, MC, V.

Restaurant or doll's house? This 18th-century cottage has been drawing wealthy Yorkshire types for 40 years and, physically, not much has changed. Stability has not extended to the kitchen – chefs have been coming and going at quite a rate. Alan Hill, the latest, arrived from Juniper in Cheshire, pledging to regain the Michelin star. His bright cooking shows real promise with wonderful dishes such as foie gras with fresh English asparagus, truffle and bacon pancake and hollandaise sauce, or wild sea bass with smoked salmon brandade, lobster bisque and ginger. The wine list starts at £13 and doesn't stop until it reaches £2,162 for a bottle of 1989 Domaine de la Romanée Conti. Service is formal but not forbidding.

Farsyde

1-3 New Brook Street, Ilkley, West Yorkshire LS29 8DQ (01943 602030). **Lunch served** 11.30am-2pm, **dinner served** 6-10pm Tue-Sat. **Main courses** £10.95-£14.95. **Set lunch** £12.95 3 courses. **Set dinner** (6-7.15pm Tue-Thur) £12.95 2 courses. **Credit** MC, V.

With bright walls and wooden tables, spruced up with tablecloths and candles in the evening, Farsyde produces simple dishes in relaxed surroundings. Start with duck and ginger dumplings with king prawns and plum sauce, or wild mushroom risotto with asparagus garnish and lemongrass dressing. Go on to lamb with a herb crust on apple rösti and creamed leeks. Finish with a toffee trio: sticky toffee pudding, toffee ice-cream and toffee brûlée. Gavin Beedham has a decent wine list and hosts fish nights and jazz brunches. A good neighbourhood bistro.

MARSDEN

Olive Branch

Marsden, West Yorkshire HD7 6LU (01484 844487). **Dinner served** 6.30-9.30pm Tue-Sat. **Meals served** 1-8.30pm Sun. **Main courses** £10.50-£17.50. **Set meals** (Tue-Thur, Sun) £13.50 2 courses. **Credit** MC, V.

The Pennine village of Marsden, the setting for a brief glorious spell of the *League of Gentlemen*'s Local Shop, can muster only one restaurant but it's a goodie. The spruced-up roadside inn – glowing fires, beams, old scrubbed pine tables – pursues its own gentle eccentricities. Pinned around the door frames, on the beer pumps and along the bar front are dozens of handwritten cards offering an eclectic repertoire: crab and lobster soup, rabbit sausage with leek mash, medallions of beef in port wine, roast duck with chilli. The cooking shows verve.

MILL BANK

The Millbank ★

Mill Bank, West Yorkshire HX6 3DY (01422 825588/www.themillbank.com). **Lunch served** noon-2pm Wed-Fri; 12.30-3.30pm Sun. **Dinner**

served 5.30-9.30pm Tue-Thur; 5.30-10pm Fri, Sat.
Main courses £10.95-£14.95. **Set meals** (5.30-7pm
Tue-Thur) £13.25 2 courses, £16.95 3 courses.
Credit AmEx, MC, V.
Spectacularly perched high above the Ryburn
Valley, this is one of the smartest pub makeovers in
Yorkshire. Outdoor decking allows fair-weather
eating with classic Pennine views over woods and a
rare surviving mill. A clean-cut contemporary
interior reflects chef Glen Futter's confident cooking.
Look out for starters like braised ham hock with
wensleydale potato cake, or belly pork in honey and
cloves. Follow up with halibut fillet with spinach
mash, mushroom and poached egg tartlet or roast
suckling pig and sauté of mushroom and potato –
robust dishes expertly cooked. Equally good
desserts, a lovely Yorkshire cheeseboard, great bar
snacks and good vibes all round.

ROYDHOUSE

The Three Acres Inn
*Roydhouse, West Yorkshire HD8 8LR
(01484 602606/www.threeacres.com).* **Lunch
served** noon-1.45pm Mon-Fri, Sun. **Dinner
served** 7-9.30pm daily. **Main courses** £10-£16.
Set meals (Sun) £17.95 3 courses. **Credit**
AmEx, MC, V.
You can't miss it. Just head towards Yorkshire's
tallest tower, the Emley Moor TV tansmitter that
famously fell down in 1969 and now has listed
building status. The hefty Three Acres Inn sits
directly in its shadow with panoramic Pennine
views and has grown into a hugely popular local
institution serving 150 covers a night, with
surprising quality for such an industrial turnover
and extensive menu. There's duck, steaks, braised
oxtail and plenty of seafood – including a dozen
Loch Fyne queenies grilled with gruyère, garlic and
mustard; oysters with horseradish salsa or grilled
with Thai butter; Whitby lobster, salmon, mussels,
Dover sole, monkfish and more. Everyone is served
with lightning speed and energy by very cheerful
young staff.

SALTAIRE

Salts Diner
*Salts Mill, Saltaire, West Yorkshire BD18 3LB
(01274 530533).* **Open** 10am-5.30pm, **meals
served** 10am-4.30pm daily. **Main courses**
£6.50-£10. **Credit** MC, V.
Saltaire, the vast Italianate mill and workers' village
created by Victorian philanthropist Sir Titus Salt,
has a definitive Hockney collection, beautiful
bookshops, drop-dead design galleries and a handy
pair of restaurants: a new fish bar (01274 531163)
and the ever-popular all-day diner. Lunch could be
Cumberland sausage and mash with braised red
cabbage, real burger and french fries, grilled ribeye
steak, duck confit or salad niçoise. And to follow,
chocolate fudge cake or New York monster cookie

ice-cream. The scope and quality of the food is pretty
reliable and the overall setting – the ultimate loft
conversion – is irresistible.

SHELF

Bentley's
*12 Wade House Road, Shelf, West Yorkshire
HX3 7RE (01274 690992/www.bentleys-
foodandwine.co.uk).* **Lunch served** noon-2pm
Tue-Fri. **Dinner served** 6.30-9pm Tue-Sat. **Main
courses** £10.50-£18. **Set lunch** £5.95 1 course,
£9.25 2 courses, £10.25 3 courses. **Credit** MC, V.
A family-run roadside bistro, where drinks are taken
in a small bar reminiscent of great granny's parlour
– except that she appears to have no dining room. All
is made plain when diners are escorted through a
narrow opening and down steps into an atmospheric
double cellar. Chef Paul Bentley cooks simply and
without pretension, and his blackboard menu derives
its British tone from regional produce: crab from
Whitby, game from the moors, rhubarb from
Wakefield. There are first-rate own-made bread and
ice-creams too. Service is friendly and concerned.

SHIPLEY

Aagrah ★
*4 Saltaire Road, Shipley, West Yorkshire BD18 3HN
(01274 530880).* **Lunch served** noon-2.30pm Mon-
Fri. **Dinner served** 5.30-11.30pm Mon-Thur;
5.30pm-midnight Fri, Sat; 4-10pm Sun. **Main
courses** £6-£9. **Set lunch** £5.95. **Set dinner**
£14-£15 2 courses. **Credit** AmEx, DC, MC, V.
The Sabir brothers opened the first Aagrah in a
Shipley side-street in 1977. It's now a prominent local
chain with eight branches across Yorkshire serving
native Kashmiri dishes and lots more. The Shipley
flagship has relocated to bigger and better premises
in a former car showroom – so ample parking and
easy to spot (there's an elephant on the roof). The
menu is vast covering several subcontinental bases
– Kashmiri, Goan and Hyderabadi – and the well-
defined cooking holds up. There's vindaloo, korma,
balti, tikka masala with all the matching vegetarian
versions. Try saag gosht, a dish of lamb and spinach
with ginger, coriander, chilli and cardomom, or murg
bangan. The lunchtime buffet is a bargain.

Also in the area
Aagrah Barnsley Road, Sandal, Wakefield, West
Yorkshire WF1 5NX (01924 242222); **Aagrah**
4 Saltaire Road, Saltaire, Shipley, West Yorkshire
BD18 3HN (01274 530880); **Aagrah** 250 Wakefield
Road, Denby Dale, Huddersfield, West Yorkshire
HD8 8SU (01484 866266); **Aagrah** Aberford Road,
Garforth, Leeds, West Yorkshire LS25 2HF (0113
287 6606); **Aagrah** 483 Bradford Road, Pudsey, West
Yorkshire LS28 8ED (01274 668818); **Bettys Café
Tea Rooms** 32 The Grove, Ilkley, West Yorkshire
LS29 9EE (01943 608029); **Nawaab** 35 Westgate,
Huddersfield, West Yorkshire HD1 1NY (01484 422775).

North East

Scotland

Scotland

0   75 miles

0   120 km

© Copyright Time Out Group 2003

North Ronaldsay
Westray
Rousay
Sanday
Stronsay
Stromness
Kirkwall
Hoy
St Margarets Hope
South Ronaldsay

WESTERN ISLES
Port of Ness
Balchrick
Durness
Skerray
Tongue
Portskerra
Thurso
John O' Groats
Pentland Firth

Outer Hebrides
Isle of Lewis
Stornoway
Culkein
Unapool
Altnaharra
Kinbrace
Mybster
Wick
Lybster

Taransay
Pabbay
Berneray
North Uist
Benbecula
Harris
Lochinver
Achiltibuie
Ullapool
Laide
Kincardine
Lairg
Dornoch
Brora
Dornoch Firth
Moray Firth
Lossiemouth
Buckie
Macduff
Fraserburgh

South Uist
Barra
Colbost
Skye
Applecross
Kishorn
Gairloch
Braemore Junction
Achnasheen
Invergordon
Cromarty
Nairn
Forres
Elgin
Keith
Mintla
Peterhead

Inner Hebrides
Canna
Kyle of Lochalsh
Drumnadrochit
Inverness
Grantown-on-Spey
Craigelliachie
Huntly
Inverurie
Ellon
Dyce
Aberdeen

Ardvasar
Mallaig
Eigg
Invergarry
Invermoriston
Aviemore
Kingussie
Newtonmore
Ballater
Braemar
Banchory
Stonehaven

Coll
Fort William
Spean Bridge
Dalwhinnie
Laurencekirk
Johnshaven

Tobermory
Glencoe
Pitlochry
Brechin
Montrose

Tiree
Mull
Oban
Aberfeldy
Blairgowrie
Forfar
Inverkeilor
Arbroath
Carnoustie
Dunkeld
Dundee
Firth of Tay
NORTH

Iona
Cairndow
Callander
Auchterarder
Perth
Cupar
St Andrews
SEA

ATLANTIC OCEAN
Colonsay
Jura
Crinan
Dunblane
Alloa
Glenrothes
Cowdenbeath
Stirling
Dunfermline
Firth of Forth

Islay
Helensburgh
Dunoon
Dumbarton
Denny
Stenhousemuir
Linlithgow
Falkirk
Livingston
Gullane
North Berwick
Dunbar
Haddington
Edinburgh
Eyemouth

Tarbert
Tighnabruaich
Greenock
Paisley
Glasgow
Hamilton
Peebles
Galashiels
Berwick-upon-Tweed

Sound of Jura
Rothesay
Bute
Dalry
Biggar
Melrose
Coldstream
Kelso

Arran
Brodick
Troon
Prestwick
Ayr
Kilmarnock
Muirkirk
Cumnock
New Cumnock
Sanquhar

Campbeltown
Maybole
Turnberry
Thornhill
Moffat
Kielder
Morpeth
NORTHUMBERLAND
Newcastle-upon-Tyne

Rathlin I.
Ballantrae
New Galloway
Dumfries
Lockerbie
Gretna
Carlisle
TYNE & WEAR

Londonderry (Derry)
Kirkcolm
Newton Stewart
Crossmichael
Annan
Alston
Durham
DURHAM

Larne
Stranraer
Glenluce
Kirkcudbright
Dalbeattie
Solway Firth

Antrim
Drummore
Whithorn
Luce Bay
Wigtown Bay
Workington
Keswick
Penrith
CUMBRIA
Darlington

BELFAST
Bangor
Windermere
Kendal
Hawes
Northallerton

Monaghan
Armagh
Ramsey
Isle of Man
Douglas
Morecambe
NORTH YORKSHIRE

Dundalk
Castletown
LANCS

Edinburgh

The Apartment

7-13 Barclay Place, EH10 4HW (0131 228 6456).
Lunch served noon-3pm Sat, Sun. **Dinner served**
5.45-11pm daily. **Main courses** £6.90-£10.60.
Credit DC, MC, V.

The Apartment arrived in autumn 1999 and 'le tout
Edimbourg' fell in love with its minimalism, menu
and super-hip staff. Its success leans on the food, but
its status as a canteen for middle-class hipsters owes
a lot to location: the upmarket areas of Bruntsfield,
Merchiston and Marchmont are right on the
doorstep. Key dishes are 'chunky healthy lines',
known as CHLs (char-grilled chunks on a skewer,
served with ample amounts of pitta and coleslaw),
and 'slabs' (thick, crunchy own-made bread with
'stuff'). A typical CHL would come with North
African spicy lamb balls, merguez and basil-
wrapped goat's cheese, while a slab might entail
melted gruyère, honey-roasted ham, cracked black
pepper and sweet mustard. It's a riot of flavour – but
if it's not your thing, there are also salads, grilled
fish, steaks and pasta. Its Old Town sister, the
Outsider, which opened in autumn 2002, is much
bigger, but the menu is the same.

The Atrium ★

10 Cambridge Street, EH1 2ED (0131 228 8882/
www.atriumrestaurant.co.uk). **Lunch served**
noon-2pm Mon-Fri. **Dinner served** 6-10pm
Mon-Sat. **Main courses** £16-£19.50. **Set dinner**
£25 3 courses. **Credit** AmEx, DC, MC, V.

Who's the daddy? One answer in this city. Andrew
Radford's flagship restaurant burst on the scene in
1993 and changed the rules of the game as far as top
Edinburgh eateries were concerned. Its design still
looks contemporary, with low-key lighting, dark
wood and copper fixtures and fittings all adding to
a real sense of atmosphere and otherness. It's in the
same building as the Traverse Theatre (downstairs)
and Radford's less formal bar-café blue (one floor
upstairs). The Atrium offers destination dining that
has stood the test of time. A typical three-course
dinner would include the likes of seared scallops and
monkfish with belly pork and spicy vinaigrette to
start, fillet of sea bass with spinach, fondant potato
and aubergine caviar as a main, and traditional
custard tart with warm poached blackberries to
finish. The wine list is one of the best. Flexible
enough to be romantic or businesslike, this is high
calibre all round.

Café Royal Circle Bar/Oyster Bar

Circle Bar *19 West Register Street, EH2 2AA*
(0131 556 1884). **Open** 11am-11pm Mon-Wed;
11am-midnight Thur; 11am-1am Fri, Sat; 12.30-11pm

Sun. **Main courses** £4-£7. **Meals served** 11am-
10pm Mon-Sat; 12.30-10pm Sun. **Oyster Bar** *17A*
West Register Street (0131 556 4124). **Lunch
served** noon-2pm, **dinner served** 7-10pm daily.
Main courses £15-£25. **Credit** AmEx, DC, MC, V.

A wonderful old island bar dominates this classic
venue where the walls are decorated with Royal
Doulton tiled pictures of famous inventors (Caxton,
Faraday, Watt and the like) – a Victorian paean to
progress. You'll usually find several cask ales on
offer, up to 20 single malts, even some wine, and if
you can't cram yourself into the leather booths
there's lots of standing room. The adjacent Café
Royal Oyster Bar beyond the partition is, if
anything, an even grander affair. A destination
restaurant before the term was coined, it prides itself
on rich, old-school fish dishes, which it does
remarkably well. Three courses might involve half
a dozen oysters on ice to start, fillet of salmon in
camembert and white wine sauce with poached
mussels and prawns as a main, and then one of the
restaurant's simply awesome brûlées (rowanberry
and elderflower, perhaps) for dessert.

Le Café St Honoré

34 NW Thistle Street Lane, EH2 1EA (0131 226
2211/www.cafesthonore.com). **Lunch served** noon-
2.15pm daily. **Dinner served** 5.30-6.45pm, 7-10pm
Mon-Fri; 6-10pm Sat, Sun. **Main courses** £13.75-
£19.25. **Set dinner** (5.30-6.45pm Mon-Fri) £13.50
2 courses, £18 3 courses. **Credit** AmEx, MC, DC, V.

Imagine if you will that Toulouse-Lautrec is still
bristling with libido, and the cancan dancers in the
corner are wrecked on absinthe. Mind you, Le Café
St Honoré being *très* middle-class, the dancers would
be politely asked to leave. This restaurant recalls
nothing more than *fin de siècle* Paris in decor, while
the food is distinctly French with an occasional
modern international twist. There might be grilled
oysters with crayfish, bacon and gruyère to start,
but also warm salad of scallops, chicken tikka and
chorizo. Mains are a little more traditional: boeuf
bourguignon with mash or lamb rump with creamed
haricots, spinach and mint sauce. There's a great
selection of house wines by the glass, and desserts
are as you might expect (crème brûlée, tarte tatin,
artisan cheeses).

Channings

12-15 South Learmonth Gardens, EH4 1EZ (0131
315 2225/www.channings.co.uk). **Lunch served**
12.30-2.30pm Tue-Sat. **Dinner served** 7-10pm Tue-
Thur; 6.30-10pm Fri, Sat. **Main courses** £11-£23.
Credit AmEx, DC, MC, V.

Channings is a smart hotel (tenemental suburban),
around 15 minutes' walk from the west end of

Princes Street. But it feels like a million miles and is valued by people who like to be close to the pulse and simultaneously discreet. It has two basement restaurants: an informal Mediterranean bistro and a fine dining room. The latter is tastefully furnished with the odd contemporary touch to buttress a wooden-fixtured classicism. Its wine list is unpretentious, service friendly, and the cooking very good indeed. Three courses might bring pan-fried scallops and ceps with bayleaf and cep foam to start; roasted Buccleuch beef with potato crisps, lardons, flageolet au jus and a shallot purée as a main; then a fabulous full dessert like crushed strawberry compote with vanilla fromage frais, crispy puffed rice, and red berry shortbread. There are excellent vegetarian options too.

David Bann

56-58 St Mary's Street, EH1 1SX (556 5888/ www.davidbann.com). **Meals served** 11am-10.30pm daily. **Main courses** £9.50-£10.50. **Credit** AmEx, MC, V.

David Bann was once the mainstay of the popular but now defunct vegetarian restaurant Bann UK in Hunter Square. He left to start up his own veggie place in St Mary's Street in late 2002 – a stylish establishment with a minimal and tasteful look, dark wood fittings and dark red decor. After a few teething troubles, the new restaurant has developed a deft touch in the kitchen and smooth service. You can choose from starters and snacks (dim sum, soup of the day), light meals, salads, mains and sides. Three courses could entail aloo bonda (spiced potato dumplings with coconut and coriander sauce and spicy tomato salsa), gorgonzola polenta with roast Mediterranean vegetables and a sweet tomato salad, then amaretto cheesecake. There are appropriate wines, good beers (Fraoch heather ale, organic lagers from Germany) and the only caveat is that this site has seen the death of a procession of restaurants – hopefully, David Bann can stay the course.

Duck's at Le Marché Noir

2-4 Eyre Place, EH3 5EP (0131 558 1608/ www.ducks.co.uk). **Lunch served** noon-2.30pm Tue-Fri. **Dinner served** 7-10pm Mon-Thur; 7-10.30pm Fri, Sat; 6.30-9.30pm Sun. **Main courses** £9.50-£20.50. **Set lunch** (12-2pm Tue-Fri) £10.70 3 courses. **Credit** AmEx, DC, MC, V.

Duck's offers an intimate and polite (but not overly so) setting on the fringe of Edinburgh's New Town, with a lot of stress put on both food and good service. The wine list is also quite a wonder to behold, with numerous affordable bottles as well as examples of top-end Bordeaux that don't even carry a price. The bargain lunch menu might involve a herb-rich tomato and rosemary soup starter and a crafted main such as cod on herb and mustard potato salad, complemented very nicely by a caper vinaigrette. Dessert? Passion-fruit parfait with coconut ice-cream is just fabulous. The à la carte menu entails a range of tastes from crispy duck, mango and cashew salad with lime and coriander dressing (as a starter) to

halibut with polenta crust on fennel and sun-blush tomato salad (as a main). The care that proprietor Malcolm Duck brings to bear has established his restaurant as a real player on the local scene.

Fishers Bistro

1 The Shore, EH6 6QW (0131 554 5666/ www.fishersbistro.co.uk). **Meals served** noon-10.30pm daily. **Main courses** £8.50-£17. **Credit** AmEx, DC, MC, V.

The nautical decor at Fishers is pretty well justified by the fact that the harbour's on the doorstep and you can see real working ships as you walk down the Shore to the restaurant. Diners can eat in the bar or in the small raised area adjacent. It's essentially a fish restaurant, although there are a few meat choices (vegetarians should phone ahead). Starters include char-grilled marlin with a spiced crust and mango sauce, cold crevettes with aïoli, and a very moist and creamy crab, mascarpone and asparagus tart. The international influences are even more apparent in mains such as whole steamed sea bass with wilted greens and soy, and halibut fillet with apricot and curry sauce and lemongrass rice. Those opting for the simple (and legendary) fish cakes get a rich, robust portion. Fishers in the City is at 58 Thistle Street; 0131 225 5109.

La Garrigue

31 Jeffrey Street, EH1 1DH (0131 557 3032/ www.lagarrigue.co.uk). **Lunch served** noon-2.30pm, **dinner served** 6.30-10pm daily. **Main courses** £14.50-£16. **Set dinner** (Mon-Thur, Sun) £15.50 2 courses, £19.50 3 courses; (Fri, Sat) £17.50 2 courses, £21.50 3 courses. **Credit** AmEx, DC, MC, V.

This restaurant sneaked quietly on to the Edinburgh scene in mid 2001 with little fanfare. Chef-proprietor Jean Michel Gauffre was formerly executive chef at the city's Sheraton Hotel, but La Garrigue allows more scope to pursue his interest in food from his home region – Languedoc in south-east France. The decor is high-class rustic, but the cooking is far from rough and ready and the ingredients are top quality and well sourced. You could start with fish soup or salted cod purée with garlic croûtons and rocket; simplicity is a key feature. Mains include leg of rabbit stuffed with Cevennes ham and juniper berries, and sea bream with chard and tomatoes on Camargue barley. Languedoc wines feature heavily. Obviously, the menu changes, but if you can catch baked figs and blackberries with muscat custard as a dessert, you'll be a happy diner.

Haldane's ★

39A Albany Street, EH1 3QY (0131 556 8407/ www.haldanesrestaurant.com). **Dinner served** 6-9pm Mon-Thur, Sun; 6-9.30pm Fri, Sat. **Main courses** £15.75-£24.50. **Credit** DC, MC, V.

If a good Scottish restaurant is one that is run by Scots, uses the best local ingredients and serves dishes with a Scots slant (but no gimmickry), then Haldane's qualifies in spades. Indeed, some regard it as the best Scottish restaurant in the city. Housed

Scotland

in the basement of the Albany Townhouse Hotel on the eastern fringes of the New Town, it has been building a steady reputation and clientele since it opened in 1997. The main dining room looks out on to the garden, and there's also a 'study' room for more intimate meals. The decor is discreet and tasteful. A full three courses could bring baked oak-smoked salmon and leek tart with white wine and mussel sauce to start; Scottish beef fillet topped with brandy and black peppercorn sabayon; then sticky toffee pudding with vanilla ice-cream for dessert. The wine list is good and there are lots of single malts. Very fine indeed.

Harvey Nichols Forth Floor

Harvey Nichols, 30-34 St Andrew Square, EH2 2AD (0131 524 8350/www.harveynichols.com). Brasserie **Meals served** 10am-6pm Mon; 10am-10pm Tue-Sat; noon-6pm Sun. **Main courses** £9-£12. **Set lunch** £14 2 courses, £17.50 3 courses. **Set dinner** £10 2 courses, £13.50 3 courses. *Restaurant* **Lunch served** noon-3pm Mon-Fri; noon-3.30pm Sat, Sun. **Dinner served** 6-10pm Tue-Sat. **Main courses** £12-£18. **Credit** AmEx, DC, MC, V.

There are few contenders for the title of 'best restaurant in an Edinburgh retail outlet' and this is certainly the leading one. The swish people's posh shop arrived in the Scottish capital in autumn 2002 with its usual expensive (Harvey) knick-knacks, but also a restaurant and bar-brasserie perched on top. Key question: would you want to eat there? Simple answer: yes. The overall impression is 1970s funky, moderated by modern panache – imagine a high-class *Space 1999* canteen – with a lot of glass and a balcony offering cool views of Edinburgh Castle and the Firth of Forth (hence the punning name). And the food? A typical three-course meal in the bar-brasserie would be prosciutto and rocket salad with celeriac and mustard remoulade, followed by an ample portion of tender lamb shank with creamy parmesan polenta, and then a good panna cotta. There's a discreet, transparent division between the all-day buzz of the bar-brasserie (the shoppers' favourite) and the more formal and expensive restaurant, where evening meals would be the appropriate choice.

Kalpna ★

2-3 St Patrick Square, EH8 9EZ (0131 667 9890). **Lunch served** noon-2.30pm Mon-Sat. **Dinner served** 5.30-10.30pm daily. **Main courses** £4-£7.50. **Set buffet** (lunch Wed) £5, (dinner Wed) £9.95. **Set dinner** £12.50 2 courses, £15 3 courses. **Credit** MC, V.

The more self-consciously vegetarian of the city's two veggie Indian restaurants, Kalpna has been plying its trade since the 1980s. The continuous stream of happy, chatty diners is testament to its enduring popularity, and the menu is far from subcontinental cliché. Proof? You could start with aloo firdoshi (potatoes stuffed with pistachios, raisins, coriander and spices) or hara kebab (fried spinach and green peas stuffed with saffron yoghurt). The

thali options give a nice spread of dishes as an alternative to starter/main/sides, but some specialities and traditional offerings on the menu are just dandy in themselves. Waiters can advise on wine and there's Indian lager on tap and some overwhelmingly sweet puds.

The Marque

19-21 Causewayside, EH9 1QF (0131 466 6660). **Lunch served** 11.45am-2pm Wed-Fri; 12.30-2pm Sat, Sun. **Dinner served** 5.45-10pm Wed, Thur, Sun; 5.45-11pm Fri, Sat. **Main courses** £12.50-£18. **Set dinner** (5.45-7pm, 9.30-10pm) £11.50 2 courses, £14 3 courses; (5.45-10pm Wed, Thur, Sun) £14 2 courses, £17 3 courses. **Credit** AmEx, MC, V.

The Marque isn't a great trumpet-blowing example of restaurant bombast. It's neat, has an understated class and quietly does its thing at its original premises in Causewayside. It's very modern/international: a typical three-course meal might start with sea bass tempura, vine tomatoes and warm smoked salmon crostini, move on to corn-fed chicken with crispy ham, parsley mash and choucroute garni, then finish with iced passionfruit and mango parfait, with pineapple sauce and coconut tuile. Local opinion has the Marque among Edinburgh's top dozen restaurants – local opinion is right. The younger Marque Central (more central, obviously, and next door to the Lyceum Theatre at 30B Grindlay Street; 0131 229 9859) hits the same high standards and offers good-value pre- and post-theatre menus.

Martins

70 Rose Street North Lane, EH2 3DX (0131 225 3106). **Lunch served** noon-1.30pm Tue-Fri. **Dinner served** 7-9.30pm Tue-Sat. **Main courses** £17-£23. **Set lunch** £13.50 2 courses. **Set dinner** £25 3 courses. **Credit** AmEx, DC, MC, V.

Not easy to find but worth the effort, Martin Irons's tasteful and welcoming backstreet restaurant is a showcase for Scottish produce; he realised the value of attentive sourcing and organic ingredients years before most. From the vegetables to the meat and the fish, Irons insists that, as far as possible, everything is just as nature intended. The reward for such persistence has been an enviable reputation in the city – and beyond – since opening in 1983. A typical three-course dinner would involve foie gras terrine, toasted brioche and red onion marmalade to start; seared loin of wild venison, potato and mushroom gratin, braised red cabbage, roasted root vegetables and thyme jus as a main; and dark chocolate fondant with sable biscuit, blood orange compote and espresso syrup to finish. The artisan cheeseboard is among the very finest in Edinburgh.

Number One ★

The Balmoral Hotel, 1 Princes Street, EH2 2EQ (0131 557 6727/www.roccofortehotels.com). **Lunch served** noon-2pm Mon-Fri. **Dinner served** 7-10pm Mon-Thur, Sun; 7-10.30pm Fri, Sat. **Main**

Café Royal. *See p301.*

courses £20-£25. **Set lunch** £14.50 2 courses, £17.50 3 courses. **Set dinner** £40 3 courses. **Credit** AmEx, DC, MC, V.

The Balmoral is the Victorian railway hotel at the east end of Princes Street. Number One is its flagship restaurant. Downstairs, away from the bustle of the city's main thoroughfare, you enter a placid and classy world of slick service and even more dextrous cuisine: chef Jeff Bland earned a Michelin star at the beginning of 2003, currently one of only two in the city (Restaurant Martin Wishart in Leith has the other; *see p306*). There are red lacquer walls, scalloped banquettes and a wine list to intimidate or delight depending on your level of self-esteem on the day. The food can be very good indeed, and the set lunch is actually excellent value for money. For that you might have a venison salad with truffle dressing, followed by pan-fried halibut then dark chocolate terrine and crème fraîche. If you go à la carte, you're talking a three-course extravaganza – including the likes of air-dried barbary duck, wild sea bass (none of your farmed muck) and parfait of prune d'Agen – for more than twice the price. Be brave. Step over that threshold.

Off the Wall ★

105 High Street, EH1 1SG (0131 558 1497/ www.off-the-wall.co.uk). **Lunch served** noon-2pm, **dinner served** 6-10pm Mon-Sat. **Main courses** £17.95-£21. **Credit** AmEx, MC, V.

From the moment the waitress brings an *amuse-bouche* of cream of cauliflower soup with truffle oil until the last impressions of mango and almond tart ebb from the palate, this establishment keeps its diners pretty much content. Set up by David Anderson (chef) and Aileen Wilson (front of house) in South College Street in 1997, it moved to Edinburgh's main tourist drag in 2000. Up one flight of stairs, Off the Wall is a haven of quietly tasteful decor and fine cooking completely at odds with its tartan shop neighbours. (In August, it's a particularly civilised escape from the Festival chaos outside.) A starter of tuna on puy lentil and sweet pepper salad

energises the most jaded customer, while a main such as seared sea bass on fennel and spinach with lemon butter sauce is virtually symphonic. Rabbit, pigeon, veal, venison and good old Scottish beef also feature.

Oloroso ★

33 Castle Street, EH2 3DN (0131 226 7614/ www.oloroso.co.uk). **Lunch served** noon-2.30pm, **dinner served** 7-10.30pm daily. **Main courses** £17-£49. **Credit** AmEx, MC, V.

Oloroso was one of Edinburgh's biggest restaurant openings of 2001, but its early period seemed to be affected by the illness of co-founder James Sankey,

Off the Wall. *See p305.*

who died in late 2002. His partner Tony Singh carried on, and diners should be grateful. The ground-floor entrance may be baffling – only a flat-screen video hints at what lies above – but once out of the lift everything is clear. The establishment occupies the top (fourth) floor of an office building, which means excellent all-round views. There's a very smart bar where you can drink or snack (artful Alsatian tart, fine samosas), and a restaurant space for the full dining experience. A typical starter would be seared tuna with artichoke hearts; a main might be corn-fed chicken with sage and parmesan polenta; then, to finish, espresso tart with vanilla ice-cream. The grill menu offers top-grade, and top-price, Highland beef – an 8oz fillet steak will cost £26 a head, with a choice of sauces (chilli jam or salsa verde, for instance). Food and service are right up there. Unfortunately, the self-worth of the clientele can be right up there too.

Pompadour

Caledonian Hilton Hotel, Princes Street, EH1 2AB (0131 222 8888/www.hilton.com). **Lunch served** 12.30-2.30pm Tue-Fri. **Dinner served** 7-10pm Thur-Sat. **Main courses** £19.50-£23.95. **Set lunch** £15.50 2 courses, £19.50 3 courses. **Set dinner** £19.50 2 courses, £21.50 3 courses. **Credit** AmEx, DC, MC, V.

This old Edwardian railway hotel houses the most traditionally opulent restaurant in the city. First impressions of the Pompadour leave you scrabbling for the right word ('rococo'? 'baroque'?); you browse the menu in an ante-room, then a waiter escorts you to your table, carrying any unfinished G&Ts on a silver tray. The staff glide around soundlessly and if you order something as simple as asparagus with hollandaise as a starter, the accompanying lemon wedge comes wrapped in muslin lest your fingers are sullied by citric detritus. The food is elaborate with roots in French haute cuisine. That means a typical starter being timbale of snow crab with king

prawns on watercress sauce, garnished with poached crawfish claw. A main might be cumin-roasted lamb with sweet potato sauté, aubergine confit and spiced pan jus. Crème vanilla with wild berries is one of the simpler – but almost perfect – desserts. Dining tip: dress smart.

Restaurant at the Bonham

35 Drumsheugh Gardens, EH3 7RN (0131 623 9319/www.thebonham.com). **Breakfast served** 7.30-9.30am Mon-Fri; 8-10am Sat, Sun. **Lunch served** noon-2pm Mon-Fri; 12.30-3pm Sat, Sun. **Dinner served** 6.30-10pm daily. **Main courses** £15.80-£20.50. **Credit** AmEx, DC, MC, V.

The Bonham is one of Edinburgh's more designery hotels, discreetly positioned in the West End but only a few minutes' walk from Princes Street. The ground-floor restaurant has a large window admitting lots of light (Scottish weather permitting), and there's a real aspiration to provide excellent service. Lawyers and financial services types eat at weekday lunchtimes; residents and destination diners in the evenings. A starter as simple as tomato, coconut and lemongrass soup is executed in a manner that makes you sit up and take notice, while a main like fried salmon fillet with confit of fennel and provençale dressing shows that the kitchen pays commendable attention to detail. The menu is creative without going over the top, desserts sound (own-made nougat glacé with mint crème anglaise, for example), the surroundings roomy, the house wines well chosen and the staff most capable.

Restaurant Martin Wishart ★

54 The Shore, EH6 6RA (0131 553 3557/ www.martinwishart.co.uk). **Lunch served** noon-2pm Tue-Fri. **Dinner served** 7-10pm Tue -Sat. **Main courses** £22.50-£24.50. **Set lunch** £18.50 3 courses. **Set dinner** £48 5 courses. **Credit** AmEx, MC, V.

As one of only two establishments in the city with a Michelin star, how good is this restaurant really?

In foodie terms, really very good. Wishart has worked under some terribly famous names (a brace of Roux, Marco Pierre White), and since opening in 1999 his diner has gained a stratospheric reputation. Restaurant Martin Wishart isn't large, but this means quality control is impeccable. The service is confident enough to be relaxed, and although it's generally formal it's not uptight. The menu changes all the time, as you'd expect, but you might be lucky enough to experience a three-courser like lobster and truffle ravioli with savoy cabbage and shellfish cream to start, pot roast pork cheek with char-grilled langoustine and honey-roast vegetables as a main, or Armagnac parfait with poached pear as dessert. The craft displayed is phenomenal.

Rogue

Scottish Widows Building, 67 Morrison Street, EH3 8BU (0131 228 2700/www.rogues-uk.com). **Lunch served** noon-3pm, **dinner served** 6-11pm Mon-Sat. **Main courses** £4.50-£23. **Set meal** (Mon-Thur) £10 2 courses, £13.50 3 courses. **Credit** AmEx, MC, V.

Rogue burst on to the Edinburgh scene in 2001 to acclaim from all quarters. Proprietor David Ramsden had already established his reputation with (fitz)Henry in Leith and the high design concepts of Rogue took him to another level. Given its location – firmly in the city's financial district – it's no surprise that its lunchtime clientele is drawn from local offices. Evenings are much more visually interesting for people-watchers. The menu is informal, offering everything from soups and starters to pizza, pasta, grills, seafood, meat and a few vegetarian options. If you want to sit in spacious, draped surroundings and just have a dish of spaghetti with baby clams and herbs, you can. But a fuller exploration of the menu could bring asparagus with herb vinaigrette and bacon to start, braised veal with fava beans and gnocchi as a main, then a dessert such as coconut pannacotta with lime syrup. Worth a visit.

Santini/Santini Bistro

8 Conference Square, Sheraton Hotel, EH3 8AN (0131 221 7788). **Lunch served** 12.30-2.30pm Mon-Fri. **Dinner served** 6.30-10.30pm Mon-Sat. **Main courses** (bistro) £5-£16.50, (restaurant) £5-£24. **Credit** AmEx, DC, MC, V.

Conference Square is right in the middle of Edinburgh's financial district. Scottish Widows is across the way, while the Edinburgh International Conference Centre, Standard Life and the back of the Sheraton Hotel complete the architectural claustrophobia. In all this sits Santini. It arrived in 2001 and gathered plaudits before the first char-grilled baby cuttlefish had time to yelp 'Mama!' There are actually two eateries: the more formal Santini and the adjacent designer-bistro Santini Bis. Both make excellent use of fresh ingredients. Santini offers wonders such as smoked swordfish carpaccio to start, then vegetarian options, meat and fish. These might entail pumpkin ravioli, scallops with

langoustine, beetroot, spring onion and celeriac, or grilled baby chicken with a spicy chilli and herb sauce. Ricotta mousse with fig sauce is quite a dessert. Santini Bis is every bit as accomplished.

Scalini

10 Melville Place, EH3 7PR (0131 220 2999/www.scaliniristorante.com). **Lunch served** noon-2pm, **dinner served** 6-10pm Mon-Sat. **Main courses** £7.80-£16.50. **Set lunch** £11.95 2 courses. **Credit** AmEx, DC, MC, V.

Among the traffic and hassle of the West End, you walk down Scalini's stairs into a small blue basement and immediately feel more peaceful. Proprietor Silvio Praino is one of the city's friendlier and more voluble restaurateurs, and he runs an establishment where people really care about food. The antipasti della casa will be brought over and shown to you – it always looks good – while other starters generally involve pasta (ravioli del giorno; linguine al pesto genovese). Mains might include thin-sliced salmon cooked with balsamic vinegar or calf's liver with onion and wine. Desserts are simple: lemon sorbet with vodka or pine nut and custard cake. One of the most exciting features is the wine. There's the 'normal' list – affordable – plus a range of Italians dating from the 1950s (with a 1945 Marchesi de Barolo at £485, if no one's quaffed it yet).

Skippers

1A Dock Place, EH6 6LU (0131 554 1018/www.skippers.co.uk). **Lunch served** 12.30-2pm Mon-Sat; 12.30-2.30pm Sun. **Dinner served** 7-10pm daily. **Main courses** £12-£19. **Credit** AmEx, MC, V.

Skippers has been around for more than 20 years and was a real pioneer in the pre-refurbished docklands of Leith. Through the 1980s and '90s it built a reputation as Edinburgh's best seafood bistro and the current proprietors (Gavin and Karen Ferguson) have been in charge since 1999. The decor is attractively cluttered with a nod to the sea, and dishes range from the simple to complex. You could start with six large Loch Etive oysters, or a terrine of Serrano ham, wild salmon and potato with chilli jam. Mains-wise, it's hard to beat the flavours in roasted Shetland langoustines with garlic and parsley butter, though marinated fillet of tuna with lime and coriander mayonnaise tries hard. There are some non-fish options, and the desserts are competent, though they don't really match courses one and two. But who cares? This is fishy heaven; watch for specials just pulled from the ocean.

The best	Places for...

Scottish produce in Edinburgh

Fishers Bistro (*see p303*); **Haldane's** (*see p303*); **Martins** (*see p304*); **Skippers** (*see p307*).

Scotland

Suruchi

14A Nicolson Street, EH8 9DH (0131 556 6583/
www.suruchirestaurant.com). **Lunch served**
noon-2pm Mon-Sat. **Dinner served** 5.30-11pm
daily. **Main courses** £8-£13. **Set dinner**
(5.30-7pm) £9.95 2 courses incl glass of wine.
Credit AmEx, DC, MC, V.
Easily one of the best Indian restaurants in
Edinburgh, Suruchi distinguishes itself with regular
food festivals, an eclectic menu (written in Scots) and
because it actually makes an effort – all appreciated
by its clientele. Yes, there's pakora and chicken
kebab among the starters, but also South Indian
offerings like bonda (potato dumplings with raisins
and spices in gram flour). Conservative diners might
stick to tried-and-tested mains (lamb jalfrezi,
tandoori king prawns) or they could opt for nirvana:
chicken with lemongrass, mustard seeds, curry
leaves, lemon and coconut. There's also a 'hame
produce' section drawing on key ingredients of the
Scottish larder, including salmon chi kori (salmon
with black pepper, ginger, spices and coconut) and
tandoori trout (whole trout cooked in the tandoor,
served with salad and rice). Suruchi Too can be
found at 121 Constitution Street; 0131 554 3268.

Sweet Melinda's

11 Roseneath Street, EH9 1JH (0131 229 7953).
Lunch served noon-2pm Tue-Sat. **Dinner served**
7-10pm Mon-Sat. **Main courses** £11.50-£14.80.
Credit MC, V.
Edinburgh's tenement suburb of Marchmont is
short on dining options, so this is an oasis in the
desert. It's a bright, compact establishment with
friendly-casual service and although it doesn't bill
itself as a fish restaurant, there's certainly a good
choice for fish lovers (and always something for
vegetarians too). First-time diners tend to walk in
with little expectation and walk out smiling because
of the standard of cooking. Typical starters are Thai
fish cakes with sweet dipping sauce or black
pudding with plum tomato and pear chutney. Mains
weigh in with dishes such as pan-fried fillets of red
snapper and sea bream with langoustine, clams and
cockles, in a fennel, Pernod and pepper sauce; or
roast cod with smoked haddock kedgeree. Basic
desserts (lemon tart or sticky toffee pud) round off
what you might call a real happy meal.

Thaisanuk ★

21 Argyle Place, EH9 1JJ (0131 228 8855).
Lunch served noon-3pm Fri-Sun. **Dinner**
served 6-11pm daily. **Main courses** £3.15-£8.95.
No credit cards.
A tiny restaurant in a baronial suburb south of the
Meadows, Thaisanuk has the kind of winning
attitude that captures hearts and minds – so book
ahead because it can get very busy and doesn't have
much space. The menu is simple: starters, mains and
noodles. Fresh ingredients are shipped in from as far
afield as Thailand itself, giving the traditional tom
yum soup (with lemongrass, galangal and lime
leaves) an extra zing. Other starters include

Indonesian spare ribs and Vietnamese spring rolls.
Noodles, whether dry bowls or soups, are pretty
generous and come in various versions from all over
Asia (Vietnamese, Malaysian, Japanese, Korean). For
mains there are dishes like Asian barbecue sticks
(meat or tofu with salad and sticky rice) or whole sea
bass marinated in Thai basil, served with crisped
skin and a lime and sweet basil sauce. It gets the
popular vote as Edinburgh's best Thai restaurant.
It's also BYO (£2 corkage on a bottle of wine).

The Tower ★

Museum of Scotland, Chambers Street, EH1 1JF
(0131 225 3003/www.tower-restaurant.com). **Lunch**
served noon-4.30pm daily. **Dinner served** 5-11pm
daily. **Main courses** £13-£20. **Set lunch** (noon-
6.30pm) £9.95 1 course. **Credit** AmEx, DC, MC, V.
There are few restaurants anywhere with a more
impressive setting. The Tower is on the top floor of
the Museum of Scotland, a repository of Caledonian
culture that opened in late 1998. The views over the
Old Town can transport you back in time, while the
chic interior wouldn't look out of place in a bigger
capital city. Service is slick and the wine list
affordable – but with some star bins for those
looking to blow serious money. The menu is flexible
(have a salad and side dish if you like), with a
trenchantly British feel in places, as well as smart
international flourishes. A starter like smoked onion
soup with parsley dumplings is warming; lobster
claw with pickled vegetables more of a departure.
Mains can be as traditional as fish and chips with
pea purée, or a little more contemporary: seared
salmon with lemongrass, chilli and coconut risotto.
For dessert, try the elderflower and pickled ginger
crème brûlée.

Valvona & Crolla Caffè Bar ★

19 Elm Row, off Leith Walk, EH7 4AA (0131
556 6066/www.valvonacrolla.com). **Breakfast**
served 8am-noon Mon-Sat. **Lunch served**
noon-2.30pm daily. **Main courses** £8.95-£13.95.
Credit AmEx, MC, V.
Valvona & Crolla is the best delicatessen in
Scotland, and one of the best in the whole UK. Its
café-bar is a simple and tasteful space at the rear of
the shop, a former stable block, with white walls and
wooden beams. The food draws on the quality of
raw materials sold in the deli (shipped in fresh from
Italian markets). Take breakfast, for instance.
Options include paesano sausage with smoked
bacon, fried egg, grilled polenta, tomato and bread;
or panettone in carrozza (sweet brioche dipped in
egg, fried, and served with cream). The flavoursome
verdure breakfast involves grilled courgette, red
pepper, aubergine and cherry tomato, a fried egg,
polenta and mushrooms. Later in the day, the
regular menu offers salads, snacks like bruschetta,
and excellent sandwiches (such as gorgonzola,
roasted courgette, pine kernels and rocket). The
more substantial specials (meat, fish, pizza) change
on a daily basis and there's a great selection of
Italian wines too. Peerless.

Santini.
See p307.

Vermilion

Scotsman Hotel, 20 North Bridge, EH1 1YT
(0131 556 5565/www.thescotsmanhotelgroup.co.uk).
Dinner served 7-9.30pm Tue-Sat. **Main courses**
£18-£24. **Set dinner** £35 3 courses. **Credit** AmEx,
DC, MC, V.

Although the terminally swish Scotsman Hotel
arrived in 2001, it took until spring 2002 to get its
flagship restaurant open, so Vermilion hasn't had
that long to establish itself as serious competition to
its elevated peer group (Number One at the Balmoral
– *see p304* – is just at the other end of North Bridge
and took six years to achieve Michelin star status).
All the same, expectations of excellence rise as
diners descend the hotel's grand marble staircase to
the dining room, which has the appearance of a
contemporary oenological grotto: a subterranean
space with walls covered by wine bottles in glass
cabinets, subtly back-lit. Three typical courses
would be lobster and orange ravioli, ginger jus and
honey-roast langoustines to start; sea scallops with
caramelised cauliflower risotto and jus of cocoa as
a main; and apple tart with vanilla ice-cream and
cinnamon syrup for dessert. It's already among the
very best restaurants in the city but, like any new
kid on the block, it's trying hard to impress. With a
more self-confident rhythm, Vermillion could be one
of the top three.

The Vintners Rooms

The Vaults, 87 Giles Street, EH6 6BZ (0131 554
6767/www.thevintnersrooms.com). **Lunch served**
noon-2pm, **dinner served** 7-10pm Mon-Sat. **Main**
courses £15-£19. **Set lunch** £13 2 courses, £16.50
3 courses. **Credit** AmEx, MC, V.

Housed in a highly atmospheric, 17th-century Leith
wine warehouse, the Vintners has tables by the bar
(high ceiling, lots of space) and another room
adjacent (more intimate, low-ceilinged, good for
candlelight trysts). Very traditional-looking, it's a
world away from the down-at-heel housing in the
vicinity. The daily changing menu has a French
slant, with such starters as tartelette aux crabes or

char-grilled scallops with saffron and mussel sauce.
The mains might be baked halibut with lobster
sherry broth, or braised partridge with puy lentils.
There's no holding back with flavour, and if the
cooking ever falls down on finesse, it usually makes
up for it in the sheer bravado of taste. Almond,
Armagnac and prune tart is the kind of dessert you
just don't want to miss; there's a good wine list too.
The Vintners makes it worth travelling to Leith.

The Witchery by the Castle/
The Secret Garden ★

Castlehill, EH1 2NF (0131 225 5613/
www.thewitchery.com). **Lunch served** noon-4pm,
dinner served 5.30-11.30pm daily. **Main courses**
£14-£22. **Set meal** (noon-4pm, 5.30-6.30pm) £9.95
2 courses. **Credit** AmEx, DC, MC. V.

Edinburgh doesn't have that many destination
restaurants, so it would be remiss not to mention
these two as they certainly qualify on the basis of
location, reputation and as an attraction for visiting
celebs. Often referred to as just 'the Witchery', we're
actually talking about two dining rooms: the
Witchery itself is a high-class, leathery/wooden
establishment just yards from Edinburgh Castle
Esplanade. Meanwhile, the adjacent Secret Garden
oozes even more atmosphere (tapestries, arched
windows, candles) and is very popular for major
romantic occasions. Both have the same menu, and
awesome wine list, which runs to more than 130
pages. A typical meal might involve roast mallard
breast to start, pan-roasted monkfish as a main, and
white peach tarte tatin for dessert. In recent years it
hasn't always delivered at the giddy heights you'd
expect, and it is very expensive – although brilliant
when on form. For an economical 'look-see', try the
bargain lunch or theatre supper.

Also in the area

The Living Room 113-115 George Street, EH2 4JN
(0870 442 2718); **Malmaison** 1 Tower Place, EH6
7PB (0131 468 5000).

Scotland

Glasgow

Air Organic

36 Kelvingrove Street, G3 7SA (0141 564 5200).
Meals served noon-10pm Mon-Thur, Sun; noon-10.30pm Fri, Sat. **Main courses** £4.25-£16.95.
Set lunch £9.95 2 courses, £12.95 3 courses.
Credit AmEx, MC, V.
An inventive menu that uses only organic produce is just part of the appeal of Air Organic, a funky, futuristic restaurant and bar situated a block from Kelvingrove Park. Its off-white and ecru decor and space-age furniture were the hippest thing going when it opened in the mid 1990s. Since then, many have copied but few have captured the place's groovy, 1960s airport lounge ambience. The menu – divided into earth, flora, ocean and carnivore sections – looks like an airline ticket, but there is nothing of the synthetic in-flight meal about the prawn and lemon linguine, barbecue sticky pork salad with mango and jumbo cashews or pan-fried chicken breast with creamy chive mash. The ground-floor bar is an attraction in its own right, offering an assortment of superior sandwiches and pizzas, plus specialities such as organic beefburger and red Thai watermelon curry to a fashionable but casual student and club-bound crowd.

Amaryllis ★

1 Devonshire Gardens, G12 0UX (0141 337 3434/www.amaryllis@gordonramsay.com). **Lunch served** noon-2pm Wed-Fri, Sun. **Dinner served** 6.45-9.30pm Wed-Sun. **Main courses** £10-£14.
Set menu £35 3 courses, £45 6-course tasting menu.
Credit AmEx, MC, V.
Don't expect simply to turn up and get a table: this hugely successful French restaurant, run by bona fide celebrity chef Gordon Ramsay – the first Scot to win three Michelin stars – often has waiting lists of up to three months. But it may be worth it, for the quality of the eating experience is as high as you'd expect. Housed in the graceful classical dining room of one of Glasgow's most exclusive hotels, everything about Amaryllis says luxury treat. The prix fixe menu features subtle modernist dishes, such as venison with braised parsnips and carrots with bitter chocolate sauce. The divinely decadent desserts are hard to resist and the wine list is also fabulous, though pricey. Definitely a venue to take someone you wish to impress. You'll have a better chance of getting in at short notice at lunchtime.

Amber Regent

50 West Regent Street, G2 2RA (0141 331 1655/www.amberregent.com). **Lunch served** noon-2.15pm Mon-Fri. **Dinner served** 5.30-11pm Mon-Thur; 5.30-11.30pm Fri. **Food served** 11am-midnight Sat. **Main courses** £9.95-£25.95. **Set lunch** £7.95

2 courses, £9.95 3 courses. **Set dinner** £27.95 4 courses. **Credit** AmEx, DC, MC, V.
The Amber Regent enjoys a reputation as one of Glasgow's finest Chinese restaurants. In some respects, the cuisine is not so vastly superior to its rivals. But the luxurious, rather old-fashioned surroundings and the little touches, such as the brass spoon rests, are a badge of its class. The expansive menu offers some refreshingly original choices at higher than average prices. The seafood selection is prodigious, with king prawns available in every conceivable incarnation. Other tempting dishes include chicken in garlic and plum sauce, and grilled fillet steak Chinese-style (with honey and wine sauce). Service is highly attentive if a little brisk. And there is certainly one area in which the Amber Regent conforms to average Chinese restaurant standards – terrible background muzak.

Arisaig

24 Candleriggs, G1 1LD (0141 552 4251). **Meals served** noon-midnight daily. **Main courses** £9.95-£16.95. **Set dinner** (5-7pm Mon-Thur, Sun) £9.95 2 courses, £12.95 3 courses. **Credit** AmEx, MC, V.
Once upon a time, these premises were the city-centre branch of café-bar Oblomov, which didn't make much of a dent – so let's hope Arisaig's mellow environment and scrummy food prove a recipe for success. The new owners have switched from Eastern European to modern Scottish cuisine, but kept the refined interior of rich dark wood. A long, elegantly curved bar leads to the dining area with its well-judged muted lighting. The seasonal menu is not extensive – no more than half a dozen choices per course – but some creativity has been exercised in the combination of flavours across the game and seafood dishes. Unusually for a Scottish restaurant, vegetarians are imaginatively catered for; nettle cakes and lavender loaf might sound like rabbit food, but are as satisfying as the filling potato mashes that accompany most dishes. Service is pleasingly unobtrusive.

Arthouse Grill

129 Bath Street, G2 2SZ (0141 572 6002/www.arthousehotel.com). **Meals served** noon-11pm daily. **Main courses** £10.50-£18. **Set lunch** £9.50 2 courses, £12 3 courses. **Set dinner** (5.30-8pm daily) £12.50 2 courses, £14.50 3 courses. **Credit** AmEx, DC, MC, V.
The Arthouse is one of Glasgow's hip hotels, ideally located to capitalise on the burgeoning dining/drinking scene along Bath Street. But its own basement restaurant is easily the equal of its neighbours, and gives non-guests the opportunity to wallow in the hotel's classy, ultra-modern interior

Amaryllis

and goggle at the waterfall feature that sluices down the middle of the main stairwell (take a look en route to the loo). Although the name might suggest a meatfest, it's actually seafood at which the Grill excels, offering tantalising starters such as smoked salmon, lobster and asparagus terrine and mains that include shellfish linguine or pan-fried red snapper with pine nut coulis. There are also numerous vegetarian options. Eminently suitable for entertaining friends, partners or business associates, the Arthouse offers aspirational dining at affordable prices and in congenial surroundings.

The Ashoka ★

108 Elderslie Street, G3 7AR (0141 221 1761/ www.ashokaflame.com). **Meals served** noon-midnight Mon-Sat; 5pm-midnight Sun. **Main courses** £7-£15. **Set lunch** £6.95 3 courses. **Credit** AmEx, DC, MC, V.

It's easy to get confused when it comes to Glasgow's many curry restaurants, some of which have very similar names – but this Ashoka is not, in fact, related to others of the same name around the West End owned by the Harlequin chain. Dating back to 1978, this one really kick-started the whole trend, and has a loyal local clientele. The grandly opulent decor is largely traditional, and the menu presents the usual Indian and Kashmiri dishes, plus some unusual ones – fruit pakora in batter, for instance. They're proud of their special 'abpaz' cooking technique, which involves flash-frying meat to seal in the juices before adding sauces. There's also a good takeaway menu. A rather trendier offshoot, Ashoka Flame, recently opened in the basement.

Brian Maule at le Chardon d'Or ★

176 West Regent Street, G2 4RL (0141 248 3801/ www.lechardondor.com). **Lunch served** noon-2.30pm Mon-Fri. **Dinner served** 6-10pm Mon-Sat. **Main courses** £16.50-£19.50. **Set menu** £14.50 2 courses, £17.50 3 courses. **Credit** AmEx, MC, V.

The story is now well told: Ayrshire lad Brian seeks out his fortune in France, ends up as head chef at

Le Gavroche in London, then returns triumphant to Scotland to open le Chardon d'Or (the golden thistle) in central Glasgow. Foodwise, it was the most exciting thing to happen in the city during 2002 and the restaurant is now established as one of the best in these parts. The decor is subtle and modern, with some interesting art. You can start with simple fried scallops, rocket salad and basil dressing; or perhaps ravioli of ceps with thyme and mushroom cream. Mains include roast sirloin with a gratin of smoked spinach and mushroom, or corn-fed chicken with olives, tomatoes and peppers flavoured with garlic. So, Franco-Scottish? Yes, but with a more eclectic spin. Finish with a deft crème brûlée or a chocolate fondant and fresh mascarpone ice-cream.

The Buttery

652 Argyle Street, G3 8UF (0141 221 8188). **Lunch served** noon-2pm Tue-Fri. **Dinner served** 6-9pm Tue-Fri; 6.30-10pm Sat. **Set lunch** £12 2 courses. **Set dinner** £34 2 courses, £38 3 courses. **Credit** AmEx, MC, V.

The grand old lady of Glaswegian dining (dating back in some form or other to 1869), this solidly respectable scion of the establishment recently survived a threatened closure. Housed in a traditional tenement, its dining room decor is sombre, dark and elegant, all stiff tablecloths and crystal glasses. There's also a cocktail bar. The menu is firmly posh Scottish nosh, with the finest local ingredients (cullen skink, Aberdeen Angus, Arbroath smokies and so on) in unthreatening but masterfully prepared dishes. The sort of place that you can see where the money goes: sheer luxury.

Café du Sud

8-10 Clarendon Street, G20 7QD (0141 332 2054). **Dinner served** 5.30-10pm Tue-Sat. **Main courses** £9.95-£13.95. **Set dinner** (5.30-7pm) £16 2 courses, £18 3 courses. **Credit** MC, V.

A lovely, wee, family-run restaurant slightly off the beaten track that combines provençal and classic

French cuisine. Small, intimate and very friendly, it has an endearingly casual atmosphere. Richly painted on the outside, it's candlelit and very French indoors. The food is excellently pungent and nicely presented, with the likes of roast red pepper mousse with baby spinach, parmesan and pine kernels, or duck cassoulet in a rich red wine and bean ragoût. Plenty of nice French wines too. The owners also run the more Italian Bistro du Sud (87 Cambridge Street; 0141 332 2666), which caters mainly to a lunchtime and weekend crowd.

Café Gandolfi

64 Albion Street, G1 1NY (0141 552 6813). **Meals served** 9am-11.30pm Mon-Sat; noon-11.30pm Sun. **Main courses** £7-£14. **Credit** AmEx, MC, V.
This cosy bistro, occupying the former site of the city's cheese market, is where Glasgow's Merchant City taste renaissance began back in 1979 – and it has wisely stuck to its winning formula ever since, serving canny Caledonian cuisine. Sculptor Tim Stead's now iconic wooden furniture and fittings, the barely audible classical music and the unobtrusive service are all part of its relaxed charm. Gandolfi standards, such as Stornoway black pudding with mushrooms and pancakes or delicate smoked venison, are legendary. The seasonal menu also lends itself to quirkier combinations, such as seared duck breast topped with plum sauce and crisp fried onions. It's also kind to veggies: the sumptuous gorgonzola, pine nut and red pepper linguine is the king of pasta dishes in a city not short of reputable Italian joints. Breakfasts are hearty, no-nonsense affairs, and somewhat oriented towards the stalwart Scottish scone. Gandolfi is also an ideal setting for coffee and a chinwag. If you're after a light lunch, a coffee or just a tipple, Gandolfi now has a first-floor bar, serving patrons a stripped-down version of the main menu in a white brick, loft-style environment.

Café Mao ★

84 Brunswick Street, G1 1ZZ (0141 564 5161/ www.cafemao.com). **Meals served** noon-11pm Mon-Sat; 1-10pm Sun. **Main courses** £7.95-£10.95. **Set lunch** (noon-5pm Mon-Fri) £7.95 2 courses, £9.95 3 courses. **Credit** AmEx, MC, V.
Mao is a great example of clued-up Glaswegian dining, as proved by the fact that its two floors are frequently packed. The food is a hip, imaginative mish-mash of Chinese, Japanese and South-east Asian cooking, while the decor – primary-coloured furniture and Warholian prints of Mao on the walls – is as vibrant as some of the truly lip-smacking flavours. Munch on a side order of shrimp crackers to get the tastebuds up and running, or pick from unusual starter options such as chilli squid, tempura tofu or duck and lychee salad. Main courses include Penang duck curry, stir-fried tiger prawns with hokkien noodles or nasi goreng. Portions are hefty; if you do manage to hit the bottom of your noodle bowl, you can plug any remaining gap with white chocolate cheesecake or a selection of sorbets. Service is chirpy to match the zing of the food.

City Merchant

97 Candleriggs, G1 1NP (0141 553 1577/ www.citymerchant.co.uk). **Meals served** noon-10.30pm Mon-Sat. **Main courses** £7.95-£24.95. **Set lunch** £11 2 courses, £13.50 3 courses incl coffee. **Set dinner** £22.50 3 courses. **Credit** AmEx, DC, MC, V.
An upmarket, family-run joint with a vaguely Celtic theme to its warm amber decor, stained glass and wooden floors. They're particularly known for their seafood; daily fish market specials appear both as starters (the seared king scallops with couscous and tomato chilli dressing is particularly refreshing) and mains. There's a set and à la carte menu, both of which feature the odd tacky item – most restaurants have dropped prawn marie rose these days – but the standard of the steaks, haggis and lamb shank is pretty high. A lengthy wine list is backed up by blackboard bin-end bargains, and the staff are quite knowledgeable about recommendations. Popular with business types, it was one of the first restaurants to open in the Merchant City area when it began to be gentrified in the 1980s.

Fratelli Sarti

121 Bath Street, G2 2SZ (0141 204 0440). **Meals served** noon-10.30pm daily. **Main courses** £5.95-£20. **Credit** AmEx, MC, V.
There are Italian restaurants and there's Sarti's: a Glasgow institution. It all began with the cosy little café-cum-deli on Wellington Street, though for a more extensive choice and more room, the adjoining Bath Street restaurant is probably a better choice for dinner. In keeping with its unpretentious, simple Italian style – no clichéd tat, just mounds of authentic imported foodstuffs and drinks – just about anyone and everyone eats here. The staff are the real thing too and graciously helpful, whether you're rushing with limited time or need advice on the wine list. The house speciality is pizza. It's nothing like the doughy supermarket variety: thin, crusty, flavoursome and with an inventive range of fresh toppings (wild boar, anyone?) – filling and yet not stodgy. The seafood and coffees are also good.

Gamba

225A West George Street, G2 2ND (0141 572 0899/www.gamba.co.uk). **Lunch served** noon-2.30pm, **dinner served** 5-10.30pm Mon-Sat. **Main courses** £12-£22.50. **Credit** AmEx, MC, V.
If you think the only thing Glaswegians can do with fish is dunk it in batter and serve it with chips, try Gamba. They know their fish, from the most basic grilled lemon sole in butter or cod fillet with mushy minted peas, to more adventurous dishes such as tuna sashimi. Most importantly, they emphasise freshly caught fish – and you can certainly taste the difference. Although it has picked up several restaurant-of-the-year awards, Gamba is still not too self-conscious about its success; from the moment you enter the warm, clean-lined interior, you feel comfortable rather than intimidated. Of course, if you don't feel in the mood for fish, it's hardly the best choice. But perhaps you could be persuaded.

Grassroots Café ★

93-97 St George's Road, G3 6JA (0141 333 0534).
Meals served 10am-10pm daily. **Main courses**
£5.75-£6.95. **Credit** AmEx, MC, V.

For our money, this bijou – and award-winning –
café is the best veggie option in the city. It's also one
of very few places where your coffee will be made
from dandelions. Other than that, it's not especially
hippie-dippy, just a laid-back, comfy hangout. The
vegetarian and vegan menu is handled with skill and
imagination, and offers more than the standard
veggie-burger-and-chips scenario (although this
option, like the veggie bangers 'n' mash, is spot-on,
especially after a night on the West End tiles).
Equally satisfying lunch or dinner options are the
fluffy risotto cakes and the Thai green curry. For a
sugar fix, there's a robust selection of cakes.
Although it overlooks the none-too-attractive M8 at
the busy Charing Cross junction, you wouldn't know
that inside, where young mothers, aspiring writers
and students converge for a meat-free bonanza – or
just some camomile tea and a squint at the papers.

The Greek Golden Kebab ★

34 Sinclair Drive, G42 9QE (0141 649 7581).
Meals served 5pm-1am Thur-Sun. **Main courses**
£7.75-£11.45. **No credit cards.**

Although its name is redolent of a greasy takeaway
selling Glasgow's favourite post-pub grub, the Greek
Golden Kebab is actually an unassuming but very
welcoming little family-run restaurant, which has
quietly built up a glowing local reputation over its
three decades of service to eastern Mediterranean
cuisine. Glasgow is not hugely endowed with Greek
restaurants, and this is one of its best. Its busy decor
– plastic vine leaves hang on trellises and Med
ephemera adorns the walls – is kitsch but charming.
The food, covering every Greek dish known to man
plus a few less familiar creations, is generally
proclaimed to be delicious, with reliable faves such
as keftedes and dolmades available as starters or
mains. There is considerable provision for
vegetarians. And if you really can't resist a classic
chicken or lamb kebab after a night on the tiles, the
takeaway service offers many of the dishes on the
main menu.

Ichiban ★

50 Queen Street, G1 3DS (0141 204 4200/
www.ichiban.co.uk). **Meals served** noon-10pm
Mon-Wed; noon-11pm Thur-Sat; 1-10pm Sun.
Main courses £5.50-£11. **Set lunch** (Mon-Fri)
£5.50 2 courses. **Credit** AmEx, DC, MC, V.

Translating as 'number one', Ichiban could be
making its own quietly confident statement about
its position in Glasgow's Japanese restaurant stakes
– and it would not get much argument from its
mixed clientele, who willingly queue for a seat at one
of the communal canteen tables. The procedure at
Ichiban is thus: salivate over the menu and make
your choice from the starters (including sushi, wun
tuns and tempura) and the ramen and udon noodle

Ichiban

OKO

main courses, whether pan-fried or in a soup. Your waiter taps the order into a little electronic pad and, before you've had time to swig a drop of Asahi, your meal arrives direct from the open kitchen for your delectation. Don't forget some heated saké to make the experience go with a zing. Not the place for an intimate romantic meal, but it is the destination of choice for bustle, quality and incredibly good value. The West End branch (184 Dumbarton Road; 0141 334 9222) is slightly larger.

Inn on the Green

25 Greenhead Street, G40 1ES (0141 554 0165/ www.theinnonthegreen.co.uk). **Lunch served** noon-2pm Mon-Fri. **Dinner served** 6-9pm Mon-Fri; 7-9pm Sat, Sun. **Main courses** £11-£16.95. **Set lunch** £8.50 2 courses, £11.95 3 courses. **Credit** AmEx, DC, MC, V.

This place is a real charmer, and a boon for the East End, which is hardly renowned for its culinary delights. Converted from a seaman's mission to a hotel in 1984, the Inn still has a salty dog feel, but with tartan additions, original art for sale and a grand piano emitting strains of Gershwin, Irving Berlin and… Robbie Williams? Oh well, you can't have everything. Miniature plaques detail the restaurant's celebrity patrons, none of whom are among the hippest young bucks in Scottish media land anymore. But its honest-to-goodness Scottish cuisine is as excellent as ever. St Andrew's fillet steak topped with haggis in whisky sauce is Caledonian nirvana, and the fresh Scottish scallops are, thankfully, nothing like the common rubberised variety. To top it all, vanilla and passion-fruit cheesecake is a remarkable pud experience. Service is refreshingly low-key. Best to get there by taxi.

Mr Singh's India ★

149 Elderslie Street, G3 7JR (0141 204 0186). **Meals served** noon-11pm Mon-Thur; noon-midnight Fri, Sat; 2.30-11pm Sun. **Main courses** £6.95-£9.95. **Set lunch** (noon-5pm Mon-Sat;

2.30-5pm Sun) £6.95 3 courses. **Set dinner** (5-6.30pm) £8.25 3 courses. **Credit** AmEx, DC, MC, V.

To many Glaswegians, this is curry paradise. The sated customers in the impressive photo gallery at the entrance include sporting heroes Larsson, McCoist and Souness, not to mention Sir Sean. But we're not talking about some exclusive old boys' curry club; Mr Singh's India is an infectiously friendly, modern restaurant. Staff in kilts whirl around cheerily serving some of the most flavoursome Punjabi dishes in the country, not least the delicate lamb ambala and the chicken tikka with garlic chilli. Vegetarians are equally well catered for – brie pakora, anyone? Family parties and groups feature prominently, and the staff will be quick to spot and indulge a special celebration.

Mother India ★

28 Westminster Terrace, off Sauchiehall Street, G3 7RU (0141 221 1663). **Lunch served** noon-2pm Wed-Fri. **Dinner served** 5.30-10.30pm Mon-Thur; 4.30-10pm Sun. **Meals served** 1-11pm Sat. **Main courses** £6.10-£12. **Set lunch** (Wed-Fri) £8.95 2 courses. **Set dinner** (5.30-6.30pm Mon-Fri; 5.30-6pm Sat, Sun) £8.95 2 courses. **Credit** AmEx, MC, V.

You won't find the all-too-familiar tikka masala experience of the processed and radioactive variety here; Mother India offers authentic Indian home cooking at its best. The city's curry lovers have clearly taken the place to their hearts: this former tearoom in a Sauchiehall Street terrace is often packed out. The first-floor restaurant has a faded Raj air, with the original Victorian opulence smothered by the sheer mass of velvet curtains, candles and bare oak tables. Downstairs, there's more of a modern, bijou brasserie feel. Either way, it's the food that's the star. All the dishes are made to order and the result is a palpable freshness and subtlety (though you may wait a little longer than usual). Many make the pilgrimage for the vegetarian menu; the dosas with various fillings are almost worth the trip in themselves.

Scotland

OKO ★

68 Ingram Street, G1 1EX (0141 572 1500/ www.okorestaurants.com). **Lunch served** noon-3pm Tue-Fri. **Dinner served** 6-11pm Tue-Thur; 6pm-midnight Fri; 5.30-10.30pm Sun. **Meals served** noon-midnight Sat. **Main dishes** £1.70-£3.85. **Credit** AmEx, DC, MC, V.

Simple Minds' main man Jim Kerr has left behind his white leather blousons and black eyeliner and instead invested his talents and finances in this super-chic sushi restaurant. Occupying the ground floor of the eminently desirable Todd Building, its minimalist interior (designed by local trendy architects Zoo) in bare stone, natural wood and stainless steel is suitably zen, raising OKO a notch above the homogeneous look of chains such as Yo! Sushi. You still get the classic sushi dining staple of a conveyor belt from which to pluck your nigiri, sashimi and maki. If you don't see what you want going round on the belt, ask for it. Hot dishes such as chicken yakitori can be ordered separately. As with any sushi restaurant, the bill can mount up as inexorably as the colour-coded plates, but the Sunday night buffet – a choice of more than 40 dishes for £15 – is a top deal. The delightful mezzanine bar, OKO-hi, is underused; its only drawback is a tendency to use Simple Minds' greatest hits as background music.

Places for...

The best

Scottish produce in Glasgow

Arisaig (*see p310*); **The Buttery** (*see p311*); **Café Gandolfi** (*see p312*); **Inn on the Green** (*see p314*); **Rab Ha's** (*see p316*); **Schottische** (*see p317*); **Stravaigin** (*see p317*); **The Ubiquitous Chip** (*see p317*).

Otago

61 Otago Street, G12 8TQ (0141 337 2282). **Lunch served** noon-4.30pm, **dinner served** 5-9pm daily. **Main courses** £9.95-£11.95. **Set dinner** (5-7.30pm Mon-Thur, Sun; 5-6.30pm Fri, Sat) £10.95 2 courses. **Credit** MC, V.

Hidden slightly from view, though only two minutes from Great Western Road, this little bistro is regarded with much affection by the bohemian and student populations of the West End. Its plain tables, chairs and wooden floor give it a clean, airy feel, and there are newspapers to browse. Dishes might seem rather basic, but are beautifully presented and seasoned; a simple bruschetta and salad is done so well, you'll relish it more than overly complicated options. Vegetarians will be happy, with plenty of interesting items like asparagus risotto topped with red chard and taleggio – though the kitchen can stretch to main meat courses such as roast supreme of guinea fowl in a mustard and white wine sauce. The food can be rich, but there are plenty of starter options for lighter meals, plus a takeaway service. A wee gem.

Papingo ★

104 Bath Street, G2 2EN (0141 332 6678/ www.papingo.co.uk). **Lunch served** noon-2.30pm Mon-Sat. **Dinner served** 5-10.30pm Mon-Sat; 5-10pm Sun. **Main courses** £12-£19. **Set dinner** (5-6.30pm Mon-Thur, Sun; 5-6pm Fri, Sat) £10.95 2 courses, £12.95 3 courses. **Credit** AmEx, MC, V.

The name means parrot (and some subtle parrot motifs appear amid its cosy, intimate decor), though that doesn't give you much of a clue to the nature of this smart basement restaurant. It caters mainly to older couples and business types, who appreciate its slightly formal air. The oft-changing menu features fine Scottish produce like venison and Angus beef, often with an exotic twist in the dressing or spicing. Typical starters include fish soup with mussels, prawns and lemongrass and mains such as roast lamb and braised fennel with redcurrant and tarragon jus. The service and wine list are good, if unimaginative. Papingo is owned by Alan Tomkins who's also behind Gamba (*see p312*).

Quigley's

158-166 Bath Street, G2 4TB (0141 331 4060). **Lunch served** noon-3pm, **dinner served** 5-10.45pm Mon-Sat. **Meals served** 1-9pm Sun. **Main courses** £10.50-£29.50. **Set lunch** (Mon-Sat) £10.50 2 courses, £12.50 3 courses; (Sun) £11.50 2 courses, £14.50 3 courses. **Set dinner** (5-6.45pm Mon-Sat) £12.50 2 courses, £15.50 3 courses. **Credit** AmEx, MC, V.

A relatively recent addition to the plethora of eateries on Bath Street, and probably the one that Glaswegians would most like to see succeed, as it signals the fulfilment of a 20-year dream for local celebrity chef John Quigley. He's come a long way since cooking for Bryan Adams's on-the-road entourage. Unlike his former employer, Quigley has certainly hit the style pulse, restoring this former

Scotland

tempus

Tempus@CCA

auction house to its original Victorian grandeur, while adding a contrasting kick of minimalism in the wooden floors, mirrored walls and sleek banquette seating. The food reflects this unorthodox alliance of styles; traditional organic burgers sit side by side with Pacific Rim-style dishes. The menu changes frequently and the chef revels in inventive combos. Quigley's is not at its most atmospheric when thinly booked, but general word of mouth, as well as hopes for the place, remain strong.

Rab Ha's

83 Hutcheson Street, G1 1SH (0141 572 0400). Bar **Meals served** noon-10pm Mon-Sat; 12.30-10pm Sun. *Restaurant* **Dinner served** 5.30-10pm daily. **Main courses** £10. **Set dinner** (5.30-7.45pm) £10.95 2 courses. **Credit** AmEx, DC, MC, V.
A bit of history: Rab Ha was a famous Glasgow glutton who ate himself to death in 1843 after a diet that involved gobbling three chickens at once or a whole calf in one meal. No one expects you to follow in his bulky wake, but this cheerfully foodie-centric place is willing to help you try. The restaurant is slightly old-fashioned, with touches of tartan. Rab Ha's is known for its haggis (possibly one of the most renowned in the city), but the menu is mostly a mixture of restaurant classics from various genres. The French roast chicken is satisfyingly rich and the soups are filling and well flavoured. There's also a good organic selection, possibly because of sister restaurant Air Organic (*see p310*). The attached bar offers daytime food, which includes some dishes from the restaurant menu, as well as the standard burgers, chips and the like.

Rogano ★

11 Exchange Place, off Buchanan Street, G1 3AN (0141 248 4055/www.rogano.co.uk). Bar **Meals served** 11am-11pm Mon-Sat; 12.30-11pm Sun. *Café* **Meals served** noon-11pm Mon-Thur, Sun; noon-midnight Fri, Sat. *Restaurant* **Lunch served** noon-2.30pm, **dinner served** 6.30-10.30pm daily. **Main courses** £17.95-£33.50. **Set lunch** £16.50 3 courses. **Credit** AmEx, DC, MC, V.

The fabulous art deco dining room at Rogano, one of the city's most enduring restaurants, recalls the Clyde-built Cunard liners. When John Byrne shot his 1989 TV series *Your Cheatin' Heart* here, the great and the good of Glasgow were a permanent fixture over champagne and oysters. These days, Rogano's star has begun to fade a little as newer, slightly less stuffy restaurants have taken the limelight and its once-legendary fish menu seems to have become fairly passé in a city now swimming in decent cullen skinks. Still, faded glamour has a certain curiosity value and Rogano remains a highly respectable venue for an important meal (booking is advisable). Staff are discreetly, efficiently excellent.

Saint Jude's ★

190 Bath Street, G2 4HG (0141 352 8800/ www.saintjudes.com). **Lunch served** noon-3pm Tue-Fri. **Dinner served** 6-10.30pm daily. **Main courses** £11.50-£18.50. **Set lunch** £11.50 2 courses. **Set dinner** (6-7.15pm) £11.50 2 courses. **Credit** AmEx, DC, MC, V.
Another chic Bath Street eaterie, offering much the same pan-global cuisine as Quigley's (*see p315*) and the Arthouse Grill (*see p310*) in refined, minimalist surroundings, but with slightly less choice: the seasonal menu typically offers three options per course. Saint Jude's is also a boutique hotel with five smart bedrooms and – arguably its main attraction – a basement bar with a super-stylish but unimposing decor and a backroom lounge that resembles a set from *2001*. It's popular with the art school set, who hoover up under-£6 lunch options such as beefburger on focaccia and asparagus tortellini. The drinks aren't especially cheap, but watch the pretty things converge when cocktail happy hour arrives.

Schottische

16-18 Blackfriars Street, G1 1PE (0141 552 7774/ www.babbitybowster.com). Bar **Meals served** 11am-10pm Mon-Sat; 12.30-10pm Sun. **Dinner served** 6.30-9.30pm Tue-Sat. **Main courses** £12.50-£14.50. **Credit** AmEx, MC, V.

Scotland

No, not someone with a speech impediment trying to pronounce 'Scottish'; this restaurant is named after a German dance influenced by the Highland fling. But the theme is certainly local enough. This was one of the first places in town to really exploit the new wave in Scots cuisine, proudly casting off the old habits of slavish adherence to French cooking to celebrate the country's own traditions and produce. However, that doesn't mean just mince 'n' tatties: the kitchen takes top-drawer ingredients (venison, seafood, haggis) and cooks them with European techniques to show that Scottish food can be as sophisticated as anything. The restaurant is upstairs from legendary Glasgow pub Babbity Bowster.

Stravaigin ★

28 Gibson Street, G12 8NX (0141 334 2665/ www.stravaigin.com). Café **Meals served** 11am-11pm Mon-Thur, Sun; 11am-midnight Fri, Sat. *Restaurant* **Lunch served** noon-2.30pm Fri, Sat; 12.30-2.30pm Sun. **Dinner served** 5-11pm Tue-Sun. **Set lunch** (Mon-Sat) £18.95 2 courses, £21.95 3 courses; (Sun) £16.95 3 courses. **Set dinner** (5-7.30pm Tue-Fri, Sun; 5-7pm Sat) £12.95 2 courses, £14.95 3 courses; £22.95 2 courses, £28.95 3 courses. **Credit** AmEx, DC, MC, V.

A festoon of awards adorn this Gibson Street stalwart, one of the daddies of them all when it comes to great local food with an exotic twist. 'Think globally, eat locally' is the Stravaigin mantra, taking good Scottish produce and plunging it into exotic combinations, such as West Coast mussels with sweet chilli, coriander and oyster sauce. The bare yet cosy basement has the feel of an old ship's cabin, while the bar upstairs also offers superior pub grub (fab fish and chips). At Stravaigin's offspring, Stravaigin 2 (8 Ruthven Lane; 0141 334 7165), there's a modern, clean look of polished wood and big windows. The adventurous menu includes a good choice of tapas and a seafood cocktail described as 'Pacific Mexico meets Kinlochbervie' – where else are you going to find that, eh? The Bloody Marys have been voted one of the five best in Scotland.

Tempus@CCA

Centre for Contemporary Arts, 350 Sauchiehall Street, G2 3JD (0141 332 7959/www.aureliusgroup.co.uk). **Open** noon-11pm Mon-Wed; noon-midnight Thur; noon-1am Fri, Sat; 11am-4pm Sun. **Lunch served** noon-2.30pm daily. **Dinner served** 5-9.30pm Mon-Sat. **Main courses** £6.95-£11. **Set dinner** (5-7pm Tue-Thur) £9.95 2 courses; (5-7pm Fri, Sat) £10.95 2 courses. **Credit** AmEx, DC, MC, V.

Glasgow's arts venues don't tend to house especially memorable restaurants, but Tempus is a notable exception, largely due to its impressive setting in the vertiginous atrium of the coolly reinvented Centre for Contemporary Arts. The restaurant, though it may not exemplify intimate dining, has merit. Sleek wooden tables and cream banquettes are laid out with symmetrical precision, and the very reasonably priced menu reflects the exacting standards of the polished modernist architecture. The food can take a while to arrive, but is tasty, offering an imaginative slant on the fail-safe checklist of game, fowl, fish, veg and snacks. Options include beetroot risotto or Thai beef salad for starters, baked hake with mussel and veg cassoulet for main and apple crumble crème brûlée for pud. Tempus is principally patronised by conceptual art fans, Sauchiehall Street shoppers and all-round hipsters.

The Ubiquitous Chip ★

12 Ashton Lane, G12 8SJ (0141 334 5007/ www.ubiquitouschip.co.uk). Brasserie **Meals served** 11am-11pm Mon-Sat; 12.30-11pm Sun. **Lunch served** noon-2.30pm Mon-Sat; 12.30-3pm Sun. **Dinner served** 5.30-11pm Mon-Sat; 6.30-11pm Sun. **Set lunch** £21.50 2 courses, £26.50 3 courses. **Set dinner** £32.50 2 courses, £37.50 3 courses. **Credit** AmEx, DC, MC, V.

In 2002, as the Chip was celebrating its 30th birthday, it collected a Taste of Scotland award for best city restaurant in Scotland. Not bad for this grande dame of Ashton Lane. In fact, the Chip just seems to get better with age. The main restaurant is housed in a lush and leafy converted mews, the menu is seductively Caledonian, the wine list is one of the city's best – and booking is essential. Sunday lunch is a tradition. The starters, such as still-sizzling pan-fried scallops on a roasted potato cake with stewed garlic and vermouth sauce, are a hard act to follow. But the main courses, such as juicy venison in a gin and juniper berry sauce, manage to top them. The bar is sometimes busy with the city's movers, shakers and well-known faces (and voices); look out for the murals painted by literary giant Alasdair Gray. Connected to the Chip, but with its own separate entrance, newish spin-off the Wee Bar is small, opinionated and very, very Glasgow.

The Wee Curry Shop ★

7 Buccleuch Street, G3 6FJ (0141 353 0777). **Lunch served** noon-2pm, **dinner served** 5.30-10.30pm Mon-Sat. **Main courses** £5.50-£6.95. **Set lunch** £4.75 2 courses. **No credit cards**.

From the people who brought you Mother India (*see p314*), this hidden gem does exactly what it says on the label. A snug (as in sardines), no-frills Indian restaurant, it enjoys great word of mouth for its simple, flavoursome home-style cooking. Unlike many of its curry cousins, this dinky establishment doesn't overpower you with an overlong menu; it's pakora or poori to start, while the mains are dominated by chicken dishes and some classic veggie choices, all prepared in the open kitchen. The two-course lunch represents almost indecent value for money. Bring your own bottle and some balti-loving chums – but don't forget to book in advance as there's only room for 22 curry buffs at one time. There's a branch at 29 Ashton Lane; 0141 357 5280.

Also in the area

Malmaison 278 West George Street, G2 4LL (0141 572 1000).

Scotland

Aberdeenshire

ABERDEEN

Silver Darling Seafood Restaurant
*Pocra Quay, North Pier, Aberdeen, AB1 5DQ
(01224 576229).* **Lunch served** noon-2pm Mon-Fri.
Dinner served 6.30-9.30pm Mon-Sat. **Main
courses** £18-£20. **Credit** AmEx, DC, MC, V.
Sitting at the entrance to Aberdeen harbour, the
Silver Darling is a first-floor dining room with wide-
reaching views. To the north is the city's beach, to
the south the working port. Oil rig supply boats and
other vessels pass by day and night. A silver darling
is a herring and seafood is the star of the show here,
presented mostly in a French style. Grilled tiger
prawns to start come with Pernod, olive oil and herb
dressing, and a provençal tian. A main could involve
rock turbot stuffed with crab and scallop mousse,
accompanied by curry and saffron cream velouté.
Sweet ravioli stuffed with Agen prune cream, with
caramel Armagnac sauce and vanilla pod parfait,
might round off a meal, though not all the desserts
are this rich. The best restaurant in Aberdeen, and
in a suitably totemic location. In summer 2003 an
oyster bar added further attraction.

BALLATER

Darroch Learg Hotel
Braemar Road, Ballater, AB35 5UX (01339 755443).
Lunch served 12.30-2pm, **dinner served** 7-9pm
daily. Closed Christmas, last 3 wks Jan. **Set lunch**
(Sun) £19.50 3 courses. **Set dinner** £36 3 courses,
£42 6 courses. **Credit** AmEx, DC, MC, V.
The River Dee runs from the heart of the Grampians
to Aberdeen. Queen Victoria built Balmoral Castle
on its banks during the 1850s, just west of Ballater.
Spending time in these parts was an essential
element of later Victorian chic and local villages,
Ballater included, tend to have a 19th-century
granite hunting lodge look – the essence of 'Royal
Deeside', along with pine trees and mountains. The
Darroch Learg Hotel fits in with this splendidly. It's
a polite establishment, with the dining space in the
conservatory, and over many years the Franks
family and chef David Mutter have built up an
excellent reputation for food. That could see three
courses like moist crab and langoustine tortellini to
start, venison on Puy lentils as a main, followed by
a classic but well-executed dessert like crème brûlée
or lemon tart with a berry compote. They also have
a daytime café, called the Station at Station Square,
Ballater (01339 755050).

STONEHAVEN

The Tolbooth
Old Pier, Stonehaven, AB39 2JU (01569 762287).
Lunch served noon-2pm, **dinner served** 6-9.30pm
Tue-Sun. **Main courses** £12.95-£19. **Set lunch**
(Tue-Fri) £12 2 courses, £15 3 courses. **Credit** MC, V.
Stonehaven is an old fishing village that serves as a
resort for the citizens of Aberdeen just 15 miles
north. At the harbour sits the Tolbooth, the oldest
building hereabouts, dating from 1600 or so. The
restaurant occupies its upper storey. New owners
took over in summer 2003 – the Cleavers – and they
gave the interior a fresher look. It has a light wooden
floor, white and aqua walls, plus artwork. The staff
are amiable, wines are generally sub-£20 and the
menu leans towards seafood. When fishermen are
landing lobster a few yards away, that's the day's
special. Otherwise three courses might entail
Arbroath smokie broth to start (Scotch broth with
smoked fish); medallions of monkfish on sloe gin and
leek sauce as a main; then fresh berry crème brûlée
for dessert. It's more of an ambitious standard of
good home cooking than Michelin star fare, but
certainly an interesting place to eat near Aberdeen.

Angus

INVERKEILOR

Gordon's
*32 Main Street, Inverkeilor, DD11 5RN (01241
830364/www.gordonsrestaurant.co.uk).* **Lunch
served** noon-1.30pm Tue-Sun. **Dinner served** 7-9pm
Tue-Sat. **Set lunch** £16.50 2 courses, £18.95 3 courses.
Set dinner £30.50 3 courses. **Credit** MC, V.
Halfway between Arbroath and Montrose sits the
Angus village of Inverkeilor. The most exciting
thing about Inverkeilor is definitely Gordon's – and
has been ever since Gordon and Maria Watson
opened the restaurant way back in the mid 1980s. It
has a faintly medieval look with leaded stained
glass, wooden fittings, yellow paintwork and an
exposed stone gable wall. The food is mostly Franco-
Caledonian in style. A typical four courses could
bring roasted whole boneless quail with black
pudding on Puy lentils to start; then a cappuccino
of artichoke, cauliflower and white truffle velouté;
roasted halibut and sea bass with Arbroath smokie
risotto and red pepper and tomato fondue as a main;
then lemon and ginger pudding with lemon curd ice-
cream and raspberry purée for dessert. Short wine
list, friendly people, this is the best stand-alone
restaurant between Aberdeen and Dundee.

Silver Darling Seafood Restaurant

Argyll & Bute

CAIRNDOW

Loch Fyne Oyster Bar

Clachan, Cairndow, PA26 8BL (01499 600264/ www.lochfyne.com). **Meals served** *winter* 9am-7.30pm, *summer* 9am-8.30pm daily. **Main courses** £4.95-£25. **Credit** AmEx, DC, MC, V.

The Loch Fyne brand is now widely known, thanks to the rash of eponymous restaurants that opened in recent years across South-east England. But the original Loch Fyne Oyster Bar beats them all for glorious setting. At the head of a major sea loch in the mountains of Argyll, it is reached after an impossibly scenic drive of not much more than an hour from Glasgow, via the shores of Loch Lomond. The premises are modern-basic (white walls and wood) and it certainly isn't somewhere to come for a lengthy romantic dinner. But for a lively lunch for crustacean enthusiasts? Ideal. Raw materials here are top quality and you don't even have to do three courses. You can just pop in for a small plate of bradan orach (strongly smoked salmon) or go mad with a shellfish platter (queen scallops, langoustines, oysters and a whole crab). All manner of marine life is here, as well as the odd meat or vegetarian dish. If you're still hungry for more, there's an adjacent shop from which you can purchase the raw ingredients.

CRINAN

The Crinan Hotel ★

Crinan, PA31 8SR (01546 830261/ www.crinanhotel.com). Bar **Dinner served** 6.30-8.30pm daily. *Restaurant* **Lunch served** noon-2.30pm, **dinner served** 7-8.30pm daily. **Main courses** £11.95-£14.50. **Set dinner** £42.50 4 courses. **Credit** MC, V.

The Crinan is a canal connecting Loch Fyne with the Atlantic. It's still a working waterway and at its west end is the Crinan Hotel: a social and tourist hub. The dining room here, the Westward under the command of chef Ben Tish, is excellent. Seafood is a key component (landed just yards from the kitchen), but also there are traditional Scottish meats like lamb and venison. Dishes can be as elaborate as grilled scallops with pickled vegetables and vanilla foam, or as simple as an attention-grabbing bowl of fresh prawns. The bitter chocolate soufflé dessert is a classic. Nick Ryan is your voluble proprietor and wine enthusiast.

TARBERT

The Anchorage

Harbour Street, Tarbert, PA29 6UD (01880 820881). **Dinner served** 6.30-9.30pm daily. **Main courses** £10-£17. **Credit** MC, V.

Any restaurant that has a mural in the gents of a mermaid with an ice-cream cone reading an Iris Murdoch novel has got to be worthy of anyone's attention (reliable reports describe a small aquarium in the ladies). But site this establishment on the harbourfront in arguably Argyll's loveliest village (perched at the end of East Loch Tarbert, at the top of the Mull of Kintyre) and it's no wonder that cosmopolitan critics hop with excitement. It's small, neatly decorated and even has a tiny 'garden' where (two) diners can go alfresco should they want to brave Scotland's legendary midges. Seafood is the mainstay of chef Clare Johnson's menu, although beef and lamb are typical alternatives. Three courses could start with an immensely flavourful smoked haddock and sweetcorn chowder, leading on to juicy grilled sea bass with preserved lemons and spicy couscous, then finishing with a simple Tunisian orange and almond cake with Greek yoghurt.

TIGHNABRUAICH

The Royal Hotel

Tighnabruaich, PA21 2BE (01700 811239/ www.royalhotel.org.uk). Brasserie **Lunch served** noon-3pm, **dinner served** 6-9pm daily. *Restaurant* **Dinner served** 7-9pm Wed-Sat. **Main courses** £17.95-£26. **Credit** AmEx, MC, V.

The Cowal peninsula isn't that far from Glasgow but feels splendidly isolated; getting there involves either a scenic and convoluted drive or a short hop on a ferry (Gourock to Dunoon). Occupying one of the most picturesque spots on Cowal is the Royal

Scotland

Hotel, sitting on the coast looking over to Bute. The McKie family have been in charge here since 1997 and have made quite an impact. This is an attractive establishment, with interesting art on the walls and fine food on the plate. Typical starters are langoustines in creamed garlic with oysters on ice or cauliflower cheese soufflé. The options for mains might include cod with Loch Fyne scallops, fennel purée, wilted spinach and a seafood reduction. A dessert like confit of orange and praline soufflé with chocolate sauce rounds matters off beautifully.

Ayrshire

BRODICK

Creelers
Home Farm, nr Brodick, Isle of Arran, KA27 8DD (01770 302797). **Lunch served** noon-2.30pm, **dinner served** 6-9.30pm daily. **Main courses** £10.50-£16.95. **Credit** MC, V.
Welcome to the original Creelers. Restaurant-goers in central Edinburgh may be familiar with the name as there are two incarnations of this seafood bistro, both run by Tim and Fran James. This first one was set up back in 1990. It's a little way north of the main town on one of Scotland's more accessible islands: take the train from Glasgow to Ardrossan, then it's an hour on the ferry to Brodick. The eaterie adjoins a smokehouse and shop, and seafood is the menu mainstay – although red meat fans and vegetarians are also catered for. What's on offer depends on what's been pulled out of the sea lately but mussels, salmon and bouillabaisse are dependable regulars. A more ambitious dish would be a 'rendezvous' of seafish and shellfish with Pernod. Crowd-pleasing desserts round off a rolling holiday atmosphere.

DALRY

Braidwoods ★
Drumastle Mill Cottage, Dalry, KA24 4LN (01294 833544). **Lunch served** noon-1.45pm Wed-Sun. **Dinner served** 7-9pm Tue-Sat. **Set lunch** (Wed-Sat) £16 2 courses, £19 3 courses; (Sun) £25 3 courses. **Set dinner** £32 3 courses, £36.50 4 courses. **Credit** AmEx, DC, MC, V.
Even though this restaurant – contained within a tidy little country cottage – is only 25 miles south-west of Glasgow, it's well off the beaten track (phone for directions). Both Keith and Nicola Braidwood are accomplished chefs with wide experience (Keith was Scottish Chef of the Year in 1999), and this shows in their imaginative but non-faddy menu that makes the most of quality local ingredients. Typical starters are chicken liver and foie gras parfait with gooseberry chutney, and whole roast boneless quail stuffed with black pudding; mains might be roast venison loin and breast of squab pigeon in wild mushroom jus or baked fillet of west coast turbot on a smoked salmon risotto; while desserts are the likes of vanilla panna cotta with passion fruit, pineapple

and mango soup or iced caramelised pecan parfait with a sharp raspberry coulis. Braidwoods is quite small, so book. One of Scotland's finest.

TROON

Lochgreen House Hotel
Monktonhill Road, Troon, KA10 7EN (01292 313343/www.costleyhotels.co.uk). **Lunch served** noon-2pm, **dinner served** 7-9pm daily. **Main courses** £6-£13. **Set lunch** (Sun) £19.95 3 courses. **Set dinner** £32.50 4 courses. **Credit** AmEx, MC, V.
Lochgreen House is one of a small group of hotels and inns around Ayrshire run by the Costley family. These range from a splendid roadside pub (the Cochrane Inn at Gatehead near Kilmarnock) to a full-on Rabbie Burns country romance hotel (the Brig o' Doon at Alloway outside Ayr). However, the foodie star in the firmament is this one and it's also the most formal and upmarket. The elaborate table d'hôte dinner could start with a warm monkfish salad with foie gras, chorizo and white onion; then throw in a sorbet or a refreshing soup; offer a main like a medallion of beef with roast vegetables and red wine sauce; then finish with chocolate marquise with caramel sauce and white chocolate ice-cream.

Dumfries & Galloway

CROSSMICHAEL

The Plumed Horse
Crossmichael, DG7 3AU (01556 670333/ www.plumed-horse.co.uk). **Brasserie Lunch served** 12.20-1pm Tue-Fri. **Dinner served** 7-8.30pm Tue-Sat. **Set lunch** £18 2 courses, £22.50 3 courses. *Restaurant* **Lunch served** 12.20-1pm Tue-Fri, Sun. **Dinner served** 7-8.30pm Tue-Sat. **Main courses** £18. **Credit** MC, V.
The Plumed Horse, which opened in 1998, is now widely recognised as one of Scotland's top dining spots. The food can best be described as Franco-Caledonian style. That means you can have a ballotine of duck and goose foie gras with muscat-spiked calves' feet jelly to start, then a pavé of local Scottish beef with root vegetables, mushrooms, pomme tatin and veal jus as a main, and round off dinner with apple bread and butter pudding with calvados caramel and cinnamon ice-cream. Or order an assiette of mini desserts for the table. July 2003 saw the opening of a new brasserie.

East Lothian

GULLANE

Greywalls
Muirfield, Gullane, EH31 2EG (01620 842144/ www.greywalls.co.uk). Apr-Oct **Dinner served** 7-9.15pm daily. **Set dinner** £40 3 courses. **Credit** AmEx, DC, MC, V.

Designed by Sir Edward Lutyens at the end of the 19th century, set amid beautiful gardens and right next to the legendary Muirfield golf course, Greywalls is the kind of place that can make grown adults weep at the sheer beauty of life on a warm summer's evening. It is formal (jacket and tie for gents), and lives and breathes golf (lots of British Open winners have stayed here when Muirfield has hosted the tournament), but not overwhelmingly so. The dining room – hung with botanical drawings rather than old clubs – overlooks the tenth tee. It's an elegant setting in which to enjoy head chef Simon Burns's assured daily-changing set price menu (with five choices at each course). A typical meal might start with an escabeche of sea bass with pickled baby fennel, followed by smoked Eyemouth lobster with lemon and chive butter, and then a splendid green apple bavarois with toasted walnut sabayon. Nice cheeseboard too.

HADDINGTON

Bonars Restaurant

Poldrate Mill, Haddington, EH41 4DA (01620 822100). **Lunch served** noon-2pm, **dinner served** 6.30-9.30pm Wed-Sun. **Main courses** £16.45-£17.95. **Set dinner** £25.95 4 courses. **Credit** MC, V.
Haddington is a pleasant market town, less than 20 miles outside Edinburgh. Among its small complement of restaurants, Bonars stands out as the most ambitious and accomplished. Within an old mill building you'll find a neat, tidy interior with much bare stone in evidence and some nice decorative flourishes (decent art, a rocking horse). The food has a French slant. A starter like crown of melon with sorbet and angel hair has so much spun sugar (intricate but ostentatious) that heads turn. The sorbets are excellent, though. The mains can be very rich: beef fillet wrapped in pancetta with port, shallot and foie gras ravioli or venison loin with sage and honeyed Armagnac sweetbreads. There's the likes of Baileys and white chocolate mousse cake with treacle ice-cream for dessert. Traditional it may be, but Bonars' desire to please is thoroughly endearing.

Fife

CUPAR

The Peat Inn

Peat Inn, nr Cupar, KY15 5LH (01334 840206/ www.thepeatinn.co.uk). **Lunch served** 12.30pm, **dinner served** 7-9.30pm Tue-Sat. **Set lunch** £17-£19. **Set dinner** £30 3 courses. **Credit** AmEx, MC, V.
The Peat Inn was serving great food when many of today's celebrity chefs were wondering what David Bowie would do after Ziggy Stardust. Main man David Wilson has created so many signature dishes that its website has a recipe section. It opened in 1972 and has the feel of a well-appointed coaching inn. The kitchen prides itself on the quality of the

raw materials (excellent beef, local game, vegetables and seafood from nearby fishing villages like Anstruther and Pittenweem). Three courses might entail roasted scallops on leek, smoked bacon, potato and pea purée, then whole lobster in herb broth with fresh pasta, and to finish a legendary little pot of chocolate and rosemary. The wine list is extensive and includes a particularly noteworthy selection of champagnes. The location, between Methil and St Andrews, and not far from Cupar (there are rooms so you can stay), is a little out of the way. Note that lunch is only available as a set price meal and at one sitting (12.30pm seated for 1pm meal).

DUNFERMLINE

Town House Restaurant & Bistro

48 East Port, Dunfermline, KY12 7JB (01383 432382/www.townhouserestaurant.co.uk). **Food served** 10am-10pm, **lunch served** noon-6pm, **dinner served** 6-10pm daily. **Main courses** £14. **Set lunch** (Mon-Fri, Sun) £9.85 2 courses. **Set dinner** (Mon-Thur, Sun) £15.95 2 courses. **Credit** AmEx, MC, V.
As the crow flies, Dunfermline is less than 15 miles from central Edinburgh, but until Paul and Diane Brown opened the Town House at the end of 2000, the local restaurant scene was surprisingly limited. This establishment introduced a flexible menu and a riot of cosmopolitan colour with its stone walls, wrought-iron fixtures and designer chairs. It does 'quick bites' during the day (such as wild boar sausages with mustard mash) and bargain lunches. In the evening à la carte could offer own-dried tomato tart with tomato and balsamic vinaigrette to start; then mains like lamb with pea mousse and rosemary scented jus or a 10oz sirloin steak with pickled walnut sauce; with sticky date and sultana pudding to finish.

Highland

ACHILTIBUIE

Summer Isles Hotel

Achiltibuie, IV26 2YG (01854 622282/ www.summerisleshotel.co.uk). **Bar Meals served** noon-8.30pm. *Restaurant* **Lunch served** 12.30-2pm, **dinner served** 8pm daily. Closed mid Oct-Easter. **Main courses** £7.50-£30. **Set dinner** £45 5 courses. **Credit** MC, V.
There's the back of beyond, then there's the heart-stoppingly more scenic bit a few miles further along: that's where you'll find the excellent Summer Isles Hotel. Ten miles north of Ullapool, you turn west on a minor road into the Inver Polly nature reserve. If you manage not to drive into Loch Lurgainn while gawping at the view, you'll reach Achiltibuie. The actual Summer Isles are before you and the hotel kitchen is on hand to demonstrate how it has cooked its way to Scottish top ten status. Dinner is a set five-course affair and the fantastic local seafood a central feature of Chris Firth-Bernard's menu (such as spiny

Scotland

Inverlochy Castle Hotel

lobster and langoustine with hollandaise as a second course). But there is meat (Aberdeen Angus with red wine sauce or duck with plum compote as mains), solidly crafted desserts, an awesome wine list and top cheeseboard.

APPLECROSS

The Applecross Inn

Shore Street, Applecross, IV54 8LR (01520 744262). **Meals served** noon-9pm daily. **Main courses** £6.75-£12.95. **Credit** MC, V.
The drive over the peninsula to the Applecross Inn must be among the most dramatic of approaches to any eaterie in these islands. Roughly 50 miles west of Inverness as the crow flies, you start climbing above Loch Kishorn to an old cattle pass, more than 2,000ft above sea level. Then you drop back down to

the coast opposite the isles of Raasay and Skye. Applecross itself is a tiny hamlet on that coast; its Inn has a homely feel, effectively a bar with a few rooms attached, but don't let that fool you. They've got access to excellent ingredients here and take their cooking very seriously. There's no metropolitan fuss about the dishes but whether you choose a bar snack (a half-pint glass filled with prawn tails) or a main meal (dressed crab pulled from Applecross Bay with salad and bread, or battered monkfish and chips with peas), the freshness of the seafood shines.

COLBOST

The Three Chimneys

Colbost, Isle of Skye, IV55 8ZT (01470 511258/ www.threechimneys.co.uk). **Lunch served** *Apr-mid Oct* 12.30-2pm Mon-Sat. **Dinner served** 6.30-9.30pm

daily. Closed last 3 wks Jan. **Set lunch** £17.50
2 courses, £24 3 courses. **Set dinner** £42 3 courses,
£48 4 courses. **Credit** AmEx, MC, V.
The Three Chimneys is a pocket of excellence.
People travel in expectation rather than hope.
Shirley Spears is the award-winning chef and the
'restaurant with rooms' is crofter cottage style, sited
in the north west of Skye, an island with imposing
mountains and Bonnie Prince Charlie associations.
Local seafood's the thing, although not exclusively.
A four-course dinner could start with Bracadale crab
risotto cake with herb salad and crab dressing; six
oysters in between; grilled west coast cod with grain
mustard mash, braised fennel, and chive and lemon
butter sauce for main; then hot marmalade pudding
with Drambuie custard for dessert.

FORT WILLIAM

Inverlochy Castle Hotel ★

Nr Fort William, PH33 6SN (01397 702177/
www.inverlochycastlehotel.com). **Lunch served**
12.15-1.30pm, **dinner served** 7-9pm daily. **Set
lunch** £23.50 2 courses, £28 3 courses. **Set dinner**
£52.50 5 courses. **Credit** AmEx, MC, V.
If you had to pick one archetypal Scottish country
house hotel, then this would surely be it. A medieval
castle once stood on the site, but the current building
is a Victorian fantasy dating from the 1860s. It sits
at the southern end of an impressive geological fault
known as the Great Glen, with Ben Nevis providing
the backdrop. The decor is sumptuous, and the
kitchen – under head chef Matthew Gray – has
gathered more accolades in recent years than a Real
Madrid midfielder. A typical three courses might
bring carpaccio of black pudding with white truffle
scrambled eggs and roast veal sweetbreads,
followed by a crisp fillet of sea bass with jerusalem
artichoke ravioli and fish velouté, then caramelised
rice pudding with apricot milkshake. The
atmosphere is very formal, but the food is exemplary
and the overall experience is something else.

INVERNESS

The Mustard Seed

16 Fraser Street, Inverness, IV1 1DW (01463
220220). **Lunch served** noon-3pm, **dinner**
served 6-10pm daily. **Main courses** £7.95-£12.75.
Set lunch £5.95 2 courses. **Set dinner** £10.95
2 courses. **Credit** AmEx, DC, MC, V.
The Mustard Seed came along in 2001, in an old
church on the banks of the River Ness. The interior
has been tricked out with a designer flourish – a fine,
airy space with yellow walls. There are also big
plants and artworks: quite a departure for a centre
whose tourist trade had traditionally featured too
much Caledonian kitsch. Three courses could kick
off with steamed rope mussels in white wine with
coriander cream, or asparagus, mozzarella and
tomato bruschetta. Mains typically include the likes
of pork fillet with sunblushed tomatoes and marsala

cream or simple sea trout with wilted spinach and
parsley butter. Vegetarians get a reasonable choice,
while dessert could be white chocolate and
raspberry charlotte. Wines are affordable.

KISHORN

Kishorn Seafood Bar

Kishorn, IV54 8XA (01520 733240). **Meals
served** *Sept-June* 10am-5pm Mon-Sat; *July-Aug*
10am-9pm Mon-Sat; noon-5pm Sun. **Main courses**
£3.50-£15.25. **Credit** MC, V.
Around 50 miles due west of Inverness, the hamlet
of Kishorn isn't really near anything, except
spectacular scenery and big sea lochs. It's on the
A896 at Loch Kishorn, part of the route from Kyle of
Lochalsh (and Skye) north to Torridon and the most
remote bits of Scotland. But Kishorn is home to a
seafood bar, courtesy of Viv Rollo: a sort of shellfish
café. The assorted edibles are displayed on the
counter and cooked to order: fresh and simple. It's
possible to do three courses here (such as own-made
soup, a plate of langoustines, then some chocolate
fudge cake), although they'll run to a burger for that
recalcitrant crustacean-resistant child, and people
pop in during the afternoon for tea and a scone. But
the shellfish are the real mainstay: the seafood platter
involves scallops, prawns, oysters, mussels and
anything else that's handy. It's licensed and you can
sit outside in good weather. Basic but brilliant.

LAIDE

Old Smiddy Guest House

Laide, IV22 2NB (01445 731425/www.oldsmiddy.
co.uk). **Breakfast served** 8.30-9.30am daily.
Dinner served 8.30pm Mon-Fri. **Dinner, bed
& breakfast** £65-£75. **Credit** MC, V.
You have to stay here to eat, but as Kate and Steve
MacDonald's place is way up in the wilds of Wester
Ross (roughly 80 miles north-west of Inverness) and
it has knockout food, you'll want to. Breakfast is
special: local grilled kippers and grilled tomatoes, or
fabulous smoked haddock and a poached egg are
just a couple of the choices. Evening meals are even
better. It's unlicensed, so you can bring your own
wine, and a typical dinner would involve red and
yellow pepper soup with sesame toast to start, then
a quick lemon and blue curaçao sorbet, Highland
lamb with rosemary and a red wine reduction on
wild mushrooms as a main, then pear and almond
tart with mascarpone for dessert. It's a set menu, but
if vegetarians call ahead Kate will cater.

NAIRN

Boath House Hotel

Auldearn, Nairn, IV12 5TG (01667 454896/
www.boath-house.com). **Lunch served** 12.30-2pm,
dinner served 7-8.30pm daily. **Set lunch** £29.50
4 courses. **Set dinner** £39.50 5 courses. **Credit**
AmEx, DC, MC, V.

The bedrooms are stunning, the architecture is Grade I listed Georgian, the grounds are extensive and there's even some decent contemporary art. But this building was in a bit of a state back in the early 1990s when Don and Wendy Mathieson decided to embark on a labour of love to first restore it, and then open it as a hotel. They succeeded on both counts and the food at Boath House Hotel – courtesy of chef Charles Lockley – triumphantly lives up to its surroundings. Both lunch and dinner are table d'hôte; the latter might start with a sweetcorn and Parma ham soup, followed by an entrée of scallop, lobster and salmon tortellini poached in lobster bisque with pea velouté. There's a choice of two mains – perhaps roasted haunch of venison on celeriac purée with spiced red cabbage and red wine jus. The cheese course typically entails a British artisan selection, then dessert might offer slow-roasted white peaches with a golden mango ice-cream. Vegetarians can be catered for, but should ideally call ahead.

SPEAN BRIDGE
Old Pines ★
Spean Bridge, PH34 4EG (01397 712324/www.old pines.co.uk). **Lunch served** 12.30-2.30pm Tue-Sun. **Dinner served** 8pm Tue-Sun by appointment only. **Main courses** £3.50-£10.50. **Set dinner** £34 5 courses. **Credit** MC, V.
The acme of hippie good taste in the heart of Lochaber. Old Pines is more than just a restaurant – often it seems like a mission, on the part of proprietors Sukie and Bill Barber, to promote a lifestyle featuring family-friendliness, informality and a love of good food. They've got an enormous poly tunnel where they grow many of the ingredients, and the building has a well-appointed cabin-in-the-woods look. A typical set dinner would involve: mussel broth; squat lobster and crab from the Isle of Muck, with salad, herbs and flowers from that poly tunnel; roast venison as a main with spiced red cabbage, wild mushrooms and thyme sauce; hazel-nut meringue with raspberries, raspberry ice-cream and berry sauce for dessert; and finally some unpasteurised artisan cheese to finish. Vegetarians are more than welcome (although they should call ahead) and the Barbers are also pretty good with wines.

Orkney Islands

ST MARGARETS HOPE
The Creel
Front Road, St Margarets Hope, KW17 2SL (01856 831311/www.thecreel.co.uk). **Dinner served** *Apr-Oct* 7-8.30pm daily. **Main courses** £16.80. **Credit** MC, V.
By the time you get to the Creel, set on the seashore of a pretty fishing village, you will already be enthralled by the empty, treeless, wide-sky

magnificence of Orkney. But you'll probably also be bemoaning the fact that, gastronomically, the islands are as barren as their landscapes. The Creel is your salvation. Its two elegant dining rooms serve a sensibly short seafood and fish-inclined menu (though there's also excellent Orkney beef and seaweed-fed lamb from North Ronaldsay on offer). The locally caught queen scallops baked in garlic butter are sublime, and the rock turbot fish cakes with tartare sauce and parsley dressing good, though they would be improved with coarser breadcrumbs and more interesting veggies on the side. Make sure that you leave some space for the Creel's divine own-made ice-cream – the passion fruit is particularly fine – and the Orkney fudge served with coffee.

Perth & Kinross

AUCHTERARDER
Andrew Fairlie at Gleneagles ★
Gleneagles Hotel, Auchterarder, PH3 1NF (01764 694267/www.gleneagles.co.uk). **Dinner served** 7-10pm Mon-Sat. **Main courses** £27. **Set dinner** £55 3 courses, £75 5 courses. **Credit** AmEx, DC, MC, V.
Everyone has heard of Gleneagles, the grand country pile in Perthshire that is synonymous with golf (three championship-standard courses). It was built in the 1920s and has been one of Scotland's nodes of pomp and circumstance ever since. However, it had to wait until 2001 for the talented Andrew Fairlie to open his restaurant and bring a more sophisticated metropolitan dining style to bear, both in terms of the food and the quietly contemporary decor. As with most other top-end eateries in Scotland, the approach is very much

Andrew Fairlie at Gleneagles

Franco-Scottish (raw materials come from both local and French suppliers). That means kicking things off with a starter like foie gras terrine with baby leek and truffle salad, moving on to braised line-caught sea bass with black olive crust and creamed polenta, then finishing off with hot blackcurrant soufflé with coconut sorbet or perhaps an assiette de fruits rouges. The wine list doesn't disappoint either. Andrew Fairlie's restaurant is certainly one of the priciest in Scotland, but it's also assuredly among the best.

DUNKELD

Kinnaird

Kinnaird Estate, nr Dunkeld, PH8 0LB (01796 482440/www.kinnairdestate.com). **Lunch served** 12.30-1.45pm, **dinner served** 7.15-9.30pm daily.
Set lunch £30 3 courses. **Set dinner** £50 3 courses.
Credit AmEx, MC, V.
Generally, no one 'drops by' Kinnaird. This Edwardian mansion with its 9,000-acre estate is a few miles along a B road off the main A9 from Perth to Inverness (the turning is around two miles north of Dunkeld). Anyone looking for an informal roadside café would tend to be put off by what looks like (and is) one of Scotland's top country house hotels. As a result, diners tend to be guests – but non-residents can eat here and the food is an absolute blast, very well presented by chef Trevor Brooks. Ingredients are top quality and they have their own kitchen garden and smokehouse. A typical starter can be as simple as hand-dived scallops with peas and pancetta, while a main might feature Angus beef fillet with foie gras, potato rösti, root vegetables, spinach and Madeira sauce. Since you've come by car, the assiette of Valrhona chocolate desserts will compensate for having to resist the extensive wine list.

PERTH

Let's Eat

77-79 Kinnoull Street, Perth, PH1 5EZ (01738 643377/www.letseatperth.co.uk). **Lunch served** noon-2pm, **dinner served** 6.30-9.45pm Tue-Sat.
Main courses £9-£16.75. **Credit** AmEx, MC, V.
Chef Tony Heath and front-of-house supremo Shona Drysdale improved the food scene in this neck of the woods no end when they opened here in late 1995. Since then, Let's Eat – with its distinctive green exterior paint job – has established itself as an award-winner and a real favourite in Perth and further afield. The interior decor looks contemporary but welcoming, with comfortable sofas to one side for browsing the menu. That menu could bring terrine of pigeon, chicken and black pudding with spiced apple and Cumberland sauce as a starter; mains include fillet of Angus beef on a truffled wild mushroom potato cake with button onions, creamed spinach and a Madeira and red wine sauce or grilled fillets of sole with chive mash and sorrel sauce. For dessert, how about baked chocolate pudding with chocolate fudge sauce and cappuccino ice-cream? No highfalutin' attitudes here: just good food and an affordable wine list.

63 Tay Street Restaurant

63 Tay Street, Perth, PH2 8NN (01738 441451/ www.63taystreet.co.uk). **Lunch served** noon-2pm, **dinner served** 6.30-9pm Tue-Sat. **Main courses** £14.95. **Credit** AmEx, DC, MC, V.
The Wares opened this excellent little eaterie by the side of the River Tay in early 2001, giving Perth a major culinary shot in the arm. Shona does front of house, Jeremy looks after the kitchen. The decor is light, the linen white, chairs blue and artwork on the walls occasionally adventurous. Lunchtime sees provincial legal eagles drop by from the nearby sheriff court, while evenings are more mixed. A

typical lunch might be pork and pistachio terrine with toasted brioche and onion chutney to start, then herb-crusted cod fillet with spinach, sautéed potatoes and a chive beurre blanc, and a chunky rhubarb crème brûlée with rhubarb ice-cream for dessert. It may be a small restaurant, but 63 Tay Street maintains consistently high standards.

PITLOCHRY

Old Armoury Restaurant & Tea Garden

Armoury Road, Pitlochry, PH16 5AP (01796 474281). Apr-Oct **Meals served** 12.30-8.30pm, **lunch served** noon-2.30pm, **dinner served** 6.30-8.30pm daily. *Nov-Mar* **Meals served** 12.30-8.30pm, **lunch served** noon-2.30pm, **dinner served** 6.30-8.30pm Fri-Sun. **Main courses** £9.95-£16.25. **Set meal** (noon-2.30pm; 5.30-6.30pm) £18.25 2 courses, £21.25 3 courses. **Credit** MC, V.

Pitlochry is a tourist town in the Perthshire hills. As the name suggests, this restaurant occupies an 18th-century armoury, formerly used by the Black Watch (tablecloths are in the distinctive regimental tartan). There are tables outside and a couple of neat dining rooms inside, one with anomalous African ornaments. Dining is flexible: afternoon teas, light lunches, and à la carte in the evenings. The dinner menu offers salmon cheesecake as a starter (a nice touch), and draws heavily on local ingredients such as Aberdeen Angus, venison and lamb. But one of the most refreshing elements here is the effort made with vegetarian dishes. One main course entails field mushrooms topped with mascarpone and mozzarella, with a polenta and olive cake, an aubergine and tomato muffin, and garlic and balsamic dressing with roasted pine kernels. To finish, typical desserts would be cranachan parfait or date and sticky toffee pudding.

Port-Na-Craig

Pitlochry, PH16 5ND (01796 472777/ www.portnacraig.com). **Lunch served** 12.30-2pm Tue-Sat; 1-2.30pm Sun. **Dinner served** 6-9pm Tue-Sat. **Main courses** £9-£15. **Credit** MC, V.

On the other side of the River Tummel from the centre of Pitlochry, this former 17th-century inn has been a fixture on the town's restaurant circuit for many years – and very handy for the Festival Theatre. But it was taken over in 2002 by the Thewes family, who gave the interior a major makeover. Port-Na-Craig is now a bright space with two adjacent dining rooms, a light wooden floor and off-white walls, plus plans for a bar (hence going back to its inn roots). The modern bistro-style menu offers a starter like caramelised scallop salad with chilli and coriander; pork fillet with red pepper and oregano sauce, turmeric rice and salad as a main; then a big, chunky gooseberry and elderflower fool with home-made shortbread as dessert. There are vegetarian choices and the majority of wines weigh in at under £25. A friendly choice in the hills.

Stirling

CALLANDER

Roman Camp Country House Hotel

Main Street, Callander, FK17 8BG (01877 330003/ www.roman-camp-hotel.co.uk). **Lunch served** 12.30-2pm, **dinner served** 7-8.30pm daily. **Main courses** £18-£28.95. **Set lunch** £16.50 2 courses, £20 3 courses. **Set dinner** £35 5 courses. **Credit** AmEx, DC, MC, V.

Callander smacks of twee tourism – you'll not want for shortbread should you visit. By contrast, the upmarket setting of Roman Camp – in Callander but with 20 acres of gardens – couldn't be more different. This is a well-run country house hotel with a formal, classy dining room and a kitchen that can knock your socks off. At dinner, chef Ian McNaught offers both à la carte and a superb daily-changing tasting menu. From the former, a meal might start with pressed ham knuckle, duck confit and sweetbreads with cep chantilly, before moving on to pan-fried calf's liver with garlic confit and sage jus, and finishing with iced honey and lavender parfait with raspberry coulis. A vegetarian menu is also available. Not cheap, but a real treat and an easily accessible escape from Scotland's populous central belt.

West Lothian

LINLITHGOW

The Champany Inn ★

Nr Linlithgow, EH49 7LU (01506 834532/ www.champany.com). Chop & Ale House **Lunch served** noon-2pm Mon-Fri. **Dinner served** 6.30-10pm Mon-Sat. **Meals served** noon-6.30pm Sat; noon-10pm Sun. **Main courses** £7.95-£19.95. *Restaurant* **Lunch served** 12.30-2pm Mon-Fri. **Dinner served** 7-10pm Mon-Sat. **Main courses** £19.50-£35.50. **Set lunch** (Mon-Fri) £16.75 2 courses. **Credit** AmEx, DC, MC, V.

Leave Linlithgow on the A803 northbound, cross over the M9 motorway and the Champany Inn is on the next corner. This is no discreet roadside dinette – more a complex of buildings that includes the main rotunda dining room and the Chop & Ale House (a bistro offering world-class hamburgers among other things). The whole operation – with its country-house-meets-farmhouse feel – is run by Clive and Anne Davidson and has an award-winning wine cellar. The central attraction in the main dining room, however, is most definitely the meat: prime Aberdeen Angus hung for three weeks and cooked to order on a specially designed grill. It is undeniably excellent. There are alternative mains (such as duck or langoustines), but committed carnivores won't want to miss something like the porterhouse steak with fried potatoes. That would come after a starter like salmon hot smoked in the kitchen over woodchips. Room for pudding? As if.

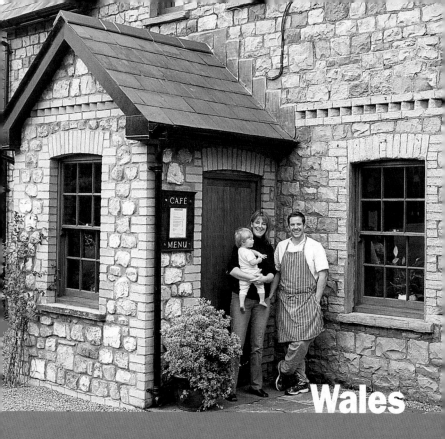

Wales

Wales

Irish Sea

Liverpool Bay

ISLE OF ANGLESEY

Caernarfon Bay

CONWY

GWYNEDD

Cardigan Bay

Bardsey Island

CEREDIGION

POWYS

DENBIGH-SHIRE

FLINT-SHIRE

WREXHAM

SHROP-SHIRE

HEREFORD-SHIRE

PEMBROKE-SHIRE

CARMARTHENSHIRE

MONMOUTH-SHIRE

NEATH & PORT TALBOT

RHONDDA CYNON-TYDFIL

MERTHYR TYDFIL

BLAENAU GWENT

TORFAEN

CAER-PHILLY

BRIDGEND

VALE OF GLAMORGAN

NEWPORT

Swansea Bay

Carmarthen Bay

St. Govan's Head

Bristol Channel

Nash Point

DEVON

SOMERSET

Lundy

Southport · Ormskirk · Wigan · Bootle · St Hele · LIVERPOOL · MERSEYSIDE · Birkenhead · Ellesmere Por · Chester · CHESHI · Mal · Wrexham · Grosford · Overton · Penley · Wem · Shrewsbury · Church Stretton · Bishop's Castle · Ludlow · Knighton · Presteigne · Leominster · Kington · Hereford · Hay-on-Wye · Talgarth · Skenfrit · Monmo · Whitebe · St Arva · Chepst · BRIS · Portishead · Weston-super-Mare · Burnham-on-Sea · Watchet · Glastonbu · Bridgwater · Taunton · Minehead · Ilfracombe · Bideford

Amlwch · Holyhead · Holy Island · Gwalchmai · Rhosneigr · Llanerchymedd · Benllech · Llandudno · Colwyn Bay · Rhyl · Prestatyn · Dyserth · Holywell · Flint · Connah's Quay · Queensferry · Buckley · Mold · Denbigh · St Asaph · Rhuddlan · Abergele · Deganwy · Conwy · Penmaenmawr · Beaumaris · Llangefni · Bangor · Llanfairfechan · Ty'n-y-Groes · Bethesda · Caernarfon · Llanrwst · Betws-y-coed · Ruthin · Llandegla · Bala · Corwen · Llangollen · Ruabon · Oswestry · Chirk · Glyn Ceiriog · Llanrhaeadr ym-Mochnant · Llandrillo · Llanuwchllyn · Llanfyllin · Welshpool · Montgomery · Newtown · Llanbrynmair · Pontdolgoch · Llanidloes · Rhayader · Llandrindod Wells · Builth Wells · Llanwrtyd Wells · Llyswen · Felin Fach · Brecon · Llanfrynach · Crickhowell · Abergavenny · Llangattock Lingoed · Llanthewy Skirrid · Rock · Clytha Hill

Bangor · Llanberis · Capel Curig · Pen-y-Gwryd · Capel Garmon · Llandwrog · Penygroes · Beddgelert · Blaenau Ffestiniog · Ffestiniog · Trawsfynydd · Porthmadog · Criccieth · Pwllheli · Nefyn · Morfa Nefyn · Efailnewydd · Llanbedrog · Abersoch · Talsarnau · Harlech · Llanbedr · Dyffryn Ardudwy · Barmouth · Dolgellau · Tywyn · Aberdyfi · Machynlleth · Eglwysfach · Aberystwyth · Devil's Bridge · Llanrhystud · Aberaeron · New Quay · Tregaron · Lampeter · Aberporth · Cardigan · Newcastle Emlyn · Llandysul · Llandovery · Llandeilo · Nant-ddu · Llanwrtyd Wells

Goodwick · Fishguard · Llangloffan · Dinas Head · Newport · St David's · Haverfordwest · St Bride's Bay · St Brides · Welsh Hook · Whitland · St Clears · Laugharne · Pendine · Carmarthen · Nantgaredig · Glanaman · Ammanford · Johnston · Narberth · Kidwelly · Pontardawe · Milford Haven · Neyland · Pembroke Dock · Saundersfoot · Tenby · Pembroke · Caldey Island · Oldwalls · Reynoldston · Llanelli · Burry Port · Gorseinon · Pontardulais · SWANSEA · Neath · Port Talbot · Maesteg · Aberdare · Nant-y-derry · Llandenny · Pontypool · Cwmbran · Pontypridd · Caerphilly · NEWPORT · CARDIFF · Penarth · Barry · Porthcawl · Cowbridge · Bridgend · Merthyr Tydfil

0 ——— 50 km
0 ——— 25 miles

© Copyright Time Out Group 2003

Wales

Cardiff

The Armless Dragon
*97 Wyeverne Road, Cathays, Cardiff, CF24 4BG
(029 2038 2357/www.thearmlessdragon.co.uk).*
Lunch served noon-2pm Tue-Fri. **Dinner served**
7-9pm Tue-Thur; 7-9.30pm Fri, Sat. **Main courses**
£10-£19. **Set lunch** £8 2 courses, £10 3 courses.
Credit MC, V.
Under new owner Paul Lane, the dining room has
been painted a pleasing burgundy and the menu
blackboards never fail to delight. The carte has such
choice: potted rabbit with pear chutney; lamb's
kidney with a gratin of potato and leek; turbot
with samphire; cider-soused skate. Mouthwatering
veggie options include leek and asparagus tarte fine
with Welsh rarebit. Produce is mainly from small
suppliers in Wales. Butter the colour of egg yolk is
brought from near Aberystwyth. Welsh Black beef
from Llandeilo combines soft texture with fabulous
taste. Saltmarsh lamb from Laugharne is wonderful.
The global wine list offers bottles from under a
tenner to around £40 and some by the glass. People
should come to Cardiff just to eat here.

Bosphorus
*31 Mermaid Quay, Cardiff Bay, Cardiff, CF10 5BZ
(029 2048 7477/www.bosphorus.co.uk).* **Lunch
served** noon-3pm, **dinner served** 6pm-midnight
daily. **Main courses** £15-£18. **Set lunch** £4.95
2 courses. **Set dinner** £17 3 courses. **Credit** MC, V.
Occupying a glass box at the end of a pier, this could
be one of the greatest restaurant locations in the
world if it overlooked the sun-drenched Golden Horn
or Bosphorus. But Cardiff Bay? Anyway, for those
travelling west of Bristol, this is as good as Turkish
food gets. Set menus include a meze of small dishes
– the usual houmous, taramasalata, falafel –
followed by lamb or chicken kebabs. From the à la
carte menu Turkey's most popular kebab, the
Adana, is minced lamb with peppers served off the
skewer with grilled tomato, green pepper and rice –
substantial and delicious. The yogurtlu kebab piles
doner meat on to a bed of flat bread and yoghurt
splashed with a spicy tomato sauce. Or there's
chicken with preserved apricots. Salads are fresh,
service is friendly and attentive. The wine list has
only a couple of cheapies from Turkey – a shame as
there are some good wines coming out of Anatolian
vineyards nowadays.

Le Gallois
*6-10 Romilly Crescent, Canton, Cardiff, CF11 9NR
(029 2034 1264/www.legallois-ycymro.com).* **Lunch
served** noon-2.30pm, **dinner served** 6.30-10.30pm

Tue-Sat. **Main courses** £20. **Set meal** £30
2 courses, £35 3 courses. **Credit** AmEx, MC, V.
'Eez eet good?' asks the waiter. Very good. Foie gras
three ways, each better than the last, with perfect
brioche. Life doesn't get much better. Still, it's nice
to know that the staff in this well-established,
family-run restaurant take your dining happiness
seriously. Cardiff-born chef Padrig Jones heads a
kitchen that produces well thought out dishes using
meat, game and seafood from Wales, and offal,
poultry, cheese and wine from France. An appetiser
of cold consommé with chives and tomato prepared
the palate nicely for the foie gras that followed. Other
starters included a carpaccio of monkfish and
asparagus with egg and summer truffle dressing. A
main course of calf's liver in goujons with braised
bok choi and fondant potatoes was expertly
prepared. Or there was roasted brill with sea
scallops. Strawberries in champagne jelly sparkled
among the desserts. House wines are good value.
One of the best restaurants in Cardiff.

Gilby's
*Old Port Road, Culverhouse Cross, Cardiff, CF5
6DN (029 2067 0800/www.gilbysrestaurant.co.uk).*
Lunch served noon-2.30pm Tue-Sat; noon-3.30pm
Sun. **Dinner served** 5.45-10pm Tue-Sat. **Main
courses** £9.50-£19.50. **Set lunch** (Tue-Sat)
£11.95 2 courses; (Sun) £14.95 3 courses. **Set
dinner** (5.45-7.15pm Tue-Sat) £14.95 3 courses.
Credit AmEx, MC, V.
This tithe barn has been ruthlessly modernised. A
French graffiti artist seems to have attacked several
walls and the large dining area is broken up by what
look like bits of staircase scattered hither and thither.
But no matter, the food – especially the fish – is good.
The large open kitchens run by Anthony Armelin
offer the finest fish, shellfish and meat from Cardiff's
markets, displayed in iced cabinets. Dishes include
main courses like traditionally smoked haddock on
a bed of mashed potatoes and leek topped with a
poached egg and mustard sauce. The à la carte menu
includes best quality lobster, Welsh Black sirloin
and fillet, Gressingham duck, Glamorgan pork,
Dover sole and sea bass in season.

Izakaya Japanese Tavern
*Mermaid Quay, Cardiff Bay, Cardiff, CF10 5BW
(029 2049 2939/www.izakaya-japanese-tavern.com).*
Lunch served noon-2.30pm, **dinner served**
6-11pm Mon-Sat. **Meals served** 1-10pm Sun. **Set
lunch platter** £5.90. **Set dinner platters** £15-£25
per person (minimum 2). **Credit** AmEx, DC, MC, V.
Good, honest, everyday Japanese food served by
helpful, well-informed staff. The large menu offers

Izakaya Japanese Tavern.
See p329.

teriyaki-style items, a small sashimi selection and sushi. Whether it's raw octopus with vegetables, fried pork with boiled egg or the delicately delicious fried beancurd (tofu agedashi) with bonito flakes, items are as appealing to the eye as they are to the stomach. There is a long list of vegetarian options and the blackboard by the busy kitchen offers daily specials like chicken wings in spicy sauce or fried smelts. Drink ice-cold Japanese Asahi beer or green tea, or try your luck with the user-friendly saké list. Ideally aim for six or seven dishes between two diners – second mortgages aren't necessary as Izakaya allows you to sample and enjoy good Japanese food at reasonable prices.

Tides Bar & Restaurant

The St David's Hotel, Havannah Street, Cardiff, CF10 5SD (029 2045 4045/ www.thestdavidshotel.com). **Lunch served** 12.30-2.30pm, **dinner served** 6.30-10pm daily. **Main courses** £14.50-£27.50. **Set meal** £27.50 2 courses, £32 3 courses. **Credit** AmEx, DC, MC, V.
Perched on the waterfront, this is a great location to enjoy Daniel James's food. After four years, he is to take control of the whole eating match from the current executive chef, Marco Pierre White. A starter of carrot and coriander soup vies with ham hock and parsley terrine for your attention. For main courses, expect steamed sewin with laver bread, fish cream and cocotte potatoes; sautéed lamb with braised lentils and wild mushrooms or slow-cooked duck leg. Tarte fine was beautifully presented – a filo pastry base with ripe tomatoes and courgette, surmounted by a Scottish goat's cheese roundel that had been shown the grill long enough to melt around the edges. From the pudding list, the siren voice of a sambucca parfait could be heard. There's a good choice of wines by the glass and some great bottles at great prices: Grands Echezeaux (Domaine de la Romanée Conti 1989) at £580. But there's something for every taste and pocket. A meal here is special.

Woods Brasserie

Pilotage Building, Stuart Street, Cardiff, CF10 5BW (029 2049 2400). **Lunch served** noon-2pm, **dinner served** 7-10pm Mon-Sat. **Main courses** £9.45-£15.95. **Set lunch** £12 2 courses, £15.95 3 courses. **Credit** AmEx, DC, MC, V.
This old port building provides a great setting for the ultra-modern interior and classic British food provided by Sean Murphy. His time with Gordon Ramsay has served him well. Starters can include delicious gazpacho finished with basil and red pepper or a wonderful potted duck with grape chutney and perfectly toasted brioche. Just in case the rich, dense duck meat isn't rich enough for you, he adds a vein of foie gras throughout. Main courses are no less alluring with vegetarian Thai green curry with rice noodles or fresh yellowfin tuna in a niçoise salad, fresh off the pan, pink in the middle and crisp outside. Chocolate and caramel délice, sticky toffee pudding and pistachio and vanilla mousse with raspberry coulis have recommended pudding wines. The fine wine list is short but good.

Carmarthenshire

LAUGHARNE

The Cors

Newbridge Road, Laugharne, Carmarthenshire SA33 4SH (01994 427219). **Lunch served** *May-Sept* noon-2pm Wed-Sun. **Dinner served** 7-9.30pm Wed-Sun. **Main courses** £12.50-£17. **No credit cards.**
Settings rarely come more dramatic than here. You approach the Victorian house via a drive running along a spectacular swamp garden. Food is sourced

locally and starters can include roasted figs with gorgonzola and Parma ham, dressed crab with basil mayonnaise, char-grilled sardines with lemon and thyme or smoked haddock crème brûlée. Main courses feature local specialities such as rack of saltmarsh lamb with a rosemary and garlic crust and chilli jam, fillet of sewin fresh from the nearby River Towy (pan-fried to perfection) or a tournedos of beef fillet with green peppercorns and red wine jus. Vegetarians can try the fennel and parmesan au gratin with char-grilled tomatoes. Chef-owner Nick Priestland's interest in assertive flavours is also reflected in his wine list, which includes aromatic whites like Albariño from Spain and an excellent value spicy house red.

Hurst House

East Marsh, Laugharne, Carmarthenshire SA33 4RS (01994 427417/www.hurst-house.co.uk). **Lunch served** noon-2.30pm, **dinner served** 7-10pm daily. **Main courses** £14.95-£19.95. **Credit** AmEx, DC, MC, V.

Famous for its bibulous, bucolic bard, Dylan Thomas, Laugharne (pronounced 'Larn') has been a tourist magnet down the years and Hurst House – with its modern, rather garish interior and background rock music – will certainly attract a new generation. The bar-bistro serves liver-liquidising cocktails, bacon butties and croque monsieurs, while the restaurant offers a more substantial menu. Starters can be pea and ham soup or tian of avocado and Cajun-spiced crab with mango and chilli salsa. A main course of Welsh beef with fondant potato and spinach has a hint of decadence with deep-fried lobster ravioli. Seared sea bass comes with saffron potatoes, asparagus and crab tortellini. Vegetarians are offered cannelloni of goat's cheese and sweet peppers. Summer pudding with vanilla chantilly, dark chocolate and griottine cherry clafoutis and crisp cannelloni of white chocolate parfait with raspberry compote should satisfy the sweetest of teeth. Modern styles dominate the wine list. Service is friendly but strangely metropolitan.

Ceredigion

CARDIGAN

Abdul's

2 Royal Oak, Quay Street, Cardigan, Ceredigion SA43 1HR (01239 621416/www.abduls.co.uk). **Meals served** 5-11.45pm daily. **Main courses** £6.50-£12.95. **Credit** MC, V.

Ask anyone in Cardigan to recommend a place to eat and we bet they'll direct you to this sparkling Indian. This tired little town has virtually nowhere else half decent to refuel. Despite Abdul's obvious pole position, staff remain helpful, attentive and welcoming. Starters include fabulous chicken sekwa, a whole breast of chicken marinated in spiced and herbed lemon juice with ginger, garlic and fenugreek. Alternatively, the vegetable shashlik,

with Indian cottage cheese, is a real no-meat treat. Some pointers from the long list of mains: karahis (baltis by any other name) are fresh, meaty and perfectly seasoned, as is the lamb pasanda. King prawn chilli garlic is also a sure-fire bet. There's a good wine list, and some Indian lagers.

Conwy

BETWS-Y-COED

Ty Gwyn

Betws-y-Coed, Conwy LL24 0SG (01690 710383/ www.tygwynhotel.co.uk). **Lunch served** Feb-Dec noon-2pm daily; *Jan* noon-2pm Thur-Sun. **Dinner served** 7-9pm daily. **Main courses** £6.25-£13.95. **Credit** MC, V.

Enjoy an appetiser in the bar at this rambling old roadside halt, but a word of warning – the armchairs are so squishy that you may need assistance getting up again. But then the joy of Ty Gwyn is its 'lived-in' feel. The restaurant – whitewashed, rough stone walls, black beams and uneven flagged floors – is comfortably worn in too. The food, however, is fresh and inventive. Starters might feature expertly seasoned sautéed king prawns kung po. Chef's pâté maison, roughly bound, is the perfect mix of flavours. Vegetarians are well cared for too. At the other end of the food chain, the fillet steak tower block with salami, black pudding and cheddar gratin is enough to stun the captain of the Welsh rugby team. Fresh Conwy trout, however, is supremely delicate. Desserts are scrummy and the decent wine selection is honestly priced.

CAPEL GARMON

Tan-y-Foel ★

Capel Garmon, Conwy LL26 0RE (01690 710507/ www.tyfhotel.co.uk). **Dinner served** 7.30-8.15pm daily by appointment only. **Set dinner** £34 3 courses. **Credit** AmEx, DC, MC, V.

Tan-y-Foel is a stone-built, solid country house hotel but within a zen-like sense of space and calm pervades the restaurant, thanks to an inspired overhaul using hessian fabrics, floor-to-ceiling mirrors and cool white walls. The semi-set menu (two choices for each course) is a treat that only 12 or so lucky diners can sample each evening. Standards are everything here and, according to chef Janet Pitman, lofty ambitions suffer when diner numbers increase further. Starters may feature crisp and delicious tempura of red mullet, or pink seared tuna with red onion: precise and world-class. The sea bass main with salmon roulade set on a leek and potato cake is stunning, but meat dishes such as char siu marinated loin of Welsh pork with kale and vegetable fritters equally impress. Cheeses are the end-of-the-meal highlight but you may also be tempted by the trio of chocolate desserts. Wines are carefully chosen but rather pricey. The restaurant is no-smoking throughout.

COLWYN BAY

Café Niçoise

124 Abergele Road, Colwyn Bay, Conwy LL29 7PS
(01492 531555). **Lunch served** noon-2pm Wed-
Sun. **Dinner served** 7-10pm Tue-Sat. **Main
courses** £9.75-£13.95. **Set lunch** (Sun) £12.75
2 courses, £15 3 courses. **Credit** AmEx, MC, V.
A relaxed bistro-style restaurant, Café Niçoise offers
a dependable, French-leaning menu. Within its
intimate, salmon-coloured walls, diners can sample
dishes that, on the whole, follow the classic route –
with the occasional surprise. The perky starter of
cured ham with avocado and pink grapefruit is a
prime example. Dishes are usually presented without
fuss and fiddling and seafood is a particular strength.
Assiette of seafood with roast fennel and a vermouth
sauce could be called a signature dish, if there weren't
plenty more like it, such as the pink and beautiful
loin of lamb with baked garlic. Desserts are great fun.
The chocolate truffle cake with chocolate and Baileys
ice-cream is just this side of illegal. Service is spot on
and wines are great value.

DEGANWY

Sands Brasserie

59-63 Station Road, Deganwy, Conwy LL31 9DF
(01492 592659). **Lunch served** noon-2.30pm,
dinner served 6-10pm Tue-Sat. **Main courses**
£7.75-£12.95. **Credit** AmEx, MC, V.
Sands is incongruously situated bang in the middle
of a Victorian shopping esplanade, complete with
wrought iron awnings. The small, summery dining
room is clutter-free and populated with a genial
crowd and smiley staff. Many starters seem a touch
heavy (crispy duck leg with butter bean purée or
warm chorizo and red onion), so it's no surprise
there's the option to super-size them into main
courses. Spiced lamb skewers with garlic houmous,
on the other hand, were expertly seasoned and not
too filling. Mains can include a wonderfully fresh
tiger prawn spaghetti with roasted shellfish sauce,
or a decadent veal T-bone with tomato, basil and
balsamic aubergine. Flavours are precise and clean.

LLANDUDNO

Bodysgallen Hall

Llandudno, Conwy LL30 1RS (01492 584466/
www.bodysgallen.com). **Lunch served** 12.30-
1.45pm, **dinner served** 7.30-9.30pm daily.
Set lunch (Mon-Sat) £17 2 courses, £19 3 courses;
(Sun) £22 3 courses. **Set dinner** £36 3 courses.
Credit MC, V.
Hushed, stately and dramatic, Bodysgallen Hall is a
feast for the senses – and that's before you set foot
in the suitably well-dressed dining room. Menus are
dependent on the availability of seasonal game and
garden produce, and tend towards the familiar. So,
starters follow a comfortable format of warming
soups and country favourites, such as braised rabbit

with savoy cabbage – fine but fiddly. Sorbet seen
off, you're on to a main course selection featuring
a choice of around ten or so well-assembled
combinations. Roast fillet of cod with pickled
cucumber and scallops is so good it reminds you
why this poor fish is being driven to near extinction.
Alternatively head for the divine breast of partridge
with pan-fried foie gras. Fabulous desserts may
feature the likes of baked raspberry soufflé. Wines
are pricey, but there are a few decent bottles around
the £20 mark.

St Tudno Hotel

North Parade, The Promenade, Llandudno, Conwy
LL30 2LP (01492 874411/www.st-tudno.co.uk).
Lunch served 12.30-1.45pm Mon-Sat; 12.30-1.30pm
Sun. **Dinner served** 7-9.15pm Mon-Sat; 7-9pm Sun.
Main courses £16-£19. **Set lunch** (Mon-Fri) £13
2 courses, £16 3 courses; (Sat) £16.50 3 courses; (Sun)
£17.50 3 courses. **Credit** AmEx, DC, MC, V.
The Garden Room restaurant at this elegant seaside
hotel is aptly named. Rattan chairs, trellis-effect
wallpaper and lots of light lend this cluttered room
a conservatory calm. That said, it's all a little too
hushed and service, while efficient, isn't always
warm. Similarly, the hotel's cooking is interesting
and ambitious, but not without gremlins – although
you'd be unlucky to leave St Tudno's without having
sampled at least one special dish. Seafood is treated
with mastery and care – a starter of fish soup with
fennel and herbs was spot on. Mains such as seared
fillet of turbot with Mediterranean prawns, white
wine and parsley sauce are also dependable, as is
the juicy fillet of Welsh beef with mushrooms,
tomatoes, straw potatoes and a béarnaise sauce.
Desserts such as shortbread biscuits layered with
strawberries and chantilly cream can't fail to
impress. The wine list offers good choice at all levels.

TY'N-Y-GROES

Groes Inn

Ty'n-y-Groes, Conwy LL32 8TN (01492 650545).
Lunch served noon-2pm, **dinner served** 6.30-9pm
daily. **Main courses** £7.95-£15.95. **Set dinner** £25
4 courses. **Credit** AmEx, MC, V.
The oldest licensed house in Wales is still going
strong, thanks to loads of charm and a knockout
position in the plump, duvet-like folds of the
Conwy Valley. When you're a higgledy-piggledy old
coaching inn with crackling fires, it's easy to pull the
crowds. To keep them coming back, however, you
must work hard. Sure, the pub area is textbook olde
worlde, but the fresh, bright restaurant offers a
dining experience that's more guidebook than
textbook. Starters include a moreish deep-fried
devilled whitebait with garlic mayo. Straightforward
mains spotlight market-fresh, quality ingredients,
making run-of-the-mill dishes such as sirloin steak
and game casserole more rewarding than they might
sound. Seafood is equally dependable. Good house
wines start from £9.

Tyddyn Llan

Denbighshire

LLANDEGLA

Bodidris Hall

Llandegla, Denbighshire LL11 3AL (08707 292292/ www.bodidrishall.com). **Lunch served** noon-4pm, **dinner served** 7-9.30pm daily. **Set lunch** (Mon-Sat) £19.95 4 courses; (Sun) £17.50 4 courses. **Set dinner** £29.95 5 courses. **Credit** AmEx, DC, MC, V. This ivy-covered medieval manor has an excellent setting in a relatively untramelled corner of Denbighshire. The elegant dining room (faux-flame torches aside) overlooks a pretty lake with great views beyond. Food is traditional but of a reassuringly high standard. Service can be slow, but this isn't a place to clock-watch. You'll soon relax into the swing of things, perhaps with a drink in the gothic bar. Over the dinner's many courses you may sample a delicate langoustine cappuccino with

horseradish sauce and chives. After a cool sorbet, main courses may include a fabulously meaty shark steak simply served on a squeakily fresh green bean salad or Welsh beef fillet with Welsh rarebit and black pudding. Desserts run from pannacotta with orange and nutmeg to iced pistachio terrine with raspberry coulis. Wines offer some surprises.

LLANDRILLO

Tyddyn Llan

Llandrillo, Denbighshire LL21 0ST (01490 440264/ www.tyddynllan.co.uk). **Lunch served** 12.30-2.30pm Thur-Sun. **Dinner served** 7-9pm daily. **Set lunch** £14.50 2 courses, £19.50 3 courses; (Sun) £19.50 3 courses. **Set dinner** £27 2 courses, £32 3 courses, £35 4 courses. **Credit** MC, V. Although it's in the featureless (almost peopleless) hinterlands of North-east Wales, the exuberant, gutsy cooking at this wonderful, pocket-sized

Wales

Penhelig Arms. *See p333.*

country house hotel is a must-try. There's nothing fusty about the Tyddyn Llan experience as you'll see from the bright, Scandinavian-inspired dining room and the relaxed, chatty service. The menu offers a clever, effortless melding of Welsh produce and European ambition. This can result in starters like salad of stuffed pig's trotter with sweetbreads, Carmarthen ham, celeriac remoulade and quail's egg. Mains tend towards the simple. So you could enjoy calf's liver with beetroot or a fabulous fillet of sea bass with laver bread butter sauce. Desserts of the calibre of cherry and almond tart with vanilla ice-cream whisk you back to your childhood, and the extensive, fairly priced wine list transports you back again. Well worth the detour.

Gwynedd

ABERDYFI

Penhelig Arms

Aberdyfi, Gwynedd LL35 0LT (01654 767215/ www.penheligarms.com). Bar **Lunch served** noon-2pm, **dinner served** 6-9.15pm daily. *Restaurant* **Lunch served** noon-2pm, **dinner served** 7-9.30pm daily. **Main courses** £8.95-£11.50. **Set dinner** £25 3 courses. **Credit** MC, V.
With superb food, attentive staff and a wonderful wine list, topped off with blindingly white linen on tables with a view of the Aberdyfi (Aberdovey) estuary, Penhelig is close to perfection. This sublime harbourfront hotel offers fabulous seafood and the best produce from local farms in its cosy dining room – and, with a little less drama, in its great bar area too. Starters such as smoked haddock chowder are wonderfully fresh, as you'd expect in a place where gulls preen themselves on the window ledges and boats bob in the gulleys. Landlubbers will be

equally sated with mains such as roast breast of Gressingham duck with a sweet and sour sauce, or grilled lamb's liver and bacon. But it's the seafood that'll make you return to Penhelig. Desserts are as delicate (apricot frangipane tart) or decadent (chocolate roulade) as you like.

CRICCIETH

Tir a Mor

1 Mona Terrace, Criccieth, Gwynedd LL52 0HG (01766 523084). **Dinner served** 7-9pm Mon-Sat. **Main courses** £11.95-£16.95. **Credit** MC, V.
The homely corner bistro of Tir a Mor doesn't look much. The dining room, which opens on to the street, is strictly farmhouse pine chairs and dried flowers, but it's usually full nonetheless. The short carte is strongest when it keeps things simple: pan-fried john dory with a warm salad is a case in point. Not that we can't allow the folks here some free rein, especially when the ingredients are so good. Hence Llyn rose beef with sweet potato and Parma ham ravioli is an unqualified success. There's always a good selection of caught-that-day fish too. Starters can be even more poetic – a twice-baked cheese mousseline with pickled walnut salad is as fluffy as can be. The wine list offers bottles at all budgets, but is strongest around the £20-£30 mark.

DOLGELLAU

Dylanwad Da

2 Ffos-y-Felin, Dolgellau, Gwynedd LL40 1BS (01341 422870/www.dylanwad.co.uk). **Open** 10am-4pm. **Dinner served** 7-9pm Thur-Sat (Tue-Sat in holiday periods – phone to check). Closed Feb. **Main courses** £9.40-£14.50. **No credit cards.**

Wales

Bringing a splash of colour into the unmistakably Welsh grey stone town of Dolgellau, Dylanwad Da offers a sparkling menu of well-handled prime materials and deft saucing. The setting is simple. A calm, unfussy dining room (blond wood chairs, cool cream walls) offers a welcome note of restraint in this chintzy tourist spot, and young, light-hearted staff buzz around. Starters may include a wonderful chicken, basil and tomato terrine – nothing here that shouldn't be. Mains are uncomplicated too, but all the better for it. Local shopping sprees may have brought succulent sirloin steak to the kitchen, served with a roquefort red wine sauce, or maybe a sesame fillet of sole with a sweet plum sauce. Puddings of the order of white chocolate cheesecake only make you wish you'd saved enough room, while wines are treated with respect, not reverence, and come in at remarkably good value.

EFAILNEWYDD

Plas Bodegroes ★

Efailnewydd, Gwynedd LL53 5TH (01758 612363/ www.bodegroes.co.uk). **Lunch served** 12.30-2.30pm Sun. **Dinner served** 7-9.30pm Tue-Sat. **Set dinner** £35 3 courses. **Credit** MC, V.

Plas Bodegroes has been painstakingly restored and now offers Michelin-starred dining. Chef-owner Chris Chown cooks and his wife, Gunna, does front of house. Tasty appetisers of crostini with pâté or a tartlet of blue cheese were followed by a choice of starters such as carrot and ginger soup or pan-fried pigeon breast with root vegetable purée and Madeira sauce. Many restaurants at this level make a big thing of presentation. Here simplicity is the name of the game: main courses might be roast cutlets of local lamb with Welsh onion cake, mustard and rosemary or tenderloin of pork with black pudding, apple and Calvados. Best of all is the local fish – whether it's seared sea bass and scallops or baked turbot with a herb crust. The trio of chocolate that followed was memorable, comprising a light but sumptuous mousse, a rich dark chocolate brownie and ice-cream in a chocolate dish. Quady's Elysium Black Muscat from California, from the extensive and keenly priced wine list, completed the dream. Service is up with the best.

LLANDWROG

Harp Inn

Llandwrog, Gwynedd LL54 5SY (01286 831071). **Lunch served** noon-2pm, **dinner served** 6.30-8.30pm Tue-Sun. **Main courses** £3.95-£14.95. **Set lunch** (Sun) £9.95 4 courses. **Credit** MC, V.

In the quiet backwaters of Llandwrog village you'll find this unstuffy little pub serving honest food to walkers, holidaying families and, well, food lovers who know when they're on to a good thing. If plastic tablecloths offend, don't bother booking in the small restaurant area – stick to the bar unless it's too smoky. There's no restaurant meal/bar meal divide

in the comforting, take-no-prisoners menu: own-made lasagne, local bangers with onion potato cakes and gravy or big battered cod all scoring top marks. The Celtic menu is a nice touch (weekends only out of season), featuring classic one-pot and rustic meals from all corners Celtica. Stand-out dishes include Pembroke fish pie and, from Brittany, roast chicken breast on a haricot bean garnish. Geography lessons have never been so tasty. Welsh-made ice-cream is the only way to finish your meal at the Harp.

PEN-Y-GWRYD

Pen-y-Gwryd Hotel

Pen-y-Gwryd, Gwynedd LL55 4NT (01286 870211/ www.pyg.co.uk). **Lunch served** noon-2pm, **dinner served** 7.30-8pm daily. **Set dinner** £20 5 courses. **No credit cards**.

Hearty food is the order of things at Pen-y-Gwryd, a lofty mountaineers' inn on the foothills of Snowdon. PYG was base camp for Hillary's Everest training sessions and it flaunts its credentials with ancient mountaineering paraphernalia. Bar lunches are first rate and would set you up handsomely for an attempt on the summit. Warming soups (spicy summer vegetable is a favourite), a great wedge of quiche with tonnes of vibrant salad or serious shepherd's pie all hit their mark. Evening meals (one sitting at 7.30pm) are a five-course affair in the inn's atmospheric little dining room (dark oak dressers, flickering candles). Starters may feature an aromatic Greek tomato salad, followed by divine Welsh lamb stew with dumplings and roasted veg. Portions are solid, but leave space for puds such as warm walnut tart or blueberry and cinnamon sponge. There's a good wine list and some excellent hand-pulled cask ales.

TALSARNAU

Maes-y-Neuadd ★

Talsarnau, Gwynedd LL47 6YA (01766 780200/ www.neuadd.com). **Lunch served** noon-1.45pm, **dinner served** 7-8.45pm daily. **Set dinner** £31 3 courses, £35 4 courses. **Credit** AmEx, DC, MC, V.

Maes-y-Neuadd means 'house in the meadow' – an accurate enough description for the sweeping lawns that lead you to this country house hotel, dating from the 14th century, in the hills above Porthmadog. The kitchen uses produce from the handsome walled garden to create a fascinating roll call of small-scale dishes, excitingly presented. Starters may include a piquant salad of local lobster, ginger and cucumber in a herb mayonnaise, followed by a fish course of, say, silver bream poached with sugar snaps. Mains are similarly small but perfectly judged, such as a soft and juicy pot-roasted chicken, and there's a creative lamb course. Dessert is a dramatic three-course affair and you're invited – no, encouraged – to sample all three. The wine list is suitably encyclopaedic, offering a few bottles under £20 but lots more over £40.

Isle of Anglesey

BEAUMARIS

Ye Olde Bulls Head Inn

*Castle Street, Beaumaris, Isle of Anglesey LL58
8AP (01248 810329/www.bullsheadinn.co.uk).*
Brasserie **Lunch served** noon-2pm, **dinner
served** 6-9pm daily. *Restaurant* **Dinner served**
7-9.30pm daily. **Main courses** £20. **Set dinner**
£25 2 courses, £30 3 courses. **Credit** AmEx, MC, V.
This beautifully decorated restaurant has a
reputation for using the best local seafood. Starters
might include a terrine of sea trout with rocket salad
and caper mayonnaise or a tartare of local sea bass
with lemon and chervil. Other options might include
a sweet potato, ginger and coriander soup or
carpaccio of Welsh beef with pickled walnuts and
hazel oil. Mains are no less alluring: cod fillet with
spinach, plum tomato confit and caper beurre blanc;
Welsh beef fillet with basil crust, shallots,
chanterelles and local Wennol beer. Cooking is
precise and the flavours expertly handled. These
admirable traits extend to the puddings, especially
the chocolate fondant served with mint ice-cream.
Needless to say, the wine list maintains the standard.

Monmouthshire

CHEPSTOW

The Wye Knot

*18A The Back Riverbank, Chepstow,
Monmouthshire NP16 5HH (01291 622929).*
Lunch served 12.30-3pm, **dinner served** 7-10pm
Wed-Sun. **Main courses** £12.50-£17.50. **Set meals**
£14.95 2 courses, £17.95 3 courses. **Credit** MC, V.
Kevin Brookes's restaurant occupies a great
riverside location in the old heart of Chepstow. In
the 19th century, Chartist organisers were housed
here before being transported to Van Diemen's Land.
Nowadays the traffic is reversed with lots of fresh
antipodean sauvignon blancs and chardonnays on
the wine list. The menu, on a blackboard in the bar,
has starters ranging from sliced melon to mousseline
of salmon or crab cakes full of best-quality Cornish
crab served with a sweet chilli sauce. Main courses
included roasted local venison served with root
vegetables or Cornish turbot fillet. Their £17 price
tag may appear high, given the rudimentary dining
room, but these dishes are rich, complex and time-
consuming. The turbot appeared with a butter and
fennel sauce garnished with slices of lobster. To
finish, try a rich date and walnut sponge.

CLYTHA

The Clytha Arms

*Clytha, Monmouthshire NP7 9BW (01873 840206/
www.clytha-arms.com).* **Open** noon-3.30pm, 6-11pm
Tue-Fri; noon-11pm Sat; noon-10.30pm Sun. **Lunch**

served 12.30-2.15pm Tue-Sat; 12.30-2.30pm Sun.
Dinner served 7.30-9pm Tue-Sat. **Main courses**
£12-£17.50. **Set meal** £15.95 2 courses, £17.95
3 courses. **Credit** AmEx, DC, MC, V.
This award-winning inn offers accommodation, a
public bar with wonderful local atmosphere and
gastropub-style food. But the dining room is
unattractive; the lounge bar is a better place to eat.
Furthermore, the menu fluctuates in size, dishes
sometimes lack balance and service can be slow as
the young staff are often overcome by the volume of
trade (a good wine list eases the wait). Own-made
pork faggots with peas, local mushrooms and gravy
or translucent carpaccio of tuna with soy and wasabi
appear as starters. Local roast duck, and loin of lamb
mains are served with vegetables on the side but
wonderful new potatoes were let down by poor
red cabbage. Beef fillet teriyaki arrived complete
with green noodles, wasabi horseradish and
ornamentally carved carrot and cucumber slices.
The Welsh Cider and Cheese Festival takes place
here in May each year – owner Andrew Canning
makes an excellent dry perry, which should be
sampled if available.

LLANDENNY

Raglan Arms

*Llandenny, Monmouthshire NP15 1DL (01291
690800).* **Lunch served** noon-3pm Tue-Sat; noon-
2.30pm Sun. **Dinner served** 7-9.30pm Tue-Sat.
Main courses £8-£13. **Credit** MC, V.
Over the past 18 months, Ian and Carol Black have
transformed the Raglan Arms into a vibrant local
with comfortable sofas, outside tables and good
food. There's no fussy presentation, just quality
ingredients. Starters include rillettes of pork,
asparagus in season with butter or hollandaise, and
king prawns in garlic sauce. Dishes such as four fish
grill follow – an excellent selection of grilled cod,
hake, salmon and sea bass. Delicious. Steaks and
own-made steak and kidney pie are also on offer and
– for real carnivores – an enormous plate of roast
wild boar with black pudding and mash. There's an
excellent choice of cheese from McBlains in Usk. The
wine list is short but varied, with house wine at
around £11 a bottle. A wonderful place for a laid-
back summer weekend lunch.

LLANGATTOCK LINGOED

Hunter's Moon Inn

*Llangattock Lingoed, Monmouthshire NP7 8RR
(01873 821499/www.hunters-moon-inn.co.uk).*
Lunch served noon-2.30pm Tue, Thur-Sun.
Dinner served 6-9pm Mon, Tue, Thur-Sun.
Main courses £10-£14. **Credit** AmEx, MC, V.
Situated on the Offa's Dyke footpath, this 13th-
century inn with rooms is run by Helen Barratt, with
food by chef Mark Peters. Lunch comprises well-
prepared local produce ideal for walking folk who
need to keep their strength up: the huge bowl of

The Foxhunter

roasted tomato soup with pecorino cheese could have fed a small family. Duck liver pâté and chutney, another vast dish, was all own-made. Main courses include locally supplied steak and sausages (Hancocks of Monmouth). Even the seafood salad uses fresh herbs from the inn's own garden. The dinner menu offers more sophisticated dishes in keeping with Mark Peters's training at Nobu and with Marco Pierre White. Rump of Welsh saltmarsh lamb with red pepper dressing is developing a local following, as are the ribeye of veal and penne with rocket. Bottles of house red and white are both under a tenner and very acceptable. The rest of the list is well chosen.

LLANTHEWY SKIRRID

The Walnut Tree
Llanthewy Skirrid, Monmouthshire NP7 8AW (01873 852797/www.thewalnuttreeinn.com). **Lunch served** noon-3.30pm Tue-Sat; noon-2.30pm Sun. **Dinner served** 7-10.30pm Tue-Sat. **Main courses** £9.75-£32.50. **Set lunch** (Tue-Sat) £16.50 2 courses, £19.50 3 courses. **Credit** MC, V.
Francesco Mattioli has taken over this famous restaurant near Abergavenny. Gone are the cast-iron garden tables – the interior has a cleaner, less cluttered feel. The à la carte retains old favourites such as Lady Llanover's salt duck with fresh figs or Vinci's Grassi Macaratese – a sumptuous, funghi-filled pasta dish. A glass of refreshing Orvieto with ricotta and spinach panzerotti appetisers can be followed by grilled pancetta, local rabbit, dolcelatte, rocket and fennel salad; locally smoked salmon; or prosciutto San Daniele with melon. Main courses include own-made Gloucester Old Spot pork sausages with polenta chips and braised lentil sauce, a bollito misto of brisket, gammon, chicken and tongue or a superb veal osso bucco Milanese. Warm figs with Welsh honey, balsamic vinegar and mascarpone or panettone bread and butter pudding

follow. Large espressos and petits fours close the event. The Walnut Tree is in safe hands and at £50 a head, it's good value.

NANT-Y-DERRY

The Foxhunter
Nant-y-derry, Monmouthshire NP7 9DN (01873 881101). **Lunch served** noon-2.30pm, **dinner served** 7-9.30pm Tue-Sat. **Main courses** £12.95-£17.95. **Set lunch** £17.50 2 courses, £20 3 courses. **Credit** MC, V.
This village 'local' has been converted into a cool, modern restaurant with natural surfaces and minimal wall decoration. Matt Tebbutt worked with Alastair Little, Marco Pierre White and Sally Clarke before moving to Wales. The menu is modern British with a strong emphasis on local produce. Starters include deep-fried sand eels, elvers (in season) or pizzetta bianca – a thin-crust pizza filled with sliced new potato, parmesan and mozzarella and drizzled with truffle oil. In addition to wonderful steaks, main courses include papardelle of veal sweetbreads or pan-fried calf's liver served with creamed potato, mangetout and a rich reduction. Seafood dishes range from char-grilled sea bass with orange braised chickory and citrus velouté to sea-fresh sashimi with wasabi horseradish and sweet dill-pickled cucumbers. For pudding, there's an incredible hot pear clafoutis. Most wines are priced below £30. Staff are friendly and knowledgeable.

NEWPORT

The Chandlery
77-78 Lower Dock Street, Newport, Monmouthshire NP20 1EH (01633 256622/www.chandleryrestaurant.com). **Lunch served** noon-2pm Tue-Fri. **Dinner served** 7-10pm Tue-Sat. **Main courses** £9.50-£16.95. **Set lunch** £8.95 2 courses, £11.95 3 courses. **Credit** AmEx, MC, V.

Wales

Newport has been known for many things, but fine dining was never one of them until Simon and Jane Newcombe launched modern British food on an unsuspecting city. Tian of Pembrokeshire crab and avocado with mango salsa; Pembrokeshire lobster, quail's egg and asparagus salad; and a foie gras and chicken liver parfait with prune and apple chutney vie for attention as starters. Main courses include grilled hake fillets with vegetable spaghetti, tomato mash and shellfish jus, roast breast of Gressingham duck – every so often – the mysteriously named 'organic chicken reared in Usk'. It's a bruiser, but when served with fondant potato, bok choi and sage and lemon gravy it's much more approachable. The short wine list is keenly priced. House bottles start at under a tenner. Ginger pudding with rhubarb compote and honey ice-cream or a chocolate fondant bring matters to a close.

ROCKFIELD

The Stone Mill

Steppes Farm Cottages, Rockfield, Monmouthshire NP25 5SW (01600 775424/www.steppesfarm cottages.co.uk). **Lunch served** noon-2.30pm, **dinner served** 6-10pm Tue-Sun. **Main courses** £10.50-£18. **Set lunch** (Tue-Sat) £7.50 2 courses, £9.90 3 courses. **Set dinner** (Tue-Thur) £10.95 2 courses, £12.95 3 courses. **Credit** MC, V.
An old cider mill converted into an intimate and rustic dining space with tall ceilings and beams in profusion, the Stone Mill is one of the emerging generation of Welsh establishments that offer fixed-price menus at incredibly low prices. Fixed-price dinner menus are slightly more expensive but the strong emphasis on local food producers remains. Chef Simon Kealy's carte includes seasonal starters like asparagus bruschetta with taleggio; poached duck egg and truffle oil; own-smoked tomatoes with rocket and parmesan; and poached chicken with purple sprouting broccoli and roast beetroot. Main courses might comprise breast of corn-fed chicken with spinach, new potatoes, raisins and pancetta with Marsala wine or fillet of hake with welsh rarebit on warm tomato salad with lemon dressing. The predominantly French (plus the odd heavyweight antipodean) wine list starts from £11.

ST ARVANS

The Piercefield

Chepstow Road, St Arvans, Monmouthshire NP16 6EJ (01291 622614). **Lunch served** noon-6pm Mon-Sat; noon-5.30pm Sun. **Dinner served** 6-9.30pm Mon-Sat. **Main courses** £7.95-£14.95. **Credit** AmEx, MC, V.
This roadside inn, close to Chepstow racecourse, now belongs to Noble House and is one of the chain's top-end bar-restaurants. Dishes are aimed at a young clientele and at the racegoing fraternity. Starters might include hand-made crab fish cakes,

oriental duck salad and black pudding. Main courses are substantial, such as smoked haddock with curry sauce and potato dauphinoise or mushroom ravioli in cream, tomato and herb sauce. Tiramisu, apple and pear crumble, and sticky toffee pudding follow. For the racing folk, there's the all-day mixed grill or the excellent eggs benedict. Theme nights take place every week and provide a great introduction to rarely seen dishes such as lao larb moo (minced fried pork), Vietnamese pho (beef broth) and Thai tom yum goong (spicy prawn soup). The wine list is short but global. A welcome change to the traditional soggy beefburger at the racecourse.

SKENFRITH

The Bell at Skenfrith ★

Skenfrith, Monmouthshire NP25 8UH (01600 750235/www.skenfrith.co.uk). **Open** 11am-11pm Mon-Sat; 11am-10.30pm Sun. **Lunch served** noon-2.30pm daily. **Dinner served** 7-9.30pm Mon-Sat; 7-9pm Sun. **Main courses** £6.95-£15.10. **Set meals** £25 2 courses, £30 3 courses. **Credit** AmEx, MC, V.
The riverside location, airy bar with flagstones, sofas, log fire and sumptuous dining room provide a great setting. William and Janet Hutchings have won a bevy of awards and new chef Denis Guillemin will no doubt continue to use seafood from St Mawes and beef and game from the Hereford Beef Company. Starters might include a salad of seared Scottish scallops with balsamic and parmesan, locally smoked chicken Caesar salad or lamb and foie gras terrine. Main courses can range from an artichoke and leek gratin with caramelised shallots and mustard dressing to butter-like Welsh Black sirloin with a classic sauce béarnaise. Individual bread and butter puddings are served with local crème fraîche, and the warm dark chocolate fondant comes with clotted Jersey cream. The wine list is extensive and catholic. Whether you choose to sample a Languedoc house wine at £12 or a 1991 Chateau d'Yquem at £149, mark-ups are very reasonable. The young, local staff are polite, enthusiastic and efficient.

WHITEBROOK

The Crown at Whitebrook

Whitebrook, Monmouthshire NP25 4TX (01600 860254/www.crownatwhitebrook.co.uk). **Lunch served** noon-1.45pm Tue-Sun. **Dinner served** 7-8.45pm daily. **Set lunch** (Tue-Sat) £11.95; (Sun) £17.50 3 courses. **Set dinner** £23.95 2 courses, £29.95 3 courses. **Credit** AmEx, DC, MC, V.
Ignore the Artex and false beams in the dining room and the sofas in the bar, as Mark Turton's cooking is sophisticated: skills learnt from his time with the Roux brothers are evident in the scale, design and balance of each dish. From the bargain lunch, millefeuille of smoked lamb fillet with lamb's lettuce and frisée salad and honeyed dressing is topped with

a perfectly cooked lamb's kidney. Fried supreme of guinea fowl with kumquat tatin is exemplary. Delicate crêpes with tangy orange and Grand Marnier add £3.95 to the bill. The award-winning wine list includes good clarets and burgundies alongside exotics such as the Lebanese Chateau Musar, and a range of half-bottles.

Pembrokeshire

FISHGUARD

Three Main Street

Main Street, Fishguard, Pembrokeshire SA65 9HG (01348 874275). **Dinner served** 6.30-9pm Tue-Sat. **Set dinner** £24 2 courses, £30 3 courses. **No credit cards**.

Marion Evans and Inez Ford capitalise on a wealth of local produce: sea bass, monkfish and turbot from the nearby Atlantic, lamb and beef from the Preseli Hills. Breads and pastas are prepared daily in-house. In the Georgian dining room overlooking Fishguard's old harbour, start with mild oak-smoked Irish salmon with crème fraîche and sweet pickled cucumber, a pasta case with a duxelle of local mushrooms, truffle oil and parmesan gratin or a superb double-cooked crab meat soufflé. Main courses comprise breast of guinea fowl with delicate lovage and citrus glaze, a huge turbot fillet with sweet buttered leeks and a rich vermouth sauce or a substantial roast best end of Welsh lamb with roast garlic, redcurrant and mint jellies and a port sauce. For pudding, how about a divine hazel-nut cream meringue with raspberry purée? Presentation is faultless, and the service is friendly and efficient.

LLANGLOFFAN

Tides

Llangloffan Farm, Llangloffan, Pembrokeshire SA62 5ET (01348 891383/www.welshcheese.com). **Meals served** noon-5.30pm daily. **Dinner served** from 7pm Thur-Sat by appointment only. **Main courses** £11.95-£16.50. **Credit** MC, V.

Located in a converted barn, Tides shares the same farmyard as the famous Llangloffan cheese dairy. A tearoom by day serving excellent farmhouse produce, Tides offers a simple but well-executed menu in the evening. Starters might include a wonderful tomato and basil soup, smoked salmon, lobster and avocado with sauce marie rose or moules marinière. To follow there's organic fillet steak, grilled whole Abercastle lobster with herb butter, sea bass with lemongrass, coriander and butter or locally caught plaice with a red pepper and tomato sauce. Puddings include summer fruits set in champagne and elderflower, cheesecake or pine nut and honey tart. Cheeses are mostly made on the premises and a decent wine list favours Australia. More and more places like this are springing up along the Pembrokeshire tourist trail, providing excellent farm cooking.

ST DAVID'S

Morgan's Brasserie

20 Nun Street, St David's, Pembrokeshire SA62 6NT (01437 720508/www.morgans-in-stdavids.co.uk). **Dinner served** *June-Sept* 6.30-9pm Mon-Sat. *Oct-Dec, Mar-May* 6.30-9pm Mon-Fri. **Main courses** £12.50-£17.50. **Credit** AmEx, MC, V.

This small family-run brasserie has provided quality dishes to visitors and residents of the UK's smallest city for a decade now. Ceri Morgan and his team are especially proud of their seafood. Local sewin, bream, salmon, turbot and Dover sole are all exceptionally good, as is crab from nearby Porthgain. To start expect crab soup, terrine of duck confit and duck flavoured with Armagnac or Menai mussels with tomatoes, garlic and herbs. As well as the carte, there's also a board of seafood recommendations. So if the confit of Welsh lamb with garlic and rosemary doesn't appeal the roast turbot with bouillabaisse sauce might. Pear tarte tatin with honey and whisky ice-cream and chocolate framboise should keep your blood sugar at record levels. The wine list is wide-ranging and fairly priced.

The Warpool Court Hotel

St David's, Pembrokeshire SA62 6BN (01437 720300/www.warpoolcourthotel.com). **Lunch served** noon-1.45pm, **dinner served** 7-9.15pm daily. **Main courses** £24. **Set lunch** (Mon-Sat) £24 2 courses, £29 3 courses; (Sun) £19.50 2 courses, £25 3 courses. **Set dinner** £45 4 courses. **Credit** AmEx, DC, MC, V.

Despite a wonderful location overlooking a beautiful bit of Pembrokeshire coastline, there's an uncertain feeling about this hotel and restaurant. Service ranges from charming and helpful to Fawlty-esque. Starters can include leek and potato soup, smoked chicken salad with caramelised apple and crispy bacon or carpaccio of beef with parmesan and caper sauce. Main courses might include best end of lamb with fondant potatoes, aubergine purée, roast courgette, pepper and rosemary jus or spinach and parmesan ravioli, vegetable panache and roast tomato sauce. The casserole of guinea fowl on mustard creamed potato, braised vegetables and chorizo was OK. The guinea fowl was cooked well, retaining juiciness, but there was too much mustard in the potato. The crème brûlée with shortbread biscuits and rosewater syrup was excellent, as was the warm pear and almond flan with honey ice-cream. The wine list is good but can't be described as keenly priced.

WELSH HOOK

Stone Hall

Welsh Hook, Pembrokeshire SA62 5NS (01348 840212/www.stonehall.mansion.co.uk). **Dinner served** 7-9pm Tue-Sat. **Main courses** £14.50-£16. **Set dinner** £22 4 courses. **Credit** AmEx, DC, MC, V.

Stone Hall's French owners have provided delightful rooms and food for over 20 years. The building is 600 years old and the dining room has a huge old fireplace. Menu, wine list and staff are unashamedly Gallic. Starters include snails in garlic butter, goat's cheese salad or tartlet with own-cured duck baked with potatoes, shallots and rosemary. Wild boar à la Normande with apple cider and cream sauce joins darne of salmon with cucumber sauce, corn-fed chicken breast stuffed with mustard and cream cheese on the list of mains. Vegetarian options include roast aubergine and pepper parmigiana with sun-dried tomatoes. To follow there's a luxurious crème brûlée, OTT profiteroles and a good choice of French cheeses. Finding this place is easier when it's light. You also get to see the magnificent hybrid rhododendra.

Powys

BRECON

Tipple 'n' Tiffin

Theatr Brycheiniog, Canal Wharf, Brecon, Powys LD3 7EW (01874 611866/www.brycheiniog.co.uk). **Lunch served** noon-2.30pm, **dinner served** 7-9pm Mon-Sat. **Main courses** £6-£8. **Credit** AmEx, DC, MC, V.

Richard and Louise Gudsell moved their business from Hay-on-Wye to this theatre setting in Brecon in spring 2003. There's almost a French café feel to this place that serves coffee and refreshments during the day and feeds diners and theatre-goers by night. Dishes are designed to share, each one halfway between a starter and a main course. Most ingredients are sourced locally and they are organic where possible. Lighter dishes include delicious deep-fried cockles from Penclawdd with crispy bacon, salad and salsa or tiffin chips with a melted Welsh cheese dip and laver bread. Local charcuterie and smoked fish also figure on the menu. For more robust appetites there are game sausages and root mash with claret gravy, and slow-roast ribs of Tamworth pork marinated in hoi sin noodles. There's also a good-value short, modern wine list. Hay's loss is certainly Brecon's gain.

CRICKHOWELL

Gliffaes

Gliffaes Country House Hotel, Crickhowell, Powys NP8 1RH (01874 730371/www.gliffaes.com). **Dinner served** 7.30-9.15pm daily. **Main courses** £10-£15. **Set dinner** £24 2 courses, £28 3 courses. **Credit** AmEx, MC, V.

Built in 1885, Gliffaes has been run by the Brabner family for over half a century. A supporter of the admirable Slow Food Movement, Gliffaes has a policy of sourcing three-quarters of its fresh produce from within 25 miles of the hotel. Starters can include a salad of asparagus and Parma ham with a pesto and balsamic reduction or spring pea soup with crisp bacon and crème fraîche. Main courses could be Perigord duck with red cabbage and sweet plum sauce, roast Gloucester Old Spot pork with fondant potatoes and baby vegetables or pan-fried fillet of sea bass atop a lemon risotto with spinach. The glory of this robust food is in the details. Puddings might include warm chocolate tart or hot raspberry soufflé. In keeping with the country house ethic, the ever-changing wine list includes an impressive range of fine clarets and burgundies built up over the years.

The Nantyffin Cider Mill Inn

Breacon Road, Crickhowell, Powys NP8 1SG (01873 810775/www.cidermill.co.uk). **Lunch served** noon-2.30pm Mon, Wed-Sun. **Dinner served** 7-9.30pm Mon, Wed-Sat. **Main courses** £10-£14.95. **Credit** AmEx, MC, V.

The Felin Fach Griffin

This traditional drovers' inn retains its pink-wash frontage and is a local institution with comfortable, warm dining rooms in winter and tables outside for summer. The menus reflect seasonal change and local produce availability (organically reared duck, chicken and lamb from their own farm at Llangynidr). A summer menu might consist of a starter of substantial Greek salad or open ravioli with goat's cheese, sweet potato and spring onion. Main courses include own-made Old Spot pork sausages with shallot and mustard mash and onion gravy, and sautéed monkfish niçoise with fresh beans, olives, waxy new potatoes and egg. Not bad for a tenner. Daily specials might feature starters of Cornish crab cakes followed by half a grilled lobster. Real ale and real cider (Addlestones Cloudy) retain the pub feel, but there's also an excellent and diverse wine list.

EGLWYSFACH

Ynyshir Hall

Eglwysfach, Powys SY20 8TA (01654 781209/ www.ynyshir-hall.co.uk). **Lunch served** 12.30-1.30pm, **dinner served** 7-8.45pm daily. **Set lunch** £13.50 1 course, £20-£22 2 courses, £28.50 3 courses. **Set dinner** £20 1 course, £28.50-£32.50 2 courses, £42 3 courses; £55 7-course taster menu. **Credit** AmEx, DC, MC, V.

The strict no-smoking policy and the vivid colour schemes may not be to everyone's liking but with a location, hospitality, food and wine like this, who cares? Michelin-starred food doesn't come cheap, nor is it that expensive considering the quality of the food on offer and the culinary skills of the chef Les Rennie. To start, you can expect a choice of wild mushroom and truffle velouté with wun tuns of red pepper and crème fraîche or ballotine of corn-fed chicken with a cauliflower purée and pan-fried foie gras. Ravioli of local Borth prawns, pak choi and avruga caviar was superb. Seared fillet of brill, chive noodles, wild rocket and prosciutto salad was a combination of wonderful textures. New season Jacob lamb is served with an onion bhajia, pea purée and lamb jus. There's a wide choice of perfectly kept Welsh, Irish and French cheeses. Puddings include a wonderful hot caramel soufflé with Jack Daniel's ice-cream and roasted marshmallow. Service is friendly and efficient.

FELIN FACH

The Felin Fach Griffin

Felin Fach, Powys LD3 0UB (01874 620111/ www.eatdrinksleep.ltd.uk). **Lunch served** 12.30-2.30pm Tue-Sun. **Dinner served** 6.30-10.30pm daily. **Main courses** £10.50-£14. **Credit** MC, V.

This roadside restaurant with rooms has been completely renovated and now provides some of the best food in Mid Wales. The menus feature much local produce. Starters might include fresh Welsh

goat's cheese, organic leaves and roasted pine kernels; smoked salmon with crème fraîche; or boudin blanc, asparagus and roasted ceps. Sometimes a traditional dish like leek and potato soup (hot or cold) will sit happily next to an escabeche of mackerel with beetroot mayonnaise. Mains could include wild mushroom risotto with lemon thyme butter or roast salmon with crushed ratte potatoes and spinach with a chive beurre blanc. The asparagus with new potatoes, parmesan and béarnaise foam is a simple but wonderful combination served with a small glass of chilled gazpacho. Puddings are mouthwatering and good Welsh cheeses are also available. The wine list has a good range of New and Old World items. If the weather permits, a table outside affords breathtaking views of the Brecon Beacons.

HAY-ON-WYE

Old Black Lion

Lion Street, Hay-on-Wye, Powys HL3 5AD (01497 820841/www.oldblacklion.co.uk). **Lunch served** noon-2.30pm, **dinner served** 6.30-9.30pm daily. **Main courses** £8.25-£15.95. **Set lunch** (Sun) £8 1 course, £10.50 2 courses, £12 3 courses. **Credit** MC, V.

Just over the border from England, Hay-on-Wye's bookshop-filled streets make this handsome town a day-tripper's delight. But linger after the crowds have gone and you'll find a number of places to enjoy a memorable meal – particularly this sturdy 17th-century coaching inn. Bar meals are justifiably popular, featuring spicy venison casserole or award-winning bangers, but the restaurant is the place to head (wonderfully snug in sumptuous crimson with exposed beams). Dishes utilise the best South Wales farm produce and Cornish seafood – the roast monkfish wrapped in bacon with rosemary and garlic butter is worth the trip alone. Vegetarians are offered a couple of choices, with many ingredients sourced from organic growers. Desserts are indulgent and often tipple-laced, such as the gorgeous Tia Maria meringue. The New World-biased wines are fine, but the real ale is great and, we're reliably informed, the cider is even better.

LLANFRYNACH

The White Swan

Llanfrynach, Powys LD3 7BZ (01874 665276). **Lunch served** noon-2pm Wed-Sat; noon-2.30pm Sun. **Dinner served** 7-9pm Wed-Sat; 7-8.30pm Sun. **Main courses** £10.95-£13.95. **Credit** MC, V.

There's been a sympathetic refurb with old wood and stone at the White Swan. The bar and dining rooms are warm and comfortable with log fires in winter and garden tables in summer – Welsh weather permitting. Try Moroccan spiced chicken with couscous and harissa to start or curried parsnip soup. Main courses are substantial and presentation is simple. Oriental poached pork shoulder with bok choi, star anise, potatoes and peas was enormous. There are lighter, less scary dishes such as grilled salmon fillet with potato and parmesan mash. Puddings include a delicious panna cotta with mango coulis or local cheeses (especially the superb farmhouse cheddar) with own-made digestive biscuits and a delicious sweet chilli jam. The wine list covers much ground in terms of price and geography. Try the 1995 Château Musar (Gaston Hochar, £23.95). Staff are very polite but rather annoyingly insist on double-checking with the kitchen on most questions.

LLANWRTYD WELLS

Carlton House
Dolecoed Road, Llanwrtyd Wells, Powys LD5 4RA (01591 610248/www.carltonrestaurant.co.uk). **Dinner served** 7-8.30pm Mon-Sat. **Main courses** £22-£25. **Credit** MC, V.
This Michelin-starred restaurant and hotel is not difficult to find. Its pink façade shines out like a gastronomic beacon. Fine table settings, a catholic wine list and hospitable front of house service by Dr Alan Gilchrist set the scene for Mary Ann Gilchrist's food. The menu is restricted to whatever is freshest and best on the day and there are rarely more than two or three options. Starters can include Carmarthen ham with slices of melon and goat's cheese or seared scallops with buttered courgettes and a shellfish velouté. The scallops were sweet and firm; the shellfish velouté was a dish in its own right. Main courses included roast canon of local lamb with crushed new potatoes, courgettes and a pearl onion sauce or grilled wild sea bass, given a Mediterranean twist with preserved lemon couscous, baby spinach, roast plum tomatoes and a vibrant lime and caper vinaigrette. The apricot and amaretto fool didn't escape the chef's eye for detail either – the amaretti biscuits gave the rich fool a subtle crunch.

LLYSWEN

Llangoed Hall
Llyswen, Powys LD3 0YP (01874 754525/ www.llangoedhall.com). **Lunch served** noon-2pm, **dinner served** 7-9pm daily. **Set lunch** £28.50 3 courses. **Set dinner** £43 3 courses. **Credit** AmEx, DC, MC, V.
Lavish is the adjective that best describes the location of Llangoed Hall, the fin-de-siècle interior decoration and food. Chef Richie Herkes's lunch menu might include local oak-smoked salmon, followed by Gressingham duck with a balsamic reduction. Puddings could include strawberry soufflé with white chocolate and truffle ice-cream and strawberry and cassis sauce. Dinner is an impressive affair and so it should be at £43 a head. Cornish lobster, Scottish scallops or guinea fowl sausages could appear as starters, with substantial main course offerings of tournedos of Welsh Black

beef or rod-caught turbot. Puddings verge on the OTT – rose champagne jelly with clotted cream, roasted peach with lemon thyme ice and peach syrup and a good selection of cheeses. The wine list is lengthy.

NANT-DDU

Nant Ddu Lodge Hotel
Nant-ddu, Powys CF48 2HY (01685 379111/ www.nant-ddu-lodge.co.uk). **Lunch served** noon-2.30pm, **dinner served** 6.30-9.30pm daily. **Main courses** £8-£14. **Credit** AmEx, MC, V.
It's rare to find a menu that features the likes of delicate boned quail with apricot stuffing alongside that old British staple, gammon and pineapple. But this bar-bistro sits where the industrial valleys of South Wales meet the wilderness of the Brecon Beacons, attracting and catering for customers from both. Traditional soups of the day and bar snacks like ploughman's lunch with local cheeses jockey for attention with exotica such as Jamaican prawn cocktail with toasted pine nuts. Cockles are given a modern twist – heavily spiced, deep-fried and served with mussels and chilli jam. There's daube of local beef with shallots and celeriac crisps or slow-roast pork belly on parsnip purée with Calvados and the lighter spring vegetable risotto or garganelli pasta with courgettes, marinated sultanas and pine nuts. Puddings include old favourites like baked custard with raspberries and shortbread. The wine list is good value but a little too thin. However, good real ale is available.

PONTDOLGOCH

The Talkhouse ★
Pontdolgoch, Powys SY17 5JE (01686 688919/ www.talkhouse.co.uk). **Lunch served** noon-2pm Tue-Sun. **Dinner served** 7-9pm Tue-Thur; 7-9.30pm Fri, Sat. **Set lunch** (Tue-Sat) £21.50 3 courses; (Sun) £26 3 courses . **Set dinner** £21.50 2 courses, £26 3 courses. **Credit** AmEx, DC, MC, V.
What happens when you become disillusioned with living in Bermuda and working as a wine buyer? Co-owner Stephen Garratt bought and overhauled a roadside inn in Powys. The bar and dining rooms have been upgraded; the keg bitter has been replaced with a list of Belgian beers; the wine list has been well thought out and is notable for the number of items from small producers not generally available. Talented South African chefs Peter and Elsie Innes seem to be having fun with the local produce. Starters include a robust mix of grilled local rainbow trout with braised leeks, sautéed smoked bacon and black pudding. Mains include local beef with thyme-roasted vegetables, red wine jus and béarnaise sabayon and organic duck with caramelised apples and a date and balsamic sauce. The selection of British cheeses is impressive. Those wishing to make a night of it can stay upstairs – not a bad idea given the twisting nature of the A470.

Wales

Swansea

REYNOLDSTON

Fairy Hill ★

Fairy Hill Hotel, Fairy Hill, Reynoldston, Swansea,
SA3 1BS (01792 390139/www.fairyhill.net). **Lunch**
served 12.30-2pm daily. **Dinner served** 7.30-9pm
Mon-Sat; 7.30-8.15pm Sun. **Set lunch** (Mon-Sat)
£14.95 2 courses, £18.95 3 courses; (Sun) £21.50
3 courses. **Set dinner** £29.50 2 courses, £37.50
3 courses. **Credit** MC, V.

Owners Paul Davies and Andrew Hetherington have
turned this 18th-century house into a comfortable,
informal hotel. It's set in 24 acres of idyllic woodland,
with a walled kitchen garden that provides many
of the restaurant's vegetables and herbs. Other
ingredients are sourced locally where possible:
Welsh Black beef, Gower-bred lamb and excellent
cockles, available year round. In season there's
skate, sewin, sea bass and mackerel. Meanwhile,
appetisers of deep-fried cockles and quail's egg can
be followed by laver bread and cockle cakes with
crispy, thick Carmarthen bacon and a piquant
tomato chutney; a luxurious combination of textures
and flavours. Main course turbot fillet was perfectly
steamed and served simply with new potatoes and
a rich butter sauce. Puddings are torture for the
weak-willed: poached peach sabayon, white and
dark chocolate terrine or steamed chocolate pudding.
Another glory of this restaurant is the splendid wine
list. It's vast, fairly priced and encompasses
producers from as far afield, viticulturally speaking,
as India.

SWANSEA

La Braseria

28 Wind Street, Swansea, SA1 1DZ (01792
469683/www.labraseria.com). **Lunch served**
11am-2.30pm, **dinner served** 7-11.30pm Mon-Sat.
Main courses £9.95-£14.25. **Set lunch** £7.50
2 courses. **Credit** AmEx, DC, MC, V.

White and glaring outside, dark and cool within,
this wine bar-restaurant is Swansea's own bodega.
The set lunch might include that Spanish staple,
hake cooked any number of ways. The à la carte
menu is even more interesting. To start, try fresh
Spanish asparagus with melted butter or huge
gambas cooked with tomato and garlic before
ruining your afternoon's work by tackling the
suckling pig or Dover sole. Come to think of it, you
might want to take the next day off as well: the
blackboards boast some of the UK's best choices of
Spanish wine and vintage clarets (Petrus, Margaux,
Lafite among others touching the 500 quid mark).
Finally, on leaving, you might notice that the
Spanish obsession with Cognac has migrated to
Swansea. There is an enormous range on offer.
Service also covers a lot of ground. Some staff are
the epitome of Spanish charm, others look at you in
something of a stern manner.

Didier & Stephanie's

56 St Helens Road, Swansea, SA1 4BE (01792
655603). **Lunch served** noon-2pm, **dinner**
served 7-9.30pm Tue-Sat. **Main courses** £11.90-
£13.90. **Credit** MC, V.

The Didier of this simple, tasteful restaurant is from
Lille and Stephanie from Burgundy. Three years ago
they opened for business offering lunches and
dinners that fuelled their childhood years. Old pine
predominates the romantic dining room, which was
once the ground floor of a Victorian house. The short
wine list, on which most items are around £20, is
designed to complement the menu. For starters,
expect perfectly cooked omelette with prawns and
herbs or roast goat's cheese with almonds. Main
courses include a superb rabbit cooked with Dijon
mustard, guinea fowl with red port sauce or confit of
duck's leg with shallots and cassis – rich, sweet and
savoury. Puddings include clafoutis or poached
plums with fresh fruit coulis. The cheeses – imported
from France each week – are faultless. A small piece
of provincial France transplanted in Swansea.

Hansons

Pilot House Wharf, Trawler Road, Swansea Marina,
Swansea, SA1 1UN (01792 466200). **Lunch**
served noon-2pm daily. **Dinner served** 6.30-
9.30pm Mon-Sat. **Main courses** £9.95-£17.
Set lunch £10.95 2 courses, £13.95 3 courses.
Credit MC, V.

Given its location in Swansea's new marina
development, it's hardly surprising that the fish
dishes in this intimate restaurant are extremely
good. The eponymous chef-owner ensures there's a
good seasonal selection of lobster, sea bass, Dover
sole, turbot, scallops, sewin and salmon. Starters
usually include smoked salmon or haddock fish
cakes with tartare sauce. Non-fishy options might
feature duck liver parfait or a cherry tomato and
goat's cheese tarte. Main courses can be grilled
organic chicken on a bed of tagliatelle flavoured with
smoked, dry-cure bacon, or slow-roasted lamb
chump on a bed of crushed new potatoes with a
redcurrant jus. Still, it's difficult to ignore the list of
fresh fish. The fish and chips are wonderful: hake in
batter atop a lattice of hand-cut chips. If you survive
this onslaught, consider traditional puddings such
as treacle sponge. The wine list is well chosen and
sensibly priced. Service is quietly efficient.

Morgans

Somerset Place, Swansea, SA1 1RR (01792
484848/www.morganshotel.co.uk). **Lunch served**
noon-2.15pm, **dinner served** 7-10pm daily. **Set**
lunch (Mon-Sat) £10 2 courses, £12.50 3 courses;
(Sun) £14.50 3 courses. **Set dinner** £25 3 courses.
Credit AmEx, MC, V.

Once Swansea's Port Authority, this imposing
piece of early Edwardian architecture has been
transformed by Martin and Louisa Morgan into an
eponymous hotel with a bar and two restaurants.
The main restaurant – in the old boardroom – has
an extensive menu and wine list. Starters could

Wales

include an excellent spring salad with asparagus, Jerusalem artichoke, Welsh goat's cheese and mixed leaves or a tarte fine of pancetta and gruyère. Main courses include garlic chicken with green beans and a jus or pavé of salmon on a bed of mash with cream sauce. The carte is full of tried and trusted combinations – fillet of Welsh Black with herb crust is an enduring favourite. To finish, try panna cotta with strawberry champagne jelly or mascarpone crème brûlée. The Plimsoll Bistro downstairs has a shorter version and set weekday lunch menus.

The Ottoman ★

20-21 Wind Street, Swansea, SA1 1DY (01792 459979/www.ottomanrest.co.uk). **Lunch served** noon-2.30pm, **dinner served** 7-11pm Mon-Sat. **Main courses** £6.95-£12.95. **Credit** AmEx, DC, MC, V.
This old shop has been cleaned out and turned into a high-ceilinged, airy place, full of Turkish-style tables and chairs and offering startlingly good value. Starters of soup or seafood salad, spicy Turkish sausages or liver and onions are followed by robust dishes of rump steak, lamb chops, chicken, salmon or hake. The Turkish set menu includes meze: french beans in spicy tomato sauce, good houmous, tsatsiki two ways, tabouleh and a fabulously tasty chilli salad. Meat dishes include kofte izgara – dense savoury meatballs cooked over charcoal with a good barbecue flavour. To finish, there's a choice of baklava or fresh fruit. Service is friendly and the wine list well priced.

Vale of Glamorgan

PENARTH

Tomlins ★

46 Plassey Street, Penarth, Vale of Glamorgan CF64 1EL (029 2070 6644/www.tomlinsvegetarian restaurant.co.uk). **Lunch served** noon-3pm Fri, Sat; noon-2.30pm alternate Sun. **Dinner served** 7-9pm Tue-Sat. **Main courses** £11.50-£12. **Set lunch** (Sun) £9.90 2 courses, £11.90 3 courses. **Credit** AmEx, DC, MC, V.
This Victorian corner shop has been stripped back to bare boards to provide a good, well-lit dining area. The menu caters for all grades of vegetarian and vegan. For starters, salad of fig and mozzarella was beautifully presented with a small salad and apricots, and decorated with pesto. The figs were barely ripe but the mozzarella was top quality. Other offerings included a tomato pudding – bread dipped in a tomato and raspberry vinaigrette encasing tomato, shallot and thyme. Main courses included a Middle Eastern medley with falafel, roast vegetables, fresh herb tabouleh, harissa sauce; green pea blinis with wild mushroom salsa; or a pasta parmigiana pie. All were very good. Puddings included cherry and ricotta cheesecake, plum sorbets and a lemon posset. The drinks list scores major brownie points: organic beers, cider, perry and wine. Service was excellent.

Tomlins

Wrexham

GRESFORD

Pant-yr-Ochain

Old Wrexham Road, Gresford, Wrexham LL12 8TY (01978 853525/www.brunningandprice.co.uk).
Meals served noon-9.30pm daily. **Main courses** £6.95-£12.95. **Credit** AmEx, MC, V.
Hidden on a side road near Gresford (look for signs to 'The Flash' – a lake, not a roadside exhibition), Pant-yr-Ochain is a vibrant gastropub with a great, unfussy approach. The tables and chairs are more bric-à-brac than pied-à-terre and shelves are lined with the sort of books you buy as a job lot from a scout sale. But who cares when the food's this good? Starter of asparagus and gorgonzola tartlet with sunblush tomato dressing was delicious. Mains are equally dependable, whether you opt for the free-form, mountainous chicken and shiitake mushroom lasagne or warming Moroccan spiced lamb casserole. The young staff are friendly and informal, and whizz the wine over to you (starting at £9 for a bottle of house white) before you've even taken your coat off. Now that's service.

Wales

Ireland

Ireland

NORTHERN IRELAND

Carndonagh
Dunfanaghy
Giant's Causeway
Rathlin Is.
Greencastle
Portrush
Coleraine
Aran Is.
Letterkenny
Limavady
ANTRIM
Londonderry
Glencolumbcille
DONEGAL
LONDONDERRY
Larne
Donegal
Ballymena
Killybegs
Omagh
Bangor
Donaghadee
Dunkineely
Donegal Bay
Ballyshannon
Belfast
Holywood
Kircubbin
LEITRIM
Portadown
Enniskillen
Glaslough
Armagh
Gilford
DOWN
Sligo
Blacklion
FERMANAGH
ARMAGH
Dundrum
Ballina
Monaghan
Newry
Warrenpoint
Achill Is.
SLIGO
Ballinafad
MONAGHAN
Carrickmacross
Dundalk
MAYO
Cavan
LOUTH
Dundalk Bay
Castlebar
Carrick-on-Shannon
Knock
ROSCOMMON
CAVAN
Clare Is.
Clew Bay
Westport
Longford
Drogheda
Roscommon
LONGFORD
Kells (Ceanannas Mor)
Clifden
Tuam
MEATH
Oughterard
Connemara
Athlone
Mullingar
GALWAY
Ballinasloe
WESTMEATH
REPUBLIC OF
Galway
DUBLIN
Galway Bay
OFFALY
KILDARE
Dún Laoghaire
Aran Islands
The Burren
Doolin
IRELAND
Bray
Cliffs of Moher
Ballinderry
Birr
Kildare
Kilmacanoge
Lahinch
Port Laoise
Wicklow Mtns
CLARE
Dunlavin
Roscrea
Wicklow
Ennis
LAOIS
Athy
Grangecon
WICKLOW
Ballina
Carlow
Aughrim
Limerick
Thurles
Kilkenny
CARLOW
Arklow
Adare
Listowel
TIPPERARY
KILKENNY
Tipperary
LIMERICK
Irish Sea
Abbeyfeale
Cashel
KERRY
WEXFORD
Tralee
Dingle
Killorglin
Wexford
Killarney
Mallow
Rosslare
Dingle Bay
WATERFORD
Waterford
Valentia Is.
Cahirciveen
CORK
Lismore
Cappoquin
Tramore
Kenmare
Macroom
Dungarvan
Sneem
Cork
Midleton
Youghal
Glengarriff
Bandon
Cloyne
Shanagarry
Bear Is.
Bantry
Clonakilty
Kinsale
Ballycotton
Dursey Is.
Durrus
Kilbrittain
St George's Channel
Bantry Bay
Skibbereen
Butlerstown
Ross Carbery
Baltimore
Clear Is.

0   50   100 Km
0   60 miles

© Copyright Time Out Group 2003

Northern Ireland

BANGOR

Shanks ★

The Blackwood, Crawfordsburn Road, Bangor, County Down BT19 1GB (028 9185 3313/ www.shanksrestaurant.com). **Lunch served** 12.30-2.30pm Tue-Fri. **Dinner served** 7-10pm Tue-Sat. **Set lunch** £17 2 courses, £21 3 courses. **Set dinner** £38 3 courses. **Credit** AmEx, MC, V.

While the coolly furnished, avant-garde building divides opinion, everyone who visits Shanks, including Mr Michelin, celebrates Robbie Millar's culinary prowess. The restrained formality of the room and service doesn't encourage diners to let their hair down, but the intense flavours and original combinations of Millar's painterly food will make your taste buds somersault. Foie gras on toasted brioche comes with a ginger and coriander-infused carrot purée, poached grapes and orange muscat jus. Seared scallops come with Thai fragrant rice, spiced aubergine chutney and a light curry cream. With the irresistible temptations presented by sublime and pretty desserts, an oozingly ripe cheese-board and top-notch wine list, Shanks isn't a restaurant for the price-sensitive, but you won't regret the spend.

BELFAST

Aldens

229 Upper Newtownards Road, Belfast, County Antrim BT4 3JF (028 9065 0079/www.aldens restaurant.com). **Lunch served** 12.30-3.30pm Mon-Fri. **Dinner served** 6-10pm Mon-Thur; 6-11pm Fri, Sat. **Main courses** £8.95-£16.95. **Set meals** (Mon-Thur) £16.95 2 courses. **Credit** AmEx, DC, MC, V.

Numerous awards frame the doorway at Aldens and this smart, friendly neighbourhood brasserie offers consistent, all-round satisfaction. The menu is modern European, with concise, classic, full-flavoured dishes – Caesar salad, chicken liver pâté with hot toast and red onion marmalade, sirloin steak with black pepper butter – offered alongside less conventional fare such as warm salad of smoked mackerel, mustard and cucumber cream or calf's liver with beurre noisette and capers or sea bass with shredded mangetout and cucumber and tarragon sauce. Straightforward desserts – soft summer fruits with clotted cream or roast banana crème brûlée – are sophisticated. Meanwhile the wine list offers everything from the cult to the classic, the fascinating to the fine.

Café Renoir & Café Renoir Pizza ★

95 Botanic Avenue, Belfast, County Antrim BT7 1JN (028 9031 1300). **Lunch served** 11am-4.30pm Mon-Sat. **Dinner served** 5-9.30pm

Mon-Thur; 5-10.30pm Fri, Sat; 5-8pm Sun. **Meals served** 10am-5pm Sun. **Main courses** £7.95-£12.95. **Credit** MC, V.

With acres of oak, architectural foliage and earthy colours, this modern Australian-inspired, light-filled café and pizzeria is at the hub of university life. It pleases students and lecturers with everything from sticky, sweet own-baked cakes and excellent coffees to interesting sandwiches (bacon and brie with mango chutney on toasted foccaccia), pastas (wood-fire baked vegetarian lasagne) and salads (warm Cajun chicken with coconut and sweet chilli dressing). Next door you'll find gourmet wood-fired pizzas (such as lamb with sweet potato base, garlic and rosemary roasted potatoes, caramelised onion and mint salsa). Consistently good food and constantly changing menus guarantee queues at lunch when the café is self-service, although its success puts even the most willing antipodean staff at full stretch. A concise list of great Australian wines is also offered. There's a branch on Queens Street (028 9032 5592) too.

Cayenne ★

7 Ascot House, Shaftesbury Square, Belfast, County Antrim BT2 7BD (028 9033 1532/www.cayenne restaurant.com). **Lunch served** noon-2.15pm Mon-Fri; 1-3pm Sun. **Dinner served** 6-10.15pm Mon-Thur; 6-11.15pm Fri, Sat; 6-8.45pm Sun. **Main courses** £8-£20. **Set lunch** £12 2 courses, £15.50 3 courses. **Set dinner** (6-6.45pm Mon-Thur) £12 2 courses, £15.50 3 courses. **Credit** AmEx, DC, MC, V.

Pride and joy of Paul and Jeanne Rankin, Cayenne attracts an eclectic, star-studded audience. Hidden on scruffy Shaftesbury Square, behind frosted glass, it's easy to miss. But those with an eye for style, a nose for wine and a taste for culinary creativity find it without difficulty. A well-priced, cross-cultural menu of inventive dishes echoes the casual, cosmopolitan sophistication of its charcoal grey interior. Orange overhead lights pulse in tune with the heady party atmosphere. Try indigenous ingredients such as char-grilled Lough Neagh eel with a palate-cleansing salsa rossa; skip overseas with fragrant laksas, dreamy risottos or spicy salads; and don't miss desserts such as caramel pot au crème with banana jam. Service is spot on, although Cayenne offers only limited time-slots on weekend nights.

Graffiti ★

258 Ormeau Road, Belfast, County Antrim BT7 2FZ (028 9069 3300). **Meals served** 9am-6pm Mon; 9am-10pm Tue-Sat; 11am-6pm Sun. **Main courses** £7-£10. **Credit** AmEx, MC, V.

Porcelain

Going strong for over 15 years, Graffiti is a teeny-weeny, polka-dot bikini of a neighbourhood café, whose homespun interior of glittering chandeliers and pastel-painted furniture attracts a bohemian set in search of decent food to go with their BYO wine. Service, although friendly, can sometimes meander, letting down a switched-on kitchen team of self-taught cooks. Menus are short. Dishes are simple, substantial and seriously tasty: roast garlic chicken with chilli butter and roast root vegetables; Glenarm organic salmon with warm potato and green bean salad; Moyallon pork sausages with cheese, onion and potato pie, and balsamic roast cherry tomatoes. A blackboard choice of daily-changing pasta, fish dishes and mega-desserts takes food up a notch and ensures repeat business.

Nick's Warehouse

30-35 Hill Street, Belfast, County Antrim BT1 2LB (028 9043 9690/www.nickswarehouse.co.uk). **Lunch served** noon-3pm Mon-Fri. **Dinner served** 6-9.30pm Tue-Thur; 6-10pm Fri, Sat. **Main courses** £7.95-£16. **Credit** AmEx, DC, MC, V.

Located among the cobbled streets of the Cathedral Quarter, Nick's Warehouse is a stalwart of the Belfast restaurant scene. Its popular wine bar – red brick walls, bar stool seating, chalk boards – is a throwback to its 1980s origins, and to eat you can choose between the buzz of the industrially chic 100-seater ground-floor canteen (The Anix), or the padded serenity of the smarter upstairs restaurant. The quality of the food tends to ebb and flow. However the local ingredients, like the wines, are carefully sourced and when dishes such as fried spiced squid on a mixed bean and mushroom salad or grilled fillet of sole with

sautéed potatoes and creamy tartare sauce hit the mark, you can understand this restaurant's enduring popularity.

Porcelain

Ten Square, 10 Donegall Square, Belfast, County Antrim BT1 5JD (028 9024 1001/www.ten-sq.com). **Lunch served** noon-2.30pm Mon-Fri. **Dinner served** 6-10.30pm Mon-Thur; 6-11pm Fri, Sat. **Main courses** £9-£18.50. **Set lunch** (Fri) £15 3 courses. **Credit** AmEx, MC, V.

In a city of dour hotels, Ten Square, Belfast's only boutique hostelry, brings a refreshing slice of metropolitan glamour, cocktail colour and accomplished cuisine with its must-see dining room, Porcelain. Peppered seared beef salad with lime, ginger and jalapeño or crisped fillet of sea bream with citrus fruits, baby fennel and chicory are typical of the menu's light, invigorating food. However, you will also find dishes of exotic warmth and luxury: peppered wild venison with hot 'n' sour red cabbage, parsnip and salsify chips or steamed sponge pudding with passion fruit curd. (The Friday set lunch is a carvery-style roast.) It's a pity that the service, like the pricey wine list, veers awkwardly and inappropriately from the overfamiliar to the downright pretentious.

Rain City Café & Grill ★

33-35 Malone Road, Belfast, County Antrim BT9 6RU (028 9068 2929). **Breakfast served** 8-11.30am, **lunch served** noon-3pm Mon-Fri. **Dinner served** 5-10.30pm daily. **Brunch served** 8am-3pm Sat, Sun. **Main courses** £6.50-£13. **Credit** AmEx, MC, V.

Heaving with families, thanks to its cheap and cheerful food and kid-friendly focus, Rain City offers a glimmer of California sunshine with

Ireland

authentic US diner staples: buffalo wings with apple and celery slaw or corned beef hash with home fries and eggs over easy, alongside a regular pizza-pasta-burger menu. This culminates in typical Stateside desserts – deep-dish apple pie, double chocolate brownie and baked vanilla cheesecake. Specials provide lighter, more innovative alternatives – char-grilled tuna with white bean, avocado and tomato salsa, basil and lemon oil. Brunches with dishes such as rare roast beef salad, potatoes, green beans and blue cheese cream or superlative buttermilk pancakes hit the spot. Young staff, an accessible wine list and great coffees are further pluses.

Restaurant Michael Deane ★

36-40 Howard Street, Belfast, County Antrim BT1 6PF (028 9033 1134/www.deanesbelfast.com). **Dinner served** 7-10pm Wed-Sat. **Set dinner** £32 2 courses. **Credit** AmEx, DC, MC, V.
Michael Deane is the proud recipient of Belfast's only Michelin star. Unlike the dated marble-effect, lattice-trimmed room, his conservative menu has few frills. He worships unashamedly and admirably at the temple of unadorned, individual flavours, holding back on everything but pure protein and handling Rolls-Royce ingredients with reverential perfectionism: squab and foie gras; scallops and black pudding; beef fillet, carrot and horseradish; roast prawn raviolo; coconut bisque. Chocolatier-precise truffles and delicious coffee end an intense experience that is enlivened by a captivating wine list and the boy-band looks and good humour of an attentive team. An extravagant night out. (The brasserie, on the same premises – open noon-3pm, 5.30-11pm Mon Sat – is an altogether more casual affair.)

Shu

253 Lisburn Road, Belfast, County Antrim BT9 7EN (028 9038 1655/www.shu-restaurant.com). **Lunch served** noon-2.30pm, **dinner served** 6-10pm Mon-Sat. **Main courses** £8.50-£16. **Set lunch** (Mon-Sat) £11.50 2 courses. **Set dinner** (Mon-Thur) £11.50 2 courses. **Credit** AmEx, MC, V.
Housed in a Georgian terrace, Shu is an elegant, modern brasserie with a basement cocktail bar. Chocolate velvet drapes, gentle lighting and occasional Asian 'antiques' soften the minimalist design, which glitters with polished veneer, mirrors and candlelight. The menu also has the odd injection of Asia – with dishes such as sashimi of cured salmon, dill and nori – but these are outnumbered by more typical brasserie items displaying flair and comfort: salmon tartare with white crab, avocado and lime crème fraîche; steak served with Jenga-style chips, roast tomato and excellent parsley hollandaise; apple and rhubarb fool. The multi-layered hierarchy of staff sport naval-style uniforms, but are friendly and relaxed.

Sun Kee ★

38 Donegall Pass, Belfast, County Antrim BT7 1BS (028 9031 2233). **Dinner served** 5-11pm daily. **Main courses** £8-£11. **Set dinner** £18-£22 3 courses. **No credit cards.**
Despite its unprepossessing frontage and unfortunate location, the Sun Kee is constantly thronged. Popular with the Chinese community, this modest shoebox of a restaurant has a warm family atmosphere and ultra-friendly staff. With the exception of the chef's specials, the menus are fairly repetitive, but the close-knit tables lend themselves to displaying what you really want – what your neighbours are eating: delicate steamed turbot with a ginger soy dressing, hot-pot of monkfish with char siu, tender green shoots of kai lan with ginger sauce, caramelised aubergine in a chilli-flecked black bean sauce. With a BYOB policy, dinner rarely costs more than £15 a head.

Tong Dynasty ★

82 Botanic Avenue, Belfast, County Antrim BT7 1JR (028 9043 9590). **Meals served** noon-midnight daily. **Main courses** £3-£16. **Credit** MC, V.
Ignore Tong's appearance: it's favourite with the Chinese community. Ask for the Chinese menu – to avoid the more diluted 'local' version – and a translation of the blackboard specials such as comforting sticky rice with shredded crab, scallops and scallions. Or, better still, leave the decision-making to owner Oliver Tong, who delights in sharing the authentic tastes and traditions of his spiritual home. Sophisticated, honest Cantonese fare – crisp roast platters, terracotta hot-pots (aubergine with minced pork and salted fish or lamb flank with bean curd and bamboo shoot) – and dynamite fish dishes like braised turbot with Chinese white turnips are offered alongside exquisite dim sum.

Ireland

Water Margin

159-161 Donegall Pass, Belfast, County Antrim BT7 1DT (028 9032 6888). **Meals served** noon-11pm Thur-Sat; noon-2am Mon-Wed, Sun. **Main courses** £8.50-£30. **Set meal** £20 5 courses. **Credit** AmEx, MC, V.

This huge church conversion has two floors, six private karaoke rooms, a bandstand, a massive bar and a team of black-suited managers in headphones controlling crowds of up to 250 people. Refreshingly, the Water Margin has made very few concessions to western style or fashion: purple beams clash with peach tablecloths and the Chinese menu introduces a more intriguing array of dishes than you'll find elsewhere: fried frogs' legs with bitter melon; crispy fried stuffed pork intestine with salt and chilli; poached chicken feet with sweet and sour sauce. But there's plenty of tamer fare. Service and food vary dramatically and can be disappointing when the kitchen is overstretched on weekend nights.

DERRY

Browns Restaurant

1 Bonds Hill, Derry, County Derry BT47 6DW (028 7134 5180/www.brownsrestaurant.com). **Lunch served** noon-2.15pm Tue-Fri. **Dinner served** 5.30-10pm Tue-Thur; 5.30-10.30pm Fri, Sat. **Main courses** £8.50-£15.95. **Credit** AmEx, MC, V.

Within easy reach of numerous businesses, Browns is ideal for a working lunch: service is speedy and the light, reasonably priced daytime menu provides everything from own-made soup to more substantial food – such as boiled bacon with spiced sauerkraut on buttery mash. The dinner menu offers more adventurous grub: fennel and lime-marinated sea bass with chilli chickpeas and baby plum tomatoes; char-grilled fillet of rare beef with kohlrabi purée and creamed confit of mushrooms; lasagne of smoked haddock with garden pea and vermouth cream. In the evening you're also more likely to enjoy the loquacious charm of Browns' chef-owner, whose talent for design has made this an interesting, welcoming restaurant. Only the brewery-led wine list disappoints.

DONAGHADEE

Grace Neill's

33 High Street, Donaghadee, County Down BT21 0AH (028 9188 4595). **Lunch served** noon-2.45pm Tue-Sat; 12.30-3pm Sun. **Dinner served** 6-9.30pm Tue-Sat. **Main courses** £10-£15. **Set lunch** (Sun) £15 2 courses, £21.50 3 courses. **Credit** AmEx, MC, V.

The low ceilings and miniature space of the oldest pub in Ireland lead to a bright, breezy, contemporary brasserie and a sheltered outdoor terrace where you can dine alfresco on summery days. Jazz, often live on a Sunday, and friendly, competent waiters enliven the ebullient atmosphere

Bar crawl: Belfast

We're good at drinking in Belfast. In fact we could probably drink the rest of you under the table – if there was any traditional pub furniture left, that is. In the last five years Belfast, like every other UK city, has seen the emergence of the super-bar phenomenon – Tardis-like structures of retro chic decor, sprawly sofas, DJ pulpits, Aussie bar staff, cocktail consultants and seared tuna and salsa verde sandwiches.

While these bars have added a touch of cosmopolitan glamour to the city and have regenerated the centre, the downside is the disappearance of many small pubs and local character. Licences are concentrated in the hands of a few major players, which exaggerates the impression of sameness. However, the fierce competition between rival bar barons ensures that interiors, services and standards are constantly shifted up a gear and that nightlife is never dull.

Customer loyalty is low and the 'in' place to be changes with every new opening or re-design, but **Apartment** (2 Donegall Square West; 028 9050 9777), with its fab views of the City Hall, kitschy **Irene and Nan's** (12 Brunswick Street; 028 9023 9123), **Northern Whig** (2-10 Bridge Street; 028 9050 9888), with its extraordinary statues of Czech revolutionaries, and **Ta Tu Bar & Grill** (701 Lisburn Road; 028 9038 0818) attract the most Ben Sherman shirts and belly tops out on the razz. While these places heave with twentysomethings drinking bottled beers and lurid liquids at night, by day they attract all ages with smart menus, decent coffees and clean, air-conditioned spaces.

For smaller, more intimate, darkened drinking dens – and the closest you'll get to urban cool – try the Morrocan makeover of **Bar Bacca** (43 Franklin Street; 028 9023 0200), which is handy for late-night drinking and dancing upstairs at **La Lea**.

created by the local golfing-sailing-tennis brigade who appreciate Grace Neill's relaxed style and astutely crafted menu. Local seafood is celebrated with sophisticated risottos and fine classic dishes such as sea bass with baby fennel, roast garlic pomme purée and sauce vierge. However, meat dishes such as rump of lamb with cinnamon-infused confit of carrots and jus of Irish honey won't disappoint either. Seasonal, traditional desserts are prettily presented. The wine list offers only two bottles by the glass and there's a surprisingly limited beer selection.

Alternatively, the oriental red, black and bamboo of **Opium** (3 Skipper Street; 028 9023 2448) has a good fusion menu pre-9pm and **am:pm** (38-42 Upper Arthur Street; 028 9024 9009) has tropical fish tanks and a regular crowd. However, when they're busy, movement and conversation are impossible at these places.

The best entertainment is to be found at **Auntie Annie's Porterhouse** (44 Dublin Road; 028 9050 1660) and the **Limelight** (17 Ormeau Avenue; 028 9032 5968), which host eclectic line-ups of rock, indie and pop bands and credible singer-songwriters. The **Errigle Inn** (312-320 Ormeau Road; 028 9064 1410) adds new country to this mix, while the **Empire Music Hall** (40-42 Botanic Avenue; 028 9024 9276) fills the rest of its programme with comedy, cover bands and salsa nights, and the **Kremlin** (96 Donegall Street; 028 9080 9700), a gay bar, puts on bingo and sing-a-longs. The **Menagerie** (130 University Street; 028 9023 5678) and the **Mandela Hall** (QUB Students' Union, Univesity Road; 028 9027 3106) attract grungy students and bands. **Maddens** (74 Berry Street; 028 9024 4114) and the **Hatfield House** (130 Ormeau Road; 028 9043 8764) specialise in traditional music, although they're not quite as welcoming as rural session pubs.

Late beverages and loud sounds can be found in **Milk** (10-14 Tomb Street; 028 9027 8876), which attracts the best touring DJs, **La Lea** (43 Franklin Street; 028 9023 0200), with three floors of sweaty, writhing bodies, and **Thompson's Garage** (3 Patterson's Place; 028 9032 3762), which is a stone's throw from the City Hall. The 'premier' hotels, such as **Ten Square** (10 Donegall Square South; 028 9024 1001), with its boutique design and extensive champagne selection, and the **Europa** (Great Victoria Street;

028 9027 1066), with impersonal lobby furniture and a great first-floor view, also provide late-night refuge and star-spotting opportunities.

You can also find nice views and alfresco drinking at the **Cutter's Wharf** (Lockview Road, off Stranmillis Road; 028 9066 3388), located on a leafy bend of the River Lagan, **Pat's Bar** (19-21 Princes Dock Street; 028 9074 4524) and the **Rotterdam** (54 Pilot Street; 028 9074 6021), two neighbouring pubs that spill out on to cobbled docksides. Or try the **Waterfront Hall** (2 Lanyon Place; 028 9033 4400) where you can admire art and fantastic panoramas of the Belfast cityscape. If you'd prefer to watch sports screens, then the **Botanic Inn** (23-27 Malone Road; 028 9050 9740), the **Chelsea** (346 Lisburn Road; 028 9068 7177), the Errigle and **Morrison's** (21 Bedford Street; 028 9032 0030) have every age and angle covered. **Bar 7** (Odyssey Pavilion, Queen's Quay; 028 9046 7070) is best to watch live sport (namely the Belfast Giants) or a concert at the Odyssey.

However, if it's Belfast charm, pubby warmth or local heritage you're after, head straight for the **John Hewitt** (51 Donegall Street; 028 9023 3768), a convincing reproduction with a solid sense of community, the **Oak Bar** at the Errigle (bow ties and table service), the **Kitchen Bar** (16-18 Victoria Square; 028 9032 4901), which has plans to move at some point, the **Duke of York** (7-11 Commercial Court; 028 9024 1062), which is all stone walls and antique pine snugs, or probably the most gorgeous pub in the world, the **Crown Liquor Salon** (46 Great Victoria Street; 028 9027 9901). Here you should spend at least one afternoon attempting to drink the friendly folk of Belfast – and your fellow travellers – under the table.

DUNDRUM

Buck's Head

77-79 Main Street, Dundrum, County Down BT33 0LU (028 4375 1868). **Lunch served** noon-2.30pm, **high tea served** 5-7pm, **dinner served** 7-9.30pm daily. **Set lunch** £14.50 3 courses. **Set dinner** (Sun) £24.50 3 courses. **Credit** AmEx, MC, V.
Both a cosy pub and smart, relaxed modern restaurant, this family-run establishment is a great stop-off point for the Mourne Mountains. Seriously

tasty comfort food is served at lunch and in the early evening, when the local tradition of 'high tea' is encouraged: smoked haddock and salmon fish cakes with sweet chilli jam, crispy fried Kilkeel cod with mushy peas and chips – accompanied by lashings of tea (or beers) and baskets of delicious wheaten bread. Come later and the menu of dazzling local ingredients shifts up a gear – oysters tossed in pinhead oats, shallow-fried and served with a curry sabayon perhaps, or Moroccan-spiced Mourne lamb with roast pepper and mango couscous – with delicate desserts and a decent wine list to match.

Ireland

The Harbour Bar and Bistro at...

ENNISKILLEN

Gallery at Le Chateau

139 Irvinestown Road, Ferndale Cross, Enniskillen,
County Fermanagh BT74 4RN (028 6632 8374).
Lunch served noon-2.30pm, **dinner served**
5.30-9.30pm Wed-Sun. **Main courses** £8.95-
£14. **Set dinner** £18 3 courses. **Credit** AmEx,
DC, MC, V.

Forget the pretentious name and grandiose Italian-
themed design, this polished, family-run restaurant-
with-rooms has friendly staff and a chef who spent
10 years training in Australia, as well as a spell at
culinary boot camp with Gordon Ramsay. Modern
fusion food is as delicious as it is visually stunning.
An intensely aromatic Thai chicken chowder is
theatrically poured around a 'sandcastle' of couscous
crowned with a 'starfish' of baby corn. A bulb of
dark green pak choi and vibrant orange pumpkin
purée accompanies fine pale pink slices of home-
smoked bacon, rösti potato and curried cabbage.
The glossy, caramelised lemon tart is citrus heaven.
Unfortunately the chef's overseas insight seems to
be missing from the predictable wine list.

Restaurant No.6

At Blakes the Hollow, 6 Church Street, Enniskillen,
County Fermanagh BT74 7EJ (028 6632 0918).
Lunch served noon-2.30pm Sun. **Dinner served**
7-9.30pm Tue-Sat. **Set lunch** £13.95 3 courses.
Set dinner £29.50 3 courses. **Credit** MC, V.

Restaurant No.6 is the jewel in the crown of the
Tardis-like building hidden behind the entrance to
Blakes Spirit Grocers. While no expense has been
spared, it lacks the ostentation and theme design
evident elsewhere and the graceful style of its formal
rooms works in harmony with its connoisseur wine
list and the succinct, meticulous menus. Original

starters – smoked haddock brandade with grilled
sardine and caramelised fruit chutney – precede
more familiar but equally well-executed modern
classics: honey-roasted loin of free-range pork with
Asian greens, ginger and coriander jus; vanilla
panna cotta with poached pear and almond biscuits.
Service is clipped, polite and pleasant; children are
welcomed at Sunday lunches.

GILFORD

Oriel ★

2 Bridge Street, Gilford, County Down BT63 6HF
(028 3883 1543/www.orielrestaurant.com). **Lunch**
served 12.30-2.30pm Sun. **Dinner served** 5.30-
9.30pm Tue-Fri; 6.30-9.30pm Sat. **Set lunch** £16
3 courses. **Set dinner** (Tue-Fri) £12 2 courses,
£15 3 courses 5.30-7pm; (Tue-Sat) £23.95 3 courses.
Credit AmEx, MC, V.

Owned by an ambitious but self-effacing young
chef, the Oriel, while not the prettiest restaurant,
offers acutely sophisticated food and an erudite
wine list. However, extraordinary value for money
and a friendly, professional front-of-house team
makes this restaurant accessible to all. The menu
oozes richness, intricacy and top-gear ingredients
with meat, seasonal game and fish dishes just
winning out over vegetarian choices: langoustine-
stuffed rabbit with pomme fondant, petit chou farci
and liquorice; wild venison with Chinese five-spice,
seared foie gras, morels and chocolate jus; or
roasted turbot with velouté of celeriac, fennel and
ginger purée, and roasted artichoke. Perhaps too
generous with complimentary canapés, appetisers
and petits fours, dinner at the Oriel is an intense
experience requiring a healthy appetite and plenty
of time.

Ireland

... Ramore Wine Bar. *See p354.*

HOLYWOOD

Bay Tree ★

118 High Street, Holywood, County Down
BT18 9HW (028 9042 1419). **Breakfast served**
8-10.30am Mon-Fri. **Lunch served** noon-2.30pm
Mon-Sat. **Dinner served** 7-9.30pm Fri. **Main
courses** (lunch) £3.20-£7. **Set dinner** £17.50 2
courses, £25.50 3 courses. **Credit** MC, V.

The wait in the queue that forms punctually at
noon is a small sacrifice for the outstandingly good
food in this café, which attracts the lion's share of
the silver pound in Holywood and an appreciative
following of young mothers. The delicious
simplicity of savoury dishes such as pan-fried
plaice with mellow champ and pure parsley butter
or grilled goat's cheese with dressed puy lentils and
toasted walnuts may make you want to linger.
However, be careful not to miss the coffee-tinged
banoffee, strawberry and rhubarb crumble or
mountainous caramelised meringues: the Bay
Tree's owner, Sue Farmer, has to be one of the best
pastry cooks in the land. There are great coffees,
lovely staff and a clean, bright space to boot.

KIRCUBBIN

Paul Arthurs

66 Main Street, Kircubbin, County Down
BT22 2SP (028 4273 8192/www.paul-arthurs.co.uk).
Lunch served noon-2.30pm Tue-Sun. **Dinner
served** 5-9pm Tue-Sat. **Main courses** £10-£15.
Credit AmEx, DC, MC, V.

The strong, bright Matisse-esque splurge of colours
on the banners that flutter outside Paul Arthurs's
bistro/chip-shop combo aptly describe this cheery
lough-side restaurant and the audacious confidence
of its chef. Kircubbin is Arthurs's home town. While
his loyalty to locals curbs the ambitious cookery of
his apprenticeship with Michelin-starred luminaries
Deane and Millar, the exquisitely simple food on his
sparky menu – sautéed crab claws in garlic and
chilli, Dover sole with hazel-nut butter – is never
mundane. With bold brush strokes he dusts down
familiar dishes – Portavogie prawn cocktail, ribeye
steak with chips, bread and butter pudding – giving
them a modern sheen and his own nifty signature.

LIMAVADY

Lime Tree

60 Catherine Street, Limavady, County Derry
BT49 9DB (028 7776 4300/www.limetreerest.com).
Lunch served noon-2pm Wed-Fri, Sun. **Dinner
served** 6-9pm Wed-Sun. **Set lunch** £6.95 2 courses,
£8.50 3 courses. **Set dinner** £15 2 courses, £19.95
3 courses. **Credit** AmEx, MC, V.

Humble, cosy and welcoming, the Lime Tree is one
of the few options on the north coast for decent food.
A converted front room in a terraced house,
furnished on a shoestring budget, the charm of
the modest dining room lies with its hosts – the
precise Maria who provides textbook-perfect
service, and the flamboyant Stanley who emerges
periodically in his chef's whites to enthuse about
the wines or deliver his refreshingly unfashionable
food. Greek lamb patties are squat hand-rolled baby
meatballs with a fresh, raw tomato salsa and a
vinaigrette-dressed mixed leaf salad. Dover
sole, served on the bone with a simple parsley
butter, comes with a dappled golden skin and
faultlessly cooked firm, juicy white flesh. The sticky
toffee pudding is light, springy, treacly and big
enough for two.

Ireland

PORTADOWN

Yellow Door Ruggers Bistro

*Portadown RFC, Chambers Park, Portadown BT62
1JD (028 3839 4860/www.yellowdoordeli.com).*
Lunch served noon-2.30pm Thur-Sun. **Dinner
served** 6.30-9.30pm Wed-Sat. **Main courses** £11-
£14. **Set lunch** £7 1 course, £12 2 courses; (Sun)
£15 2 courses, £16.95 3 courses. **Credit** DC, MC, V.
Portadown RFC has broken the mould by opening
its doors to the outside world with a contemporary
culinary oasis in the midst of its brown and
burgundy bars and clubrooms. Bright whites, blond
wood, tongue and groove panelling, sculptural
blooms, and the dramatic baked earth triptychs that
decorate the restaurant walls echo the New World
freshness, colour and sunshine of the menu. Savvy,
seasonal, stylish comfort food is on offer – fusilli with
seared beef, dolcelatte and fire-roasted peppers; chilli-
spiced monkfish with Madras cream and a rich ochre
mash of sweet potato; caramelised pear and chocolate
gateau. The children's menu is good. Further pluses
are a user-friendly wine list and cheery service.

PORTRUSH

Ramore Wine Bar ★

*The Harbour, Portrush, County Antrim BT56 8BN
(028 7082 4313).* **Lunch served** 12.15-2.15pm
Mon-Sat; 12.30-3pm Sun. **Dinner served** 5-10pm
Mon-Sat; 5-9pm Sun. **Main courses** £4.95-£12.95.
Credit DC, MC, V.
A trio of eating venues, the packed Ramore provides
modern pizzas and pastas at Coast, and sophisticated,
fashionable fast food at the theatrical Harbour
Bistro or in the contemporary room-with-a-view

Harbour Bar. All operate an efficient order-pay-and-
wait system. All provide value-for-money wines and
a reliably tasty feast of good-quality, cheap tucker:
from the Neapolitan pasta to the peppered rump pizza
at Coast; and from the steak and slaw burgers to the
more extravagant tempura of prawns with lobster
mayonnaise at the Harbour Bistro. The Wine Bar
offers a please-all menu with an Italian and oriental
focus. Prepare to queue.

WARRENPOINT

Duke's Restaurant

*7 Duke Street, Warrenpoint, County Down BT34
3JY (028 4175 2084/www.thedukerestaurant.com).*
Dinner served 6-10pm Tue-Sun. **Main courses**
£10-£14. **Set dinner** (Tue-Thur) £12.95 3 courses.
Credit AmEx, MC, V.
Where the beautifully soft Mourne foothills meet
Carlingford Lough, you'll find an ordinary-looking
bar in an ordinary seaside town, but the Duke is no
ordinary restaurant and its popularity is explained
by two parallel menus. One offers comfort-seekers
the familiarity of real, fresh retro food – chicken liver
pâté and melba toast; garlicky, crisp chicken kiev.
The other offers the most creative seafood menu in
Northern Ireland. Packed most nights of the week,
the Duke is a humdinger at the weekends, when
timorous, bright-eyed school children wobblingly
present dishes: fresh prawns with chilli, garlic and
basil followed by grilled turbot with wilted bok choi
and prawn bisque cream; or roast barramundi with
lemon and basil risotto, and sweet pea broth. There's
a fab fish-friendly wine list and the place might soon
be open for lunch on Sundays – phone to check.

Ireland

Republic of Ireland

County Cavan

BLACKLION

The MacNean Bistro ★
Main Street, Blacklion, Co Cavan (072 53022).
Lunch served 12.30-1pm, 3.15-3.30pm Sun. **Dinner served** 6.30-9pm Wed-Fri; 6-6.30pm, 9.15-9.30pm Sat; 6.30-7.30pm Sun. **Main courses** €21-€25. **Set lunch** €25 4 courses. **Set dinner** €55 6 courses. **Credit** MC, V.

Every weekend Neven Maguire packs out his small dining room and cooks up some of the most inspired food to be found in Ireland. Blacklion is remote, but this little hamlet is already a place of culinary pilgrimage. Maguire is still a twentysomething, but half a lifetime has already been spent honing culinary skills that are wondrously controlled. Eat the degustation menu here – at such fantastic value it's unmissable. The cooking is as balanced as it is brilliant: scallops with crab and saffron risotto; loin of lamb with confit lamb shoulder; belly pork with five-spice; and don't miss those extraordinary desserts, in particular warm strawberry millefeuille.

County Clare

BALLINA

The Cherry Tree ★
Lakeside, Ballina, Co Clare (061 375688). **Dinner served** 6-10pm Tue-Sat. **Main courses** €23.50-€32.50. **Credit** AmEx, MC, V.

Harry McKeogh's waterside restaurant is one of those great success stories that proves that God is in the detail. Yes, McKeogh and his chef Mark Anderson produce sophisticated, wise cooking, but it is their unrelenting quest for perfection that really places the CT apart. Every detail of every dish has been thought through, polished and primed. After a few visits to this colourful, comfortable room, you realise that the only competition the CT has is with itself: was tonight's turbot with a truffle butter sauce better than last time's hake with a crab crust? The duck confit better than the crab spring rolls? Service, by local youngsters, is efficient.

LAHINCH

Barrtra
Lahinch, Co Clare (065 7081280). **Dinner served** *July-Aug* 5-10pm Tue-Sun. **Main courses** €19. **Set dinner** (5-6.30pm) €20 3 courses; (6.30-10pm) €35 6 courses. **Credit** AmEx, MC, V.

Paul and Theresa O'Brien cook classic fish dishes. Then they serve them with quiet charm in this simple room, with its jaw-dropping views out over lovely Liscannor Bay, add in a great wine list that reflects Mr O'Brien's keen interest in vinous matters, and do their darndest to make sure you have a night to remember. And you will surely remember that haddock baked with orange and ginger, the char-grilled cod with chilli and lime or that fine poached wild salmon with white wine sauce. Fish and shellfish are the stars, as you would expect from a restaurant overlooking the sea.

County Cork

BALLYCOTTON

Grapefruit Moon
Main Street, Ballycotton, Co Cork (021 4646646). **Dinner served** 7-9.30pm Tue-Sat. **Main courses** €17-€28. **Credit** AmEx, MC, V.

In an elegant room smack in the centre of Ballycotton village, Ivan Whelan and his partner Jean Manning belie their youth with food that is winningly professional and delicious. A watermelon salsa served with fillets of john dory is clever, and the superlative freshness of the fish itself is beyond argument. And alongside the classics that adorn the menu – lambs' kidneys flamed in brandy; slow-cooked lamb shanks; black sole on the bone; fillet of beef with french-fried onions – Mr Whelan cooks a fine dish of Cantonese noodles with duck and red peppers. Desserts are a comfort zone of bread and butter pudding and crème brûlée.

BALTIMORE

The Customs House ★
Baltimore, Co Cork (028 20200). **Dinner served** *Apr-June, Sept* 7-10pm Thur-Sun; *July-Aug* 7-10pm Wed-Sun. **Set dinner** €25 3 courses, €35 4 courses. **No credit cards.**

Susan Holland's cookery has a very simple aim: to present the integral flavours of the Atlantic sea fish in the most pristine, perfect way imaginable. She will start by serving the fish as a ceviche – some lightly cured with coconut milk – and served with razor-thin shaved fennel and red onion. Then there might be one of her wonderful signature partnerships – perhaps roast turbot with a simple salmoriglio sauce or red mullet with a savoury-bitter tapenade. Desserts such as poached pears with roasted almond ice-cream, or a mi-cuit chocolate fondant, show the same mastery.

BANDON

Otto's Creative Catering ★

Dunworley, Butlerstown, Bandon, Co Cork
(023 40461/www.ottoscreativecatering.com).
Lunch served 1.30-3.30pm Sun. **Dinner served**
7.30-10pm Wed-Sat. **Set lunch** €30 4 courses.
Set dinner €45 5 courses. **Credit** MC, V.

Here is what Otto Kunze cooked for a weekend lunch
one afternoon: nettle soup; sea spinach and goat's
cheese lasagne; cured pork with salad leaves;
Ummera smoked salmon with garnishes; rhubarb
gratin with the creamiest custard ever made. Then
Mr Kunze appeared to say hello. To a man and
woman, the party stood up and gave the chef a
standing ovation. That's what Otto Kunze can do:
cook food the like of which you simply will not find
anywhere else. The pork is from his own pigs. The
fish is landed locally. He grows his own vegetables.
He is a master of wild foods, collecting leaves and
mushrooms. It all makes for one of the most holistic
culinary experiences anyone can enjoy.

CLOYNE

The Cross of Cloyne

Church Street, Cloyne, Co Cork (021 4652401).
Dinner served 6-9.30pm Wed-Sun. **Main courses**
€17.95-€25. **Credit** DC, MC, V.

Whitewashed walls, a casually stylish themed
interior in black-and-blue, simple but delicious food,
and a big buzz. Set in unspoiled, medieval Cloyne,
Colm Falvey's restaurant and adjoining bar are
direct and straightforward. No fancy faux-French
fussiness here; just super-fresh, local ingredients
prepared with skill and verve. You can have a big
char-grilled steak on a bed of champ potatoes,
meltingly delicious poached Blackwater wild
salmon with a cucumber hollandaise sauce, or
maybe a big, fat juicy pan-fried fish cake with a
lemony coriander mayonnaise dressing.

CORK

Café Paradiso ★

16 Lancaster Quay, Western Road, Cork, Co Cork
(021 4277939/www.cafeparadiso.ie). **Lunch served**
12.30-3pm, **dinner served** 6.30-10.30pm Tue-Sat.
Main courses €18.50. **Credit** AmEx, MC, V.

Chef-proprietor Denis Cotter has managed to achieve
the impossible – taking vegetarianism out of its
ghetto and planting it in the mainstream restaurant
culture – simply by being such an outstanding cook.
With something as delicious as fresh noodles in a
ginger broth with stir-fried pak choi, cauliflower, egg
roll, scallions, coriander and aduki bean wun tuns,
you don't ask what's missing. And that's the
Paradiso secret: great cooking, beautifully realised
from starters such as the beetroot mouse with
watercress, pear and walnut salad, through to
desserts such as plum and raspberry fool with
shortbread biscuits.

Ivory Tower

Exchange Buildings, Princes Street, Cork, Co Cork
(021 4274665). **Dinner served** 6.30-10pm Wed-Sat.
Set dinner €50 5 courses. **Credit** AmEx, MC, V.

Seamus O'Connell is a performance artist in the
kitchen and even though he has been cooking in the
Ivory Tower for the best part of a decade, he shows
no signs of letting his cooking settle down. The Ivory
Tower is a walk on the culinary wild side: a soufflé
of crozier blue sheep's cheese served in a globe
artichoke with a port beurre rouge; carpaccio of
wood pigeon; a guinea fowl and popcorn broth
matched with Asian greens; pheasant cooked 'under
pressure' with Aqua Libra; a cherry crème brûlée
spiced with saffron. It's exhilarating cooking.

Jacobs on the Mall ★

30A South Mall, Cork, Co Cork (021 4251530).
Lunch served 12.30-2.30pm, **dinner served**
6.30-10pm Mon-Sat. **Main courses** €14.80-€30.
Credit AmEx, DC, MC, V.

Mercy Fenton has been weaving her delicate magic
in the elegant Jacobs since the restaurant opened five
years ago but, despite producing food of the highest
calibre, she remains Cork's best-kept secret. She is a
quiet woman, whose energy goes into creating
dishes with sublimely nuanced flavours. Dishes that
read as if they might offer a pretty similar template
of tastes – seared squid with crisp vegetable salad
and a hot and sour dressing; confit duck leg with hot
and spicy prawn broth, vegetable confit and fine
noodles – instead demonstrate a remarkable
panoply of tastes and flavours.

DURRUS

Good Things Café ★

Ahakista Road, Durrus, Co Cork (027 61426). **Food
served** 10am-5pm daily. **Lunch served** *summer*
noon-4pm daily; *winter* noon-4pm Mon, Thur-Sun.
Dinner served 7-8.30pm Mon, Thur-Sat. **Main
courses** €5.50-€15.50. **Set dinner** €32.50 2 courses,
€38.50 3 courses. **Credit** MC, V.

Carmel Somer's open-plan café has a Californian
headiness about it – just look out at the waters of
Dunmanus Bay – and it's a headiness which her
cooking hammers home. The menus read like a road
map of local producers – Durrus cheese pizza with
spinach and nutmeg; Fingal's ham with eggs and
potato cake; West Cork ploughman's with a glass of
Carlow stout; West Cork fish soup with Desmond
cheese – with world-class artisan foods raised to a
new pitch thanks to classy cooking.

KILBRITTAIN

Casino House

Coolmain Bay, Kilbrittain, Co Cork (023 49944).
Lunch served 1-3pm Sun. **Dinner served** 7-9pm
Mon, Tue, Thur-Sun. **Main courses** €16.90-€24.50.
Set dinner €30 3 courses. **Credit** MC, V.

Michael Relja may well be one of the most technically
accomplished cooks working in Ireland right now.

Café Paradiso

His menus in the lovely Casino House pose him a set of stern challenges – just think of the demands of quail on a black olive and balsamic risotto. But the stern challenges are effortlessly surmounted. So, once you have admired the technical beauty, just tuck in and savour the work of a chef who delivers haymaker flavours: ricotta, vegetable and tofu in filo on a red paprika sauce; turbot poached in a lobster and vegetable bisque; desserts such as gratinated lemon sabayon with strawberries.

KINSALE

Fishy Fishy Café ★
Guardwell, Kinsale, Co Cork (021 774453).
Lunch served *Apr-Oct* noon-3.45pm daily;
Nov-Mar noon-3.45pm Mon-Sat. **Main courses**
€12-€18. **No credit cards**.
Martin Shanahan gets up at 5am to source his fish, then he brings it back to Kinsale and cooks it and sells it. That's what this single-room restaurant and fish shop is all about. He loves to pair a sweet chilli sauce with shellfish, and he likes to throw chickpeas into a dish, but for the most part Mr Shanahan lets the flavour of the fish do the talking. And if some fine fillet on the wet slab takes your fancy, then he will happily cook it for you. With some white wine and a table out under the awning, you won't care about queueing.

Toddies
*Eastern Road, Kinsale, Co Cork (021 4777769/
www.toddieskinsale.com).* **Dinner served**
7-10pm Tue-Sun. **Main courses** €21-€28.
Credit AmEx, MC, V.

Pearse and Mary O'Sullivan's restaurant is a bright spark, despite being one of the new kids on the block in Kinsale, a town with numerous undistinguished places to eat which still continues to trade on former glory as 'Ireland's gourmet capital'. The cooking is very fine – an Atlantic fish bouillabaisse is a clever reworking of the original dish; a fine leek, gruyère and chervil tart has light-as-a-feather pastry; and gutsy, sweet Angus beef with a Perigordine sauce is polished and deeply satisfying. The rooms are also excellent and showcase the couple's interest in modern Irish paintings. This is a bright destination.

MALLOW

Longueville House ★
*Mallow, Co Cork (022 47156/www.longueville
house.ie). Bar* **Meals served** 12.30-5pm daily.
Main courses €12. *Restaurant* **Dinner served**
6.30-8.15pm daily. **Set dinner** €50 5 courses.
Credit AmEx, DC, MC, V.
William O'Callaghan is one of the modern Irish masters. There are few better country cooks, nor more sophisticated country cooks, anywhere in Ireland. His pâtés and terrines are made using Longueville pork; the lamb is from their 500 acres, the fish is Blackwater river salmon; the fruits are grown in the garden as are the vegetables, and in a good year they even manage to make a little white wine. This self-sufficiency gives Mr O'Callaghan's cooking a profundity that is the glory of this grand, capacious, birthday-cake pink country house. Service at Longueville House is immaculate and dinner is excellent value for money.

Ireland

MIDLETON

O'Donovan's

58 Main Street, Midleton, Co Cork (021 4631255).
Lunch served 12.15-2.30pm, **dinner served**
6-9.30pm Mon-Sat. **Main courses** €18.95-€27.
Credit AmEx, MC, V.

O'Donovan's used to be a pub that served food, but
it has slowly become a full-blown restaurant. Eat Ian
Cronin's excellent cooking and you will understand
why they have changed focus: Toulouse sausage and
flageolet beans is delicious comfort cooking; barbary
duck with a beetroot and horseradish tapenade is
judged just right; roast salmon with deep-fried cherry
tomatoes and chive hollandaise is funky and fun. It's
a calm, casual room, and the pricing and excellent
service are further encouragement to return.

ROSS CARBERY

O'Callaghan-Walshe ★

Ross Carbery, Co Cork (023 48125). **Dinner served**
summer 6.30-9.30pm Tue-Sun; *winter* 6.30-9.30pm Fri,
Sat. **Main courses** €26.50-€45. **Credit** MC, V.

Everyone rates Sean and Martina's O'C-W. What's
so special? The room for a start, which looks more
like a stage set of a restaurant than a real restaurant.
Then there's the service by Sean Kearney. And then
there's Martina O'Donovan's cooking: spicy fish
cakes with chermoula or hot prawns with lemon
and garlic to begin. Then some scallops with basil
crème fraîche, or john dory with a cider and mussel
sauce. Don't miss the rainwater syllabub or the
fantastic Trinity burnt cream.

SHANAGARRY

Ballymaloe House

Shanagarry, Co Cork (021 4652531/www.bally
maloe.com). **Lunch served** 1-1.30pm, **dinner**
served 7-9.30pm daily. **Set dinner** €55 5 courses.
Credit AmEx, DC, MC, V.

Myrtle Allen's Ballymaloe House is the most famous
culinary address in Ireland, its reputation for great
cooking spanning the globe. Yet many people turn
up here, stay and eat, and just don't get it. 'Where's
the glamour?' they ask. 'Where's the slickness, the
cosmopolitanism?' Ballymaloe doesn't do any of
those things. It serves the food of the farm, and the
food of the area, cooked with elegant simplicity, and
it has been doing this since 1964. This is traditional
cooking, using traditional ingredients, and is some
of the greatest you can encounter anywhere.

SKIBBEREEN

Island Cottage

Heir Island, Skibbereen, Co Cork (028 38102/
www.islandcottage.com). **Dinner served** *15 May-*
15 Sept 8pm-midnight Wed-Sun. **Set dinner** €30
4 courses. **No credit cards.**

To get to Island Cottage, you must drive down to the
sea and take a little boat along with your fellow
diners to Heir Island. Then you walk for a mile or so
to this tiny cottage. There is one tiny dining room, a
set menu with no choices, and a tiny selection of
wines. Sounds crazy? It is. Sounds magical? It most
certainly is. John Desmond and Ellmary Fenton's
restaurant is unique, and offers an experience that is
sublime. Part of the sublimity is the cooking: perfect
duck; lovely salads; great vegetables; marinated
mackerel which Mr Desmond has probably caught
himself; gubbeen farmhouse cheese. There is
nowhere else quite like it.

County Donegal

CARNDONAGH

The Corncrake

Millbrae, Carndonagh, Co Donegal (074 9374534)
Dinner served 6-9pm Tue-Sat. **Main courses**
€17-€23. **No credit cards.**

L'Ecrivain. See p360.

Ireland

People don't just like Brid McCartney and Noreen Lynch's restaurant in Carndonagh, they love it. They love the new room just as much as they loved the old room; they love Brid's sassy, upfront cooking; they love the value for money. They order the same dishes every time they eat here: that crab vinaigrette, for example. Ditto spring lamb with rosemary and redcurrant, and cracking desserts such as classic orange panna cotta or rhubarb ice-cream. A one-off.

DUNFANAGHY
The Mill Restaurant
Figart, Dunfanaghy, Co Donegal (074 36985/ www.themillrestaurant.com). **Lunch served** 12.30-2pm 1 Sun a mth. **Dinner served** 7-9pm Tue-Sun. **Set dinner** €34 3 courses. **Credit** AmEx, MC, V.

You can't get much further north than Dunfanaghy, but it's worth the trip for Derek Alcorn's delicious food and a night at this charming mill, with its beautiful views across New Lake. The cooking is polished, but not precious: a lobster ragoût will match with Sheephaven Bay salmon; Doe Castle mussels are cooked with Smithwicks ale and sage; pommes Anna with fillet of Hereford beef; fried anchovies will join with sea bass in a salad. Vegetarian choices are imaginative and serious. A lot of attention is paid to sourcing ingredients, so don't miss the scarce local farmhouse cheeses.

DUNKINEELY
Castlemurray House
St John's Point, Dunkineely, Co Donegal (073 37022/ www.castlemurray.com). **Lunch served** 1.30-3.30pm Sun. **Dinner served** 7-9.30pm Mon-Sat; 6.30-8.30pm Sun. **Main courses** €34-€46. **Set lunch** (Sun) €22.50. **Credit** MC, V.

Castlemurray House has one of the most outstanding locations of any restaurant in Ireland, with views that sweep down the hill and out into the wild Atlantic waters. The restaurant is set up to take maximum advantage of the views, but the cooking will quickly drag your gaze back to the plate: lobster risotto with morels, red mullet with saffron vinaigrette, sea bass with fennel and dill salsa, steamed lobster or buttery turbot with chanterelles. Fish is obviously the speciality, but the meat cookery is no slouch either.

GREENCASTLE
Kealy's Seafood Bar
Greencastle, Co Donegal (074 9381010). **Lunch served** *winter* 12.30-3pm Fri-Sun; *summer* 12.30-3pm Wed-Sun. **Dinner served** *winter* 7-9.30pm Thur-Sun; *summer* 7-9.30pm Wed-Sun. **Main courses** €15-€50. **Set dinner** €35 4 courses. **Credit** AmEx, MC, V.

A little bar with a little restaurant serving fresh fish, just a stone's throw from the little pier in the harbour of Greencastle. James Kealy's seafood bar is a dreamy little spot, comfortable rather than stylish, and quietly unselfconscious. They cook fresh fish and shellfish, they do it accurately and they serve it with charm. Cod with stilton is an innovative dish, but there are classics aplenty: lemon sole with mustard beurre blanc; oysters pearl of the Foyle; john dory with anchovies; haddock florentine.

County Dublin

DUBLIN
Bang Café ★
11 Merrion Row, Dublin 2 (01 6760898/ www.bangrestaurant.com). **Lunch served** 12.30-3pm Mon-Sat. **Dinner served** 6-10.30pm Mon-Wed; 6-11pm Thur-Sat. **Main courses** €10.55-€23.95. **Credit** AmEx, MC, V.

All that modern food that so many restaurants do badly – the fig and prosciutto salad; the cod in beer

batter; the crème brûlée? Well, in the tiny but perfectly formed Bang, Lorcan Gribbin and his team do that sort of food to perfection. In fact, they elevate it to a modest glory by treating their ingredients, their own work and their customers with such respect. Bangers and mash with an onion gravy is a pure thrill. Bang is now one of the key Dublin city centre destinations, and drop-dead cool to boot.

Chapter One

18-19 Parnell Square, Dublin 1 (01 8732266/ www.chapteronerestaurant.com). **Lunch served** 12.30-2.30pm Tue-Fri. **Dinner served** 6-10.30pm Tue-Sat. **Set lunch** €24.50 2 courses, €27.50 3 courses. **Set dinner** (6-7pm) €27 3 courses; €28.50 3 courses. **Credit** AmEx, DC, MC, V.
Ross Lewis has worked away patiently during the last decade, establishing his reputation as master chef of Dublin's northside, further refining his distinctly Irish cooking, building a crack team around him, and making Chapter One one of the city's most reliable restaurants. Expect the unexpected from this intelligent cook. Expect braised venison to have an intriguing chocolate sauce; expect a strawberry confiture with the winningly refulgent ardrahan cheese from North Cork; expect a little foie gras sausage with pheasant.

Dish

146 Upper Leeson Street, Dublin 4 (01 6642135). **Lunch served** noon-4pm, **dinner served** 6-11pm daily. **Main courses** €15-€26. **Credit** AmEx, DC, MC, V.
Everything about Dish, from its splendidly succinct title to the excellent food and service, is trimmed, modest, efficient, sleek. Everything works, from the fine cocktails to the well-mannered, contemporary cooking from Gerard Foote, with its easy Mediterranean wanderings: Basque fish soup with tomato, saffron and chilli is as comfortably achieved as roast loin of kassler with mustard mash, apple relish and a sharp calvados jus; seared salmon with asparagus is as flavourful as lamb cutlets with minted pea purée, or superb organic beef with fondant potato; vanilla panna cotta is a typically ace dessert. The lovely room and polite service make this a favoured haunt.

L'Ecrivain ★

109 Lower Baggot Street, Dublin 2 (01 6611919/ www.lecrivain.com). **Lunch served** noon-2pm Mon-Fri. **Dinner served** 7-11pm Mon-Sat. **Main courses** €29-€36. **Set lunch** €30 2 courses, €35 3 courses. **Set dinner** €57.50 3 courses. **Credit** AmEx, MC, V.
Derry Clarke has become the pre-eminent Dublin chef. He's done it by being a very open individual, generous with his time and his talents, and by steadily and surely honing and refining a modern cooking style which takes classic dishes and gives them a very Clarkeian twist. He will pair quail with black pudding and braised lettuce, and make that trio seem like they were made for one another. This ability to find synergies of flavour makes for cooking that is supremely satisfying. L'Ecrivain also offers one of the very best dining rooms in the capital.

The Elephant & Castle

18-19 Temple Bar, Dublin 2 (01 6793121). **Breakfast served** 8-11.30am Mon-Fri. **Brunch served** 10.30am-5pm Sat; noon-5pm Sun. **Dinner served** 5-11.30pm Sat, Sun. **Main courses** €7.50-€22.95. **Credit** AmEx, DC, MC, V.
The E&C is the original Temple Bar institution, and while it is surrounded by indifferent eateries of every hue and cry, this stalwart continues to deliver. Good food is produced throughout the day, from great breakfast waffles to the must-have spicy chicken wings that made the restaurant's reputation back in the late 1980s. Indeed, for many folk, a visit to the E&C must involve a sticky encounter with that basket of wings and its splendid accompaniments of crunchy celery and cool yoghurt dipping sauce. But the pastas are equally fine, the savoury cooking reliable, and the energy in the room is palpable.

Halo ★

The Morrison Hotel, Ormond Quay, Dublin 1 (01 8872421/www.morrisonhotel.ie). **Lunch served** 12.30-2.30pm, **dinner served** 7-10.30pm daily. **Main courses** €24-€36. **Set lunch** €25 2 courses, €29 3 courses. **Set dinner** €35 2 courses, €38 3 courses. **Credit** AmEx, DC, MC, V.
Head chef Jean-Michel Poulot and his team are cooking some of the most exciting food you can eat in Dublin. Everything they create, right from the stupendous white bread rolls through to dazzling desserts, is touched with culinary magic. Add in a John Rocha-designed room, a great service team and excellent value, and Halo shines all round. The food is beautifully presented, in a style that borrows from Japan but focuses on gutsy succulence. A cappuccino of Dublin Bay prawns is intense yet light, sea bass with braised scallions and yam mash works perfectly. Then there are the desserts: try their version of the Dublin Spire, a foot-tall chocolate tower stuffed with lime mascarpone.

Jacob's Ladder

4-5 Nassau Street, Dublin 2 (01 6703865/ www.jacobsladder.ie). **Lunch served** 12.30-2.30pm, **dinner served** 6-10pm Tue-Sat. **Main courses** €29. **Set dinner** €32 3 courses. **Credit** AmEx, DC, MC, V.
Adrian Roche, chef-patron of Jacob's Ladder, is an imaginative and distinctive chef, who remains one of the best-kept secrets of Dublin. A sauce of orange and rhubarb with salmon is beautifully realised. He makes a pesto of celery to pair with tuna, he matches crisp fritters of prune and apricot to partner terrine of foie gras, and he moves into culinary overdrive with desserts such as strawberries with a sweet tomato and black olive confit and a basil sorbet. Cooking this complex is almost mathematical in its rigour, but Roche never overworks his food: flavours are pure, tastes aren't tortured. A great destination.

Halo

The Mermaid Café ★

69-70 Dame Street, Dublin 2 (01 6708236/
www.mermaid.ie). **Lunch served** 12.30-2.30pm
Mon-Sat. **Brunch served** noon-3pm Sun. **Dinner
served** 6-11pm Mon-Sat; 6-9pm Sun. **Main courses**
€18.95-€29.95. **Set lunch** (Mon-Sat) €14.95 1 course,
€18.95 2 courses, €22.95 3 courses. **Set dinner**
(6-7.15pm) €30 2 courses. **Credit** MC, V.
The Mermaid is one of the hottest and most
distinctive restaurants in Ireland, and it's the star of
Temple Bar. Head chef Temple Garner's cooking
style shines through in dishes such as an arrestingly
tart salad of confit fennel with rocket, orange and
feta; perfect beef skewers with horseradish cream,
char-grilled tuna with olive and caper ratatouille;
and a stonking venison stew with mustard mash.
Great cooking, fantastic value, and the staff are as
singular as it gets.

O'Connell's ★

Merrion Road, Ballsbridge, Dublin 4 (01 6473304/
www.oconnellsballsbridge.com). **Lunch served**
12.30-2.30pm Mon-Sat; 12.30-3pm Sun. **Dinner
served** 6-10.30pm Mon-Sat; 6-9.30pm Sun. **Main
courses** €16.45-€18.95. **Set dinner** €25 3 courses.
Credit AmEx, DC, MC, V.
What's the secret of success of Tom O'Connell's

bustling basement brasserie? Great vegetables.
Mighty vegetables. Brilliant roast potatoes. Sweet
carrots. Great turnips. Yep, that's right: great
turnips. When that dish of vegetables arrives with
your main courses, it is time to celebrate, time to get
stuck in. Tom O'Connell and his crew consider every
single detail of this great room, from service to
wines, from value – the value for money is the best
in the city – all the way down to getting the very
best out of those turnips. It's loud, busy, fun and
simply brilliant.

101 Talbot

101 Talbot Street, Dublin 1 (01 8745011).
Dinner served 5-11pm Tue-Sat. **Main courses**
€10-€19. **Set dinner** (5-8pm) €20 2 courses. **Credit**
AmEx, MC, V.
The evergreen 101 is one of the most bustling rooms
in the city. Clamber up the stairs to this big, square
eating arena, push back the door and the energy of
the place hits you smack in the face. It's irresistible.
101 is one of the great creations of Dublin dining,
and that energy is created by the generosity of the
staff, their hard work, their joie de vivre. Along with
the comfort cooking and the good wines, you can't
resist any part of 101. Excellent vegetarian cooking

One Pico

5-6 Molesworth Place, Schoolhouse Lane,
Dublin 2 (01 6760300/www.onepico.com). **Lunch
served** 12.30-2.30pm, **dinner served** 6-10.30pm
Mon-Sat. **Main courses** €19-€29. **Set dinner**
(6-6.30pm) €27 2 courses, €35 3 courses. **Credit**
AmEx, DC, MC, V.

Eamonn O'Reilly's grown-up and glamorous One
Pico is just the sort of space that every capital city
needs. You can come here to do business at
lunchtime; you can return in the evening to smooch
with your beloved; you can enjoy the room as a
visitor to the city. The food is kind of fussy – sauce
vierge is curried; béarnaise with salmon has red
onions; leek and saffron risotto has a poached egg.
But O'Reilly makes this complexity work and the
food is always as satisfying as it is intriguing. The
room is one of the best in the city, and prices are very
keen for the quality of the ingredients and slickness
of the service.

The Tea Room

The Clarence Hotel, 6-8 Wellington Quay,
Dublin 2 (01 4070800/www.theclarence.ie).
Lunch served 12.30-3pm Mon-Fri; noon-3pm
Sun. **Dinner served** 6.30-10.45pm daily.
Set lunch €24 2 courses, €28.50 3 courses.
Set dinner €41.50 2 courses, €52.50 3 courses.
Credit AmEx, DC, MC, V.

Everything about the Clarence Hotel is blue-chip
cool, particularly the glorious, intelligent cooking
which Antony Ely and his crew produce in the
knock-out luxury of the dining room. Like the room
itself, Ely's cooking is stylish, but never overdone.
Here is a chef who will cook such maternal fare as
braised neck of lamb with creamed potatoes, baby
carrots and button mushrooms. Value for money
here is truly exceptional, and the Tea Room is one
of the most romantic spots you will find in the city:
a big date restaurant.

Thornton's

128 St Stephen's Green, Dublin 2 (01 4787008/
www.thorntons.com). **Lunch served** 12.15-
2.30pm, **dinner served** 7-10.30pm Tue-Sat.
Main courses €49. **Set lunch** €30 2 courses,
€40 3 courses. **Set dinner** €65 5 courses. **Credit**
AmEx, DC, MC, V.

Prices are high in Kevin Thornton's eponymous
restaurant, situated up in the Fitzwilliam Hotel on
St Stephen's Green in the heart of the city. Indeed,
the size of the bill you can find yourself holding,
should you stray into the à la carte, has become a
staple of city lore. Is it worth it? The answer is
unequivocally yes. Thornton's is an experience
unlike any other, a place where the chef and his crew
aim for the stars. Every detail in the simplest things,
such as the array of vegetables paired with black leg
chicken, or the choron sauce with scallops and the
little shot of squid ink, is almost multi-dimensional
in its impact: amazing to look at, extraordinary to
eat, impressive to ponder. And the set menus do
offer fine value.

DUN LAOGHAIRE

Cavistons ★

59 Glasthule Road, Sandycove, Dun Laoghaire,
Co Dublin (01 2809245/www.cavistons.com).
Lunch served noon-1.30pm, 1.30-3pm, 3-5pm daily.
Main courses €13-€28. **Credit** AmEx, DC, MC, V.

Most restaurateurs are happy with one lunchtime
service. In Cavistons they do not one, not two, but
three services of lunch. Six days a week equals 18
lunch services, and 18 squadrons of happy fish
lovers who bless the day the Caviston brothers
decided to start cooking the fish the family shop had
been selling for decades. Noel Cusack mans the
stoves, and the secret of their success lies in cooking
the freshest fish they can get: crab claws in tempura
batter; fresh haddock with toothy tartare; lobster
with garlic and herb butter; the trademark seafood
pie; char-grilled swordfish with mojo picon; salad of
Boston shrimps.

County Galway

BALLINAFAD

Ballynahinch Castle

Recess, Ballinafad, Co Galway (095 31006/
www.ballynahinch-castle.com). **Lunch served**
12.30-3pm, **dinner served** 6.30-9pm daily. **Main
courses** €30. **Set dinner** €45 5 courses. **Credit**
AmEx, DC, MC, V.

Ballynahinch Castle is grand, gracious and rather
forbidding. But step inside and the warmth of the
welcome, and the lack of pretension, is instantly
winning. The rich, the not so rich, the young and the
old all feel at home thanks to manager Patrick
O'Flaherty's bonhomie, and chef Robert Webster's
fine cooking. Mr Webster cooks the classics with
panache: rod-caught salmon with hollandaise; fillet
of beef with confit of shallots; Cleggan lobster with
garlic and herb butter; risotto of spring vegetables
– all of it judged just right by a cook who shows
respect for his ingredients. The dining room is
swooningly romantic.

CLIFDEN

High Moors ★

Dooneen, Clifden, Co Galway (095 21342).
Dinner served 7-9.30pm Fri-Sun. **Main courses**
€20-€25. **Set dinner** €35 3 courses. **Credit**
AmEx, MC, V.

Hugh and Eileen Griffin's restaurant is situated in
the sitting room of their bungalow. It's an unusual
place which takes the concept of 'home-grown' to
new heights. Hugh serves the food at dinner, but also
grows most of the vegetables and fruits in his
polytunnel and vegetable patch. Eileen cooks on the
Aga in her neat kitchen – dreamy and delicious
domestic cooking brought to a new nobility: terrific
herb-stuffed mussels; local Connemara lamb as a
sweet-roasted loin; their trademark spicy lamb

shanks or Carna Bay scallops with a basil sauce. And while you think you will never eat that big dish of vegetables, see if there isn't so much as a pea pod left when the plates are lifted.

The Signal

Station House, Clifden, Co Galway (095 22946). **Dinner served** 6.30-9.30pm Wed-Sun. **Main courses** €20-€26. **Set dinner** €39 4 courses. **Credit** MC, V.

Chef-proprietor Stefan Matz leaves the running of his upstairs restaurant to his team while he holds down the job of head chef in the posh Ashford Castle, a little further north in Cong, County Mayo. But the Signal works like clockwork and is *the* destination address in pretty Clifden. Matz's signature of very light, highly flavoured cooking is triumphant: a lovely tartlet of own-smoked duck breast is sharpened with a raspberry vinegar; prawn tails are wrapped in fine strands of potato and served with fresh asparagus; turbot has smoked oysters and the strong scent of wild mushrooms. Vegetarian choices are always imaginative, and while the Signal is not cheap, prices are fair.

GALWAY

Goya's

2-3 Kirwan's Lane, Galway, Co Galway (091 567010/www.goyas.ie). **Food served** 9.30am-6pm, **lunch served** 12.30-3pm Mon-Sat. **Main courses** €3.65-€7.75. **Credit** MC, V.

Emer Murray is one of the very best patissiers in Ireland, and for many Goya's is the ultimate destination for a sweet fix: just try those lemon madeleines, the poppyseed and blueberry muffins, the best-ever carrot cake. But the savoury cooking here during the day is just as accomplished. Ms Murray makes a mean bowl of celery and sage soup, her quiche Lorraine shows just why the dish became a classic, and the char-grilled Mediterranean pie is as good as it gets. The room is elegant, the staff are hip-as-it-gets Galway girls, and the punters themselves cool Galwegians.

Nimmo's

Long Walk, Spanish Arch, Galway, Co Galway (091 561114). **Lunch served** 1-3.30pm Fri-Sat. **Dinner served** 6-10pm Tue-Sun. **Main courses** €10-€21. **Credit** MC, V.

In a city that remains more devoted to drinking than eating, Harriet Leander's funky restaurant down by the Spanish Arch offers the sort of spontaneous, creative cookery that is all too rare. Galwegians tend to gather in the wine bar downstairs, preferring this gadabout space to the slightly more formal upstairs. But – this being Galway – what unifies Nimmo's is a very distinct bohemianism. Bistro classics such as coq au vin and boeuf bourguignon are the staples they produce with ease, but they also make a fine fish soup, and everything seems to have half an eye on matching to perfection some particular bottle from the fine wine list. Bohemian bliss.

County Kerry

DINGLE

The Chart House

The Mall, Dingle, Co Kerry (066 9152255/ www.charthousedingle.com). **Dinner served** 6.30-9.45pm Wed-Mon; *July-Sept* 6.30-9.45pm daily. Closed 8 Jan-16 Feb. **Main courses** €14.75-€24.95. **Set dinner** €30 2 courses. **Credit** MC, V.

Jim McCarthy's Chart House restaurant is one of those spaces and places you dream about finding. A simple, stone-clad cottage, at the edge of the road just as you drive into Dingle, it's the sort of room in which you want to kick off your shoes. And Mr McCarthy takes care of everyone in such a witty way, always focused on making sure everyone has a great time. The cooking is, once again, the stuff of dreams: local Annascaul black pudding; roasted cod with basil mash; fillet of pork with brandied apricots. Feel-good food in a feel-good place.

KENMARE

Mulcahy's

16 Henry Street, Kenmare, Co Kerry (064 42383/ www.mulcahys.com). **Dinner served** 6-10pm Wed-Mon. Closed 10 Nov-10 Dec; 10 Jan-10 Feb. **Main courses** €14.95-€27. **Set dinner** €55 5 courses. **Credit** DC, MC, V.

Fusion cooking and a postmodern room – clashing colours, holes in the wall, waves of candles – might sound a bit like a step too far, but Bruce Mulcahy's restaurant is a place of culinary discipline. It would have to be to succeed in Kenmare, a town with the highest culinary standards in Ireland. The fusion notes arrive with dishes such as scallops with red grapes and leeks, or a green tea anglaise with panna cotta. There are also more conventional dishes such as john dory with a mussel cream or crispy duck confit. Don't miss the desserts, though: the French lemon tart is as good as it gets. Professional service and fair prices complete the picture.

Packie's Food & Wine

Henry Street, Kenmare, Co Kerry (064 41508). **Dinner served** 6-10pm Mon-Sat. Closed Jan-Feb. **Main courses** €15-€27. **Credit** AmEx, DC, MC, V.

Packie's is one of the benchmark Irish restaurants, a room where for more than 40 years Maura Foley cooked some of the most delicious – and deliciously simple – fish and shellfish you could enjoy in these islands. Martin Hallissey has now assumed charge of the kitchens, following a long tenure working alongside Mrs Foley, so it's business as usual with sparklingly fresh Atlantic fish still holding sway: smoked cod fish cakes; plaice with coriander, orange and lime butter; monkfish with chermoula; steamed lobster. Meanwhile, starters and desserts are marvellously old-fashioned – especially dishes such as potato cakes with garlic butter or their memorable trifle. Lovely room, excellent service.

Ireland

KILLARNEY

The Killarney Park Hotel ★

Kenmare Place, Killarney, Co Kerry (064 35555/ www.killarneyparkhotel.ie). **Breakfast served** 7.30-10am Mon-Fri; 8-11am Sat, Sun. **Meals served** *Bar* 12.30-9pm daily. **Dinner served** *Restaurant* 7-9.30pm daily. **Main courses** *Bar* €8-€17.50; *Restaurant* €28. **Set dinner** €50 5 courses. **Credit** AmEx, MC, V.

The Killarney Park has a claim to being the best run hotel in Ireland. The entire place gleams and the cooking is sparkling too. Both the food served in the bar (where the locals all head) and the restaurant shows real panache. Asparagus tips with sauce gribiche, and a risotto of pea and crab with a base of shellfish bisque are fine starters, while their delicacy is a stark contrast to the ruddiness of roast stuffed saddle of rabbit or herb-crusted canon of lamb, which has some ace potato dumplings to set off the sweetness with something starchy. The sheer elegance of the food, right through to the superb chocolate desserts, is marked with a confident understatement that is the hallmark of this place.

TRALEE

Restaurant David Norris

Ivy House, Ivy Terrace, Tralee, Co Kerry (066 7185654). **Dinner served** 6-10pm Tue-Sat. **Main courses** €15-€26. **Credit** AmEx, MC, V.

David Norris has made a big splash since coming back to his home town and creating this notable eating room in Tralee. His cooking has a precision and a depth of experience that makes it both impressive and enjoyable. They try extra hard in this restaurant, and it really does show: this is a crew working at full tilt. So relish that splendid home-made fettuccine with wild mushrooms and onion velouté, enjoy the chilli-roasted pineapple with duck confit, savour the exactitude of Kerry beef with colcannon, admire the care of braised summer vegetables with chicken, and don't miss those desserts. Value for money is very good indeed.

County Kilkenny

KILKENNY

Fleva

84 High Street, Kilkenny, Co Kilkenny (056 70021). **Lunch served** 12.30-3.30pm Tue-Sat; 12.30-4pm Sun. **Dinner served** 6-10pm Tue-Fri, Sun; 6-10.30pm Sat. **Main courses** €16.50-€24. **Set lunch** (Tue-Fri) €14.50 2 courses, €17.50 3 courses. **Set dinner** (Mon-Thur, Sun) €28.50 3 courses. **Credit** AmEx, MC, V.

Michael Mee's menus in the first-floor Fleva are an eclectic read: Cajun spiced chicken, Shanghai noodles, monkfish wrapped in Parma ham, Asian duck – culinary postcards from a global tour. But Mee's skill pulls these diverse dishes together and

makes them work successfully. If he has a particular strength, it is game cooking: Canadian goose with sliced potatoes is delicious; warm slices of pigeon breast with mango is very fine indeed. All of which makes Fleva a good choice for wholesome winter dining. But the Mediterranean touches, such as monkfish with black olive tapenade, are no less deft. It's a comfortable room, demurely lit by candles and indirect lighting, and value for money is very keen.

Zuni ★

26 Patrick Street, Kilkenny, Co Kilkenny (056 7723999/www.zuni.ie). **Lunch served** 12.30-2.30pm Tue-Sun. **Dinner served** 6.30-9.30pm daily. **Main courses** €17-€25. **Set dinner** (Mon-Thur, Sun) €30 4 courses. **Credit** AmEx, MC, V.

Kilkenny has always had a certain confident cosmopolitanism about it, and the super-stylish Zuni is the Kilkenny restaurant that shows that confidence off better than anywhere else. Maria Raftery's elegant and savvy cooking lifts such dishes as Moroccan lamb shank or chicken caesar salad. Gutsy and generous, they hit the spot time after time. At weekends, the energy in the room is intoxicating and Zuni has been one of the most impressive new arrivals in Irish hospitality.

County Leitrim

CARRICK-ON-SHANNON

The Oarsman

Bridge Street, Carrick-on-Shannon, Co Leitrim (078 21733/www.theoarsman.com). **Lunch served** noon-3.30pm Mon-Wed; noon-2.30pm Thur-Sat. **Dinner served** 7-9.30pm Thur-Sat. **Main courses** €17-€23. **Credit** MC, V.

Brothers Conor and Ronan Maher have created *the* destination address in Leitrim with this fine old pub. There is splendid gastropub cooking during the day – vegetable rice with beef stroganoff, marinated chicken salad, grilled brie and smoked bacon on own-made brown bread, minced beef with cumin and cayenne in pitta – and at weekends they open the upstairs for some more serious cooking: terrine of smoked chicken, bacon and savoy cabbage; corn-fed chicken with red pimento mousseline; loin of venison with morel stuffing; sirloin of beef with potato dauphinoise. Excellent staff are powering the Oarsman steadily.

County Limerick

ABBEYFEALE

Whyte's on the Square

The Square, Abbeyfeale, Co Limerick (068 32917). **Dinner served** 4-9pm Wed-Sun. **Main courses** €10.95-€25. **Credit** MC, V.

They are really putting out some fantastic food in Whyte's. Flavours are totally precise, beautifully in tune with one another, the work of a really smart

La Marine. *See p369.*

team. That salmon, cod and mussel fish cake with chive hollandaise? Knockout food, superbly achieved. Lamb's liver with champ and a brown onion gravy? This is the dish that gives offal a new respectability. Lemon tart with Thai basil cream? Really excellent. Whyte's is a dynamic arrival, and a blessing for Abbeyfeale: everyone driving the main road down to Kerry should make sure this is their lunchtime destination.

ADARE

The Wild Geese ★

Main Street, Adare, Co Limerick (061 396451/ www.wild-geese.com). **Lunch served** 12.30-2.30pm Sun. **Dinner served** 6.30-10pm Tue-Sun. **Main courses** €25. **Set lunch** €19 2 courses, €24 3 courses. **Set dinner** €30 2 courses, €34 3 courses. **Credit** AmEx, DC, MC, V.

Is this the prettiest restaurant in Ireland? It's certainly every bit as pretty as its location, in exquisite Adare, and owners David Foley and Julie Randles manage the feat of making sure everything they do in this gorgeous space chimes with a precise aesthetic. Ms Randles' service is apt, and Mr Foley's cooking assured. The lavishly described cooking – ravioli of crab meat and fine herbs served on a barigoule of jerusalem artichoke, lemon and thyme; grilled fillet of blackened salmon served on roasted peppers and rice noodles with a mango and ginger dressing – is simpler than it sounds, and is as delicious as it is descriptive. This is great modern Irish cooking.

LIMERICK

Copper & Spice

2 Cornmarket Row, Limerick, Co Limerick (061 313620). **Dinner served** 5-10.30pm Mon-Sat. **Main courses** €8.50-€16. **Set dinner** (Mon-Wed) €19 3 courses. **Credit** AmEx, MC, V.

Indian restaurants in Ireland compromise their cooking – 'to suit the Irish palate', they will tell you. Brian and Seema Conroy's cooking makes no such compromises. Copper & Spice is the real thing, Indian food in all its multi-faceted glory: complex, subtle, delicate, fiery, intense. Keema matar – minced lamb with tomatoes, peas, yoghurt and spices – is a fine dish, while the muttar paneer, using own-made cheese in a curry with peas, is vegetarian heaven. Unusually, the Thai dishes are equally expert, thanks to the fact that a Thai chef works alongside Mrs Conroy in the kitchen. The room is swish and modern. All in all, Copper & Spice is the best thing to have happened to Limerick in yonks.

LISTOWEL

Allo's

41 Church Street, Listowel, Co Kerry (068 22880). **Meals served** noon-7pm Tue-Sat. **Dinner served** 7-9pm Tue-Fri. **Main courses** €15.50-€26.50. **Set dinner** (Thur) €22.50 3 courses. **Credit** AmEx, MC, V.

Ireland

Allo's is one of the loveliest bars in Ireland, and with Helen Mullane taking care of service and head chef Theo Lynch in charge of the kitchen, this beautiful bar also produces some pretty perfect food. Allo's was the gastropub before gastropubs were ever thought of, so the food is informal but serious and well crafted: garganelli pasta with an excellent herb and garlic sausage from Tralee and a light mustard cream; lovely salmon and mussel potato cake with tarragon hollandaise; breast of duck with roast onion mash; beef fillet with sweet potato chips; seared tuna with bok choi, all delivered with confident panache.

County Monaghan

CARRICKMACROSS

Nuremore Restaurant

Nuremore Hotel, Carrickmacross, Co Monaghan (042 9661438/www.nuremore.com). **Lunch served** 12.30-2.30pm Mon-Fri, Sun. **Dinner served** 6.30-9.30pm Mon-Sat; 6.30-8.45pm Sun. **Set lunch** (Mon-Fri) €19.50 2 courses, €25 3 courses; (Sun) €28 4 courses. **Set dinner** €42.50 5 courses. **Credit** AmEx, DC, MC, V.

Ray McArdle is one of the most ambitious young chefs in Ireland. He is already garnering accolades for his cooking in Julie Gilhooly's grand Nuremore Hotel, where he is allowed the luxury of cooking only for the restaurant. The food is seriously cheffy, but not too self-indulgent. The menus are rich with rich ingredients – truffles, foie gras, lobster, Madeira, game birds – but Ray McArdle's skill can take even a simple thing like braised rabbit and wild mushrooms and make it unforgettable. Value for money is exceptional considering the quality of the ingredients and the distinctiveness of the cooking.

GLASLOUGH

Castle Leslie

Castle Leslie, Glaslough, Co Monaghan (047 88109/www.castleleslie.com). **Dinner served** 6.30-9.30pm daily. **Set dinner** €48 5 courses. **Credit** MC, V.

Everything is oversize and oversize is the word for Castle Leslie's reputation these days, ever since Paul McCartney had his wedding reception here and the word about this behemoth of a country house went all around the world. The man carrying that reputation is chef Noel McMeel, and the reputation is in good hands. McMeel is one of Ireland's most original cooks, making delicate magic with a little gateau of crab cakes with pickled beetroot and spiced couscous, making Monaghan fillet of beef with spring onion mash sublime. He cooks an imaginative vegetarian menu too, with signature dishes such as spinach bavarois with woodland mushrooms or aubergine gateau with black pepper tuile. Strange place. Great food.

County Tipperary

BALLINDERRY

Brocka on the Water ★

Kilgarvan Quay, Ballinderry, Co Tipperary (067 22038). **Dinner served** 6.30-9pm Mon-Sat by appointment only. **Main courses** €25. **Set dinner** €40 3 courses. **No credit cards.**

Regulars in Anne and Anthony Gernon's gorgeous restaurant not only have favourite tables, they also have favourite cutlery and crockery. Home from home; that's Brocka. And with Anne's mum, Nancy, cooking up a storm, this beautiful restaurant serves food with a sense of style all its own: soulful winter vegetable soup with a hint of mint; smoked seafood platter with a Mediterranean marinade; sea bass stuffed then baked and served with a dill hollandaise; superb pork medallions in a herb crust with a wholegrain mustard sauce; cracking desserts. It's a terrific location beside the lake, and an unforgettable experience all round.

CASHEL

Chez Hans

Moor Lane, Cashel, Co Tipperary (062 61177). **Dinner served** 6-10pm Tue-Sat. **Main courses** €27-€35. **Set dinner** (6-7.30pm) €23 2 courses, €29 3 courses; (7.30-10pm) €45 3 courses. **Credit** DC, MC, V.

Chez Hans is so much a part of the culinary landscape of Ireland – more than 30 years old and counting – that it is easy to take for granted the superb cooking Jason Matthiae and his crew put out. But this isn't cooking to be taken for granted: starters such as risotto of wild mushrooms with duckling and chorizo or tagliatelle of spinach with chives, smoked salmon and crab meat are powerful showcases of flavour, subtlety, earthiness and downright smart cookery. And what a sweet ending to the evening a steamed chocolate pudding with white chocolate ice-cream delivers. The room is one of the very best, and while service could be a tad more affable, Chez Hans remains a prime destination.

Legends

The Kiln, Cashel, Co Tipperary (062 61292/ www.legendsguesthouse.com). **Dinner served** 6.30-9.30pm Tue-Sat. **Main courses** €22-€30. **Set dinner** €43 3 courses. **Credit** AmEx, MC, V.

Michael O'Neill is a pro, a cook with deep background, acres of experience, a true journeyman professional. Pick anything off his menus in Legends – it doesn't matter if it's crème brûlée or rabbit stuffed with mushrooms – and what you will get, and what you will enjoy, is a dish which is measured, confident, smart, pleasing, and perfectly understood. No histrionics, no archfulness, no silliness, just cracking food, food that defines the art and craft of the professional chef, served with professional grace. It is just as well that Mr O'Neill

Avoca. *See p369.*

is so good, because he has some competition: Legends is perched right under the Rock of Cashel. Forget the big stone: once the food arrives, there is only one attraction in this town.

County Waterford

CAPPOQUÌN

Richmond House

Cappoquin, Co Waterford (058 54278/www.richmond house.net). **Dinner served** *summer* 7-9pm daily. *Winter* 7-9pm Mon-Sat. **Set dinner** €45 5 courses. **Credit** AmEx, DC, MC, V.

Richmond House looks like a comfortable but unremarkable old country home. But Richmond's secret lies in the fact that Paul Deevy is currently knocking out some of the best country house cooking in Ireland. Cassoulet of monkfish and Rossmore mussels is allied with coconut milk; fillets of brill with butternut squash and tartare sauce are hopping with flavour. Main courses are a showcase for meat cookery of the highest class: Waterford lamb with own-made mint jelly and Puy lentils; Waterford fillet of beef with roast shallots and béarnaise. Everything cooked here shows the signature of a mature, thoughtful man who enjoys his work almost as much as you do.

DUNGARVAN

The Tannery ★

10 Quay Street, Dungarvan, Co Waterford (058 45420/www.tannery.ie). **Lunch served** 12.30-2.15pm Tue-Fri, Sun. **Dinner served** 6.30-9.30pm Tue-Sat. **Main courses** €20-€28. **Set dinner** (6.30-7.30pm) €25 3 courses. **Credit** AmEx, DC, MC, V.
You need courage to go against the grain of contemporary cooking, but Paul Flynn has not only the courage to cook his own way, he has a confidence born of experience. Eating in the Tannery offers a culinary treat that takes you from the cutting-edge all the way through cooking's back pages. He cooks in an old-fashioned way, despite the glamour and minimalist style of this lovely room. Grilled ox tongue with potato terrine; amazing tournedos of slow-cooked pork with colcannon and a French onion broth; rump steak with creamed peas; warm poached apple with mincemeat ice-cream. All rendered in a very convincing manner.

LISMORE

Buggy's Glencairn Inn ★

Glencairn, nr Lismore, Co Waterford (058 56232/ www.lismore.com). **Dinner served** 7.30-9pm daily. **Main courses** €19.95. **Credit** MC, V.
Ken and Cathleen Buggy's country inn is like something out of a dream: picture-postcard pretty, in the middle of nowhere, an oasis of good food, great comfort and great craic. Mr Buggy is a supremely witty man, and his cooking is as free-form as his sense of humour. He likes to cook braises and stews, he likes to make crisp salads, and he likes to pan-fry fish. All of these things he does superbly. His food tastes true and natural, thanks to knowing when to leave things well alone. And if you get lucky and eat here on a night when he does make them, Mr Buggy makes the best chips you have ever eaten. A dreamy, magical little inn.

TRAMORE

Coast

Upper Branch Road, Tramore, Co Waterford (051 393646/www.coast.ie). **Lunch served** 1-3pm Sun. **Dinner served** 6.30-10.30pm Tue-Sat; *July, Aug, bank hols* 6.30-10.30pm Tue-Sun. **Main courses** €18.50-€26. **Set lunch** €24 3 courses. **Set dinner** (6.30-7pm) €26.50 3 courses. **Credit** AmEx, MC, V.
Tramore is one of those seaside resorts that seem to specialise in dreariness and rain, but Coast is pure gorgeous, one of the smartest, most comfortable restaurant spaces in Ireland. And Turlough McNamara and his team deliver with the food as well. Their smart take on prawn cocktail – the lettuce and shellfish sandwiched between thin slices of piquillo pepper, with more prawns resting on top – is a treat, but savoury mains such as perfect barbary duck with cassis sauce are just as confident

and handsome. Stir-fried vegetables could do with more consideration, but gorgeous desserts such as caramel meringues are right on the money.

WATERFORD

Bodéga!

54 John Street, Waterford, Co Waterford (051 844177/www.bodegawaterford.com). **Lunch served** noon-2.30pm Mon-Fri. **Dinner served** 6.30-9.30pm Mon, Tue; 6.30-10pm Wed, Thur; 6.30pm-12.30am Fri, Sat. **Main courses** €10-€20. **Credit** AmEx, MC, V.
Bodéga! is fun. Loud, cramped and sweaty fun. This is Waterford's party place. The staff will bring you menus: ignore them. In Bodéga! you eat the specials chalked on the blackboard, for this is where you find the real meat of this restaurant, and that meat is usually the fish dishes: sea bass with French beans and asparagus and a ratatouille sauce is superb; a fish medley offers salmon and cod, a crab ravioli and mussels. Desserts – chocolate soufflé or a fine crème brûlée – and espressos are good, and if some things can dip below the bar, you forgive them every time.

Dwyer's Restaurant

8 Mary Street, Waterford, Co Waterford (051 877478/www.dwyers.com). **Dinner served** 6-10pm Mon-Sat. **Main courses** €20.50-€27.50. **Set dinner** (6-7pm) €27.50 3 courses. **Credit** AmEx, DC, MC, V.
Martin Dwyer has been around for a fair few years now, but the flavour in his cooking seems more like the work of a kid newly intoxicated by food. His restaurant is stylish and comfortable, just the right sort of theatre for dishes that have a sophisticated rusticity. He likes the deep impact of dishes such as game terrine with caramelised red onions, or beautiful venison served with an expert celeriac mash, hip country cooking that you never tire of. But there is a finesse in the sweet cuisine that is unarguable: a lime tart or hazel-nut praline ice-cream with cinnamon sauce. Confident, experienced and calming, and proof that the old guys can mix it with the new kids.

County Westmeath

ATHLONE

Left Bank Bistro

Fry Place, Athlone, Co Westmeath (064 94446/ www.leftbankbistro.com). **Lunch served** noon-5pm, **dinner served** 5.30-9.30pm Tue-Sat. **Main courses** €18-€27. **Set dinner** (Tue-Fri) €21 2 courses, €25 3 courses. **Credit** AmEx, MC, V.
Annie and Mary's groovy bistro is the toast of the Midlands, a sleek, slick room that rocks with the energy of a kitchen and service team having a whale of a time. The cooking is simple, funky and moreish: Thai-spiced chicken with egg noodles; chicken with black turtle bean salsa; oysters baked with coconut and sweet chilli; grilled swordfish with tomato and

coriander salsa. But smart cooking and great service don't give the full picture of the Left Bank. It's the spontaneity and joie de vivre of this room that makes the place such a success.

County Wexford

ROSSLARE

La Marine ★
Kelly's Resort Hotel, Rosslare, Co Wexford (053 32114/www.kellys.ie). **Lunch served** 12.30-3pm, **dinner served** 6.30-9.30pm daily. Closed Dec-Feb. **Main courses** €15.95-€22. **Set lunch** (Sun) €21 3 courses. **Credit** AmEx, MC, V.

Eugene Callaghan's cooking has no pretentions: goodness is his aim, whether he is rustling up some moreish grub for kids – creamy seafood chowder; roast leg of lamb with creamed potato; chocolate and hazel-nut torte with vanilla ice-cream – or producing the serene and understated style of food for adults that allows him to bring to bear the trademark melding of flavours which he loves: rocket and bell pepper relish with almond-crusted goat's cheese; a fennel and orange compote with roast fillet of salmon; a fantastic coffee and cardamom crème brûlée. Allied with the unpretentious style of the place, La Marine is one of the most enjoyable rooms in which to eat in Ireland.

WEXFORD

Forde's Restaurant
The Crescent, Wexford, Co Wexford (053 23832). **Lunch served** noon-6pm Sun. **Dinner served** 6-10pm daily. **Main courses** €15-€25.50. **Set dinner** (6-7pm) €22 2 courses. **Credit** AmEx, MC, V.

Liam Forde's smart restaurant formula, mixing a calm and very atmospheric dining room with its bistro-like style, but serving classical cooking with imaginative twists, pulls in the diners big time. This is a busy and successful first-floor operation, and very much the key Wexford town destination. Forde's cooking can really hit the spot. Dublin Bay prawns with roasted garlic and lovage are a pure sensation; sirloin with garlic butter is deeply satisfying; beignets of fresh crab meat with ginger and basil hit the spot. The wine list is imaginative and good value for money, and service is fleet and sociable. You'll be back.

County Wicklow

AUGHRIM

The Strawberry Tree
Brook Lodge, Macreddin, Co Wicklow (040 236444/ www.brooklodge.com). **Lunch served** 1-7pm Sun. **Dinner served** 7-10pm Mon-Sat. **Set lunch** €30 4 courses. **Set dinner** €48 5 courses. **Credit** AmEx, DC, MC, V.

Housed in the new and stylish Brook Lodge Hotel, the Strawberry Tree offers a menu devoted to wild and organic foods, and it also offers a dazzlingly romantic room in which to swoon with your date as you admire the excellent cooking of chef Frederic Souty. Wild rabbit comes with wild mushroom risotto and rich thyme and red wine gravy; monkfish is wrapped in dilisk seaweed and served with gently poached fennel; venison chops have a ruddy purée of swedes and roasted vegetables. It's smart, optimistic cooking with vivid, dramatic flavours thanks to the use of great ingredients, and the hotel itself, with its refined comfort, is the new chill-out capital of County Wicklow.

DUNLAVIN

The Grangecon Café ★
Grangecon, nr Dunlavin, Co Wicklow (045 403982). **Meals served** 10am-5.30pm Tue-Sat. **Prices** €1.85-€7.95. **No credit cards**.

The Grangecon Café has two tables. That's it. And by the look of them, they must have set owners Richard and Jenny Street back, oh, at least €30. For the pair, that is. Does anyone care? Do they, hell. You come to Grangecon to eat Mrs Street's sublime cookery. Start with cannellini bean soup with cavalo nero, move on to their awesome potato and parsley pie, then have a piece of pecan pie with good coffee to finish. The Grangecon Café is not just simple: it's simply amazing. The only problem is booking one of those two tables.

KILMACANOGE

Avoca ★ ★
Kilmacanoge, Co Wicklow (012 867466/www.avoca.ie). **Meals served** 9.30am-5pm Mon-Fri; 10am-5pm Sat; 10am-5.30pm Sun. **Main courses** €9.45. **Credit** AmEx, DC, MC, V.

There are several Avoca shops throughout the Republic, and they produce good food for more people every day than any other operation in Ireland. The shops also sell lots of other stuff – such as dinky garden gear, cute kids' fashions, smart designer foods – but many devotees of the Avoca cuisine never look at anything other than the menus. The cooking here is true, spirited and imaginative, though it reads simply enough: roast tomato soup with pesto; broccoli and chicken gratin; shepherd's pie; Santa Fe pork. But the enormous amount of care and precision shown by this inspiring crew mean that everything they produce is delicious. This is a don't-miss-it destination.

Also in the area
Avoca Suffolk Street, Dublin (01 6726019); **Avoca** Powerscourt, Enniskerry, Co Wicklow (012 046070); **Avoca** Avoca Village, Co Wicklow (040 235105); **Avoca** Moll's Gap, Co Kerry (064 34720); **Wagamama** South King Street, Dublin 2 (01 478 2152).

Advertisers' Index

Please refer to relevant sections for
addresses/ telephone numbers

Index

A-Z Index

Index

Index

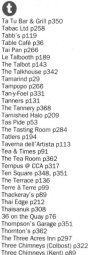
Index

Subject Index

Ales, real
The best food pubs for **p281**
Berks: George & Dragon p153, Swan Inn p152; *Bristol*: Cornubia p113; *Bucks*: Crooked Billet p158, Green Dragon p157; *Cambs*: Old Fire Engine p186; *Cornwall*: Springer Spaniel p123; *Cumbria*: Drunken Duck p244; *Derbys*: Chequers p214; *Devon*: Drewe Arms p124; *Dorset*: Royal Oak p135; *Durham*: Manor House Inn p272; *Edinburgh*: Café Royal p301; *Gloucs*: Churchill Arms p163; *Hants*: Red House p82, Wykeham Arms p83; *Kent*: Spotted Dog p87, Three Chimneys p89; *Leeds bars* p276; *Lincs*: Black Horse p221, Wig & Mitre p223; *Liverpool*: Baltic Fleet p255; *London bars* p71; *Manchester*: Mr Thomas's Chop House p262, Ox p264; *Norfolk*: Crown p196, Darby's

Free House p196, Lifeboat Inn p196, Ostrich Inn p195, Three Horseshoes p196, Walpole Arms p193, White Horse p191; *Rutland*: Olive Branch p229; *Shrops*: Warehouse Restaurant p232; *Suffolk*: Bell Inn p204, Crown Hotel p202, Star Inn p199; *Sussex*: Fox Goes Free p102; *Wales*: Nant Ddu Lodge p342, Nantyffin Cider Mill p340, Old Black Lion p341; *Warwicks*: Fox & Goose p236, Howard Arms p233; *Wilts*: Beckford Arms p179
Microbreweries: the best p224; *Cumbria*: Queens Head (Tirril) p248; *Kent*: Swan on the Green p90

American food
(*See also* South American food)
Bristol: Firehouse Rotisserie p111; *Liverpool*: Panamerican Club p257; *London*: Arkansas Café p44, Christopher's p37, Dexter's

Grill p61, Eagle Bar Diner p30, Prospect Grill p43; *Northern Ireland*: Rain City Café p348; *Surrey*: Zinfandel p92

Asian food
See Pan-Asian food

Austrian food
Dorset: Stock Hill p136

Bar crawls
Belfast pp350-351; *Birmingham* p209; *Bristol* pp112-113; *Leeds* p276; *London* pp40-41; *Nottingham* p226; *Manchester* p263

Beers
See Ales, real; Organic produce (beers)

Belgian food
Bucks: La Chouette p158

Breakfast or brunch
Birmingham: Bank Restaurant p208; *Cornwall*:

Alba p120, OnShore p121; *Cumbria*: Lucy's on a Plate p245; *Devon*: Alf Resco p126, Blue Walnut p132, Cat in the Hat p127, Hobbs p126, Pig Finca p128; *Durham*: Hide Café Bar p271; *Edinburgh*: Restaurant at the Bonham p306, Valvona & Crolla p308; *Glasgow*: Café Gandolfi p312; *Hants*: Baywatch Beach Restaurant p77, George Hotel p77, Sian Elin's p78; *Irish Republic*: Elephant & Castle p360, Killarney Park Hotel p364, Mermaid Café p361; *Jersey*: Longueville Manor p121; *Kent*: Harbour Street Café p90, Sandgate Hotel p88, Tea & Times p91; *Lincs*: Wig & Mitre p223; *Newcastle*: Barluga p278, Cluny p278; *Norfolk*: Walpole Arms p193; *Northern Ireland*: Bay Tree p353; *Oxon*: Fleece p176, Old Parsonage p174; *Scotland*: Old Smiddy Guest House p323; *Somerset*: Demuths p141; *Suffolk*:

Index

Index